BUSINESS CYCLES

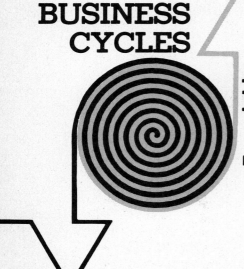

AND FORECASTING

FIFTH EDITION

CARL A. DAUTEN
Late Executive Vice Chancellor
 and Professor of Finance
Washington University

LLOYD M. VALENTINE
Professor of Economics
University of Cincinnati

Published by

H53 **SOUTH-WESTERN PUBLISHING CO.**

CINCINNATI   WEST CHICAGO, ILL.   DALLAS   PELHAM MANOR, N.Y.   PALO ALTO, CALIF.

ISBN: 0-538-08530-4

Library of Congress Catalog Card Number: 76-57109

2 3 4 5 6 Ki 3 2 1 0 9 8

Printed in the United States of America

PREFACE

The economy of the United States, like that of every industrialized nation, is characterized by fluctuations in economic activity. These fluctuations affect not only the operations of business, the welfare of labor, and the policies of government, but also the everyday life of all of us as consumers and citizens. *Business Cycles and Forecasting* attempts to explain the nature of fluctuations and the factors which produce them to help you, as individuals, analyze plans that are proposed to mitigate the effects of these fluctuations or to eliminate them.

The analysis of current and prospective levels of national income is one of the major concerns of today's economists, who are called upon more and more frequently to recommend policies that will promote economic growth and stability. They can recommend appropriate action only if they thoroughly understand the factors that promote growth as well as those which lead to fluctuations in the level of economic activity. Economists are also being called on with increasing frequency to forecast the future state of economic activity, so as to provide the economic background for developing governmental, business, and labor policies.

The business executive has a special interest in business fluctuations: the level of economic activity affects the volume of business and the ability to operate profitably. Executives must make the best possible projections of future sales when buying goods for inventory, when hiring labor, and when expanding plant and equipment. In fact, modern business planning is based on a forecast of business conditions in the immediate future and for longer periods of time.

This book provides the background which is needed by individuals, economists, and business people to understand the factors which contribute to economic growth and stability and to the level of national income. This book also surveys the techniques which may be used to analyze current economic conditions and to forecast future levels of activity. The authors believe that the factors which affect the level of economic activity and national income and the techniques of forecasting them should be studied as a unit. Prediction of future events in any field of knowledge is possible only when the causal factors that produce changes are fully understood. The factors at work to produce changes in economic activity and in the level of national income are not completely understood in all of their ramifications, but many of the basic factors at work are clear. The business cycle is no longer a completely unsolved riddle, and there exists a large measure of understanding of the factors that promote economic growth and determine the level of national income. As the knowledge of the causal factors at work steadily increases, forecasting will become more accurate.

This book is intended for senior or graduate courses in the field of business cycles or national income analysis and in forecasting. These courses do not have uniform content or titles, but they are given under such titles as *Business Cycles* or *Business Cycles and Forecasting, Business Conditions Analysis, National Income Analysis,* or *Forecasting.*

The earlier editions of this book studied the factors which led to economic growth and to fluctuations in such growth and used this material as a background for forecasting. This fifth edition has continued the integration of the knowledge in this field but has carried it further. The introductory section discusses those factors which affect economic development and summarizes the major characteristics of American economic development. Chapter 3 is devoted to relating the basic processes of the economy to national income accounting and to measuring changes in production and prices. The next segment of the book, which deals with an analysis of the causal factors at work in business cycles and in the determination of the levels of national income, is divided into two parts. Part 2 discusses the causal factors at work in the cyclical process. The chapter entitled "Classical Aggregate Economics" serves as a basis for understanding theories of the cycle. This part serves as a basis for understanding the factors at work in determining the levels of national income. The integration of business cycle analysis and national income analysis is again a major feature of this edition. Part 3 is devoted to national income analysis using the contributions of John Maynard Keynes as the basic framework.

The discussion of the statistical and historical record of business fluctuations remains much as it was in the fourth edition. The material on the measurement of business fluctuations, on the behavior of the cycle and of other fluctuations in economic activity, and the history of recent cycles is covered in Part 4. The history section has been revised to cover cycles in the post-World War II period. The recession of 1973–1975 has been analyzed at some length because of its severity and also because it is based on some unusual factors.

Part 5 deals with forecasting aggregate economic activity. The material about building an expenditure model of GNP is treated in two chapters and is followed by a chapter entitled "Forecasting Price Changes." Part 6, "Forecasting Sales," has been designed for use primarily by students in business administration. Part 7, "Proposals for Achieving Economic Growth and Stability," has been revised to cover new developments.

The authors wish to express their appreciation to their colleagues and to their friends in business and government. Without their help in discussing what is being done and can be done to analyze and forecast national income and business conditions, this book could not have been written. Professors Merle Welshans, Jack Wolff, Henry Guithes, Arthur Vieth, Robert Virgil, and others have offered valuable suggestions based on classroom use of earlier editions of this book. Professors David G. Davies, of Duke University, and John M. Kuhlman, of the University of Missouri, also kindly read and discussed sections of the manuscript of an earlier edition.

Carl A. Dauten

Lloyd M. Valentine

Postscript

It is with deep sadness and sincere regret that I must write a postscript to this Preface with the announcement of the death of Dr. Carl A. Dauten. With his characteristic thoroughness and concern for others, he completed his responsibilities toward this fifth edition before his death. His influence will continue in his several books, in the University he so ably served, and in the lives of the thousands of his former students. We are all better off for that influence.

Lloyd M. Valentine

CONTENTS

Part 1

INTRODUCTION

This book is about fluctuations in economic activity. Changes are continually taking place in prices, in wages, in the level of employment, and in other economic factors; and these changes affect the fortunes of all of us, not only in our country but in the world. The early pioneers on the frontiers of civilization could largely ignore economic changes since they built their own homes from native timber, raised their own food, and made their own clothes. However, in an economy of interdependence in which almost everyone works for a living and uses the money received to buy goods and services, the state of economic activity is of primary concern to all.

Periods of depressed economic activity, which have occurred from time to time, have caused untold deprivation and suffering for many people. In fact, the argument has been made with some appeal that the free-enterprise system is unacceptable because of such suffering during major periods of depressed economic activity. Those who favor a controlled economy have promised an end to periods of economic depression. Thus, one of the challenges for our society is to cure this problem within the framework of a free society and, at the same time, to continue to raise the standard of living of our people. The struggle for power in our modern world is in part a struggle between two competing economic systems, each claiming that it can raise the standard of living of its people and of those of the rest of the world more rapidly than the other.

This introductory part presents the background (1) for the study of business fluctuations and of procedures for forecasting them and (2) for understanding policies to stabilize economic activity. Chapter 1 describes the nature of economic fluctuations and forecasting. It identifies the major types of fluctuations in economic activity in a preliminary way. This is followed by an introduction to the nature of forecasting of economic fluctuations. Chapter 2 discusses the salient features of the American economy as it operates currently and the major characteristics of American economic development. Consideration is first directed to the record of growth in the American economy and then to the characteristics of major cyclical variations in such growth.

This discussion provides a review of the background needed to understand what is happening in the economy during cyclical fluctuations. These features of the American economy will be used in the explanation of why the cycle develops as it does. If the economy were changed materially, the cycle would be changed or perhaps even eliminated in the form in which it has occurred. Chapter 3 is devoted to the conceptual foundations of aggregate economic activity and the measures used to describe this activity.

CHAPTER 1

NATURE OF ECONOMIC FLUCTUATIONS AND FORECASTING

The volume of economic activity in America has been increasing since early colonial days. This has been true not only because population has increased but also because our productivity has increased as methods have been developed to turn out more and more goods with a given amount of labor. This growth of economic activity has not taken place, however, at a steady rate. It was very rapid during World War II and the early postwar years and much slower in the 1930s. Nor has growth taken place without interruption. There have been several periods of minor decreases in economic activity even in the prosperous years since the end of World War II. From time to time there have been much more serious and protracted interruptions in the forward push of economic progress. This happened from 1929 to 1933 and also in several earlier periods in our history.

NATURE AND SIGNIFICANCE OF ECONOMIC FLUCTUATIONS

Several fluctuations in production, employment, prices, and other phases of economic activity are of primary importance as economic, social, and political factors. They not only affect the economy and society at large but also the living standards and styles of individuals of all ages and in all walks of life.

Depression Periods in Economic Activity

It is difficult to comprehend the full effect on the lives of individuals of periods of severe depression in economic activity. Those who are unable to find employment in a period of depressed activity are forced to curtail consumption of goods and services to such an extent that real want and privation often exist. The psychological impact on their lives is more difficult to measure, but it is certainly great. The effect on the attitudes of young people who are just entering the labor force and cannot find employment can be highly detrimental to the social framework of the nation. This is especially true of young people who are members of minority groups since these groups have in the past been hit hardest by unemployment. Older workers who lose their jobs during the decline in business activity on the downswing of the cycle may find it almost impossible to find gainful employment again on a regular basis.

Depression periods have also often been periods of declines in the general level of prices, that is, of deflation. In a period of deflation debtors find their loans and the interest payments on them more difficult to repay since it takes more purchasing power to do so than it did at the time the loan was made. This creates problems for business people and farmers who mortgaged their property in a period of high prices and must pay off mortgages and meet interest payments in a period of falling prices. The same is true for individuals buying a house on which they have a substantial mortgage. Not only does it take additional real income to repay the loan and interest on it, but problems arise when an individual is forced to move. More dollars may be owed than the house will bring on the market and, as a result, there will still be some debt remaining after the sale, so nothing would remain for a payment on a new home.

Business fluctuations also create problems for the total economy and for society at large. From the economic standpoint there is the loss of goods that might have been produced during the period of less than full employment. This will amount to billions of dollars even in relatively minor downturns and is staggering in major depressions. There is also a loss of capital equipment which deteriorates faster than it is replaced. As a result, it is more difficult to achieve high levels of production in the ensuing prosperity period, and the nation is permanently poorer than it would have been if capital had been replaced and expanded at more normal levels.

Business failures increase rapidly during periods of depressed business activity, especially in major depressions. This not only involves losses for the owners, but generally also for creditors. Such losses to creditors have been substantial even in minor downturns. Business failures also have an adverse effect on the employees of the concerns that fail and on the communities in which they are located.

Depressions also create social problems that become especially severe during protracted periods of large-scale unemployment. The crime rate increases, especially among the younger people who have not been firmly established in their jobs and homes or who are just entering the labor force and find it impossible to get jobs. Marriages are postponed and birth rates drop with resulting social problems. This also intensifies the depression since demand for housing and consumer goods related to homemaking and rearing a family is further reduced.

The political repercussions of business fluctuations are also of great importance. When large numbers of people are unemployed, they are easily swayed by demagogs who promise them food and shelter in exchange for some freedoms. At least part of the rise of communism and fascism, especially the latter, can be traced to such situations in periods of greatly depressed business activity. In democratic nations there is tremendous pressure on the government during times of subnormal business activity to do something about unemployment and its problems with the result that the trend toward government regulation and public ownership of business is greatly accelerated.

Boom Periods in Economic Activity

Problems of a severe nature also occur when demands that are beyond its ability to supply are made on the economy. Increasing output in itself creates no economic problems, but the effect of demand in excess of the ability to supply leads to an increase in the general level of prices. Prices do not change uniformly but do so at different rates in different sectors of the economy, and this creates problems. It leads to inequities between individuals and groups and thus to a less than optimum allocation of resources.

Inflation creates serious problems for the individual. Debts become easier to pay off, but problems in planning insurance, investment, and retirement programs increase. The face value of life insurance policies remains unchanged, but the proceeds buy less. The same is true of pension programs guaranteeing a fixed dollar amount as most of them do. Personal investment also becomes a problem since bonds and savings and loan shares lose purchasing power as prices go up, and the average individual does not have the necessary analytical ability to invest in common stocks in such a way as to keep up with inflation to some degree.

Many groups in society suffer a loss in real income during inflationary periods and try to use political pressure to stop it. The pay of government workers, teachers, employees in regulated industries, and others lags behind the rise in prices, and this makes it difficult to recruit and hold good workers. The teaching profession is likely to be hard hit since, when income fails to keep up with prices, fewer students, especially the good ones, plan to become teachers and thus a shortage exists for several years.

In the American economy the desire to avoid the undesirable consequences of economic fluctuations led to the enactment of the Full Employment Act of 1946, which stated that it was the policy of the federal government to plan its activities affecting the economy so as to promote full employment. The government is also under continuing pressure to use its powers and influences to control inflation as well as deflation. Government programs in agriculture have been directed toward stabilizing agricultural income and in housing toward stabilizing overall economic activity.

TYPES OF VARIATIONS IN ECONOMIC ACTIVITY

Economists recognize different types of variations in economic activity. These are the trend, business cycles, seasonal fluctuations, and irregular and random fluctuations.

Trend

Even though economic activity does not proceed smoothly but is interrupted by periods of decline followed by increased activity, there is an underlying long-run tendency for economic activity to increase that is referred to as the trend. *Trend* is the persistent underlying movement that takes place in economic activity in general or in a sector of the economy over a period of years. It is the basic growth or decline that would exist if there were no periods of boom or depression or less pronounced variations in economic activity.

The trend in total economic activity is a linear one; that is, activity has grown at a more or less constant rate over a period of years. This trend in the United States has been upward due to many factors. The development of a new continent was a major factor until around 1900. The rapid increase in population, the increasing stock of capital goods, technological progress, the increased education and skills of the labor force, increased managerial skills, and the discovery of new sources of raw materials have also been significant.

The trend of total economic activity is the combined result of the trends of individual industries and businesses. A successful new industry usually grows rapidly in its early stages. Growth then levels off to a more gradual rate, and after a time the industry becomes integrated with the economy and its growth is largely governed by the growth in the general economy. The trend of growth of such a new industry is a curvilinear one; that is, it resembles an elongated S. As the demand for goods and services changes, some industries may pass their peak and decline. This may be a gradual downward movement, as in the case of coal furnaces, or a rapid decline, as in the case of a product which has become obsolete, such as wagon wheels.

Business Cycles

Changes in the level of economic activity caused by the trend are overshadowed by continually recurring variations in total economic activity. Several years of expansion in total economic activity are followed by a period of slower growth or of contraction in such activity. These fluctuations occur in total economic activity, not just in a particular industry or sector of the economy. Such expansions and contractions in the level of activity occur at about the same time in most sectors of the economy. This sequence of fluctuations is a recurring one, but it is not periodic; that is, such variations do not occur at regular time intervals and do not last for the same periods of time. The amplitude of movement from the low point of activity to the high point of activity is not the same. These fluctuations have become known as *business cycles*. Any connotation of regularity, however, which the term "cycles" may give does not exist in data on total economic activity, production, employment, prices, or any other major economic series.

Seasonal Fluctuations

Seasonal fluctuations are changes in economic activity during the course of a year that occur in a more or less regular pattern from year to year. Such changes are related to the changing seasons of the year, to holidays, or to the calendar. The canning or freezing of fruit, for example, must take place during that season of the year when the fresh fruit is available and, therefore, this economic activity follows a seasonal pattern. Other seasonal patterns are related to customs in our society, such as sales arising out of Christmas gift exchanges and the Easter parade. The changing date of Easter leads to a changing seasonal pattern in those sectors of economic activity which are affected.

Other seasonal variations occur because of the unequal number of days in the month in our calendar and the unequal distribution of holidays that are generally observed.

Irregular and Random Fluctuations

Economic activity in various sectors of the economy, and to some degree in the total economy, is also affected from time to time by such exogenous factors as a widespread drought, a major flood, or a political disturbance. It may also be affected by a major strike. Some minor variations in economic activity are due to more or less unpredictable factors, such as unusual absenteeism due to a flu epidemic. Others may be due to purely random factors, such as the bunching of large orders from several major customers in one month or quarter. These various factors are known as *irregular and random fluctuations*.

PRICE LEVEL CHANGES

The changes in economic activity involved in the trend, the business cycle, seasonal factors, and irregular and random fluctuations affect the general level of prices. For example, there is some tendency for prices to rise during the upswing of a business cycle as the demand for goods and services grows faster than the ability of the economy to provide goods and services; there is also some tendency for prices to decline during the downswing of the cycle. Changes in the price level from time to time may also be primarily related to changes in the money supply or the money standard, rather than to real changes in the level of economic activity. For example, during the Vietnam War, the money supply was increased greatly by the methods used to finance the war and prices rose until the supplies of money and of goods were in balance. At other times (although not in recent years) the basic movement of prices has been downward. This was true in the 1870s and 1880s because economic activity was expanding and the money supply was more or less fixed.

FORECASTING AND ECONOMIC FLUCTUATIONS

When making decisions about the future course of a business, management must take into consideration all of the factors that are likely to affect it, both external and internal. Business fluctuations are among the major external factors that affect a business and are therefore of prime importance in making management decisions.

The Relationship of Economic Changes to Business Management

The primary function of management in a business is to determine the objectives of the business in the long run and short run. Then management must make plans to carry out these objectives, organize human and material resources to put the plans into action, implement the plans, and control the activities of the business to be sure that all is going according to plan. Economic analysis and forecasting are involved in all of these steps in management, but primarily in determining objectives and in developing long-range and short-range plans to carry out these objectives.

In determining its objectives each business must decide on the commodities it plans to produce and sell, the price range of its products or services, the geographic region in which it plans to sell, the potential market for the products, the share of the market it can realistically hope to get, the prospective return on capital, and the like. Such objectives can only be realistic and well-balanced if management has analyzed trends in the economy and has forecast the demand for its products in both the long run and short run, the prices at which it will sell, the cost of the factors of production, and so on. Thus, an analysis of trends and current developments in the economy and a forecast of such trends and current developments is basic to establishing sound business objectives and in developing long-range and short-range plans to carry out such objectives.

The Need for Forecasting in Business

Some business people and economists still feel that forecasting is impossible in their businesses or at best is so indefinite as to be hazardous as a basis for business decisions. The statement is frequently made that forecasting may have succeeded well for others but "our business is different." The fact remains, however, that in any business in which raw materials must be purchased before orders are received or in which substantial capital equipment is used, some form of forecasting is being done, even if unwittingly.

If a business plans to continue to operate at present levels, the forecast implicitly made is that present levels of business are predicted for the future. For most businesses this is not true for any period of time since they are continually affected by changing business conditions. Another frequent basis for business decisions is that past trends will continue. If, for example, business has been increasing at a rate of about 5 percent a year, that rate of increase is expected to continue for the next year or several years. This can be a hazardous assumption because growth does not continue at the same rate for an indefinite period of time in a dynamic economy.

In many concerns in which the top officials feel that forecasting cannot be done, someone is actually doing the forecasting. For example, a manufacturer of appliances used in home construction felt that the level of business could not be forecast successfully. The manufacturer believed that current orders were the only real guide to follow in planning production. Since orders usually were received several weeks ahead of the requested delivery date and since the appliances could be assembled in several days, this looked like a reasonable procedure. Some of the raw materials, however, had to be ordered as much as five months in advance to allow for delivery and fabrication. Since no one would venture a forecast, not even the purchasing agent, the clerk who did the ordering had to decide when to order materials. The clerk tried to follow production but, of course, got behind on an upswing due to the time required to obtain materials. As pressure increased for raw materials when business increased, the clerk ordered faster. As business turned down, the firm received large stocks when they were no longer needed.

What was happening in effect was that the order clerk was forecasting. The clerk knew little about the prospects of the business and acted in response to pressure from superiors to either obtain materials in a hurry or reduce excess stocks. The manufacturer finally called in outside consultants for advice on reorganizing the purchasing department and was surprised when told that top management was to blame because no forecast existed.

Nature of Forecasting

Business has no alternative to some type of forecasting, since aimless drifting is unthinkable in a well-managed organization. The basic question really concerns the approach that is to be used in forecasting. It can be done in a mechanical way as, for example, predicting a 5 percent increase in sales since this has been the average experience over the last few years. Or it can be done by relying on one of several series that have generally led business in the past, such as using changes in stock prices to predict changes in business activity. On a somewhat more sophisticated level it can be done by studying the economic and business situation and then intuitively deciding what will happen.

The scientific approach in this field is the same as in any field. It involves a knowledge and understanding of what has happened in the past, what is currently happening in the economy, and why it is happening. Only when phenomena are understood is it possible to predict accurately what will happen and take action in the light of such predictions.

Our knowledge of the causal factors at work in business fluctuations is not comprehensive enough to make it possible to forecast with complete accuracy. But it is advanced enough to make possible more reliable indicators of future events than can be done with unscientific approaches. The forecasts which can be made more than justify the time and money spent on them. As knowledge increases in this field, better and better results will be forthcoming.

Benefits from a Forecasting Program

The only thing certain about any specific forecast is that it will be wrong, at least to a degree or in some particular. With the present knowledge of business fluctuations it is impossible to gauge all variables exactly. As a rule, however, it should be possible in most businesses to forecast total sales for a quarter of a year ahead within a range of 5 percent above or below the actual figure, and for a year ahead within a range of 10 percent. Such results are usually accurate enough to be of real aid in managing a business, even if sales and production forecasts of individual products are off somewhat more. Such forecasting is a valuable managerial tool for business planning.

Consideration of Every Contingency. A forecasting program should help a business to meet any eventuality. A good forecast considers all factors that might influence a business, including remote possibilities. If management studies the forecasts carefully, it will at least not be caught unaware when the unexpected happens. It is impracticable to prepare in advance for every contingency, but knowing what can happen and spotting unusual situations early will go a long way toward preventing serious difficulties.

Study of Past Record. Forecasting forces a business to study its past record carefully. This must be done to determine past trends and the most likely pattern in the future. A study of the past is also necessary to determine if any regular seasonal pattern exists. Furthermore, an analysis of past cyclical movements should be made in developing data for future forecasting. The determination of the trend, cycle, and seasonal pattern requires the recognition of all sporadic or unusual factors. An analysis of these compared with a study of the past policies of the business will often reveal both good and bad courses taken by management. Such study can provide the basis for avoiding the same mistakes in the future and for continuing the policies that have proved successful.

Study of Outside Factors. Another important benefit of forecasting is that it forces management to look at all the outside factors affecting the business. In this way executives are kept informed of the governmental and social environment in which they make decisions. Favorable trends may be discerned and developed, or action may be taken to combat unfavorable aspects of a situation before they develop too far. Such awareness of the social and governmental milieu in which business operates is important for the preservation of free private enterprise in a democratic system.

Limitations and Problems of a Forecasting Program

Several problems are likely to be encountered in a forecasting program. One problem is that top management may expect a greater degree of accuracy from a forecast than is possible with the present knowledge of business and economic factors. Many top executives, especially in smaller concerns, feel that a forecast which is made once a year should be accurate enough to use as a basis for planning a year ahead with no further review or change. Such accuracy is seldom possible, however, since the numerous factors affecting business are changing constantly. Forecasting must be a continuous process.

Another problem is to obtain cooperation among various groups that participate in developing and using the forecast. At times sales departments are inclined to be overpessimistic when sales are bad. Other departments may argue for levels of production that are too high to make per unit costs look more favorable. This emphasizes the need for an independent forecasting group rather than one under direction of sales or production planning departments.

Small businesses have a special problem in the forecasting area. Their forecasting problems may not keep one trained person occupied, and they cannot afford to pay for the required background and experience. They are also at a disadvantage in finding a good forecaster since the number of persons qualified in this area is small. A possible solution is to have forecasting services set up locally, serving clients in a manner similar to law offices or tax consulting services.

The Need for Forecasting in the Government

The many activities of the federal government and its widespread obligations in the economic sphere cannot be carried on without an analysis of current economic activity and a forecast of future economic activity. This has to be done to carry out governmental responsibilities under the Full Employment Act, and the Council of Economic Advisers has been established for this purpose. The level of economic activity must also be forecast to develop the annual budget of the federal government. To estimate receipts of the federal government, which come to a large degree from personal and corporate income taxes, it is necessary to forecast personal income and corporate profits. This, of course, cannot be done without forecasting the level of total economic activity and the level of prices.

The Department of Agriculture must forecast the prospective supply of farm products, the level of farm prices in general, and the supply and prices of particular commodities to plan its crop control and price support programs. The Board of Governors of the Federal Reserve System must forecast the demand for money and credit and the basic supply and demand factors at work in the economy to develop and carry out its monetary policies.

The various housing agencies must forecast supply and demand in developing their programs. In fact, every agency that deals with economic matters must analyze the factors at work in the economy and forecast future economic conditions. State and local governments, too, are finding that forecasting is an absolute necessity. Forecasting has become one of the important activities of government, and the skill and accuracy with which it is done are major factors in the success or failure of government programs.

THE PLAN OF STUDY

This book is designed to give the student of economics and business administration an understanding of some of the major factors which affect the economy and in turn decisions in business, labor, agriculture, and government. It is necessary to understand these factors to make intelligent decisions —decisions that will help shape the destinies of an organization and the total economy rather than allow them to be buffeted by forces which are not understood. For example, a decision on plant expansion, including the size and timing of such an expansion, can only be made intelligently in light of the trend of the economy and the industry and seasonal and cyclical factors. The student should also gain an understanding of techniques that are available to measure and forecast levels of total economic activity and the level of sales in an individual business. Such study will provide an understanding of present programs for stabilizing economic activity and a framework for analyzing such programs that may be proposed in the future.

Introduction

This first chapter has introduced the nature of economic fluctuations and their significance for individuals, the economy, and society. The nature of forecasting has also been considered in a preliminary way. The second chapter in this part will provide additional background on the basic characteristics of economic development and economic fluctuations in the United States and the nature of the American system of capitalistic enterprise. Chapter 3 will analyze the conceptual foundations of aggregate economic activity and the measures used to describe this activity.

Causal Factors in the Cyclical Process

Using the record of past trends and cycles as a background, an analysis is made in Part 2 of the causal factors at work in the business cycle. Consideration is given to individual factors, such as monetary expansion and contraction, and the relationship between saving and investment; but major emphasis is placed upon a study of the interrelationships of all the factors at work in the cycle. Chapter 4 is devoted to a survey of the theoretical foundation of aggregative activity as understood by the classical school of economics. A summary of the main strands in the development of business cycle thought is found in Chapters 5 and 6.

National Income Analysis

Part 3 presents a study of national income analysis which integrates all the factors affecting the level of economic activity. National income analysis is based on an analysis of the economy as it has developed over the past 45 years and on the theory of cyclical movements. Chapter 7 considers the contribution to national income analysis of the British economist John Maynard Keynes and develops the basic framework of the analysis. The other chapters in Part 3 develop the analysis further and present the main analytical tools constructed to aid in our understanding of how the many aspects and components of the system mesh. The theories of aggregate demand and aggregate supply are developed in some detail and in the process we determine saving, investment, consumption, taxes, government spending, imports and exports, money supply, interest rates, wages, employment, aggregate output, and the price level.

The Record of Business Fluctuations

To forecast future levels of activity, it is necessary to know the extent of changes in economic activity. Consideration is given in Chapter 11 (the first chapter of Part 4) to the statistical techniques for breaking down an economic time series into the trend, seasonal, cyclical, and irregular components, since such a data breakdown is a necessary prerequisite to analysis and forecasting.

Before forecasting can be done effectively, it is necessary to summarize what is known about past fluctuations, especially the quantitative data available about such fluctuations. Chapter 12 includes data on the cycle in general economic activity and in major sectors of the economy. The pattern of events during the business cycle is also traced briefly from the beginning of the revival in activity, through the upswing, the peak, the downswing, and the trough at the end of the cycle.

Chapter 13 summarizes data on trends, seasonal factors, building cycles, agricultural cycles, and other fluctuations in economic activity. Some attention is also given to long swings in economic growth and to long-run fluctuations in price.

Chapter 14 covers the record of business fluctuations from the pre-World War II period to the present, including major and minor cycles. This period is discussed in some detail because the recent past is most significant in predicting what is most likely to happen in the future, and also because events in this period still have a profound influence on the thinking of persons in business and government today.

Forecasting Economic Activity

Scientific forecasting must be based on an understanding of the nature of fluctuations and of the causal factors which produce them. This understanding is developed in Parts 1 through 4 of this book. Procedures for analyzing economic conditions and forecasting them are considered in Part 5. Chapter 15 discusses methods used to project the trend of economic activity. Chapter 16 is a summary of forecasting techniques used by practitioners of the art and discusses problems that forecasters face. Chapters 17 and 18 detail a widely used method of forecasting aggregate economic activity by the construction of an expenditure model. This approach is based on the kind of economic analysis constructed in Part 3. Chapter 19 considers the special problem of forecasting price changes.

Forecasting Sales

In many situations in government and business a forecast of the trend of economic activity and the level of general economic activity for the next year can serve as the basis for sound decisions. If business planning and budgeting is to be done effectively, however, it is necessary also to forecast the sales of a business. In Part 6 methods of forecasting industry sales are discussed, along with methods of forecasting for an individual business.

Proposals for Achieving Economic Growth and Stability

The last part discusses proposals for stabilizing general economic activity and for promoting desirable economic growth. The emphasis is placed on aggregative policy, primarily monetary and fiscal policy toward the ends of achieving a high employment and low unemployment goal, a relatively stable price level, a reasonable balance of payments equilibrium, and a rising standard of living. The theoretical and institutional perspectives gained in the earlier chapters are prerequisites to full appreciation of these last two chapters.

QUESTIONS

1. Review the nature of our economic development.
2. How do business fluctuations affect individuals? Society at large? Governments?
3. What is the trend of economic activity?
4. Describe the nature of the trend in an industry.
5. Describe the business cycle. Comment on the use of the word "cycle" in describing this type of economic fluctuation.
6. Describe seasonal variations in business activity.
7. Give several examples of irregular fluctuations which may affect the level of economic activity.

8. Explain how economic analysis and forecasting are related to determining business objectives.
9. Describe the role of forecasting in business planning.
10. What is the nature of forecasting as it is used in business planning?
11. Discuss the advantages and limitations of forecasting in business.
12. Discuss the role of forecasting in government activities.

SUGGESTED READINGS

Butler, William F., and Robert A. Kavesh (eds.). *How Business Economists Forecast.* Englewood Cliffs, N.J.: Prentice-Hall, Inc., 1966. Part Five.

Chisholm, Roger K., and Gilbert R. Whitaker Jr. *Forecasting Methods.* Homewood, Ill.: Richard D. Irwin, Inc., 1971. Chapter 1.

Economic Report of the President. Various issues. Washington: U.S. Government Printing Office.

"Forecasting Sales," *Studies in Business Policy,* No. 106. New York: National Industrial Conference Board, 1963.

McClelland, Peter D., *et al.* (eds.). *Focus Macroeconomics.* Guilford, Conn.: The Dushkin Publishing Group, Inc., 1975.

McKinley, David H., Murray G. Lee, and Helene Duffy. *Forecasting Business Conditions.* New York: The American Bankers Association, 1965. Chapter 1.

CHAPTER 2

AMERICAN ECONOMIC DEVELOPMENT AND BUSINESS CYCLES

This chapter begins with general observations about some characteristics of the American economy which have relevance for an understanding of the causes of instability. The economies of the world differ in greater or lesser degree with respect to these characteristics. Changes in features that occur in any nation's economy make the analysis of business conditions take on different nuances. What may be very important at one time and place may be quite insignificant at another. Accordingly, one needs some understanding of the institutions and historical forces at work in the economy being studied.

Since we are using the American economy as our example, the remainder of the chapter is devoted to a review of some of the salient characteristics of the system, a brief historical overview of secular economic trends, and a look at the major depressions which have afflicted our economy.

CONSUMER FREEDOM OF CHOICE

Consumer sovereignty is a fundamental principle of democratic capitalism. By and large, freedom of the individual to make economic choices is characteristic of the economy of the United States. Consumers are free to spend their income as they see fit. Choices are made among various types of goods and services, and the timing of the purchases is left to the consumer. If the individual elects not to spend on commodities in the immediate period, a further decision must be made as to the form in which the increased wealth will be held: money, bonds, insurance, equity securities, and so on, or the reduction of debt. While this kind of freedom is priceless, it is also one of the factors that gives the economic system some of its unstable characteristics.

When consumers, businesses, peoples of other countries, and governments are free to determine their purchases, total spending can sometimes be inadequate to employ all the resources that are available for use, or sometimes total spending is more than the value of the goods that can be produced. Consumers are vital in determining the rate of economic growth of the system since capital expansion, which is the essence of growth, is limited by the amount of saving.

Classical economists admitted some temporary difficulties as consumer preferences shifted from certain goods to other goods, but believed that flexible prices and mobility of the factors of production would eliminate them. It was inconceivable, however, to Ricardo and later classicists that less total spending by consumers could result in any excess of labor or other resources. Their way of phrasing this proposition was that a general glut was impossible. The reasoning was that the interest rate would fall, causing investors to increase their demand for resources and leading households to revise their spending plans upward so that total resources would be employed but with a lower percentage of them devoted to present or consumption goods. This line of analysis, known as Say's Law, has played such an important role in the development of the understanding of how economic systems work that we shall come back to it again and again. In particular, Chapter 4 is devoted to an exposition of the classical model of the aggregate economy.

PROFIT MOTIVE

In our system most production is done for the market. Most business firms cannot wait until the orders come in to produce precisely the amount needed. Instead, they try to estimate what the demand will be when the goods are ready for the market, and what the costs will be when they are actually incurred in the production process. The possibility of error is great. Both revenue and cost forecasts can be wrong so that undesired inventory accumulation or attrition, or conversely, serious price changes, may easily arise. Unexpected outcomes provoke responses by the business community that cause further changes in the important variables of the economy. The problems arise because production takes time. If output could be created instantaneously, no inventories would be maintained, and no possibility of error in expectations would exist.

Sometimes government officials and other observers admonish business people to make decisions "for the good of the nation" rather than on the self-interest principle or profit motive. During depressions business is asked to expand; and when inflation appears to be the problem, restraint is in order. In general, if there is a conflict between the larger good and self-interest, business decision makers are well advised to ignore and, in fact, do ignore such admonitions. By relying on the profit motive, we get into difficulties, but it is not clear that any alternative criterion would be superior or as good.

Business decisions concerning such items as price, production, and investment may be made upon the basis of careful, rational appraisals of all factors in the business situation. They may also be influenced by psychological factors, such as waves of optimism or pessimism; the desire to follow in the footsteps of competitors; or fear of the future outlook because of international uncertainties, governmental policies, and the like.

The bases on which decisions are made have changed somewhat as the economy has developed so that the role of business decisions in the cycle is not necessarily the same today as it was a generation ago. More and more firms are taking a longer-range point of view, realizing that it is better to maximize long-run profits than short-run profits. This often means that in the short run prices are set at a lower level than the market will bear in order to maximize long-run profits. This tends to narrow the range of price fluctuations over the cycle in those fields where such a policy is followed and thus to change the characteristics of the cycle to this extent.

In many cases modern management decides inventory policies, working capital policies, and the timing and amount of investment in new plants and equipment on the basis of careful studies of the long-range demand for its product. As such actions reach sizable proportions, it eliminates excessive accumulation of inventory and the building of unnecessary plants and equipment and thus, by reducing activity somewhat during the boom, changes some of the characteristics of the cycle.

THE INDUSTRIAL STRUCTURE

Elements of great importance in the analysis of business fluctuations are the degree of price flexibility and output responsiveness to changing conditions. According to the traditional theory of the firm, both purely competitive firms and unfettered monopolies respond immediately to changes in supply or demand by altering price and output. Only casual observation is needed, however, to observe that the prices of some goods and services seem to remain quite stable even though cost conditions and demand change markedly.

Competitive prices become rigid when governments impose controls over them, as under price control or agricultural price supports, when government is the sole or major buyer, and in other cases where it is deemed in the public interest, as with milk. Monopoly prices are rigid when set by government or when they must be approved by a governmental agency, which, of course, describes public utilities. Monopolies might also maintain constant prices to avoid more direct and pervasive involvement by government. Most firms in the real world are somewhere between the poles of pure competition and pure monopoly, and here our micro theory is less helpful.

There are a number of explanations for the price stability that is fairly characteristic of these oligopolistic markets. One is that collusion, tacit or overt, exists; in this situation any change in price or other policy could precipitate a falling out among the members. This is a way the firms can live together without damaging price wars or extreme price fluctuations. Another explanation involves the kinked demand curve which is established if each firm believes that if it raises its price, other firms in the industry will not raise their prices; and if the firm lowers its price, the others will follow suit. Under these circumstances variations in costs will not change price or output unless the cost changes are extreme. In some activities the cost of changing prices is considerable and, consequently, will not be done unless circumstances have definitely changed and are expected to be relatively permanent. Sometimes price stability has as its source the organizational structure of the firm, and internal political considerations may lead to the no-change decision. If the firms are large, as they frequently are in the oligopoly case, fear of government involvement in one way or another may induce the firms to leave well enough alone; that is, to keep prices where they are.

In general, where prices are relatively inflexible the response to changes in demand or cost conditions is a more pronounced change in output than where prices are flexible. In unrestricted agricultural markets, for example, price varies considerably as demand changes and output variations are less pronounced. In contrast, automobile sales and output vary directly as demand varies, and price changes are more moderate. This relationship between price and output variability in particular industries and the differences in this respect among industries has a great deal to do with the character of business fluctuations, and so we shall come back to this question later.

LABOR UNION POLICIES

Another important factor in shaping the cycle in present-day America is the position of labor unions. When workers were largely unorganized, wages were cut rapidly in a period of declining business to bring costs into line with declining prices. This is what one would expect to happen under any perfectly competitive system in which workers compete with each other for the available jobs. With the advent of powerful labor unions, however, the wage is fixed by collective bargaining between union negotiators and representatives of management. The wage rate is usually set for a specified period, though in some contracts it is tied to a cost-of-living index. When wage rates are fixed through union contracts or by minimum-wage laws, a reduction in the demand for a product will result in a greater reduction of employment in that industry than would otherwise occur.

In business cycle analysis it is important to distinguish between real wages and money wages. Constant money wages during a period of rising consumer goods prices result in falling real wages. Real wages rise if the consumer price index falls at a faster rate than money wages; and if money wages and prices rise or fall at the same rate, real wages remain constant. We raise a question to be taken up later: Are business decisions, and the decisions of workers, based on the real wage or on the money wage?

PERSONAL INVESTMENT PATTERNS

According to national income determination theory, saving that is not matched by concurrent, voluntary investment expenditures brings about a reduction in aggregate economic activity. Financial institutions have evolved over the years to aid in the process of accepting funds from those who are willing to give up their ability to command goods currently (savers), and to make the funds (and therefore the ability to command resources) available to investors. In this sense financial institutions are intermediaries between savers and investors. They are also intermediaries between savers and dissavers, and to some extent between disinvestors and investors. To serve this important function, they must tailor their liabilities to the manifold needs and personalities of savers; on the other hand, the nature of the credit granted must be such as to fit the needs of those who wish to use the funds. As economic conditions change, financial institutions and financial instruments must also change if serious problems are to be avoided.

A very familiar class of financial institution or financial intermediary is the life insurance company. Life insurance as it is generally sold in America represents a combination of protection and investment. The growth of life insurance has resulted in a large volume of assets in the hands of life insurance companies. In early 1976, life insurance companies had about $300 billion in assets.[1] Since the major concern of a purchaser of insurance and of the insurance company is protection rather than maximum investment return, life insurance funds are invested on a conservative basis. Legal requirements have in most cases restricted insurance company investments to mortgages, real estate, high-grade bonds, a few well-protected issues of preferred stock, and a small proportion of high-grade common stocks.

Large sums are also deposited in savings banks and put into trust accounts in banks and trust companies. There are also legal restrictions on the use which such institutions may make of funds. Such institutional investment makes large sums of money available for debt financing. This creates no problem so long as sufficient demand for debt capital exists. It may, however, make it more difficult to raise equity capital that is also needed if business is to maintain a sound capital structure.

A problem may arise in periods of recession in keeping all funds invested. Especially in life insurance purchases, savings go on year by year, in good years and bad, since the major aim is protection. This means that savings are available in large quantities when demand has fallen off due to the lower level of business. Economic activity would hold up better if less were saved and more spent on consumption, but institutional arrangements prevent this.

There has also been a phenomenal growth in the postwar period in savings accounts in savings and loan associations. The total in such savings accounts was about $7.5 billion in 1945 and had increased to $308 billion by mid 1976.[2] Many savers put money into these institutions because the rate of return is somewhat more favorable than in alternative uses offering the same degree of liquidity and safety. This restricts a large volume of savings for use in financing residential real estate. It may also create problems because large liquid assets have been built up while the proceeds have been invested in long-term assets. Even though it is legally possible to require a time period for withdrawing savings, in practice they are paid on demand. This makes it possible for savers to withdraw funds for consumption purposes almost at will and without penalty.

A large amount of personal investment is also made in government bonds, especially savings bonds. The volume of savings bonds outstanding in June, 1976, was $70 billion,[3] and a substantial amount of marketable government securities was also held by individuals. These huge amounts of liquid assets could seriously affect the economy if the public attempted to convert large amounts into cash to use for consumption expenditures.

Thus, the trends in personal investment patterns create additional problems of economic balance. On the one hand, savings are made available to limited

---

[1] *Federal Reserve Bulletin* (October, 1976), p. A31.
[2] *Ibid.,* p. A31.
[3] *Ibid.,* p. A34.

sectors of the economy which may not be the sectors of greatest need. On the other hand, savers have a large degree of liquidity which makes it possible for them to shift funds to consumption expenditures with little or no delay and with little or no penalty.

THE ROLE OF GOVERNMENT IN THE ECONOMY

The role of government in the economy is a very large subject, and we cannot do justice to the topic here. The consensus of what the proper role of government is has changed considerably over the history of our nation. It always has been, and no doubt always will be, the subject of widespread debate; but the range of disagreement is narrowed by the understanding of how the economic system operates. But whether we agree or disagree with the actions taken by government, we must know what they are and take account of them in our analysis.

When our country was first established, the basic attitude was "that government is best which governs least." Interferences with the functioning of the economy arose primarily out of war financing, or out of government changes in banking rules and regulations such as those that occurred in the period of "wildcat" banking during the administration of Andrew Jackson prior to the crash of 1837. As time went on, government assumed a larger and larger role in the economic system. Beginning with the passage of the Interstate Commerce Act in 1887, which regulated railroad rates, government regulation has spread to many sectors of the economy, and the government has engaged in business on a large scale in such projects as the production of electrical energy and atomic energy.

The role of the government in pricing agricultural products also has decided effects on the course of the business cycle. Before the advent of the New Deal, agricultural production was left almost entirely to the decisions of individual farmers, although some attempts were made to stimulate production during World War I and to take surpluses off the market during the Hoover administration. Since 1933, however, various aspects of agricultural production and pricing have been controlled by the government.

The prices of some commodities are regulated by means of marketing agreements, as in the case of milk. The prices of basic commodities have a floor set by the prices at which the Commodity Credit Corporation will make loans to farmers on these commodities as collateral. These loans are in effect purchases by the CCC if the price does not rise above the loan value, since there is no legal recourse against the farmer if the loan is not repaid. Such loans, therefore, set a lower limit to farm prices.

In past cycles agricultural prices and food prices in general usually dropped rapidly and gave the cycles some of their characteristics. With government control of some agricultural prices, this characteristic of the cycle has changed and past price-quantity interrelations have been altered.

While there has been some movement away from direct agricultural controls in recent years, the federal government has turned its policy attention to the areas of environmental controls, health and safety regulations, and the broad class of activities referred to as consumerism. Many of these activities have serious effects on the operations of business enterprise and in some cases have had significant impact on the overall performance of the economy.

We could continue to enumerate the points at which government impinges upon the operations of the different segments of the economy. This kind of government policy might be termed *structural economic policy*, since it alters the relationships among the basic units of the system. Increasingly the viewpoint has been growing that the government should not restrict its influence to structural policy, but should take as its responsibility the assurance that the level of total economic activity behaves in a desirable manner. We might refer to this kind of policy as *aggregative economic policy*. In this connection the role of the government includes full employment policy, anti-inflationary policy, economic growth policy, and a balance of payments policy. The tools used are monetary and fiscal policy. Part 7 is devoted to the study of these aggregative tools.

MAJOR TRENDS IN ECONOMIC ACTIVITY

The story of American economic development is one of dramatic growth in total output as a new continent was being populated and developed. It is also a story of increased output per capita and the development of many new goods and services to meet the needs and wants of consumers. This growth has not been continuous because it has been interrupted by many periods of decline in economic activity. Most of these have been short and mild, but several have been severe and protracted.

Economic activity from the end of the War of Independence to the present can be divided into several periods in which the factors at work were somewhat different from what they were in the period taken as a whole. The first such period runs from 1783 to the beginning of the Civil War in 1861. The Civil War marked a distinct political turning point in our history and in many phases of activity also an economic turning point.

The second period starts at the outbreak of the Civil War and ends at the beginning of World War I in Europe. It was a period of rapid growth in which manufacturing replaced agriculture as the dominant American industry. The end of the period has been set at 1914 because World War I had a pronounced influence on the American economy, especially in its relationships to the rest of the world, and also because the passage of the Federal Reserve Act in 1913 materially changed the nature of banking and credit in the American economic system.

The third period begins with the outbreak of World War I in Europe in 1914 and runs to the present. The American economy was affected by this war from its beginning, even though this country did not enter the war until fighting had gone on for several years. The economy of the world was so profoundly affected by World War I that it did not return to many prewar relationships.

From 1783 to 1861

The period from the end of the Revolutionary War in 1783 to the beginning of the Civil War in 1861 was one of rapid development on an extensive scale.

The population of the country grew rapidly and pushed westward past the Eastern mountain ranges to the Mississippi River and beyond.

When the first census of the United States was taken in 1790 the nation had a population of just under 4 million people. In each 10-year period from 1790 to 1860 population increased more than 30 percent.[4] Part of this population increase was due to natural growth in a new country; part of it to an increased life span that, according to the best estimates, increased 10 to 15 years during this period; and part of it to an influx of immigrants.[5] This rapidly growing population provided an expanding market for consumer goods and services.

The growth in population was not uniform in all sections of the country. Between 1790 and 1860 it was most rapid in the territory between the Alleghenies and the Mississippi River. The portion of this area north of the Ohio River had a rapid increase in population after the development of steamboat transportation on inland rivers and newly constructed canals in the period from 1825 to 1837. During this period migration westward began.

In the period ending in 1861 basic changes took place in the methods of producing goods. The factory system was begun shortly after the turn of the century. Textile factories were set up which for the first time combined all phases of spinning and weaving under one roof. The flour milling and leather industries made rapid strides, and there were beginnings of the canning and liquor industries. Advancement also took place in the iron industry with the replacement of charcoal by coke as blast furnace fuel.

A revolution occurred in agricultural technology during this period. In 1790 the average farmer did the work with a clumsy axe, a plow with a wooden moldboard, a wooden-toothed harrow, a hoe, a scythe, a sickle, and a flail. By the time of the Civil War the typical farmer in the northern states had a seed drill, a reaper, a mower, a portable thresher, a grist mill, and modern plows, cultivators, and harrows. The economy of the South was affected profoundly by the invention of the cotton gin by Eli Whitney in 1792. The use of the gin made it possible to handle large quantities of cotton, which almost immediately became the leading southern crop.

Far-reaching changes in transportation occurred before 1860. Early in the period road building went on at a rapid rate, so that by 1820 all the major cities in the eastern and northern states were connected by a fairly good system of surfaced roads.

Between 1800 and 1840 there was also a large amount of canal building. After the invention of the steamboat in 1807, there was rapid development of transportation on rivers. According to one estimate over 1,000 steamboats were built between 1830 and 1840.[6] Railroad development did not take place to any large extent until after 1835, but from that year on development took place rapidly, especially between 1850 and 1860.

Foreign trade was an important factor in the economy of this period since large quantities of raw materials were exported and many manufactured goods

---

[4] U.S. Dept. of Commerce, *Statistical Abstract of the United States: 1976* (Washington: U.S. Government Printing Office, 1976), p. 5.

[5] Harold F. Williamson (ed.), *The Growth of the American Economy* (New York: Prentice-Hall, Inc., 1947), p. 339.

[6] *Ibid.*, p. 180.

were bought from abroad. Trade was affected by wars that began in Europe before the turn of the century and that continued, with only brief periods of peace, until the final defeat of Napoleon by the English in 1814. The volume of trade in war goods increased materially despite some interference with our commerce by the warring powers. After the depression following this war, trade again increased substantially and continued to do so for the remainder of the period.

The fields in which income was produced shifted materially between 1799 and 1859. Whereas agriculture accounted for about 40 percent of total income in 1799, it accounted for 30 percent in 1859. Manufacturing increased its contribution from 5 to 12 percent during the same period. There was also a significant increase, from 5 to 12 percent, in income arising from trade. The same thing was true to a lesser degree of service income, which increased from 10 to 14 percent of total income from production of goods and services.[7]

The young country suffered through difficult times while evolving a banking system and a money supply process. Throughout most of the period the major problem was the instability of money. The country used a welter of coins, mainly the issues of foreign governments. Bimetalism was tried and failed because of establishing legal price ratios for gold and silver which were different from the market ratios and so first one, then the other was driven out of circulation. Congress simply didn't know how to create a currency and coin system that would work.

The history of banking prior to the Civil War was colorful. Two experiments with nationally chartered banks, The First Bank of the United States, (1791–1811) and the Second Bank of the United States (1816–1836), provided periods of some soundness, but state-chartered banking dominated the period. These state banks issued currency but much of it circulated at prices well below par, and some of it was worthless. Waves of bank failures occurred periodically.

The long-term trend of prices during this period was downward except for a period of inflation during and after the War of 1812. On the average prices were about one-third lower at the end of the period in 1860 than they were in 1800.[8]

Statistics on national income during this period are, of course, not too meaningful if they are to be used in comparison with more recent data, but one estimate gives per capita annual income in terms of 1926 prices at $216 in 1799 and $296 in 1859.[9] This is a 37 percent increase in 60 years.

From 1861 to 1914

The period from 1861 to 1914 was one of continued rapid growth in population and in total economic activity. It was a period in which manufacturing and trade increased rapidly and surpassed agriculture in their contributions to the total production of goods and services in the economy.

---

[7] Robert F. Martin, *National Income in the United States, 1799–1938* (New York: National Industrial Conference Board, 1939), p. 60.

[8] Jesse M. Cutts, "One Hundred and Thirty-Four Years of Wholesale Prices," *Monthly Labor Review* (July, 1935), p. 250.

[9] Martin, *op. cit.,* p. 6.

The rate of increase in population after 1860 was slower than it had been before that period, dropping to about 25 percent per decade until 1890 and 20 percent per decade between 1890 and 1910.[10] The westward movement of population was so rapid that by 1900 the frontier had all but disappeared. As a result, unemployment in the cities during depression periods became a more serious problem since, as long as free land had existed, many of the unemployed had moved to the West to begin life anew.

In 1859 agriculture accounted for 30 percent of the total realized private production income; by 1914 it had declined to 20 percent. Manufacturing became more important, increasing from 12 percent of the total to 21.5 percent, and trade increased from 12 percent to 20 percent.[11]

In 1860 the most important manufacturing industries were the production of flour and meal products, cotton goods, lumber, and boots and shoes. By 1914 the slaughtering and meat-packing industry was at the head of the list, iron and steel production were second, flour and mill production third, and foundry and machine shop production fourth.

Changes in agriculture that affected the whole economy took place during this period. In 1860 agriculture was based on the use of "cheap land," which could always be deserted for new land. By 1900 the frontier was gone and a period of intensive development of available land was begun. The development of machinery to harvest cereal crops, such as the combined harvester and thresher, made it possible to produce more food at a lower cost. It meant, however, that farming was becoming a business that required a high degree of managerial skill and sizable amounts of capital. Lowered costs and increased production also meant lower prices for farm products.

A major development in the field of transportation was the rapid growth of the railroad network. In 1860 there were 30,000 miles of railroad in the United States; by 1916 the railroad network had increased to 260,000 miles.

The volume of foreign trade increased significantly from 1860 to 1914, and its composition also changed. In 1860 agricultural products accounted for 80 percent of total exports and finished manufactures accounted for about 10 percent; by 1914 agricultural products constituted 40 percent of total exports and finished manufactures 30 percent.[12]

During the Civil War Congress passed legislation authorizing the establishment of banks with a national charter. These banks were permitted to issue bank notes, using government bonds as collateral. A tax was placed on state bank notes that drove them out of circulation and left national bank notes as the most important form of money except for small change. Since the debt of the federal government was not increasing, the volume of national bank notes was restricted by the amount of available government bonds for collateral. This led to a shortage of currency, especially in the fall of the year when crops were being marketed, and created problems in several depression periods.

[10] U.S. Department of Commerce, *Statistical Abstract of the United States: 1976* (Washington: U.S. Government Printing Office, 1976), p. 5.

[11] Martin, *op. cit.,* p. 60.

[12] Ernest L. Bogart and Donald L. Kemmerer, *Economic History of the American People* (New York: Longmans, Green & Co., Inc., 1943), p. 635.

The level of national income showed a decided rise during this period. In 1859 realized national income was $4.3 billion; by 1914 it had reached $31 billion, an increase of 626 percent. Measured in terms of constant dollars based on the 1926 cost of living, the increase was 508 percent. On the basis of the cost of living as it was in 1926, the 1859 per capita income was worth $296 and the per capita income of 1914 was worth $565, an increase of 91 percent.[13]

From 1914 to the Present

The period from 1914 to the present has been marked by wide variations in economic activity. The early years were boom years due to the demands for goods arising out of World War I. The decade of the 1920s was a period of boom and speculation, and that of the 1930s one of worldwide depression. This was followed by a new boom period during World War II and a period of prosperity during most of the 1940s, 1950s, and 1960s as international tensions and large-scale military expenditures continued. The first part of the 1970s was marked by problems of inflation, both at home and abroad, and a series of crises in the international money markets due to balance-of-payments problems in the United States and in some other major trading countries.

The rate of increase in population in this period has been slower than in the preceding periods, especially in the years before World War II. Between 1910 and 1920 population increased 15 percent and between 1920 and 1930, 16 percent, but in the decade of the 1930s only 7 percent.[14] In the 1940s population increased 15 percent and continued to increase in the 1950s at a somewhat faster rate, by 19 percent. The rate of increase slowed in the 1960s to 13 percent when the number of births started falling while the number of marriages increased. This pattern of a decreasing rate of population increase was still in evidence in the 1970s.

These changing birth-rate patterns changed the composition of the population by age groups. Before 1960 there were large increases in the age groups under 20 and little change in the age groups between 20 and 40. Between 1960 and 1965, the 15-to-25 age group increased most rapidly; and between 1965 and 1970, it was the 20-to-30 age group that showed the most significant rate of increase. The number of persons over 65 years of age increased faster than the total population during this entire period and especially after 1945.

The rapid increase in population after 1945, following the low birth rates of the 1930s, affected materially the economic situation in the 1950s. The large number of children demanded increases in children's products and housing. Schools also had to be expanded to take care of the large number of youngsters. At the same time the number of people entering the labor force was relatively small because of the abnormally low birth rates at the depth of the depression in the 1930s. This combination of a strong demand because of increased population and a relatively small addition to the labor force gave the economy underlying strength to help prevent prolonged unemployment.

---

[13] Martin, *op. cit.*, p. 6.
[14] *Statistical Abstract of the United States: 1976, op. cit.*, p. 5.

This situation changed somewhat during the 1960s. The number of persons of working age increased sharply in the mid-1960s as children born after the end of World War II reached age 18. An increasing proportion of these young people went to college, thus greatly increasing the demands upon the nation's colleges and universities. The number of new workers to be integrated into the labor force also increased materially in a period when the pool of executive and management talent in the age group of 35 to 50 was not increasing materially. The employment of teenage workers became a major economic challenge of the mid-1960s and early to mid-1970s.

The trends in manufacturing in this period continued in the same pattern as in the previous period. The rate of output of manufacturing industries increased rapidly when measured either in terms of absolute output or on a per capita basis. The trend toward large establishments also continued, and their efficiency increased because of scientific management and industrial research.

The period since the end of World War II has been marked by large-scale capital investment in almost all major industries. Automation has become a household word in our economy. In some fields, such as textiles and the production of automobile engines, factories have been established that use practically no direct labor in production. In those fields which have not gone so far in automation, there has also been a steady increase in the amount of work done by machines. From 1955 to 1970 output in manufacturing increased by about 70 percent, but employment increased by less than 16 percent. In mining, output also increased substantially and total employment decreased as more and more work was done by machinery.

The trend toward mechanization in agriculture also progressed at a faster rate in this period. The most significant development in the early part of this period was that of the gasoline tractor, which replaced horses and mules to draw farm machinery. Power machinery was also developed for harvesting and threshing. This mechanization reduced the amount of labor needed to produce farm products and freed labor for jobs in industry. Use of tractors and self-propelled machines also materially reduced the number of horses and mules on farms, and this reduction freed millions of acres used to raise animal feed for other crops.

Agricultural productivity increased even more rapidly in the post-World War II period than it did earlier. This rapid increase in productivity was due to the use of more and better machinery, fertilizers, and chemical weed killers, of improved seed, of scientifically developed feeds for farm animals, and the like. Between 1914 and 1970 the output per worker-hour of farm work more than tripled. About half of this increase in productivity occurred in the 10-year period from 1949 to 1958.[15]

A revolution in transportation also took place in the early part of this period with the development of the automobile. The automobile was a luxury for the few in 1914, but by 1929 over 5.6 million cars were sold. The automobile was brought into the price range of the middle-income group by the introduction of

---

[15] U.S. Department of Agriculture, *Agriculture Outlook Charts* (Washington: U.S. Government Printing Office, 1959), p. 65.

assembly-line production, which cut costs drastically. The airplane was developed as a major form of transportation in the late 1920s and early 1930s and continued to increase in importance throughout the remainder of the period, especially in the 1950s and 1960s with the development of jet planes.

The foreign trade of the United States increased rapidly and its composition changed materially during this period. In 1914 exports of goods and services were somewhat above $2 billion and they increased to almost $75 billion in 1972. The composition of exports also changed during this period. In 1914 agricultural products were more significant than manufactured goods, but by 1972 agricultural products were only about a fifth of the total of all merchandise exported.[16]

During the depression that began in 1929 the role of government increased markedly. The role of government also increased spectacularly during and after World War II. Federal government purchases of goods and services grew from $17 billion in 1941 to $133 billion in 1976. Even more spectacular was the growth in transfer payments (welfare, unemployment benefits, veterans' benefits, medical payments, etc.) from $2.6 billion in 1941 to $191 billion in 1976. State and local governments outdid the federal government, increasing their expenditures on goods and services from $8 billion in 1941 to $232 billion in 1976. With this growth in the outlays by governments, obviously taxes also had to become a more important consideration to the people and firms in the economy.[17]

The difficulties with the currency system led to the establishment of the Federal Reserve System in 1913. Provision was made for an elastic currency that would increase with the demands of industry and commerce. The total resources of the banking system increased materially during this period, but the number of banks decreased markedly.

One of the outstanding developments during this period was the growth in consumer credit, especially in installment financing of the sale of durable consumer goods. Such financing was begun before the turn of the century to finance the sale of sewing machines, pianos, books, and a few other types of goods, but it had not reached any sizable proportions by the time of World War I. It grew rapidly after the end of World War I as a method of financing the growing sales of automobiles and other consumer durables.

Wholesale prices experienced a rapid rise during World War I, a marked decline during the postwar depression that began in 1920, a period of stability during the 1920s, and another decline during the 1929 depression. Consumer prices increased gradually in the 1920s, then declined during the 1929 depression. They then increased gradually in the 1930s after reaching a depression low point in 1932. They increased somewhat during World War II and went up rapidly following the war before stabilizing in 1949. They increased again during the Korean War and continued to rise slowly through the remainder of the 1950s and the first half of the 1960s but began rising rapidly in the late 1960s and especially in the early 1970s when the government tried on- and off-again price controls.

---

[16] Bogart and Kemmerer, *op. cit.*, p. 803, and *Survey of Current Business* (July, 1973), p. 511.
[17] *Federal Reserve Bulletin* (April, 1973), pp. A68-A69; and (July, 1977), pp. A52-A53.

National income and personal income increased materially during this period. In dollars of constant purchasing power, based on the Department of Commerce price deflators using 1958 as 100, per capita personal income went up from an estimated figure of $1,065 in 1914 to $1,274 in 1929 and $3,650 in 1975.[18]

Gross national product increased from $38.6 billion in 1914 to $1,516 billion in 1975. Per capita GNP in terms of 1958 prices went up from $1,267 in 1914 to over $4,000 in 1975, an increase of over three times in this period of approximately 60 years.[19]

CHARACTERISTICS OF FIVE MAJOR DEPRESSIONS

The business cycles that have interrupted economic growth have varied widely in length and severity. The most frequent type of cycle is one that is about four years long and results in changes in the level of economic activity no more severe than those experienced in the post-World War II economy. Several cycles, however, have been much more severe than all others and have led to depressions which lasted for several years. Other cycles led to depressions which were less severe than the long, deep depressions, but were much more pronounced than the minor recessions in the post-World War II period. Five depression periods in our history stand out as being more severe than the others. These were the depressions following the Revolutionary War, the War of 1812, and those which began in 1837, 1873, and 1929. Each of these will be considered in turn, the last only briefly since it is covered in more detail in later chapters.

Post-Revolutionary War Depression

The first major depression began at the end of the Revolutionary War in 1783. It arose out of the events of the preceding years in which America successfully waged a war for independence.

Background and Character of the Depression. In 1783 the American economy was in an unsettled political and economic condition. It was necessary to shift from a wartime status under the Second Continental Congress to a peace-time government for the new nation. The economy suffered from the inflation of currency during the Revolutionary War, which was due in large measure to the issuance of paper money without backing of any kind. The use of depreciated paper money drove specie out of circulation and, as a result, trade had to be carried on in currency of doubtful value. The government of the United States was also heavily in debt to foreign countries and to citizens at home, and it found itself substantially in arrears in the payment of interest on the domestic debt. As a result, business activity declined substantially from wartime levels for a period of several years.

---

[18] *Long-Term Economic Growth 1860–1965* (Washington: U.S. Government Printing Office, 1966), pp. 218, 224, 225, 228; and *Survey of Current Business* (July, 1976).
[19] *Long-Term Economic Growth 1860–1965, op. cit.,* pp. 166, 167, 169; *Survey of Current Business* (June, 1971), p. S-1; and *Business Conditions Digest* (June, 1976).

This depression lasted until 1787 when recovery began in various sectors of the economy. Business remained in an unsettled state until the early 1790s when the new government provided for in the Constitution was firmly established and the financial situation stabilized. This first depression was different from all later depressions because of the almost complete collapse of former trade relationships and the breakdown of the financial system. In many ways it was a complete breakdown of the economy rather than a depression of the type experienced in later years.

Causes. The immediate cause of this depression was the ending of the Revolutionary War. The economy had been geared to the production of goods needed to carry on the war, and the demand for such goods suddenly ceased to exist. Conditions were much too unsettled to effect a smooth transition to the production of peacetime goods and, as a result, economic activity declined sharply.

Unsettled political conditions prevented normal economic development, but other serious problems existed, the most acute being an imbalance in foreign trade. During the colonial period a large part of our trade — both exports and imports — was with England. These trade relations were interrupted during the war and it was impossible to restore normal relations in the immediate postwar period. During 1784 and 1785 American merchants bought more goods from England than they were able to pay for. Before the war the colonists had exported large quantities of tobacco, bread, flour, dried fish, rice, and indigo to England. The war, however, practically destroyed the fishing industry, military operations in the Southern colonies destroyed a large part of the rice fields, and indigo could not be produced profitably without British subsidies that had been paid previously.

This serious imbalance of trade led first of all to an export of specie on a large scale. The loss of specie would normally have resulted in a rapidly declining price level and did in fact have this tendency. Several of the states, however, issued paper money to take the place of the vanishing specie. Since such paper money had no backing, there was some question about its value and prices in terms of it tended to increase.

Monetary problems were not the only problems in this period. New manufacturing industries, which had sprung up during the war, suffered serious losses because English merchants dumped excess goods into the United States at low prices in an attempt to win back American markets, which had been lost as a result of the war.

Depression Following the War of 1812

The second major depression was also related to an end of hostilities — this time the War of 1812. It likewise arose out of events in the preceding period of wartime boom.

Background and Character of the Depression. War in Europe affected the American economy during the first part of the 19th century. Business activity was at a high level as a result of sales of goods to England, France, and other warring powers, except during the period from 1807 to 1809 when the Embargo Act made it illegal for American vessels to sail to the ports of any foreign power.

The period during and shortly after the war was one of inflation and boom. The War of 1812 was financed to a large extent by borrowing and by the issuance of Treasury notes. The deficit of the government was large in each of the war years and in the first postwar year, 1815, resulting in an increase in money. The banking system also added to the flow of inflationary purchasing power. This period of inflation during the war was followed by a depression in 1815, when the inflationary pressure of war finance was removed. The depression was severe and protracted, from 1815 to 1822, and the economy remained at a fairly low level for two more years. This depression was accompanied by a period of financial chaos. Prices of commodities and securities dropped drastically and business failures were at a high level. This was due in part to the attempts of British merchants to flood the American market with cheap goods as they had done at the end of the Revolutionary War.

Causes. The immediate cause of the decline in business activity was the rapid decline in prices that occurred when wartime inflationary finance was halted. The economy, however, had more serious readjustments to make than the correction of imbalance due to inflation. Since the turn of the century, business had been geared to European wartime purchases. Peace was finally achieved in Europe in 1814, and the American economy had to readjust to a new pattern of production based on peacetime demands for goods. The war demands had lasted for over 15 years, and the economic system had become adjusted to such a pattern.

Depression of 1837

The third major depression was not related to the cessation of wartime activities as were the first two. It occurred during a period of rapid development in the economy and interrupted that development for several years.

Background and Character of the Depression. The depression which began in 1837 was the result of activities in the economy during the 1820s and 1830s. Especially significant was the inflation of the money supply that took place because of President Andrew Jackson's action in regard to the Second Bank of the United States. Jackson vetoed the bill to renew the charter of this bank and made it an issue in the campaign of 1832. Since he was reelected, he decided that the people had voted against the bank and began to remove the deposits of the United States government from it. As a result, the bank was forced to contract its loans and a panic developed in 1833. After the bank had adjusted to the loss of government deposits and these federal funds were deposited in other banks, the money shortage was relieved. The government placed its funds in state banks that were friendly to the administration and this action gave them the basis for issuing additional paper money.

The increase in the number of banks and in bank-note circulation helped cause the inflation of the period, but that inflation was also in part the result of speculative development in many parts of the economy as internal improvements were constructed at a rapid rate. Expenditures by the federal government on roads and canals were increased materially, especially after 1832. New York led in this development with the construction of the Erie Canal, which cost over $10 million, and a series of other canals, which cost almost as much. Massachusetts, Pennsylvania, and South Carolina were among the other states that spent large sums on internal improvements. The building of canals and turnpikes opened up new land for development, which in turn led to large-scale land speculation. Deposit of the receipts from the sale of public lands in banks in the western states provided the reserves for a further inflation of the money supply and thus reinforced the speculative boom.

The depression that began in 1837 was one of the most severe in our history. Unemployment was extensive and business failures were numerous. Prices dropped disastrously and this added to the panic of the period. Cotton, for example, fell from 20 cents a pound to 10 cents, causing some of the largest financial institutions in New Orleans, as well as some large plantation owners, to fail. In all, over 600 banks failed during the 1837 depression.[20] With the resumption of specie payments by most banks in the latter half of 1838, business revived somewhat; but it collapsed completely with the failure of the Bank of the United States, which had been rechartered with a Pennsylvania charter.

Causes. The immediate factor that led to the end of the speculation in land and to the end of the boom was the issuance by President Jackson in July, 1836, of his now famous "specie circular," which required that all public land had to be paid for in specie rather than in the notes of state banks. The resulting demand for specie restricted the operations of the western banks and led to a good deal of opposition; but despite pressure on President Van Buren, who succeeded Jackson, the order was allowed to stand.

Another source of difficulty was the transfer of funds of the federal government from one section of the country to another when Congress voted to deposit with the several states part of the surplus that had developed from the sale of public land. The resultant scarcity of money in those sections of the country from which funds were withdrawn necessitated the suspension of specie payments by New York banks and by banks in many other cities.

The situation was further aggravated because credit had been created in large amounts by privately owned banks chartered on a basis of political favoritism. The banks issued notes with little or no backing and, at least in the West, with little regard to the needs of business. The result was again a period of inflation followed by one of deflation.

The immediate cause of the depression of 1837 is to be found in the financial situation. The severe nature of this depression cannot be accounted for, however, by the financial situation. It was due in large measure to the nature of the economic development in the 1820s and 1830s. Canals were constructed at a rapid rate, and transportation was also developed on all important rivers. This was made possible by the development of the steamboat and the rapid building

---

[20] Bogart and Kemmerer, *op. cit.,* p. 369.

of such boats to haul freight and passengers. These changes made it possible to settle new areas rapidly and led to the large-scale development of western areas, which created a demand for new houses and also for new towns and cities with all of their facilities.

Additional production capacity was needed to build steamboats and the equipment needed to make them run. This created a demand for more iron and steel and more machine tools. Plants and equipment were also needed to meet the demands of the construction industry for materials to build houses and other buildings.

By 1837 this phase of economic activity had run its course. Canals had been built wherever it was feasible in the northern part of the country, and a few were also built in the South. Most of them did not turn out to be profitable ventures, and this slowed down new building. Some railroads had been built and had sufficiently demonstrated their capacity so that enthusiasm for more canal projects was dampened.

After this burst of development, the economy had to adjust itself to a less spectacular form of growth. The long depression was due to the readjustment from an economic pattern geared to the rapid development of the northern part of the country west to the Mississippi to one based on the more gradual growth of population and real income.

Depression of 1873

The fourth major depression was similar in some respects to the one which began in 1837. It too occurred during a period of rapid development in the economy and interrupted such development for almost six years.

Background and Character of the Depression. A financial crisis began in the fall of 1873, when several important financial institutions were forced to suspend operations. The first of these was the New York Warehouse and Security Company, which was organized to make advances on grain but which had been persuaded to tie up its funds in financing the Missouri, Kansas, and Texas Railroad. Several large brokerage firms failed in the next few days, and these failures led to a rapid recall of loans by the banks. To meet these demands to repay loans, investment houses attempted to sell stocks to obtain cash to pay the banks and these sales broke the price of securities. On Saturday of the crisis week several of the large banks and trust companies were forced to suspend operations, and before the day was over stock prices were declining so rapidly that the stock exchange was closed.

The depression that followed this panic was long and severe. Business declined until the middle of 1879, a period of almost six years. This is the longest period of contraction in any cycle in American history. Business failures were not as spectacular during the downturn as they were during the panic, but they increased slowly year by year. Unemployment also increased and became a serious problem, especially in the industrial centers in the eastern part of the country. Prices declined steadily until they were at much lower levels than in 1873 and this led to distress in agricultural communities.

Causes. The financial crisis of 1873 was due in part to unsound commitments by the financial institutions and also in part to the operation of the money and banking system of that period. The banks had not engaged in any large-scale credit expansion before 1873 nor were their reserves unusually low. One of the factors leading to the financial crisis was the concentration of deposits from a large number of banks in seven large New York banks. Under the National Banking Act, national banks were required to keep a set percentage of reserves against deposits and could keep part of them in other banks. Between 70 and 80 percent of these deposits were concentrated in seven large New York banks. There was normally a demand for funds late in the fall to meet the needs of the crop-moving period. As a result of this demand, these seven banks had a sizable deficiency in the required 25 percent reserve of legal tender notes and specie against their deposits by mid-September of 1873. They were forced to call in some of their loans to meet reserve requirements. This happened at the same time that several brokerage houses failed and banks called in loans in this field. A financial panic and runs on the banks followed, and they were forced to suspend specie payments. Despite the financial panic and the suspension of specie payment, most of the national banks were sound since only a few of them failed during this period.

The basic cause of the 1873 depression was the overexpansion of the preceding period, especially in railroads. The years from 1868 to 1872 witnessed extraordinarily rapid growth, especially in the upper Mississippi valley.

The real cause for the decline was the completion of most of the railroad network that could be operated profitably at this time. The eastern part of the country had fairly adequate railroad coverage. There was still room for development, especially west of the Mississippi River; but railroads in this area found it difficult to operate profitably without being tied in with the eastern network of railroads. The lack of bridges across the Mississippi River made this impracticable. It was not until several years later that such bridges were successfully built and business increased sufficiently to resume profitable railroad development in the western part of the country.

Depression of 1929

The 1929 depression will be covered in some detail in Chapters 11 and 14. Its nature is similar in many respects to the earlier major depressions. Business declined from 1929 to 1933 and less than full employment levels persisted throughout the 1930s. Industrial production dropped 50 percent and employment 25 percent. The basic causes of this depression are to be found on both the international and domestic scenes. Attempts during the 1920s to reestablish some of the pre-World War I economic relationships, especially in the monetary area, proved unsuccessful. Financial and trade problems arising out of the war were not solved successfully, and as a result international trade collapsed during the depression.

On the domestic scene a major shift in production patterns took place during the 1920s due to the rapid development of several new industries, especially the mass production of automobiles. The general use of the automobile for transportation changed living and shopping habits. Other consumer durable goods were also developed during this period, especially electrical appliances such as refrigerators and radios. The electric utility industry also experienced rapid growth in the 1920s. By 1929 the automobile had become a standard part of the living pattern of middle-income families, and the rapid developments accompanying its introduction slowed down. The shift to a new pattern based on more intensive development of needs and resources rather than on the rapid expansion of major new industries was made slowly.

Summary of the Major Depressions

The study of the causal factors at work in major cycles shows that protracted depressions have occurred at the time of a basic shift in the nature of capital investment in the economy. A long depression followed the end of the Revolutionary War when a shift had to be made not only from a wartime economy to a peacetime economy, but also from an economy of a colony dependent on England to one of an independent nation with no assured markets or sources of raw materials not available at home. A long depression followed the War of 1812 as the economy of the United States and of the world shifted from a protracted period of war to one of relative peace. The depression that began in 1837 was severe and prolonged because a rapid period of development based on canals and the steamboat had been completed. In 1873 the railroad network had been largely completed in the portion of the country east of the Mississippi River, and it took some time to cross this natural barrier and resume railroad building. In 1929 a large part of the capital investment needed to make the automobile and some electrical appliances a part of the American way of life had been committed, and it took time to develop a new pattern of investment. Therefore, a study of the current investment pattern and of the trends in the major areas making it up is an integral part of any analysis of current business conditions and future prospects.

QUESTIONS

1. How would the susceptibility to business fluctuations differ in an economy such as ours where consumer freedom of choice exists as contrasted to a controlled economy where the state decides what commodities the people will get?
2. The level of employment and unemployment can be affected by structural economic policy and by aggregate economic policy. Under what conditions would you expect each of these policies to be most effective?
3. Discuss the trend of prices from 1783 to the present. Does this record of prices substantiate the proposition that prosperity can only take place when the price level is rising?
4. Describe the changes in the sources of production income by industries between 1800 and the present. How were changes in manufacturing, agriculture, transportation, banking, foreign trade, employment, and productivity related to such changes?

5. (a) Why was there a protracted depression after the end of the Revolutionary War?
   (b) How did this depression differ from all later depressions?
6. (a) What caused a long and severe depression after the end of the War of 1812?
   (b) How was it related to the development of the economy in the 15 years preceding the war?
7. (a) What was the immediate cause of a downturn in business in 1837?
   (b) What basic causal factors were at work?
8. Why was the depression following 1837 one of the most severe in our history?
9. In what respects were the depressions that began in 1815 and 1837 due to similar causal factors?
10. Describe the immediate and basic causal factors at work in the 1873 depression.
11. Why was the depression which began in 1929 a long and severe one?

SUGGESTED READINGS

Bretzfelder, Robert B. "Variations in National Output." *Survey of Current Business* (November, 1960), pp. 14–20.

Cole, A. H. "Statistical Background of the Crisis of 1857." *Review of Economic Statistics,* XII (November, 1930), pp. 170–80.

Dewey, Davis Rich. *Financial History of the United States.* New York: Longmans, Green & Co., Inc., 1931. Chapters 12–21 inclusive.

Frickey, Edwin. *Production in the United States, 1860–1914.* Cambridge: Harvard University Press, 1947.

Hyndman, H. M. *Commercial Crises of the Nineteenth Century.* London: Swan Sonnenschein & Co., 1902.

Kuznets, Simon. *Modern Economic Growth: Rate, Structure, and Spread.* New Haven: Yale University Press, 1966.

McGrane, Reginald Charles. *The Panic of 1837.* Chicago: University of Chicago Press, 1924.

Mitchell, Wesley Clair. *A History of the Greenbacks.* Chicago: University of Chicago Press, 1903.

Rezneck, S. "Distress, Relief, and Discontent in the United States during the Depression of 1873–78." *Journal of Political Economy,* LVIII (December, 1950), pp. 494–512.

Smith, Walter Buckingham, and Arthur Harrison Cole. *Fluctuations in American Business, 1790–1860.* Cambridge: Harvard University Press, 1935.

Sprague, O. M. W. *History of Crises under the National Banking System.* Washington: U.S. Government Printing Office, 1910.

Stigler, George J. *Trends in Output and Employment.* New York: National Bureau of Economic Research, 1947.

CHAPTER 3

AGGREGATE ECONOMIC CONCEPTS AND MEASUREMENTS

In this chapter we discuss the meanings of the most important terms and concepts used in aggregative economics, the interrelationships among them, and the statistical approximations which have been developed to measure them. The most fundamental of these terms which are subject to misunderstanding are wealth, income, production, consumption, saving, investment, capital, and profit.

It is worth considerable effort to understand the meaning of these terms, since a great deal of confusion and disagreement have, as their source, different understandings of what a particular term involves. It would be very easy to give a half dozen different concepts embodied in such words as capital, consumption, saving, profit, and many other words that belong in the popular domain and are used by economists. Since each of these concepts represents a significant feature of economic behavior, they need to be incorporated in our analysis. We should use qualifying adjectives or explain which notion we have in mind, and we often do, but frequently we simply hope that the concept intended is clear from its context.

One of the serious stumbling blocks in the understanding of economic relationships is the confusion between flow variables and stock variables. In popular discourse this distinction is often glossed over, but in the study of economics it should not be. For instance, the word "investment" to an economist is strictly a flow, and the associated stock is called wealth or capital. A flow variable can be measured only over a period of time, while a stock variable can be measured only at a point in time. Similarly, saving is an act that can be performed only over a period of time. The associated stock that results from saving is popularly called savings. A better practice would be to refer to the accumulated stock simply as assets.

In national income analysis, as in most of economics, there is usually a difference between the definition of a term designed to permit its measurement and the definition designed for purely analytical purposes. For example, the idea of consumption has been the "using up" of goods and services, or the destruction of utility or value. Since this notion is measurable only in the aggregate, we usually find it expedient to define consumption as purchases by households for current use. Sometimes the two definitions are very close, but under other conditions they diverge so much that if a person's analysis is based upon the one idea and the empirical evidence is based upon the other idea, that person may be seriously misled. The definition of consumption as the destruction of value implies that it would be desirable to minimize consumption. However, there is the other side of consumption, which is the receipt of utility by the consumers. Also, the goal of the economy, of course, is to maximize the utility of its people.

Another source of difficulty is that economics deals with transactions and every transaction is two-sided — the buyer's and the seller's. Sometimes our terms put the emphasis on the one side, and it is forgotten that forces are also operative on the other side. For this reason newspapers frequently report a wave of selling on the stock exchange and ignore the "wave" of buying that is necessarily taking place simultaneously.

A long debate over the equality of saving and investment culminated in the warning of the necessity of distinguishing between planned or intended magnitudes on the one hand and actual or measured magnitudes on the other. It is always necessary to be clear in discussion and analysis whether one is referring to planned magnitudes, which are usually of most interest but difficult, if not impossible, to measure, and actual magnitudes, which are usually of less interest, but are measurable.

CONCEPTS OF PRODUCTION, INCOME, CONSUMPTION, SAVING, AND INVESTMENT

In this section we will look first at the most fundamental meaning of these terms. *Production* is the creation of value. Thus, any activity that results in someone being willing to pay more for a good or service than the value of the materials used has produced something. Defined in this way, production is the same thing as income, since all the value created must be allocated or distributed to someone. Under capitalistic principles, the rule is that the income will be distributed to the factors of production responsible for the production. In a complex process this is difficult to achieve, but we have a large body of thought, called income distribution theory, which attempts to explain this allocative process. It is customary to use the income categories of wages, rent, interest, and profit, even though a rigorous theoretical division of them is not possible. From the point of view of the business sector, wages, rent, and interest are elements of cost, and profit is a pure residual between total revenues from the sale of goods and services and contractual costs. From the factor-owner side, wages are the payment for human services; and rent, interest, and profit are derived from the provision of the services of property.

In the aggregate, *income* is the amount of goods and services that could be consumed during a period of time, leaving the stock of wealth of the society at the end of the period the same as it was at the beginning.[1] From this it follows that income is equal to consumption plus capital accumulation, where *consumption* is defined as the destruction of value; and *investment,* or capital accumulation, is the act of adding to the stock of capital or wealth. *Saving* is the process of not consuming as much as was produced during the time period.

Now, if we let Y stand for national income, which we have said is equal to aggregate production, and let C stand for consumption, or destruction of value, the difference between them is what was produced and not destroyed. The result of destroying less than the amount produced is an increase in the stock of physical goods. This is what we defined to be investment, which we label I. But by definition this is also saving, S, since it is the amount by which income exceeds consumption. Therefore, $Y \equiv C + I$ and $Y \equiv C + S$, or $I \equiv Y - C$, $S \equiv Y - C$, and $I \equiv S$.

We should keep in mind that these fundamental notions are what we are really interested in, since questions of economic welfare, growth possibilities, and so on must be evaluated in these real terms. There are some analytical and statistical reasons for using approximations to these concepts, however. Consumption, for example, cannot be accurately measured so we use, as a close estimate of it, expenditures on consumer goods. The difficulty here is to define *consumer goods,* and we do this by including all goods purchased by households that are normally destroyed during the period in which we are interested. Likewise, we can't tell what part of the expenditures of government add to the society's wealth and what part are currently consumed for present utility. In this case we devote our attention simply to government expenditures *in toto.* Expenditures by business units on capital account becomes our measure of investment.

Production

In the study of the business firm, we are used to thinking of production as simply the output to be sold. But in the aggregate economy, we are interested in the output of all the firms. It would be serious multiple counting if the sales of all firms were simply added up, since the output of any single firm will necessarily include the value of the output of other firms which were used as intermediate goods. It also can occur that the goods and services sold in the current period were produced in an earlier period and therefore should not be counted as part of current production.

Production is defined as the creation of value (or utility) during a specified time period. The *value added* of a particular producing unit is the value of its sales minus the purchases from other firms, minus any decrease in inventory or capital depreciation during the period of measurement. Notice that our

---

[1] This notion of income is discussed in J. R. Hicks, *Value and Capital* (2d ed.; London: Oxford University Press, 1946), Ch. XIV.

definition of production makes no reference to the physical processes. Much production does involve a physical conversion in which the final product may have little resemblance to the raw materials, as is the case in manufacturing and agriculture. But production takes place even when no physical or tangible commodity is involved. For example, by increasing the demand for the product and hence its price or value measure, advertising can create value or utility. So can crop storage, the holding of art works, making music, or transporting goods.

The sum of all of the values added in all of the producing units of the economy equals the net output or production of that economy. That same total can be found by ignoring all of the intermediate production steps and counting only the "final" product values. By *final goods* we mean those which will not be resold nor will be embodied in other goods or services. This is required to avoid double counting.

The measure of the amount of final goods can be taken from the side of the sellers or from the side of the buyers. The buyers are classified into sectors called households, governments, business, or the rest of the world; i.e., buyers located in other economies. The expenditures by these four sectors are called, respectively, consumption, government expenditures, investment, and net foreign exports.

Income

We stated earlier that production and income are equal to each other since income is defined as the earnings of the factors of production for their contribution to current production. An individual may think of his or her income as simply the inflow of funds, but it must be remembered that our concern here is with the income of the aggregate of all individuals. Thus, the receipt of any funds which are not associated with production in the current time period will not be counted. For example, a person who receives a gift, gambling winnings, an inheritance, a welfare benefit, stock market gains, proceeds from a robbery, etc., may think of those funds as income, but in each case the income of someone else is reduced by the same amount so that no net income is involved. These are all examples of what are called "transfer payments." On the opposite side of the issue, an individual may not think of the services received from living in an owner-occupied home, food taken from the garden or farm, the services of a refrigerator or automobile, or the value of a do-it-yourself project, etc., as income; but they are. Since they are not money receipts they are called "income in kind." Notice that in these and in all other cases, income and production are simultaneous occurrences.

NATIONAL INCOME ACCOUNTING VERSUS BUSINESS ACCOUNTING

A system of accounting is necessary to understand fully the nature and extent of changes that take place in aggregative economic activity. Such a system was developed by the National Bureau of Economic Research and is now under the National Income Division of the United States Department of Commerce, Bureau of Economic Analysis (BEA). Data on national income and related items are published regularly in the *Survey of Current Business*. These data, which give a complete and reliable record of events in the American economy, are available for 1929 to the present.

The basic principles on which national income accounting is based are similar to those used in accounting for an individual business. At the present time the only data that are available regularly on a national basis are income data, since no detailed balance sheet for the total economy is regularly prepared. Furthermore, since information on many phases of economic activity is not available in income statement form, national income figures are developed by estimating some of the items used.

The form in which national income data are presented is different, however, from that used in reporting business income. The usual income statement of a firm begins with a statement of gross sales from which expenses of various types are subtracted to arrive at the net profit or loss. Such a statement is illustrated in Table 3-1. This form of the income statement can be revised somewhat to show the identity between current receipts from sales on one side and the allocations of these receipts on the other side. An income statement so revised is shown in Table 3-2.

Table 3-1
Income Statement of the ABC Corporation for 1978

Sales		$35,000,000
Less Cost of Goods Sold		15,000,000
Gross Profit		$20,000,000
Wages and Salaries	$9,000,000	
Social Security Taxes	500,000	
Taxes, Other than Income	1,000,000	
Depreciation	1,000,000	
Interest	500,000	
		12,000,000
Net Income before Taxes		$ 8,000,000
Income Taxes		2,400,000
Net Income after Taxes		$ 5,600,000
Dividends Paid		2,000,000
Added to Retained Earnings		$ 3,600,000

Production, i.e., value added, in this firm is its sales ($35,000,000) minus its purchases from other firms ($15,000,000) minus depreciation ($1,000,000), which equals $19,000,000. The earnings or income of the individuals supplying factor services to the firm are also $19,000,000: wages and salaries,

Table 3-2
Income Statement for the ABC Corporation for 1978

Allocations of Sales Receipts		Receipts from Sales	
Goods and materials purchased from other firms	$15,000,000	Sales to Co. A	$ 5,000,000
Wages and salaries	9,000,000	Sales to Co. B	10,000,000
Social security taxes	500,000	Sales to Co. C	15,000,000
Taxes, other than income	1,000,000	Sales to other	
Depreciation	1,000,000	companies	5,000,000
Interest	500,000		
Corporate profit taxes	2,400,000		
Dividends	2,000,000		
Undistributed profits	3,600,000		
	$35,000,000		$35,000,000

$9,000,000; Social Security taxes, $500,000; taxes, other than income, $1,000,000; interest, $500,000; corporate profits taxes, $2,400,000; dividends, $2,000,000; and undistributed profits, $3,600,000. The tax amounts and the undistributed profits are included because these amounts have been earned, even though they have not been received by the factor owners.

An income—expenditures—production statement can be visualized for the economic system by aggregating the information found in the statements of all the producing units. Table 3-3 is such a (simplified) consolidated statement. Notice that sales of intermediate goods and services among firms have been cancelled from both sides of this statement except for that portion which is added to the stock of capital or inventory.

Table 3-3
Consolidated Income-Expenditures-Production Statement

Uses	*Sources*
Wages	Sales to households = Consumption
Rent	Sales to governments = Government expenditures
Interest	(Net) Sales to the rest of the world = Exports minus imports
Profit (includes capital consumption allowance)	Sales to business units on capital account plus increase in inventory = Investment (including replacement expenditures)
INCOME = EXPENDITURES	

The right half of the statement measures the total production in the economy during a period of time by measuring final sales. The Department of Commerce publishes its estimates of these magnitudes in the form shown in Table 3-4. The total is called the *gross national product* (GNP).

Table 3-4

Sources of GNP, 1976
(In Billions of Dollars)

Personal consumption expenditures	**1,094.0**
Durable goods	158.9
Nondurable goods	442.7
Services	492.3
Gross private domestic investment	**243.3**
Fixed investment	230.0
Nonresidential	161.9
Structures	55.8
Producers' durable equipment	106.1
Residential	68.0
Change in business inventories	13.3
Net exports of goods and services	**7.8**
Exports	162.9
Imports	155.1
Government purchases of goods and services	**361.4**
Federal	130.1
National defense	86.8
Nondefense	43.3
State and local	231.2
GROSS NATIONAL PRODUCT	**1,706.5**

Source: *Survey of Current Business* (July, 1977), p. 16.

Sources of GNP—Definitions

Since forecasts of aggregate economic activity are frequently made by estimating gross national product from the sales or sources side of the statement, it is desirable to define each of these terms more precisely.

Personal consumption expenditures, as the term is used in national income accounting, consist of the purchases of goods and services at market value by individuals and nonprofit institutions and the value of food, clothing, housing, and financial services received as income in kind. They do not include the purchase of dwelling units, which are classified as capital goods, but do include an estimate of the rental value of owner-occupied houses.

Gross private domestic investment includes capital goods that are newly produced by private business and nonprofit institutions; all private new dwellings including those acquired by owner occupants; commissions arising in the sale and purchase of new and existing fixed assets, principally real estate; and the value of the change in the volume of inventories held by business.

Net exports of goods and services are the net differences between exports and imports of goods and services that have taken place in international transactions, excluding transfers under military grants. They measure the excess of exports of goods and services over imports of goods and services, net transfer payments from the United States government to foreigners, and net personal transfer payments to foreigners.

Government purchases of goods and services consist of the net purchases of goods and services by governmental bodies, except the acquisition of land and the current outlays of government enterprises.[2] Thus, this item consists of general governmental expenditures for the compensation of employees, purchases from business (net of sales by government of consumption goods and materials), net government purchases from abroad, and the gross investment of government enterprises. It excludes transfer payments. It also excludes government interest, subsidies to business, loans, and other financial transfers. These items are excluded because they do not represent payments to the factors of production for current production. Government interest payments are put into this category because most government debt has arisen out of war expenditures that are not, in the usual meaning of the word, productive. Private interest payments are included in the selling price of goods because they are one of the costs involved, representing a payment to capital used in production, and, therefore, they are included in the total of government purchases of goods and services.

Charges Against GNP—Definitions

The left half of Table 3-3 represents charges against GNP in that these payments to factor owners constitute the charges or costs of producing the goods sold on the right-hand side. These charges from the point of view of the people of the economy are their incomes. The Department of Commerce reports these estimates in the form shown in Table 3-5.

Most of the factor payments making up the national income categories are self-evident, but additional comments on some of them may be in order.

---

[2] The purchase of land is excluded since it is a national resource on which productive resources were not expanded. The current outlays of government enterprises are excluded since these do not involve purchases of goods but payments to the factors of production to produce goods and services sold to consumers. The value of these goods and services is included at the time of sale.

Table 3-5

Uses of GNP, 1976
(In billions of dollars)

Compensation of employees	**1,036.3**
Wages and salaries	891.8
Disbursements	891.8
Wage accruals less disbursements	.0
Supplements to wages and salaries	144.5
Employer contributions for social insurance	68.6
Other labor income	75.9
Proprietors' income with inventory valuation and capital consumption adjustments	**88.0**
Rental income of persons with capital consumption adjustment	**23.3**
Corporate profits with inventory valuation and capital consumption adjustments	**128.1**
Profits before tax	156.9
Profits tax liability	64.7
Profits after tax	92.1
Dividends	35.8
Undistributed profits	56.4
Inventory valuation adjustment	−14.1
Capital consumption adjustment	−14.7
Net interest	**88.4**
NATIONAL INCOME	**1,364.1**
Business transfer payments	8.1
Indirect business tax and nontax liability	150.5
Less: Subsidies less current surplus of government enterprises	.8
Statistical discrepancy	5.5
CHARGES AGAINST NET NATIONAL PRODUCT	**1,527.4**
Capital consumption allowances with capital consumption adjustment	179.1
CHARGES AGAINST GROSS NATIONAL PRODUCT	**1,706.5**

Source: *Survey of Current Business* (July, 1977), p. 16.

As the term is used in national income accounting, *supplements to wages and salaries* include such items as employer contributions for social insurance, contributions to private pension and welfare funds, compensation for injuries, doctors' fees, pay for the military reserve, and a few other minor items.

    Proprietor's income in unincorporated businesses is shown as one sum, since it is not ordinarily broken down on the books of such enterprises into wages of management, rent, interest, and profit. An inventory valuation adjustment is made in arriving at the income figure for this sector of the business community. Such an adjustment is necessary because, under most accounting systems, profits are taken inclusive of inventory profits or losses because of price changes, whereas only the value of the change in the physical quantity of inventories is considered in national income accounting.

The *rental income of persons* consists of the monetary earnings from the rental of real property, the imputed net rentals to owner occupants of nonfarm dwellings, and the royalties received from patents, copyrights, and rights to natural resources.

Corporate profits are measured without a deduction for depletion charges and exclusive of capital gains and losses, neither of which is related to the production of goods and services. Intercorporate profits are eliminated and the net receipts of dividends and profits from branches abroad are added. An inventory valuation adjustment is also made for corporations. It includes the profits of stock life insurance companies and of mutual financial institutions.

Net interest includes all interest accruing to the nation's residents except interest payments from the government and interest paid by consumers. Such payments are not included in the concept of national income because they do not add to the value of goods and services, since most government debt has arisen out of military expenditures and consumer expenditures are not considered productive. An item of imputed interest is added, which consists of the value of financial services received by individuals from banks and other financial institutions that render financial services free of charge rather than pay interest on balances on deposit and make specific charges for services rendered. Also included is imputed interest on reserves held for individuals by life insurance companies and similar financial intermediaries.

It was argued above that aggregate production is identically equal to aggregate income, but in Table 3-5 it is seen that what the Department of Commerce calls gross national product is significantly greater than what it calls national income (by some $342.4 billion). An explanation is called for. First, GNP is a larger concept than our definition of aggregate production because it includes all production of plant and equipment without subtracting the amount of plant and equipment destroyed in the production process during the year. To the extent that capital is destroyed in producing goods and services, the value of the capital has been transferred, so to speak, to the produced goods. That amount of value was not produced during the year in question. For example, if a farmer harvests 1,000 bushels of corn after having planted ten bushels of corn, the production of corn during the year would be 990 bushels. Likewise, if 100 lathes are worn out in producing widgets this year and 100 new lathes are produced during the year, total production should be just the value of the widgets.

Net national product is GNP minus *capital consumption allowances.* Net national product comes closer to our notion of aggregate production, but has the shortcoming of depending on a very crude approximation of depreciation or capital consumption. The figure for capital consumption allowances is not necessarily very close to the true amount of capital consumption. So while

NNP (net national product) is a better welfare concept, GNP is more accurately measurable. Another reason for the greater popularity of the GNP figure is the belief that it may be more closely related to employment demand than is NNP, though this is not necessarily so.

NATIONAL INCOME

GNP and NNP are estimates of aggregate production or income valued at *market prices*. The accounting term *national income* is an estimate of the aggregate output or income valued at *factor prices*. This income concept focuses on income earned in producing current output, as opposed to income received, be it disposable or any other criteria.

Again referring back to Table 3-5, it can be seen that there is a quantitative difference between net national product and national income. This too needs explanation, and the clue is that NNP (and GNP) are measured at output prices and national income is measured at input prices.

Since the data is gathered from different sources and from a different perspective, one would expect a *statistical discrepancy*—and there always is. However, the substantive reasons for the difference between NNP and national income are accounted for by the existence of *business transfer payments, indirect business taxes and nontax liabilities,* and *subsidies less current surplus of government enterprises.*

Business Transfer Payments

Receipts from business firms to individuals for which the recipient has made no contribution to current production are called business transfer payments. Examples are pensions to retired employees, scholarships, robberies, bad debts, gifts, etc. The value of these payments are covered by the revenues of the firms, so they are included in the price of the product and therefore are also included in the calculation of NNP. However, they are not a part of national income since the owners of the factors of production were not compensated to the extent of the transfer payment.

Indirect Business Taxes and Nontax Liabilities

Those taxes or fees paid to governments which are assumed to affect the price of the product are indirect business taxes. Included in this category are sales taxes, excise taxes, property taxes, license fees, fines, etc. (Income or corporate profit taxes are direct taxes and it is assumed that they do not effect the price of the product.) Since indirect business taxes are included in the price of the product, the NNP is affected. However, no factor owners receive income from this portion of the value of the product, so indirect business taxes are subtracted from NNP to arrive at national income. For example, if a package of cigarettes retails for 60 cents, the value of the product (NNP) is 60 cents, but if the sales and exise taxes are 40 cents, the suppliers of services and materials to the cigarette industry would earn only 20 cents (national income) per pack.

Subsidies Less Current Surplus of Government Enterprises

A subsidy is a payment by government to producers, whereas a transfer payment is a payment to non-producers. With a subsidy, income earned in the production process is greater than the value of the product produced. For example, suppose the market price of peanuts is ten dollars per bushel and the farmer is paid a one dollar subsidy per bushel. The farm income from the production of one bushel of peanuts is $11 (national income) but the value of the output is just $10 (NNP). Thus, subsidies are added to NNP to arrive at national income.

The surpluses of government enterprises are combined with subsidies in the national income accounts because they are, in a sense, opposites. A good example is the Tennessee Valley Authority (TVA) and the sale of electricity. The electricity is sold at its market value, but the income earned in its production is only wage income. The TVA does not pay interest, rent, or profit to the public. The difference between the TVA's receipts from the sale of electricity and its wage bill and payments to other firms is absorbed by the U.S. government. Thus, the surplus of government enterprises is subtracted from NNP to arrive at national income.

PERSONAL INCOME

For some purposes, a somewhat different concept of income than the one we have been using is of value. This concept, called *personal income* by the Department of Commerce, is described as income received by households. Recall that national income is income earned in current production. This means that personal income differs from national income to the extent that some income received by households is not earned in production during the current time period, but some income earned is not received. The items included by the Department of Commerce which are earned in current production (and therefore included in national income, NNP, and GNP) but not received by households are as follows: (1) *Contributions for social insurance* by both employers and employees are considered to have been earned by workers, but none of those earnings are received by the households. (2) Similarly, *wages accrued* (earned) during the current year but not paid during the current year are deducted from national income. This would arise, for example, if the last day of the year would fall on Thursday and payday would be on Friday, or if there were a payments lag such that paychecks were based on income earned in the week or month preceding the current one. On the other hand, at the beginning of the year the opposite situation would arise, so that this circumstance is always a trivial item.

The receipts of households during the current accounting period which have not been earned in this period are *transfer payments by government and by business*. Thus, these two items are added to national income to get personal income.

Profit and interest present somewhat more complex situations. Dividends are the portion of corporate profits which are received by stockholders. The difference between corporate profits and dividends is the amount not received by households (i.e., undistributed profits and corporation income taxes) although it has been earned. Thus, the BEA (Bureau of Economic Analysis) subtracts *corporate profits* and adds *dividends* when going from national income to personal income.

Personal interest income includes interest received by households from business and government. Part of this is made up of transfer payments (e.g., interest on the national debt and interest on consumers' debt to business). The account *net interest* is interest paid by business firms on debt presumed to be incurred in adding productive facilities. For this reason net interest is included in national income (as well as NNP and GNP). What the BEA does is to add personal interest income to national income and subtract net interest (since it is already included in national income) to get the transfer payment portion of interest, which is then added to national income to arrive at personal income.

Table 3-6 summarizes the relationships among GNP, NNP, national income, personal income, and one additional concept, *disposable personal income*. Disposable personal income is simply personal income minus personal tax and nontax payments, a concept of considerable interest in analyzing consumer behavior.

WEALTH

Despite the great importance of wealth in influencing activity in an economy and its value as a measure of welfare, no adequate estimates of wealth on a national or sectoral level are constructed.[3] The practical difficulties of measurement are immense. Nevertheless, the idea of wealth is extremely important, and economists regularly use proxy (substitute) variables to approximate wealth or changes in wealth.

The definition of wealth is simple: wealth is defined as any tangible thing of monetary value. It must be tangible because wealth is a stock (as opposed to a flow) concept. It must have monetary value in order to be measured.

---

[3] As Martin Gainsbrugh has said, "The lack of a current and continuing set of wealth and balance sheet estimates is perhaps the most serious omission in our current system of economic intelligence." "Measuring the Nation's Wealth," in U.S. Department of Commerce, Office of Business Economics, *The Economic Accounts of the United States: Retrospect and Prospect,* a supplement to *Survey of Current Business* (Washington: Vol. 51, No. 7, Part II, July, 1971), pp. 72–73.

Table 3-6

Relation of GNP, NNP, National Income, Personal Income, and Disposable Personal Income, 1976
(In Billions of Dollars)

Gross national product		**1,706.5**
Less:	Capital consumption allowances with capital consumption adjustment	179.1
Equals:	**Net National Product**	**1,527.4**
Less:	Indirect business tax and nontax liability	150.5
	Business transfer payments	8.1
	Statistical discrepancy	5.5
Plus:	Subsidies less current surplus of government enterprises	.8
Equals:	**National income**	**1,364.1**
Less:	Corporate profits with inventory valuation and capital consumption adjustments	128.1
	Net interest	88.4
	Contributions for social insurance	123.8
	Wage accruals less disbursements	.0
Plus:	Government transfer payments to persons	184.7
	Personal interest income	130.3
	Dividends	35.8
	Business transfer payments	8.1
Equals:	**Personal income**	**1,382.7**
Less:	Personal tax and nontax payments	196.9
Equals:	**Disposable personal income**	**1,185.8**

Source: Adapted from *Survey of Current Business* (July, 1977), pp. 21, 27.

The nature of any piece of wealth (its particular characteristics, its special productive abilities, and so on) depends on what has gone on in the past — how intensely and in what ways the wealth has been used, the changes that have been made over time, etc. At the instant of measurement, however, the piece of wealth is whatever it is at that moment, and its value depends strictly on the expected future, as bygones are bygones. The original cost of production is completely irrelevant at that point. (This is one of the most difficult of all lessons in economics.) The value of anything is the anticipated future net benefits to be derived from its ownership discounted to the present moment to reflect the fact that (1) benefits (which might be money earnings, but could be subjective utilities with monetary values placed on them) in the future are worth less than the same benefits currently, and (2) the further into the future the benefits are, the less valuable they are. This calculation, which is called the present value determination, is demonstrated in a more rigorous way in Chapter 8.

For most analytical purposes, the economic value of human beings (human capital) should be included as a part of the individual's wealth and therefore also as a part of national wealth. The reason for sometimes excluding human wealth is that, in general, it is not marketable.

All income flows from wealth, either human or property wealth. On the other hand, wealth arises out of income (production) which has not been consumed—what earlier was called investment (which is equal to saving). And, as was just pointed out, the value of wealth depends on expected future income.

The measurement of wealth starts at the level of the household, or individual. The individual's balance sheet might look like Table 3-7.

Table 3-7

Hypothetical Personal Balance Sheet

Assets			Liabilities and Net Worth	
Financial Assets	Cash (currency, coin, demand deposits)	$ 1,000	Mortgage on home	$ 40,000
	Savings Accts. in S&L	$ 6,000	Broker's Loan	$ 3,000
	Gov't. Bonds	$ 4,000	Dept. Store Debt	$ 700
	Corporate Bonds	$ 2,000	Auto loan	$ 2,000
	Common Stock	$ 14,000	Total Liab.	$ 45,700
	Insurance (Surrender value)	$ 20,000		
Real Assets	Home	$ 60,000		
	Furnishings	$ 9,000	Net Worth	$338,300
	Automobiles	$ 5,000		
	Other personal items	$ 13,000		
	Present Value of Myself	$250,000		
	Total Assets	$384,000	Total liabilities and Net Worth	$384,000

The wealth of the individual is that individual's net worth. For the individual, wealth includes both financial assets and real assets, but for the society as a whole only real wealth (plus net claims on other societies) is included. The reason, of course, is that financial assets owned by individuals are offset by financial liabilities of other individuals. Corporations are intermediaries. The net worth of a corporation is already included in the assets of the individuals who own the shares of the firm. Thus, if we sum the net worth of all individuals, this sum would be equal to the value of all the real wealth of the society—the land, the buildings, the capital equipment, inventories, and household goods.

A question which has not been completely resolved in the calculation of wealth is whether money should be included. If the society uses a full-bodied money, that is, a commodity such as gold, silver, or wheat, there would be no question that it would be wealth. However, the question would still remain of whether it should be valued at its value as a commodity or as money. To the individual owning any kind of money it is surely wealth, but fiat money (non-commodity money) is a liability either of the government, the central bank, or private commercial banks. Most economists conclude that money which is a liability of the government or central banks (called outside money) is a part of wealth. Their reasoning is that while this money is a liability, it need never be paid off nor (usually) must interest be paid. Demand deposits in commercial banks (called inside money) are usually not included in wealth.[4]

Money performs such tremendously important functions in the economic system that its real value must also be great. But if the stock of money were to double, for example, would we all be better off in real terms? Money has total utility but its marginal utility may be nil. It may be best to act as if the real value of money is already embodied in the real value of all the physical wealth of the society.

In some analyses, economists separate the private sector from the government sector, noting that while the government has liabilities which are ultimately liabilities of the public, the public acts as if the liabilities were not its concern. On the other hand, the individuals or firms who hold these government liabilities as assets treat them as they would any other assets. For example, when the government issues a bond, this establishes the necessity of interest payments and repayment of principle in the future, possibly requiring higher taxes in the future. Thus, while the bond is a part of the holder's wealth, the expected increase in future taxes reduces everyone's current net worth. The point here is that people don't act as if their liabilities had increased, but they do act as if their assets had increased when they have more government bonds (and not less of any other asset).

PRICE LEVEL COMPLICATIONS

The national income and product accounts and their component parts must be measured in dollar values in order for any summations to be made. Everyone recognizes that some distortion of the significance of the figures can occur if changes in the price level take place. For example, if it is observed

---

[4] Among economists who do include demand deposits as part of wealth are Boris Pesek and Thomas Saving, *Money, Wealth, and Economic Theory* (New York: The Macmillan Company, 1967).

that GNP has increased, it cannot be known whether the increase was entirely due to (1) a change in the output of goods and services, (2) a change in their prices, or (3) some combination of changes in output and prices.

Price indexes are attempts at measuring the degree to which prices in general (or prices in a grouping of commodities) have changed. If an estimate of price change can be made, then an estimate of the amount of change in the real variables can be made.

Before discussing the construction of price indexes, it may be advisable to mention some of their shortcomings since misinterpretation seems to be rampant in the world, especially the reporting of price index changes in the popular media. While it is of great value to have a good price index, a perfect one is inconceivable. Any price index should, therefore, be used with caution and an awareness that "the price level" may not be accurately reflected by the price index.

One important problem with price level estimations is that the commodities in one time period are never the same as the commodities produced, purchased, and used in another time period. This is the quality problem and becomes more serious with the length of the time period over which an index is used. While there are some goods you might buy this year which are identical to those your parents bought at your age, the vast majority are quite different, though we may use the same word to describe them (such as automobile, razor blade, or paint). Since most manufacturers are constantly striving to improve their products, we should expect continual quality enhancement of most products. In many cases the changes are subtle qualitative improvements which defy any attempts to rigorously quantify; yet we would know that if we pay the same price for a gallon of paint today that we paid five years ago, the price per quality unit of paint has gone down.[5] Where it is possible to quantify quality improvements (or quality deterioration), the constructors of index numbers do attempt to make those adjustments.

Two opposing approaches can be taken to the quality problem. One is to insist upon using the identical or nearly identical product whose price is to be included in the index. The problem with this approach is that buyers will move to purchase the product whose quality has improved, and over time the product in the index may become one which is no longer significant in the consumers' budgets. In addition, the products replacing it are not included in the index. Another approach is to keep changing the composition of the commodities included in the index so that the more important ones are in it. The difficulty with this approach is that comparisons of the prices of essentially different goods and services at two different points in time become nearly meaningless. Besides, this approach would be prohibitively expensive. Therefore, the Bureau of Labor Statistics does the best it can by compromising, using both approaches in some measure.

---

[5] An interesting experiment has been suggested which you might like to try: get a copy of a mail order catalog such as that of Sears, Roebuck & Co. of ten years ago and ask yourself whether you would prefer to make all of your purchases from that catalog at prices listed there, or from the current issue at current prices.

Most economists seem to agree that the quality issue and its handling lead to an upward bias in the price index with the degree of bias estimated at from $\frac{1}{2}$ percent to $1\frac{1}{2}$ percent. That is to say that if the Consumer Price Index rose $\frac{1}{2}$ percent to $1\frac{1}{2}$ percent in a year, the conclusion would be that the price level had remained approximately constant (excluding all other factors).

A second very important problem with price indexes which also results in an upward bias is the fixed weight problem. Since prices of different commodities vary at differing rates and in different directions even when prices in general move in one direction, relative prices change. It is an article of faith with economists that when relative prices change, buyers will demand more of the products whose relative prices have fallen and less of those whose relative prices have risen. Thus, more importance or weight should be given to the lower priced (larger quantity) goods and less weight to those whose prices have risen, but this is not done since the weights are fixed either at base year figures or at ending year figures.

As a simple example, consider two substitute commodities with the same base weights, for example, butter and margarine. Suppose the price of one rises 50 percent and the price of the other falls 50 percent. The index including these two goods would show no change, but the true price level has fallen since people would shift heavily to the lower priced spread and get more utility with the same income.

The degree of the upward bias caused by changing relative prices in a fixed weight index is difficult to gauge since factors other than relative prices determine quantities demanded, but it too has been estimated to range from $\frac{1}{2}$ percent to $1\frac{1}{2}$ percent per year.

Another problem which is quite severe at times but minimal at other times is that of getting the actual prices at which exchanges take place. Anyone who has shopped for a new automobile with a trade-in involved will recognize one dimension of the problem. When certain prices are illegal (under price control for example), it is again difficult to know what prices really are. Secret price concessions, discounts, tie-in sales, etc., all occur at times to bias the price index one way or another.

In recent years an additional obstacle to any attempt to measure general price level movements has taken on serious proportions. It is that much current production is being sold at zero price and the cost of production is being borne by some marketed good or service. For example, if you were to pay $50 per month for electricity (generated by coal), you would really be buying some electrical service and some units of cleaner air, water, and landscape. You would also be buying some statistical information for the government and a number of other services for yourself and others. The point here is that if the price of the electricity had increased by 10 percent, for example, it would not be clear whether the price of the electricity plus the other services had gone up at all.

This particular bias of price indexes has been important in making the appearance of inflation greater than the fact during the early 1970s. It is important to point out that the bias is relevant only during the time period that the events (usually, laws) are being phased into the economy. Once they are incorporated into the productive process, no index bias would appear. Another point worthy of some note is that no value judgment has been made about the worth of the zero-priced products — the cleaner environment, better health, better information, etc. Clearly, judgments would differ on the particulars of such goods or services.

NATIONAL INCOME IN CONSTANT DOLLARS

One important use of a price index is to interpret the national income accounting figures as to whether the changes in them are real changes or if the changes are attributable to price level changes. Thus, the real GNP is equal to the GNP at current dollars divided by the price index. Similarly, real (or constant dollar) consumption is equal to nominal (i.e., current dollar) consumption divided by the price index, and so on for any variable.

The GNP in constant and in current dollars is shown in Figure 3-1 for the years 1960–1975 and in Table 3-8, page 56, for the years 1946–1976. From these, one can get a good impression of the degree to which the growth in the nominal GNP has overstated the real increase in economic activity.

USE OF INDEX NUMBERS

In developing index numbers for production or prices, several problems require solution. One is to determine the items that are to be included in the index, since it is impossible to include more than a fraction of the universe being studied. A decision must also be made concerning the sources from which the data are to be collected and the methods of collection to insure accuracy and uniformity over a period of time. It is also necessary to determine the relative importance of the various items that have been selected for inclusion in the index and then to assign proper weights to those items. Furthermore, a decision must be made concerning the base year or period for the index. A fairly recent year or period that is reasonably representative of the years covered by the index should be chosen.

It is also necessary to select the method of computing the index number. Two basic methods are available — the aggregative and the average of relatives. A simple example will be used to illustrate the basic principles involved in calculating indexes. A fruit merchant sells 20 bushels of apples and 500 pounds of bananas each year. Prices change over the next three years as follows:

	Average Price	
Year	Bushel of Apples	Pound of Bananas
1	$1.50	$0.04
2	1.20	0.12
3	.75	0.16

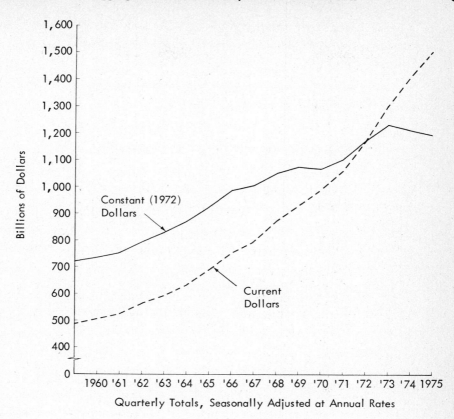

Figure 3-1

GNP in Current and Constant (1972) Dollars
1960–1975

To obtain a weighted aggregative type of index, the average price of each fruit each year is multiplied by the quantity weight. These products are then added. The values for the second and third years are expressed as percentages of the first or base year, taken as 100. These figures become the index numbers.

Year	Apples	Bananas	Total	Index Number
1	$30	$20	$50	100
2	24	60	84	168
3	15	80	95	190

The same result may be achieved by an alternative method known as the average of relatives type of index number. The first step is to reduce the price for each year to a percentage of the price in the base year as is shown on the following page.

Table 3-8
Gross National Production in Current and Constant Dollars
1946–1976
(Billions of Dollars)

Year	Current Dollars	Constant (1972) Dollars
1946	209.6	477.6
1947	232.8	468.3
1948	259.1	487.7
1949	258.0	490.7
1950	286.2	533.5
1951	330.2	576.5
1952	347.2	598.5
1953	366.1	621.8
1954	366.3	613.7
1955	399.3	654.8
1956	420.7	668.8
1957	442.8	680.9
1958	448.9	679.5
1959	486.5	720.4
1960	506.0	736.8
1961	523.3	755.3
1962	563.8	799.1
1963	594.7	830.7
1964	635.7	874.4
1965	688.1	925.9
1966	753.0	981.0
1967	796.3	1,007.7
1968	868.5	1,051.8
1969	935.5	1,078.8
1970	982.4	1,075.3
1971	1,063.4	1,107.5
1972	1,171.1	1,171.1
1973	1,306.6	1,235.0
1974	1,413.2	1,214.0
1975	1,516.3	1,191.7
1976	1,706.5	1,274.7

Source: Adapted from *Survey of Current Business* (January, 1976), Part II, pp. 6–9, and (July, 1977), p. S-1.

Year	Price Relatives	
	Apples	Bananas
1	100	100
2	80	300
3	50	400

These relatives are then weighted by multiplying them by the total value of each commodity in the base year; that is, $30 for 20 bushels of apples at $1.50 and $20 for 500 pounds of bananas at 4 cents. The value for the base year is again taken as 100 and the values for subsequent years is expressed as a percentage of the base year.

Year	Apples Price Relatives × 30	Bananas Price Relatives × 20	Total	Index
1	3,000	2,000	5,000	100
2	2,400	6,000	8,400	168
3	1,500	8,000	9,500	190

In this simple form these two methods of calculating index numbers give identical results. However, the methods may be modified in calculating more complicated indexes in which cases the results obtained will differ somewhat.

Federal Reserve Board Index of Industrial Production

The Federal Reserve Board of Governors has developed an index of industrial production including manufacturing, mining, and utilities. It is computed for all three areas from 1947 to the present, and for manufacturing and mining only from 1919 to 1947. The index is available on two base periods: 1957–1959 and 1967.

The items in the index are grouped in two different ways, by industry and by market. The first industry grouping is by manufacturing, mining, and utilities. Manufacturing is divided into two major subgroups, durable and nondurable manufactures. Each group is further subdivided as shown in Table 3-9. Index numbers are available monthly for each subgroup, both with and without seasonal adjustment.

The first market grouping is by final products and materials. Final products are divided into two groups, consumer goods and equipment (including defense equipment). Consumer goods are further divided into automotive products, home goods, clothing, and consumer staples. Materials are divided into three basic groups—durable goods materials, nondurable goods materials, and energy materials. Each of the subgroups is further divided as shown in Table 3–9. Monthly indexes are available for each of these groups and subgroups, both with and without seasonal adjustment.

Figures for the Index of Industrial Production by industry groupings in 1975 and 1976 are shown in Table 3-10 on page 59.

Whenever possible, physical production units are used as the basis for measuring changes in production. In about half of the industries included in the index, however, changes are measured by the use of series on worker-hours worked in each field. In order that these series may measure changes in production, it is necessary to adjust them for changes in the output per worker-hour. The use of worker-hour series makes it possible to get a better measure of changes in such fields as machinery, furniture, chemicals, baking, canning, and shipbuilding, where quantity figures are not too meaningful because the product is not homogeneous and there is no convenient unit in which output can be expressed directly.

Table 3-9

Major Groupings in the Federal Reserve Board Index of Industrial Production and Their Relative Importance

Industry Grouping	1967 proportion	Market Grouping	1967 proportion
Total index	**100.00**	**Total index**	**100.00**
		Products	**60.71**
		Final products	*47.82*
Mining and utilities	**12.05**	Consumer goods	27.68
		Equipment	20.14
		Intermediate products	12.89
Mining	6.36	**Materials**	**39.29**
Utilities	5.69	**Consumer goods:**	
Electric	3.88	*Durable consumer goods*	*7.89*
		Automotive products	2.83
		Autos and utility vehicles	2.03
		Autos	1.90
		Auto parts and allied goods	.80
Manufacturing	**87.95**	Home goods	5.06
		Appliances, A/C, and TV	1.40
Nondurable	35.97	Appliances and TV	1.33
Durable	51.98	Carpeting and furniture	1.07
		Misc. home goods	2.59
		Nondurable consumer goods	*19.79*
		Clothing	4.29
Mining:		Consumer staples	15.50
		Consumer foods and tobacco	8.33
Metal mining	.51	Nonfood staples	7.17
Coal	.69	Consumer chemical products	2.63
Oil and gas extraction	4.40	Consumer paper products	1.92
Stone and earth minerals	.75	Consumer energy products	2.62
		Residential utilities	1.45
		Equipment:	
		Business equipment	*12.63*
Nondurable manufactures:		Industrial equipment	6.77
		Building and mining equip.	1.44
Foods	8.75	Manufacturing equipment	3.85
Tobacco products	.67	Power equipment	1.47
Textile mill products	2.68	Commercial transit, farm equip.	5.86
Apparel products	3.31	Commercial equipment	3.26
Paper and products	3.21	Transit equipment	1.93
		Farm equipment	.67
Printing and publishing	4.72	*Defense and space equipment*	*7.51*
Chemicals and products	7.74	**Intermediate products:**	
Petroleum products	1.79	Construction supplies	6.42
Rubber & plastic products	2.24	Business supplies	6.47
Leather and products	.86	Commercial energy products	1.14
		Materials:	
		Durable goods materials	*20.35*
		Durable consumer parts	4.58
Durable manufactures:		Equipment parts	5.44
		Durable materials n.e.c.	10.34
Ordnance, pvt. & govt.	3.64	Basic metal materials	5.57
Lumber and products	1.64	*Nondurable goods materials*	*10.47*
Furniture and fixtures	1.37	Textile, paper, and chem. mat.	7.62
Clay, glass, stone prod.	2.74	Textile materials	1.85
		Paper materials	1.62
		Chemical materials	4.15
Primary metals	6.57	Containers, nondurable	1.70
		Nondurable materials n.e.c.	1.14
Iron and steel	4.21	Energy materials	8.48
Fabricated metal prod.	5.93	Primary energy	4.65
Nonelectrical machinery	9.15	Converted fuel materials	3.82
Electrical machinery	8.05	**Supplementary groups:**	
		Home goods and clothing	9.35
		Energy, total	12.23
Transportation equip.	9.27	Products	3.76
Motor vehicles & pts.	4.50	Materials	8.48
Aerospace & misc. tr. eq.	4.77		
Instrument	2.11		
Miscellaneous mfrs.	1.51		

Source: *Federal Reserve Bulletin* (January, 1977), pp. A48 and A49.

Table 3-10

Federal Reserve Board Index of Industrial Production by Industry Groupings, 1975–1976 (1967 = 100)

Industry Grouping	1967 proportion	1975 average	1976 average
Mining and utilities	**12.05**	**128.5**	**131.9**
Mining	6.36	112.8	114.1
Utilities	5.69	146.0	151.7
Electric	3.88	160.8	....
Manufacturing	**87.95**	**116.3**	**129.4**
Nondurable	35.97	126.4	141.0
Durable	51.98	109.3	121.4
Mining:			
Metal mining	.51	115.8	122.8
Coal	.69	113.4	116.9
Oil and gas extraction	4.40	113.3	112.0
Stone and earth minerals	.75	107.0	118.3
Nondurable manufactures:			
Foods	8.75	123.4	132.0
Tobacco products	.67	111.8	117.2
Textile mill products	2.68	112.3	135.9
Apparel products	3.31	107.6	126.1
Paper and products	3.21	116.3	133.1
Printing and publishing	4.72	113.4	120.7
Chemicals and products	7.74	147.3	169.4
Petroleum products	1.79	124.1	132.7
Rubber & plastic products	2.24	166.7	199.8
Leather and products	.86	76.5	82.0
Durable manufactures:			
Ordnance, pvt. & govt.	3.64	76.6	71.7
Lumber and products	1.64	107.6	125.1
Furniture and fixtures	1.37	118.2	132.8
Clay, glass, stone prod.	2.74	117.9	135.8
Primary metals	6.57	96.4	108.0
Iron and steel	4.21	95.8	104.4
Fabricated metal prod.	5.93	109.9	123.3
Nonelectrical machinery	9.15	125.1	134.7
Electrical machinery	8.05	116.5	131.7
Transportation equip.	9.27	97.4	110.6
Motor vehicles & pts.	4.50	111.1	140.7
Aerospace & misc. tr. eq.	4.77	84.5	82.2
Instrument	2.11	132.3	148.2
Miscellaneous mfrs.	1.51	128.3	143.5

Source: *Federal Reserve Bulletin* (January, 1977), p. A49, and (June, 1977), p. A49.

In weighting the various factors to be included in the index, the importance of the individual series is measured by the value added by manufacture as shown in the Census of Manufactures and Minerals and by annual census surveys and other benchmark data. The most recent census years are 1972, 1967, 1963, 1958, and 1954.

In order to present an accurate index, allowances must be made for the number of nonworking days in a year. This has been done by a study in each field of the regular weekly closing days, if any. Seasonal factors, including holidays, have also been studied so as to develop a seasonally adjusted index for each component as well as for the total index. These seasonal factors are studied continuously and changed as the seasonal changes in any field are made.

Bureau of Labor Statistics Wholesale Price Index

Several indexes are available for measuring changes in prices. One of the most comprehensive is the Wholesale Price Index of the Bureau of Labor Statistics. This index is based on the prices of 2,650 commodities and is classified into 15 major product groups and numerous subgroups by stage of processing, by durability, and other special groupings. The index for all commodities and several of the major groups for the years 1969 through 1976, and monthly from May, 1976, through May, 1977, is shown in Table 3-11.

The wholesale price index measures price changes in primary markets; that is, at the level of the first commercial transaction for each commodity. Most of the prices are those quoted by producers rather than by wholesalers in the strict sense. The term "wholesale" in the index refers to sales in sizable quantities, not to prices at which goods are either sold to or by wholesalers.

For almost all of the items in the monthly index three or more price quotations are averaged. Detailed specifications are drawn up for each item on which prices are collected. Some of the wholesale prices are obtained by mail from individual reports, others are obtained from trade journals, a few from boards of trade or commodity markets, and several from federal and state agencies.

Each price used in the index applies to only one day each week, but the day varies for different commodities. The monthly price is the average of the four or five one-day-a-week prices that fall within the month.

Indexes for the subgroups are first computed and then the total index is developed from these indexes. When necessary, adjustments are made because of major changes in the specifications of commodities, shifts in the relative importance of sales to different types of purchasers or by different types of sellers, and alterations in the distribution pattern of the industry.

In using this index several limitations should be borne in mind. It is not a measure of the general price level or of the purchasing power of the dollar, since it does not include changes in the price of real estate, securities, services, etc. It does not cover transactions at all levels of marketing. In addition, prices used in computing the index are those prevailing in national markets and are therefore not effective in any specific locality.

Table 3-11

Wholesale Price Index, 1969–1976

(1967 = 100)

Period	All commodities	Farm products and processed foods and feeds	Industrial commodities	Farm products	Processed foods and feeds	Crude materials[1]	Intermediate materials[2]	Producer finished goods	Special groupings — Consumer finished goods excluding foods — Total	Durable	Non-durable
Unadjusted											
1969	106.5	108.0	106.0	109.1	107.3	110.6	106.1	106.9	104.6	104.0	105.0
1970	110.4	111.7	110.0	111.0	112.1	118.9	109.9	112.0	107.7	106.9	108.3
1971	114.0	113.9	114.1	112.9	114.5	122.7	114.3	116.6	111.2	110.8	111.7
1972	119.1	122.4	117.9	125.0	120.8	131.1	118.9	119.5	113.5	113.2	113.6
1973	134.7	159.1	125.9	176.3	148.1	155.2	128.1	123.5	118.6	115.8	120.5
1974	160.1	177.4	153.8	187.7	170.9	219.1	159.5	141.0	138.6	126.3	146.8
1975	174.9	184.2	171.5	186.7	182.6	225.1	178.6	162.5	153.1	138.2	163.0
1976	182.9	183.1	182.3	191.1	178.0	250.0	189.4	173.2	161.7	144.3	173.2
Seasonally adjusted											
1976: May	181.9	184.8	180.5	194.3	181.1	244.1	187.4	171.8	159.5	143.3	170.3
June	183.2	187.4	181.5	195.3	181.6	246.8	188.2	172.5	160.7	143.9	171.8
July	184.4	188.1	182.7	194.2	180.5	252.7	189.1	173.1	161.5	144.2	173.1
Aug	183.8	181.7	183.8	187.7	175.9	254.4	190.3	173.6	162.5	144.9	174.2
Sept	184.8	182.9	184.8	189.2	176.0	253.1	192.0	174.5	163.7	145.7	175.6
Oct	185.3	179.5	186.3	188.2	174.9	262.4	193.3	176.3	164.6	146.5	176.7
Nov	185.6	178.3	187.1	187.1	175.6	271.6	194.3	177.0	165.5	146.8	178.0
Dec	187.1	183.9	187.4	191.9	178.9	265.8	195.3	178.5	165.8	146.9	178.4
1977: Jan	188.0	184.8	188.4	194.0	178.6	262.6	196.3	179.2	167.4	148.0	180.3
Feb	190.0	188.4	189.9	198.3	181.9	273.0	197.4	180.1	167.9	148.8	180.7
Mar	191.9	190.9	191.6	203.3	185.4	279.3	199.1	180.8	169.2	149.4	182.5
Apr	194.3	195.9	193.2	210.2	190.1	280.1	200.3	181.8	170.4	150.5	183.7
May	195.2	196.8	194.2	205.3	193.5	282.4	200.9	182.8	171.2	151.1	184.6

Source: *Economic Indicators* (June, 1977), p. 22.

[1] Excludes crude foodstuffs and feedstuffs, plant and animal fibers, oilseeds, and leaf tobacco.

[2] Includes supplies and components; excludes intermediate materials for food manufacturing and manufactured animal feeds.

Bureau of Labor Statistics Consumer Price Index

In addition to measuring changes in a comprehensive series of prices, such as is done in the Wholesale Price Index, it is desirable to have special price indexes for more restricted segments of the economy. One such index that measures changes in the purchasing power of consumers was initiated during World War I by the Bureau of Labor Statistics and is currently available as the Consumer Price Index. It measures changes in prices that are paid for goods and services usually bought by moderate income families in large urban centers of the United States. In addition to the composite index, figures are also available for the following groups of commodities:

Food
Housing—Total and rent, home ownership, fuel oil and coal, gas and elec-
    tricity, furnishings, and operation
Apparel and upkeep
Transportation
Health and recreation—Total and medical care, personal care, reading and
    recreation, other goods and services

This index is based on the average of 1967 as 100. Weights are based on surveys of family expenditures determined by an extensive study of family consumption. Prices are gathered by part-time and full-time employees by means of shopping trips and personal interviews. A few prices, such as those for fuel, are obtained directly from dealers, and electric power rates are obtained from the Federal Power Commission. Table 3-12 is a recent example of the Consumer Price Index.

It is again necessary to note some of the limitations in the use of this index. It does not show changes in the amounts that urban families spend for living, since to develop such a measure, it would be necessary to have information reflecting changes in income and the manner of living. It also does not show changes for any group other than typical moderate income families. It does show changes in the prices of a representative aggregate (or market basket) of goods and services bought by city wage-earner and clerical-worker families.

Implicit Price Indexes

What index should be used if one is interested in the general price level or the value of the dollar? Most of the readily available price indexes are more or less specific; that is, they measure the price behavior of a particular class of commodities or services such as farm products, transportation, lumber, or consumer goods. While it is usually the case that when general inflation is taking place these indexes will also be rising, it is not necessarily so. We need an index that reflects price movements in all segments of the economy.

Table 3-12

Consumer Price Index, 1969–1976
(1967 = 100)

Period	All items	Food	Commodities less food	Services	All commodities	Food			Commodities less food			
						All	Food at home	Food away from home	All	Durable	Non-durable	Services
		Unadjusted							*Seasonally adjusted*			
1969	109.8	108.9	108.1	112.5	108.4	108.9	108.2	111.6	108.1	107.0	108.8	112.5
1970	116.3	114.9	112.5	121.6	113.5	114.9	113.7	119.9	112.5	111.8	113.1	121.6
1971	121.3	118.4	116.8	128.4	117.4	118.4	116.4	126.1	116.8	116.5	117.0	128.4
1972	125.3	123.5	119.4	133.3	120.9	123.5	121.6	131.1	119.4	118.9	119.8	133.3
1973	133.1	141.4	123.5	139.1	129.9	141.7	141.4	141.4	123.5	121.9	124.8	139.1
1974	147.7	161.7	136.6	152.1	145.5	161.7	162.4	159.4	136.6	130.6	140.9	152.1
1975	161.2	175.4	149.1	166.6	158.4	175.4	175.8	174.3	149.1	145.5	151.7	166.6
1976	170.5	180.8	156.6	180.4	165.2	180.8	179.5	186.1	156.6	154.3	158.3	180.4
1976: May	169.2	180.0	155.5	178.4	164.4	180.8	179.6	185.0	155.6	153.7	156.9	178.9
June	170.1	180.9	156.5	179.5	165.0	181.2	179.9	186.1	156.2	154.2	157.6	179.9
July	171.1	182.1	157.1	180.7	165.5	181.4	179.9	187.2	156.9	155.0	158.4	181.1
Aug	171.9	182.4	158.0	181.8	166.2	181.8	180.2	188.0	157.8	155.6	159.3	182.2
Sept	172.6	181.6	158.9	183.2	166.6	181.9	180.1	188.7	158.3	156.1	159.9	183.2
Oct	173.3	181.6	159.6	184.1	167.1	182.2	180.3	189.0	159.0	156.6	160.6	184.0
Nov	173.8	181.1	160.3	185.1	167.4	181.7	179.6	189.5	159.6	157.3	161.3	184.8
Dec	174.3	181.7	160.6	185.8	168.0	181.9	179.7	190.4	160.5	158.4	162.0	185.5
1977: Jan	175.3	183.4	160.6	187.5	169.4	183.5	181.3	192.0	161.6	159.9	162.8	187.2
Feb	177.1	187.7	161.6	188.7	171.4	187.1	185.4	194.0	162.7	161.4	163.7	188.4
Mar	178.2	188.6	162.6	190.0	172.2	188.2	186.4	195.4	163.4	162.4	164.2	189.9
Apr	179.6	190.9	163.6	191.3	173.6	191.0	189.3	197.5	164.0	163.2	164.7	191.4
May	180.6	191.7	164.7	192.3	174.5	192.4	190.7	199.5	164.7	163.5	165.6	192.7

Source: *Economic Indicators* (June, 1977), p. 23.

The best index for overall price movements is constructed by the Department of Commerce and is called the implicit GNP deflator. The deflator itself is found very simply by dividing the actual GNP (GNP in current dollars) by real GNP (GNP in constant dollars) and multiplying by 100. For example, in Table 3-8 on page 56, we have shown GNP in current and in constant (1972) dollars for the years from 1946 through 1976. GNP in 1976 was $1,706.5 billion and in 1972 dollars was $1,274.7 billion, which means that the implicit price deflator was $\frac{1,706.5}{1,274.7}$ (100) or 133.9. In other words, the general price level rose 33.9 percent from 1972 to 1976.

The important thing to understand is the method the Department of Commerce uses to construct the series of GNP in constant dollars. This series is extremely important in its own right, being our best estimate of what we are interested in: namely, the total output of goods and services corrected for price level changes.

The GNP is broken down into the smallest groupings for which specific price indexes are available. The total output of the particular commodity or group of commodities is then corrected to reflect the price changes in those specific commodities. This yields a figure of output in constant dollars, or in base year prices. If this is done for all the components of GNP, all categories corrected for price changes can be summed to the corrected GNP. The deflators used for the various subgroups are also available in the *Survey of Current Business*.

There are still some shortcomings in this price index. Some gaps remain in that more refined subgroup indexes could be used. Estimates in the government sector, the service sectors, and in the construction industries are thought to be particularly subject to error. Furthermore, its method of construction leads to a chronic bias toward the overstatement of inflation. The index is available only quarterly and with a lag so it is not usable for month to month or other short-run purposes. In spite of these weaknesses, the implicit price index is still clearly superior to any other available index in measuring general price movements.

OPTIMUM PERFORMANCE OF THE ECONOMY

As a last issue to be discussed in this chapter, we take up the question of the degree to which the economy is operating at the optimal level. Usually that optimum is thought to occur when the human factor of production is employed in the numbers wishing to work; i.e., full employment. Thus, the concepts of employment, full employment, unemployment, and their measurements are very important. Another way of looking at the issue is to ask what the capital stock level of utilization is. Here, both the notion of full capacity and the capacity rate become important.

Both the unemployment level and the unused capacity figures are significant from the point of view of the economy producing less than it is capable of producing, and both may be of importance in gauging the degree of inflationary pressures from any increase in aggregate demand. A difference between the two concepts is that the loss of productive activity by humans cannot be captured later, whereas in some part the loss of use-time of capital can be made up later.

A much more important difference, of course, is that workers are also human beings who may suffer severe psychological distress from the fact of unemployment, the feeling of worthlessness, familial problems, crime, alcoholism, the feeling associated with accepting charity or welfare, and many other very human concerns, as well as the loss of employment skills and attitudes due to disuse.

In summary, when the economy is performing at less than its potential, output is lost and the incomes of both workers and capital owners are reduced or eliminated. In addition, the social impact on the unemployed persons and on the society may be an even more serious consequence of this situation.

EMPLOYMENT, FULL EMPLOYMENT, AND UNEMPLOYMENT

The Bureau of Labor Statistics is an agency within the Department of Labor of the U.S. government. The Bureau gathers statistics on the many dimensions of the labor force; its composition in terms of sex, age, race, and other demographic characteristics; the skill and industry composition; and the employed-unemployed status.

The *labor force* is made up of the employed and the unemployed. Considerable debate surrounds the definition of the unemployed. At the present time, according to the BLS rules, persons aged 16 and over are *unemployed* if they:

1. Did not have a job and thus performed no work at all in the survey period (a full week). (Any work at all classifies a person as employed, regardless of any job-seeking activity.)
2. Actively looked for work sometime during the prior 4 weeks, as evidenced by the use of one specific job-search method or more (visited a public or private employment office, visited an employer directly, and so on). Persons on layoff or waiting to start a new wage or salary job within 30 days need not meet the job-seeking requirement.
3. Are currently available for work (excluding temporary illness).[6]

There is probably no ideal way to define unemployment statistically. It may depend on the purpose for which the figure is to be used. Thus, if the goal is to measure the hardship suffered by the unemployed, or the need for assistance to

---

[6] John E. Bregger, "Establishment of a New Employment Statistics Review Commission," *Monthly Labor Review* (March, 1977), p. 15.

individuals or localities, a different definition may be needed than one that is to be used to judge the impact of fiscal or monetary policy on inflation or aggregate economic activity. In the current measurement people who have quit looking for work because of despair of not finding a job ("the discouraged worker") are not counted as unemployed nor as a part of the labor force. There are also persons working at jobs below their capacity, such as a graduate engineer pumping gas ("disguised unemployment"). There are many other such issues which indicate that no single concept will be completely satisfactory.

The unemployment figure is often used as the measure of how well the economy is performing, but frequently this is misleading.[7] For example, during the decade from 1967 to 1976 unemployment grew from about 3 million (3.8 percent of the labor force) to over 7 million (7.7 percent of the labor force); yet during that same period employment grew from 74 million to 87 million. The relevant population grew over this period by about the same percentage (17 percent) as the growth in jobs, but the growth in the labor force was about 20 percent. In other words, the economy was generating new jobs for the new population, but the labor force was growing more rapidly as people who were not previously in the labor market joined it. These new workers were primarily women whose employment grew from 27 million in 1967 to 35 million in 1976, an increase of 30 percent.

Full employment is an elusive concept which does not have a rigorous definition. Most economists and others consider a condition where about 4 or 5 percent of the labor force is not working as full employment. Even in the most ideal situation, some of the labor force will not be at work during the survey period. Some will have quit a job, or been laid off or fired; some will be new entrants or reentrants into the labor market; and some will prefer the alternative of some kind of welfare to gainful employment.

There will inevitably be a period of time during which a worker will be unemployed while looking for a position. The individual looking for employment would want to find the most attractive job in terms of pay, working conditions, challenge, etc. Since no one has perfect knowledge about the openings available, the unemployed person will have to engage in a time-consuming search process. During this time, the searcher is counted as unemployed even though that person could have a job. In economic theory the individual job seeker is viewed as making the marginal comparison between the expected marginal benefits (higher pay, better work situations) and the marginal costs (primarily loss of income during the search). As economic conditions change, the average length of time the search for work continues will also change; and as this time changes, so does the "natural" unemployment figure.

---

[7] An excellent discussion of the major reasons for the misleading nature of employment-unemployment figures is contained in: Stewart Schwab and John J. Seater, "The Unemployment Rate: Time to Give it a Rest?" the Federal Reserve Bank of Philadelphia's *Business Review* (May–June, 1977), pp. 11–18.

QUESTIONS

1. Explain why the value of final goods production in the whole economy is equal to the sum of the "values added" in all of the producing units of the economy, and in turn, is equal to the incomes earned by all of the factors of production.
2. How does the accounting concept of national income differ from gross national product?
3. Explain how each of the following are related to personal income:
   a. Personal income taxes.
   b. Personal and real property taxes.
   c. Personal saving.
   d. Contributions for social insurance.
   e. Net interest paid by the government.
   f. Government payments to veterans.
   g. Corporate contributions to the American Red Cross.
   h. Dividend payments.
   i. Corporate income taxes.
4. Explain how wealth and income are related.
5. Consider whether each of the following are included as a part of wealth of an individual and of the whole society. Explain your reasoning.
   a. Corporate bonds.
   b. Government bonds.
   c. Corporate common stock.
   d. Houses.
   e. Money.
   f. The shoes you are wearing (if any).
   g. The shoes in a department store.
6. Discuss the difference between "the price level" and a price index.
7. What is the difference between the "cost of living" and the "standard of living" (not discussed in text)?
8. Describe the construction of the GNP deflator.
9. Explain what is meant by the cost of unemployment.

SUGGESTED READINGS

McKenna, Joseph P. *Aggregate Economic Analysis,* 5th ed. Hinsdale, Illinois: Dryden Press, 1977. Chapter 2.

Morton, J. E. "A Student's Guide to American Federal Government Statistics." *Journal of Economic Literature,* Vol. 10, No. 2 (June, 1972), pp. 371–397.

Poindexter, J. Carl. *Macroeconomics.* Hinsdale, Illinois: Dryden Press, 1976. Chapters 2 and 3.

Stewart, Kenneth. "National Income Accounting and Economic Welfare: the Concepts of GNP and MEW." Federal Reserve Bank of St. Louis *Review,* (April, 1974).

Stockton, John R., and Charles T. Clark. *Introduction to Business and Economic Statistics,* 5th ed. Cincinnati: South-Western Publishing Co., 1975. Parts 3 and 4.

The National Income and Product Accounts of the United States, 1929–1974 Statistical Tables, A supplement to the *Survey of Current Business* (1976).

U.S. Department of Commerce, Office of Business Economics. "The Economic Accounts of the United States: Retrospect and Prospect." A supplement to the *Survey of Current Business*, 50th Anniversary Issue, Vol. 51 (July, 1971).

PROBLEMS ON PART 1

1. Calculate the average percentage increase per year in income per capita in the 1799–1859, the 1859–1914, and the 1914 to the present periods in American economic history. Make a table for each of the three periods of economic development showing the major factors that may have led to an increase in economic activity and the major factors that may have slowed it down. On the basis of your data, account for differences in the rate of growth.
2. (a) Develop a chart showing similarities and differences in the factors at work in the depressions that began in 1815, 1837, and 1873.
   (b) How might the pattern of business fluctuations in the 1790–1860 period have been affected if the steamboat had been perfected after a good system of roads had already covered the section of the country north of the Ohio River and east of the Mississippi River?
   (c) Suppose Henry Ford had begun assembly line production of automobiles in 1926 rather than before the United States entered World War I. Discuss the possible effects on economic fluctuations from 1920 to 1939.

PART 2

CAUSAL FACTORS IN THE CYCLICAL PROCESS

In the description in Chapter 2 of the major depressions that occurred in the economic development of the United States, some of the factors that were at work in these periods were pointed out. No attempt was made, however, to fully explain these causal factors. A discussion of the factors that cause the economy to grow in a cyclical fashion has been reserved for Part 2.

Chapter 2 also reviewed some of the salient features of the American economy as it operates currently. It provided a review of the background needed to understand what happens in the economy during the cycle. These characteristics also help explain why the cycle develops as it does. If the economy were changed materially, the cycle would be changed or perhaps even eliminated in the form in which it has occurred.

Part 2 begins with Chapter 4, which is devoted to a study of the basic framework and overview of the system of economic thought called *classical aggregate economics*. Some understanding of this theory is helpful in appreciating the contributions to the development of the history of business cycle theories covered in Chapters 5 and 6. This theory also serves as a counterpoint to the Keynesian and post-Keynesian analysis of aggregate economics, which is the subject matter of Part 3. Furthermore, Chapter 4 should give the reader a feel for the interdependence of macroeconomic variables and for what is meant when we refer to an economic system.

Chapters 5 and 6 present various aspects of cycle theory, beginning with theories which explain the cyclical behavior of some forces outside the economy. There is no attempt to analyze all possible theories, nor are the theories presented in the chronological order of their formulation. The major types of theories are considered to emphasize the role in the cyclical process of the main points stressed by each group of theorists. These theorists give us insights into the workings of the whole economy and how particular events or developments lead to responses by economic actors that produce fluctuations in total activity.

CHAPTER 4

CLASSICAL AGGREGATE ECONOMICS

Attempts to understand the functioning of the economy have been carried on for several centuries and it is stimulating to realize that there is a great deal yet to be learned. Anyone who is likely to contribute to our further understanding will be one who has a knowledge of what has gone before. Some past economists were brilliant scholars whose ideas deserve serious study.

This chapter will present the outline of a body of aggregate economic thought known as the "classical model." It is not necessarily a true representation of the views of any individual economist. It is, rather, a synthesis of orthodox economists' theories prior to the publication of John Maynard Keynes' *General Theory*.[1] Many contemporary economists feel that the classical model is a more useful approach than present alternatives.

Chapters 5 and 6 discuss the business cycle theories of the classical model. Part 3 covers the contributions of Keynes and post-Keynesian economic theory.

FUNDAMENTALS OF CLASSICAL THOUGHT

Classical economists held certain fundamental beliefs about the nature of the economy, most importantly the pervasiveness of competition and the laws of diminishing returns. Also, they thought that households seek to maximize their utility and business units consistently seek to maximize their profits.

From these assumptions the following conclusions were reached:

1. Prices and wages are flexible and respond readily to changes in demand or supply conditions.
2. Money is a veil which makes it necessary to look behind activities expressed in money terms to discover the fundamental behavior underlying them. Relative prices are important in directing the activity of the economy.
3. The quantity theory of money explains how the stock of money determines the absolute level of prices, the only important variable determined by money.

---

[1] John Maynard Keynes, *The General Theory of Employment, Interest, and Money* (New York: Harcourt, Brace & World, 1936).

4. The total demand for the output of the economy is equal to the amount of goods and services produced (Say's Law).
5. Full employment of labor is assured in the sense that anyone wishing to work at prevailing wages is able to do so.
6. The interest rate is determined by the willingness of households to save and of business firms to invest.
7. The rate of growth of the economy is related to the rates of saving and investment.
8. The size of the population of an area is related to the ability of its economy to support the populace.
9. The economic role of government should be minimal. Government use of resources can take place only at the expense of private use.

In the pages that follow, the theoretical structure which produces these conclusions will be explained and the ramifications discussed.

SAY'S LAW

Because of the confining interpretation of Say's Law, the mainstream of classical economic thinking was not directed toward the study of business fluctuations. The usual statement used to explain Say's Law is that "supply creates its own demand." This means that the total value of goods produced during a period of time (supply) is an amount sufficient to purchase (demand) all that was produced during the period. Our national income accounting is based on this law, although in that connection we usually state the fact in a slightly different way; namely, the total income earned in a period by the factors of production is equal to the total value of all the goods and services produced by those factors of production. Thus, we speak of Say's Law as a truism; supply of and demand for the total output of the economy are equal by definition.

There is an exciting question that is raised by Say's Law. That is, does the amount of goods and services that producers wish to produce and sell equal the amount of goods and services buyers want to buy? Since this question involves intentions of people, it certainly is possible that supply and demand in this sense are not necessarily equal. In fact, their equality is a condition of equilibrium. Classical economists, with their basically hedonistic view of the nature of human motivation, believed that departures from equilibrium would be transitory and of only short duration. Their argument was that saving was unpleasant or onerous; that since present goods were valued more highly than future goods, a reward or premium would have to be paid to induce the public to save, which is to say, abstain from present consumption. This reward is the interest paid to those who save, and the higher the interest rate, the more people will be willing to save. While high interest rates encourage saving (thrift) and low interest rates discourage saving, just the opposite is true of investment. A high interest rate makes it more costly to borrow or to use one's own funds for investment purposes, whereas a low rate of interest lowers the cost and is a stimulus to more investment. Briefly, then, the savings function, that is, the supply of resources available for investment, is positively sloped with respect to interest, and the investment demand for these resources is negatively sloped with respect to interest. Interest rate adjustments assure the equality of savings and investment and, hence, assure equilibrium of aggregate demand and supply.

To understand the classicist viewpoint, consider the implications of disequilibrium in Figure 4-1. At the interest rate r_a, which stands for any interest rate above the equilibrium rate, saving of S_a is greater than investment of I_a. Since investors are willing to invest (or pay r_a to use saved resources) in just the amount I_a, some savers would be unable to lend their surplus funds at all and, therefore, their reward for saving is zero. Rather than accept this state of affairs, the disappointed savers would offer to lend at lower interest rates, but the lower interest rates would encourage investors to invest more and induce some savers to save less. In this way saving and investment come into equality and the interest rate falls toward r_e.[2]

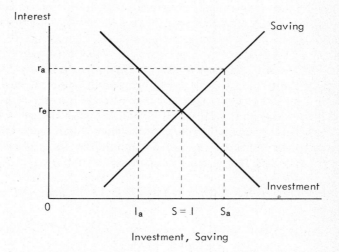

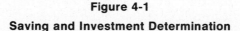

Figure 4-1

Saving and Investment Determination

If you were to question this analysis, as later economists did, by noting that people might be willing to forego the interest income from saving by holding money instead of making it available to investors, the classicist would have made two counter arguments. First, the assertion probably would have been made that there is no advantage in holding money; therefore, no one would be willing to do it. Second, even if there were such a thing as a demand for money to hold in idle balances, the only result would be lower commodity prices and a redistribution of goods and services from the foolish money

---

[2] We resist the temptation to explain the forces at work if the interest rate is below equilibrium so the reader can use this case as an exercise in understanding.

holders to the more reasonable members of the society who want money only because it can be used to purchase things.

David Ricardo (1772–1823) was the strongest adherent of Say's Law and the power of his logic was so great that few economists were bold enough to challenge it. One who did was his contemporary and friend, the Reverend T. R. Malthus. Ricardo was interested in demonstrating the nature of the forces included in Adam Smith's "invisible hand," the forces that insured equilibrium in all economic activity.[3] The fascination of this study caused him to be impatient with observations that the real world did not always coincide with his description of it. His interest was in the long run, not in the temporary aberrations. Malthus, on the other hand, lived in the short run. He saw unemployment and overproduction and wanted to explain them, even though according to Ricardo's theory they couldn't exist.

Malthus was not convinced that all the resources being saved were automatically flowing into investment demand. In fact, he thought oversaving was a chronic problem in an economy where the demand for capital building was limited by the decisions of private entrepreneurs. The excessive saving was due to the unequal distribution of income in favor of the landlords and other wealthy individuals. His solution to the problem was to advise this group to spend more on nonproductive or intangible output, such as the services of armies, clergy, teachers, and other retainers whose output is not storable.

It cannot be said that Malthus' position was accepted by any considerable number of economists, but his was one respected voice questioning the unquestioned acceptance of Say's Law, and it opened the way for others to make some attempt to explain fluctuations in economic activity.

REAL OUTPUT AND EMPLOYMENT LEVELS

The study of the determination of national income involves an analysis of supply and demand. It is an important characteristic of the classical school that the major emphasis is on supply or the output of goods and services; because of Say's Law, demand is expected to be sufficient to purchase all that has been produced. Furthermore, since real income (i.e., output) is used as a measure of the welfare of the people, the classicists devoted most of their time to the analysis of the behavior of the supply side in aggregate economics.

The Austrian school of economists classified the economic factors of production as land, labor, capital, and entrepreneurship. Associated with these were rent as the payment for land, or "nature," (the nonaugmentable or God-given resource); wages, the payment for human effort; interest, the reward for waiting or saving embodied in capital goods; and profit, the return to the risk-taker and organizer of business activity. While there is no rigorous way to distinguish among these factors, as there is no way to demonstrate the correspondence between classes of factor payments and the individual factors, we have continued to use the terminology as a matter of convenience.

---

[3] Adam Smith, *An Inquiry into the Nature and Causes of the Wealth of Nations*, Modern Library edition, edited by Edwin Cannan (New York: Random House, Inc., 1937).

In the long run, or in a growth context, the total volume of output of goods and services the economy is capable of producing depends on the quality and on the quantities of all these factors. At the moment our analysis is focused on the short run where, given both the state of the arts and the nonhuman resources as fixed, real national output depends on the level of employment.

The law of diminishing returns states that if all other resources are constant, the total product will increase at a decreasing rate as employment increases. This means that the marginal physical product of labor declines as hours worked increases, both at the level of the firm and at the level of the total economy. Figure 4-2 shows the application of this important principle.

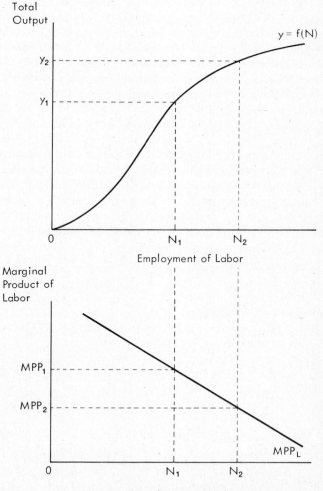

Figure 4-2

Application of Law of Diminishing Returns

The upper portion of the graph shows the aggregate production function where real output y depends on the amount of labor used N. The law of diminishing returns is reflected in the declining slope of the curve (concave from below). The same thing is shown in the lower half of the diagram since the line labeled MPP_L, the marginal physical product of labor, is precisely the slope of the production function.

The *marginal physical product of labor* is defined as the change in total output per unit change in the input, labor. Mathematically, it is the first derivative of the production function, $\frac{\partial y}{\partial N}$. Note carefully that the vertical scale of the upper portion of the graph may be many millions of times larger than the scale on the vertical axis of the lower portion. Thus, if total production in the economy were the equivalent of 500 billion bushels of wheat per year ($y_1 = 500,000,000,000$), the marginal physical product of labor might be the equivalent of 2,000 bushels per worker year ($MPP_1 = 2,000$) when N_1 workers are employed. If employment increased to N_2, total output might be y_2 or 700 billion (bushels of wheat equivalent) and the marginal physical product of labor might be MPP_2 or 1,200 (bushels equivalent).

The Demand for Labor

We will continue the hypothetical example of the preceding paragraph to show that the marginal physical product of labor becomes the demand for labor curve. For this we have to turn to the individual firm. This particular firm (farm) finds that its output is 25,000 bushels of wheat when it employs 10 workers full time for the year along with particular amounts of land, seed, equipment, and other resources. If the manager determines that by employing one more worker (and not changing anything else) the output will increase to 27,000 bushels, the marginal physical product of labor is estimated to be 2,000 bushels for those conditions. If the expense of hiring another worker is less than the value to the firm of the 2,000 bushels, it would be profitable to employ the additional worker.

The law of diminishing returns implies that if this manager continues to add workers, the increase in the total product will be smaller each time another worker is added. Thus, if the wage per year per worker were the value equivalent of 2,000 bushels of wheat, the farm would employ not more than 11 workers. On the other hand, if the wage were equal to 1,200 bushels of wheat, this firm might employ 20 workers if the output increased by 1,200 when the 20th worker is added to the work force.

For this business unit the demand curve for labor is its marginal physical product curve because, whatever the wage, the number of workers the firm will wish to employ is that number at which the wage and the marginal physical product of labor are equal.

Extending the analysis to the whole economy, the marginal physical product curve derived from the aggregate production function is society's demand for labor. This is also the summation of the individual firm's demand for labor curves.

The Supply of Labor

Like the demand for labor function, the explanation of the supply of labor is found in microeconomic theory foundations. Every potential worker is viewed as having a preference function relating the conflicting desires for income and the things it will buy on the one hand and leisure on the other hand. The point of this is that to get the income, the worker will have to expend effort and tolerate the onerousness of work, but to enjoy the leisure some income will have to be given up.

The form of the function implies that the more one works in any given period of time, such as a week or a year, the more distasteful work becomes, the more attractive an additional hour of leisure becomes, and the less utility is attached to any additional income. It can be inferred from this that the utility maximizing individual will be willing to work more hours per time period at a higher rather than a lower wage rate. Some individuals enter the labor force only when wage rates reach a certain height so that the higher the wages the larger the labor force will be. This seems to be particularly characteristic of younger people (especially students), older people who remain in the labor force longer before retiring, and homemakers. In a completely open society higher wages would also attract workers by way of immigration.

The upshot of all this is the assertion that the supply of labor curve is upward sloping. Many economists, however, believe that at some relatively high wage any further increases in wage rates will decrease the total hours of labor offered. This proposition seems plausible by the observation that when wages are high, family income becomes large enough so the family can "afford" to enjoy the choice of sending the children to college and having the homemaker remain at home rather than work for wages.

It would appear to be unquestionable that the supply curve of labor for a particular firm, industry, or occupation is positive since workers would be attracted from other firms, industries, or occupations as the wages of one grew while others did not. It would, of course, be fallacious to infer that this necessitates a positive aggregate labor supply curve. Nevertheless, empirical evidence seems to support the positive supply function hypothesis, and in any case, classical economists accepted it. Indeed, all economists treat the "backward bending" portion as an exceptional case.

Wage and Employment Determination

A fundamental tenet of classical economics is that both the demand and supply of labor depend on the real wage rather than the money wage rate. The real wage is defined as the money wage divided by the price level, $w = \dfrac{W}{P}$.

Real wages change when there is a change in the money wage rate or in commodity prices; real wages remain the same if both money wages and the price level change in the same direction and proportion. Real wages rise if the rate of increase in money wages exceeds the rate of rise in the general price level, or if prices fall more rapidly than wage rates fall. Similar observations are pertinent to the case of declining real wages.

The equilibrium real wage and the amount of employment are determined simultaneously at the point where labor supply and demand are equal. Figure 4-3 shows the picture.

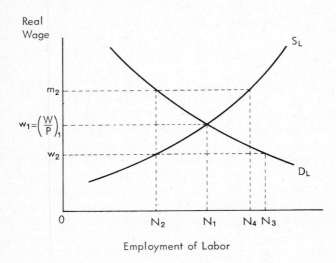

Figure 4-3

Demand and Supply of Labor, and the Real Wage

If both parties in the labor market are price takers, that is, if competition prevails, the wage will be $w_1 = \left(\frac{W}{P}\right)_1$, and employment will be N_1. N_1 represents one concept of full employment, but not one that agrees with employment statistics. N_1 is full employment in the sense that everyone who wishes to work at the prevailing wage $\left(\frac{W}{P}\right)_1$ can do so. If the demand curve were to shift continuously to the left, the equilibrium level of employment would continuously decrease but we would still be at full employment. Fewer people would be working because fewer would wish to work at the lower wages.

As long as the wage and employment combination are on the supply curve, the labor force is in equilibrium. Laborers will be at their optimum if the wage is $\left(\frac{W}{P}\right)_1$, or at any lower wage. For example, at a wage of w_2, workers would wish to work at the level N_2. Since there is nothing to prevent them from being employed at that level, they are in equilibrium—they are in fact doing what they wish to do *given the real wage*.

At any wage below w_1 it is the employers who are out of equilibrium. Employers *wish* to employ N_3 if the wage is w_2, but since workers will only supply N_2 amount of labor the employers will be unable to employ as many as they wish. In this circumstance it is evident that some producers would be willing to raise wages since, at N_2 employment, the marginal physical product of labor (m_2) is greater than the price of labor (w_2). As the wage rises two things happen: (1) workers are induced to increase their provision of labor (moving upward on the supply curve), and (2) the marginal physical product decreases (moving down the demand curve). Whereas at wage w_2 employers wish to employ N_3, at wage w_1 they wish to employ N_1, which is exactly the amount of employment workers wish to render.

At all wages above w_1 the business units would be at their optimums since they would be able to employ the number of workers they wish to employ (N_2 if the wage were equal to m_2). However, the workers would not be in equilibrium. More of them would wish to work (N_4) than employers would be willing to hire. The unemployed workers would then be expected to offer to work at lower wages. Lower wages would then increase the number of workers that business would employ, and at the same time reduce the labor time offered by at least some workers.

Thus, given the demand and supply curves as drawn on Figure 4-3, the wage will be w_1 and employment will be N_1. As an exercise in understanding this system, visualize an ongoing process of inflation in which workers and their employers are raising wages faster than the prices of commodities are rising. The real wage will go above w_1, resulting in unemployment. This situation could persist, bring about inflation and unemployment concurrently, a situation which seemed so perplexing to many people in the early 1970s. Of course, one would expect that the pressure of unemployment would slow the rate of increase in money wages and restore equilibrium.

Suppose the opposite situation of inflation of commodity prices more rapid than increases in money wage rates was in effect. In this circumstance where prices are rising faster than wages, the real wage would fall below w_1, employers would be unable to employ as many workers as they would like, and they would thus offer higher money wages. The real wage would thus return to w_1 and employment would be N_1 again.

We must emphasize that the labor market we have been describing is of the greatest significance to the classical school since it is here that the real national income and output are determined. The money supply has nothing to do with it. Fiscal policy has nothing to do with it. Saving and investment have nothing to do with it. Those things are of some importance but they do not determine real national income or product. The roles played by these variables in the classical model will now be discussed.

MONEY IN THE CLASSICAL SYSTEM

The role of money in classical economics is simply to determine the absolute price level. By absolute price we mean the price of a commodity in terms of the unit of account. For example, if a loaf of bread costs 30 cents and a particular shirt has a price of $3.00, these are the absolute prices. Their relative prices are determined by supply and demand and are one to ten, and ten to one, with respect to each other. At another time the absolute prices of these same goods might be, respectively, 60 cents and $6.00, in which event their relative prices haven't changed. The classical economist would say that the really important prices are the relative prices and that money has no influence on them.[4]

The quantity theory of money is the classical explanation of the general price level or, in other words, the value of money. The quantity theory is the oldest, and also perhaps the newest, monetary theory. Of course, it has evolved with greater sophistication over a period of time. Its earliest statement was based on the simple observation that when currency in a country increased, the prices of commodities also increased; and when currency flowed out of the country, prices fell. Later versions introduced refinements that involved the rapidity with which the money was spent and the volume of production.

The equation that is the starting point of any discussion of the quantity theory is called the *equation of exchange: MV = Py*. In the equation, M stands for the money supply, V stands for the velocity of circulation of that money, P stands for the general price level, and y is a measure of the production of goods and services.

There is never any debate over whether the equation is true or not. If the components are carefully defined, it is a tautology, a truism, or an identity. Looking at the left side, we multiply the number of units of money by the average number of times each unit was spent to buy the things included in y during a specified period of time. MV, then, is the total spending of that money for those things which were purchased in that period. If y is the total number of units of goods and services sold and P is their average price, then Py is the total value of those goods and services. No one questions that total spending for a particular group of commodities is equal to the total money received from the sale of those same commodities. In itself this is a good disciplinary device. We must be careful not to say anything that contradicts a true statement. We can choose any set of goods, such as those which are included in the gross national product, or all goods and services, to define y. But once y has been defined, for the equation to be true, P and V must have reference to the same set.

An alternative statement, called the Cambridge equation, which involves the same variables is $M = kPy$. The only new symbol introduced here is k, and the only one not included is V. The relationship between V and k is very simple. From $MV = Py$, it can be seen that $V = \dfrac{Py}{M}$. From $M = kPy$, obviously $k = \dfrac{M}{Py}$. Thus, $V = \dfrac{1}{k}$ and $k = \dfrac{1}{V}$. For example, if $V = 4$, it means that on the average each piece of money is spent four times per period (assume it to be one year). In that event $k = \dfrac{1}{4}$, which means that on the average each piece of money is not spent on y for one fourth of the year, or three months. Another way of

---

[4] This dichotomy in the classical system between the determination of absolute and relative prices has been the subject of considerable debate in recent years. For a convenient summary of the issues involved, see Robert L. Crouch, *Macroeconomics* (New York: Harcourt Brace Jovanovich, Inc., 1972), Ch. 15.

looking at k is to observe that it is the portion $\left(\frac{1}{4}\right)$ of annual spending (Py) that is held in cash balances (M).

Looked at in this last way, $M = kPy$ can be viewed as a demand for money function. But if it is that, it is no longer a truism; and if it is no longer a truism, we need a new definition of k. Now, instead of k being the portion of total spending held in the form of money, it is the portion of total spending that economic units *wish* to hold in the form of money. To see the difference, let us take an example in which the monetary system determines the money supply originally at \$100 billion; the money value of national income is in equilibrium at \$400 billion. Since equilibrium exists, k of the identity (call it k') is the same as k of the equation (call it simply k). Both have a value of $\frac{1}{4}$: $\$100 = \frac{1}{4}$ (\$400).

Now, suppose the operations of the monetary system act to double the money supply to \$200 billion. The truism reads: $\$200 = \frac{1}{2}$(\$400). k' has doubled from $\frac{1}{4}$ to $\frac{1}{2}$ because people are holding one half of total spending in the form of money. Since the money exists, someone must hold it, but our demand for money equation says that people wish to hold only \$100 billion when income is \$400, so $\$200 \neq \frac{1}{4}$(\$400) — a disequilibrium condition. Economic units are holding twice as much money as they wish to hold, and we would expect them to take steps to reduce their money balances until they hold the desired amount. But by our assumption that only the monetary system can control the money supply, any individual can reduce cash balances only by inducing others to increase their balances. This can be accomplished by buying more things at the old prices or paying a higher price for the same number of things. In other words, either y or P will increase. If everyone holds rigidly to their original judgment on the portion of their income they should hold in money balances, and if no change in income distribution occurs, Py will continue to rise until it reaches \$800. Only then will equilibrium exist where both k and k' are $\frac{1}{4}$: $\$200 = \frac{1}{4}$(\$800). Notice that if real output remained constant so that all of the expansion were accounted for by the increase in the price level, then the real value of money holdings would not change even though more money was held.

The example we have just covered is, of course, too extreme. No contemporary quantity theorist believes that k is quite as rigid as the one in our example. There is the opposite extreme view that is characteristic of those whom we might call antiquantity theorists who believe that in certain circumstances, notably in a severe depression, k will change proportionately with any change in the money supply so that money supply changes have no effect on national income. Going back to our example, where the original equilibrium situation was $\$100 = \frac{1}{4}$(\$400), a doubling of the money supply would cause both k and k' to become one half, $\$200 = \frac{1}{2}(\$400)$. This says that people are willing to hold any additional amounts of money the monetary system creates, and that they will not increase their rate of spending because of these increased amounts.

These two examples should make it clear that the usefulness of the quantity theory depends upon the degree of stability of k or its reciprocal, V, and even more importantly upon their independence of M. This is not as simple to determine as it might appear, since k itself cannot be measured directly. Statistically, we can measure only k', and even in the example above, where k was rigidly fixed, k' did vary. Quantity theorists, especially Irving Fisher, believed that the size of cash balances was mainly determined mechanically by institutional arrangement for payments in the system. Thus, the frequency of receipts and disbursements and the degree of correspondence between them would be important, as would the efficiency of the transportation and communication systems, the degree of specialization and integration of industry, population changes, habits of thrift and hoarding, and the use of trade credit. These are all factors that would change only slowly over time, and furthermore would not seem to be related in any systematic way to the money supply. A modern critic might point out that several important influences have been neglected, such as expectations of future price level and interest rate changes and the relative attractiveness of substitutes for money, such as savings accounts, bonds, and potential borrowing sources.

It has been observed recently that it would be consistent with classical thought to include the interest rate as an argument in the demand for money relation even if the transaction motive is the only reason for holding money. The point of this is that the (opportunity) cost of holding money is the interest income foregone; thus, the higher the interest rate, the greater will be the incentive for more efficient cash management. At lower interest rates it would not be profitable to incur the costs of economizing on cash balances.

If k is assumed to be a constant for the moment, then an increase in the money supply must increase Py proportionately; however, the question remains, will P increase, or will it be y, or might both increase? To the rigid classicist the answer has to be that P alone will increase since y is always at its practicable maximum through the efficiency of the free market system and is determined in the labor market (as discussed earlier in this chapter). Real income, of course, would be expected to rise secularly as the state of the arts advances and as capital and population grow; but in the short run, these could be assumed to be fixed. For this reason the quantity theory was, above all, the explanation of the absolute level of prices and was a supplement to the explanation of relative prices through micro supply and demand analysis. To some business cycle theorists, however, the quantity theory was used to explain variations in both output and prices. In contemporary analysis the point is usually made that the closer the economy is to full employment or "full capacity," the less y can change so that increases in M result in significant changes in P; but when large-scale unemployment or "excess capacity" exists, the increase in M can increase y with negligible effects on P.

The graphic analysis in Figure 4-4 ties together some of the ideas developed so far in describing the classical system. Part (a) graphs the strict quantity theory. If the stock of money is M_0, the nominal level of national income will be $(Py)_0$. The slope of the line is the value of V, the income velocity of money, or the reciprocal of k. Thus, if $V = 4$, Py is simply four times as large as the money supply. If the quantity of money in the economy is increased by $10 billion, the money value of national income will increase by $40 billion.

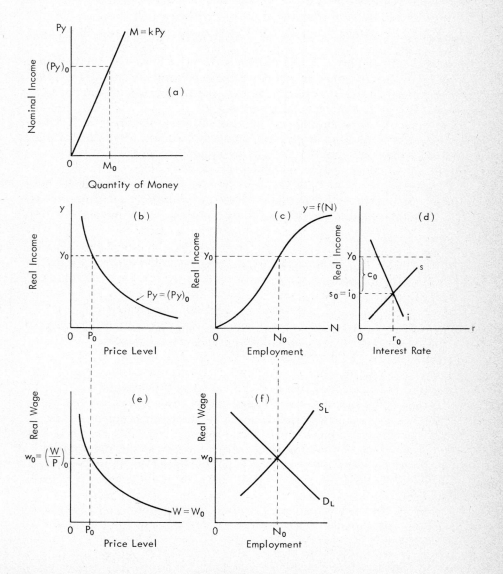

Figure 4-4
The Classical Aggregate System

Part (b) shows the combination of y's multiplied by P's to give the product $(Py)_0$ [as determined in Part (a)]. The curve is a rectangular hyperbola.

Part (c), the aggregate production function, was explained earlier. Here, given employment of N_0, the level of real national income is y_0. If the volume of production of goods and services is y_0 and [from Part (a)] Py is $(Py)_0$, then Part (b) shows that the price level must be P_0.

The level of employment is derived in the labor market (also explained earlier), and shown as Part (f). The real wage is seen to be the money wage (W) divided by the price level (P).

This real wage $\left(\dfrac{W}{P}\right)_0$ is consistent with an infinite number of combinations of money wages and price levels, but since the price level was determined (in our figure) in Part (b), only one money wage is possible. This is shown in Part (e). The curve $W = W_0$ shows the points of w and P_0 consistent with the money wage W_0. It, too, is a rectangular hyperbola.

To complete the picture that is usually described as the classical system we have repeated the saving-investment graph as Part (d). Since the total real output is shown to be y_0 in Part (c) and investment is i_0 in Part (d), the production and sale of consumption goods and services is $y_0 - i_0 = c_0$.

Many of the implications of the classical system can be shown with the aid of this set of diagrams. Notice that one can trace the effects of changes in any of the variables on all of the others. These can be listed in the following way:

From Part (a)
1. M can change—move left or right on the abscissa.
2. k (or V) can change—rotate the function clockwise (if V falls) or counterclockwise (if V rises).

From Part (c)
3. The production function can shift upward (if productivity increases) or downward (if productivity decreases) as the quantities and/or qualities of the nonlabor factors change, or as the quality of labor changes.

From Part (d)
4. The investment function can shift or rotate as the expected profitability of capital changes because of innovations, or by changes in the quantities or qualities of the other factors of production.
5. The saving function can shift or rotate as the public changes its relative preferences between present and future goods.
6. If government is included in the model the s function can incorporate taxes and the i function can incorporate government spending, thus shifting either of the functions whenever government spending or taxation changes.

From Part (f)
7. The relative preferences of the population among work, leisure, and income change, or the population changes via immigration or increased or decreased birth and death rates, causing the supply of labor curve to shift and/or rotate. (Note that the demand for labor curve can change only if the production function changes as mentioned in 3 above.)

A complete taxonomy would require us to perform two further chores. First, we should list all of the possible real world events which could cause the variables to change as specified above, and secondly, we should trace the implications of each variable shift on the total system. Since this would be a lifetime of analysis, we will have to be content with an example or two.

CHANGES IN THE SUPPLY OF OR DEMAND FOR MONEY

Our first example is designed to trace the impact of a change in either the supply of money or in the demand for money on the various endogenous variables included in this analysis. The conclusion is reached that the nominal

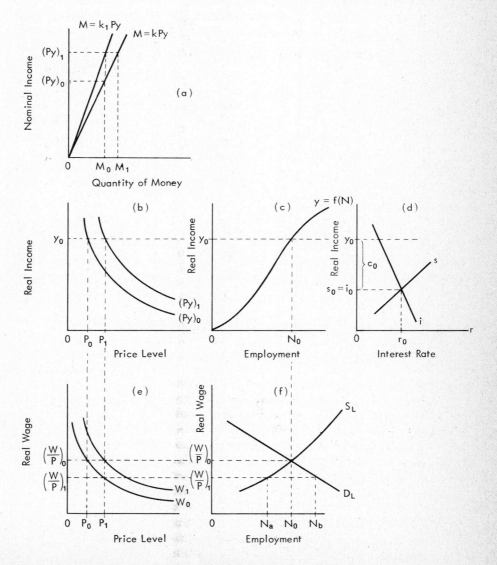

Figure 4-5

Monetary Changes and the Classical System

variables (i.e., those expressed in money prices, namely nominal income, nominal consumption, nominal savings, nominal investment, the price level, and the nominal wage) change, but that the real variables (output, real wage, employment, the interest rate, real consumption, real saving, and real investment) all remain the same. The explanation follows.

In Part (a) of Figure 4-5, page 85, nominal national income is caused to be increased to $(Py)_1$ by either an increase in the stock of money to M_1 or a decrease in the demand for money (a decrease in the numerical value of k to k_1, which is an increase in V).

Since the money value of national income has increased, a new higher rectangular hyperbola has been drawn in Part (b) and labeled $(Py)_1$. Production of goods and services (y_0) has not changed so the price level must increase to P_1. Our problem is to find out if y will change. If the money wage remains at W_0, the real wage will fall to $\left(\dfrac{W}{P}\right)_1$, as shown in Parts (e) and (f). But at that real wage the demand for labor (N_b) exceeds the supply of labor (N_a) and employers will have to raise the money wage to get all the workers they wish to employ. Clearly, the money wage will rise until the real wage returns to $\left(\dfrac{W}{P}\right)_0$. That money wage will be W_1, a new rectangular hyperbola, as shown in Part (e). The money wage had to increase in exactly the same proportion as the price level for the ratio $\dfrac{W}{P}$ to remain the same.

Since the real wage did not change (because of the originating change in the money supply or demand), the level of employment did not change. Therefore, real output (y) did not change either, which is what the classicists wished to prove. The real system is not affected by the money system. Money is a veil.

CHANGE IN THE PRODUCTIVITY OF LABOR

Figure 4-6 shows how changes in the productivity of labor brought about by (for example) changes in the amount of capital with which laborers have to work affect the variables in the system.

In Part (d) we show a positive amount of investment taking place. This means that in the next time period, the stock of capital goods will be larger than it was. Any given amount of labor employed should produce a larger amount of output than before. As shown in Figure 4-6, the aggregate production function of Part (c) has shifted upward. So has the demand for labor in Part (f) shifted upward to D'_L.

From our earlier arguments we know that the real wage will have to go to the new equilibrium of $\left(\dfrac{W}{P}\right)_1$, and employment to the larger level of N_1. Real output then increases to y_1 on Part (c). Since nothing has happened to cause any change in Py on Part (a), the price level will fall in the same proportion as y increased. In the particular case drawn here the money wage has fallen, but it might have risen or remained the same. The new money wage curve in Part (e) must intersect the point determined by the coordinates of the new real wage and the new price level.

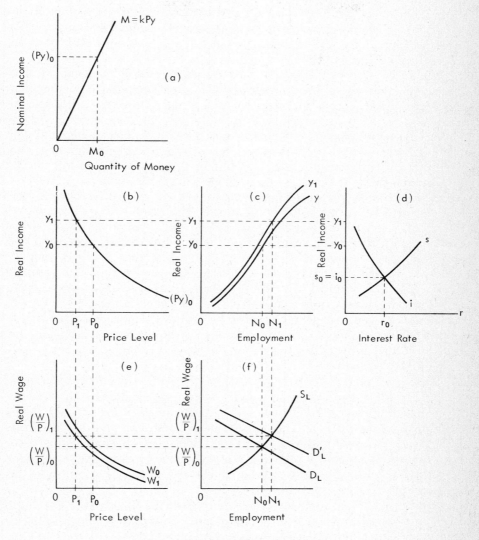

Figure 4-6

Effect of an Increase in Labor Productivity on the Economic System

CLASSICAL THEORY OF ECONOMIC GROWTH

Economic growth theory is covered in a more substantial way in Part 7. At this point we wish merely to present the basic elements of the classical analysis of growth. Referring again to the set of diagrams in Figure 4-6, economic growth is a process of rising national output, shown by an upward shift of the production function in Part (c) and/or a movement to a higher point on the same aggregate production function.

The discussion that follows is restricted to the growth which is unquestionably desirable; that is, growth in per capita national income. This means that we are dealing with a shifting production function which, in turn, implies an upward shifting demand for labor function as in Part (f).

Such shifts are expected to arise via expansion of the stock of capital; that is, positive investment. Since investment can only occur to the extent that saving takes place, economic growth requires the willingness of people to abstain from present consumption. The rate of growth, then, depends on the saving propensities of the population and on the productivity of capital. Each individual is viewed as deciding his or her own personal growth plans. The interest rate is determined in the total market so the individual takes the interest rate as given. The individual determines that at the given rate of interest a certain amount of current income will be saved and a larger amount of purchasing power will be received in the future. The individual will receive the larger future income as payment for having made resources available to business units (by buying bonds or stock, or by direct investment) who use them for productive investment.

It would seem that there is no role for government to play in the growth process other than assuring that society possesses the necessary social capital, such as transportation and communications systems, a legal environment conducive to the encouragement of business activity, a stable government, and so on. The "right" rate of growth depends solely on the conditions governing the productivity of resources and the rate of savings of the population *in toto* as determined by individual decisions.

Classical economists stressed the economic growth associated with population growth, but their conclusion was that while aggregate income increased with population, per capita income declined. The reason for this, once again, is that pillar of the classical school, the law of diminishing returns. The pessimistic view of Ricardo and Malthus on the implications of population growth superseded Adam Smith's principle that economic activity becomes more efficient as specialization and division of labor develops in response to the expansion of the market as population grows.

The Ricardo-Malthus analysis is summarized in Figure 4-7. The horizontal axis shows population or, what amounts to the same thing, the labor force. Real output appears on the vertical axis, and the curve drawn shows the declining marginal physical product of labor.

As explained earlier in this chapter, if the population is N_0, the real wage will be w_0. If the population increases, the real wage, which really stands for the standard of living, will fall along the curve MPP_L. In this analysis the population will grow until the wage falls to the subsistence level, w_0. Were the population to increase beyond the point consistent with the subsistence wage, the standard of living would be so low that the population-labor force would decline through ill health, earlier deaths, fewer births due to later marriages, higher infant mortality, and so on.

Thus, if w_0 is the subsistence level, any wage higher than this (such as w_a, which would exist if population were N_a) will encourage growth in population and the labor force through better health, longer life, more births, earlier marriages, lower infant mortality, and so on. Since a wage of w_b would cause a reduction of the population from N_b toward N_0, there would be a tendency for the population always to move toward that level at which the wage would be at the subsistence level, and population would be N_0.

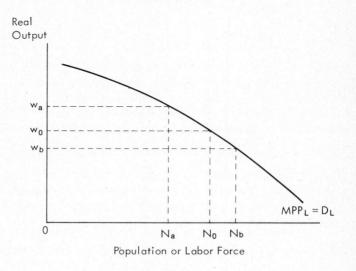

Figure 4-7

Population Growth and Wages

An important issue in this analysis is the connection between population growth and economic well-being as represented by per capita national income. Empirical evidence does seem to support the hypothesis that the two are indeed related, though the correspondence is not as close as implied by the theory. An immediately related consideration involves the meaning of the term, subsistence wage. Does the concept imply some physiological minimum standard of life sustenance? If so, the evidence in the developed economies contradicts the expectations derived from the theory, though in underdeveloped societies the analysis appears to be a not unreasonable description.

If we abandon the absolute notion of subsistence, the subsistence wage can be defined simply as that real wage at which population would be constant — or in equilibrium. This could be a relatively high wage in some societies where, if the wage fell below the equilibrium, the people would make the conscious decision to reduce the population by lowering the number of children per family, by reducing the number of families by later marriage, or by restricting immigration or increasing emigration. In other words, the population and labor force would not decline because of the inadequacy of diets, housing, medical care, etc., but because of the judgment that the marginal benefits of additions to the population are less than the marginal costs.

The later classical economists, neoclassicists, rejected the hypothesis of population as a function of real per capita income; they considered the growth rate of population to be exogenously determined for the purpose of analysis. The problem lies in the relationships among the rate of growth in the labor force, the rate of growth of the productivity of capital, and the rate of saving.

If the labor force is growing at the rate n $(n = \dfrac{\Delta S_L}{S_L}$, and S_L stands for the supply of labor), the real wage will fall unless the rate of growth of national income $\left(m = \dfrac{\Delta y}{y}\right)$ is equal to or greater than n. As shown in Figure 4-8, for the standard of living (real wage) to remain at the current level (w_0), as the labor force increases from N_0 to N_1 the marginal physical product of labor schedule will have to shift to $MPP_{L(1)}$. For this to happen the stock of capital must increase in the same proportion as the increase in the labor force (with no change in the average productivity of capital). That is, $\dfrac{\Delta K}{K}$ must also equal $n = m$. But ΔK is investment and so the rate of saving must be equal to ΔK. Thus, for a steady state of growth the rate of increase in saving must equal the rate of growth in investment which, in turn, must equal the rate of growth in the labor force.

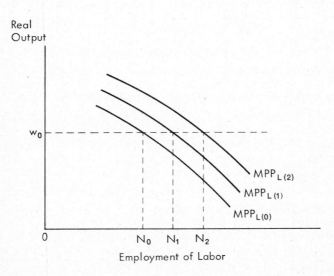

Figure 4-8

Labor Force Growth and Productivity Changes

Any independent change in any of these growth rates necessitates adjustments by the others. This is not the place to get involved in all the possible adjustments and repercussions of these changes. Suffice it at this point to observe that, according to the reasoning of the neoclassicist, since the rate of population change is fixed, the other variables will ultimately return to equality with that rate.

GOVERNMENT IN CLASSICAL ECONOMICS

The role of the state in classical economics was very limited. In general the proposition was that the system, left alone to operate as a system, produced results that were superior to any results which could be foreseen from governmental interferences with the free market forces. The economy was viewed as having a host of self-adjusting mechanisms which produced harmony in the world of commerce. The price system was seen as a way of resolving conflict peaceably.[5]

A set of "rules of the game" was necessary however. A framework was considered necessary, and it was thought to be a proper function of government to provide the legal framework detailing the meaning of private property and human rights. Classical economists frequently have been maligned as hardhearted, laissez-faire advocates, but in point of fact, most of them were very concerned about the human condition of their fellows. They were quick to propose laws making consumer fraud illegal, to favor regulations to control monopoly, and to suggest protective labor legislation.[6]

Aside from establishing the legal environment for the operation of the economic system, the classicists determined other legitimate functions of government, which we shall now briefly review.

Public Good

National defense may be the outstanding example of a public good. It is indivisible. If one person or group buys defense for themselves, it is impossible to exclude others from the enjoyment of that service, and it is impossible to charge for the service what it is worth to the recipients. This might be called the "freeloader" principle. The individual would have to be compelled to pay through the power of the state if the service is to be provided. Adam Smith specifically charged the state with the responsibility of protecting society from external and internal threats of violence.

Externalities or Neighborhood Effects

A principle familiar to students of microeconomics is that an individual is advised to purchase an item if the marginal utility or benefit exceeds the

---

[5] See Armen Alchian and William Allen, *University Economics* (3d ed.; Belmont, California: Wadsworth Publishing Co., Inc., 1972).

[6] See Warren J. Samuels, *The Classical Theory of Economic Policy* (Cleveland: World Publishing Co., 1966).

marginal cost. There are some goods or services where the benefits to other people, or the society, are large in addition to the utility of the decision maker. In this case it might be advantageous to the whole community to bear at least some of the cost. Immunization from communicable diseases and some categories of education are outstanding examples of this situation. These are called "neighborhood effects" or external benefits.

Conversely, there are instances when the market cost to the individual making the decision does not reflect all the costs involved in providing the good or service. Dramatic examples are provided by all forms of pollution where costs are imposed on individuals without regard to the amount of their consumption of the product. These, too, are referred to as "neighborhood effects" or external costs, and may provide justification for governmental interference with the free market system.[7]

Public Works

Classical and neoclassical economists also felt that there was a category of public works proper for government to establish even though it would be feasible for private enterprise to do so. Private enterprise did not because of the great capital requirement, the high risk involved, or the expense of collecting the price. A network of streets and highways might involve all these reasons for private firms not to undertake such a project. The Tennessee Valley Authority is often cited as an example of a project which the federal government initiated because private firms seemed unlikely to be capable of providing such a service (in addition to the contention that great social benefits would be a concomitant).

The private sector will not produce where the probability of profit is not present. In some instances (where externalities are significant) the public sector should provide goods or services, rather than have the community do without them. This argument is often used in support of public transit systems.

Monopoly

Where one firm can operate profitably but two or more firms in the industry could operate only at a loss, a monopoly situation usually arises. This is often due to decreasing costs as output is expanded within the range of the demand for the product, though it sometimes occurs by virtue of ownership of certain unique factors of production, including patents and other forms of governmental protection. Three possibilities in response to such circumstances are possible, and classical economists as well as others have differed in their decisions as to the best approach. The three possibilities are mentioned here without elaboration. They are: (1) to socialize, that is, to accept public ownership and control; (2) to allow private ownership regulated by a governmental authority as we do in our public utilities; and (3) to allow private ownership unfettered by government in the hope that competitive products or services will develop over time.

---

[7] There is a growing body of literature developing on this topic. See, for example, Henry G. Manne (ed.), *The Economics of Legal Relationships* (St. Paul: West Publishing Co., 1975).

Taxation

Government, to be able to perform its functions, must finance its expenditures and normally this will be done through taxation. The principle of a balanced budget was generally viewed as a virtue until the mid-1930s. Taxation was not thought of as a positive force for influencing aggregate economic activity, but as a necessary evil. Indeed, since real income was determined in the labor market and nominal income was determined by the money supply and velocity, government spending could occur only at the expense of private expenditures. The idea is that since the total pie is fixed in size, if one sector takes a larger slice, there will be less available to the remaining groups.

QUESTIONS

1. Explain the difference between Say's Law viewed as an identity and Say's Law viewed as a condition of equilibrium. Why is this distinction important?
2. Using classical interest rate theory, explain why the interest rate would rise if it were below the intersection of the saving and investment curves. It is not enough to say that aggregate demand is greater than aggregate supply, although that is true.
3. Show that a firm should employ the number of workers at which the marginal physical product of labor is equal to the additional expense of hiring one more worker.
4. The general proposition is that the supply of labor offered in the economy increases as the real wage increases. Explain why this statement seems plausible.
5. What would be the impact on the classical labor market situation if some outside agent forced nominal (money) wages to be higher than the equilibrium wage rate? Demonstrate graphically that in this case the problem could be cured by the inflation of prices of other goods and services.
6. Explain the difference between relative prices and absolute prices. What is the importance of each concept?
7. Some writers state the Cambridge form of the equation of exchange as $\frac{M}{P} = ky$.

   Review the meaning of the terms, and interpret this equation.
8. "Labor unions (or monopolies) are the cause of inflation." Using the tautology $MV = Py$, what arguments would be necessary to defend such a statement?
9. Graph the complete classical system and show that an autonomous increase in investment (or government expenditures) will redistribute the output of the economy, but (in the absence of any change in the money stock) will not increase real output or the absolute price level.
10. Write an essay explaining why you think classical economists minimized the role of government in the economic system, and explain what principles were used to justify government involvement.

SUGGESTED READINGS

Ackley, Gardner. *Macroeconomic Theory.* New York: The Macmillan Co., 1961. (Part II).

Heilbroner, Robert L. *The Worldly Philosophers,* rev. ed. New York: Simon and Schuster, 1972.

Kuhn, W. E. *The Evolution of Economic Thought,* 2d ed. Cincinnati: South-Western Publishing Co., 1970.

Laidler, David E. W. *The Demand for Money: Theories and Evidence.* Scranton, Penn.: International Textbook Co., 1969.

Miller, Merton H., and Charles W. Upton. *Macroeconomics: A Neoclassical Introduction.* Homewood, Ill.: Richard D. Irwin, Inc., 1974.

Pigou, Arthur C. *The Theory of Unemployment.* London: Macmillan and Co., Ltd., 1933.

――――. *Employment and Equilibrium,* 2d ed. New York: The Macmillan Co., 1952.

――――. "Some Considerations on Stability Conditions, Employment, and Real Wage Rates." *Economic Journal,* Vol. LV, No. 220 (December, 1945).

Samuels, Warren J. *The Classical Theory of Economic Policy.* Cleveland: World Publishing Co., 1966.

CHAPTER 5

AN INTRODUCTION TO BUSINESS CYCLE THEORIES

In the next two chapters we deal with theories of the business cycle. Before embarking on this project, it might be well to ask why we take the time to study different and even conflicting theories rather than devoting all our effort to the presentation of "the" theory of the business cycle. Fluctuations in economic activity are far too complex to be incorporated into a single universal theory applicable to every historical period. There is a great deal to be learned from each theory that is relevant to today's student even though the theory might have been developed many years ago. Each theory stresses certain forces or aspects of the economy and necessarily slights others. A complete theory would have to incorporate all of these important causal factors in a systematic way. Even those ideas that may be considered errors of earlier writers are valuable to us because they teach us not to make the same mistakes and point out which alleys are blind.

Virtually all economic theory has been developed with the concept of equilibrium at its core. Movement or changes in any variables are viewed as returns to equilibrium (either to a new one or to an old one) following some exogenous or outside change. It is very difficult to break out of this method of comparative statics to the kind of theory needed to explain the continuity of successive rises and falls in economic activity resulting in cyclical behavior. This has been one of the stumbling blocks to the development of a satisfactory theory of economic fluctuations.

This chapter begins with an explanation of the "cobweb theorem" as an example of the way equilibrium analysis can be made dynamic, thus explaining fluctuations. It is also an example of a "specific cycle" as opposed to the "general cycle" on which we spend most of our time. Other specific cycles which are taken up are the building cycle, hog and cattle cycles, the coffee cycle, and seasonal cycles in a number of industries (all in Chapter 13). In contrast to these the general cycle is measured by variations in more aggregated variables, such as GNP, employment, unemployment, and price levels.

THE COBWEB THEOREM

The business cycle is a phenomenon that occurs over a span of time. Most economic activity, such as production and consumption, usually cannot take place instantaneously. A development may inspire a change in some action, but usually only with a lag in time.

Perhaps the clearest example of the way time lags are responsible for fluctuating economic behavior is to be seen in the "cobweb theorem." It is demonstrated here on a micro level of analysis, although it also has applications in macroeconomic theory.

In the usual price theory, quantities supplied and demanded of a particular commodity are said to be determined by the current price of that commodity and certain other factors. The analysis is termed "static" because it is essentially timeless. Implicitly, all activity takes place instantaneously. In dynamic analysis, the fact that an activity takes time is taken into account, and the results are sometimes considerably different from that flowing from static theory.

In the case of the cobweb theorem, it is assumed that the quantity demanded of a good depends upon the price existing at the time the decision to purchase is made. The notation is $Q_{D_t} = f(P_t)$. (In words: quantity demanded in time period t is a function of price in period t.) This isn't always the best assumption, but for many, perhaps most, commodities it is accurate. It is on the supply side where the most obvious time lag would seem to exist—the production lag. In the cobweb theorem the assumption is made that the decision of the producers to sell different amounts of the good depends on the price of that good at some critical time in advance of the time of sale. A farmer, for example, must decide early in the spring how many acres of land will be devoted to the production of a certain crop that will be harvested in the fall. The amount of fertilizer and water and other care to be applied must also be determined. In any event, these decisions which determine the quantity that will be produced must be made in some time period before the sale can take place. In other words, $Q_{S_t} = f(P_{t-1})$. (Quantity supplied in period t is a function of the price of the product in period $t-1$).

Figure 5-1 has been drawn with the supply function slightly steeper than the demand function (ignoring the signs). We can suppose that the example is potatoes, and the current price (P_0) is above the equilibrium price (P_E) because of a severe drought last year. Potato farmers and potential potato growers, observing this relatively attractive price, decide to produce relatively large quantities of potatoes, $Q_{S(1)}$. When this size crop comes on the market, however, buyers of potatoes will be willing to purchase the entire crop only if the price falls considerably, namely to P_1. P_1, being a price at which little or no profit can be expected, will induce farmers to plan on smaller crops next spring. Many will shift to more promising crops. Thus, the output in time period 2 will be expected to be just $Q_{S(2)}$, a very small output which, when it is grown and harvested, will bring the higher price (P_2). That higher price will induce a larger output ($Q_{S(3)}$) in the next time period, which, in turn, can be sold only at the lower price, (P_3), and so on. A cycle is in operation, represented on the conventional time diagram on the right side of Figure 5-1. If we were to plot the output figures, they would be inverse to the price figures; that is, when price is high, output is low, and vice versa.

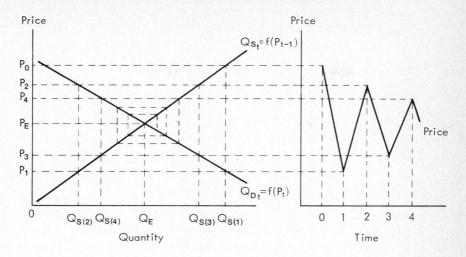

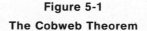

Figure 5-1

The Cobweb Theorem

The cyclical process shown in Figure 5-1 is a convergent cycle, so-called because the variables converge toward equilibrium. If the reader will experiment a bit with different shapes of the demand and supply schedules, it will be discovered that if the demand curve is steeper than the supply curve, the result will be an explosive cycle, that is, one in which price and quantity move farther away from equilibrium each time period. If the two curves are drawn with the same slope, the cycle will be one of constant amplitude. When both functions are relatively steep, price will fluctuate widely and the output cycle will be within a more narrow range; whereas if both curves are relatively flat, the greatest fluctuation will be in output, and the price variation will be mild.

In most industries considerable qualifications to this simple framework would be necessary to make a realistic picture; but in spite of these, the general theory goes a long way toward explaining many of the cycles that do exist in particular products. One of those qualifications is the ability to store the commodity, but the higher the cost of storage the closer does the cobweb theorem approach reality. Closely connected with storability is the existence of speculation in the market for the commodity. The extreme swings in price would probably be evened out where a well-developed futures market exists. Perhaps the most important qualification to the theory is the questioning of the hypothesis that the decision to produce is based blindly on present price instead of the more realistic (but impossible to discover) expected future price. Where government sets a minimum or maximum price or where noncompetitive conditions hold, further qualifications are necessary.

We proceed now to a summary statement of a number of theories that have been advanced to explain the phenomenon of general business cycles. The classification of theories will be that suggested by Gottfried von Haberler in his definitive study, *Prosperity and Depression*.[1]

OUTSIDE FORCE THEORIES

Theories in which the cyclical nature of business activity is explained by the cyclical behavior of some outside force are known as outside force theories or exogenous theories of the business cycle. What is an exogenous or outside variable is sometimes difficult to say. We might all agree that the economic system has no influence on sunspot activity, but what of war, or the discovery of gold, or innovations? A Marxist would probably consider wars to be endogenous (or internal) to the economy, something to be explained by the economist. Cassel[2] argued that gold discovery was an endogenous variable in that lower prices and costs would encourage the prospecting for and mining of gold, the value of which would be high when other prices were low. Schumpeter's theory depends heavily upon the argument that the volume of innovations is strictly dependent upon the stage of the business cycle and is therefore endogenous.[3]

Thus, there is no rule that tells us which factors are really exogenous or endogenous. It depends completely on the theory or the theorist. In general, the procedure is to agree that there is no way for us to know which variables are really exogenous, so we adopt the convention that if the value of a variable is to be explained by the theory, it is endogenous; and if we are not concerned with explaining the behavior of the variable, we call that variable an exogenous one. A variable may actually be both exogenous and endogenous in the same theory. For example, spending by government might be increased for political reasons, in which case the economist will consider that an exogenous change; whereas, if the increased spending were caused by an increase in national income, it would be counted as endogenous.

The appeal of exogenous explanations of the business cycle is easy to understand. We observe fluctuations in business activity. Business activity responds to outside forces. If an outside force behaves cyclically, cycles in business are explained by the cycle in the outside force. Even today, many people are involved in the search for statistical series which are so highly correlated to business conditions that they can be used as forecasting guides. If the movement in the series is not explained by theory, this amounts to an exogenous theory of the business cycle. In an earlier day when agriculture dominated the economy and variations in crop yields were dominated by the weather, it was natural to look for cycles in weather to account for cycles of good and bad trade.

---

[1] Gottfried von Haberler, *Prosperity and Depression* (3d ed.; Geneva: League of Nations, 1941).

[2] Gustav Cassel, *Theory of Social Economy* (New York: Harcourt, Brace & Company, Inc., 1932).

[3] Joseph Schumpeter, *Theory of Economic Development* (Cambridge, Massachusetts: Harvard University Press, 1934).

Changes in Agricultural Yields

Some students of cycles claim to have found a high degree of relationship between cycles in agricultural yields and business cycles. In particular, W. S. Jevons[4] and Henry L. Moore[5] searched for periodicity in meteorological phenomenon consistent with the periodicity in business fluctuations. Jevons found it in sunspot activity and Moore in the peculiarities of the orbit of the planet Venus. Both went on to explain the connection between weather and agricultural activities, and between agricultural activity and general business conditions.

Other scholars, however, have come to exactly opposite conclusions, and in several cases shortcomings were found in the statistical techniques used to establish the relationship between agricultural and business cycles.

This is not intended to imply that changes in agricultural production have no effect on business conditions. When crops are bountiful, prices of agricultural commodities drop and costs in the industrial fields using them as raw materials are reduced. If prices are not reduced in the same proportion, profits increase and higher profits tend to stimulate further capital investment. If prices are reduced and the demand for the product is elastic, consumers buy larger quantities of such goods and thus industrial activity in that field expands. Higher agricultural prices resulting from small crops have just the opposite effect.

Changes in agricultural yields may also affect the income of agricultural areas. The income of agriculture is not changed at the same rate as the change in agricultural yields because prices of most farm products increase sharply when crops are small and drop markedly when crops are large. In those cases in which the demand for a product is quite elastic, however, farmers may get a larger total income in periods of large crops than they do when crops are small. This is especially true when crops are large in a year in which consumer income in general is increasing. More money is also paid to operators of farm services, such as combine crews for harvesting wheat when crops are large, and railroads and trucking companies get more revenue for hauling the products to market.

If exports are increased materially when crops are large, there is also a tendency for business activity to increase. Exports will reduce, in part, the price decline that would occur if all of the crop had to be marketed at home, and so the total income in the domestic economy is increased. As foreign funds flow into the country to pay for the larger exports, there is also a tendency for money supplies to increase and for interest rates to decline. This lowering of interest rates has a stimulating effect on business activity. Just the opposite effect takes place when crops are small and exports are reduced.

---

[4] W. S. Jevons, *Investigations in Currency and Finance* (London: Macmillan and Co., Ltd., 1884).

[5] Henry L. Moore, *Generating Economic Cycles* (New York: The Macmillan Company, 1923). See also his earlier *Economic Cycles: Their Law and Cause* (New York: The Macmillan Company, 1914).

It is not clear, however, from modern records of agricultural production and business fluctuations that such relationships exist between total agricultural yields and general business activity. This situation can be accounted for in several ways. In the first place, agricultural production does not move up and down as a unit. In the same year there may be a good cotton crop and a poor corn crop. The effects on business in general of a large crop of one commodity may thus be offset by the effects of a small crop of another commodity.

There have also been some farmers, especially those who operate on a large scale, who have held their crops in storage in years of low prices and sold them later when prices have been more favorable. This has helped to mitigate the effects of changes in crop yields. Since the early 1930s until quite recently this practice of storing crops has been done on a large scale by the government.

As our industrial economy has expanded, agriculture has accounted for a smaller and smaller proportion of total income so that its influence on business has become less and less. Therefore, its role in initiating changes in economic activity has also become less important. Changes in agricultural yield cannot alone explain the cycle since such changes do not correspond to the regularly recurring cycles of recession and recovery in business.

Sunspots

One of the earliest of the outside force theories of the cycle, and in fact one of the earliest explanations offered for business cycles, was the sunspot cycle theory proposed in 1875 by an English economist of note, W. Stanley Jevons. From the available data on major English business cycles and from fragmentary data on sunspot cycles, he was led to believe that there was a correspondence between them. He reasoned that sunspot cycles must cause changes in agricultural yields and these in turn cause business cycles. This thesis was refuted when research showed that the sunspot cycles were longer than Jevons thought, and that changes in agricultural yields did not correspond closely to business cycles.

The sunspot idea, however, continues to find support from time to time. Different measurements have been made of solar activity, especially of the total area of "bright spots" on the sun, and claims of a high correlation between such measurements and business activity have been made in recent years. An explanation of the relationship suggested in a recent book is that sunspot changes cause changes in the quantity of ultraviolet rays reaching the earth and that this affects the emotional responses and general health of human beings.

A quite sophisticated chain of analysis was forged by Henry L. Moore relating the conjunctures of the sun, Venus, and earth to the weather conditions on earth, particularly in the amount of rainfall. The cycle of favorable and unfavorable weather conditions results in a cycle of high and low crop yields, which, in turn, generates a cycle in the prices of basic raw materials, which then produces a cycle in industrial production and general economic activity.

War Cycles in Population

Some students of cycles, especially in Germany, have reasoned that major cycles can be traced to changes due to major wars, especially population changes. The heavy casualties suffered during a war, especially in the wars preceding World War II, were primarily among young men and so reduced the size of the labor force. The birth rate was also reduced while the men were on the fighting fronts, but it increased sharply when the war was over. Such changes in the number of births affect the birth rate a generation later because many young people marry at about the same time, have some effect two generations later, and gradually disappear.

Some geopolitical theorists have carried the analysis further by arguing that this growth in population exerts such pressure on the limited national territories of some countries that the governments seek relief in attempting to claim the territory of other nations, which precipitates new wars. Thus, war itself is a periodic phenomenon and produces cyclical economic responses.

The effect of wars on population seems well established, and the high birth rates in the years after World War II will affect the American economy for some time to come. The time intervals involved, however, are too long to account for business cycles in general, and certainly this factor cannot account for American cycles in the past.

UNDERCONSUMPTION THEORIES

Underconsumption theories of the cycle are about as old as the discipline of economics itself. These theories have appeared in various forms and have frequently been expounded by writers who lacked formal training in the field of economics. They lend themselves well to the justification for such political schemes as the Townsend Plan of large pensions for old people. The views of many underconsumptionists really do not constitute a complete theory of the cycle since most of them have attempted only to explain the downturn of the cycle and the depression period. A complete analysis of the cycle cannot be based upon such underconsumption theories.

Another difficulty in describing these theories is that the term "underconsumption" is not used in the same sense by all of them. Some of them use underconsumption to mean that the economic system does not pay out sufficient funds to purchase all of the goods that are produced. This point of view should be distinguished from a periodic hoarding of money or slowing down of the velocity of money, which are integral parts of a monetary theory of the cycle. Others use underconsumption to describe a situation in which too large a proportion of income is saved in relationship to that amount which is spent on consumption.

Insufficiency of Purchasing Power

Major C. H. Douglas of England has received considerable publicity for an underconsumption explanation of the cycle based on deficiency of payments.

Douglas tries to make this point by means of his *A plus B theorem.*[6] *A payments* are payments made to individuals, such as wages, salaries, or dividends; while *B payments* are payments made to other organizations, such as those for machinery, raw materials, and the payment of interest on bank loans. *A* payments, of course, automatically and directly become purchasing power for consumers. The difficulty arises with *B* payments, which do not go to consumers directly. These payments are made some time before they are spent by the organizations that receive them. They are thus not available for spending on the present output of goods. In other words, the gap between the value of current output and income that is currently distributed constitutes a deficiency of purchasing power.

Since both *A* and *B* payments are costs and enter into the price, there is a deficiency of purchasing power equal to *B* payments that must be made up. This deficiency can be overcome for a period of time through bank credit. Difficulty soon arises because, as businesses receive the *B* payments, they must be used to pay off earlier bank loans and are not returned to the income stream. If new loans were continuously made as old ones were extinguished, there would be no problem; but Douglas holds that this will not be the case under modern banking practice. This is partly true because interest is charged on each round and also because there are limits to bank credit expansion.

Past cycles do not indicate that the amount of bank credit continuously falls short of the needs of society. In fact, the opposite appears to have been the case more frequently since the Federal Reserve System was established.

The underconsumption thesis is at times based on the failure of the money supply to keep up with the increased demands placed upon it. Improvements in technology and increases in population lead to an increase in the supply of goods that is not accompanied by an increase in the quantity of money, and this in turn leads to a deficiency of purchasing power for consumption. Such an explanation by itself cannot explain the cyclical process since it is based on a long-run imbalance between production and the money supply. There can be a cycle due to monetary factors only if the supply of money moves in a cyclical fashion; and this is, of course, the essence of the purely monetary explanation of the cycle.

Underconsumption as Oversaving

If we were tracing the chronological history of underconsumptionist thought, we would probably start with Malthus (recognizing his roots in Adam Smith's *Wealth of Nations*) and end with the theory of John Maynard Keynes. We could go further and include a later Keynesian such as Professor Alvin Hansen, late of Harvard. Probably the most important stop between Malthus and Keynes would be John A. Hobson, the British economist who presented a persuasive case both for underconsumption as the cause of depression and for a theory of cyclical instability based on underconsumption principles.

Hobson challenged Say's Law directly, asking why, in a world in which human wants are said to be insatiable, large amounts of unsold commodities

---

[6] C. H. Douglas, *Social Credit* (New York: W. W. Norton & Co., Inc., 1933).

appear at the beginning of a business downswing. His answer is that a kind of cultural lag exists. Productivity increases today at a relatively rapid rate. There are no important deterrents in instituting new production methods or innovations that will increase the rate of output. Competition in capitalistic systems forces producers to introduce production-enhancing methods as quickly as possible.

Consumption, on the other hand, is, according to Hobson, a very conservative art. Tradition, custom, and habit dominate. Most consumption is done in private and, Veblen[7] to the contrary notwithstanding, the pressures to increase consumption when income increases are relatively mild. Society is faced with a problem of rapidly increasing powers of production with lagging willingness or ability to consume the increasing output.

In this view of things, if production and income are increasing faster than consumption, savings are growing. This would seem to present no problem if there is sufficient investment demand to absorb this additional output. But if all the additional savings go into new productive capacity by way of investment, the problem becomes still more acute when this new capital begins to add more goods and services to the aggregate supply. Unless one can conceive of a world in which capital goods are continuously being produced to produce more capital goods, a crisis must be pending. The additional productive capacity must either result in inventories of goods unsalable at current prices or in drastic price reductions. In either case the demand for investment will decline sharply and total production will be reduced to a level that can be sustained by consumer demand. This means idle workers and plants—a recession.

We can see in Hobson the beginnings of a dynamic theory of growth. The rate of savings must be just the amount needed to add to the capital stock the productive power to produce increased goods and services at the rate of increase consumers will demand. As we have just seen, if the rate of savings is greater than this a recession will inevitably ensue. When will the downward movement stop? The answer is when excess capacity has been eliminated by depreciation or capital consumption, and when consumers have learned to consume a larger portion of their income, which will happen as incomes fall.

Typically, underconsumption theorists argue that the problem can only be eliminated by a redistribution of wealth and income. Hobson pointed out that most economists believe that the average level of saving is high for high income groups and low for low income groups. This means that a redistribution of income away from the high-saving, high-income recipients in favor of low-saving, low-income workers would result in a lower ratio of savings to spending or income. Therefore, there must be some distribution that would produce a rate of savings compatible with the rate of increase in productivity. He recognized that if the redistribution were carried too far in the direction of equality, the rate of savings could be so low that economic progress would be impeded. On the other hand, he pointed out that progress was also slowed by the intermittent periods of depressed business conditions under the present income distribution.

---

[7] Thorstein B. Veblen, *The Theory of the Leisure Class* (New York: The Modern Library, 1934).

It must be conceded that the underconsumption theory, as presented by its most capable adherents, is highly convincing. It is not something out of the dead past. It is present doctrine for many, and aspects of it are accepted by virtually all economists. New Deal policies as well as many current government policies imply the acceptance of the basic hypothesis. Anyone who thinks that our economy would be in serious difficulty if the defense budget were slashed is an underconsumptionist.

It would be a mistake for the reader at this stage to accept the underconsumptionist position. What is intuitively so plausible may not be true. Actually, the relationship of consumption and saving to income is not as simple and straightforward as it may seem at this point.

Outline of the Underconsumption Cycle

The expansion phase of the business cycle is characterized by underconsumptionists as a period when, as income rises, wages tend to lag behind the growth in other incomes, especially the profit component. Since it is contended that wage earners spend a larger proportion of their income on consumer goods than do the higher income profit recipients, saving grows at an increasing rate during the upswing of the business cycle. The rate of growth in saving must reach a point where it is in excess of the amount of investment that can feasibly be justified on the basis of the current amount of consumption. This brings about the crisis, or upper turning point.

During the resulting contraction phase incomes fall, but now profit incomes fall more rapidly than the incomes of wage earners. Since profit earners have high saving to income ratios relative to wage earners, saving declines more rapidly than consumption and income. In the early stages of the downswing, the supply of capital is large relative to the need for it as expressed by the demand for consumption. For this reason investment will fall off very sharply and will remain depressed until the forces of depreciation reduce the stock of capital to a level consistent with the current rate of consumer goods output. The downswing is supposed to stop when consumption stabilizes, and consumption will stop falling as income is transferred from the low consumption group of profit recipients to the high consumption group of laborers. The stage is then set for a reversal of direction of economic activity, which will happen when investment increases.

PSYCHOLOGICAL THEORY OF THE BUSINESS CYCLE

We shall next consider the theories of economists who consider psychological factors as the dominant forces causing oscillations in economic activity. One should not get the impression from this that other economists ignore the psychology of decision makers in their theories. Since any economic decision has its psychological aspects, every economist is concerned with them to some degree. Those who are not included as psychological theorists, however, generally take the state of mind of the economic unit as given. Their usual reaction is that changes in psychology are very important, but that they have no ability to predict the cause of these changes beyond what is already incorporated in their theory. When prices have been rising for some time, for example, some people will expect them to continue to rise; others will feel that since they have gone up so long they are sure to fall soon. It is relatively easy, after the fact, to say that expectations were such and such. It is very difficult, if not impossible, to say what they are or what they will be.

In the study of economics, most of the important decisions that are analyzed involve forecasts of the future. If the period of time is relatively long, the outcome depends on many possible events that simply cannot be accurately forecast at the moment the decision is made. The business person, or the homemaker, or the government official is forced to fall back on a judgment as to whether important innovations will occur, whether war or peace will be the environment, whether depression or prosperity will characterize the period, or whether more or less government intervention will take place. Pessimism and optimism will bias the judgment when few objective grounds are available on which to base a forecast.

The economist who is best known for his stress upon emotional responses in business decisions is the great Cambridge economist, Arthur C. Pigou, and it is his theory that we shall summarize.[8] Wesley Clair Mitchell, the outstanding American student of business cycles, quoted Pigou approvingly in this regard, and is, himself, considered an adherent of the psychological theory. The key features of Lord Keynes' explanation of business fluctuations are psychological in origin, as we shall see when we look in depth into his contributions. Though these economists subscribe to the general thesis that the psychological reactions of business people are important causal factors in the cyclical process, they do not ignore other important objective events. They hold, however, that even though changes in the supply of and demand for the factors of production can bring about fluctuations in economic activity, they are not sufficient to bring about business cycles in the absence of psychological factors.

They believe that the causal factors in the cyclical process are to be found in the ways in which changes in real underlying factors cause changes in the attitudes of business people. Pigou, for example, recognizes five real causes of business change: (1) changes in agricultural yield, (2) changes in the rate of investment, (3) discovery of new mineral resources, (4) industrial disputes, and (5) changes in consumer tastes. Changes in the first three of these have similar effects since they lead to an increase or a decrease in supply with no change in labor input, or at least to a change in the supply per unit of labor expended. The impact of any of these three factors on the economy may be illustrated by considering the effect of a change in agricultural yield. Changes in agricultural yield are believed to stimulate or retard business activity since an increase in yield promotes business expansion, while a decrease in yield discourages expansion or may even lead to a contraction. If there is an increase in the yield of an agricultural commodity and if the demand for that product is such that the total amount spent on it is larger than before, total demand for all goods will

---

[8] A. C. Pigou, *Industrial Fluctuations* (London: Macmillan and Co., Ltd., 1927) and *The Theory of Unemployment* (London: Macmillan and Co., Ltd., 1933).

tend to be increased. Farmers will have more money to spend, and this fact will lead to increased sales and production of goods demanded by them. A decrease in agricultural yield will have the opposite effect. Such changes lead to fluctuations in business activity, but not to a business cycle. The same is true of increased production due to the discovery of new resources or to inventions that reduce costs.

The last two of the real causes, namely, industrial disputes and net changes in consumer tastes, are not considered important factors causing business fluctuations. Industrial disputes in basic industries, if prolonged, could lead to a downturn in the economy; but this does not happen very often, if at all, and net shifts in consumer tastes are not likely to be important enough in the short run to affect the economy seriously.

Errors of Business People

When any of these real changes occurs, there will be a dual effect. There will be the direct effect of the change that has taken place and also an indirect effect caused by the reactions of business people to the change. These reactions will not always be consistent with the facts because they may be based on errors in evaluating the situation. The scope or range of the errors of business people will be determined primarily by two basic factors, the capacity of business forecasters and the accessibility of information.

In a capitalistic system, with its interdependent processes of production, forecasting is a difficult procedure. The economic response of business people to real changes will depend in part upon the skill developed in forecasting the effects of these changes. Some error, however, will always be involved in such forecasts.

Probably more important as a source of error is the lack of information about all of the factors that will be affected by the change. Under a competitive system individual producers have no real way of knowing what the demand for their product or the supply of productive factors will be in the future. Each producer endeavors to supply a part of the market without knowing the portion of the increased demand that other producers are preparing to meet. The result is that producers tend to overestimate the quantity they can sell and the price at which they can sell their output during an expansion period and to underestimate these same items during a period of declining business. They likewise underestimate the costs of production during the upswing and overestimate them during the contraction. This is also true in regard to the cost of capital; that is, the interest rate.

A second reason for the lack of adequate knowledge on the part of business people is the tendency to order more goods than are really wanted during periods of rising prices to insure the receipt of at least those quantities that are needed. Such duplication of orders makes it impossible to know what the true state of demand is and causes producers to turn out goods in excess of the quantity demanded at current prices.

A third reason for the lack of knowledge of all pertinent factors is the large geographical area of the market. Raw materials are frequently purchased from various parts of the nation and from foreign countries. Production is also carried on for regional, national, and international markets. Under such conditions it is difficult to properly appraise future supply and demand conditions.

The basic reason for the lack of satisfactory knowledge of the market is the length of time required to produce a commodity, especially a capital good. Pigou places great emphasis on what he calls the *period of gestation*. This is the length of time required for the new output to come on the market after the decision to increase production has been made. Different commodities have different gestation periods. Very long gestation periods would characterize commodities that are produced with large amounts of complex capital goods. If capital goods are produced without the expansion of bank credit, nothing happens normally that should give rise to any serious errors. If, as actually happens, an expansion of bank credit takes place during the gestation period, however, there is an overall increase in purchasing power without a corresponding increase in the volume of consumer goods. This excess purchasing power leads to higher prices until the capital goods are completed and the output of consumer goods increased. As a result, business decision makers are misled about the real demand for their products. As the gestation period ends and the new consumer goods begin to flow onto the market, the errors come to light. The length and severity of the expansion phase of the cycle is dependent upon the length of the gestation period.

Mutual Generation of Errors

These errors can only lead to a cyclical process if they are predominantly in the same direction. If they are made on a more or less random basis, they will tend to neutralize each other as errors of optimism are canceled out by errors of pessimism. The latter situation does not occur because of an existence among business people of a tendency toward common action.

Several factors cause errors of either optimism or pessimism to become general throughout the business world. One of these is the tendency for people in business to influence each other's thinking. The continuous contact during the course of business and in the meetings of business organizations spreads feelings of optimism and pessimism widely. Furthermore, errors in forecasts of business conditions tend to create their own justification. An error on the optimistic side by one producer results in an increased demand for goods and services, thus brightening the prospects of other businesses. Thus, the errors of some producers lead other producers to commit errors in the same direction.

The debtor-creditor relationship also disperses errors through the various parts of the business system. If one optimistic business person makes credit more easily available to customers or relaxes terms of credit, this in turn stimulates others to do likewise so as not to be at a competitive disadvantage.

The cycle occurs because errors on the optimistic side inevitably lead to errors of pessimism, and these in turn to errors of optimism, and so on in a continuous cycle. In a period of expansion errors of optimism do not become apparent during the period of gestation because the creation of credit and the length of time required to produce various goods prevent the realization that part of the demand is fictitious and that the shortage of consumer goods is only temporary. When the errors of optimism are revealed at the end of the period of gestation, the expansion comes to a halt and a recession begins. Optimism then gives way to pessimism as firms realize that their forecasts of the situation were wrong and, as business turns downward, errors of pessimism spread. As expenditures are curtailed, there is an oversupply of consumer goods and, as a result, producers underestimate the real demand for their products. As capital goods again need replacement, the errors of pessimism come to light and the stage is set for revival. This process by which errors of optimism lead to errors of pessimism and errors of pessimism to those of optimism is referred to as the *mutual generation of errors*.

Evaluation

Even though the psychological theorists have stressed psychological factors, their explanation of the cycle includes many factors that relate to investment and bank credit creation. They have made a valuable contribution to business cycle theory by showing how waves of optimism can lead to waves of pessimism and these in turn to waves of optimism. Since these are based upon real changes that have taken place in the economy, however, it can hardly be maintained that the cycle is due entirely to psychological factors. These factors help explain the cumulative nature of expansion and contraction, but are of little or no help in explaining turning points. Psychological factors should be considered in a complete explanation of the cycle, but they should not be given the only position of importance.

SERIES OF OUTSIDE FACTORS

Some economists contend that the cycle is caused by the many outside forces which are continually affecting the economy. These not only include weather changes, cycles in farm yields, wars, and war-induced changes in population, but also new inventions and discoveries. Since these occur in a more or less random fashion, they lead to cycles of different time intervals. Sometimes several factors occur at about the same time and thus lead to more severe cycles. Even though such outside influences do affect business activity, they alone cannot account for the cycle because they cannot explain the cumulative nature of the expansion and contraction. These explanations must be sought in the operation of the economic system itself. More recent work in this field involves the creation of formal economic models which incorporate the behavior relations of the economic system. When random disturbances or "shocks" are introduced into such a system, the response of the economy is to generate cyclical movement. We shall consider this variety of business cycle theory in a later chapter. The theories of Wesley Clair Mitchell, considered next, attempt to explain the cumulative nature of expansion and contraction.

MITCHELL'S THEORY OF THE CYCLE

In his classic volume on business cycles published in 1913, Mitchell presented a synthesis of cycle theory based on the evidence available to him at that time.[9] He founded the National Bureau of Economic Research where he made the study of business cycles an empirical science. It was Mitchell's profound belief that the study of business cycles was no less than the study of the total operation of the capitalist system. Understanding the cycle phenomenon was not based on broad general aggregates but on the complex interrelationships among all of the parts of the economy.

Using this principle, Mitchell examined over eight hundred time series, observing that when the preponderance of the individual production and price series were rising a business expansion was in progress. Likewise, a general contraction was made up of contractions in most individual industries. But not all series behaved alike; some series of data tended to lead general activity, some usually followed, and some activities varied inversely to the business cycles. Mitchell looked for clues to the explanation of the cyclical nature of business in these diverse movements.

Mitchell concluded that there were some features which seemed to be common to all the cycles he was able to study, but that each cycle was unique. Thus, one does not find dogmatic assertions in the writings of Wesley Mitchell about what happens during business cycles. His last book, published after his death and summarizing the work of many years, still described the results as "tentative and subject to change as the investigation proceeds."[10] The remainder of this chapter is a brief overview of Mitchell's conception of the nature of the business cycle.

Upswing

According to Mitchell, a revival in business activity begins with a legacy from the depression period. Prices during a depression are low in comparison to prices during prosperity. Business costs have been drastically reduced, profit margins are narrow, bank reserves are liberal, the policy in regard to the extension of credit is conservative, stocks of goods are moderate, and buying is cautious. The upturn is slow at first, but the process is cumulative. It has often been speeded up by some propitious event, such as unusually profitable harvests, large government purchases of goods, or a large increase in exports.

The revival begins at first in just a small sector of the economy but soon spreads to all fields. This is true because those concerns experiencing an increase in business buy materials from other enterprises, these latter from still others, and so on. As incomes increase, expansion increases in a cumulative fashion. Price increases and the expectation of future price increases lead to an increase in orders to beat the price rise, and this accelerates the upward spiral.

This would be of little interest if all prices rose in the same proportion. For instance, if the price of the product a firm sells were to increase by 10 percent, and the prices of all the services and materials that go into the product were also to increase by 10 percent, the profit rate would be as it was before the price rise. Mitchell's statistics indicated, however, that finished goods prices rise more rapidly during the business expansion than do the prices of those

---

[9] Wesley C. Mitchell, *Business Cycles* (Berkeley: University of California Press, 1913).
[10] Wesley C. Mitchell, *What Happens During Business Cycles: A Progress Report* (New York: National Bureau of Economic Research, Studies in Business Cycles [5], 1951), p. 5.

items entering into costs of production, particularly wage rates, rents under leases, and interest on bonds. Thus, profits increase and investment expenditures are encouraged, which leads to further expansion of the physical volume of production and puts further pressure on prices.

Downturn

This cumulative process also sets in motion stresses which undermine prosperity. The lag in supplementary costs ceases when the limit to the business that can be handled with the present equipment of a firm is reached. A rise in costs begins when the expiration of contracts forces renewals at higher rates of interest, rent, and salaries. At the same time other costs rise rapidly because less efficient equipment is brought into use, more overtime is paid, and prices of raw materials rise faster than selling prices on the average. Waste and inefficiency occur and increase the cost of doing business.

Stresses also develop in the investment and money markets as the supply of funds available fails to keep pace with the rapidly swelling demand. Tensions in the money markets are unfavorable to the continuance of prosperity. This is true because high rates of interest reduce prospective margins of profit and thus reduce the demand for additional capital goods for further expansion. As new orders fall off and as old contracts are completed, there is a serious reduction in the volume of production of capital goods and workers are laid off in this field.

Increases in prices at different rates also lead to an imbalance in the system. Some prices cannot be raised sufficiently to prevent a reduction in profits because they are set by public commissions, by long-term contracts, or by custom. Consumer demand does not remain the same in all fields as money income increases and, as a result, prices rise faster in some fields than in others. In some cases prices do not rise as fast as costs, and profit margins are reduced. As profits decrease, cautious creditors fear for the safety of their loans and stop making new loans and refuse to renew old ones as they come due. Thus, prosperity ultimately brings about a liquidation of the huge credits piled up during expansion.

The process of contraction is cumulative, just as expansion was. The same factors that work to increase business on the upswing are also at work depressing business activity during the downswing. Depression spreads over the whole field of business and grows more severe as it spreads.

The rapid decline in business, however, sets into motion the very factors from which a revival will emerge. Prices fall, but again not uniformly in all fields. Wholesale prices drop faster than retail, the prices of producer goods faster than those of consumer goods, and the prices of raw materials faster than those of manufactured goods. Not only are the day-to-day costs of doing business reduced, but supplementary costs are also reduced by the reduction in rents, the refunding of loans, the charging off of bad debts, and the writing down of depreciable properties. Accumulated stocks left over from prosperity are gradually exhausted, after which current consumption requires current production. Consumer and producer durable goods wear out and must be replaced and, as population continues to grow, more food, clothing, and shelter are needed. The environment for investment also becomes more favorable as pessimism gives way to cautious optimism. New methods of production are developed, and these call for additional capital investment. As a result, revival begins and the cumulative cyclical process is once more under way.

This synthesis by Mitchell is still a reasonable explanation of the cyclical process. It does not give sufficient emphasis, however, to the factors at work in the investment process. In the next chapter we consider the theories which place primary emphasis on the role of investment in the business cycle. This prepares the way for the later study of the contributions of Keynes and his followers.

QUESTIONS

1. Draw three charts depicting the cobweb cycle as (a) convergent, (b) explosive, and (c) of constant amplitude.
2. What is the basic difference between an exogenous and an endogenous theory of the business cycle?
3. Explain the conflict between the acceptance of Say's Law and the development of business cycle theory.
4. Explain the relevance to Mitchell's theory of the business cycle that some categories of prices react more quickly than others to changing economic conditions.
5. According to the underconsumption theory, what makes the collapse of an economic expansion inevitable?
6. Explain why a business cycle expansion would be of long duration if the gestation period for key commodities is long.
7. What do you see as the principal difficulty in constructing a theory of the business cycle based on waves of optimism and pessimism?

SUGGESTED READINGS

American Economic Association. *Readings in Business Cycle Theory,* Vol. III. Homewood, Ill.: Richard D. Irwin, Inc., 1965.

Clark, John J., and Morris Cohen (eds.). *Business Fluctuations, Growth and Economic Stabilization,* A Reader. New York: Random House, 1963.

Douglas, C. H. *Social Credit.* New York: W. W. Norton & Company, Inc., 1933.

Estey, J. A. *Business Cycles, Their Nature, Cause, and Control.* Berkeley: University of California Press, 1941.

Ezekiel, Modecai. "The Cobweb Theorem." *Quarterly Journal of Economics,* Vol. LII, No. 1 (February, 1938).

Hansen, Alvin H. *Business Cycles and National Income.* New York: W. W. Norton & Company, Inc., 1964.

————, and R. W. Clemence. *Readings in Business Cycles and National Income.* New York: W. W. Norton & Company, Inc., 1953.

Jevons, W. S. *Investigations in Currency and Finance.* London: Macmillan and Co., Ltd., 1884.

Mitchell, W. C. *What Happens During Business Cycles: A Progress Report.* New York: National Bureau of Economic Research, Studies in Business Cycles [5], 1951.

————. *Business Cycles.* Berkeley: University of California Press, 1913.

Moore, Henry L. *Generating Economic Cycles.* New York: The Macmillan Company, 1923.

————. *Economic Cycles: Their Law and Cause.* New York: The Macmillan Company, 1914.

Pigou, A. C. *Industrial Fluctuations.* London: Macmillan and Co., Ltd., 1927.

————. *The Theory of Unemployment.* London: Macmillan and Co., Ltd., 1933.

Schumpeter, Joseph. *Theory of Economic Development.* Cambridge, Mass.: Harvard University Press, 1934.

von Haberler, Gottfried. *Prosperity and Depression,* 3d ed. Geneva: League of Nations, 1941.

CHAPTER 6

MONETARY AND INVESTMENT THEORIES OF THE CYCLE

The structure of the monetary and credit system of the economy has an important influence on the nature of business fluctuations. In fact, since Say's Law would be true in a barter economy, business cycles as we know them could not exist. The important role of monetary factors led early business cycle theorists to give major emphasis to them in their analysis of the causal factors at work in the cycle. One group of monetary theorists held that changes which occur in this system are sufficient in themselves to produce cycles. Another group thought that the interaction of the monetary system with changes in investment activity leads to cyclical fluctuations. Most of the writers who held these theories were quantity theorists along with the majority of all economists of their day. Chapter 4 includes a review of the quantity theory, so it will not be repeated here.

In this chapter consideration will be given also to those theorists who hold that the basic cause of the cycle is found in the process of investment rather than in the operation of the monetary system. One group of investment theorists has stressed a shortage of capital as the basic cause of the cycle; another, fluctuations in the investment process that are produced by innovations; and a third, changes in consumption that lead to magnified changes in the demand for producer goods and thus lead to imbalance.

THE PURELY MONETARY THEORY

Considering the pervasive role of money in modern economic systems, it would be strange indeed if it were not included in an important way in the explanation of business fluctuations. In fact, the only disagreement lies in the particular way and the degree of importance attached to money in generating business cycles. Even those theories that are called nonmonetary implicitly require the necessary response of the money supply to bring about the cycles described. These theorists argue that the initiating or causal force is something other than monetary, whereas the monetary theories place the monetary system in this critical position. The purely monetary theory takes the polar position that variations in money are the necessary and sufficient conditions for variations in economic activity. This is essentially the position taken by

Ralph G. Hawtrey, a British economist whose name is virtually synonymous with the purely monetary theory.[1]

Without question the kinds of cycles that have occurred in the economies of industrial nations could not exist in an economy with an inelastic monetary system. An increase in business activity could not develop in a cumulative fashion for any period of time under such a monetary arrangement. As the demand for goods increased in some sectors of the economy, more money would be used to make sales in these fields. With inelastic money and credit, this would leave fewer funds for other fields of business activity and prices would fall in these areas. Velocity could increase to some extent, but a cumulative expansion of sales in many fields at the same time would be impossible.

Such a cumulative expansion of sales, however, is one of the major characteristics of the cycle in the United States and other industrial countries. Both the volume of goods sold and the prices of goods normally expand during prosperity. On the upswing the quantities of goods sold expand somewhat faster than do the prices at which they are sold. During the downswing both the prices of goods sold and the quantities sold usually contract.

The usual situation in the case of individual products or services is for the quantities sold to increase as prices are lowered and to decrease as prices are raised. Prices of goods and quantities sold can only move together in the upswing and downswing of a cycle because the total supply of purchasing media is expanding and contracting as business goes up and down. This change in the supply of purchasing media is primarily due to a change in the volume of demand deposits that are expanded and contracted as borrowing from the banking system increases and decreases during the cycle.

The Upswing

It is not unusual in cycle analysis to have the turning points brought about by the conditions created in the phase just preceding them. Hawtrey's theory is a good example of this. The period of downswing develops a situation of the banking system accumulating excess reserves and of growing desires on the part of bankers to make loans. Accordingly, interest rates fall and other credit terms and standards for borrowing are eased. The depression has also gone on long enough to eliminate any excess inventories that might have existed early in the downswing, and weaker firms may also have been eliminated so that even though general business conditions are depressed, conditions for the remaining business units are at least stabilized. Lower interest rates obviously make borrowing more attractive, but the firm must expect the borrowed funds to add to its earning power enough to more than cover the costs of the borrowing.

Who will borrow during the depths of a depression? The business person who overcomes the pessimism of the times and anticipates an imminent period of good times will do so. Most economists would expect borrowing to increase

---

[1] Ralph G. Hawtrey has written many books and articles detailing his view of the cycle. Two representative books are: *Trade and Credit* (London: Longmans, Green & Co., Ltd., 1928) and *Capital and Employment* (London: Longmans, Green & Co. Ltd., 1937).

during the downswing if innovations create expectations of improved sales or lower costs. The general opinion has been that lower interest rates have the greatest effect on borrowers whose use for funds is very long term. Hawtrey, however, concentrates his attention on the merchants who have the carrying of inventories as a major expense. Since a major portion of the variable cost of maintaining inventories is the interest, any lowering of interest rates reduces these costs. If larger inventories are advantageous, we would expect their lower costs to induce merchants to add to their holdings. Larger stocks of inventories provide greater selection by customers and quicker service and delivery of large orders. Thus, even if aggregate sales are low, a seller can gain some competitive advantage by increasing the company's inventory.

So, in Hawtrey's version of the monetary theory of the trade cycle, as he calls it, the upswing begins when excess reserves build up sufficiently for interest rates to fall enough to cause merchants to borrow to increase their inventories. For the new orders to be additions to total demand, the purchasing power must come from new or idle money that would not decrease demand elsewhere. The new demand produces added income for the producers, and the upswing is in progress.

After the process of expansion has been started, it is cumulative for a period of time. As more goods are ordered, more are produced, more income flows into the hands of consumers, and consumer expenditures are increased. Traders, finding their stock of goods decreased because of the growth in sales to consumers, increase their orders for merchandise, which in turn increases production, consumer income, and consumer outlay. As this cumulative process develops, there is a rise in the general level of prices because output in certain areas cannot be increased readily due to a scarcity of plant capacity, labor, or intermediate inputs. The rise in prices adds further impetus to the expansion that is underway since it increases the profits of entrepreneurs and therefore makes them willing to increase the amount of credit used in their business. This credit expansion accelerates the expansion process and in turn adds to the pressure on prices and reinforces the upward movement.

According to Hawtrey, the expansion is reinforced by the expectation of rising prices that causes people to reduce the size of their cash balances relative to the amount of their transactions—that is to say, that k in the equation $M = kPy$, falls (or, alternatively, velocity in the equation $MV = Py$ increases) during the expansion if rising prices are expected.

The Contraction

Prosperity comes to an end when the banks restrict the expansion of credit. Banks take such action because their excess reserves are being depleted by the increase in loans and deposits and by the withdrawal of cash for hand-to-hand circulation. The central banks could continue to supply additional credit, but they have usually felt that it was their function to prevent excessive expansion and therefore have refused to do so.

Some monetary theorists believe that, if the restriction of credit did not occur, the expansion phase of the cycle could be continued indefinitely although that would mean an indefinite rise in prices. The continuous increase in prices leads to an increasing demand for cash for hand-to-hand circulation, for till cash and petty cash funds by business concerns, for working cash balances by financial institutions, and for cash needed in day-by-day operations of banks. These increased demands for cash, being a drain on reserves, not only cause banks to stop expanding credit but also to contract the amount outstanding.

The upper turning point is brought about, according to Hawtrey, because of a lag between the growth in bank deposits and the outflow of currency into circulation. While Hawtrey was referring to a gold standard system in which gold served both in the capacity of reserves for the banking system and as circulating currency, the general ideas are applicable to our present system. At the time the expansion begins, the skeleton balance sheet of the banking system might look something like this:

Commercial Banking System

Gold (reserves)	$ 20	Demand deposits	$150
Earning assets	$130		

British banks did not have legal reserve requirements, but tradition did dictate a minimum reserve ratio. For purposes of our example, let us assume this to be 10 percent of deposits, so that in our initial situation the amount of excess reserves is $5 billion. At this stage the banks are lowering their interest charges, and merchants begin to borrow for the purpose of adding to their stock of inventory. Earnings assets increase, and at the same time demand deposits are increasing *parri passus*. While this is happening, the incomes of workers who are producing the goods are growing, although with a lag. In Hawtrey's time workers kept their cash balances in the form of currency rather than demand deposits. Thus, gold specie will be accumulating in the hands of the workers, leaving the banks; so the balance sheet of the banking system might approach a position like this:

Commercial Banking System

Gold (reserves)	$ 18	Demand deposits	$180
Earning assets	$162		

At the 10 percent reserve ratio limit, the banks are loaned up at this point; but because of the lag gold will continue to flow into circulation, which throws the banks into a deficient reserve position. This, of course, will force the contraction of earning assets. Interest rates will rise to encourage borrowers to get out of debt to the banks. Some forced liquidation of inventories will be imposed. Merchants will find the interest costs high enough to induce them to decrease the size of their inventories. Now the contraction is in process.

When bank credit is contracted, business firms must reduce their stocks of goods to retire bank loans and thus they place orders for a smaller amount of goods than they are selling currently. This starts business on a downward movement, which is cumulative just as the upward movement was. As prices begin to fall, merchants expect them to fall further and therefore try to reduce their stocks. As producers receive smaller orders, they cut down production, consumer income is cut as are consumer expenditures, so the reduction in stocks will be less than intended. The same lags which were observed in the expansion appear in the contraction phase. Income reductions of workers lag behind the reduction in loans and demand deposits, and the inflow of currency into the banks which becomes bank reserves lags behind the decline in incomes. If people expect the continuance of the price declines, the velocity of money will fall and cash balances will increase, accentuating the downswing.

Periodicity

According to the monetary theory, there are pronounced business cycles rather than minor oscillations around a level of equilibrium because of the cumulative, self-sustaining nature of the processes of expansion and contraction. These processes go on for a period of time because the expansion of bank credit and the use of the increased cash balances of the community are not instantaneous. It takes time for economic activity to expand to the point where increased cash balances are needed and for this loss of cash by the banks, along with increased borrowing, to put pressure on bank reserves. Likewise, during contraction, it takes time for these cash balances to return to the banking system and to increase bank reserves above normal levels.

When most of the commercial nations of the world were operating on the gold standard, this process took place with some regularity since the central banks acted to maintain the gold reserves. Since the abandonment of the automatic gold standard, however, the regular periodicity is no longer apparent because the intricate mechanism that produced regular periods of expansion and contraction has been altered materially.

Evaluation

Monetary factors are certainly active factors in the cyclical process. It is difficult, however, to agree that the cyclical phenomenon is entirely a monetary one. Changes in economic activity may be due to changes in demand, to new inventions, to changes in the cost structure, to changes in the methods of doing business, and so forth, which are not monetary factors but which, of course, affect monetary factors. The monetary theorists have well described the cumulative processes of expansion and contraction that such factors set into motion. Their explanation of the turning points, however, is not a completely satisfactory one.

It is highly doubtful that business people generally are as sensitive to small changes in interest rates as the monetary theorists maintain they are. The most important factors affecting investment decisions generally are present and prospective levels of sales, and price, cost, and profit expectations rather than minor variations in interest rates. It is true that under any given state of expectations some firms may gain by increasing inventories and are encouraged to do so by lower interest costs, but this is not likely to be quantitatively important in bringing about an expansion unless expectations are favorable for increased business activity. A complete explanation, then, must account for changed expectations, not lower interest rates alone. The explanation of the upper turning point is likewise not fully satisfactory. Turning points have occurred when bank credit was easily available, and prosperity has continued when credit was severely restricted.

THE MODERN MONETARIST THEORY

The monetary theory of the business cycle has made something of a come-back in recent years, after the period of the 1930s, '40s, and '50s when the majority of economists felt that money really wasn't very important. The resurgence can be attributed to the keeping of the flame at the University of Chicago, mainly by Professor Milton Friedman. The majority of economists today have been persuaded that money does matter. Debate revolves around questions such as how much money matters and the nature of the transmission mechanism by which money stock changes are translated into changes in other economic magnitudes.

A great amount of empirical work has been done in recent years to assess these questions. The evidence of close correspondence between money and general economic activity is impressive. Friedman and Schwartz found that over a period of almost one hundred years, the stock of money generally increased during both expansion and contraction phases of the business cycle.[2] However, during the most severe contraction periods, the stock of money did decline absolutely. They found that not only were the rates of change in the money stock closely associated with general business conditions, but that the severity in the rate of change in money stock and the magnitude of cyclical movements in business were highly correlated.

The money series normally leads the general business cycle, but the length of the lead varies. This variability in the presumed response of the economy to changes in the quantity of money has not been entirely adequately explained and, until it has been explained, the skeptics will have some justification for their doubts.

It is recognized, of course, that the fact that two statistical series vary together is no proof that one causes the other. An explanation is needed for the monetarist case to show that the direction of causation is from money to business activity, and that, while it is recognized that feedbacks from economic activity to variations in money stock exist, it is the money stock variation which triggers the change.

Friedman and Schwartz visualize the basic process in the following way. Suppose the economy to be proceeding in a moving equilibrium in which real income per capita, real wealth per capita, the money stock, and the price level are all increasing at constant rates. The example they use assumes that the income elasticity of the demand for money δ is 1.5; that is, if real income increases by 2 percent, the demand for money will increase by 3 percent. Thus, if the rate of growth of real income (a_y) is 2 percent per year, and the rate of growth of the nominal money stock (a_M) is 4 percent per year, the rate of growth of the price level (a_P) will be 1 percent per year: $a_P = a_M - \delta a_y = 1\% = 4\% - 1.5(2\%)$.[3] Now, if the Federal Reserve were to engage in open-market operations and cause the rate of growth in the money supply to go to 5 percent per

---

[2] Milton Friedman and Anna J. Schwartz, "Money and Business Cycles," *The Review of Economics and Statistics,* Vol. XLV, Supplement (February, 1963), pp. 32–64.

[3] *Ibid.,* p. 59. Friedman and Schwartz state that the values given here are approximate averages over the 90 years between 1870 and 1960.

year, the price level would increase at the rate of 2 percent annually. Thus, an increase of 1 percentage point in the rate of money stock growth resulted in a 1 percentage point increase in the rate of price level growth.

How do we move from increased open-market purchases by the Federal Reserve to the increased growth in the price level? First, the open-market agent buys (for example) from a government securities dealer who deposits the check received into a commercial bank. The dealer has more money and fewer securities now. Presumably, the dealer's inventory of securities would be replenished by purchasing other securities from customers who might be financial institutions, other corporations, or individuals. Like others, security dealers try to buy at lower prices and sell at higher prices. This buying activity, first by the Federal Reserve and then by the dealers, has the effect of raising security prices (and, hence, lowering the interest yield) somewhat.

In the meantime the reserves of the commercial banks will have been increased by the open-market purchase and they will have more excess reserves than desired, so they too will be in the market for securities and/or loans to local customers. This also forces financial asset prices to rise, and as banks expand their assets the money supply increases. Most of the entities who have received money in exchange for their assets, or who have borrowed from the banks, will have uses for the money other than simply holding it dormant. Some of this money will be spent for bonds to replace those that were sold; some will be spent for real goods, such as plants and equipment, homes, and automobiles. Some of the spending will be for equity securities, the prices of which are also bid up, encouraging firms to increase real capital and causing the price of real capital to increase.

In summary, the open-market purchase and the response of the banking system to the purchase increase the amount of money and decrease the financial assets held by the nonbank public. Portfolios are out of adjustment until prices of financial and nonfinancial assets rise. The adjustment process describes the expansion phase of the business cycle. The forces would be reversed if the initial impulse were a reduction in the growth rate of money stock.

This theory implies that the stock of money must provide the expansive and the contractive impulses which propel the business cycle. After study of the major business cycles in the United States, Friedman and Schwartz conclude that each cycle can be explained by such monetary forces, but its systematic character is elusive. Each significant change in the growth rate of money stock is accounted for in a different way. There is one feature common to many of the historical incidences but not to all of them. That is the occurrence of runs on banks, which increase the currency-deposit ratio and, hence, decrease the rate of growth in the money stock.

THE NONMONETARY OVERINVESTMENT THEORY

One group of investment theorists stresses overinvestment as a basic cause of the cycle and assigns only a subordinate role to monetary factors. Therefore, their theory has been referred to as the nonmonetary overinvestment theory.

It is a fact that investment spending fluctuates more severely than do the other major components of total spending in the economy over the course of the business cycle. This can be explained either as the response of investment to other forces at work in the system, as it was in the purely monetary and the psychological theories; or investment spending can be viewed as the causal factor that provokes the other elements to behave in a cyclical fashion. The nonmonetary overinvestment theory focuses upon investment as the factor that has an inherent tendency to fluctuate and causes the whole economy to react in a cyclical manner. These economists describe the monetary system as a passive agent in the cycle, expanding during the upswing and contracting during the downswing. In other words, the money supply is not an originating force but a response variable. Changes in the money supply are a necessary but not a sufficient condition for cycles.

The earliest writer of this group we have called the nonmonetary overinvestment theorists was Tugan-Baranowsky.[4] In his version, the most important feature of the cycle was the conversion of free capital into fixed or real capital during the expansion and the opposite movement of fixed into free capital during the contraction. Free capital, which today we would call loanable funds, is converted into fixed capital, or capital goods, by the act of investment. Fixed capital is converted into free capital by the capital producing the receipt of funds, which are not used to replace the depreciating machine but are available for future spending. Free capital also builds up during the downswing because of people on fixed incomes whose savings accumulate without acceptable outlets for the use of these funds. Of course, investment in plant and equipment absorbs these funds during the expansion phase. A downswing comes to a halt, and the direction of the economy is reversed, when free capital has accumulated in large enough amounts that great pressure to employ these funds is felt, and the fixed capital, which was too large at the beginning of the downswing, has been reduced by way of depreciation in use over this time. The low interest rate in effect at this time is further encouragement to the initiation of investment activity. The upper turning point is explained by the absorption of all of the available free capital by real capital. Investment must stop because there are no longer funds to pay for the new equipment and buildings.

Professor Arthur Spiethoff[5] improved upon Tugan-Baranowsky's explanation of the overinvestment theory, especially of the turning points. Spiethoff agreed with Tugan-Baranowsky that the lower turning point would be initiated by the push of free capital, but he was of the opinion that the pull of real capital might be a more powerful force. This demand for capital goods would arise from innovations that would open up new profit possibilities. Spiethoff's addendum to the theory of the upper turning point is to observe that the expansion will stop if the society runs out of loanable funds, as Tugan suggested; but it will also come to an end if the investment possibilities inherent in the innovations are exhausted. Thus, Spiethoff has added the force of the pull of investment

---

[4] Michel Tugan-Baranowsky, *Les Crises Industrielles en Angleterre,* 1913.
[5] Arthur Spiethoff, *Business Cycles,* International Economic Papers, No. 3 (New York: The Macmillan Company, 1953).

demand or real capital at both the upper and lower turning points to the reliance that Tugan-Baranowsky had made on the push of free capital.

It remained for Professor Joseph A. Schumpeter [6] to explain why innovations would occur with sufficient regularity to explain the periodicity of the business cycle. The Schumpeter schema will be considered immediately after we have summarized the events of the cycle according to the nonmonetary overinvestment school.

The Upswing

The nonmonetary overinvestment theorists describe the upswing and the cumulative process of expansion in the following way. After a period of depression, there are again profit possibilities and an increase in investment activity. This revival of investment generates income and purchasing power, which leads to an increase in the demand for capital goods and also for consumer goods. The increased demand for consumer goods stimulates further investment, and the increase in profits arising from larger volumes of business and a rising price level provide a psychological stimulus for further expansion. Thus, prosperity arises out of this cumulative process of expansion.

To describe the maladjustment, which develops in this expansion period, theorists in this group divide goods into four categories: nondurable consumer goods, durable and semidurable consumer goods, durable capital goods, and materials used to produce durable goods. Disequilibrium arises among these categories of goods during the upswing of the cycle. What actually occurs is a shortage and abundance at the same time, since there is too much of one type of good and too little of another. Because of the development of new types of durable capital goods that can be used to reduce costs of production, a larger proportion of the factors of production are allocated to the making of durable capital goods and the materials used to produce such goods. As a result, insufficient resources are available for the consumer goods industries that are counted on to use the new capital goods.

Also contributing to the imbalance is the long interval between the construction of a plant or factory and the time when it begins to turn out products. This situation makes a correct forecast of demand very difficult. Additional income is being paid to workers and to capital owners in the field of producer goods, and this increased income leads to more demand for consumer goods. The increased demand cannot be satisfied until the new producer goods go into production and, as a result, prices rise. This rise in prices is temporary to the degree that the supply of new producer goods will increase to an extent large enough to meet demand. It is difficult for individual producers to determine the industry's increase in capacity and also the price that will exist after production is in full swing. The higher prices may also lead to some expansion projects based on profit expectations at these prices, which will turn out to be unsound when supply is increased and prices return to lower levels.

---

[6] Joseph A. Schumpeter, *Business Cycles*, Vol. 1 (New York: McGraw-Hill Book Company, 1939); also his *Theory of Economic Development* (Cambridge, Massachusetts: Harvard University Press, 1934).

The development of new durable consumer goods may also attract the factors of production to this field and away from the production of nondurable and semidurable consumer goods. The imbalance among the various types of production cannot be corrected because to do so would require additional labor and additional consumer goods to satisfy the demand of such labor. Since all resources are in use, the additional labor and consumer goods are not available.

The Downturn

The expansion continues until either a shortage of loanable funds develops, which forces investment to decrease, or because of the virtual completion of profitable investment projects. The capital goods industry becomes depressed and the downswing is under way. After a long period of high activity and high incomes the people who receive their incomes from this industry find their incomes, and hence their ability to purchase consumer goods, reduced at about the same time that the new plants and machinery are ready to turn out larger volumes of consumer goods. Now it can be seen that overinvestment has taken place. Projects, which would have been profitable had they been available when incomes were rising and resources were being devoted to capital building rather than consumer goods, are now excessive when large amounts of resources are available for the production of consumer goods and incomes are insufficient to buy them. Prices of consumer goods fall and a cumulative contraction is under way.

During the downswing conditions are being created that make the lower turning point possible. The capital wears out over time and is not replaced so the stock of capital is reduced. The costs of building capital equipment are lowered, wages are reduced, prices of raw materials are cut, and interest rates are lowered as loanable funds accumulate in the system. The contraction will continue until investment is again stimulated by these conditions and/or until the occurrence of an innovation requiring capital expenditures.

Evaluation

This form of the overinvestment theory is hardly satisfactory as a complete explanation of the business cycle. It has made a contribution, however, by pointing out that imbalance can occur among different categories of consumer goods as well as between producer and consumer goods. There is no completely satisfactory explanation given of the reasons for the imbalance among the different categories of goods. The minor emphasis on monetary factors cannot be fully accepted since changes in the monetary system have played an active role in many past cycles. The explanation of the factors that initiate an upswing after business has declined during a recession period is inadequate in that it does not sufficiently explain why innovations occur at just the right time to produce the regularity of the business cycle. For this we turn to the work of Professor Schumpeter.

INNOVATIONS

The most thorough analysis of the role of innovations and the process by which they generate economic fluctuations was developed by Joseph A. Schumpeter. Changes in economic activity may be initiated by external factors, such as war, changes in tariffs, damage due to earthquakes, and changes in agricultural yield. Such external influences disturb economic equilibrium, but they do not of themselves lead to cyclical fluctuations of business activity. Fluctuations may also be due to internal changes in the economic system, such as changes in consumer tastes, changes in the quantity or quality of factors of production, and innovations in the ways of producing commodities.

The movement is cyclical because of the cumulative process that takes place. Conditions in a period of prosperity are unbalanced and therefore lead inevitably to depression; and in turn conditions in the depression become favorable to a revival of investment; and thus the cycle goes on in a regular fashion. After there has been an initial boom in capital construction, replacements tend to assume a cyclical character since much of the equipment must be replaced at about the same time in the future.

Crucial to the understanding of the Schumpeterian analysis is the distinction between inventions, or discoveries, and innovations. The invention of new techniques, processes for production of new capital goods, new consumer products, and the discovery of new markets or new sources of raw materials are the major categories. These would seem to happen at any time, perhaps in a random fashion. The presumption is that individuals and organizations engaged in research to discover or invent do so at a fairly continuous rate but that there is no regular pattern to the actual occurrences. Innovations are the economic exploitation of these inventions or discoveries, which is the introduction of them into the economy so that they are effective in causing the system to respond as it does in the business cycle. Innovations are introduced because a few business leaders see possibilities that are not generally seen by the rank and file. At first they must strive hard to overcome inertia and introduce the innovation. After a time others see the prospects for profits and they too get into the new field.

Schumpeter uses the construct of the "stationary state" or "static flow," an idealized situation of equilibrium that is as complete an equilibrium as can be imagined. In it there is no uncertainty because there are no changes, and no changes because there are no innovations. There is no reason to invest except to replace worn-out equipment, so there is no saving. All output and all spending are on consumption. The lack of uncertainty assures that no profit will exist. Management, having no risk to take, simply repeats what was done in the past and so receives only its wages. There would be no borrowing or lending between households and business because capital would earn no net return. Everything else is constant, including the money supply, the velocity of money, prices, output, and full employment.

Into this euphoric environment rides the dynamic entrepreneur, Schumpeter's hero. The entrepreneur is the risk taker, the innovator, the creator of change and uncertainty. Inventions or discoveries that may have been developed in the past are introduced by this entrepreneur.

Since this analysis starts with an economy that is in a state of equilibrium and has no unemployed factors of production, any new production must be financed by bank credit. This introduction of bank credit causes prices to rise, and it also causes an increase in money income.

If most of the great obstacles to change are conquered and the innovation is successful, profit will arise and hosts of imitators will be attracted into the new field and into peripheral areas. This expansion of investment will be paralleled by credit and monetary expansion, and savings will be forced to increase to equal the investment.[7] Since the expansion started from a condition of full employment there can be no net increase in total output. As a result, when more labor and capital are devoted to the production of additional capital goods, output of consumer goods must fall. At the same time, the demand for consumer goods will increase as the additional money arising through bank credit is paid out in wages, thus putting additional pressure on prices.

This situation is changed as soon as the capital goods have been produced and the new consumer goods arising from putting them into production flow into the market. Since the innovations are more efficient than the processes they replaced, the volume of consumer goods will be greater than it was before the process began. Old plants will be modernized to keep up with competition from the efficient plants or will be forced out of business. The turning point in this process will come when entrepreneurial activity in introducing innovations ceases. This slowing down in the activity of the entrepreneurs will cause uncertainty in business, and for a time new projects will not be planned. This process, however, is not cyclical in the sense in which business cycles have occurred in our economy. It describes the disturbance from equilibrium and the expansion, and then the return to equilibrium. The return to equilibrium is a period of the adjustment of industry to the new innovations. Some old firms will go out of business as they are unable to compete with the new. Others will curtail the scale of their activity or in other ways readjust their output or ways of production. Some of the old firms whose products are complementary to the new innovation will adapt by expansion or other adjustments.

The cycles that we have experienced in the past are described as due to a secondary wave of speculation. When business is in the process of readjustment because innovations are being introduced, many feel that the boom which is being produced, especially in the capital goods industries, will be permanent. As a result, the already established firms borrow money to increase their operations, and consumers also go into debt to buy additional goods. General expansion of inventories also takes place due to expected price increases. The excessive indebtedness built up during this speculative wave causes trouble.

When the additional goods and services that are made possible by the new capital equipment enter the markets, prices gradually drop. This leads to difficulties for businesses and consumers who have gone into debt because they

---

[7] The process of "forced saving" is detailed in the next section on the monetary overinvestment theory.

contracted their obligations under the impression that the boom would be permanent. When prices fall, many cannot meet their obligations and a depression results. During the expansion overoptimism and overextension of debt took place. During the downswing overpessimism takes over and forced liquidation of inventories and indebtedness go on. This situation can easily lead to a panic.

THE MONETARY OVERINVESTMENT THEORY

One group of theorists stresses deviations in the structure of production that are caused by an expansion in economic activity which is initiated by monetary factors. During a boom a basic maladjustment occurs in the structure of the economy. Not only is there a shortage of bank credit, but also the production of capital goods is increased to a larger extent than is justified by the demand for consumer goods.[8]

The structure of production that exists at any period of time is not an accidental or an arbitrary one. It has been built up by entrepreneurs who have invested in plant and equipment for the purpose of producing those goods that consumers demand. The amount and types of machinery used depend in part upon the stage of technology in the economy. Also of primary significance is the amount of savings that is available for investment in business plant and equipment and the rate of interest that must be paid to get the holders of savings to invest them. The relative costs of capital and labor are also significant because firms combine these factors of production so as to achieve the best possible combination from a cost standpoint.

To keep the economy in equilibrium, it is necessary that the factors of production be utilized so as to produce a pattern of production which corresponds to the pattern of consumption. The pattern of consumption is, in a general way, determined by the decisions of the population to spend or save its income and by the decisions concerning the distribution of expenditures among various types of goods. If, as production increases, the division between the making of new producer goods and of new consumer goods does not correspond to the division of income between saving and spending on consumption, a vertical maladjustment occurs. If the pattern of production of consumer goods of various types does not correspond to the pattern of consumer expenditures for such goods, there is a horizontal maladjustment.

The terms "vertical maladjustments" and "horizontal maladjustments" are used because of the nature of the relationships of the industries to each other. Consumer goods industries are considered as being on one plane, and producer goods industries are thought of as being on a higher plane. There are also stages in the producer goods field since some plants produce consumer goods directly, some produce machinery for such plants, some produce machine tools needed to make production machinery, some the basic metals for the tools, and so on.

---

[8] For an excellent presentation of this point of view, see F. A. Hayek, *Monetary Theory and the Trade Cycle* (New York: Harcourt, Brace & World, 1933), and *Prices and Production* (London: George Routledge & Sons, Ltd., 1935).

The stages closest to the consumer have been referred to by the monetary over-investment theorists as the "lower stages of production"; those further removed, as the "higher stages of production."

Also basic in the monetary overinvestment theory of the cycle is the concept of the *natural rate of interest*. This is the rate at which the demand for loan capital is just equal to the supply of savings. It should be distinguished from the *money* or *market rate*, which is the actual going rate of interest at any time. If banks lower the market rate below the natural rate, the demand for credit will rise and exceed the available supply of savings. The supply of credit is supplemented by the creation of bank credit, which leads to inflation. If the market rate is above the natural rate, the demand for credit will fall and, as a result, part of the supply of savings will not be used and deflation will occur.

The Upswing

The monetary overinvestment theorists have stressed an important economic phenomenon called "forced saving." Hayek, in particular, has made great use of the concept and feels that this is the essence of the expansion process in the business cycle. To explain how forced saving occurs we shall first show how investment can increase *without* forced savings, that is, when savings are increased voluntarily. Figure 6-1 shows this case.

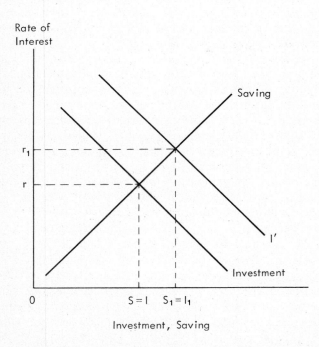

Figure 6-1

Investment Increase and Voluntary Saving

The original equilibrium condition is represented by the intersection of the savings and investment functions, where $S = I$ at the interest rate r. Now, for example, we assume an increase in the demand for resources to produce capital goods because of an important innovation. This increased demand means that business units wish to increase investment spending and are willing to pay higher interest costs to do so. In this case investors *persuade* savers to increase saving (that is, reduce their consumption spending) by offering a higher reward for saving in the form of interest. In fact, households voluntarily relinquish their right to use resources for consumption in exactly the amount needed to satisfy the investors' demands. Saving increases (consumption decreases) from S to S_1, and investment increases from I to I_1. The rise in the rate of interest from r to r_1 induced the higher rate of saving and caused investors to invest less than they would have invested had the interest rate remained at r. There is nothing disruptive in this process. Total income and output in the economy will not change since neither M nor V of the equation of exchange has changed. Only the composition of output has been altered — more capital goods are produced, and in equal amount, less consumer goods are produced. Austrian economists describe this alteration in output as a lengthening of the stages of production. When it happens in the manner just presented, no business cycle expansion occurs.

To demonstrate the contrast between the situation involved in Figure 6-1 and what happens in a business cycle, the monetary overinvestment theorists utilize the Wicksellian analysis involving the notions of the market rate of interest versus the natural rate of interest.[9] The natural rate is the rate that equates savings and investment and maintains equilibrium of the price level. In Figure 6-1 the market rate, which is the rate actually in existence, is the same as the natural rate. Divergence between the two occurs if an increase or decrease in hoarding, that is, a decrease or increase in velocity, V, or an increase or decrease in the money supply takes place. An increase in the money supply or the release of funds from "hoards" can make resources available to buyers of capital goods just as surely as if the resources were derived from saving.

Figure 6-2 includes on the supply side savings plus changes in the money supply. For simplicity we have not incorporated increases in velocity, but the analysis would be basically the same. To start the analysis, we can take $S_e = I_e$ at interest rate r_n (natural rate) as the original equilibrium position, and some event causes the banking system to find itself in a position of having excess reserves that bankers want to lend. To get all the available funds borrowed, the interest rate will fall to r_m, the market rate of interest. Now, the market rate is below the natural rate. Investors can now command resources valued at I_1 amount. Of this total S_1 is supplied by savers and $I_1 - S_1$ is supplied by the expansion of the money supply. Notice the difference between this case and the case depicted in Figure 6-1. When investment increased in Figure 6-1 saving increased, that is, the use of resources for consumption purposes decreased. In Figure 6-2 when investment increased, planned saving actually decreased, which is to say that consumption demand increased at the same time that the quantity of investment demanded increased.

---

[9] Knut Wicksell, *Interest and Prices* (London: Macmillan & Co., Ltd., 1936).

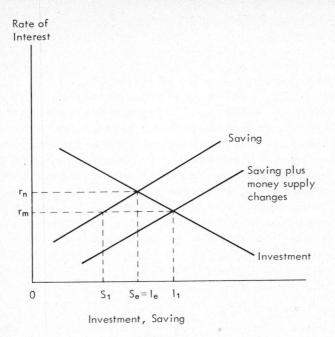

Figure 6-2

Investment Increase and Forced Saving

At this stage we must point out that Hayek assumes that we started from a position of full employment so that the total supply of output cannot increase. This being the case, if investors are successful in increasing the output of capital goods, they must lure resources away from their current employment in the production of consumer goods. This can be done only by raising factor prices and, therefore, also the prices of final goods. In other words, consumers are forced to decrease their real consumption by way of price inflation. This is what is meant by the term *forced saving*. Actual saving is equal to I_1, even though desired or intended saving is just S_1.[10]

The market rate of interest will continue to be below the natural rate as long as the money supply continues to expand; and as long as the rates differ in this way, the upswing of the business cycle will persist. But what happens when the source of expansion of the money supply dries up? Then, again, the supply of loanable funds will be limited to the desired amount of current saving and the market rate of interest will rise to become equal to the natural rate. At this point, in the Austrian terminology, a shortage of capital exists. Investment projects, which were expected to be profitable when evaluated in terms of the lower market rate of interest, cannot be justified at the higher rate. It is now

---

[10] This description should be qualified to observe that new investment demand would be expected to drive up prices of resources used in both consumption and capital goods industries so that some forced reduction of investment will take place as well as some reduction in consumption. The amount of the reduction in each industry will depend largely on the length of the lag in receipts of wages and other income payments behind money supply expansion.

the households whose desires are fulfilled. They will save the amount they wish to save, and investors will be able to invest just that amount. Investment must decline to I_e and savers will plan to increase their saving to S_e. Now there is a decrease in aggregate demand, since both investment and consumption demands have decreased and national income will fall.

The Downturn

According to the overinvestment theory, the process of monetary expansion and heavy investment must always end in a collapse. Here let us review very briefly the sequence of events of the expansion leading to this collapse. The artificial lowering of the interest rate causes business firms to invest in capital equipment at a rate that cannot be maintained because it is out of balance with consumer demand. The effective demand for consumer goods is reduced by forced savings at the same time that additional capital is invested to produce consumer goods. In other words, the structure of production has become top-heavy since it is now out of balance with too many facilities in the higher stages of production in the capital goods field.

Forces that tend to reverse this pattern are then set in motion. As money is paid out to laborers, who are producing capital goods, the demand for consumer goods rises and the consumer goods industries become more profitable. This, in turn, entices the factors of production away from the higher stages of production back to the production of consumer goods. This demand for the factors of production in all fields causes an increased demand for bank credit and further inflation.

The immediate cause of the breakdown of the boom is almost always the inability or unwillingness of the banking system to continue the process of credit expansion. This is due to monetary reasons, that is, either the pressure on the reserve requirements of individual banks or to central bank policy.

When pressure develops on bank reserves and bank credit is restricted, the producers of capital goods can no longer obtain the funds to pay the higher prices and wages needed to bid raw materials and labor away from the consumer goods field. At the same time increased costs force these producers to charge higher prices for their products. These higher prices of capital goods lower the return to be received from investment in capital equipment at the same time that interest rates are rising because banks have used up most of their excess reserves and are no longer anxious to increase their loan volume. This combination of factors leads to reduced activity in the capital goods field. As workers are laid off, total income is reduced and the downward spiral sets in. The real cause of the collapse, however, is the shortage of real capital. It is not merely a shortage of investment funds but a real shortage of capital in the lower stages of production, which is needed to achieve a new balanced pattern of production in line with the additional investment in the higher stages.

During the depression the structure of production is again brought into balance. This is a lengthy and painful process of readjustment during which workers are thrown out of work in the higher stages of production and gradually reabsorbed in the lower stages as a new pattern of equilibrium is developed. The depression is intensified by the general deflation that accompanies the decrease in the velocity of circulation brought about by hoarding on the part of businesses and households. Now, the market rate of interest will rise above the natural rate because of the increase in hoarding and the possible decrease in the money supply. If total output did not decrease, something like "forced consumption" would take place because the price level would decrease, and since investment has decreased consumption would have to increase. While this is apparently the assumption that Hayek makes, a more realistic position would be that unemployment does occur and total output falls and results in a decline in both investment and consumption during the contraction phase of the cycle. The depression comes to an end when the money supply ceases to decline and when the pessimism that caused the hoarding dissipates. At this point, the natural rate and the market rate would again come into equality, and the stage would be set for another expansion phase that would take place whenever the banking system again finds it profitable to create more money.

Evaluation

There are several shortcomings to this theory as the sole explanation of the cycle. The thesis that credit, which is created when the market rate of interest differs from the natural rate, goes to the higher stages of production and leads to an imbalance between consumption and investment would be generally true under conditions of continuous full employment. However, the upswing of the cycle starts at a time when the economy has unused resources, and the production of both producer goods and consumer goods can be expanded before full employment of resources is reached. At full employment, if credit continues to be expanded to meet the demands of producers, forced saving and imbalance result. But imbalance also results if credit is created to meet the demands of consumers or of government.

The stress upon changes in interest rates as a determinant in the investment process may also obscure other factors that are at work. Investment decisions are based upon the interaction of the demand for funds with the supply of and cost of funds. The demand for funds at various stages in the cyclical process is affected materially by changes in prospects of sales and profits. An analysis of the reasons for the changes in these prospects is an integral part of an understanding of the cyclical process.

Answers to this question supplied by a group of theorists stressing changes in investment activity will be considered in the next section. The monetary overinvestment theorists have stressed an important factor in their analysis of imbalance during the cycle between producer and consumer goods and between different types of producer goods.

THE ACCELERATION PRINCIPLE

Both the monetary and the nonmonetary overinvestment theories, as well as the innovation theory, hold that the initiating force in the cyclical process comes from the investment sector of the economy. There is, however, a point of view which has been used in explaining the cyclical process which holds that the initiating impulses come from changes in consumer demand. According to this point of view, changes in consumption expenditures can lead to a cycle because slight changes in the demand for consumer goods can produce much more violent fluctuations in the demand for investment goods. This principle, known as the *acceleration principle,* has been used by many theorists as part of their explanation of the cycle, notably by the French economist Albert Aftalion, the American economist J. M. Clark, and the British economist R. F. Harrod.[11]

In its broadest aspect the principle of acceleration states that changes in the absolute rate of change in the demand for and production of finished goods and services tend to give rise to much more pronounced changes in the demand for and production of the producer goods that are needed for their production. This principle applies not only to finished consumer goods but to all intermediate goods with respect to their preceding stages of production. It also applies to changes in demand resulting from other factors than changes in final demand, such as changes in technology calling for the use of more machinery to produce a given level of output. It also holds true to a degree in the production of durable and semidurable consumer goods.

Producer Goods

The relationship in the case of producer durable goods may best be illustrated by means of a hypothetical example. Let us suppose that in a given economy 1,000 units of consumer goods are produced in a year and that it takes 100 units of producer durable equipment to turn out the consumer goods. If the producer equipment lasts 10 years, there is an average demand for 10 units of equipment each year to replace those that are wearing out so as to keep the stock of equipment intact.

Let us suppose, further, that there is an increase of 10 percent in the demand for this particular consumer good so that 1,100 units are now desired by consumers. To produce these additional 100 units, it will be necessary to have 10 more units of equipment. Even though this equipment will be useful for a period of 10 years, it is needed immediately. As a result, there is now a demand for 20 units of equipment, the 10 needed for replacement and the 10 additional units needed to take care of the increased consumer demand. Thus, an increase of 10 percent in the demand for consumer goods has been magnified into an increased demand of 100 percent in the producer goods field.

The degree of this acceleration in the derived demand for capital goods depends upon the life of the capital equipment. If the machines in our example lasted only 5 years, there would be a normal demand for replacement of 20 per year. In this case a 10 percent increase in the demand for consumer goods would result in a 50 percent increase in the demand for producer goods since 10 additional machines would be needed and 20 are being produced regularly. On the other hand, if the machines lasted 20 years, the normal replacement demand would be only 5 per year and the 10 percent increase in the demand for

---

[11] Mr. Harrod makes use of the acceleration principle in his analysis of the business cycle but following his own terminology calls it "the relation."

consumer goods would lead to a 200 percent increase in the demand for producer equipment.

At the one extreme, if a machine would last indefinitely and was capable
of producing an unlimited number of commodities, there would be no activity
in the replacement business and so any increase in primary demand would
result in an increase in the demand for new equipment only. In that case the
total demand for equipment would be represented in Table 6-1 by our column
headed "Demand for New Equipment." There would be no demand for
replacement. This is the most volatile case. At the other extreme, suppose the
durability of the machines was just one period, that is, capable of producing
just 10 units of commodity output. In that case, the replacement industry
would be producing the existing stock of capital each period, and any increase
in primary demand would result in exactly a proportional increase in total
demand for equipment.

It is possible for the demand for new equipment to slow down while the
demand for consumer goods is still increasing. If the demand for the consumer
goods increases from 1,000 to 1,100 units, the demand for equipment increases
by 10, or 100 percent. However, while the demand for the consumer goods
continues to increase to 1,150 units, the total demand for equipment has
already been cut to 16 units, a reduction of 20 percent. If in the next period
the demand for the commodity remains constant, the only equipment demand
is for replacement and, as a result, demand falls still further. This can be seen
clearly from the example in Table 6-1.

Table 6-1
Changes in the Demand for Producer Goods
Resulting from Changes in Consumer Goods Demand*

Period	Commodity Demand	Equipment Stock (Beginning of Period)	Demand for Equipment for Replacement	Demand for New Equipment (Net Investment)	Total Demand for Equipment (Gross Investment)
1	1,000	100	10	0	10
2	1,100	100	10	10	20
3	1,150	110	11	5	16
4	1,150	115	11.5	0	11.5
5	1,000	115	11.5	−15	−3.5

* Assumptions:
  1. Commodity demand figures are arbitrarily selected.
  2. One piece of equipment produces at the rate of 10 units of the commodity per period.
  3. The equipment has a life of 10 periods, that is, its depreciation rate is 10 percent per year.
     In reality, the assumption is that in its lifetime the equipment is capable of producing 100
     units of the commodity.
  4. No depreciation occurs in the year in which equipment is added.

Thus, it can be seen that increases in the absolute rate of change in demand
for consumer goods when an industry is at or near capacity will lead to an

accelerated derived demand for producer goods, but this demand will be sharply curtailed as the rate of increase slows down.

Durable and Semidurable Consumer Goods

The second case of the principle of acceleration is similar to the first except that it pertains to durable and semidurable consumer goods. Identically the same example can be used with modifications in terms. Instead of the production of a consumer good, it is necessary to substitute the service received from it (as, for example, the service received from a house) and to substitute the supply of houses for the equipment used to produce consumer goods. An increase in the demand for housing accommodations leads to a greatly magnified demand for new houses because houses last for a long period of time.

The same situation is true in the automobile field where the basic demand is for transportation service. Since cars last for several years, there is a basic demand for automobiles for replacement and an increase in the demand for transportation service leads to an accelerated increase in the demand for new cars. This relationship will be elaborated on more fully in a discussion of the methods of forecasting the demand for consumer durable goods in Part 6.

Inventories

The third case of the acceleration due to derived demand occurs in the case of inventories. Let up suppose that it is the practice of a dealer in men's suits to adjust the store's inventory to sales in such a way that the usual stock on hand is about equal to the sales during two months, and that sales are normally 100 suits a month. Because of an increase in demand, sales rise to 110 suits a month. As a result, it is necessary to increase orders for suits by more than the increase in sales if the regular relationship of inventory to sales is to be maintained. If the increased demand for suits is permanent, 20 extra suits must be added to the stock to maintain past inventory relationships.

This principle works on the downturn as well as on the upswing. It is, however, subject to some very definite qualifications. It is by no means clear that a relatively fixed relationship will be maintained at all times between sales and stocks, especially in the short run. In addition, the volume of stocks is subject to speculative changes that may easily overshadow any changes due to the acceleration principle.

Evaluation

The acceleration principle has been used as part of the explanation of the cycle by various theorists. It is another factor that explains the accelerated increase in demand in the upswing of the cycle. It is especially significant in a highly developed economy in which large amounts of capital equipment are in use, with much of the equipment having a long period of usefulness. As has already been demonstrated, the longer the life of the equipment, the greater the acceleration due to derived demand. Since some of the new capital equipment is financed out of credit expansion, the additional credit intensifies the upswing. The acceleration in demand for durable goods and in demand for inventories also offers a further explanation of the factors leading to the cumulative nature of the expansion.

The acceleration principle also adds a new possibility for an explanation of the downturn. Instead of being due to a shortage of money or of equipment, the downturn may occur because the rate of increase in the demand for consumer goods has slowed down, thus reducing the demand for new equipment and leading to unemployment in the producer goods field. This further reduces the demand for consumer goods which still further reduces the demand for producer goods. As this cumulative process of contraction takes place, the boom must come to an end.

Attempts to verify the acceleration principle statistically have not always met with success. This is to be expected since it is only a greatly simplified statement of a principle, not an explanation of a phenomenon which happens in just that way in the real world. In the case of producers' durable equipment, for example, it is very unlikely in an economy which experiences marked fluctuations in demand that there will be any regularity in the replacement of equipment. Most replacement is likely to occur in prosperity periods when the demands for new equipment must also be met. Furthermore, when an expansion of business begins, there is usually unused capacity in an industry so that the first effect of an increased demand for consumer goods is a fuller utilization of existing capacity. As demand expands further, it is also possible in many plants to utilize existing equipment more fully by adding additional shifts of workers. Beyond that point it becomes necessary to place orders for new equipment, which will show the accelerated effect of derived demand.

As the economy approaches full employment of workers and other resources, however, it is no longer possible to increase production in all fields. The major result will be a bidding up of prices, especially those of basic raw materials utilized in both the producer and consumer goods fields. Thus, the acceleration principle cannot hold completely as full employment of labor and resources is achieved. This explanation is in harmony with the record of business fluctuations as developed by the National Bureau of Economic Research. The most rapid rate of increase in the production of capital goods occurs early in the cycle, but the most rapid rate of increase in price does not occur until the last segment of expansion. This relationship is much too complex to be measured effectively in all of its ramifications and therefore it is not surprising that the evidence on this point is at variance. It is, however, an integral part of the explanation of the cyclical process, especially the more pronounced fluctuations in demand for durable goods of all kinds rather than for nondurable goods.

Here we have discussed the acceleration principle as it applies on the micro or industry level. The principle has also been integrated into the general theory of national income analysis, and this will be discussed in Chapter 8.

QUESTIONS

1. Show the balance sheet changes of the commercial banking system over a complete business cycle as implied in Hawtrey's analysis. Use successive T-accounts. The only items needed are reserves, earning assets, and demand deposits. Assume a 10 percent customary or required reserve ratio.

2. Trace the development of a full business cycle according to the purely monetary theory within the framework of the equation of exchange, either $MV = Py$, or $M = kPy$.
3. What weakness in Tugan-Baranowsky's theory did Spiethoff correct? What was Schumpeter's contribution to this same problem?
4. Would the nonmonetary theory of the cycle be an acceptable theory if the money supply were held completely constant? Defend your answer.
5. In the overinvestment theories, the upper turning point is associated with a decrease in investment. Why, then, are the theories called "overinvestment"?
6. Explain how inflation of the general price level operates to produce the phenomenon called "forced saving."
7. Explain why the acceleration principle is more pronounced the more durable the capital equipment.

SUGGESTED READINGS

Hawtrey, Ralph G. *Trade and Credit.* London: Longmans, Green & Co., Ltd., 1928.
———. *Capital and Employment.* London: Longmans, Green & Co., Ltd., 1937.
Hayek, Friedrich A. *Monetary Theory and the Trade Cycle.* New York: Harcourt, Brace & World, 1933.
———. *Prices and Production.* London: George Routledge & Sons, Ltd., 1935.
Schumpeter, Joseph A. *Business Cycles,* Vol. 1. New York: McGraw-Hill Book Company, 1939.
———. *Theory of Economic Development.* Cambridge, Mass.: Harvard University Press, 1934.
Spiethoff, Arthur. *Business Cycles,* International Economic Papers, No. 3. New York: The Macmillan Company, 1953.
Tugan-Baranowsky, Michel. *Les Crises Industrielles en Angleterre,* 1913.
Wicksell, Knut. *Interest and Prices.* London: Macmillan & Co., Ltd., 1936.

PROBLEMS ON PART 2

1. Construct a table from data in the *Federal Reserve Bulletin* showing the following for the years 1955 to the present:
   (a) Gross National Product
   (b) Wholesale Commodity Price Index
   (c) Money supply (i.e., currency in circulation plus demand deposits)
   (d) Velocity of money (i.e., (a) divided by (c))
   (e) Index of Industrial Production
   Relate the behavior of these series to the equation of exchange and the quantity theory of money.
2. (a) Assume that the economy is in a state of equilibrium in which the market rate of interest is equal to the natural rate. Analyze the changes, if any, that would be likely to occur if the following happened:
   (1) The Federal Reserve bought $3 billion of bonds in the open market.
   (2) A large new gold deposit was discovered and $2 billion added to the monetary gold stocks in a year.
   (3) There was a rapid development of automatic factories requiring large amounts of new capital.
   (4) A law was passed requiring steel mills to use more machinery around furnaces to eliminate hazardous jobs. Total costs of producing steel remain about the same.

(5) Banks changed their credit standards so as to make it easier to get term loans for 15 years to build new plants.

(b) Business has been improving for several years. Bank credit has been increasing in volume and prices have moved upward. Analyze the possible effects that could result from the following actions:

(1) The Federal Reserve raises reserve requirements 2 points, and a month later the rediscount rate is increased 1 percent.

(2) The federal government has been operating at a deficit during the upswing in business. A new administration cuts expenses drastically, but maintains tax rates so as to have a surplus for debt retirement.

(3) The Federal Reserve supplies the banking system with $5 billion of added reserves.

(4) The rate of consumer saving increases from 7 percent of disposable income to 9 percent.

(c) There is reasonable balance between the production of nondurable consumer goods, semidurable and durable consumer goods, durable capital goods, and materials used to produce durable goods. Analyze the possible effects of the following:

(1) A small, safe helicopter that can be sold for the price of a small car is developed. Consumer demand for this new means of transportation is strong.

(2) New machines are developed at a reasonable price to replace most workers on assembly lines for durable goods. Industrial demand for such machines is far in excess of supply.

3. In a textile factory one unit of machinery and equipment is required to produce 20 lots of cloth a day. The average life of the machinery and equipment is 10 years. Develop a table similar to Table 6-1 showing the demand for equipment for replacement, the demand for equipment resulting from increased consumer demand, and the total demand for equipment when the output of textiles varies as follows:

Year	Average Production per Day
1	2,000 lots
2	2,200 lots
3	2,360 lots
4	2,360 lots
5	1,700 lots

4. (a) Assume that business is operating at a level of full employment except for a normal amount of frictional unemployment. Several of the independent appliance companies are combined into an integrated company. Their forecast of demand for their appliances turns out to be decidedly overoptimistic, even though many of the executives thought it might be correct. How will business in general adjust to such an error in forecast according to the psychological theorists?

(b) The economy is fairly well adjusted at full employment levels. Consumers are spending 92 percent of disposable income and saving 8 percent. As a result of bank and savings and loan thrift campaigns, savings increase to 10 percent of disposable income. Discuss the possible effects on the economy in the short run and long run of such a shift.

PART 3

NATIONAL INCOME ANALYSIS

This part presents the core of modern national income analysis or the essentials of what is taught in intermediate macroeconomics courses. The chapters preceding this part have familiarized the reader with earlier systems of thought and have dealt with the major variables involved in the study of aggregate economics. The chapters that follow Part 3 build on this theoretical foundation by extending the study to the measurement and application of the concepts and then proceed into forecasting the behavior of the economy and its components.

In Chapter 7 the familiar basic Keynesian national income determination model, including the multiplier, is reviewed. This model is presented verbally, geometrically, and in the arithmetic of period analysis. Chapter 8 considers the nonconsumption elements of the market for goods and services, primarily investment but also government expenditures and net foreign demand for the national output. The equilibrium situation of the aggregate market for goods and services is summarized in an *I-S* curve. Chapter 9 covers the monetary aspects of the economy: the theory of money supply behavior, the demand for money, and the equilibrium situation in the money market summarized by the *L-M* curve. The goods market and the money market are then integrated, and the level and the importance of inflation and deflation are considered.

Chapter 10 deals with a number of important topics in national income analysis such as taxation, alternative theories of consumption, the stagnation thesis, and economic growth theories.

CHAPTER 7

THE BASIC FRAMEWORK OF NATIONAL INCOME ANALYSIS

The next four chapters develop the modern theory of national income analysis. This chapter begins with some comments on the contributions of Lord Keynes, who was mainly responsible for initiating interest in this form of analysis, and then continues by presenting the basic framework of the theory. Chapter 8 extends the analysis by integrating the market for goods and services, develops the theory of investment, and includes a presentation of a multiplier-accelerator model that shows how business cycles can occur because of the form of the investment demand function. Chapter 9 is concerned with the distinction between real values such as physical quantities of goods and services, their nominal or dollar values, and the connection between them, namely, the level of prices. Chapter 10 concludes this part with some important topics in national income analysis.

THE KEYNESIAN CONTRIBUTION

The expression "Keynesian Economics" is employed in recognition of the influence of John Maynard Keynes in contributing an alternative approach to aggregate economic analysis. While Keynes was a member of the neoclassical school as a Professor at Cambridge University, he became dissatisfied with certain aspects of neoclassicism. He has had great influence both as an academic economist and as an adviser on public policy. Few, if any, economists, at least since the days of Adam Smith, have had as pronounced an effect on economic theory as did Lord Keynes. In his *General Theory of Employment, Interest, and Money,* he analyzed what he considered to be the weaknesses of classical economics and presented a new set of tools for economic analysis and a new formulation of the factors that determine the level of employment of labor and other resources. As is the case with any new approach to a problem, his work generated a great deal of discussion and controversy, some of which continues to this day. Those who refused to accept his general approach to economic analysis were forced to reexamine their concepts and to define them more accurately and more clearly. His followers were given the tools which led them to develop a greatly increased understanding of our economy, especially the factors that determine the level of consumption, saving, investment, and interest rates.

Keynes not only attained a standing as an economist held by few individuals, but he also achieved a place as an adviser on public policy in the economic area that has seldom, if ever, been equaled. In his early twenties he was an adviser to the government of India on financial matters; in his early fifties governments in all parts of the world sought his advice on matters of economic policy. His position of preeminence as an economic adviser continued until his death. In his last years he was one of the leading advisers responsible for the agreements that led to the establishment of the International Monetary Fund.

Another reason for devoting so much space to the work of J. M. Keynes is that he analyzed the factors determining the level of investment and consumption and developed the relationships between them in a fuller and different way from that of earlier cycle theorists. Since Keynes' analysis of these factors has become the wellspring of modern aggregative economic analysis, we use this chapter as the introduction to the basic elements of national income determination theory. A mastery of the material in this chapter will permit comprehension of the later developments in macroeconomic theory and contemporary business cycle thought discussed in later chapters.

AGGREGATE DEMAND

In Chapter 4, where classical macroeconomics was discussed, we had little need for the analysis of *aggregate demand*. The classicists, in accordance with Say's Law, reasoned that whatever the rate of output might be in an economy, there would always be sufficient aggregate demand. In stark contrast, Keynes' position was that the demand side was the active determinant of how much would be produced. It may be simplifying too much to put the matter as bluntly as this, but the general emphasis is valid to say that the classical school said that when you determined how much would be produced, you knew how much would be demanded; whereas, Keynes said that if you knew how much would be demanded, you would know how much would be produced.

Aggregate demand is the sum of final goods and services that decision-making units intend to buy. The usual procedure is to group the decision-making units into the various sectors of the economy. In general, it has been found helpful to use the categories of households, business, government, and the rest of the world. There are three reasons for this particular breakdown: (1) the decision-making process is somewhat different for each of the categories, or at least is handled differently in the theory explaining their behavior; (2) the impact of the expenditures of the various sectors on the future may be different; and (3) value judgments about the welfare effects of the expenditures of the several sectors may differ.

Households

Households include all of the human beings in the domestic economy. The *raison d'etre* of the economy is to improve the welfare, in some sense, of this sector. Consumption takes place to satisfy the desires of households, so that in the fundamental meaning of the term only households consume. A large and well-developed theory of household behavior exists in the literature where each consuming unit is viewed as an expected utility maximizer. A household is in equilibrium when the marginal utilities of all commodities relative to their prices are equal; that is, $\dfrac{MU_A}{P_A} = \dfrac{MU_B}{P_B} = \ldots = \dfrac{MU_N}{P_N}$.

Macroeconomic theory does not concern itself in any important way with the allocation of income among commodities, but it does concern itself with the allocation of income between present goods as a group and future goods as a group. In other words, in aggregative economic theory the decision of households to spend a part of current income on present consumption implies a decision to save the remainder. On partial equilibrium grounds, then, the household is in equilibrium when the marginal utilities of all present goods relative to their prices are equal to the marginal utilities of all future goods relative to their current prices.[1] An increase in a consumer's income would be expected to increase the consumer's demands for both present and future goods. The precise manner in which a change in income will influence this decision is the subject of considerable controversy, as will be seen in our review of consumption function studies. To the extent that households opt for more saving, they have, at once, increased the demand for future goods and made resources available for future use.

All income from production accrues to the household sector in the sense that all factors of production are owned by members of that sector, either through personal, direct ownership or indirectly through the intermediary of a corporation or government. In national income accounting, reference is made to business saving and government saving, but even in these instances where retained corporate earnings or government surpluses exist, saving will occur only to the extent that consumers acquiesce in the decision.

It stretches credulity too much to declare that consumption and household spending are identical. What should be included in consumption spending is the spending on goods and services that is normally destroyed in value during the period under analysis. The purchase of a new home or new automobile, for example, should be excluded since the largest part of the expenditure is not for current consumption but for future use. Thus, spending for these items should be included in investment demand. Such spending should also be included in the category of investment because the decision to purchase is based on the same elements as the process of decision making by business firms. Since investment is the act of adding to the stock of capital, the purchase of a home or auto is an act of investment which increases the supply of future income.

The Business Sector

In the circular flow analysis all productive activity takes place at the level of the business sector. Business firms employ the services of the factors of production owned by the households. Microeconomic theory asserts that business units

---

[1] The future price of commodities is, of course, unknown. If the price level were expected to remain constant, then the interest rate could be used in calculating the current price ratios of present and future goods. Similarly, the marginal utility of future goods in the future is unknown; our reference must be to the present utility of future goods, which, too, involves a forecast.

utilize resources in such proportions as to maximize expected profits. The equilibrium of a firm occurs when an additional dollar spent on any given resource is expected to yield a return equal to that of the dollar spent on any other resource.

In the manner of price theory textbooks, $\dfrac{MP_A}{P_A} = \dfrac{MP_B}{P_B} = \ldots = \dfrac{MP_N}{P_N} = 1$,

where MP is the marginal product of the factors of production $A, B, \ldots, N$ and P is the per unit price of factors $A, B, \ldots, N$. This means that the employment of any resource will increase if its productivity increases or if its cost decreases.

From the side of aggregate demand, the most important decision of the business firm is the amount of investment to be undertaken. The investment decision is based on the expected returns from dollars invested compared to the expected cost of engaging in the investment. Chapter 8 contains a lengthy discussion of this principle.

If investment takes place, the stock of productive resources increases and the ability of the economic system to produce goods and services in the future has increased. In the case of investment in inventory, the physical supply of goods available for future consumption has increased directly. The type of investment that takes place makes a great deal of difference to future employment and to future price prospects. If the investment is primarily in increased inventories of finished consumer goods, in finished producer goods, in raw material stocks, or in the many types of plant or equipment, the implications for the future are clearly different. It is easy to conceive of cases in which the investment expenditures would be of the type that would put pressure on wages to move in one direction and prices of finished goods to move in the other direction. On the other hand, the investment might be of a kind that created an unemployment problem, or it might create an imbalance between agricultural versus industrial production. Such problems are discussed in greater detail at later stages of our study.

A major question may arise in the reader's mind concerning the demand for replacement expenditures and for maintenance and repair of the existing capital stock. Some aggregate economic models do include gross investment rather than net investment as we shall do. These economists argue that replacement expenditures generate a demand for workers and other resources just as much as do expenditures for increasing the capital stock. Since that is true, one should be aware of the situation involving the rate of actual destruction and deterioration in the capital stock compared to the actual amount of replacement. At certain times, during wars and depressions, for example, the capital stock is allowed to deteriorate without replacement. At other times, in the aftermath of wars and in the recovery stage of the business cycle, for example, replacement expenditures will be in excess of the current rate of capital consumption. Net investment is the concept that takes these issues into consideration, so if our concern is with national income as a measure of welfare, we want net investment as the business sector's contribution to aggregate demand. On the other hand, for short-run analysis of employment and price-level behavior, gross investment may be the more useful figure.

The Government Sector

The theory of government behavior has not been as well developed nor as generally accepted as has the body of theory on the private sector. On one hand, we have the welfare-oriented theory which states, in general terms, that marginal social benefits should be equal to marginal social costs. The problem of determining what these benefits and costs are to a society made up of individuals with different preference patterns is, of course, controversial. Theoretical analysis of actual government behavior runs the gamut from the extremely naive to the extremely cynical. One approach, which has attracted a number of adherents, runs in terms of votes gained from a particular action weighed against the number of votes lost by the action. It is at least conceivable that the two approaches lead to the same action, although at this stage in the development of the analysis, it cannot be proved nor disproved.

The place of the government sector in the circular flow depiction of the economy is to absorb purchasing power from the household sector by taxation and to direct this purchasing power to the business sector (including government employees therein) as governments purchase goods and services.[2] Some of the expenditures by government will result in current satisfactions of the public (thus being consumption-type expenditures), and some expenditures increase the wealth of the society (thus being investment-type expenditures). Classification of particular government spending into either category would involve us in serious philosophical debate, so we restrain ourselves, but it should be pointed out that the question which needs to be answered is whether the expenditures have the effect of increasing the stock of wealth of the society or simply increasing current services.

For purposes of short-run analysis of national income behavior, it is insignificant whether government spending is classified as consumption or investment. All such spending acts as an injection of demand for the output of the economy and becomes income for the owners of the factors of production responsible for the production of the goods and services.

The main reason for handling the government sector apart from the others is that its behavior is subject to political control, and its taxing and spending can be adjusted to bring about what are believed to be desirable goals. The most important reason, ultimately, that the federal government differs from the other sectors is that it has the sovereign power, which makes its receipts from taxes different from the receipts of units that must sell a product or service; its borrowing power is unlimited, as long, of course, as the general public has confidence in the monetary system.[3]

---

[2] Government also distributes funds to some households without requiring any current goods and services in exchange. This is what is meant by "transfer payments," and we include transfer payments as negative taxes since the amount of taxes offset by transfer payments constitutes no net outflow from the household sector.

[3] This statement may sound shocking, but it must be remembered that issuing money is the prerogative of all national governments, and money is a noninterest-bearing form of debt. We are not yet ready to discuss whether, or under what conditions, government should borrow at interest or at no interest.

The Rest of the World

Exports of goods and services result in an injection of demand by other economies for output and an increase in the incomes of the factors that produced the commodities. Imports into this economy can be looked upon as an outflow or withdrawal from the income stream, since these expenditures do not return purchasing power to our business sector. The international transactions are almost always handled as a net figure called *net foreign investment* or net exports of goods and services, which is the difference between what our nationals sell to foreigners and the amount foreign nationals sell to citizens of this country.

Selling goods or services to peoples of other countries is akin to other investment activities since it increases the future consumption abilities of our nationals, while purchasing goods from the rest of the world decreases our ability to consume in the future. Another important reason for dealing with the net amount by which exports exceed imports is that it is impossible for us to measure directly the amount of foreign and domestically produced goods and services bought by our households, government, and our business sector. Many goods said to be "made in America" may actually contain raw materials from foreign countries, or perhaps foreign machines were used to produce the raw materials in this country.

The demand to import goods and services depends primarily upon national income and the prices of foreign goods as represented by the exchange rates among currencies. The demand for exports depends on the incomes in other countries and the exchange rates. In addition to these factors, exports and imports are heavily influenced by various government policies, such as quotas, tariffs, taxes, subsidies, and many others usually designed to encourage exports and discourage imports of the country.

THE CIRCULAR FLOW

The process by which income is generated through production and sales, and sales are made possible by income, is called the *circular flow*. Business firms receive receipts from the sale of goods and services to all of the four sectors we have just described: households; governments; the rest of the world; and the business firms themselves, which buy whatever was not sold to the other three sectors. It is important to understand that what business units buy may be voluntary purchases by one firm from another, or the producing firm may not sell to other buyers so that its inventory of its own product will increase. This increase in inventories may be intentional or unintentional. Such unintentional investment is of critical importance in the study of national income because, when it occurs, business units can be expected to attempt to reduce the unplanned accumulation by decreasing production, and therefore incomes, or by maintaining the old level of sales by lowering prices and thus also reducing incomes. Unintended real investment also can take place when a firm uses up less of its capital equipment than it had planned because output was less than intended, while planned investment remained the same.

The receipts of business units accrue as income to household owners of the factors of production. Households allocate their incomes among the following uses: purchasing goods and services directly from business units (consumption); paying taxes to governments; purchasing goods from other countries (imports); or if the households do none of these, we say they have saved (personal saving). This saving is a definitional residual, and whatever else might be done with the money does not alter the fact that saving took place.

Like investment, saving can be viewed as taking place either voluntarily or involuntarily. Involuntary saving might occur because earners of income during a period do not receive it until some future period. The payment lag is quite short for wage earners, but for property income recipients it might be considerable. Professor Modigliani has pointed out that the strictly Keynesian analytical framework implicitly assumes that consumers have their way so that intended saving is always the same as actual saving and that unintended saving never occurs.[4] This assumption has the logical corollary that the impact of a disequilibrium income is always on the business sector. It always appears as a condition where unintended investment or disinvestment exists. These statements will be made clearer when we demonstrate the income equilibrating mechanism.

Symbolically, the circular flow can be described in the following identity:

$$Y \equiv C + G + I_B + (X - M) \equiv C + T + S_P$$

where

Y = income
C = consumption
G = government spending
I_B = business investment
X = exports
M = imports
T = taxes
S_P = personal saving

As a first approximation, it is convenient to reduce $G + I_B + (X - M)$ to I = injections; and $T + S_P$ to S = savings in the inclusive sense. In this way a simpler model can be constructed where the supply side or value of goods and services produced is equal to $C + S = Y$, and the demand side is $C + I$.

The condition of equilibrium is that supply equals demand; that is, $Y = C + I$. It is necessary to see why equilibrium exists only if aggregate supply and demand are equal. First, suppose the total value of goods and services produced is greater than the demand for them. In that event unintended inventories accumulate and business will attempt to reduce them by laying off workers and buying fewer materials and services from other firms. In other words, if income is greater than the equilibrium level, income will fall. If, instead of reducing production, firms with excess inventory lower the prices of the unsold goods, the profits of the sellers (which are their incomes) will fall. In later production the incomes of the other factors of production will also fall.

---

[4] F. Modigliani, "Liquidity Preference and the Theory of Interest and Money," *Econometrica* (January, 1944).

In the preceding paragraph the case of aggregate supply exceeding aggregate demand was discussed. Now consider the case where demand is greater than supply: $C + I > Y$, or $C + I > C + S$. Since $C = C$, it follows that $I > S$. It is also true that since purchases of goods and services $(C + I)$ are greater than the value of goods and services produced $(C + S)$, some of the goods sold must have been produced in prior time periods. In other words, the stock of capital, most importantly inventories, must have been reduced. This is described as involuntary disinvestment or negative investment. In this situation, where business is in fact investing less than it intended to invest, we can expect the firms to try to build back their inventories to the desired level. This will necessitate the employment of additional workers and other resources or an increase in the prices of goods and services as well as factor prices. Thus, when income is less than the equilibrium level ($C + I > C + S$, and $I > S$), income will rise.

Parenthetically, it is worth noting that even in the disequilibrium situations where $S > I$ or where $I > S$, it is still the case that *actual* saving and *actual* investment are exactly equal in amount. In this framework it is usually assumed that savers do save the amount they intend to save. If this is so, then when $S > I$, involuntary investment in the amount $S - I$ must take place; and conversely, when $I > S$, involuntary disinvestment in the amount $I - S$ must take place.

The Simple Algebraic Model

What has just been verbalized can also be put in the form of a formal model. Certain propositions can be more easily demonstrated with such a model; but more importantly, more complete models or models closer to reality simply cannot be handled, or cannot be handled efficiently, verbally.

The first model to consider is the simplest that can be constructed. It is composed of the following three equations containing three unknowns:

$$Y = C + I.$$
$$C = a + bY.$$
$$I = I_o.$$

The first equation is the condition of equilibrium. Our goal is to "solve" for Y, that is, to find the equilibrium value of Y in terms of the "knowns," (a, b, I_o).[5] The second equation is the "consumption function." It is a behavior equation, which is to say that it describes the expected behavior of households that consume specific amounts at specific levels of income. The third equation asserts that the amount of investment is exogenously determined. For purposes of this model, investment is not to be explained. We get the value of I_o from some other theory, or we simply ask all business people their intentions. For our present purpose it is most important to observe that intended investment does not depend on the level of current income.

---

[5] The meaning and significance of these terms are detailed later.

Now solve for Y by substituting into the first equation. First, the unknown C can be replaced by $a + bY$ and the unknown I can be eliminated by using the known I_o.

Thus: $Y = a + bY + I_o$.
Subtract bY from both sides of the equation: $Y - bY = a + I_o$.
Factor out Y from the left side: $Y(1 - b) = a + I_o$.

Divide both sides by $(1 - b)$: $Y = \dfrac{a + I_o}{1 - b}$.

We now have one equation and one unknown (Y). If we know the values of the knowns (the parameters), we can determine the value of the unknowns. Thus, if $a = \$20$ billion, $b = 8/10$, and $I_o = \$30$ billion, then $Y = \dfrac{\$20 + \$30}{1 - 8/10} = \dfrac{\$50}{2/10} = \$250$ billion. Since $C = a + bY$, $C = \$20 + 8/10 (\$250) = \$20 + \$200 = \$220$ billion.

No equation for S was given, but since we know that $S = Y - C$, we can derive the equation for S by substituting $a + bY$ for C.

Thus: $S = Y - a - bY$,
and factoring: $S = -a + (1 - b)Y$,
and $S = -\$20 + \left(1 - \dfrac{8}{10}\right) \$250 = -\$20 + \$50 = \$30$ billion.
Since $I = I_o = \$30$ billion, $S = I$.

The Geometry of the Simple Model

This model can now be demonstrated graphically (see Figure 7-1). In general, the geometric approach is not as powerful as the equations approach since the charts get cluttered up quite quickly when many refinements are added. It is, however, a very handy method for attacking certain problems.

Each line on the graph is now to be explained. First consider the Z line (Figure 7-2). It is drawn at a 45° angle from the origin, so that triangles such as $0YX$ and $0XZ$ are identical right triangles. This is significant in that it assures that $0Y = 0Z$. In this way distances measured along the horizontal axis can be compared to distances measured along the vertical axis, since the equation for any straight line is a constant, which measures the intersection of the line with the vertical axis [call it α (alpha)], plus another constant which is the slope of the line [call it β (beta)], times the value on the horizontal axis. For the Z line we have drawn, its equation is: $Z = \alpha + \beta Y$ but $\alpha = 0$, and $\beta = 1$, so $Z = Y$. We know that $\beta = 1$ because the slope can be measured by any triangle such as RWX. It is $\dfrac{XW}{RW}$, but $XW = RW$ (by construction, again) so $\dfrac{XW}{RW} = 1$, so the equation for the Z line collapses to $Z = Y$.

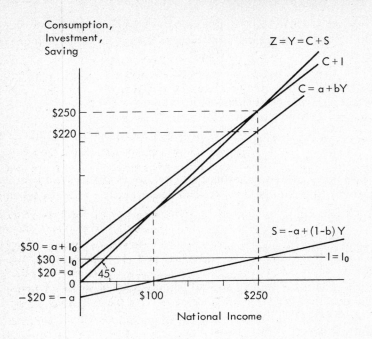

Figure 7-1

Basic National Income Determination

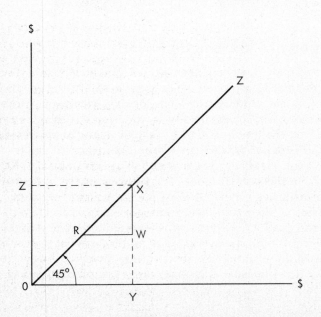

Figure 7-2

The Z Function

The Consumption Function

The C line (Figure 7-3, see below) has the equation $C = a + bY$, which makes it a straight line. The consumption function is the heart of the Keynesian system, and books have been written about it. It has been thought by some to be Keynes' most important contribution to the methodology of aggregate economic theory.

The C line is drawn on the basis of the past behavior of comsumption and income. It is the line which represents the best single estimator of what consumption was at various levels of income. Statistically, it is the least squares simple regression of consumption on income. When income is Y_1, the best prediction for consumption is C_1; and when income is Y_2, the best prediction for consumption is C_2. Furthermore, the line shows that if income is expected to increase from Y_1 to Y_2 (i.e., by ΔY_1), consumption would be expected to increase from C_1 to C_2 (i.e., by ΔC_1).

The ratio of $\frac{\Delta C}{\Delta Y}$ is a very important element in the analysis. It is the *marginal propensity to consume,* the slope of the consumption function, and is equal to b of our equation. In a straight line the slope is a constant; that is, it is the same wherever it is measured. Keynes reasoned that the marginal propensity to consume would get smaller as income gets larger; that is to say,

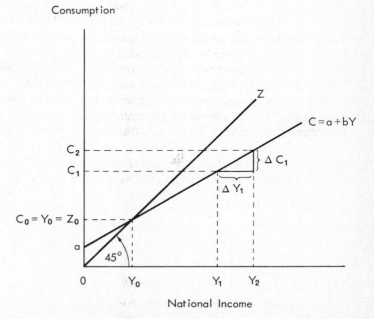

Figure 7-3

The Consumption Function

he thought a curved line, rather than a straight line, would be a closer approximation to the real world consumption function. More will be said about the realism of the function in the next chapter.

Less important than the marginal propensity to consume is the *average propensity to consume,* defined as $\frac{C}{Y}$. On a linear consumption function the marginal propensity to consume (MPC) is constant, but the average propensity to consume (APC) declines as income gets larger. For this to be true, the intercept, a, must be positive. This is easy to see. Since $APC = \frac{C}{Y}$, and $C = a + bY$, $APC = \frac{a + bY}{Y}$.

If a were equal to zero, the APC would be equal to $\frac{bY}{Y} = b$, and b is a constant. At very small incomes (Y), the APC would be dominated by a; in fact, if $Y = 0$, then $APC = \frac{a}{0}$, which is customarily known as infinity. At that level of income at which $C = Y$ (Y_o in Figure 7-3), of course the $APC = 1$. At all smaller incomes $C > Y$ so $APC > 1$, and at all incomes larger than this, $Y > C$ so $APC < 1$ and falling. As a minimum, the APC approaches the MPC. This can readily be seen since in the expression $\frac{a + bY}{Y}$, as Y gets extremely large, the significance of a diminishes to nothing and for all practical purposes the APC becomes $\frac{bY}{Y}$, which reduces to b, the MPC.

It should be clear how important the consumption-income relation is to the entire analysis. In all economies, consumption is by far the largest component of national income; thus, if income is to be accurately forecast, consumption must also be predictable. The analysis collapses if the consumption function is not relatively stable or at least if the shifts in it are not predictable.

A word of warning. Students are frequently tempted to argue that a somehow represents the minimum standard of living for the economy. It does not! We have no idea how much consumption would be if income were, in fact, equal to zero. We have had no experience with such low levels of income. Thus, a should be thought of simply as the factor that establishes the height of the consumption function on the chart. Changes in the value of a can occur because of government restrictions on consumption, or because of changes in the Social Security System, or because of taxes and a number of other things; but this says nothing about what consumption would really be if income were zero.

The Saving Function

The saving function is derived from the definition of saving as the difference between national income and consumption. Since the 45 degree line labeled Z is equal to Y, we can subtract the C line from the Z line (Figure 7-4, page 151). At $Y = 0$: $S = Y - C = Y - (a + bY)$, but if $Y = 0$, $S = -a$. At $Y = Y_o$:

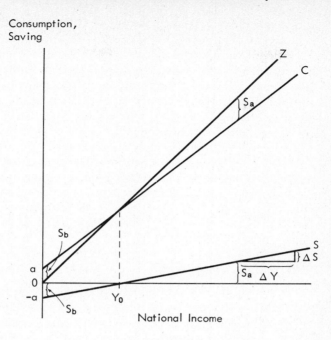

Figure 7-4

Consumption-Saving Relationship

$Y = C$ so $S = Y - C = 0$. At incomes to the left of Y_o, $C > Y$ so $S < 0$ by the vertical distance between C and Z. At incomes greater than Y_o, $Y > C$ so $S > 0$ by the amount of the vertical distance between Z and C. Thus, on the graph $S_a = S_a$, $S_b = S_b$, etc.

It has already been shown that the equation for S is $S = -a + (1 - b)Y$. Thus, the intercept is $-a$, and the slope of the S function is $1 - b$. Therefore, if b, the MPC, is 8/10, the slope of the saving function is $1 - 8/10 = 2/10$.

In this example, if income were to increase by 20, consumption would increase by 16 and saving would increase by 4. Analogously to the consumption function, the slope of the saving function $(1 - b)$ is the marginal propensity to save (MPS) and is defined as $\dfrac{\Delta S}{\Delta Y}$.

Another way to demonstrate this is to start with the definition of $S = Y - C$ and observe that it is also true that $\Delta S = \Delta Y - \Delta C$. Now, dividing through by ΔY gives $\dfrac{\Delta S}{\Delta Y} = \dfrac{\Delta Y}{\Delta Y} - \dfrac{\Delta C}{\Delta Y}$; so, $\dfrac{\Delta S}{\Delta Y} = 1 - \dfrac{\Delta C}{\Delta Y}$, which shows that the $MPS = 1 - MPC$.

The Investment Function

The investment function used in our present model is $I = I_0$, which appears graphically as a straight line parallel to the horizontal axis. Its intercept is I_o, a constant amount of investment. It has a slope of zero, which means that investment does not change as income changes. There are two reasons for adopting this functional form. (1) Logically, current income should be irrelevant in the decision to invest. A decision to purchase investment goods for future production should be based on expected future income, which may only be influenced by present income. A theory of investment behavior using this proposition will be developed in the next chapter. (2) A statistical problem of discovering the investment-income relationship exists. If a regression of the actual amounts of investment and income were computed, the resulting function would be the same as our saving function because measured saving and investment are identical amounts. The justification for claiming that the regression is in fact the saving function and not the investment function lies in the belief that intended saving is relatively less volatile than intended investment, that investment is the active agent for change, and that saving is relatively passive.

The Multiplier

The concept of the multiplier, the notion that a given increase in investment or government spending would result in a multiplied effect on national income, was one of the most startling conclusions drawn from the Keynesian revolution. It is hoped that the section that follows will dispel any notions that any magic is involved, and that what happens to bring about this result is actually quite ordinary behavior by quite ordinary people. The procedure here will be to demonstrate the multiplier algebraically, graphically, and in tabular form.

The Algebra of the Multiplier

We begin by defining multipliers in general as the change in a dependent variable per unit change in an independent variable. In aggregative economic analysis, the principal dependent variable is national income, so we shall derive income multipliers. In the simple model we are using in this chapter, income would change if I changed, if a changed, or if b changed. What is usually referred to as the "investment multiplier" is the amount by which income changes when investment changes, i.e., $\frac{\Delta Y}{\Delta I_0}$. Recall the model presented earlier:

$$Y = C + I,$$
$$C = a + bY,$$
$$I = I_o,$$

and the solution, or reduced form: $Y = \dfrac{a + I_0}{1 - b}$.

Now, if this same economy experiences an increase in the rate of investment of ΔI_0, the model appears as follows:

$$Y' = C' + I'.$$
$$C' = a + bY'.$$
$$I' = I_0 + \Delta I_0.$$

The solution to this system is $Y' = \dfrac{a + I_0 + \Delta I_0}{1 - b}$.

We want to know the change in income (ΔY) which resulted from the change in investment (ΔI_0).

$$\Delta Y = Y' - Y = \frac{a + I_0 + \Delta I_0}{1 - b} - \frac{a + I_0}{1 - b}.$$

Subtracting: $\Delta Y = \dfrac{\Delta I_0}{1 - b}$. If we now divide both sides of this statement by ΔI_0, we have discovered the multiplier: $\dfrac{\Delta Y}{\Delta I_0} = \dfrac{1}{1 - b}$. Remembering that $1 - b = MPS$, we can say that this multiplier is the reciprocal of the marginal propensity to save.

Using the same numerical values of the parameters as before: $a = \$20$ billion, $b = 8/10$, $I_0 = \$30$ billion, and adding $\Delta I_0 = \$10$ billion, we get the following results:

$$Y = \frac{a + I_0}{1 - b} = \frac{\$20 + \$30}{1 - 8/10} = \$250 \text{ billion.}$$

$$Y' = \frac{a + I_0 + \Delta I_0}{1 - b} = \frac{\$20 + \$30 + \$10}{1 - 8/10} = \$300 \text{ billion.}$$

$$\Delta Y = Y' - Y = \$50 \text{ billion.}$$

$$\frac{\Delta Y}{\Delta I_0} = \frac{50}{10} = 5 = \frac{1}{1 - b} = \frac{1}{1 - 8/10} = 5.$$

The change in income of $50 billion is composed of the $10 billion of added new investment and $40 billion of added consumption. Our consumption function, $C = a + bY$, tells us that the original amount of consumption was $20 + 8/10\ (\$250) = \$220$, and at the new equilibrium it is $20 + 8/10\ (\$300) = \$260$. Since the MPC is 8/10, we can determine immediately that a change in income of $50 billion would induce 8/10 of $50 billion of additional consumption or $40 billion. The change in saving (ΔS), we know, must be 2/10 of $50 billion or $10 billion, which is the amount necessary for saving to equal investment. The change in investment (ΔI_0) of $10 billion is thus equal to the change in saving (ΔS) of $10 billion.

The Graphics of the Multiplier

Now we will show the same events graphically. Figure 7-5 is the same as Figure 7-1, but with the addition of the new larger investment function.

The original position of equilibrium income is at $250 billion, with consumption of $220 billion, and saving and investment equal at $30 billion. Now the demand by business for investment increases by $10 billion per period. This means that aggregate demand is $260 billion, still $220 billion of consumer demand plus the $40 billion of investment demand, whereas the current production of goods and services totals just $250 billion. Y is no longer an equilibrium income. The increased demand for investment creates new income, the recipients of which will increase their demand for consumption. In turn, this new demand for consumption generates new income which again stimulates further

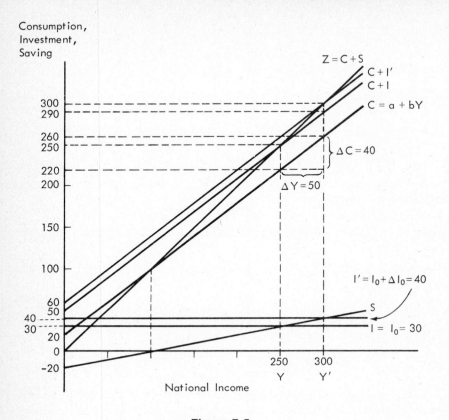

Figure 7-5

The Multiplier Graphics

consumption. This process continues as long as demand $(C + I')$ exceeds output $(C + S)$. It will stop when demand and output are equal at Y', which is where the Z line intersects with the $C + I'$ line and where $S = I'$.

That the multiplier is the reciprocal of the slope of the saving function can be seen directly from Figure 7-5. Remembering the definition of the multiplier as $\dfrac{\Delta Y}{\Delta I_0}$, ΔY is the distance between the new and the old levels of equilibrium income $(Y' - Y)$, and ΔI_0 is equal to ΔS; i.e. $(I' - I)$. The MPS is $\dfrac{\Delta S}{\Delta Y}$, which is the reciprocal of $\dfrac{\Delta Y}{\Delta S}$, but this is equal to $\dfrac{\Delta Y}{\Delta I_0}$.

If the S line is drawn very flat, that is, with a very low MPS and hence a very large MPC, the change in income would be very large. Conversely, a steep S function generates only a small change in Y. This is easily seen in Figure 7-6, where the same change in investment (ΔI_0) generates a very large change in income when the saving function is S''' and a very small change in income when the saving function is S''. In each case, the change in saving is

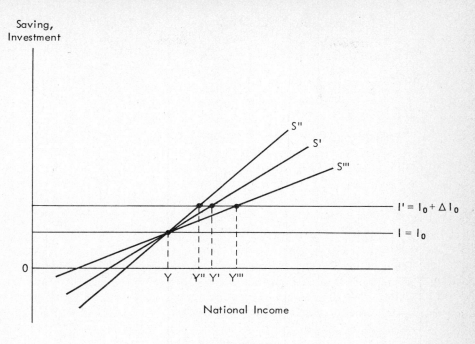

Figure 7-6
The Change in Income Depends on the Slope of the S Curve

the same ($\Delta S = \Delta I$), but the change in income needed to bring about that change in saving varies with the slope of S.

The Movement to a New Level of Income

All of the preceding can be shown by means of a simple table, but it is now necessary to introduce explicit statements about the timing of the events. For this we attach time subscripts to the variables in the following way:

$Y_t = C_t + I_t.$
$C_t = a + bY_{t-1}.$
$I_t = I_{0t}$ and $I'_t = I_{0t} + \Delta I_{0t}.$

Paul Samuelson has taught us the wisdom of checking up on our model in this way to be sure that the movement of the system is, in fact, toward the equilibrium position.[6] It would be a good exercise to test your understanding of this analysis by graphing a model in which the investment function has a steeper slope than the saving function. Now shift the investment function upward and find the new equilibrium. The next part of the exercise would be to construct a table similar to Table 7-1.

---

[6] This involves what Samuelson calls the correspondence principle. See Paul A. Samuelson, *Foundations of Economic Analysis* (Cambridge, Massachusetts: Harvard University Press, 1947).

Table 7-1

Income Adjustment to a Change in Investment

Period	Y	C	I	S	Actual Investment	Actual Saving
0	250	220	30	30	30	30
1	260	220	40	30	40	40
2	268	228	40	32	40	40
3	274.4	234.4	40	33.6	40	40
4	279.5	239.5	40	34.9	40	40
.	.	.	"	.	"	"
.	.	.	"	.	"	"
.	.	.	"	.	"	"
.	.	.	"	.	"	"
n	300	260	40	40	40	40

Source: Hypothetical Data (see pages 152–153).

The adjustment from the original equilibrium in Period 0 to the new equilibrium at Period n is a process of consumption increasing by continuously decreasing increments. Each increase in consumption is 8/10 (the MPC) of the preceding change in income. But each change in income (except the first one) is just the change in consumption, so each change in income is 8/10 of the change in income of the period before.[7]

Saving increases in every period also, but it increases by 2/10 of the preceding change in income. Intended saving is the same as actual saving only in the two rows representing equilibrium income. In the interim periods, intended saving is less than actual saving, and, of course, less than intended investment.

Notice that in this presentation it is the household sector—not the business sector—that makes all of the adjustments. Consumers are saving more than they intend to save because of our assumption that consumption spending lags behind the earning of income ($C_t = a + bY_{t-1}$). This can be justified by the observation that in this economy, income earned in a period is received at the end of the period, and hence is available for spending only in the next period.[8]

QUESTIONS

1. Explain the concept of the sectoral demand components of total demand for the output of the economy in the circular flow.
2. Explain why income will move toward the equilibrium level when total demand exceeds total supply and when total demand is less than total supply.

---

[7] Another way to see the multiplier process is to observe that the summation of the changes in income are made up of the following series: $10 + 8/10(10) + (8/10)^2(10) + (8/10)^3(10) + (8/10)^4(10) + \ldots + (8/10)^n 10 = \dfrac{10}{1 - 8/10} = 50$, which is the same as $10 \times \dfrac{1}{1 - 8/10}$, or the change in investment times the multiplier.

[8] This is the technique contributed by Professor D. H. Robertson.

3. Consider the following model:

$$C = a + bY \qquad a = \$30 \text{ billion}$$
$$I = I_0 \qquad b = 9/10$$
$$Y = C + I \qquad I_0 = \$25 \text{ billion}$$

(a) What are the equilibrium values of Y, C, S, and I?
(b) What is the numerical value of the investment multiplier?
(c) What would be the equilibrium values of Y, C, and S, if I_0 became $30 billion?
(d) What would be the equilibrium values of Y, C, S, and I if a became $35 billion? (Assume $I_0 = \$25$ billion.)

4. Draw question 3 on graph paper.
5. Complete the following table for question 3.

Period		Y	C	I	S	Actual Saving
Equilibrium	(0)			25		
	1			30		
	2			30		
	3			30		
	4			30		
	5			30		
	.	.	.	.	.	.
	.	.	.	.	.	.
	.	.	.	.	.	.
Equilibrium	(n)			30		

SUGGESTED READINGS

Hicks, J. R. "Mr. Keynes and the 'Classics': A Suggested Interpretation." *Econometrica*, Vol. 5 (April, 1937).

Keynes, John Maynard. *The General Theory of Employment, Interest, and Money.* New York: Harcourt, Brace & Co., Inc., 1936.

Lancaster, Kelvin. *Modern Economics: Macroeconomics.* Chicago: Rand McNally and Co., 1973. Chapter 22.

Modigliani, F. "Liquidity Preference and the Theory of Interest and Money." *Econometrica* (January, 1944).

Ritter, L. S. "The Role of Money in Keynesian Theory," in Deane Carson (ed.). *Banking and Monetary Studies,* sponsored by the U.S. Comptroller of the Currency. Homewood, Illinois: Richard D. Irwin, Inc., 1963.

Shapiro, Edward. *Macroeconomic Analysis,* 3d ed. New York: Harcourt Brace Jovanovich, Inc., 1974. Chapters 7 and 8.

CHAPTER 8

INVESTMENT AND
THE I-S FUNCTION

The basic framework of the modern approach to national income determination was presented in Chapter 7. The model demonstrated there was silent about the role of money, and investment demand was simply assumed to exist. In this chapter a theory of investment behavior is developed which then permits us to present the analysis of equilibrium in the market for commodities in a framework called the Hicks-Hansen *I-S* function. Within the same framework, the market for money and bonds is built up into an equilibrium relation called the *L-M* function in Chapter 9.

THE GOODS MARKET

A modern economy is made up of a large number of different markets, a market being any situation in which demand and supply relations can be distinguished. In macroeconomics we aggregate many markets to reduce the number to a manageable few in order to generalize about large classes of events. The markets generally utilized in macro models are the goods market, the money market, the bond market, and the labor market. All markets are interrelated as noted in the frequently used statement, "In economics, everything depends on everything else." More formally, Walras' Law states that if three of the markets mentioned above are in equilibrium, the fourth is also in equilibrium; or alternately, if one of the markets is not in equilibrium, then at least one of the others is also in disequilibrium. Some of these interrelationships should become clear as the analysis proceeds.

What is called the *goods market* is the market in which goods are exchanged for money, but money is merely the vehicle by which the exchange is effected. What is really involved is the exchange of goods and services for other goods and services. Productive goods and services are purchased by producing units and are converted into final goods and services, which, in turn, are sold to those whose incomes were derived from the sale of the productive services.

On the supply side of the goods market lies the production of the great variety of commodities available from the business sector. The demand side includes the demand for goods and services by households, governments, foreign nationals, and the business sector itself. Equilibrium in this market occurs when all of these buyers wish to buy all of the commodities the business units wish to produce and sell. As shown in Chapter 7, this happens when saving (or aggregate withdrawals from the income stream) is equal to investment (or aggregate injections into the income stream). All of this is incorporated in the *I-S* function that is developed in this chapter. Before the *I-S* curve is explained, however, a theory of investment must be considered.

The Marginal Efficiency of Capital and the Theory of Investment

It is now appropriate to ask the question: What will cause the investment function to shift upward or downward? Such a question can be answered only if one has a theory of investment behavior. The purpose of this section is to develop such a theory.

Decisions to invest are made by individual business units, not by business as a whole. Thus, the theory explaining investment expenditures must be based on the micro theory of the business firm. The firm's decision to invest in a physical asset will be affirmative if that asset is expected to yield a return greater than the return on alternative uses of funds. Presumably, business people would be able to rank the opportunities available to them at any moment according to their expected yields.

In this comparison it is necessary to evaluate assets of differing durabilities. How, for example, would one choose between an asset expected to return $100 per year for 5 years with an asset expected to yield $20 per year for 30 years if they both cost the same amount of money? This brings up the more basic question of how one values any asset, the returns of which are to be received in the future. The answer depends upon what future returns are worth at the time the decision is made — in general, today. What, for example, is the value at this moment of $100 that is to be received one year from now, or of $100 to be received 50 years from today? In a society in which borrowing and lending take place and in which positive interest rates exist, everyone adjusts to that rate. The value of $100 one year from today is $\frac{\$100}{1+r}$, where r is the interest rate, and the value of $100 fifty years from today is $\frac{\$100}{(1+r)^{50}}$. This says that if the interest rate remains at r, the present value of a sum of money in the future is the amount needed today to produce that sum in the future.

We can look upon any physical asset as the present embodiment of returns that will accrue in the future. Its worth in the present, then, is the discounted value of all of its expected future returns. The usual formula for the determination of present value is:

$$PV = \frac{a_1}{1+r} + \frac{a_2}{(1+r)^2} + \frac{a_3}{(1+r)^3} + \ldots + \frac{a_n + S}{(1+r)^n}$$

where

PV is the present value of any durable asset,

a is the expected annual returns in dollars,

r is the interest rate used to discount those returns, and

S is the expected value of the asset at some date in the future, usually what is thought of as the "lifetime" of the asset, that is, the salvage value.

A very significant portion of the fields of accountancy and managerial economics is involved in the calculation of the a's. For most physical assets, $a_1, a_2, \ldots, a_n$ are different; i.e., $a_1 \neq a_2 \neq a_3 \neq \ldots \neq a_n$. Each a is calculated as the expected net return from owning the asset over not owning the asset. This means that the additional revenue and the additional costs must all be estimated in all future periods. These, necessarily, will all be forecasts since they involve the future in an uncertain world. The most important cost to be included, from the point of view of our development of the theory, is the cost of uncertainty. This can be handled as a premium similar to an insurance premium, but it is the essence of business profit that certain risks cannot be insured against, so the firm must absorb them in its calculation of cost. This cost must include a subjective estimate on the part of the firm's major decision makers, but, in part, it can be scientifically computed.[1]

Sometimes there is a question about which rate of interest to use as the discounting factor. We hope we have avoided this problem by including all the risk and other costs in the numerators of the equation so that the interest rate should be the pure rate, the rate reflecting only time preference. In the real world, probably the closest we can get to this is the rate on short-term Treasury bills.

We have just seen how the value of any asset can be calculated. The firm will find it profitable to invest in any asset whose value to the firm is greater than its cost. It is now to be demonstrated that where the value is greater than the cost, the marginal efficiency of capital is greater than the rate of interest.

The *marginal efficiency of capital* (*MEC*) is to be defined with reference to the following equation:

$$C = \frac{a_1}{1+m} + \frac{a_2}{(1+m)^2} + \frac{a_3}{(1+m)^3} + \ldots + \frac{a_n + S}{(1+m)^n}$$

where m is the *MEC*, the a's and S are defined exactly as before, and C is the price to the firm of the asset being considered — what Keynes called the supply price of capital. It should be obvious that since the a's are the same for a given asset, if *PV* is greater than C, then m is greater than r. This leads to the assertion that firms will find it advantageous to purchase a unit of capital as long as the *MEC* is greater than the rate of interest.

The following paragraphs will develop the analysis of the investment decision by individual firms and then expand the theory and its application to the aggregate economy.

---

[1] There are a number of ways that risk can be handled in these calculations, but it would take us too far afield to develop any of them properly.

The Investment Decision

The firm has a demand for capital goods derived from its demand for the productive services of capital. The demand for capital services can be thought of as being completely analogous to the producer's demand for labor services. The price of a unit of labor service is a person's wage per hour or other time period. The price of a unit of capital service is the cost (or rent) per hour or other time period of a machine. Both human workers and machines are extremely heterogeneous categories, so it is a gross simplification to speak of a unit of labor or a unit of capital. We will, nevertheless, have to think of "standard" units of labor and capital and mentally make adjustments for differences in productivity of different specific units.

Labor and capital are complements in the productive process but are, in greater or lesser degree, substitutes for each other as well. From microeconomic theory we know that if the price of one service increases relative to the other, the firm will employ more of the lower priced one and less of the more costly service. In the following discussion we will assume the real wage of labor to remain constant.

Because of the law of diminishing returns, the marginal product of capital services declines as the quantity of such services increases. We would further expect that as a firm increases its use of capital, it would proceed by choosing the most productive forms of capital first and use less and less productive types as it expands. In Figure 8-1 we show the marginal physical product curve declining as the stock of capital (and therefore the services of capital) increases.

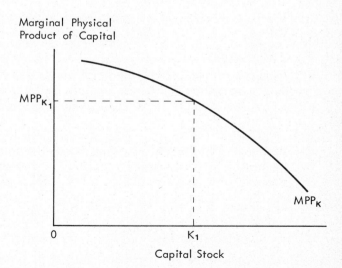

Figure 8-1
Productivity of Capital

This curve, the MPP_K curve, is at once the basis of the demand for capital services and the demand curve for the stock of capital. The assumption is made that all of the other factors of production and the state of the arts are given because any change in these would cause the curve to shift. If a firm owns (or rents) the number of machines denoted by K_1 (say 20 machines), it uses these machines for a total of 40,000 hours per year and the total output of the firm is 400,000 widgets. The purchase (or rental) of one more machine might increase the annual output to 406,000. In that case the marginal physical product of capital (MPP_{K1}) would be 6,000 widgets.

Suppose the price of a widget is $2.00. Then the value of the marginal product of capital is $12,000 per year. If the firm were able to rent a machine for a net cost less than $12,000 per year, it would pay the firm to do so; and, of course, if the cost were greater than $12,000 per year, it would not pay to use the 21st machine.

The rental cost (which would be the same whether the firm rented the machine from another firm or owned the machine and, in effect, rented it from itself) depends upon the price of the machine, the durability of the machine, and the interest rate. For example, if each machine lasts three years and is worthless at the end of that time, the rent (or annual cost) would be $12,000 per year if it costs about $32,678.97 with an interest rate of 5 percent to acquire the machine. This can be seen from the present value formula explained earlier.

$$PV = \frac{a_1}{1+r} + \frac{a_2}{(1+r)^2} + \frac{a_3}{(1+r)^3}$$

$$PV = \frac{\$12,000}{1.05} + \frac{\$12,000}{(1.05)^2} + \frac{\$12,000}{(1.05)^3}$$

$$\$32,678.97 = \$11,428.57 + \$10,884.35 + \$10,366.05$$

Thus, the $12,000 annual return would be sufficient to replace the machine (or repay the debt if the money were borrowed) at the end of the three years and still yield the required 5 percent interest return. Put another way, the value of the marginal product per machine per year is equal to the interest cost per year of $1,633.95 (.05 × $32,678.97) plus the depreciation cost per year ($10,367.08).[2]

Summarizing this example, VMP_K, the value of the marginal product of capital, is $12,000 per machine. Expressed as an annual rate per dollar's worth of capital, it is $\frac{\$12,000}{\$32,678.97}$ or 37 percent. Annual depreciation is $10,367.08 which, expressed as an annual rate per dollar's worth of capital, is $\frac{\$10,367.08}{\$32,678.97}$ or 32 percent. The annual interest cost is $\frac{\$1,633.95}{\$32,678.97}$ or 5 percent.

Since 5 percent plus 32 percent equals 37 percent, this is an equilibrium situation. The marginal cost of buying a unit of capital (the interest rate plus

---

[2] The depreciation figure is the amount that would have to be set aside each year and invested at 5 percent interest in order to have $32,678.97 to buy a new machine at the end of the three years.

the depreciation rate) is equal to the additional revenue from adding that unit of capital, which is the rate of the marginal product of capital.

Now if the rate of interest were to change, the optimal stock of capital would change. (In our example that would mean a change in the number of machines the firm would wish to own or rent.) An increase in the interest rate would decrease the number of machines desired if the price of machines and the rate of depreciation both remained the same, because the increased rate of interest plus the rate of depreciation cost would be greater than the marginal product of the machines. The firm would then allow some machines to wear out without replacing them in order to decrease the value of the stock of capital. On the other hand, if the interest rate were to fall while other things remained the same, the marginal returns per machine would be greater than the interest and depreciation costs so it would be profitable to add machines.

Notice that the rate of investment does not depend on the rate of interest (though it does depend on the change in the rate of interest), but that the stock of desired capital is determined by the level of the interest rate. This is due to the fact that whatever the interest rate, once the firm has the amount of capital it wishes to have, there is no need for investment or disinvestment. (Remember that investment is the act of adding to the stock of capital.) Investment takes place only after the interest rate has fallen and the firm is in the process of expanding its capital stock. Once it has reached the desired level, investment would again be zero. The firm would be in equilibrium and only the replacement expenditures (or depreciation) would take place.

What would happen if the price of capital goods increased? In that event the firm would want fewer machines and would substitute labor for capital. The marginal efficiency of capital (the marginal product of capital minus depreciation, both expressed as a ratio to the price of capital) would then be less than the rate of interest. Referring once again to the present value formula, this implies that the machines are worth less than they cost.

Anything that would increase the marginal productivity of capital would increase the demand for capital. This would happen if the quality of the capital itself were improved, if its durability were increased, if the quality or the quantity of other factors of production were enhanced, or if the technology of production were somehow improved.

Aggregate Investment

The discussion up to now has dealt with the decision process involving the demand for capital and the resulting act of investment by the individual firm. With that background we turn to the study of investment behavior in the aggregate economy.

It is usually assumed that a single business unit is not large enough to perceptibly change the price of the product it produces by changing its output, nor is it able to change the price of its inputs when it changes its purchases of them. This is what differentiates the micro from the macro approach, since if all firms change their output, the price of the products sold will change as will the prices of the resources used.

We can construct a demand relationship for capital as a function of the price of capital goods by aggregating or summing the individual firm's demand curves. Recall that these were derived from the marginal product of capital curves. Figure 8-2 shows the aggregate demand for capital curve where K is the total amount of capital desired at all possible prices of capital (P_K). The curve has a negative slope (1) because of the declining marginal product per unit of capital service as the capital stock is enlarged; (2) because the price of the goods produced by this capital would decline as the amounts produced are increased; and (3) because the firms could afford to utilize less productive kinds of equipment as the price of that equipment falls.

At a price of capital goods of P_{K_1}, the amount of capital all firms wish to have is K_1. If the price were just a little higher, say P_{K_2}, less capital would be desired. How would they adjust to this new situation? Presumably, they would reduce their capital holdings to K_2 by allowing some machines to depreciate without replacement, or they would be willing to sell the amount $-X_1$ (equal to $K_1 - K_2$). The demand for machines to add to the stock of capital is therefore negative; that is, the demand for investment is negative in the amount of $-X_1$.

At prices below the equilibrium price P_{K_1}, the demand for new capital (investment) would be positive. Thus, at price P_{K_3}, K_3 amount would be desired. In order to increase capital from K_1 to K_3, new machines would have to

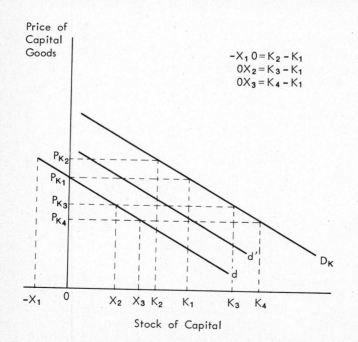

Figure 8-2

The Demand for Capital

be purchased from the producers of such machines. There would then be demand to buy new capital in the amount $0X_2(=K_3 - K_1)$. At a still lower price, say P_{K_4}, the demand for investment would be the difference between the desired stock of capital (K_4) and the actual stock of capital (K_1). This is shown as the amount $0X_3$ in Figure 8-2. In this fashion we can construct the demand for (net) investment as a function of the price of capital and label it d. The D_K curve can be thought of as the demand to *hold* capital and the d curve as the demand to *buy* capital.

Recognizing that machinery wears out over time, there will be a demand to buy new machines to replace the worn-out ones. With the stock of capital at K_1, the depreciating amount will be a constant. We have arbitrarily chosen $0X_2$ to represent that amount. Adding $0X_2$ to the d curve, we have the d' curve, which is then the demand curve facing the machine-producing industry.

To keep things in perspective, keep in mind that a very small change in the D_K curve, say a shift of 1 percent, would have a very large impact on the d curve, perhaps 50 percent.

If the interest rate were to fall, the present value of the machines would rise. In that event the firms would demand a large number of machines at any given price of machines. This is shown in Figure 8-3 where, at the original interest rate, the quantity of capital desired is K_1 when the price per unit of capital is P_{K_1}; and at the new lower interest rate the firms would wish to have K_2 amount of capital. Thus, the lower the rate of interest, the higher the demand curve for capital; and conversely, the higher the rate of interest, the lower the demand curve for capital.

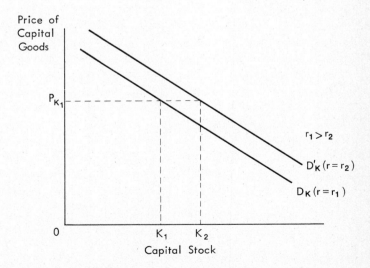

Figure 8-3

A Shift in the Demand for Capital
Due to a Decrease in the Interest Rate

Since the situations we are considering are supposed to be general throughout the economy, a decrease in the interest rate would leave the business community with a smaller stock of capital than desired, so we presume that the
firms will order more capital goods. We know that the machine-producing
firms, too, are subject to the law of diminishing returns so that the marginal cost
of producing machines increases as output increases. Micro theory also shows
that the sum of all the marginal cost curves of the individual firms becomes the
supply curve for the industry. Figure 8-4, shown below, graphs the supply
curve of the machine-producing industry.

Starting from a position of equilibrium where all firms have the number of
machines they wish to have, the machine-producing industry will be producing
just the number of machines needed to replace those that are wearing out. In
Figure 8-4 this is designated as $0R$. The equilibrium price is $0P_1$ when $0R$ is the
rate of output of machines.

When the machine-using firms want more machines because the interest
rate has fallen, the additional output of machines will force the price of machines to rise. For instance, if the demand for machines increases such that the
total output of machine producers is $0X_1$, the price per machine would have to
go up to $0P_2$. The number of new machines added to the existing stock per
time period would then be RX_1. Gross investment would be $0X_1$ and net investment would be RX_1.

The increased prices of capital goods reduce the yield per dollar spent on
them. In other words, the marginal efficiency of investment is lessened as
investment increases because the price of capital increases as the output of the
capital goods industry increases.

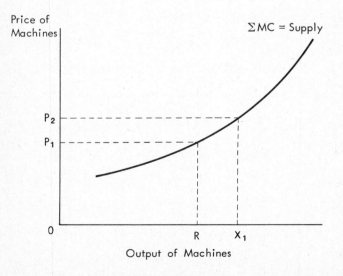

Figure 8-4

The Supply of Capital

Reverting to our numerical example, let us assume that the interest rate falls from the earlier rate of 5 percent to 3 percent. Immediately, the present value of the machines rises to PV_1 where

$$PV_1 = \frac{\$12,000}{1.03} + \frac{\$12,000}{1.03^2} + \frac{\$12,000}{1.03^3}$$

$$\$33,943.61 = \$11,650.49 + \$11,311.15 + \$10,981.97$$

If the price of the machines stays at the original level of $32,679, the firm will buy more machines. As the number of machines increases, however, the value of the marginal product will decline. The number of machines the firm will wish to add to its stock will be that number at which the VMP, when discounted to the present by the 3 percent interest rate, will equal the price of the machines. Thus,

$$C = \frac{VMP}{(1+r)} + \frac{VMP}{(1+r)^2} + \frac{VMP}{(1+r)^3}$$

$$\$32,679 = \frac{VMP}{1.03} + \frac{VMP}{1.03^2} + \frac{VMP}{1.03^3}$$

$$\$32,679 = \frac{\$11,550.62}{1.03} + \frac{11,550.62}{1.0609} + \frac{11,550.62}{1.0927}$$

But since all of the firms would be demanding more machines, the price of the machines will go up. As the price of the machines rises, the yield, or the marginal efficiency of capital, declines. Thus, if the machine price were to rise to $33,000, the firm would buy the number of machines at which the VMP, discounted at the 3 percent rate of interest, would equal $33,000.

$$\$33,000 = \frac{VMP}{1.03} + \frac{VMP}{1.03^2} + \frac{VMP}{1.03^3}$$

$$VMP = \$11,664.00$$

Investment is a dynamic process. In a static equilibrium, whatever the rate of interest or whatever the level of national income, firms would have adjusted the stock of capital to the desired level and no investment would take place. Investment occurs only when the interest rate, the level of income, or other determinants change or are expected to change. Thus, it is not true that investment will be larger the lower the interest rate, but it is true that investment will increase as the interest rate falls. Gross investment will be larger the lower the interest rate since a low interest rate implies a large stock of capital and, hence, a larger rate of capital consumption and replacement expenditure.

Investment and the Rate of Interest

Keynes could argue that the rate of investment spending was inversely related to the interest rate in the short run because he assumed that the increase in the stock of capital was negligible compared to the existing stock. Many other assumptions were implicitly made but we submerge them here in order to summarize the theory as developed by later writers following Keynes' general guidelines.[3]

The demand for capital as a function of the price of capital is shown in part (a) of Figure 8-5. A lower rate of interest will shift this function upward or to the right because the present value of capital increases when the interest rate falls so that for any current price of capital, a larger stock would be wanted. This indicates that firms using capital are willing to pay more than the current price for it.

According to Figure 8-5(b) the capital-producing firms are willing to produce a larger quantity at higher prices. If the marginal cost curve is relatively flat, the output will increase substantially; whereas if the curve is steep, the increased production will be less per time period.

Figure 8-5(c) then shows that investment increases as the interest rate decreases. Whatever the elasticity of this function, the total amount of investment would be the same—it would just take more time to accomplish this amount if the function is inelastic. Observe that the shape of this marginal efficiency of investment curve depends on the supply curve of capital producers rather than on the demand curve of capital-goods users.

This analysis of the interest-investment relationship leaves unanswered the most important question for business conditions analysts, since it doesn't explain the observed phenomena that while investment may fluctuate significantly, it is never near zero. This shortcoming can be traced to the essentially static nature of the theory. We have to believe that over time, the demand for capital schedule shifts to the right, sometimes more, sometimes less, independent of changes in interest rates. Given this situation, the marginal efficiency of investment (*MEI*) schedule would be such that investment would be positive at most interest rates.

The *MEI* schedule is one of the most volatile functions with which economists have to deal. Knowledge of the kinds of events which will cause the *MEI* schedule to shift upward or downward is indispensable to the business conditions analyst. The subject is far too large for an exhaustive discussion here, but we can mention certain classes of events which would affect the *MEI*. The most important category in this connection is innovation in the broad Schumpeterian sense. Innovations may increase the physical productivity of capital by lowering the cost of production, or affect the value of the output by increasing the demand for it. Outside events, such as changes in tax provisions, in other governmental policies, or in the business environment, also will have an effect in one direction or the other. The class of events that projects uncertainty into future forecasts of profits has often been emphasized, particularly by Keynes and his followers. Greater uncertainty leads to a higher risk premium being included in costs and so a downward shift. Pure optimism or pessimism, even if the cause for it cannot be found, will also shift the function.

---

[3] The explanation in this section closely follows the work of James G. Witte, "The Microfoundations of the Social Investment Function," *Journal of Political Economy* (October, 1963), reprinted in W. L. Johnson and D. R. Kamerschen, *Macroeconomics: Selected Readings* (Boston: Houghton Mifflin Co., 1970).

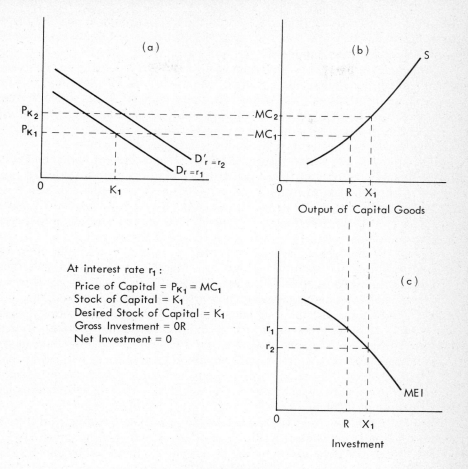

Figure 8-5
The Marginal Efficiency of Investment

GOVERNMENT AND THE NATIONAL INCOME

In this section government expenditures and taxation will be introduced into the theory of national income determination. Part 7 of the text deals with national policies to promote full employment, price stability, economic growth, and other goals; so at this juncture our concern is with the analytical framework rather than with the evaluation of such policies. Taxation, of course, is also a very important aspect of the government's impact on national income but its effect is by way of altering consumption behavior. For that reason the subject of taxation is covered in Chapter 10 where the consumption function is explored in some depth.

Purchases of goods and services by government are a portion of the total demand for the national output. They may be on capital account or on current account. They may be by state and local units or by the federal government.

From the point of view of their impact on the level of national income, these distinctions can be ignored; but in using the theory as a framework for forecasting, they are quite important.

State and local units of government do not have the spending flexibility of the federal government. Borrowing is often restricted by provision of their constitutions or charters and is otherwise more difficult to accomplish. The federal government has the power to create money, but the smaller units do not have this power. Thus, the state and local levels of government are necessarily more closely tied in their decisions to spend to their ability to tax.

The ability to tax is also restricted more for state and local units than it is for the federal government. The smaller the taxing jurisdiction, the easier it is for the public to avoid the taxes by moving to another jurisdiction. The type of taxation available to the smaller levels of government is also usually quite limited. As a rule they are forced to depend more on taxes based on property rather than income.

The many difficulties involved in acquiring funds by the smaller units of government force their spending patterns to be dictated by their receipts rather than by considerations of their counter-cyclic effect. It would probably be correct to make state and local spending a positive function of national income.

Spending by the federal government is such a large portion of aggregate demand that changes in its volume have an important impact on the national income. The national government must be concerned with the effect of its expenditures upon the economy, and we are concerned here with what that effect will be. Since it is a matter of policy, government expenditures are usually handled as an exogenous factor. The G-function is, therefore, autonomous, or not a function of income.

In Figure 8-6 government expenditures for goods and services have been added to business investment (I_B) to become the injections function $(I_B + G)$. A new, higher rate of spending by the government is indicated by adding ΔG to create a new total amount of injections. The multiplier is operative on the new spending demand in exactly the same way as it was for new investment demand. The government expenditures multiplier is defined as $\dfrac{\Delta Y}{\Delta G}$, and it would be derived exactly as the investment multiplier was in Chapter 7. Graphically, it can be seen that income would increase from Y_0 to Y_1 when government spending was increased by ΔG, so $\dfrac{\Delta Y}{\Delta G} = \dfrac{1}{\dfrac{\Delta S}{\Delta Y}} = \dfrac{1}{1 - \dfrac{\Delta C}{\Delta Y}}$. In other words, in the mechanics of income determination government spending can be handled in exactly the same manner as is investment. Since no new principles are involved in introducing government expenditures into the model, we shall delay its incorporation into an algebraic model until we have also brought in the taxation component.

The purpose of the I-S curve development is to bring together all of the elements of the demand for goods and services in the total economy and to relate them to their fundamental determinants, namely the rate of interest and

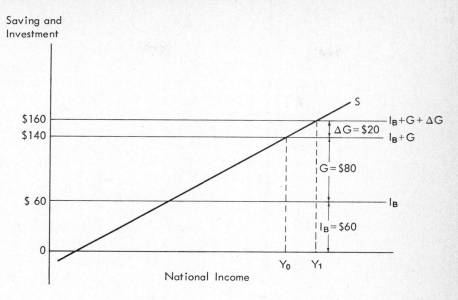

Figure 8-6
Government Expenditures Multiplier

national income. In this discussion of the *I-S* curve derivation, the interest rate is assumed to have been established. How to determine the interest rate will be discussed in the following chapter.

The supply of national income is the rate of production of commodities by the business sector, and in the Keynesian type of analysis this will be sufficient to meet the demands of buyers for these commodities. The demands are classified as demands by households for consumption expenditures, by the business community for investment, by the government for the expenditures it wishes to make, and as the net difference between the demand by foreigners for our goods and our demand for theirs, which we term net foreign investment.

In the following discussion, government expenditures and net foreign investment will be considered to be independent of interest rates and national income, or exogenous variables. This is shown in Figure 8-7 (d) where $\bar{G}_0 + \bar{F}_0$ are at their given levels no matter what the rate of interest happens to be. In the preceding section the argument was presented that the lower the rate of interest, the greater the spending on new plants, equipment, and inventories by business firms. For example, if the interest rate is r_1, government spending will be $\bar{G}_0$, net foreign investment will be $\bar{F}_0$, and investment will be I_1. The sum of the three demands are shown on the $G + F + I$ function.

A fall in the interest rate to r_2 has no effect on G nor on F but does increase investment to I_2, and the sum of the three demands would then be $\bar{G}_0 + \bar{F}_0 + I_2$, as shown.

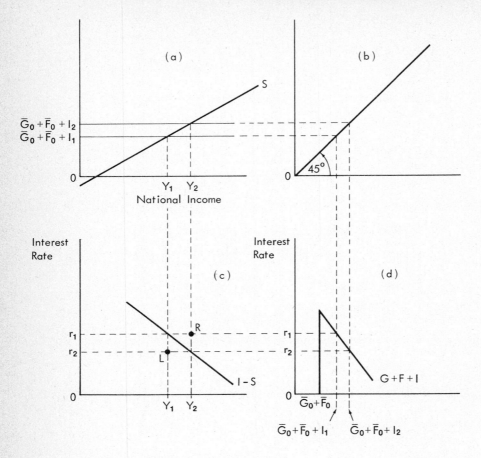

Figure 8-7

Derivation of the I-S Function

Our analysis in Chapter 7 showed that national income is in equilibrium when aggregate supply is equal to aggregate demand, that is, when $C + S_p + T = C + I + G + (X - M)$. Since the supply and demand for consumption are equal, this condition reduces to $S_p + T = I + G + (X - M)$. In the diagrams of Figure 8-7, $S = S_p + T$ and $X - M$ is labeled $\bar{F}_0$. Thus, national income is shown to be in equilibrium in Figure 8-7 where $S = \bar{G}_0 + \bar{F}_0 + I$. Part (b) of Figure 8-7 is simply a 45 degree line which allows us to "turn the corner" so that $\bar{G}_0 + \bar{F}_0 + I$, determined horizontally in (d), can be converted to a vertical measurement and then projected to (a). For an interest rate of r_1, the level of $\bar{G}_0 + \bar{F}_0 + I_1$ is found in (d). For $S = \bar{G}_0 + \bar{F}_0 + I_1$, national income will have to be Y_1 in (a). In part (c) we show the conjuncture of interest rate r_1 and national income Y_1 as an equilibrium situation. Now, if the interest rate falls to r_2, $G + F + I$ will be $\bar{G}_0 + \bar{F}_0 + I_2$ and income must rise to Y_2 in order for S to increase to equal $\bar{G}_0 + \bar{F}_0 + I_2$.

Two points on the I-S curve have been derived. The curve is a locus of such points at which the equilibrium condition holds that the aggregate supply of goods and services is equal to the aggregate demand for goods and services; or what amounts to the same condition, saving $(S_p + T)$ is equal to investment $(I + G + F)$.

What would happen if the economy had an interest rate of r_1 and income were at Y_2, that is, at point R, to the right of the I-S curve? Since r_1 is a high rate of interest, investment would be curtailed at a level of I_1. At income Y_2 saving is greater than $\bar{G}_0 + \bar{F}_0 + I_1$, so either actual saving is less than intended saving, or actual investment is greater than intended investment. In either case we know that income must fall. In this case it would fall to Y_1, which is a point on I-S. Conversely, of course, at a point to the left of the I-S curve such as L, intended injections would exceed intended saving and income would rise.

MULTIPLIER-ACCELERATOR INTERACTION

In this chapter we have looked at the foundations of investment behavior from a study of the decision processes of the firms demanding capital and those supplying capital goods. This theory makes investment depend on changes in the interest rate, given any level of national income. The acceleration principle makes investment depend on changes in the level of national income, given any interest rate. Both ideas would seem to be needed in a complete theory of investment.

In Chapter 6 the acceleration principle was seen to produce cyclical behavior in certain industries. The same sort of forces are operative on the macro level of analysis. The theory that is outlined here as the multiplier-accelerator interaction theory has become an important contemporary explanation of business cycles.

The multiplier process is capable of explaining why income and expenditures rise in a cumulative fashion once an expansive act occurs, or why economic activity declines cumulatively in response to some contractive action. The theory itself does not explain the turning points of business cycles. Other theories must be introduced for that purpose, such as Keynes' psychologically caused shifts in the marginal efficiency of capital.

The essential features of introducing the acceleration principle into the theory is that cycles are generated as a part of the response mechanism of the economy. The basic difference between a "multiplier-type" model and a model that incorporates the accelerator lies in the nature of the investment function.

A multiplier-type investment function either makes investment independent of income or associates larger investment with larger levels of national income. This implies that if income were constant at some high level, investment would also be constant at a high rate. In a business firm one would expect that if the level of production were constant, the firm would have no need for new equipment except to replace that which wears out or becomes obsolete, neither of which are a part of net investment. A firm would purchase additional capital only to meet expected increases in its rate of production.

An accelerator type investment function takes this reasoning into account, making investment depend on the change in national income and not on the level of income.[4] This implies that if national income is constant, no matter what the level, investment expenditures will be zero. The accelerator, then, is a dynamic theory where time plays an important role.

The easiest way to see why the accelerator generates cycles and why multiplier-type investment relations do not is through the use of an example. First, compare the investment functions themselves.

$I = \bar{I} + iY$ (multiplier type investment function)
$I' = \bar{I}' + A \Delta Y$ (accelerator type investment function)

In these two equations $\bar{I}$ and $\bar{I}'$ are autonomous investment parameters, the portion of investment which does not vary as income varies.

A study of Tables 8-1 and 8-2 should bring out the distinction being made between a multiplier-only model and a model that incorporates both the multiplier and the accelerator. Table 8-1 is the multiplier model constructed from the following equations and parameter values:

$Y_t = C_t + I_t$
$C_t = a + bY_{t-1}$
$I_t = I_t + iY_{t-1}$

$a = 30, b = 8/10, I_0 = 50, I_1 = 60, i = 1/10$

Table 8-1

Multiplier Model

Period	Y	C	I	I_i	I
0	800.00	670.00	50.00	80.00	130.00
1	810.00	670.00	60.00	80.00	140.00
2	819.00	678.00	60.00	81.00	141.00
3	827.10	685.20	60.00	81.90	141.90
4	834.39	691.68	60.00	82.71	142.71
5	840.59	697.51	60.00	83.44	143.44
6	846.86	702.76	60.00	84.10	144.10
7	852.18	707.49	60.00	84.69	144.69
8	856.97	711.75	60.00	85.22	145.22
9	861.28	715.58	60.00	85.70	145.70
10	865.46	719.33	60.00	86.13	146.13
·	·	·	·	·	·
·					
n	900.00	750.00	60.00	90.00	150.00

---

[4] Frequently writers relate investment to a change in consumption rather than in income, which sometimes leaves the impression that this is the distinctive feature of the accelerator. It is not! Making changes in consumption or income, the independent variable has no effect upon the cycle-generating capability of the model.

The first row is found by solving for equilibrium income in period 0, as follows:

$$Y_0 = \frac{a + \bar{I}}{1 - b - i} = \frac{30 + 50}{1 - 8/10 - 1/10} = 800$$
$$C_0 = a + bY_0 = 30 + 8/10\,(800) = 670$$
$$I_0 = \bar{I}_0 + iY_0 = 50 + 1/10\,(800) = 50 + 80 = 130$$

The latter rows are completed by first finding consumption as a function of income in the preceding period, then finding induced investment (I_i) also as a function of the preceding income, and adding $C + I$ to find Y.

In this table Y will always increase because once the rate of autonomous investment has increased, consumption and investment must both increase. Increases in consumption and investment are increases in income which, in turn, means that consumption and investment in the following period must increase. Each of the increases is smaller than the one which went before it, and all variables will approach new equilibria as shown in period n.

Table 8-2 shows the accelerator in action and was constructed from the following:

$$Y_t = C_t + I_t$$
$$C_t = a + bY_{t-1}$$
$$I_t = \bar{I}_t + A(Y_{t-1} - Y_{t-2})$$
$$a = 60,\ b = 8/10,\ \bar{I}_0 = 100,\ \bar{I}_1 = 110,\ A = 1$$

Table 8-2
Multiplier Model With Accelerator

Period	Y	C	$\bar{I}$	I_A	I
0	800	700	100	0	100
1	810	700	110	0	110
2	828	708	110	10	120
3	850.4	722.4	110	18	128
4	872.72	740.32	110	22.4	132.4
5	890.50	758.18	110	22.32	132.32
P 6	900.18	772.40	110	17.78	127.78
7	899.82	780.14	110	9.68	119.68
8	889.49	779.85	110	−.36	109.64
9	871.26	771.59	110	−10.33	99.67
10	848.78	757.01	110	−18.23	91.77
11	826.55	739.03	110	−22.48	87.52
12	809.02	721.25	110	−22.23	87.77
T 13	799.70	707.23	110	−17.53	92.47
14	800.45	699.77	110	−9.32	100.68
15	811.12	700.37	110	.75	110.75

Equilibrium income is found from $Y_0 = \dfrac{a + \bar{I}_0}{1 - b}$ at which income $C_t = a +$ $bY_{t-1} = 60 + 8/10\,(800) = 700$. Investment is 100, which is the autonomous portion ($\bar{I}$) only. Induced investment (I_A) is zero because income is at equilibrium and is therefore constant, so $Y_0 - Y_{0-1} = 0$.

Table 8-2 has been carried out to 15 periods to show that with these particular values of the *MPC* ($b = 8/10$) and "the relation" ($A = 1$), a cycle is indeed operating with a peak or upper turning point in period 6 and a trough or lower turning point at period 13. Other values of b and A would produce different behavior. This particular set creates a slightly explosive or divergent cycle; another set (different values of A and b) would lead to damped or convergent cycles; in other cases, the multiplier effect would swamp the accelerator so that income would move only in one direction.[5]

The acceleration principle is a good example for being wary of too mechanistic an approach to determining cause and effect. On the basis of the statistics alone, one might conclude that, since investment declined earliest (period 5), this was the "cause" of the ensuing depression. But why did I fall? Because the increase in income from period 4 to 5 was less than the increase from period 3 to 4. Why was this true? We already know that the reason for the cycle is the relative sizes of the response mechanism and the structure of the economy. In this case, at least, the search for direct cause and effect would be fruitless.

The accelerator relation (A) can be related to the productivity of capital by observing that $A = \dfrac{I_t - \bar{I}_t}{Y_{t-1} - Y_{t-2}}$, or if we ignore the exogenous portion:

$A = \dfrac{I_t}{Y_{t-1} - Y_{t-2}}$. Recalling that investment is the change in the stock of capital goods, and $Y_{t-1} - Y_{t-2}$ is the change in output, or income, A is almost the reciprocal of the national average of the marginal product of capital. The marginal product of capital is defined as the change in total output per unit change in the stock of capital, with all other factors held constant. The important difference between the two ideas is that in the accelerator concept, the change in income is the independent variable and the change in capital (I) is dependent, whereas in the marginal product concept income (or output) change is dependent upon the change in the stock of capital.

The marginal product of capital is a technological relation between capital input and the product output. In the theory of the firm, after some refinements, the marginal product schedule becomes the demand curve for the factor of production. In the case of capital, interest is the relevant price or wage. The accelerator, too, should be considered as an element of the demand for capital; here the quantity demanded varies as income varies. Higher or lower interest rates would be assumed to alter the size of the accelerator coefficient.

The speed with which business managers react to an increase in the demand for their product and the length of time required to construct new capital are also important elements in the determination of the size of A. The time lag involved in the model (such as that of Table 8-2) must be determined by the consumption lag; that is, the length of time for consumers to adjust their

---

[5] For more precision see the much quoted article by Paul A. Samuelson, "Interaction between the Multiplier Analysis and the Principle of Acceleration," *Review of Economic Statistics* (May, 1939).

spending to their new income. Suppose the consumption lag to be one month so that $Y_{t-1} - Y_{t-2}$ is the change in the rate of income within one month. If all businesses immediately ordered new equipment and producers of this equipment were able to produce it in less than a month, the accelerator would be very large. This is not very realistic for most industries. It would seem more likely that many investors would hesitate to evaluate the permanence of the increased demand immediately and would also require time to arrange financing. Furthermore, the cost of production of capital often dictates that a long period of time will be taken to produce it. The response will also depend in part upon the current degree of utilization of existing capital. If much excess capacity exists, firms need not increase their capital stock significantly when demand increases so A would be relatively small. On the other hand, if the capital goods producing industry is at, or near, full capacity, it may take a relatively long time to supply new equipment to the users of the equipment — again a low value of A would exist.

On technological grounds underdeveloped economies are likely to exhibit lower A values than are the well-developed, industrialized societies because the marginal product of capital relative to that of labor and land is quite high. This, in part, can be used to explain the observed phenomena that the business cycle is a greater problem in the well-developed systems than it is in the less industrialized systems.

This discussion would seem to indicate that the acceleration coefficient is complex. The lag is probably distributed over several periods. The numerical value of the relation fluctuates over a period of time, especially over the business cycle, and is different in different industries or geographical areas. Although we can find many qualifications to the simple theoretical system, it is nevertheless an important contribution to business cycle analysis.

QUESTIONS

1. Refer to the example on page 162. Figure the machine's worth if the interest rate were 4 percent. Figure its value if the interest rate were 6 percent.
2. Using the present value formulas, comment on the investment action of a firm (a) if the price of a machine it uses falls; (b) if the machine is improved to add a year to its productive life; (c) if the firm's product price increases.
3. Derive the government expenditure multiplier.
4. Choose a point to the left of the I-S function and explain why the point would have to move to the I-S curve.
5. Without a numerical example, explain why a multiplier type investment relation can produce only single-direction movements of national income while the accelerator relation generates cyclical responses to the same shock.
6. Would you expect the accelerator to operate differently when the capital stock is being used only partially and when it is being used near capacity?
7. Continue Table 8-1 through the 15th period. Will there be a turning point?
8. Continue Table 8-2 through the 21st period. Is there another turning point?
9. Derive graphically the shift in the I-S function caused by (a) a shift to the right of the MEC schedule, (b) an upward shift of the saving function.

SUGGESTED READINGS

Crouch, Robert L. *Macroeconomics.* New York: Harcourt, Brace Jovanovich, Inc., 1972.

Hirshleifer, J. *Investment, Interest, and Capital.* Englewood Cliffs, N.J.: Prentice-Hall, Inc., 1969.

Jorgenson, Dale W. "The Theory of Investment Behavior." *Determinants of Investment Behavior,* edited by Robert Ferber. Urbana, Ill.: Bureau of Economics and Business Research, 1966. Also in *Macroeconomic Theory: Selected Readings,* edited by H. R. Williams and J. D. Huffnagle. New York: Appleton-Century-Crofts, 1969.

Klein, L. R. *The Keynesian Revolution.* New York: The Macmillan Co., 1947.

Patinkin, D. "Price Flexibility and Full Employment." *The American Economic Review,* Vol. XXXVII (September, 1948).

Pigou, A. C. "Economic Progress in a Stable Environment." *Econometrica,* New Series, Vol. XIV (August, 1947).

Samuelson, Paul A. "The Simple Mathematics of Income Determination." *Income, Employment, and Public Policy: Essays in Honor of Alvin Hansen,* edited by Lloyd A. Metzler, *et al.* New York: W. W. Norton & Co., Inc., 1948.

————. "Interactions Between the Multiplier Analysis and the Principle of Acceleration." *Review of Economic Statistics* (May, 1939).

Witte, James G. "The Micro-foundations of the Social Investment Function." *Journal of Political Economy* (October, 1963).

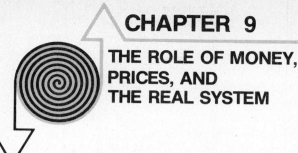

CHAPTER 9

THE ROLE OF MONEY, PRICES, AND THE REAL SYSTEM

This chapter begins with the construction of a basic theory of money supply behavior. We then develop the demand side by discussing the liquidity preference theory which was introduced by Keynes to supplement or supplant the quantity theory and to act as an alternative to classical and neoclassical interest rate theories. This allows us to construct a curve of interest rate and income levels in which the supply and demand for money are in equilibrium. Since the interest rate and income are also important in establishing equilibrium in the market for goods and services, the *I-S* curve of Chapter 8 is combined with the money market equilibrium curve to determine the interest rate and national income. The final portion of the chapter discusses the distinction between the nominal values of the elements of our system and the real values.

MONETARY AND CREDIT SYSTEM

The effect of the monetary system on the nature of business fluctuations is more significant than any other facet of our capitalistic system. Therefore, it is discussed at greater length than other institutional factors.

Monetary System

The *monetary system* of the United States is made up of the United States Treasury, the Federal Reserve System, and the system of commercial banks. All of these institutions have one feature in common that no other units of the economy have: they are capable of creating and destroying money. These institutions are peculiar in that they have money as a liability. The bulk of our money supply is in the form of demand deposits, which are liabilities of commercial banks. Our hand-to-hand money is made up of coins, a liability of the Treasury, and currency, a liability primarily of the Federal Reserve Banks, but also of the Treasury.

The stock of money at any time depends mainly on the actions of the members of the monetary system, on the constraints placed on them by the law and its administration, and on the actions of parties not included in the monetary system, such as households, business units, and the rest of the world. The significance of variation in the money supply is discussed later. Here, however, the purpose is to show how the variation comes about. In the analysis of business conditions, it is the total money supply that is important, not just the currency supply. If the money supply were, for instance, $300 billion, it would make very little difference whether it were $300 billion of currency or $300 billion of demand deposits. It is simply a matter of convenience for the nonmonetary system (the public) to have both kinds of money. The monetary system accommodates the public by dividing the total money supply into the desired proportions. In restricting our attention to the stock of money, defined in the narrow sense of demand deposits plus currency and coin, we are not denying the importance of near monies, such as savings and time deposits, government bonds, or savings and loan shares. These items are important, but in our approach their effect is considered separately from the effect of money itself.

A *commercial bank* is a firm that has the power to accept accounts which are subject to immediate withdrawal by check. Commercial banks are either members of the Federal Reserve System or they are nonmember banks. All national banks, banks that receive their charters from the Comptroller of the Currency of the United States Treasury, must be member banks. State banks, chartered by state governments, may become member banks if they meet certain standards on capital and agree to abide by FRS laws and regulations.

Member banks must keep a legally prescribed minimum amount of *legal reserves,* at present defined as deposits with the district Federal Reserve Bank or as currency and coin (vault cash). Nonmember banks are required by the state banking authorities to maintain legal reserves, which typically are defined as balances held with other commercial banks and vault cash. The definition of legal reserves and the reserve requirements have changed occasionally, causing variation in the money stock.

Currently reserve requirements for member banks depend on the volume of deposits in the individual bank. This system went into effect November 9, 1972. The requirements as currently specified (August, 1977) are as follows:

Net Demand Deposits (in millions of dollars)	Reserve Requirement
0–2	7%
2–10	$9\frac{1}{2}\%$
10–100	$11\frac{3}{4}\%$
100–400	$12\frac{3}{4}\%$
over 400	$16\frac{1}{4}\%$
Savings Deposits	3%
Other Time Deposits (in millions of dollars)	
0–5	From 1% to 3%, depending on maturity
over 5	From 1% to 6%, depending on maturity

Credit Expansion

Credit expansion refers to the process by which banks increase the money supply. One should distinguish between credit expansion and money supply expansion. Money supply expansion points to the liability side of the balance sheets of the members of the monetary system. Credit expansion points to the asset side of bank balance sheets and emphasizes the fact that bank credit normally increases as demand deposits grow. The purpose of this section is to review credit and money expansion as it takes place through the activities of commercial banks.[1]

If a customer deposits either currency or coin in a bank, the full amount is immediately included as legal reserves since vault cash is counted as legal reserves. If a deposited check is drawn on the receiving bank itself, neither its total deposits nor its legal reserves are affected. If a check drawn against another bank is deposited, the check will be sent for collection and the collection will take the form of an increase in the bank's deposit account with the Federal Reserve Bank of its district. It may take a day or two for the collection to take place; but when it does, the full amount is added to the bank's legal reserves.

The bank receiving the deposit now has 100 percent of its new deposit backed by legal reserves. If its reserve requirement were 15 percent, it could allow its legal reserves to fall by 85 percent of the new deposit and continue to operate within the legal minimum. It could expect that if it made a loan or purchased securities in the amount of the 85 percent, the borrower, or the seller of the security, would write checks on the created balance and thus withdraw the deposit and legal reserves from this bank. The bank then would have the original deposit as its liability, the 15 percent remaining in legal reserves as assets, and the 85 percent as earning assets (loans or investments). But the bank on whom the original deposited check was written would have lost reserves and deposits in the amount of the check. Its required reserves would have gone down by 15 percent of the amount of the withdrawal, so it will now have to take steps to acquire 85 percent of the check amount in reserves. It will allow loans to expire or will sell other earning assets in this amount so that the expansionary action by the one bank is exactly offset by the contractionary action of the other bank.

The key to most of the analysis of credit and money expansion or contraction comes exactly at this point. Is there or is there not an offsetting action elsewhere in the system? If, for example, currency that had been in circulation for some time was returned to the banking system, there would be an increase in reserves of the bank receiving the deposit without a corresponding loss by another bank. Similarly, if the Federal Reserve bought securities, or if the Treasury paid off some of its debts or spent some money out of its account at the Federal Reserve, some banks would receive new reserves while no other commercial bank would lose reserves.

---

[1] Although we tend to speak of expansion, the reader should realize that the contractionary process is equally important in business cycle analysis. The steps involved in the contraction are just the reverse of those cited for the expansion.

Now let us assume that the Federal Reserve buys $100 million worth of Treasury bills on the open market. The sellers will receive checks drawn against the Federal Reserve Banks and will deposit them in commercial banks, which will have new reserves as soon as the checks are sent to the Federal Reserve Banks. Since no commercial bank loses reserves in this transaction, there is a net increase of reserves in the banking system and of deposits of $100 million for the sellers of the bills. Now the affected banks have excess reserves of $85 million (assuming a 15 percent reserve requirement). Each bank could lend or purchase other earning assets by the amount of its excess reserves unless it wished to hold additional excess reserves. If, for example, banks on the average had a demand for excess reserves equal to 5 percent of their demand deposits, they would expand earning assets by $80 million rather than the $85 million that could legally be added. Borrowers would spend the proceeds by writing checks, and those who received these checks would deposit them in their own commercial banks. In this process we might expect a currency drain to take place, since, as the money supply is expanding, it is likely that the public will demand more of both kinds of money; that is, currency and coin as well as demand deposits.

To the extent that currency and coin are drawn into circulation, the banks are losing reserves. If we assume that the currency drain is 10 percent of deposit expansion, the public will withdraw $10 million since demand deposits have increased by $100 million. This means that of the $80 million of earning asset expansion by banks, $70 million will be deposited to become new reserves for depositors' banks. These banks, in turn, will have $56 million available for loans and investments (deposits and reserves increased by $70 million; required reserves went up by $70 million × .15 = $10.5 million; desired excess reserves increased by $70 million × .05 = $3.5 million). This process of banks making loans and losing reserves and deposits to other banks and to currency in circulation will continue until all of the original $100 million is absorbed into required reserves, desired excess reserves, and currency in circulation. The interesting question in monetary theory is how much the money supply will increase.

To answer this question, it is necessary to discover the size of the monetary expansion multiplier. This multiplier is the number by which the monetary base must be multiplied to equal the size of the money stock; that is, $M = KB$ where M = the amount of money in the economy, K = the multiplier, and B = the monetary base.

The Simple Multiplier

If we were to introduce all, or even most, of the complications in the real world, the model would become extremely complex. In view of this, we will present first the simplest possible multiplier and then develop one that is adequate for the analysis we shall need in this book.

1. $M = KB$
2. $B = R$ where R is the amount of legal reserves held by the Commercial Banking System (CBS).

3. $R = rD$ where r is the reserve requirement and D is the amount of demand deposits in the banking system.

4. $M = D$ which states that in this model the only kind of money is demand deposits.

$$K = \frac{M}{B} \text{ from (1)}$$

$$K = \frac{D}{R} \text{ from (2) and (4)}$$

$$K = \frac{D}{rD} \text{ from (3)}$$

$$K = 1/r$$

Thus, the simple multiplier is the reciprocal of the reserve requirement. If the reserve requirement is .20 (or 20 percent), the value of K, the multiplier, is 5. This means that if legal reserves are \$20 billion, the money supply will be $5 \times \$20$ billion or \$100 billion; and if R is increased by \$100 million, the money stock will increase by \$500 million.

A More Complete Multiplier

To use the simple model as a forecasting tool would obviously be absurd; other things would have to remain constant, and we can be quite certain that some very important things would not remain constant. For example, if the reserve base were increased and the amount of demand deposits were increasing, the public would be expected to increase their demands for currency and for time deposits, and the banks might want more excess reserves. Our next problem is to incorporate these factors into a model and to add that there are still a number of important variables which have not been included.

1. $M = KB$

2. $B = R + C_b + C_c$ where R is deposits of member banks in Federal Reserve Banks, C_b is vault cash, C_c is currency in circulation.

3. $R + C_b = rD + eD + r'T$ where e is the desired excess reserve ratio, r' is the reserve requirement on time deposits, T is time deposits.

4. $C_c = aD$ where a is $\frac{C_c}{D}$, the ratio of currency to demand deposits that the public wishes to hold.

5. $T = tD$ where t is $\frac{T}{D}$, or the ratio of time deposits to demand deposits the public wishes to hold.

6. $M = D + C_c$ The money supply is made up of demand deposits and currency in circulation.

Solving for K:

$$K = \frac{M}{B} = \frac{D + C_c}{R + C_b + C_c} \quad \text{from (6) and (2)}$$

$$K = \frac{D + aD}{rD + eD + r'T + aD} \quad \text{from (4) and (3)}$$

$$K = \frac{D(1 + a)}{D(r + e + r't + a)} \quad \text{from (5)}$$

$$K = \frac{1 + a}{r + e + r't + a}$$

$$M = \frac{1 + a}{r + e + r't + a} \quad (B)$$

To demonstrate the value of this type of model, let us assign some values to the parameters and observe the resulting consolidated balance sheet of the commercial banking system:

$a = .20$ $r' = .05$

$r = .15$ $t = .60$

$e = .02$ $B = 100$ (in billions of dollars)

Now we can insert these values into the equation for K:

$$K = \frac{1 + a}{r + e + r't + a} = \frac{1 + .20}{.15 + .02 + .05(.60) + .20} = \frac{1.2}{.40} = 3$$

Thus, the money supply multiplier, K, is 3, and since $M = KB$, $M = 3 \times$ \$100 billion = \$300 billion. Now that the money supply is known, its division into currency in circulation and demand deposits can be determined. Since $M = D + C_c$ and $C_c = aD$, $M = D + aD$ or $M = D(1 + a)$ or $D = \frac{M}{1 + a} = \frac{\$300}{1 + .20} =$ \$250 billion. Currency in circulation is the difference between the money supply and demand deposits; that is, $C_c = M - D$, or $C_c = \$300$ billion $-$ \$250 billion = \$50 billion. To check that result, compare it with (4), which is $C_c = aD$. Thus, $C_c = .20 \times \$250$ billion = \$50 billion.

Commercial Banking System (Billions)

$R + C_b$	= \$ 50	D	= \$250
Earning Assets	= 350	T	= 150
Total Assets	= \$400	Total Liabilities	= \$400

Legal reserves of deposits with the Federal Reserve plus vault cash were found by multiplying the reserve requirement r of .15 times D of \$250 billion, and the desired excess reserve ratio e of .02 times D, and r', the time deposit reserve requirement (.05) times T. T was found from equation 5: $T = tD = .60$ (\$250 billion) = \$150 billion. Earning assets are the difference between total liabilities and nonearning assets (cash); i.e., \$350 billion = \$400 billion $-$ \$50 billion.

If \$1 billion is added to the base (B) through open-market purchases by the Federal Reserve, the changes in the consolidated balance sheet of the commercial banking system would be as follows:

Commercial Banking System (Billions)

$R + C_b$	$= +\$\ .5$	D	$= +\$2.5$
Earning Assets	$= +\ 3.5$	T	$= +\ 1.5$
Change in Total Assets	$= +\$4.0$	Change in Total Liabilities	$= +\$4.0$

The new balance sheet of the banking system now looks like this:

Commercial Banking System (Billions)

$R + C_b$	$= \$\ 50.5$	D	$= \$252.5$
Earning Assets	$= \ 353.5$	T	$= \ 151.5$
Total Assets	$= \$404.0$	Total Liabilities	$= \$404.0$

The money supply increased by the multiplier ($K = 3$) times the change in the reserve base ($B = +\$1$ billion) or \$3 billion, \$.5 billion of currency in circulation and \$2.5 billion of new demand deposits. While the money supply increased by \$3 billion, credit expansion was \$3.5 billion (change in earning assets), and liquid assets of the public ($D + T$) increased by \$4 billion, which is partly offset by the fact that the public's liabilities to the banks increased and/or their holdings of other assets (such as government securities) were reduced.

Money and Business Fluctuations

In this section we shall try to demonstrate the way the model that has just been presented can be of help in the analysis of the role of money in business fluctuations and in evaluating monetary policy. Later chapters develop these topics in more detail.

A brief account of the events leading up to the crisis of 1929 and the severe depression which followed in the 1930s was discussed in Chapter 2. Here we can look at the impact on the money supply of some of the attitudes and reactions to the situation existing at the time. A quite dramatic example can be seen in the behavior of a, the currency/demand deposit ratio, which was approximately .16 in June of both 1928 and 1929 and rose to about .33 in the same month of 1933. If we insert these figures into our model, holding all other values constant, the money supply would decline by some 22 percent! Of course, other factors also changed. The ratio of time deposits to demand deposits (t) decreased from 1.28 in June, 1928, to 1.00 in June, 1933, which by itself would have increased the money supply by about 3 percent. The excess reserve ratio (e) increased over this same period from .002 to .026, sufficient to cause a 6 percent decrease in the money supply. It was after 1933 that the great increase in bank demand for excess reserves took place to put greater contractionary pressure on the stock of money. The excess reserve ratio of member banks rose to .136 in 1936 and continued to .214 in June of 1940.

Monetary policy, too, can be evaluated by means of our model. It probably is reflected in all of the variables, but the most direct relationship is in the reserve requirement parameters and in the monetary base.

Reserve Requirements

The Federal Reserve Board of Governors has the authority to vary the reserve requirements of member banks; so r (which should be a properly weighted average of the requirements of the member banks) and r' are directly under the control of the Federal Reserve System. The size of the multiplier, the money stock, and bank credit rise when r or r' is decreased and fall when r or r' is increased.

Member bank reserve requirements were unchanged from 1917 until 1936 when they were increased by approximately 50 percent. They were raised again in 1937; and on May 1, 1937, they were increased to their legal maximum and were kept at that level for some years and at relatively high levels to the present. Since this was a period of depressed economic conditions and large-scale unemployment, one might wonder why reserve requirements were kept so high. After all, we have seen that an increase in r is contractionary to the money and credit supply! Some very eminent economists have also questioned this action. Defenders of Federal Reserve policy argue that it was desirable to lower the value of the multiplier because of the growth in the monetary base that was taking place during these years. There was a great fear in the System of what would happen if e were suddenly to decrease; that is, if banks were to decide to expand their earning assets significantly, the money supply could explode. Detractors of Federal Reserve policy respond that if the money supply were to expand at too rapid a rate, open-market operations could be used to dampen the rate of growth.

Open-Market Operations

The impact of open-market operations is directly on B, the monetary base. No matter what is happening within the multiplier, the effect can be offset by changes in B. Thus, if one of the components of the multiplier is changing in such a way as to cause an increase in the money supply and the Open-Market Committee finds this undesirable, the open-market agent can be told to sell enough securities to counteract the expansion. On the other hand, if additional expansion is deemed warranted, the orders will be to purchase securities.

There is no possibility of open-market operations failing to affect B. If the Open-Market Committee buys or sells, someone must sell to them or buy from them. Since all of the firms who deal directly with the Open-Market Committee are large dealers in government securities, the checks received in payment or the checks they pay for the securities immediately result in an increase or a decrease in some member banks' reserves held at the Federal Reserve Banks. These new reserves, of course, spread pervasively throughout the system of banks.

Discount Rate

Another policy tool of the Federal Reserve that affects the money base is the *discount rate,* which is the rate of interest at which member banks may borrow from the Federal Reserve Bank of the district. When a bank borrows from the Federal Reserve Bank, it takes payment in the form of deposits at the Reserve Bank. Since no other commercial bank has lost reserves by this act, total reserves and B have increased by the amount of the loan. The borrowing is at the initiative of the individual commercial bank, but at the discretion of the Federal Reserve Bank, and is, therefore, not under the precise control of the monetary authority. The Federal Reserve can encourage borrowing by lowering the discount rate and can discourage borrowing by raising the rate.

Many writers and practitioners of central banking have concentrated their attention on what is called the "announcement effect" of discount rate changes, arguing that an increased rate is taken as a signal that the Board of Governors views the current situation as one where contractionary action is in order, and that banks ought to be more cautious in their lending policies. In terms of our model, the expectation (or hope) is that e, the excess reserve ratio, will rise somewhat, causing a slight decrease in the size of the multiplier as well as decreasing B by decreasing member bank indebtedness to the Federal Reserve.

Other Factors Affecting the Base of the Monetary System

Federal Reserve policy is not the only determinant of B. There are other important sources of variation, but it should be kept in mind that if these other sources cause undesired changes, the Federal Reserve's policy can neutralize them, although it has not always done so.

One continuously perplexing feature of the United States monetary system is that both the Federal Reserve System and the United States Treasury have powerful ability to affect the money base. Although this is consistent with the political philosophy of checks and balances, it makes for divided responsibility, inconsistent policy actions, and sometimes a stalemate. Both the Treasury and the Federal Reserve System are capable of completely offsetting the effects of the policy actions of each other.

The Treasury causes member bank reserves to vary inversely as its own deposit balances at the Federal Reserve Banks vary. A decrease in the Treasury's balance means that it has paid out money for the purchase of goods and services, transfer payments, or the retirement of its debt; the recipients have cashed the checks; and member banks have received new reserves. Reserves decrease when the Treasury's balance at the Federal Reserve increases because the reserve balance falls when the Treasury directly transfers funds from its deposits at commercial banks and when tax collections or the proceeds of government security sales are placed in its balance at the Federal Reserve Banks. The Treasury also adds to the base by its issuance of currency and coin.

Another important source of variation in the monetary base arises out of the flow of monetary gold. Purchase of gold bullion by the Treasury results in the receipt by the seller of the gold of a check drawn against the Treasury's balance at the Federal Reserve. The Treasury's balance may then be replenished by the issuance of gold certificates. In this way the reserves of commercial banks are increased without a decrease in the Treasury's Federal Reserve Bank balance.

A new item in determining the monetary base is the "Special Drawing Rights certificate account." These certificates are broadly comparable to Gold Certificates. The Treasury is authorized to issue the SDR certificates to the Federal Reserve which then allows the Treasury to use the funds to pay for the SDRs or to engage in exchange stabilization operations.[2] Thus, "paper gold" is monetized in basically the same manner as physical gold.

A table is published each month in the *Federal Reserve Bulletin* entitled "Factors Affecting Member Bank Reserves." By means of this table one can see the various factors that have caused changes in the monetary base.

Table 9-1 is a restructuring of the table in the *Federal Reserve Bulletin* to conform with the monetary base scheme being used here. This table shows very clearly that government securities held by the Federal Reserve Banks explain the bulk of the monetary base at the present time. They come into being primarily through net purchases over time in the open market. The gold stock is the next largest item, but is now less than half of what it was in the 1940s and 1950s. Treasury currency has grown quite steadily, but slowly, and so presents no serious problem. Some of the other items are important mainly in their short-run volatility such as Loans (reflecting the discount policy of the Federal Reserve and money market conditions), Float (reflecting variations in clearing and collection time, the volume of activity, and the availability schedule), and Treasury deposits at the Federal Reserve (reflecting the mechanics of Treasury cash flows). In understanding the reasons for changes in the money supply, the starting point is an analysis of the behavior of the components of the monetary base.

THE MONEY MARKET

The determination of equilibrium national income in the goods market depends upon particular interest rates being given. For the model to be complete, the interest rate must be determined; that is, the reason that the interest rate is what it is and the kind of forces that will cause it to change must be explained. It is to the money market that we look for the theory of interest.

The Theory of Interest

The interest theory to be discussed now is called the *liquidity preference theory*. It was the theory Keynes advanced, although what is to be presented here draws from the work of later contributors as well. According to this theory, interest is determined by the supply of and the demand for money. (Remember that money is defined to include demand deposits and currency.)

---

[2] For a more complete explanation of Special Drawing Rights, see "SDR's in Federal Reserve Operations and Statistics," *Federal Reserve Bulletin* (May, 1970), p. 421.

Table 9-1

Components of the Monetary Base, May, 1977
(In Millions of Dollars)

Reserve Bank Credit Outstanding		112,765
U.S. Government and Federal Agency Securities	106,282	
Loans and Acceptances	689	
Float	2,844	
Other Federal Reserve Assets	2,950	
+ Gold Stock		+11,632
+ Special Drawing Rights Certificate Account		+ 1,200
+ Treasury Currency Outstanding		+11,058
− Treasury Cash Holdings		− 443
− Deposits, Other than Member Bank Reserves, with Federal Reserve Banks		−11,878
Treasury Deposits	−10,997	
Foreign Deposits	− 332	
Other Deposits	− 559	
− Other Federal Reserve Liabilities and Capital		− 3,324
= Monetary Base		121,010
Currency in Circulation (less member bank holdings)		86,353
+ Member Bank Reserves		34,657
Deposits with Federal Reserve Banks	26,041	
Currency and Coin (Vault Cash)	8,616	
= Monetary Base		121,010

Source: Adapted from the *Federal Reserve Bulletin* (June, 1977), pp. A4 and A5.

Every dollar of the money stock must be held by someone, so there is no question of how much money people and business hold. The question asked by demand-for-money theory is how much do they wish to hold.

The demand for money is divided into two basic categories. The first we shall refer to as working balance demand or active balances, and the second category will be referred to variously as pure liquidity preference, as speculative demand for money, as asset demand for money, or as inactive balances.

Demand for Money for Working Balances

The demand for money for working balance purposes is a function of the money value of national income, $M_w^D = f(Y)$. According to classical economists, the only reason for holding money is for transactions purposes. Every economic unit needs some cash to bridge the time span between receipts of money, during which time outflows of funds take place. Everyone is familiar to some extent with this reason for holding cash. To operate effectively as a going concern or a household, one simply needs some money. How much one needs depends upon the nature of receipts and expenditures, but it is probably a correct generalization to say that the larger the level of economic activity, the more money a household or business unit would need. This would seem to be true whether the increased activity is in increased physical output or in higher prices of the same output.

Figure 9-1 demonstrates the positive relation between the amount of money demanded for working balances and the level of national income. In it, income is the independent variable and the demand for money is the dependent variable; that is, when income is Y_1, money demanded for working balances will be M_1. In the theory it is assumed that the amount of money people wish to hold for this purpose is the amount they actually do hold.

Pure Liquidity Preference

The term liquidity preference is meant to indicate that money held for the speculative motive is held in preference to other assets. This is also why some economists refer to these balances as asset balances. In some respects money is superior to other assets, and in some respects other assets are superior to money. The price of money is constant in terms of the unit of account and is, therefore, perfectly liquid. Its value, however, is variable in terms of things it will command.

Debt instruments, which shall be referred to generally as bonds, are similar to money in that the legal obligation is stated in terms of the unit of account, so bonds and money share the quality of variable value in terms of the goods and services they will buy. This means that if inflation is expected, both money and bonds would be expected to lose value; and if deflation is expected, bonds and money would both gain in real value. On this consideration alone, bonds would be preferred to money in that an interest income is attached to the bonds.

There is a risk involved in holding bonds rather than money. The risk is that interest rates will rise because a rise in interest rates is equivalent to a

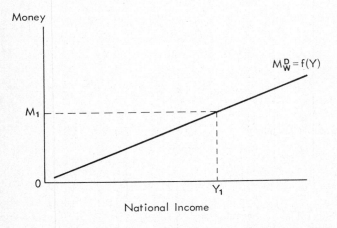

Figure 9-1
Relationship Between Income and Demand for Money

decrease in the price of outstanding bonds. One would hold money if the expected loss in the capital value of the bond is greater than the interest income
the bond yields over the relevant period of time. If the current interest rate is
very high, two factors should be noted: (1) the interest income to offset any
losses in bond prices is high, and (2) any given interest rate change (increase)
will have a relatively small effect on the price of bonds. This leads to the conclusion that when interest rates are high, the demand for money in the expectation of rising interest rates will be smaller than when the interest rate is low.

A low current rate of interest induces more holding of money because the
cost of holding it (the foregone interest income) is low. A given change in the
interest rate has a relatively large capital value effect, and the earnings to offset
such capital losses are small. Keynes and others have argued further that when
interest rates are high, expectations are likely to be that they will fall so less
money would be demanded; whereas when interest rates are low, they would
be expected to rise and thus induce more demand for money for the speculative
motive.

All of this leads to the conclusion that the demand for money as an asset
is a negative function of the current rate of interest. Its general shape seems
to be that shown in Figure 9-2. An interest rate of r_1 would induce M_1 amount
of money to be held for pure liquidity preference purposes.

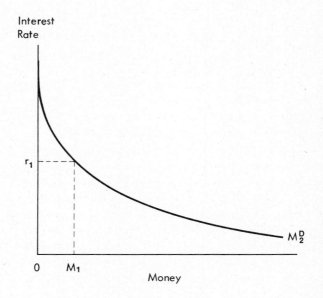

Figure 9-2

**Relationship between Interest Rates
and the Demand for Money — The
Liquidity Preference Function**

The L-M Function

Now we can combine the two types of demand for money and the supply of money to form a new function, the *L-M* curve. In the derivation of the *L-M* function, it is convenient to start at the lower right-hand part of Figure 9-3. Choose any income, such as Y_0, which indicates that the amount of money people wish to hold and, in fact, do hold for working balance purposes is M_1. The total money supply is shown on the lower left-hand part of Figure 9-3. There, a 45-degree line is drawn from the total money supply measured on the horizontal axis to the same amount measured on the vertical axis. Observe that $0M_1$ is equal to $0\bar{M}^S - 0X_2$ (by right triangles) so that $0X_2$ is the amount of the money supply not being used for working balances. This is the amount that

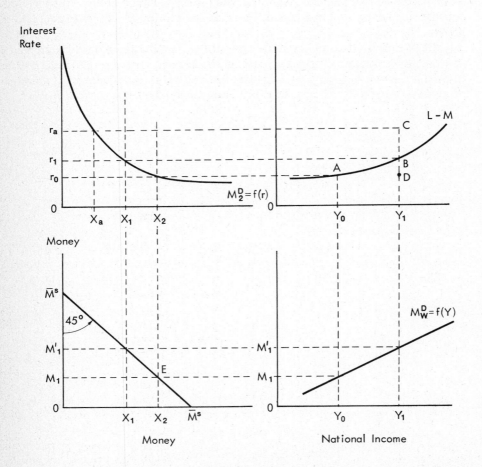

Figure 9-3

Derivation of the *L-M* Function

is available for holding for other purposes, namely, as speculative balances.[3] The interesting thing is that this money, because it exists, must be held whether people want to hold it or not. What makes them willing to hold it is a particular rate of interest. The upper left-hand part of Figure 9-3 shows that the public is willing to hold exactly $0X_2$ only if the rate of interest is r_0.

Point A on the upper right-hand part is a point of equilibrium at interest rate r_0, given an income of Y_0. Likewise, point B is a point showing that income Y_1 is compatible with interest rate r_1, and so on for all other points on L-M. Any point on L-M represents a possible condition of equilibrium in the money market where the supply of money and the demand for it are equal. As with the I-S function, any shift of the functions making up the L-M function will cause a shift in the L-M curve.

Suppose the system is not in equilibrium. What is the nature of the forces at work in the economy to drive interest rates and/or income to the position we have called equilibrium? Take a point such as C, a point above the L-M curve. Income is Y_1, so the amount of money demanded for working or transaction purposes is $0M_1'$, which means that $0X_1$ is available for speculative holdings. Point C interest rate is r_a; but if the interest rate is r_a, the amount of money the public wishes to hold is just $0X_a$, which is less than the amount they must hold. Now if more money is held than the holders wish to hold, we would expect them to try to get out of money and into bonds. The offers to buy bonds would drive the price of bonds up—thus driving current yields on the bonds, and hence current interest rates, down. Therefore, if interest rates are above equilibrium, competitive pressures in the bond markets will push the interest rates downward toward equilibrium.

To cement your comprehension of this analysis, you are invited to prove that if the interest rate and income were at the point labeled D, that is, any point below the L-M curve, the forces operative in the system would move interest rates upward toward L-M.

Both the L-M and the I-S curves represent possible points of equilibrium of income and interest rates. But there is an infinity of points on both curves so equilibrium can exist only at that point which is common to both curves, that is, at their intersection. Figure 9-4 shows this situation.

A good exercise to see why income would really be Y_e and why the interest rate would really be at r_e is to ask the question: What would the economic environment be like if a different combination of income and interest existed? To do this, select a point such as A on Figure 9-4, which is neither on the L-M nor the I-S curve. Take the analysis in steps. First, since A is above the L-M curve, by the reasoning we used above, the interest rate would have to fall to point B. Point B, however, is to the right of the I-S; and by our argument in Chapter 8, income would fall to the level represented by point C. C is above the

_____

[3] Thus, $0M_1 = X_2E$. $\triangle X_2\bar{M}^SE$ is a right triangle since $\angle X_2 = 90$ degrees and $\angle E$ and $\angle \bar{M}^S = 45$ degrees. EX_2 is therefore equal to $X_2\bar{M}^S = 0M_1$. $X_2\bar{M}^S = 0\bar{M}^S - 0X_2$. Looking at the situation the other way, note that if $0M_1$ is used for transaction balances, the rest of the money supply ($0\bar{M}^S - 0M_1$) is available for speculative balances. $0\bar{M}^S - 0M_1 = M_1E$ because triangle $M_1E\bar{M}^S$ is a right triangle. Therefore, $0X_2 = M_1E$ is the part available for speculative holdings that is transferred to the graph above.

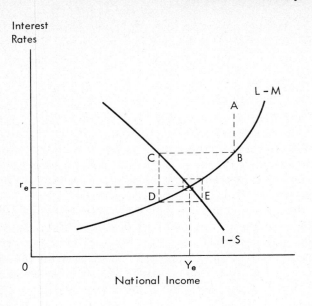

Figure 9-4

L-M, I-S Equilibrium

L-M function so the interest rate would fall to the point represented by *D;* but since *D* is to the left of the *I-S* curve, income would rise to point *E*.

As you can see, if this mechanism were continued, interest and income would oscillate in the direction of the equilibrium levels. Our approach here has been very mechanistic. The real world does not operate exactly in this step fashion, which we adopted for pedagogical reasons. A spiraling approach toward the equilibrium point might be more realistic. The exact path by which the forces at work operate to move income and interest toward equilibrium is dependent upon several time lags. To be candid about the matter, we still have a great deal to learn about these lags. Professor Hicks, who first advanced the cobweb theorem in this context, proposed some rather complicated lags in both the money and the goods markets. It takes time for consumption spending (or saving) to react to changes in income, for investment spending (or saving) to react to changes in income, for investment spending to change when interest rates change, and for money balances to change as income and interest rates change.[4]

THE DETERMINATION OF THE PRICE LEVEL

The discussion of the *I-S, L-M* analysis has been ambiguous in the definition of some of the variables by not being explicit in stating whether the variables are nominal or real. It is uncertain from this structure if any given change,

---

[4]J. R. Hicks, *A Contribution to the Theory of the Trade Cycle* (Oxford, England: Oxford University Press, 1950), Chapter 11.

in income for example, is caused by an increase in real output or is partly or wholly a change in the price level. Since this question is of considerable interest and since price level changes may have independent significance, many economists treat all variables in the framework adjusted for price level.

The following discussion will consider the question of what the impact is on real variables as the price level changes. Lower-case letters $c, i, g, ex, im, m, s,$ and t will be used to stand for real consumption, real investment, real government expenditures, real exports, real imports, the real value of money, real saving, and real taxes, respectively. The corresponding nominal values are $C, I, G, Ex, Im, M, S,$ and $T,$ each one being the real value multiplied by the price level $P.$ Therefore, the real values are also the nominal values divided by the price level $P.$

The discussion will distinguish between an expected change in the price level and an actual change in the price level. Expectations will be considered but at this time it is the actual change in the price level which is being incorporated into the structure. References to price level changes are abstracted from changes in relative prices; so if the price level changes by 5 percent, it is assumed that all prices have changed by that same rate.

Investment and Government Expenditures

It is usually agreed that real investment depends on the real rate of interest and real income. The real rate of interest is the nominal or market rate minus the expected rate of inflation. A firm would invest the same amount if the rate of interest were 4 percent and no inflation were anticipated as it would if the market rate of interest were 7 percent and 3 percent inflation were expected.

Business decision-makers are judged to be sufficiently sophisticated to be aware of the implications of price level changes so that if the demand for total output were to increase only because of an increase in prices, their investment decisions would not change. In other words, no money illusion is assumed in the market for capital goods. That is, $\frac{I}{P} = f\left(\frac{Y}{P}\right) = i = f(y).$

Consumption and Personal Saving

Our primary interest is in the real system, the actual goods and services produced, consumed, and so on. If the price level is constant throughout the time of the events included in the analysis, this would constitute no problem. If, for instance, national income in value terms increased by 10 percent, real national income would also increase by 10 percent. At very large levels of unemployment and great excess capacity of productive facilities, this situation is likely to be closely approximated. At the other extreme, that is, full employment and near capacity utilization of capital, any change in the money level of national income is likely to be almost completely a change in the price level, since real output is near its maximum.

Classical economic theory concluded that full employment was the equilibrium to which the system would always adjust. Therefore, classical economists concentrated their attention on price level behavior, and their interest in saving and investment was directed at its impact on future production rather than its determination of current income.

If the economy exhibits unemployment, it signifies that the total demand for output is less than the potential output. A classical economist would contend that unemployed workers and the owners of other unused factors would lower the prices of their services, thus making it economical for more of them to be reemployed.

Most classical theorists made the mistake of handling this question with the tools of partial equilibrium theory. They reasoned that the lower wages resulting from the pressure of unemployment would shift the firm's marginal cost curve downward, leading to increased output and lower product price. The increased output would absorb the unemployed resources, and the pressure for falling wages would continue until full employment was reached.

The great Swedish economist, Knut Wicksell, was probably the most adamant critic of this approach. He pointed out that in the total economy, the income earned by laborers and other resource owners was what they used to demand the output. Thus, the demand curve for the product of a firm could be held constant while the marginal cost curve shifted due to lower wages paid by that firm, but it is completely erroneous to do so for the entire economy.

Keynes, too, adopted this position. He believed that wages in particular, and prices, generally, were not flexible. While the upward movement of wages would take place quite easily, Keynes said that workers would vigorously resist the lowering of their nominal wages. Furthermore, he argued, lower wages would be effective in stimulating increased output only if the real wage, that is, the money wage divided by the price level, were lowered, and workers and their unions could have an influence only on the money wage rate.

Another way to see the issues involved is to observe that if labor agrees to lower the money wage rate such that the marginal cost curves of all firms decrease, the demand curve for the output of the firms will also decrease. According to Keynesians, there is no reason to believe that the marginal cost curve would shift more than the demand curve. The result of lowering money wages is shown in Figure 9-5.

The situation depicted is what Keynes referred to as "doomsday," with wages and prices falling continuously while employment and production continue at a depressed level.

The classical response to this argument was offered by A. C. Pigou; in fact, it has been titled "the Pigou effect." It is also called "the real balance effect," since it involves the real value of money balances.

Pigou said that as prices are falling in the manner just described, there is an important reason for believing that the demand curve for the firm's output will not fall as much as does the supply curve when wages fall. The reason is that holders of money become wealthier in real terms without anyone else becoming less wealthy. With debt instruments other than money, the creditors become wealthier and so would be expected to increase their real demand for goods and services. However, that increase in demand would be approximately offset by the decrease in demand of debtors who become less wealthy as prices fall,

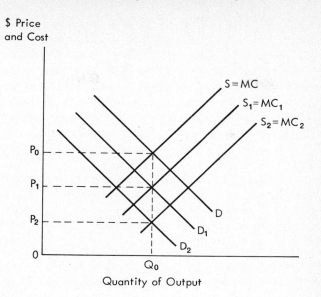

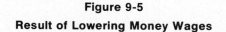

Figure 9-5

Result of Lowering Money Wages

and the real burden of their debt becomes more severe. The government and the banks are the debtors in the case of money outstanding, and neither would be expected to react to an increase in the real value of their debt as would other debtors. However, the important characteristics of money as debt are that there is no interest paid by the debtor, and money is a perpetual debt so the principal need never be repaid.

Another way to look at the significance of the Pigou effect is to consider the Keynesian national income analysis in real rather than money value terms. According to this theory, national income is determined at the intersection of the saving and investment functions, and Keynes said that this intersection could occur at a level insufficient to provide full employment. Adding the real balance effect, however, amounts to saying that saving and consumption depend not only on current income but also on wealth. Falling prices have no effect on the real value of goods nor on the aggregate real value of financial instruments, except money. The real value of money would increase, causing real consumption to increase and, therefore, causing real saving to decrease.

The Pigou effect can be included in the theory by using as the saving function: $s = f(y, m) = \dfrac{S}{P} = f\left(\dfrac{Y}{P}, \dfrac{M}{P}\right)$, where $\dfrac{M}{P}$ is the money supply divided by the price level and hence is a measure of the real value of money holdings. If P falls while M is constant, or if M rises when P is constant, real balances increase and S falls. On our familiar saving and investment graph, the classical system includes the proposition that the saving function will shift downward as long as unemployment exists.

Consider the situation shown in Figure 9-6. Income is at the Keynesian equilibrium of y_1 where s and i are equal. The Pigou effect is included to cause s to shift in the direction of s_f, at which point the economy would be in equilibrium at y_f, full employment national income.

The analysis would presumably apply also in the case of rising wages and prices as well. If, for example, the saving curve were to the right of (below) the s_f curve so that national income were greater than the full employment level, inflation would be in process. Rising wages and prices would reduce the real value of money balances $\left(\dfrac{M}{P}\right)$ so that economic units would attempt to increase their holdings of money by increasing their rate of saving. In other words, the real saving function shifts upward whenever the price level increases and shifts downward whenever the price level decreases. This, of course, implies that the real consumption function shifts downward for increases in the price level and upward for decreases in the price level.

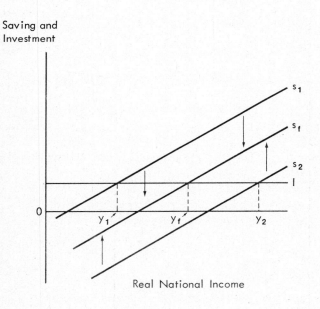

Figure 9-6

The Pigou Effect and Full Employment

If we translate this to the I-S relation, plotting real income (y) on the horizontal axis and interest on the vertical axis, the I-S function moves further to the right as the price level falls. Thus, in Figure 9-7 the I-S function with the higher price level ($P = P_0$) is to the left of the I-S function with the lower price level ($P = P_1$). Then, given any L-M curve, the lower the price level, the greater the real income demand.

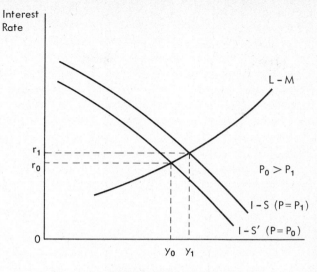

Figure 9-7

Effect of Price Level on Real Income Demand

How strong this effect is, that is, how much and how fast the curve would shift, has not been finally determined. It may take a large change in the price level to effect a relatively small change in real consumption and saving. Logically, it should assure full employment, but the time required might very well be unacceptably long.

Real Money Balances

When the price level falls, if the nominal stock of money remains the same, the real value of the money stock rises. Less of the nominal stock would be needed for transactions purposes so more would be available for speculative holdings, thus causing the interest rate to fall. This is demonstrated in Figure 9-8, where the decrease in the price level is shown as an increase in the real money stock in Part (c), causing the L-M function to shift to the right and indicating that at any given level of real income the interest rate will be lower. This lower interest rate will then induce additional investment to be initiated.

Now we have another reason to expect that aggregate demand is larger when the price level is lower, and conversely, the higher the price level, the lower the level of aggregate demand.

Foreign Trade

At any given level of real national income, a changing level of prices of domestic goods and services alters the relative prices of foreign vs. domestic

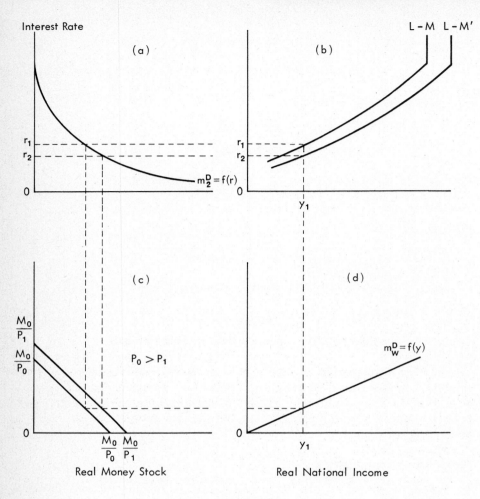

Figure 9-8

Real Money Balances

commodities. If our prices rise while foreign prices do not rise, as long as ex-change rates are fixed or less than completely flexible, the demand for do-mestically produced goods will fall relative to foreign-made products. Our exports will fall and imports will increase so that $(x\text{-}m)$ decreases. Thus, again, the $I\text{-}S$ curve shifts to the left as domestic prices rise and to the right as our prices fall, and real aggregate demand varies inversely with the price level.

Government Spending and Taxes

Taxes are collected on the basis of nominal personal income and not on real income. If our tax structure is progressive, an increase in the price level (and therefore an increase in nominal income earned) will cause the tax liability to increase by a larger proportion than the increase in income so that the real tax will increase when the price level increases, even though real income remains the same. Then, if real consumption depends on real disposable income, consumption will decline as the price level rises. This is another reason to believe that the I-S curve shifts to the left at higher prices and to the right for lower price levels, and that real aggregate demand is negatively related to the price level.

This decrease in private consumption demand could, of course, be offset by an increase in real government spending, which could neutralize the impact of real tax changes on aggregate demand. Whether government spending will increase when real tax collections increase is simply uncertain. It depends on the political forces extant at the time. It is even possible that the administration and Congress might elect to offset the increase in real taxes by lowering tax rates. In the short run it may be that changing neither spending nor taxes is feasible given the cumbersomeness of the governmental decision-making processes.

Price Expectations

All the factors considered so far lead to the conclusion that falling price levels increase the quantities demanded of the economy's output, and that rising price levels decrease quantities demanded. However, if falling prices generate the expectation in the minds of people that prices will fall further, then they might very well hold off on some of their expenditures. Similarly, inflation may precipitate expectations of further price level expansion and economic units may decide that it is advisable to shift into more goods and out of monetary assets. When price level movements generate expectations of this sort, it cannot be said with any confidence that aggregate demand is inversely related to the price level.

Such evidence as is available on the impact of changing price levels on expectations indicates that a very long time lag is involved.[5] Thus, for short-run or static analysis this effect on aggregate demand can be disregarded; and wherever it seems to be pertinent, it can be treated as a shift in the aggregate demand function.

The Aggregate Demand Function

Figure 9-9 is a graphic representation of the aggregate demand function. It simply shows the inverse relationship between price levels and the quantity of real goods and services demanded in the whole economy in conformance with the preceding discussion.

As usual, if such a tool is to be valuable, the causes of shifts in the function must be explained. Only the changes which shift the AD function upward from AD_1 to AD_2, for example, will be discussed, leaving downward shift analysis to the reader. Changes that shift the AD function upward are:

---

[5] See, for example, Milton Friedman, "Factors Affecting the Level of Interest Rates," *Savings and Residential Financing, 1968 Conference Proceedings* (Chicago: The United States Savings and Loan League, 1968).

1. An increase in the money stock shifts the aggregate demand curve by causing the interest rate to fall, inspiring an increase in the demand for national output for investment purposes and, perhaps, an increase in consumption demand (by reducing desired saving).
2. Autonomous decreases in the demand for money either for transactions or speculative purposes shift *AD* upward by decreasing interest rates and, as above, increasing investment and consumption demand.
3. An autonomous increase in the consumption function, the investment function, government spending, or export spending, or autonomous decreases in taxes or imports are all expected to shift the *AD* curve upward.

These are the reasons the real *I-S* or the real *L-M* functions can shift to the right. If either of these functions shifts to the right, the aggregate demand curve also shifts to the right, indicating that at a constant level of prices, demand for goods and services will be larger.

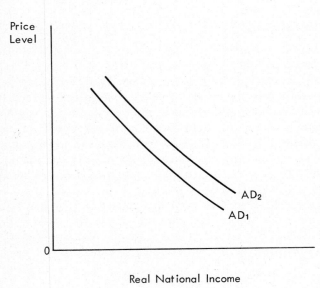

Figure 9-9

Aggregate Demand Function

Aggregate Supply

The above points are a summary of the construction of an aggregate demand curve and the factors that might cause it to shift. In the following paragraphs the aggregate supply curve, which is the quantity of real output firms will wish to supply at all possible price levels, will be discussed.

In considering the classical model in Chapter 4, it was seen that changing price levels would have no effect on output. Thus, in the purely classical case, the aggregate supply curve is a perpendicular line; i.e., output is inelastic with respect to the price level. The reason for this conclusion is that wages and prices are both considered completely flexible, and both the demand for and supply of labor depend on real wages $\left(w = \dfrac{W}{P}\right)$. Any change in the price level would be matched by a proportional change in money wage rates so the real wage would not change and, hence, the quantity of labor employed would remain the same. Since output depends only on the amount of labor used, given other constant factors, real production would be unchanged.

If the assumptions of the classical case are changed, the aggregate supply curve can take on different shapes. First, if wages are less flexible than prices of commodities, a change in the price level will result in a change in real wages. For example, assume that wages are fixed in nominal terms and the price level increases. Real wages would fall, and workers would be willing to supply fewer hours of work so output would decline. On the other hand, if the price level decreases and money wages do not change, the real wage will rise and employers will want to employ fewer worker hours and again output will fall. Thus, if wages are completely rigid, any change in the price level will decrease employment and production.

Many people have concluded that, in fact, money wages are rigid only in the downward direction but are flexible in an upward direction. If this is indeed the case, then lower price levels will reduce employment and output; however, higher price levels will be matched by higher nominal wages, and employment and production will remain the same.

If employment decisions of workers are made on the basis of the nominal wage and not on the basis of the real wage as assumed by the classicists, then the supply curve of output with respect to the price level will be positively sloped. Under these conditions, if the price level increases, the demand for labor will increase because the real wage paid to workers will decrease; or putting it another way, for any given number of workers employed, the money value of the contribution of an additional worker (the marginal revenue product) will be greater than it was before the price of the product increased. At the existing money wage, firms will wish to employ more workers so the money wage will rise. Therefore, according to the assumption that the supply of labor depends on nominal wages only, more employment and thus more output will be forthcoming. Figure 9-10 illustrates this case.

While this assumption is quite unrealistic and insulting to the intelligence of workers, it is quite plausible to say that workers might be more conscious of their own wages in dollar terms than they are aware of the prices of a multitude of other commodities. So while the "money illusion" of the labor force may not be as complete as assumed by a labor supply curve based strictly on money wages, as long as there is any degree of money illusion the labor supply curve and, hence, the aggregate supply curve will be positively sloped. Money illusion exists in this direction as long as the increase in labor supplied per unit increase in the nominal wage is greater than the decrease in labor supplied per unit increase in the price level. Figure 9-11 shows a case where money illusion exists but is less than complete.

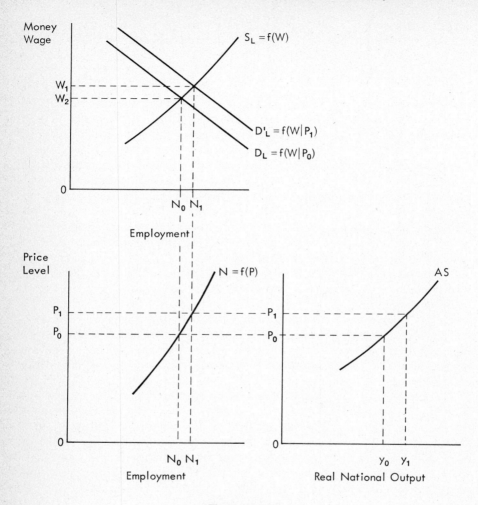

Figure 9-10

Aggregate Supply Where Labor Supply Depends on Money Wages

Here both the demand and the supply of labor curves shift upward because of an increase in the price level, but the supply curve shifts less than the demand curve. Again, the aggregate supply curve is positively sloped but is less elastic than in the pure money illusion case.

If we can accept these ideas, the aggregate supply curve (AS) is derived as shown in Figure 9-11. The original equilibrium is shown with the $_0$ subscripts; that is, employment is N_0, nominal wage is W_0, real national product is y_0, and the price level is P_0. Now if the price level increases to P_1, the demand for labor increases to N_2; but since the supply of labor curve has shifted upward due to the price level increase, employment will go to N_1 rather than to N_2 as

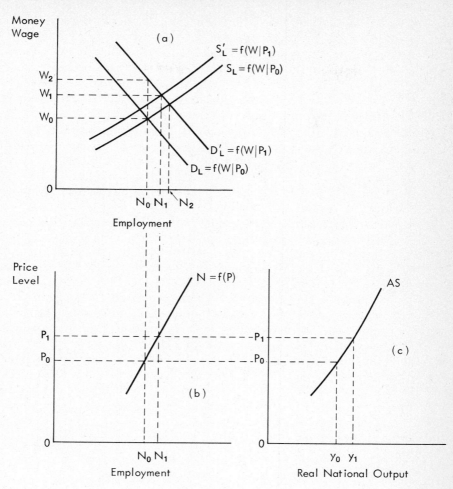

Figure 9-11

**Aggregate Supply Where Labor Supply Depends on Money Wages
more than on Price Level**

the money wage rises to W_1. (Notice here that the real wage has fallen since the money wage did not rise as high as W_2.) Since employment has increased, output will rise to y_1 on part (c) of Figure 9-11.

The AS curve will shift if the supply of labor curve shifts because laborers changed their attitudes toward work vs. income or because the labor force changed. The AS curve will also shift if the productivity of labor changes, thus changing the production function and hence the demand for labor function.

The aggregate demand and the aggregate supply relationships have now been explained, so they can be combined to show the mutual determination of

the price level and the level of national income or product. According to this
framework of analysis, inflation can take place only if aggregate demand increases or if aggregate supply decreases. In the analysis leading up to this point,
all of the events that can cause either AD or AS to shift have been described.
The underlying relations which determine the slopes of the two functions have
also been discussed in regard to what will determine whether the price level or
output will change in response to any shift in one of the relations.

Figure 9-12 shows the AS and AD curves determining the price level at
P_0 and real national output at y_0. The AD curve shifts to AD' if any of the functions making up the I-S curve shift the I-S curve to the right, such as an increase in government spending, or if any of the functions making up the L-M
function shift the L-M function to the right, such as an increase in the money
stock.

If we use the classical assumptions of (1) flexible wages and prices and (2)
labor supply determined by real wages, the supply curve will be AS' and the
shift in the demand curve will cause prices to rise with no increase in output. If
the assumptions of flexible wages and prices and of labor supply determined by
money wages are made, then AS is the aggregate supply curve and both output
and prices will increase in response to the increased aggregate demand.

An example may be helpful in demonstrating what is involved in the model
as it is now composed. The model starts from a condition of equilibrium in all
aspects of the economy, changes any variable which shifts the I-S or L-M
function and thus the AD curve, and traces the impact on the other variables;
or one of the variables which shifts the AS curve can be changed and the effects
then traced.

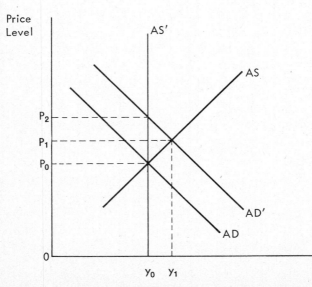

Figure 9-12
Aggregate Supply and Demand
Determine Price Level and Output

An increase in the money stock shifts the *L-M* curve to the right, reducing interest rates and increasing demand for real national income. Investment and consumption demand both increase because of the lower interest rate. This point is seen as $r_1 y_1$ in part (a) of Figure 9-13. Looking at part (b), we interpret this by noting that if the price level remained at P_0, the aggregate quantity of commodities demanded would be y_1. Thus, the *AD* curve has shifted to *AD'* and excess demand in the amount of the difference between y_1 and y_0 would

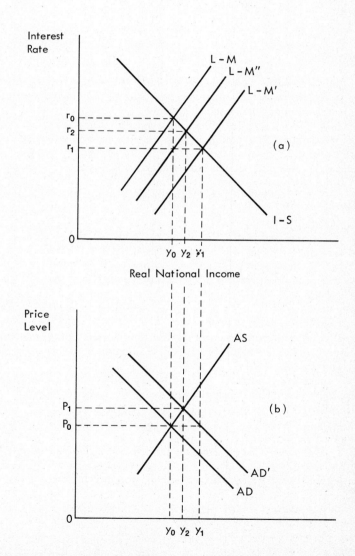

Figure 9-13

Shift in Aggregate Demand

show up. This causes the prices of products to go up because the demand has increased more than the costs of production by way of wage increases. This brings us to a price level of P_1 on part (b) and an equilibrium national income and output of y_2.

Since prices have gone up, the real value of money balances has decreased; since this amounts to a decrease in the real money stock, the L-M curve will shift upward to L-M", bringing the interest rate to r_2. This increase in the interest rate reduces investment and consumption compared to what they would have been had it stayed at r_1, which is the reason that income moves to y_2 rather than y_1.

QUESTIONS

1. The text does not define "the financial system." What do you think should be the important elements in such a definition? Explain how "the monetary system" differs from your definition of "the financial system."
2. Using the complete multiplier model on pages 183–185, show the final balance sheets of the commercial banking system and the money supply in each of the following events:
   (a) Reserve requirements on demand deposits (r) increase to 35 percent.
   (b) Reserve requirements on time deposits are eliminated altogether.
   (c) Currency in circulation increases significantly so that the value of a becomes .50.
   (d) The monetary base decreases by $2 billion.
3. Discuss the events that will increase or decrease the monetary base. Organize your answer according to the agency responsible for the change, that is, the Treasury, the Federal Reserve, and "other."
4. Refer to Figure 9-4 on page 194. Explain why a point below the L-M function and to the left of the I-S function would not be an equilibrium point. What are the forces which would cause movement of the interest rate and income in the direction of the intersection of the L-M and I-S curves?
5. Graphically derive the shift in the L-M function caused by (a) an increase in the money supply, (b) a downward shift in the M_w^D function, (c) a shift to the right of the liquidity preference function.
6. Given the following conditions, when would it be advisable to hold bonds? (Assume that the bonds available are all perpetuities and can be exchanged only on one date each year.)
   (a) The current interest rate is 1 percent and you forecast that the rate next year will be 2 percent.
   (b) The current interest rate is 2 percent and you forecast that the rate next year will be 1 percent.
   (c) The current interest rate is 30 percent and you forecast that the rate next year will be 31 percent.
   (d) The current interest rate is 10 percent and you forecast that the rate next year will be 11 percent.
   (e) The current interest rate is 10 percent and you forecast that the rate next year will be 12 percent.
7. How would you qualify your conclusions in question 6 if the forecast of future interest rate behavior was clouded with a great deal of uncertainty?

8. Explain why the Pigou effect would not be expected to operate on corporate bonds, whereas it would be operative on Federal Reserve notes.
9. Give as many reasons as you can to explain why aggregate demand for the output of the economy will rise as the price level falls.
10. Give as many reasons as you can to explain why aggregate supply of goods and services will rise as the price level rises.

SUGGESTED READINGS

Branson, William H. *Macroeconomic Theory and Policy.* New York: Harper and Row, Publishers, 1971.

Burger, Albert E. *The Money Supply Process.* Belmont, California: Wadsworth Publishing Co., Inc., 1971.

Federal Reserve Bank of Boston. *Controlling Monetary Aggregates,* Vol. I, 1969; Vol. II, 1972.

Friedman, Milton. "A Monetary Theory of Nominal Income," *Journal of Political Economy* (March/April, 1971).

Hicks, J. R. *A Contribution to the Theory of the Trade Cycle.* Oxford, England: Oxford University Press, 1950.

Laidler, David E. W. *The Demand for Money: Theories and Evidence.* Scranton, Pa.: International Textbook Co., 1969.

Patinkin, Don. *Money, Interest, and Prices: An Integration of Monetary and Value Theory,* 2d ed. New York: Harper and Row, Publishers, 1965.

Smith, Warren L. "A Graphical Exposition of the Complete Keynesian System." *Readings in Money, National Income, and Stabilization Policy,* edited by W. L. Smith and R. L. Teigen. Homewood, Ill.: Richard D. Irwin, Inc., 1971.

CHAPTER 10

TOPICS IN NATIONAL INCOME ANALYSIS

In this chapter the topic of aggregate consumption theory is pursued in some depth, beginning with the influence of taxes on consumer spending. The discussion presents a hypothesis called the stagnation thesis which, while having fallen out of favor somewhat as a forecast for the U.S. economy, is still very useful for illuminating certain economic principles. It also serves as an introduction to the last segment of the chapter on the theory of economic growth.

TAXATION

Receipts by government are looked upon as a withdrawal from the income stream. Government has the ability to absorb purchasing power from the rest of the economy by its legal power to tax. The usual procedure is for the taxing authority to set the rate of tax and other conditions and to forecast the amount of collections.

Since taxes are withdrawals, they are not a part of aggregate demand. Instead, they are a part of aggregate supply but influence aggregate demand. Some taxes or rules for computing taxes will have their impact on the marginal efficiency of capital. Others will affect the net foreign investment figure. The most important classes of taxes, however, are those that reduce the disposable income of households and thus influence the consumption function. It is these taxes that will be introduced into our national income model at this stage.

The new consumption function that is to be utilized here is $C = \alpha + \beta Y_D$. We have switched from English to Greek letters for the parameters simply to indicate that this function is the after-tax consumption function. Y_D is disposable income, equal to national income (Y) minus taxes (T_x).

For our example, a linear tax function is used: $T_x = \bar{T}_x + tY$. This relationship is similar to a proportional tax in that a change in income results in a proportional change in the tax payments; i.e., $\dfrac{\Delta T_x}{\Delta Y}$ is constant. However, $\dfrac{T_x}{Y}$ is not constant. It is declining, so in that sense it is a regressive tax. A strictly proportional tax function would have both $\dfrac{\Delta T_x}{\Delta Y}$ and $\dfrac{T_x}{Y}$ constant, which could be accomplished by setting $\bar{T}_x$ equal to zero. This tax function relates to national income, not to personal or individual incomes; therefore, we can say very little about the tax rate structure that applies to individuals. As national income changes, so may its distribution. Formally, our model looks like this:

$$Y = C + I_B + G$$
$$C = \alpha + \beta Y_D$$
$$Y_D = Y - T_x$$
$$T_x = \bar{T}_x + tY$$
$$I_B = \bar{I}_B$$
$$G = \bar{G}$$

And its solution can be shown in the following way:

$$Y = C + I_B + G$$
$$Y = \alpha + \beta Y_D + \bar{I}_B + \bar{G}$$
$$Y = \alpha + \beta(Y - T_x) + \bar{I}_B + \bar{G}$$
$$Y = \alpha + \beta Y - \beta T_x + \bar{I}_B + \bar{G}$$
$$Y = \alpha + \beta Y - \beta \bar{T}_x - \beta tY + \bar{I}_B + \bar{G}$$
$$Y - \beta Y + \beta tY = \alpha + \bar{I}_B + \bar{G} - \beta \bar{T}_x$$
$$Y(1 - \beta + \beta t) = \alpha + \bar{I}_B + \bar{G} - \beta \bar{T}_x$$
$$Y = \frac{\alpha + \bar{I}_B + \bar{G} - \beta \bar{T}_x}{1 - \beta + \beta t}$$

A tax multiplier can be constructed if it is defined as $\dfrac{\Delta Y}{\Delta \bar{T}_x}$. The meaning of $\Delta \bar{T}_x$ here is that whatever the level of national income, the amount of the tax will be $\Delta \bar{T}_x$ larger than before. Notice that it does not say that taxes will be $\Delta \bar{T}_x$ larger than before the additional tax was imposed. Since the change in taxes will change the national income, taxes will also change because income changes. The derivation of this multiplier can be accomplished by comparing the equilibrium income of the latest model with the income found to be equilibrium when the tax function includes $\Delta \bar{T}_x$. Thus, in place of $T_x = \bar{T}_x + tY$ use $T_x = \bar{T}_x + tY + \Delta \bar{T}_x$.

The new equilibrium income Y' is then $Y' = \dfrac{\alpha + \bar{I}_B + \bar{G} - \beta \bar{T}_x - \beta \Delta \bar{T}_x}{1 - \beta + \beta t}$.

Our goal is to find $\dfrac{\Delta Y}{\Delta \bar{T}_x}$. ΔY is $Y' - Y$. Subtracting the equation for Y above from the equation just found for Y' gives $Y' - Y = \Delta Y = \dfrac{-\beta \Delta \bar{T}_x}{1 - \beta + \beta t}$.

Then, dividing both sides of this equation by $\Delta \bar{T}_x$ we get $\dfrac{\Delta Y}{\Delta \bar{T}_x} = \dfrac{-\beta}{1 - \beta + \beta t}$, which is the tax multiplier.

The tax multiplier is negative. Since $\Delta \bar{T}_x$ is positive, ΔY must be negative; that is, an increase in taxes results in a decrease in national income.

Figure 10-1 shows how to develop a consumption function when taxes are imposed in the form described by the tax function $T_x = \bar{T}_x + tY$. Y_2 is disposable income (i.e., $Y - T_x$) when national income is Y_1 ($T_1 = Y_1 - Y_2$). We make

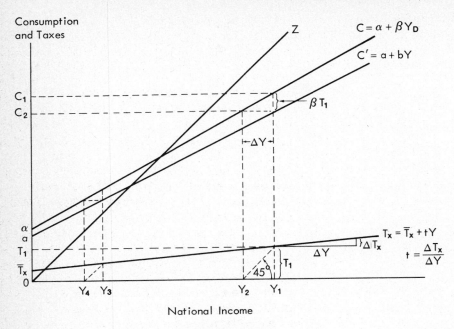

Figure 10-1

Before- and After-Tax Consumption Function

the assumption that households will spend the same amount on consumption if national income is Y_2 and no taxes are paid, or if national income is Y_1 and taxes of T_1 make disposable income Y_2. This is like saying that a person with an income of \$150 and taxes of \$50 would consume the same as if income were \$100 with no taxes to pay, acting on the basis of take-home pay rather than gross pay.

By this assumption we are able to draw an after-tax consumption function, $C' = a + bY$. At a given level of income, it is below the pretax function ($C = \alpha + \beta Y_D$) by β times the amount of the tax at that income. The individual's disposable income has been reduced by the amount of the tax so we expect the consumer to reduce consumption by the marginal propensity to consume times the reduction in income. Also, b is the marginal propensity to consume national income given this particular tax function. It will be a little smaller than β, the marginal propensity to consume disposable income. A little algebra will show that $b = \beta - \beta t$. With the given tax function, C' is the relevant consumption function. The C function is needed to derive C', so it is kept in the diagram.

Now that taxes have been incorporated, aggregate leakages or withdrawals (S) include both personal saving and taxes: $S = S_p + T_x$. $S = Y - C'$, so $S_p + T_x = Y - C'$. Therefore, $S_p = Y - C' - T_x$. The aggregate saving curve can be derived by simply subtracting the C' line from the Z line. Then the S_p line can be found by $S_p = S - T_x$. Alternatively, the S_p line can be constructed by the same reasoning by which the C' curve was derived in Figure 10-1. Then S_p and T_x sum to S.

As before, equilibrium income occurs at that level at which aggregate saving $(S_p + T_x)$ is equal to aggregate investment $(I_B + G)$. An increase in government spending of ΔG will cause income to increase by that amount (ΔG) times the reciprocal of the slope of the S function $\left(\dfrac{1}{1 - \beta + \beta t}\right)$.

A decrease in taxes by a given amount will result in an increase in income, but the increase will be somewhat less than that resulting from the same increase in government spending. Likewise, if government expenditures and taxes were both increased by the same amount, national income would not be constant—it would increase. The reason for this asymmetry of taxes and spending is that while government purchases of goods and services become a part of national income, a decrease in taxation increases consumption by less than the full amount of the tax. The change in taxes of $\Delta \bar{T}_x$ shifts the consumption function by $\beta \Delta \bar{T}_x$ and the aggregate saving function by the same amount but in the opposite direction. The shift of the saving curve can be viewed as a composite of the shift in the personal saving function and the shift in the tax function. For example, suppose the increase in the tax is \$10 billion ($\Delta \bar{T}_x = \$10$ billion) and the MPS disposable income is 2/10. Then the tax function shifts upward by \$10 billion, and the S_p function shifts downward by \$2 billion—a net increase in the S function of \$8 billion.

Figure 10-2 shows a balanced budget situation where taxes and government spending were both increased by an amount equal to $\Delta \bar{G}$. If only government expenditures had been increased, income would have risen to Y_1. If only

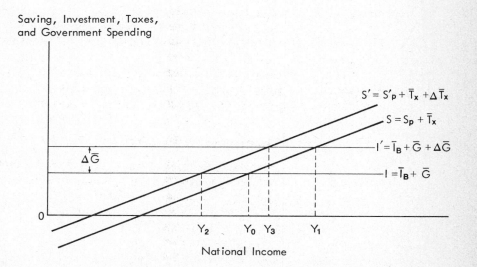

Figure 10-2
Balanced Budget Situation

taxes had been raised, income would have fallen to Y_2. Since both were raised, the net effect is for income to rise to Y_3.

Figure 10-3, see below, compares the effect of an increase in G and a decrease in T_x of equal amounts. Clearly the increase in G has a larger impact on national income than does the decrease in T_x.

RECENT CONTRIBUTIONS TO
THE THEORY OF CONSUMPTION

The statistical correlation between annual real personal consumption expenditures and annual real disposable personal income is extremely high. With the exception of the war years 1941–1945, virtually all the points from 1929 to the present fall on the regression line that has a slope of about .90, which seems to confirm the empirical relevance of the kinds of consumption functions we have been using.

Our confidence in the function is shaken considerably, however, if we go through the same procedure using quarterly or monthly data. Here the correlation is not nearly so impressive, since the points appear to be scattered almost haphazardly. Some significant errors in forecasting consumption on the basis of income have inspired many economists to probe more deeply into the nature of consumer behavior. This can be done by study of individuals or groups of individuals with different characteristics such as age, urban vs. rural, wealth, and education, or it can be done by a more sophisticated theoretical attack on the aggregate level. Both of these approaches are being followed continuously. The final answers are not yet in.

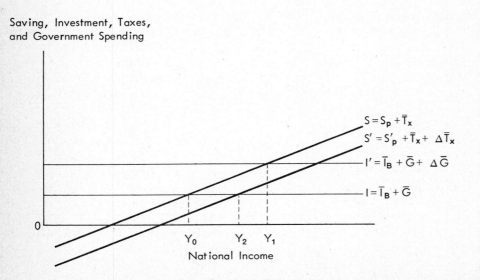

Figure 10-3

Effect of Equal Government Spending Increases and Tax Decreases

The significant errors in the short-run empirical consumption function suggest that factors other than disposable income contribute importantly to the consumption decision. Some of them will be discussed here. Some empirical evidence on them will be taken up in the chapters on forecasting.

Expectations of Changes in Income, Employment, and Prices

Households in any given income bracket would be expected to increase their current consumption if they anticipated a considerable increase in income in the near future. Such expansion of spending out of a given income is usually possible through the reduction of saving, through spending out of assets accumulated during the past, or through borrowing against future income. If a person fears the possibility of becoming unemployed, that person's spending behavior will probably become more conservative. If the feeling is widespread, the consumption function might shift downward.

We would expect that uncertainty in and of itself would be an important reason for saving, so anything creating uncertainty in the minds of the family decision makers would shift the consumption function downward. Closely connected to this idea, but independent of it, is the reasoning that volatility of income would alter consumption behavior. Imagine two families whose incomes over a long period of time would be the same, but one of them had a constant income from an annuity and the other had an income that fluctuated greatly from month to month or quarter to quarter. The short-run consumption function for the two might be quite different, even though the longer run functions might be identical. The aggregate consumption function would probably be higher as uncertainty and volatility of income were diminished. This is one of the hoped-for effects of the expansion of Social Security and other governmental economic policies.

The Survey Research Center of the University of Michigan has engaged in extensive research into consumer expectations and behavior, stressing particularly the psychological and sociological elements of the study. In general, their findings support the view that pessimism with respect to income and employment, as well as the vague feeling that "things are going to get worse," results in diminished consumer spending. The converse also seems to be true: an attitude of optimism about future income, about employment, and about the general economic and political climate acts as a stimulus to consumption expenditures.[1]

One would certainly anticipate that consumers who expect prices to rise would increase spending to take advantage of the current lower prices, and that consumers would curtail present consumption as much as possible if they expected prices to fall in the future. Apparently consumer psychology is more complex than this. It seems that when prices are rising and expected to

---

[1] Most of the Center's publications are pertinent to this discussion. See, in particular, G. Katona and E. Mueller, *Consumer Expectations, 1953–56* (Ann Arbor, Mich.: University of Michigan Institute for Social Research. Survey Research Center, 1957). Also, see G. Katona, *The Powerful Consumer: Psychological Studies of the American Economy* (New York: McGraw-Hill Book Co., Inc., 1960).

rise further, they are already higher than they were, so there is reluctance to increase consumer purchases at what are thought of as "high" prices.

Expectations of the future price level will affect the demand for some goods more than others. For example, if prices are expected to fall in the near future, families will probably choose to get along with their present automobile or household appliances, whereas their consumption of less durable items may remain about the same.

Prices

Rational consumer behavior implies that if all prices (and hence incomes) increased proportionally, consumption valued in current prices should also increase by the same proportion so that real consumption would remain constant. Frequently households suffer from a type of myopia encountered earlier in the labor supply context; economists call this the "money illusion" in the goods market. This means that the consumer might emphasize a rise in income without realizing that prices have also increased. Others might be so conscious of the higher prices of goods and services that they seemingly are insensitive to the fact that their incomes have also increased. Economists are not in general agreement as to whether a money illusion exists in dependable-enough form to include the hypothesis in their analysis.

We saw earlier that the major effect of price level changes on consumer behavior came through the Pigou effect where increases in the general level of prices reduced the real value of money balances and so inspired consumers to attempt to add to their money holdings by reducing their consumption. The Pigou effect assumes that the money illusion is not operative. In fact, it assumes a high degree of awareness of the "real" effects of price level changes, unclouded by any veil of money.

Inflations and deflations as they have been experienced are not characterized by proportional price changes. Rather, some prices change very readily while others are termed "sticky." We saw earlier that this fact alone can be quite important in generating business fluctuations as described by W. C. Mitchell. We are not prepared to make empirically meaningful generalizations about the effect of nonproportional price variability on consumption spending. We can, however, observe that if it were true that price volatility was characteristic of goods whose income elasticity of demand was high and if price rigidity were true of goods with low income elasticity, then a general price level rise would reduce consumption. Of course, such statements are of very little value until a great deal more research on the problem is complete.

There are other considerations of this sort that can be observed. For example, a general increase in prices, even if proportional, will result in a shift of real income from the private sector to government where a progressive income tax is in effect. Assume all prices to increase by 10 percent so that all money incomes also increase by 10 percent. Since the income tax is progressive, the increase in tax payments will be more than 10 percent and real disposable income will have declined. In this instance we should expect real consumption to be reduced.

Another possible source of a change in consumption could come through a systematic redistribution of income by price level changes from those with a high marginal propensity to consume to those with a low marginal propensity to consume, or vice versa. In order to make significant statements about this, we would have to know that inflation does have this redistributional effect on particular classes of consumers, and that classes so affected do, in fact, have different marginal propensities to consume. Inflation could also cause a shift from the consumption of domestically produced goods to foreign produced goods as their relative prices changed.

Interest

In a number of connections, it has been pointed out that classical economists relied on the interest rate to explain the division of income into its consumption and saving components. In the logic of utility maximization, an increase in interest rates should cause households to save more and consume less out of any given level of income. A saver whose goal is to accumulate a particular sum of wealth at a particular date in the future, however, would save less when interest rates rise, since the same sum could be accumulated by that date with smaller periodic additions. In some instances this may describe some households' behavior, but it is inconsistent with utility maximization and therefore somewhat suspect as a part of the theory.

Income Distribution

Many schemes to promote economic expansion are based on the belief that the marginal propensities to consume of low income groups are higher than those of high income groups. Consumption and income would increase if income were taken away from low MPC households and given to high MPC households. The hypothesis seems to be so intuitively appealing that many have accepted policy proposals based upon it. There are several fallacies incorporated into this position, quite aside from the most fundamental one, which is that because an act has one desirable outcome it should be done.

The simple error of confusing the marginal propensity to consume with the average propensity to consume is often discovered. It is quite well established that the APC of high income families is significantly lower than that of low income families. The evidence on the MPC by income class is an entirely different matter. It is a very difficult thing to measure, and most attempts seem to indicate that the differences in the marginal propensities to consume of the various income classes are not significant. One reason for this surprising conclusion is that low income families might have debts to pay, cash balances to build up, insurance to buy, and so on. There are many nonconsumption uses for added income.

Even if it were discovered that low income households had high marginal propensities to consume, it would be advisable to determine whether some other factor might be the fundamental reason rather than the level of income. For example, it seems to be the case that young families have a high MPC and are more likely to be lower on the income scale. Certainly there are groups in the low income category who have low marginal propensities to consume, such as farmers and certain immigrant groups. The source of income seems to have some influence on consumption behavior. Profit recipients behave differently than do wage earners and interest and rent receivers. These considerations ought to give us pause before we recommend income redistribution as the preferred solution to a slumping economy. This is not to say that income redistribution may not be defended by some as a worthwhile goal, but its defense must rest on other grounds.

Wealth

The relationship of wealth to consumption behavior is difficult to ascertain. For one thing, wealth and income are themselves so highly correlated it is difficult to determine their individual effect upon consumption. Another difficulty is that the very fact of wealth ownership may indicate that the owners saved large portions of income in the past and thus are motivated differently than are those whose wealth is small. Again, considering any given level of income, wealth holding is likely to be concentrated in the older age group whose spending patterns are different from those of younger people.

Wealth of different kinds may have different effects on consumer spending. Some consumer wealth requires additional spending if its value is to be maintained and services received. Automobiles and household appliances are in this category. On the other hand, the services of some kinds of consumer wealth substitute for new consumer goods and services. Thus, to some extent a television set may reduce spending on other forms of entertainment, and ownership of an automobile reduces spending on other forms of transportation.

The influence of financial wealth on consumer spending habits is the more serious question. It has been suggested that the unexpectedly high levels of consumption following World War II can be partially explained by the rapid accumulation of financial assets in the hands of consumers during the war years. It does seem plausible that of two families with the same income, the one with the larger holdings of financial assets would spend more on current consumption. Undoubtedly the most important consideration is the level of wealth relative to the family's aspiration level. Unfortunately this is not directly measurable.

Consumer Credit Terms

Consumption can be accomplished without regard to current income either by allowing the stock of assets to vary or by varying the amount of indebtedness over a period of time. The terms on which consumers can borrow are altered periodically. The interest rate is of some consequence in these terms, but other conditions may be of equal or even more importance. Among these conditions are the down payment requirement, the length of the repayment period, and the credit standards imposed by the lenders. Easing of these terms stimulates consumer borrowing and spending, and the tightening of the terms discourages new borrowing and spending. The major impact, of course, is on durable consumer goods, but revolving type charges involving the purchase of "soft goods" are also affected.

Short-Run Versus Long-Run Consumption Functions

The statistical evidence on the consumption-income relation suggests that the consumption function over short periods of time has a positive intercept and a relatively small slope. The long-run function derived from empirical evidence is approximately proportional; that is, it is linear and its intercept is at the origin.[2] These seemingly contradictory findings demand an explanation. In fact, any explanation of consumer behavior must be consistent with these observations. Figure 10-4 is drawn to serve as the basis for discussing the problem.

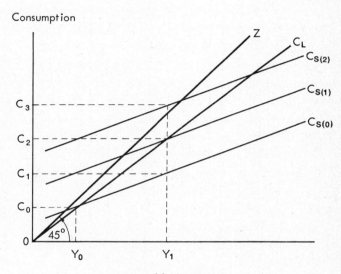

Figure 10-4

Consumption-Income Relation

The consumption function labeled C_L represents the long-run consumption-income relationship. Kuznets found remarkable stability in the average propensity to consume when he used decade figures from 1869 to the beginning of the great depression in 1929. During the 1930s the APC increased significantly when disposable income fell well below what it had been. During the

---

[2] The study on which these statements are based is Simon Kuznets, *National Income: A Summary of Findings*, (New York: National Bureau of Economic Research, Inc., 1946).

years of World War II, the APC was very low as incomes again grew very rapidly. After the war the APC again returned to figures comparable to the long-run historical norms.

The short-run consumption functions of Figure 10-4 have the subscript s. They represent the consumption behavior in response to incomes in relatively short periods of time. The argument is that the short-run consumption function has been shifting upward because of some basic changes taking place in the economy, such as developments of new consumer goods, accumulation of wealth, education to new desires, the growth of urban populations, and so on.

Start with income Y_0, at which level of income consumption is C_0. If income increases to Y_1 within a year, consumption would increase to C_1; but if the changes we spoke of took place such that the consumption function shifted to $C_{S(1)}$, consumption would increase to C_2. Many years later Y_1 might be a severe depression level of income, but since the consumption function had shifted upward considerably, consumption would then be at C_3. Arthur Smithies showed that the statistical evidence was consistent with this explanation of consumer behavior,[3] but, as we shall see, a number of other explanations are also consistent with the evidence.

One of these explanations is the "relative income hypothesis" of James Duesenberry. Where Smithies felt that the basic consumption relation was the short-run function and the long-run proportional function showed up as shifts in the short-run functions, Duesenberry believes that it is the proportional function that is the fundamental one.[4] In other words, if income were to continuously increase, consumption would increase proportionally; but since income fluctuates, consumer response is nonproportional.

This argument is based on the view that consumption is determined not simply by one's current income but, to an important extent, by one's position in society which in turn depends partly upon one's own past income and the income of one's neighbors. Thorstein Veblen, in his penetrating discussion of consumption, emphasized the degree to which people consume to impress others via "conspicuous consumption," and how socially approved consumption patterns were set by the higher ranking or higher income groups, a phenomenon called "pecuniary emulation."[5] Persons whose income is low relative to their neighbors' will spend a larger proportion of their income, whereas those with relatively large incomes can consume smaller proportions of their income. Thus, the least wealthy of the "jet set" may have a higher APC than the wealthiest persons living in a very poor neighborhood.

Duesenberry's description of consumption behavior is based on the dynamics of fluctuations and growth in income. Figure 10-5 can be used to explain the hypothesis. Consumption would be equal to C_1 if income were Y_1, and if income grew steadily, consumption would follow the C_L line so that

---

[3] Arthur Smithies, "Forecasting Postwar Demand," *Econometrica*, Vol. 13 (January, 1945).

[4] J. S. Duesenberry, *Income, Saving, and the Theory of Consumer Behavior* (Cambridge, Mass.: Harvard University Press, 1949).

[5] Thorstein B. Veblen, *The Theory of the Leisure Class: An Economic Study of Institutions* (New York: The Modern Library, 1934).

Consumption

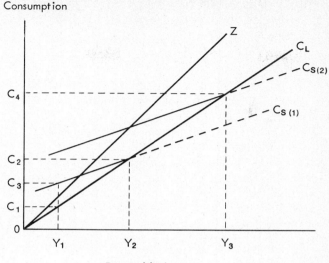

Disposable Income

Figure 10-5
Duesenberry's Hypothesis of Consumption Behavior

as income increased to Y_2, consumption would increase to C_2. But when income hits a peak of Y_2 and declines, consumption would follow the $C_{S(1)}$ line down, so that if income fell all the way back to Y_1, consumption would be C_3 rather than C_1. The reason given for making the short-run (nonproportional) function the relevant one when income falls is that households, having once reached a high standard of living (as represented by C_2), will give it up only very reluctantly. They will allow their savings to decline rather than give up the level of consumption attained during the boom. However, as income reaches its trough, say, at Y_1 and begins to rise again, consumption will increase again, but again along the $C_{S(1)}$ line. Now the argument is that, having become accustomed to the lower standard of living represented by C_3, when income rises, the desire to save seems more urgent. But when income again reaches Y_2 and continues to increase, consumption will again increase according to C_L until income reaches a new peak at, say, Y_3, at which point as income falls, consumption behavior follows a new short-run function $C_{S(2)}$.

Professor Friedman has approached the problem of the consumption-income relation in a novel way.[6] The underlying motivation and attitudes of consumers are similar to those described by Duesenberry, but Friedman makes consumption depend explicitly on what he calls "permanent income." The term "permanent" should not be taken too literally. It is measured as a weighted average of incomes of the recent past and can be viewed as an

---

[6] Milton Friedman, *A Theory of the Consumption Function,* National Bureau of Economic Research, Inc. (Princeton, N.J.: Princeton University Press, 1957).

approximation of an individual's expected future incomes. This is a long step toward making consumption depend on current wealth rather than on current income, since if expected future incomes are discounted to the present, the resulting figure is the present value of wealth. This wealth figure would include both human and nonhuman wealth.

Actual income differs from permanent income by an amount called "transitory income." Friedman believes, and his statistical evidence supports his belief, that consumers will not respond to an increase in income by a proportional increase in consumption; but if that income continues for several years, they will consume virtually all of it.

The rigid statement is that the marginal propensity to consume out of permanent income is one, and that the marginal propensity to consume transitory income is zero. Transitory income is in the nature of a windfall gain or loss, and, therefore, is not incorporated into the consuming units' budget. Instead, people tend to use transitory income to pay off debts or to accumulate assets for future use when income might fall or when heavy expenses might arise.

It is important to keep in mind when evaluating the permanent income hypothesis that the consumption variable is not synonymous with consumer outlay or spending, but is a measure of current household use of resources for utility. Thus, if an individual were to receive a significant windfall, part of it may very well be spent to purchase an automobile; but consumption would be increased only to the extent that the new car provided more or better service than the old one during the income period.

Another observation that is consistent with the permanent income hypothesis is that people with fluctuating incomes do not alter their consumption patterns to conform with the variation in their incomes. Someone with a great amount of wealth might in a particular year have a very small or even negative income. Such an individual would not be expected to reduce consumption drastically. On the other side of the issue, persons whose income is very stable and who can forecast that their future income will be roughly the same as their current income tend to consume most of their income continuously.

The Life Cycle Hypothesis

Another theory explaining consumption behavior of individuals from which an aggregate consumption function can be derived is the "life cycle hypothesis."[7] In this theory the individual is viewed as wishing to maximize lifetime utility from consumption on the basis of expected lifetime income. As in Friedman's hypothesis, short-run changes in income would not be expected to alter consumption behavior seriously. Wealth rather than current income dominates the consumption-saving decision process.

[7] The earliest presentation of this theory was in Franco Modigliani and R. E. Brumberg, "Utility Analysis and the Consumption Function: An Interpretation of Cross-Section Data," in *Post-Keynesian Economics,* edited by K. K. Kurihara (New Brunswick, N.J.: Rutgers University Press, 1954). Another important contribution came in Albert Ando and F. Modigliani, "The 'Life Cycle' Hypothesis of Saving: Aggregate Implications and Tests," *American Economic Review,* Vol. LIII, No. 1, Part 1 (March, 1963), pp. 55–84.

Over an individual's lifetime a certain pattern of income receipts can be expected. Typically, income is very small during the earliest years, rises in the middle years, reaches a peak, and then declines with a sometimes precipitous drop upon retirement from the labor force. If lifetime utility is to be maximized, consumption will have to be allocated in some rational way. The consumption pattern need not closely follow expected income flows. Imagine two contrasting extreme cases of income recipients. A young man who has just graduated from college, but who happens to be the best basketball player in the country, will have an extremely high income for a relatively short number of years. If he were to consume during those years commensurate with his salary, his ability to consume in the future would be quite low. A young woman may know that in 20 years she will be the recipient of a very large inheritance. She would not be expected to deny herself the pleasures of consumption in the years prior to the receipt of the inheritance. Both young people might have identical spending patterns over their lifetimes, with the basketball player saving in the early years and making the resources available for use by others, and the heir being a borrower (and dissaver) during the early years.

Most people are somewhere between these extremes but would exhibit the same sort of propensities. Whatever the expected income pattern may be, a person will also have a utility function relating expected utility from consumption in the present and in all future periods. In noneconomic terms one would say that very young children have fewer needs than adults, that people in their child-raising years have more needs, and that older people again have fewer needs. If this sort of pattern reflects an individual's views of future utility potentials, that person might equate a dollar's worth of present spending with a dollar and a half of spending ten years from now. An important part of this decision is that the further into the future the projection is made, the lower the probability that the person will be alive to enjoy the future consumption. On the other hand, some people may have powerful psychological fears of not having purchasing power when they get older, or others may have a strong desire to leave an estate to their heirs.

Whatever the motivation, the life cycle hypothesis predicts that consumption behavior in the aggregate will be less variable than income. Saving, of course, will then have to adjust, being large when income is unusually large and being small or negative when income is small.

A large proportion of the low-income earners are either quite young or quite old. According to the life cycle hypothesis, both groups would have low average saving (or even dissaving) whereas the large proportion of high income earners are those in their middle years who have a higher average propensity to save. Thus, the life cycle theory predicts a relatively flat cross section consumption function. It also says that saving and consumption depend partly on the age distribution of the population.

The life cycle theorists stress that current income depends on wealth and that current wealth is the result of saving in the past. This means that even though the marginal propensity to consume current income is relatively low, over the long run the average propensity to consume increases as wealth increases. The underlying rationale for this observation is that a change in current income has relatively little impact on wealth and so relatively little influence on current consumption, but in the longer run the stock of wealth increases as income increases and therefore, by hypothesis, consumption will increase proportionately.

Clearly the explanation of consumption behavior is not a simple thing. Many economists, besides those mentioned, have made important contributions to the study, and the research continues. In particular, much of the work discussed here involves consumption rather than household expenditures. For forecasting and employment analysis, the steps of developing an expenditure theory from a consumption theory are still in the works.

STAGNATION THESIS

The prolonged depression of the 1930s and some of the ideas developed by John Maynard Keynes led some economists to develop the stagnation thesis. Two factors are prominent in this point of view. The first is that investment opportunities become less attractive as an economy develops, and therefore the long-run marginal efficiency of capital declines. The second is that consumers do not spend as large a proportion of their income as incomes go up since they already have satisfied a large proportion of their wants. In other words, the long-run average propensity to consume is a declining one.

Even if the average propensity to consume does not decline, a problem may develop because of the long-run decline in the marginal efficiency of capital. As more and more capital is put into place year after year, income must also increase if unemployment is to be avoided. As income increases, savings will also increase, and this means that still more investment opportunities must be found. This is no problem in a rapidly developing economy; but it can become a problem in a mature economy, especially if innovations are not being developed, since the marginal efficiency of presently used types of capital decreases as more and more of it is built.

During the days of rapid economic development the real problem was to get sufficient savings to meet the demands for capital investment. This demand was due to several factors, one of the foremost being the necessity to provide for the needs of a rapidly growing population. More food, clothing, shelter, services, and the like were required by more people, and large-scale capital investment was required to provide these.

There was also a large demand for capital because of the development of new territories in the United States and in South America, Australia, and Africa. Means of transportation had to be developed to penetrate into the new territory. New houses had to be built, new shopping centers had to be developed, wholesale centers had to be established. Gradually manufacturing also developed, and the new territory became integrated into the total economy. At this stage the demand for new capital decreased because it now depended more on the replacement of plant and equipment and the increased demand due to gradual increases in population, changes in technology, and the like. The rapid development of new industries also led to a large-scale demand for capital. This was especially true of the durable consumer goods fields, such as automobiles, radios, and refrigerators. These industries also made use of highly developed assembly lines to manufacture their products, and these required a larger proportion of capital in relationship to output than was the case in industry in general.

Those who have argued for the stagnation thesis hold that the factors making for large-scale investment have largely disappeared as economies have become more mature. Population growth has slowed down, as was especially apparent in the 1930s. The physical frontier is gone, in the United States at least. Especially during the 1930s, new industries were not being developed as fast as in earlier periods. Moreover, in the face of reduced investment opportunities, there was a tendency for savings to increase. A larger percentage of people were receiving an income high enough to save a significant proportion of it. Saving was also taking place to an increasing degree through insurance and annuity programs. The advocates of the stagnation thesis hold that this combination of factors will result in a chronic tendency for planned saving to outrun investment opportunities except for short boom periods due to wars and speculation. The result is chronic unemployment in the labor force.

The stagnation thesis has not been as popular in recent years as it was in the 1930s. Population again grew rapidly for a time and new industries were developed on a large scale as the electronic and atomic age came into being. Automatic factories have been developed in several fields. Machines are again being developed to replace labor, and the amount of investment in capital required to produce many products is going up. Some still hold that these are temporary phenomena and that stagnation will return in a few years at the most.

During the period of the late 1950s in which unemployment was somewhat higher than in earlier postwar years, the stagnation thesis was again used by some to justify expanded government investment programs to stimulate the rate of growth of the economy. It is, of course, possible for an economy to become stagnant in the sense used in this thesis. There is, however, little evidence to indicate that the needs for capital investment are being saturated. In fact, the supply of capital goods may well be growing too slowly to meet all of the demands of our economy.

There is also no proof of any long-run tendency for the propensity to consume to decline. Demands of consumers for new goods and services have kept pace with increases in income. In fact, in many postwar years the problem was not one of insufficient consumption expenditures but of insufficient saving to meet the needs of the economy without credit expansion and inflation.

Economic Growth and Fluctuations

The stagnation thesis discussion leads us into the study of long-run economic problems. We can visualize the situation by means of Figure 10-6. First, we observe that the equilibrium levels of income where $s = i$ are only short-run equilibriums because if investment is a positive amount, it means that the stock of capital is increasing each period during which this situation holds. For short periods of time, this may not be very significant because the amount of investment may be a relatively small fraction of the total stock of capital.

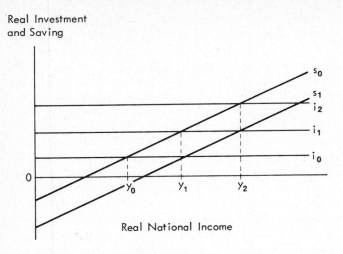

Figure 10-6

Saving, Investment, and Full Employment

But if this short-run equilibrium exists for many periods, the stock of capital grows by i amount each period and must become a significant proportion of the total.

The growth of the capital stock must have some impact because capital is productive. At this point it is necessary to be clear on whether we are speaking of real or money valued national income. If y_0 is real national income, then factors of production other than capital must be unemployed as investment takes place since the given level of output can be produced with the larger amount of capital goods and a smaller amount of labor. The severity of the unemployment of labor depends upon the nature of the new capital or how productive it is in terms of the displacement of labor.

Presumably under these conditions prices and wages would continuously fall, and if the Pigou effect is operative, the saving function would decline, causing real income to increase to absorb the unemployed. In this context the question is: Would the saving function shift downward at a rate fast enough to exactly compensate for the increased productivity of capital caused by its increase in the amount i?

To be more explicit, refer to Figure 10-6. If study would indicate that when i_0 amount of investment took place, income would have to increase to y_1 for employment of labor to remain constant, would the saving function shift to precisely the position represented by s_1? The answer depends most importantly on the degree of flexibility of prices and wages, and on the responsiveness of the public to these price changes in their saving behavior via the Pigou effect.

The stagnationists did not consider the Pigou effect. They reasoned that if income had to increase to y_1, investment would have to shift upward to i_1, but $i_1 > i_0$ so in the following period income would have to increase by more than the difference between y_0 and y_1. Income would have to increase to some level of income such as y_2 to maintain employment. The problem of economic growth then would seem to be that saving and investment must increase at exactly the right speed.

Two considerations led the stagnation theorists to conclude that government spending was the solution to the problem. First, as pointed out above, these economists were pessimistic about the ability of the economic system to find profitable investment opportunities in ever-growing amounts sufficient to keep up the necessary growth rate. Second, to the extent that government spending is included in i and does not replace labor, the problem is avoided.

Since a downward shifting saving function is also a cure for the problem, government policy directed at achieving this end is also frequently suggested. While it can be accomplished in a number of indirect ways, the direct method would be by either lowering income taxes or by increasing transfer payments.

Domar's Growth Theory

In the preceding section it was pointed out that a positive amount of investment would lead to unemployment of labor unless income continuously increased. Excess capacity of capital might also occur that would discourage any further investment. In that event national income would decline. We are forced to the conclusion that Schumpeter was correct (refer to Chapter 6) in saying that the only complete static equilibrium is one in which saving and investment are both zero.

Growth theorists search for another kind of equilibrium, a dynamic equilibrium where savings and investment will be equal at growing levels of income. The first growth theory to be presented is that of Professor Evsey Domar.[8]

Central to the Domar model is the concept of the increase in productive capacity of the economy caused by an increase in its capital stock. Domar uses the symbol σ (lower case sigma) to stand for the ratio of the change in the amount of output that can be produced in the system (ΔY^*) divided by the increase in the stock of capital which brought about the increase in potential output. The letter K is used to stand for the total amount of capital goods in the system, so ΔK (the change in that stock) is by definition the amount of investment (I). Thus, $\sigma = \dfrac{\Delta Y^*}{I}$. If $\sigma = .25$, the ability of the system to produce goods and services will increase by $25 per time period for every $100 of new investment (in constant dollars).[9]

To demonstrate the principle involved, Domar uses a very simple national income model. It is the same as the first model we presented in Chapter 7 except that he assumes that the long-run consumption function, and therefore also the saving function, are proportional. The model is:

---

[8] Evsey D. Domar, *Essays in the Theory of Economic Growth* (New York: Oxford University Press, 1957). Essay IV is a straightforward nonmathematical treatment. The same model with the mathematical derivations is found in Essay III.

[9] The value of σ incorporates the fact that some of the old capital may be retired early by virtue of the introduction of the new. In other words, the new investment might be capable of producing $30 of new output per period, but since some old capital was retired, the net increase in output per $100 of investment might be $25.

$Y = C + I$
$C = bY$, which implies that $S = (1 - b) Y$ or $S = \alpha Y$
$I = \bar{I}$

If $b = .88$, $1 - b = \alpha = .12$, and $\bar{I} = \$18$, $Y = \dfrac{\bar{I}}{\alpha} = \dfrac{\$18}{.12} = \$150$.

Since $\sigma = .25$, the addition to the stock of capital of \$18 means that in the next period potential output will be $.25 \times \$18 = \$4.5 (= \Delta Y^*)$ larger than it had been. If "full employment" of capital is to continue, national income or aggregate demand must also increase by \$4.5. Since the multiplier in this model is $\dfrac{1}{\alpha} = \dfrac{1}{.12} = 8.33$, investment must increase by \$.54 (i.e., $\Delta Y = \dfrac{1}{\alpha} \times \Delta I = 4.5 = 8.33 \times .54$). If investment increases by \$.54, saving will also increase by \$.54 because $\alpha = \dfrac{\Delta S}{\Delta Y} = \dfrac{12}{100} = \dfrac{.54}{4.5}$.

The increase in investment of \$.54 means that investment (and saving) in the second period will be 18.54, which implies that productive capacity (ΔY^*) and aggregate demand (ΔY) must both increase (by an equal amount) in the following period. To maintain full employment, $\Delta Y^* = \Delta Y$.

Since $\Delta Y^* = \sigma I$, $\Delta Y = \Delta I \dfrac{1}{\alpha}$, and $\sigma I = \Delta I \dfrac{1}{\alpha}$, multiply both sides of the equation by α: $\alpha \sigma I = \Delta I$, and divide both sides by I: $\alpha \sigma = \dfrac{\Delta I}{I}$.

The right-hand side is the rate of change of investment necessary to keep the change in potential output equal to the actual change in output or income, that is, $\Delta Y^* = \Delta Y$. The left-hand side tells us what this rate of growth must be. In our example $\alpha = .12$, and $\sigma = .25$, so the rate of growth in investment per period needed to maintain the full use of capital is $.12 \times .25 = .03$ or 3 percent.

In this example income must also increase by 3 percent.[10] Our original income was 150 and increased by 4.5 $\left(\dfrac{4.5}{150} = 3\% \right)$. This can be seen directly by observing that the rate of change of income can be expressed as $\dfrac{\Delta Y}{Y}$, and $\Delta Y = \dfrac{\Delta I}{\alpha}$, and $Y = \dfrac{I}{\alpha}$; thus $\dfrac{\Delta Y}{Y} = \dfrac{\frac{\Delta I}{\alpha}}{\frac{I}{\alpha}} = \dfrac{\Delta I}{I} = \alpha \sigma = .12 \times .25 = 3\%$.

One shouldn't take all of this too literally: our economy is much too complex to be represented by this model. However, the model does indicate that both the productivity of capital, as expressed in σ, and the habits of the population with respect to saving (and consumption), as expressed in α, influence the degree to which income must grow in order to avoid falling into a recession.

There is another side to the problem. If aggregate demand increases at too rapid a rate relative to the growth of productive capacity, inflation will result.

---

[10] This result depends upon the assumption used here that the marginal propensity to save and the average propensity to save are the same.

Thus, according to this theory, economic growth must proceed at a particular rate to maintain full employment and stable prices. A faster rate results in inflation. A slower rate results in unemployment. This problem has been described as the "tightrope" or "knife-edge" problem. We look more closely at this aspect in Harrod's growth model.[11]

Harrod's Growth Theory

In the Domar model, investment or the change in investment was treated as exogenously determined. Domar's problem was to show the required change in investment to achieve an equilibrium rate of growth in national income. Sir Roy Harrod, on the other hand, uses a version of the accelerator as the equation explaining investment: $I = A\Delta Y$. In order to switch to Harrod's symbols, we note that what we have called A, Harrod calls C_r — in other words, the "capital requirement."

In our discussion of the acceleration principle, we pointed out that the equation could be looked upon both as a behavior relation and as a technical production relation. Harrod uses both meanings. As a behavior relation, $I = C_r\Delta Y$ is the demand by business for new capital. If income increased in the last period, investment would be positive in the current period; but if income fell, investment would be negative as businesses failed to replace worn-out capital. As a behavior relation, the equation expresses the intentions to invest and may, therefore, be different from the actual amount of investment. In the Harrod model, the burden of adjustment in a disequilibrium situation is entirely on investors since Harrod assumes that savers actually save the amount they intend to save.

The rationale behind Harrod's acceleration-type investment demand function is that the change in income from the last period to the present serves as a forecast of income (aggregate demand) in the next period. In order to produce goods and services sufficient to supply the amount demanded, new plant and equipment will be needed. Hence, new investment will be proportional to the change in income, the proportion being determined by the productivity of capital; that is, $I = C_r\Delta Y$.

Like Domar, Harrod uses a proportional long-run saving function without a time lag: $S_t = sY_t$. The concept of the warranted rate of growth is central to his analysis. It is the rate of growth in national income which keeps saving and investment equal and is labeled G_w. Since (1) $I_t = C_r(Y_t - Y_{t-1})$ and (2) $S_t = sY_t$, the equilibrium condition $I_t = S_t$ implies $C_r(Y_t - Y_{t-1}) = sY_t$. Dividing both sides by s gives (3) $Y_t = \dfrac{C_r}{s}(Y_t - Y_{t-1})$. $Y_t - Y_{t-1}$ is the change in income from one period to the next (call it ΔY). The rate of change in income is $\dfrac{\Delta Y}{Y}$. From Equation (3) we find that $\dfrac{\Delta Y}{Y} = \dfrac{s}{C_r}$. This is the warranted rate of growth (G_w).

---

[11] Sir Roy Harrod, *Towards a Dynamic Economics: Some Recent Developments of Economic Theory and Their Application to Policy.* (Toronto: Macmillan Co. of Canada, Ltd., 1948).

If income grows at precisely this warranted rate, the amount of goods and services demanded will be exactly enough to employ all of the new capital as well as the previously existing stock of capital. Entrepreneurs who planned the investment expenditures made the right decisions, and will continue to plan to increase their investments in accordance with the forecasting procedure used before.

While income is growing at the warranted rate, income increases by just enough to generate the amount of saving needed to supply the resources for investment. To summarize the growth process described by the warranted rate of growth, output measured by consumption plus saving exactly balances with the demand for the output by consumers and investors.

Harrod finds no reason to believe that the economy would actually grow at the rate prescribed by the warranted rate, and herein lies the difficulty. If the actual growth rate (G) is greater than G_w, income will grow at a still faster rate, diverging farther and farther from G_w. For instance, suppose the propensity to save should suddenly decline to a figure less than equilibrium requires, which, of course, means that consumption demand would increase. This would mean that the output forecast on which investment expenditures were based was too small. Inventories would decline (unintentionally). Capital equipment would wear out faster than expected. In other words, intended investment would be greater than actual investment, so in the next planning period businesses would increase their demands for investment; however, this would aggravate the problem still more, leading to a greater rate of growth of actual income.

If income expands faster than it should to maintain G_w, output has not increased as much as has aggregate demand. The reverse case, that is, where output increases faster than aggregate demand, will occur when $G < G_w$. A higher rate of saving or a lower demand for investment would bring about this result. An increase in saving (a decrease in consumption) or a decrease in investment demand would mean that output would exceed sales, inventories would build up (unintentionally), and capital would not be fully utilized. Actual investment, in this case, would be greater than intended investment which would, in turn, reduce demand for capital still further and income would decline. In this case, too, the actual growth rate would get continuously farther away from the warranted rate.

Harrod's warranted rate of growth is the rate that will assure the full utilization of the capital stock of the economy and thereby assures the condition of equality of saving and investment. But Harrod also points out that if population and the labor force are also growing, there must be some rate of growth that will absorb all of the additions to the labor force into employment. The rate of growth needed to maintain exactly full employment — neither unemployment nor over full employment — he terms the natural rate of growth. The situation is complicated in that not only does the labor force grow but also the productivity of labor increases through the growth of capital and its quality and by the improvement of the labor force itself through education and training.

Harrod finds no systematic reason for believing that the rate of growth appropriate to both the growth of capital and labor will be the same. Indeed, he finds it highly unlikely that they would be close enough to avoid difficulties. What does happen when the natural rate and the warranted rate differ?

The actual rate of growth in output is restricted by the growth of the labor force and its productivity. Thus, if the natural rate is less than the warranted rate, actual income will grow too slowly and chronic stagnation will result. As we have just seen, under these conditions where $G_w > G$, actual investment, including unintended investment in capital and inventory, will exceed planned or intended investment.

The opposite case occurs when the labor force is growing fast enough to cause the natural rate of growth to be higher than that warranted by the need to keep capital utilized. In such a situation $G_n > G_w$ and $G > G_w$, which would lead to continuously expanding output as actual investment would be below intended investment.

QUESTIONS

1. Graph and explain the construction of an after-tax consumption function where consumption is a linear function of disposable income and taxes are an upward curving function of national income.
2. List the attributes of families or individuals whom you would expect to produce a high level of consumption relative to income.
3. List the attributes of families or individuals whom you would expect to produce a low propensity to consume.
4. Show that a high APC could be consistent with a low MPC and vice versa.
5. Consider how various types of consumer wealth might increase and/or decrease consumption out of current income.
6. Develop the thesis that the true consumption function is based on expected lifetime income rather than on current income. Remember that borrowing, lending, and repayment are always possible, and that expected future income and expenses can be discounted to the present to give a present value estimate.
7. Using the Domar growth model, determine the rate at which income would have to grow to maintain full employment of capital if the marginal (and average) propensity to consume were 8/10ths and if the ratio $\frac{\Delta Y^*}{I}$ were .20.
8. Explain the following of Harrod's terms:
   (a) Warranted rate of growth.   (c) Actual rate of growth.
   (b) Natural rate of growth.

SUGGESTED READINGS

Ackley Gardner. *Macroeconomic Theory.* New York: The Macmillan Co., Publishers, 1961.

Domar, Evsey D. *Essays in the Theory of Economic Growth.* New York: Oxford University Press, 1957.

Duesenberry, J. S. *Income, Saving, and the Theory of Consumer Behavior.* Cambridge, Mass.: Harvard University Press, 1949.

Ferber, R. A. *A Study of Aggregate Consumption Functions.* New York: National Bureau of Economic Research, Inc., 1953.

Friedman, Milton. *A Theory of the Consumption Function.* National Bureau of Economic Research, Inc., Princeton, N.J.: Princeton University Press, 1957.

Harrod, Sir Roy. *Towards a Dynamic Economics: Some Recent Developments of Economic Theory and their Application to Policy.* Toronto: Macmillan Co. of Canada, Ltd., 1948.

Houthakker, H. S., and L. D. Taylor. *Consumer Demand in the United States.* Cambridge, Mass.: Harvard University Press, 1970.

Katona, G. *The Powerful Consumer: Psychological Studies of the American Economy.* New York: McGraw-Hill Book Co., Inc. 1960.

————, and E. Mueller. *Consumer Expectations, 1953–1956.* Ann Arbor, Mich.: University of Michigan Institute for Social Research. Survey Research Center.

Kuznets, Simon. *National Income: A Summary of Findings.* New York: National Bureau of Economic Research, Inc., 1946.

Smithies, Arthur. "Forecasting Postwar Demand," *Econometrica,* Vol. 13 (January, 1945).

Veblen, Thorstein B. *The Theory of the Leisure Class: An Economic Study of Institutions.* New York: The Modern Library, 1934.

PROBLEMS ON PART 3

1. Given the following model:

$$Y = C + I + G$$
$$C = a + bY$$
$$I = I_0 + iY$$
$$G = G_0$$

$a = \$40$ billion
$b = 8/10$
$I_0 = \$30$ billion
$i = 1/10$
$G_0 = \$50$ billion

(a) Calculate the equilibrium values of Y, C, I, S.

(b) Assume that autonomous investment (I_0) changes from $30 to $40 billion. Calculate the new values of Y, C, I, S. What is the value of the investment multiplier?

(c) Draw an accurate graph reflecting the original model and the change introduced in (b).

(d) Construct a period table showing the above events over time.

2. Using the *Federal Reserve Bulletin,* account for the changes in the monetary base to the latest monthly figures from the same month one year earlier. Over this same span of time, what was the change in the money supply? The actual money expansion multiplier is M/B. What was it for your time period? Evaluate the behavior of the parameters in the money supply model on page 184 to determine whether any of them had a significant effect on the money supply.

3. (a) Using the *Survey of Current Business,* the *Federal Reserve Bulletin,* or any other reliable source, construct a table for the years 1955 to the present showing annual data for the following series:
   (1) Personal consumption expenditures.
   (2) Durable consumption goods.
   (3) Nondurable consumption goods plus services.
   (4) Disposable personal income.

(b) Using the data of (a), plot (1), (2), and (3) on the vertical axis using disposable personal income on the horizontal axis. Draw straight line approximations of each of these three sets of data. Estimate the vertical intercept and the marginal propensity to consume of each function.

(c) Visually, which functions appear to be most stable and which least stable? Calculate the APC for the personal consumption expenditures function for each year. How do the APCs compare to the MPC?

PART 4

THE RECORD
OF BUSINESS
FLUCTUATIONS

To understand the present and to face the future with any degree of assurance, it is necessary to study the past. Although history repeats itself, each period has new factors at work which lead to a somewhat different course of events than would have been predicted from a study of past events alone.

To analyze business fluctuations it is necessary to measure past changes as well as current changes. Data on total business activity and on activity in an industry or an individual business must be gathered. The basic elements of national income accounting and of measuring changes in production and prices were covered in Chapter 3. Chapter 11 is devoted to a description of the methods of measuring the various types of fluctuations in business and the relationships among them. Attention is first directed to methods of measuring seasonal fluctuations after which the various methods of estimating the trend are discussed. Two methods of arriving at the cycle are presented next. The first is the residual method in which the trend and the seasonal are removed. The second is the National Bureau of Economic Research method, which measures the cycle more directly.

To analyze the cyclical forces at work, it is necessary to study in some detail the empirical evidence on the behavior of the cycle. Such a study should determine which factors, if any, are typical and the extent of deviations from a typical pattern. Chapter 12 is devoted to a study of the statistical record of the cycle in general economic activity and in various sectors of the economy, and it also presents some data on the general cycle pattern as it develops during the expansion and contraction phases. Chapter 13 deals with the empirical evidence of other types of business fluctuations, such as those in construction and in agriculture.

Chapter 14 analyzes the record of business cycles from the beginning of World War II (1939) to the present. Most of the cycles during this period have been relatively minor when compared with the major depression which began in 1929 or even when compared with such recessions as those which began in 1920 or 1937. The recession which began in 1973, however, was longer and more severe than earlier postwar recessions.

CHAPTER 11

ANALYSIS OF TIME SERIES

In analyzing any series of economic data over a period of time, it is helpful to segregate the major types of factors that have influenced it. It may contain seasonal variations, it may have a long-term trend of growth or decline, there may be cyclical fluctuations, and it may also include irregular movements caused by strikes, droughts, floods, etc. To understand the influences that have affected a particular series, it is necessary to isolate each of these factors. These will be discussed in turn in this chapter.

MEASUREMENT OF SEASONAL VARIATIONS

Seasonal variations are the results of changes from one season of the year to the next that may be due to changes in the weather, in customs related to the seasons of the year or to holidays, or to the unequal number of days in the months in our calendar. A *seasonal variation* exists in any economic series when there is a regular pattern of variation in the series over a specific period of time, usually a year, but sometimes less than a year. This may be a regularly recurring pattern from year to year, or it may be a changing pattern in which changes are regularly taking place as, for example, an increased proportion year by year of December sales of a commodity for Christmas giving.

There are several reasons for calculating a measure of seasonal variation. The best form for data for measuring cyclical changes and for forecasting them is that in which an adjustment has been made to eliminate the effects of seasonal variations. This eliminates the effect of a regular factor and puts the major stress on the variable factors at work.

A measure of seasonal variation is also needed in developing a sales forecast for an industry, and especially for an individual business. The basic forecast is made without regard to the seasonal variation. A measure of seasonal variation is then used to put the data in the annual forecast of sales on a month-by-month basis throughout the year.

Before calculating a measure of seasonal variation, the analyst should be sure that regular variations of this type exist. The factors causing the variations should be studied to make certain which factors cause an observed variation. Random factors may at times produce variations for a period of time that appear to be regular. If a measure of seasonal variation is calculated from them, it is not only useless for analysis and prediction but also adds a source of error that may make such analysis and prediction impossible.

The most widely used measure of the seasonal variation is found by the ratio-to-moving-average method. A 12-month moving average is calculated from monthly data of sales or production for a period of several years. Since such a moving average always includes each of the 12 months of the year, it averages out the seasonal fluctuations in the data. This means that the moving average contains the trend, the cycle, and any irregular factors that may have affected the data. By dividing the original monthly data by the 12-month moving average, which includes everything but the seasonal, it is possible to obtain a measure of the seasonal variation.

The basis for this procedure may be shown in equation form, using the following symbols: T for the trend, S for the seasonal factor, C for the cyclical factor, and I for irregular factors.

The original data may then be expressed in terms of the above symbols as $T \times S \times C \times I$. The 12-month moving average averages out the seasonal factor and, therefore, contains the trend and cyclical and irregular factors. It may be expressed as $T \times C \times I$.

Dividing the original data containing trend, seasonal, cyclical, and irregular factors by the 12-month moving average containing the trend, cyclical, and irregular factors gives a measure of the seasonal factor as shown below.

$$\frac{T \times S \times C \times I}{T \times C \times I} = S$$

The following hypothetical example of the calculation of the seasonal index of the sales of the Super Ice Cream Co. illustrates the method. For simplicity a period of 4 years has been used, but in actual practice it is best to use a period of 10 or 12 years. Monthly sales from 1975–1978 are shown below.

Table 11-1
Monthly Sales of the Super Ice Cream Company,
1975–1978
(Thousands of Dollars)

	1975	1976	1977	1978
January	50	52	55	58
February	60	62	65	68
March	77	79	83	86
April	96	99	102	106
May	137	140	144	149
June	158	163	165	170
July	167	174	175	180
August	159	165	166	171
September	108	114	116	120
October	75	78	81	85
November	61	62	64	67
December	54	56	58	61

Source: Hypothetical data.

Table 11-2

Calculation of a 12-Month Moving Average of the Monthly Sales of the Super Ice Cream Company, 1975–1978

	12-Month Moving Total Centered at the 7th Month[1]				12-Month Moving Average Centered at the 7th Month			
	1975	1976	1977	1978	1975	1976	1977	1978
January		1219	1263	1297		101.58	105.25	108.08
February		1226	1264	1302		102.17	105.33	108.50
March		1232	1265	1307		102.67	105.42	108.92
April		1238	1267	1311		103.17	105.58	109.25
May		1241	1270	1315		103.42	105.83	109.58
June		1242	1272	1318		103.50	106.00	109.83
July	1202	1244	1274	1321	100.17	103.67	106.17	110.08
August	1204	1247	1277		100.33	103.92	106.42	
September	1206	1250	1280		100.50	104.17	106.67	
October	1208	1254	1283		100.67	104.50	106.92	
November	1211	1257	1287		100.92	104.75	107.25	
December	1214	1261	1292		101.17	105.08	107.67	

Source: Table 11-1.

[1] Actually the average for the first set of data from January through December, 1975, is the average for the middle of the year, that is, between June and July. For greater refinement, the July figure can be calculated by taking this figure and the figure between July and August found by averaging the data from February, 1975, through January, 1976, and averaging these two figures.

The first step is to find a 12-month moving average of the sales data. To do this, it is necessary to find a 12-month moving total and then to divide it by 12 to get the moving average. These calculations are shown in Table 11-2 on page 237.

The original data are divided by the 12-month moving average and the result is expressed as a percentage to determine the year-by-year seasonal factors. For example, the sales figure of $52,000 for January of 1976 is divided by the 12-month moving average for that month of 101.58 to get a seasonal factor of 51.2 percent. The results of these calculations are shown below in Table 11-3.

Table 11-3

Original Monthly Sales Data of the Super Ice Cream Company for 1975–1978 Divided by the 12-Month Moving Average

	1975	1976	1977	1978
January		51.2	52.3	53.7
February		60.7	61.7	62.7
March		76.9	78.7	79.0
April		96.0	96.6	97.0
May		135.4	136.1	136.0
June		157.5	155.7	154.8
July	166.7	167.9	164.8	163.5
August	158.5	158.8	156.0	
September	107.5	109.4	108.7	
October	74.5	74.6	75.8	
November	60.4	59.2	59.7	
December	53.4	53.3	53.9	

Source: Tables 11-1 and 11-2.

Since unusual factors may affect the seasonal pattern in any one year, the seasonal factors for several years are averaged to obtain a typical figure for each month. If necessary, these typical seasonal factors are then adjusted up or down proportionately to make them total 1,200 percent or an average of 100 percent a month. These steps are shown in Table 11-4 on page 239.

When a longer period of years is used, it is often desirable to find some average other than the arithmetic mean to arrive at a typical seasonal pattern. This may be done by placing the items in an array, that is, arranging them from low to high and then taking the middle item or median, or by taking an average of the middle three or five items. It is also possible to use a modified arithmetic mean, that is, to eliminate any unusually low or high items and then take an arithmetic average of the rest.

If the seasonal variation in any field changes, it is necessary to alter the procedure used in finding typical seasonal factors. Instead of calculating an average January figure, for example, the proper procedure is to plot the January

Table 11-4
Calculation of the Refined Seasonal Factors from the Crude Seasonals of the Super Ice Cream Company

	Jan.	Feb.	Mar.	Apr.	May	June
1975						
1976	51.2	60.7	76.9	96.0	135.4	157.5
1977	52.3	61.7	78.7	96.6	136.1	155.7
1978	53.7	62.7	79.0	97.0	136.0	154.8
Average Seasonal	52.4	61.7	78.2	96.5	135.8	156.0
Seasonal Index	52.4	61.6	78.1	96.4	135.7	155.9

	July	Aug.	Sept.	Oct.	Nov.	Dec.
1975	166.7	158.5	107.5	74.5	60.4	53.4
1976	167.9	158.8	109.4	74.6	59.2	53.3
1977	164.8	156.0	108.7	75.8	59.7	53.9
1978	163.5					
Average Seasonal	165.7	157.8	108.5	75.0	59.8	53.5
Seasonal Index	165.6	157.7	108.4	74.9	59.8	53.5

Source: Table 11-3.

crude seasonal figures for the period being studied and then to draw a trend line showing the change that is taking place. It is usually best to draw this trend line freehand, especially if it is being done by someone who has a thorough knowledge of the changes taking place. The trend may also be fitted by means of a formula either for a straight line or for a curve. The use of such formulas is considered more fully in the next section of this chapter on the measurement of the secular trend. The same thing is done for each of the 12 months. The current seasonal factors are then found by projecting the trend line for each of the 12 months one year ahead and then adjusting these figures on a proportionate basis to add to 1,200.

A seasonal index such as that calculated from the sales of the Super Ice Cream Company shows the percentage of each month's sales in relationship to average monthly sales as 100. For example, January sales are 52.4 percent of the average, July sales 165.7 percent, and so on. It is helpful at times to express the seasonal factor for each month as the average percentage of the business for the year done in that month. January sales in this case are $\frac{52.4}{1,200}$ of the year's business or 4.4 percent. Figures for each month as a typical percentage of the year's business are shown in Table 11-5.

Table 11-5

Typical Seasonal Factors
for the Super Ice Cream Company
Expressed as a Percentage of the Year's Business

January 4.4	May 11.3	September 9.0
February 5.1	June 13.0	October 6.2
March 6.5	July 13.8	November 5.0
April 8.0	August 13.2	December 4.5

Source: Tables 11-1 and 11-4.

MEASUREMENT OF THE SECULAR TREND

After the seasonal variation has been calculated and then eliminated from a series of data, it is possible to calculate the long-term or secular trend. This trend is the persistent underlying movement that has taken place in a series of data over a period of time long enough to cover several business cycles. It is the basic growth or decline that would be there if there were no cycle.

In the absence of the cycle the growth of any economic series, such as the production of a new product like microwave ovens, would probably approximate a curve like an elongated S. Any new industry will probably grow slowly at first, will then experience a period of rapid growth while it is becoming integrated into the economy, and will then grow more slowly in the relationship to increases in total economic activity.

The long-term trend in total economic activity in the United States has been a gradually rising one at a more or less constant rate. This is true in part because of increases in population that are continuing, although at a reduced rate. Increases in productivity and in the proportion of the population in the labor force have in all probability more than offset the decreasing rate of population growth. The quantity of capital in use has been increasing, and from all available evidence it appears that its effectiveness has also increased. American industry has likewise developed methods of economizing on materials and labor by improving design, by using by-products, by developing more efficient planning of work, and by introducing labor-saving techniques. In some fields natural resources of the highest quality are being depleted, but this factor leading to a slowdown in the rate of growth has been more than offset by the development of substitute materials and synthetic products. The system of distribution is also becoming more efficient through the introduction of self-service facilities and the development of larger, more economical units. The net result of all of these factors has been a more or less constant rate of increase in total economic activity.

There are several reasons for calculating a measure of the trend of an economic series. It can be used to project the most likely level of that series over a long period as, for example, 10 or 20 years in the future. Such a projection is only valid if the factors that led to its growth in the past continue. It is possible to calculate a measure of the trend from any series showing a significant change in magnitude over a period of time even when year-by-year changes are largely random, but projections made from such measures are useless. A measure of the trend is also useful as a means of analyzing the changes due to the business cycle in the past. In forecasting for a calendar quarter or a year ahead, the cycle may easily overshadow the trend so that a measure of the trend is of limited usefulness in short-run forecasting.

Since most economic series are in that stage in which they are growing in relationship to changes in population and national income, their current growth can be effectively measured by a straight line trend, even though an S-shaped curve would be needed to describe their total growth. The straight line that most closely approximates the growth in the total economy or in an industry which is growing in relation to increases in population and national income is the line of least squares. It is a line from which the sum of the squared vertical deviations is at a minimum. This line was not developed as a logical explanation of the growth in these series but was adapted from the physical sciences because it produces a good fit.

The following example shows the calculation of this line for the sales from 1974 through 1978 of the Super Ice Cream Company. This is much too short a period for calculating a trend, which should cover several cycles, but it is used to illustrate the method of getting the least-squares line. The formula for any straight line is $Y = a + bx$, in which Y is the trend value for each year expressed in terms of the original data. The symbol a is the average of the original data and establishes the height of the trend line in the middle year of the series. The slope of the line is determined by the value of b, which measures the annual deviation from the average value of the trend at the midpoint of the series. The following example shows its calculation.

Sales of Ice Cream for Each Year
(Thousands of Dollars)

1974	—	$1,080
1975	—	1,202
1976	—	1,244
1977	—	1,274
1978	—	1,321

Year	Production Y	Years from Midpoint x	xY	x^2
1	1,080	−2	−2,160	4
2	1,202	−1	−1,202	1
3	1,244	0	0	0
4	1,274	1	1,274	1
5	1,321	2	2,642	4
	6,121	0	554	10

The value of a is found by dividing the sum of the original data (Y) by the number of years or N; thus, $a = \dfrac{\Sigma Y}{N} = \dfrac{6,121}{5} = 1,224.2$. The value of b is found from the following formula: $b = \frac{\Sigma xY}{\Sigma x^2}$. In this case it is $\frac{554}{10}$ or 55.4. The straight line formula is then $Y = 1224.2 + 55.4x$. The values of Y (in thousands of dollars) for each year are found by adding and subtracting 55.4 for each year from the midyear, as shown below.

1974	1,113.4	(1,224.2 minus 2 × 55.4)
1975	1,168.8	(1,224.2 minus 1 × 55.4)
1976	1,224.2	(average value)
1977	1,279.6	(1,224.2 plus 1 × 55.4)
1978	1,335.0	(1,224.2 plus 2 × 55.4)

At times it may be desirable to express the long-term trend by means of a curved line rather than a straight line. This should be done, however, only if the analyst is convinced that such a curve actually represents the basic growth of the economic series at hand. Formulas are available for many types of curves such as the second degree parabola, the compound interest curve, and several different forms of S-shaped curves.[1] In most cases it is probably better to draw a trend line freehand rather than to use a formula that may not accurately express the rate of growth.

MEASUREMENT OF CYCLICAL FLUCTUATIONS

One of the most complete definitions of the business cycle has been developed by the National Bureau of Economic Research. The working concept used in its research is as follows:

Business cycles are a type of fluctuation found in the aggregate economic activity of nations that organize their work mainly in business enterprises: a cycle consists of expansions occurring at about the same time in many economic activities, followed by similarly general recessions, contractions, and revivals which merge into the expansion phase of the next cycle; this sequence of changes is recurrent but not periodic; in duration business cycles vary from more than one year to ten or twelve years; they are not divisible into shorter cycles of similar character with amplitudes approximating their own.[2]

Several important factors are included in this definition. They are listed as follows:

1. The business cycle refers to fluctuations in aggregate economic activity rather than in a particular industry or sector of the economy.

---

[1] For a discussion of the methods of deriving such curves, the reader is referred to a comprehensive text in statistics such as John R. Stockton and Charles T. Clark, *Introduction to Business and Economic Statistics* (5th ed.; Cincinnati: South-Western Publishing Company, 1975); and Werner Z. Hirsch, *Introduction to Modern Statistics* (New York: The Macmillan Company, 1959). The latter book also discusses a method of testing the significance of a measure of the trend which differentiates a measure based on random data from one based on a true trend. Such tests are also described for measures of seasonal and cyclic variations.

[2] Wesley C. Mitchell, *What Happens During Business Cycles* (New York: National Bureau of Economic Research, Inc., 1951), p. 6.

2. It is a phenomenon of an economy that has developed sufficiently to organize its activity in business units.
3. Expansions and contractions occur at about the same time in many phases of economic activity.
4. This sequence is recurrent but not periodic; that is, one cycle follows another in a continuous process but the cycles are not of equal length.
5. These cycles cannot be further subdivided into shorter cycles that have similar characteristics or the same amplitude of fluctuation from the low point of activity to the high point, and from the high point to the next low point.

A measure of the cycle is valuable for historical analysis of past cyclical movements. It cannot be used for mechanical projection into the future since cycles do not develop in a regular pattern. Some of the factors in the cycle do develop in somewhat similar ways, and there is some consistency in cycle patterns. This makes a measure of past cycles of some value as an aid in analyzing the present situation. Such elements of similarity in the cyclical pattern will be described in Chapter 12.

Several methods have been developed for measuring the business cycle. The most widely used is the residual method, in which the cycle is found by eliminating the other factors in the data. The National Bureau of Economic Research has developed a method of determining the cycle directly. It has become significant since more and more of the data from the intensive business cycle research of the National Bureau are being published in this form. These two methods will be considered in this section.

Residual Method

The residual method of calculating the cycle is based on the elimination of the trend and seasonal factors. The first step is to find a normal factor by multiplying the trend by the seasonal variation. The original data are then divided by the normal factor to obtain the cyclical and irregular factors. For example, the trend value of sales of the Super Ice Cream Company for 1974 was $1,113,400.[3] Since the trend of sales was increasing at a rate of $55,400 a year or $4,600 a month, the trend figure at an annual rate for January, 1974, is $1,088,100 ($1,113,400 minus $5\frac{1}{2} \times$ $4,600); for February, 1974, it is $1,092,700, and so on. The seasonal pattern shows that business in January is normally 4.4 percent of the business for the year. In this case normal sales in January are 4.4 percent of $1,088,100 or $47,900, normal sales in February are 5.1 percent of $1,092,700 or $55,700, and so on.

Deviations from such normal sales based on the trend and the cycle are due to cyclical and irregular factors. In the above examples actual sales for January, 1974, were $40,000 so they were $7,900 below normal due to cyclical and irregular factors.

Actual figures may also be expressed as a percentage of normal sales. Sales of $40,000 in January, 1974, for example, were 83.5 percent of normal sales of $47,900. Deviations due to cyclical and irregular factors for each month of 1974 are shown in Table 11-6.

---

[3] The trend value for 1974 is 1,113.4 expressed in thousands of dollars, or $1,113,400.

Table 11-6

Calculation of the Cyclical and Irregular Factors in the Sales of the Super Ice Cream Company for Each Month of 1974
(Thousands of Dollars)

Month	Trend (Monthly Figures at an Annual Rate)	Normal (Trend and Seasonal)	Actual Sales	Cyclical and Irregular Factors	
				Deviations from Normal	Percentage of Normal
January	1,088.1	47.9	40	−7.9	83.5
February	1,092.7	55.7	47	−8.7	84.4
March	1,097.3	71.3	64	−7.3	89.8
April	1,101.9	88.2	81	−7.2	91.8
May	1,106.5	125.0	122	−3.0	97.6
June	1,111.1	144.4	143	−1.4	99.0
July	1,115.7	154.0	154	0.0	100.0
August	1,120.3	147.9	149	+1.1	100.7
September	1,124.9	101.2	102	+0.8	100.8
October	1,129.5	70.0	71	+1.0	101.4
November	1,134.1	56.7	58	+1.3	102.3
December	1,138.8	51.2	49	−2.2	95.7

The irregular factors cannot be eliminated from the data but can be smoothed out by means of one or a series of moving averages. The most frequent procedure is to use a three-month moving average, since most irregular factors affect a series for only a few months.

This residual method leaves a cyclical pattern that is correct only if the trend and seasonal have been correctly measured. It shows the cycle completely divorced from the trend and may thus give a somewhat false impression, since the trend which has occurred during the period of the cycle is an integral part of the fluctuations that are taking place.

National Bureau Method

The National Bureau has developed a method for isolating and analyzing cyclical and irregular fluctuations directly, rather than by first calculating a normal figure and expressing these factors as deviations from the norm.

Since business fluctuations go on in a continuous process, it is necessary to agree on a consistent method of isolating individual cycles. A cycle could be considered as the interval from one peak of business activity to the next, from one trough or low point to the next, or perhaps in other ways. The National Bureau measures the cycle from trough to trough. Thus, a cycle begins at the initial trough at point *A* in the simplified pattern in Figure 11-1, develops to the peak at point *C*, and ends at the terminal trough at point *E*.

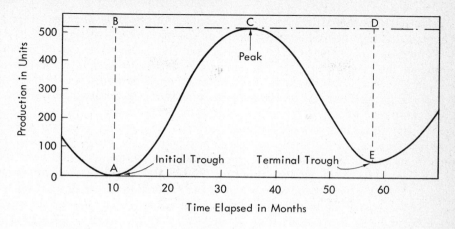

Figure 11-1

Simplified Cycle Pattern

It is also necessary to establish the dates of the initial trough and terminal trough to isolate a cycle and, for some purposes, to establish the peak. This may be done for a series by noting the low point in the cycle, the high point, and the following low point. These points should, of course, correspond in a general way to the time period of the cycle in total economic activity. Since there is no comprehensive series available that covers all economic activity, it is necessary to determine the dates of the cycle in total activity in a different way. The National Bureau has analyzed many areas of economic activity and on the basis of such study has determined when aggregate economic activity reached cyclical highs and lows. The Bureau has developed reference dates showing the time of the initial trough, the peak, and the terminal trough of cycles in aggregate economic activity. The cycle based on such reference dates measured from the initial trough through the peak to the terminal trough is called the *reference cycle*. For example, February, 1961, is the initial trough of the reference cycle in the 1960s; December, 1969, is the peak; and November, 1970, is the terminal trough.

To analyze the data for any series on economic activity the first step is to eliminate the variations due to seasonal factors. The seasonally adjusted data are then studied to find the specific cycles in the data by looking for troughs and peaks, which correspond in a general way to the reference dates for troughs and peaks. The specific cycles are measured from the initial trough through the peak to the terminal trough in those series that fluctuate in a similar manner to total economic activity. In those series that move in an inverse fashion from general economic activity, as for example commercial failures, the cycle is measured from the initial peak through the trough to the terminal peak.

To get a pattern of the cycle in any series, such as coke production, the seasonally adjusted data for each month of the specific cycle are averaged to find the cycle base. The seasonally adjusted figure for each month of the specific cycle is then expressed as a percentage of the cycle average or base. These percentage figures are referred to as specific cycle relatives.

The data on coke production are also analyzed in the same way during the period of the reference cycle. The data for each month during the reference cycle are averaged to find the cycle base, and then each month is expressed as a percentage of this average. These percentages are referred to as reference cycle relatives.

To obtain a fairly smooth-cycle pattern that is not affected materially by irregular factors, the full cycle is divided into nine stages. Stage I includes the three months centered at the initial trough; Stage V, the three months centered at the peak; and Stage IX, the three months centered at the terminal trough. Stages II to IV cover successive thirds of the expansion phase, and Stages VI to VIII successive thirds of contraction. The reference cycle relatives for Stage I are averaged to find the standing at Stage I, those for Stage II are averaged to find the standing at Stage II, and so on.

To follow the process of expansion and contraction, the cycle is also divided into eight segments. Segment 1 begins at the initial trough and runs to the midpoint of Stage II, Segment 2 runs from the midpoint of Stage II to the midpoint of Stage III, and so on. These procedures for dividing the cycle into segments are illustrated in Figure 11-2.

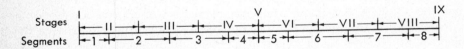

Figure 11-2

Cycle Stages and Segments

From such data it is possible to derive significant information about the cycle in any series. It is possible to calculate the timing of the cycle in any series by obtaining the number of months lead or lag of the specific cycle troughs and peaks from the reference cycle troughs and peaks. For example, the peak of the reference cycle was in June, 1929, but the peak of the specific cycle in coke production was in July, 1929, a lag of one month. The trough of the reference cycle was in March, 1933, but the trough of the coke production series came in August, 1932, a lead of 7 months.

The duration of the cycle may be calculated by finding the number of months in the specific cycle and also the time periods covered by expansion and contraction. For example, the average period of the cycle in coke production for the five specific cycles from 1914 through 1932 was 42.6 months. The average for expansion was 24.0 months and for contraction 18.6 months.

It is also possible to compare the length of the specific cycle with the length of the reference cycle, and to do the same for the expansion and contraction phases to see if any regular pattern exists. The specific cycle in coke production was 1.2 months shorter on the average between 1914 and 1932 than the reference cycle. The period of contraction was 1.6 months shorter and that of expansion .4 months longer on the average than the periods of expansion and contraction of the reference cycle. Data on the timing and duration of the cycles in coke production from 1914 to 1932 are shown in Table 11-7, page 248.

The amplitude of the specific cycle can be measured by the difference between the relatives at the initial trough and the peak, and between those at the peak and terminal trough. To reduce the influence of random factors, three-month averages centered on the troughs and peaks are used in making such calculations. For example, such an average specific cycle relative of coke production at the initial trough in November, 1927, was 105.5. The average relative at the peak in July, 1929, was 141.6 and at the terminal trough in August, 1932, it was 41.7. The amplitude of the rise was then 141.6 minus 105.5, or 36.1; the amplitude of the fall, 141.6 minus 41.7, or 99.9; and the combined amplitude of the rise and fall, 136.0. The amplitude may also be expressed on a per month basis. Table 11-8, page 249, gives an example, as calculated by Burns and Mitchell, for pig iron production showing the total amplitude of the rises and falls in this series as well as the per month amplitudes.

In a similar fashion the amplitude of the reference cycle may be calculated. For the rise, it is the difference between the reference cycle relatives at the dates of the initial trough and the peak of the reference cycle; and for the fall, the difference between the reference cycle relatives at the dates of the peak and the terminal trough of the reference cycle.

Plotting Data for Cyclical Comparisons

A visual presentation of cycle patterns may be obtained by plotting cycle relatives. This may be done for the reference cycle by plotting cycle relatives for each of the nine stages of the cycle from the initial trough through the peak to the terminal trough. Several cycles may be plotted on the same chart for cyclical comparisons. Comparison may not be easy when cycles are of varying lengths.

The most important times for cyclical comparison are often those around reference cycle troughs and peaks. As a cycle develops it is not possible to divide the cycle into stages since this can only be done when the cycle is complete. It is possible, however, to present cyclical data using a somewhat different technique. Data on such series as GNP, industrial production, or unemployment may be shown as they develop in the period immediately preceding or following a reference trough or peak. Data on a quarterly or monthly basis are expressed as percentage deviations from the level of the series at the reference peak or trough. Series presented in percentage form, such as unemployment data, are plotted directly. Figure 11-3, p. 250, shows such a chart for a composite index of coincident series around the trough of the 1973 recession.

Table 11-7

Sample of Table S1: Timing and Duration of Specific Cycles Coke Production, United States, 1914–1932

Dates of Specific Cycles Trough-Peak-Trough	Timing at Reference Peak No. of Months Lead (−) or Lag (+)	Timing at Reference Peak Date of Reference Peak	Timing at Reference Trough No. of Months Lead (−) or Lag (+)	Timing at Reference Trough Date of Reference Trough	Duration of Cyclical Movements (Month) Specific Cycles Expansion	Specific Cycles Contraction	Specific Cycles Full Cycle	Excess over Reference Cycle Expansion	Excess over Reference Cycle Contraction	Excess over Reference Cycle Full Cycle	Percentage of Duration of Specific Cycles Expansion	Percentage Contraction
Nov., 1914			−1	12/14								
Nov., '14–July, '18–May, '19	−1	8/18	+1	4/19	44	10	54	0	+2	+2	81	19
May, '19–Aug., '20–July, '21	+7	1/20	−2	9/21	15	11	26	+6	−9	−3	58	42
July, '21–May, '23–July, '24	0	5/23	0	7/24	22	14	36	+2	0	+2	61	39
July, '24–Feb., '26–Nov., '27	−8	10/26	−1	12/27	19	21	40	−8	+7	−1	48	52
Nov., '27–July, '29–Aug., '32	+1	6/29	−7	3/33	20	37	57	+2	−8	−6	35	65
Average	−0.2		−1.7		24.0	18.6	42.6	+0.4	−1.6	−1.2	57	43
Average deviation	3.4		1.9		8.0	8.3	10.3	3.5	5.5	2.6	12	12

Source: Arthur F. Burns and Wesley C. Mitchell, *Measuring Business Cycles* (New York: National Bureau of Economic Research, 1947), p. 26, Table 5.

Table 11-8

Sample of Table S2: Amplitude of Specific Cycles Pig Iron Production, United States, 1914–1932

Dates of Specific Cycles	3-Month Average in Specific Cycle Relatives Centered on			Amplitude			Per Month Amplitude of		
Trough-Peak-Trough	Initial Trough	Peak	Terminal Trough	Rise	Fall	Rise & Fall	Rise	Fall	Rise & Fall
Nov., 1914–July, '18–May, '19	55.5	119.6	74.5	64.1	45.1	109.2	1.5	4.5	2.0
May, '19–Aug., '20–July, '21	88.7	125.9	45.0	37.2	80.9	118.1	2.5	7.4	4.5
July, '21–May, '23–July, '24	44.3	144.0	82.6	99.7	61.4	161.1	4.5	4.4	4.5
July, '24–Feb., '26–Nov., '27	69.4	118.2	92.1	48.8	26.1	74.9	2.6	1.2	1.9
Nov., '27–July, '29–Aug., '32	105.5	141.6	41.7	36.1	99.9	136.0	1.8	2.7	2.4
Average	72.7	129.9	67.2	57.2	62.7	119.9	2.6	4.0	3.1
Average deviation	19.5	10.4	19.1	19.8	22.2	23.0	0.8	1.7	1.2

Source: Arthur F. Burns and Wesley C. Mitchell, *Measuring Business Cycles* (New York: National Bureau of Economic Research, 1947), p. 27, Table 6.

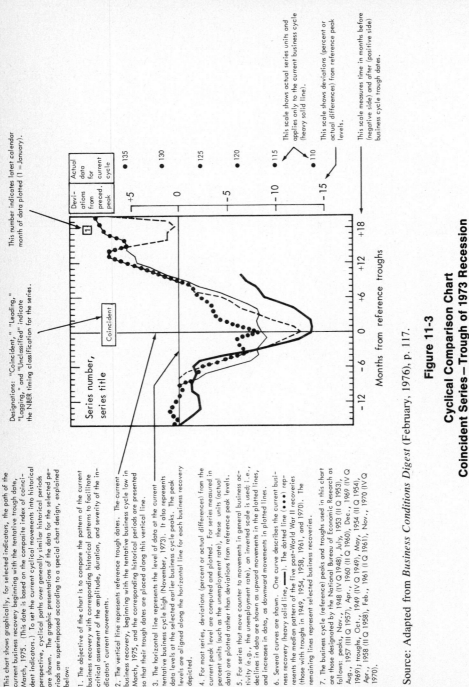

This chart shows graphically, for selected indicators, the path of the current business recovery beginning with the tentative trough date, March, 1975. (This date is based on the composite index of coincident indicators.) To set the current cyclical movements into historical perspective, cyclical paths over generally similar historical periods are shown. The graphic presentations of the data for the selected periods are superimposed according to a special chart design, explained below:

1. The objective of the chart is to compare the pattern of the current business recovery with corresponding historical patterns to facilitate critical assessment of the amplitude, duration, and severity of the indicators' current movements.

2. The vertical line represents reference trough dates. The current business recovery, beginning with the tentative business cycle low in March, 1975, and the corresponding historical periods are presented so that their trough dates are placed along this vertical line.

3. The horizontal line represents the level of data at the current tentative business cycle high (November, 1973). It also represents data levels at the selected earlier business cycle peaks. The peak levels are aligned along the horizontal line for each business cycle recovery depicted.

4. For most series, deviations (percent or actual differences) from the current peak level are computed and plotted. For series measured in percent units (such as the unemployment rate), these units (actual data) are plotted rather than deviations from reference peak levels.

5. For series that move counter to movements in general business activity (e.g., the unemployment rate), an inverted scale is used; i.e., declines in data are shown as upward movements in the plotted lines, and increases in data, as downward movements in plotted lines.

6. Several curves are shown. One curve describes the current business recovery (heavy solid line, ____). The dotted line (•••) represents the median pattern of the five post-World War II recoveries (those with troughs in 1949, 1954, 1958, 1961, and 1970). The remaining lines represent selected business recoveries.

7. The business cycle (reference) peaks and troughs used in this chart are those designated by the National Bureau of Economic Research as follows: peaks, Nov., 1948 (IV Q 1948), July, 1953 (II Q 1953), Aug., 1957 (III Q 1957), Apr., 1960 (IV Q 1960), Dec., 1969 (IV Q 1969); troughs, Oct., 1949 (IV Q 1949), May, 1954 (II Q 1954), Apr., 1958 (II Q 1958), Feb., 1961 (I Q 1961), Nov., 1970 (IV Q 1970).

This number indicates latest calendar month of data plotted (1 = January).

Designations: "Coincident," "Leading," "Lagging," and "Unclassified" indicate the NBER timing classification for the series.

This scale shows actual series units and applies only to the current business cycle (heavy solid line).

This scale shows deviations (percent or actual differences) from reference peak levels.

This scale measures time in months before (negative side) and after (positive side) business cycle trough dates.

Deviations from preced. peak | Actual data for current cycle

Series number, series title

Coincident

Months from reference troughs

Source: Adapted from *Business Conditions Digest* (February, 1976), p. 117.

Figure 11-3

Cyclical Comparison Chart
Coincident Series — Trough of 1973 Recession

QUESTIONS

1. Describe the ratio-to-moving-average method of calculating the seasonal.
2. How is a changing seasonal calculated?
3. Describe the method of calculating a trend line by the least-squares method.
4. Describe the residual method of isolating the cycle.
5. What can be done to remove the effect of irregular factors?
6. How does the National Bureau use the term reference cycle? Specific cycle?
7. How are reference cycle relatives calculated? Specific cycle relatives?
8. How can the amplitude of the cycle be determined from specific cycle relatives?
9. How do the residual method and the National Bureau method differ in handling the trend?
10. Describe cyclical comparison charts. How may they be used in studying cycles as they develop?

SUGGESTED READINGS

Burns, Arthur F., and Wesley C. Mitchell. *Measuring Business Cycles*. New York: National Bureau of Economic Research, 1946.

Gordon, Robert A. *Business Fluctuations*, 2d ed. New York: Harper & Brothers, 1961.

Kuznets, Simon. *Seasonal Variations in Industry and Trade*. New York: National Bureau of Economic Research, 1933.

Stockton, John R., and Charles T. Clark. *Introduction to Business and Economic Statistics*, 5th ed. Cincinnati: South-Western Publishing Co., 1975. Part 4.

U.S. Department of Commerce. *Business Conditions Digest*, monthly.

CHAPTER 12

BEHAVIOR OF THE CYCLE

The study of the statistical record of the behavior of the cycle will begin with an analysis of the most common length of the cycle, its expansion and contraction phases, and the extent of the deviations from these patterns. Attention will next be directed to the international conformity of business cycles, especially in the major industrial countries. The extent to which the cycle has affected all phases of American business will then be considered, followed by a study of the timing of various phases of economic activity in relationship to the turning points in the reference cycle. Special attention will be given to important series that lead and lag in the cyclical process. The varying amplitudes of different economic series in past cycles will be described and analyzed. The nature of the cycle in inventories will be described and the factors which cause it will also be analyzed. In conclusion, some aspects of the general cycle pattern will be described as the pattern develops during expansion and contraction.

LENGTH OF THE CYCLE

In forecasting changes in the level of economic activity it is helpful to know what pattern, if any, has existed in the length of the cycle and in the expansion and contraction phases of the cycle. These factors will be considered in turn in this section.

Length of the Cycle in Years

Using the definition of the National Bureau of Economic Research and measuring the length of the cycle from trough to trough, American business cycles from 1854 to the present have varied in length between 2 and 10 years. The average length of the cycle has been 4 years, and the most common length 3 years. Three fourths of the cycles have been between 3 and 5 years in length. Table 12-1 shows the length of American business cycles from 1854 to 1975.

Table 12-1

**Length of American Business Cycles
1854 to 1975**

Length in Years	Number of Cycles
1	0
2	2
3	10
4	8
5	3
6	2
7	1 (June, 1938–October, 1945)
8	1 (December, 1870–March, 1879)
9	0
10	1 (February, 1961–November, 1970)

Sources: Adapted from Willard Throp, *Business Annals;* and Burns and Mitchell, *Measuring Business Cycles;* and carried forward to date.

Length of the Cycle in Months

For cycles between 1854 and 1975 for which the National Bureau has established monthly reference dates, the full cycle varied from 28 months to 117 months, with an average of 52 months. The expansion periods varied from 10 months to 106 months, with an average of 33 months; and the contraction periods from 7 months to 65 months, with an average of 19 months. Thus, it can be seen that there is neither a uniform length of the cycle nor uniform periods of expansion or contraction.

There is no uniform relationship between the length of the expansion phase in an individual cycle and the length of the contraction phase in that cycle. In some cases the expansion period is much longer than the contraction period, as was the case in the cycle that reached its peak in May, 1937. In others, the two periods are of about equal length; and in still others the contraction phase is decidedly longer than the expansion period, as was the case in the cycle that reached its trough in March, 1879.

In the post-World War II period, expansions have been about 50 percent longer than the average and contractions have been only about half as long as the average. The six postwar contractions have been 8, 11, 10, 8, 10, and 16 months long. Since 1920, 9 of the 12 contractions have lasted 14 months or less. The contraction in the post-World War I depression, however, lasted 18 months and in the depression which began in 1929, 43 months.

The duration of expansion and contraction periods, and of the full cycle for reference cycles from December, 1854, through March, 1975, is presented in Table 12-2.

Table 12-2

Duration of Business Cycle Expansions and Contractions in the United States, 1854-1975

Business Cycle			Duration (in Months) of—		
Trough	Peak	Trough	Expansion	Contraction	Full Cycle
Dec., 1854	June, 1857	Dec., 1858	30	18	48
Dec., 1858	Oct., 1860	June, 1861	22	8	30
June, 1861	Apr., 1865	Dec., 1867	46	32	78
Dec., 1867	June, 1869	Dec., 1870	18	18	36
Dec., 1870	Oct., 1873	Mar., 1879	34	65	99
Mar., 1879	Mar., 1882	May, 1885	36	38	74
May, 1885	Mar., 1887	Apr., 1888	22	13	35
Apr., 1888	July, 1890	May, 1891	27	10	37
May, 1891	Jan., 1893	June, 1894	20	17	37
June, 1894	Dec., 1895	June, 1897	18	18	36
June, 1897	June, 1899	Dec., 1900	24	18	42
Dec., 1900	Sept., 1902	Aug., 1904	21	23	44
Aug., 1904	May, 1907	June, 1908	33	13	46
June, 1908	Jan., 1910	Jan., 1912	19	24	43
Jan., 1912	Jan., 1913	Dec., 1914	12	23	35
Dec., 1914	Aug., 1918	Mar., 1919	44	7	51
Mar., 1919	Jan., 1920	July, 1921	10	18	28
July, 1921	May, 1923	July, 1924	22	14	36
July, 1924	Oct., 1926	Nov., 1927	27	13	40
Nov., 1927	Aug., 1929	Mar., 1933	21	43	64
Mar., 1933	May, 1937	June, 1938	50	13	63
June, 1938	Feb., 1945	Oct., 1945	80	8	88
Oct., 1945	Nov., 1948	Oct., 1949	37	11	48
Oct., 1949	July, 1953	May, 1954	45	10	55
May, 1954	Aug., 1957	Apr., 1958	39	8	47
Apr., 1958	Apr., 1960	Feb., 1961	24	10	34
Feb., 1961	Nov., 1969	Nov., 1970	106	11	117
* Nov., 1970	Nov., 1973	Mar., 1975	36	16	52
Average, all cycles:					
27 cycles, 1854–1975			33	19	52
11 cycles, 1919–1975			42	14	56
5 cycles, 1945–1975			50	10	60
Average, peacetime cycles:					
22 cycles, 1854–1975			26	20	46
8 cycles, 1919–1975			29	16	45
3 cycles, 1945–1975			33	10	43

Source: *Business Cycle Developments* (February, 1976), p. 112. Based on National Bureau of Economic Research data, except for the most recent cycle.

* These dates have been estimated by the editors of *Business Conditions Digest* based on an analysis of series with coincident timing.

CONFORMITY IN BUSINESS CYCLE PATTERNS

This section will review the degree to which the business cycle pervades all areas of economic activity. Consideration will be given to the international pattern of cycles and to the domestic pattern of activity during cycles.

International Pattern

Business cycles affect all countries that have economies organized on a free enterprise-pecuniary basis. The most highly organized countries show the most pronounced cyclical patterns. Major cycles have occurred at about the same time in industrial countries such as England, France, Germany, Japan, and the United States. This was generally true in the cycles that reached their peaks in 1815, 1837, 1847, 1857, 1890, 1907, 1920, and 1929.

Minor cycles have not occurred at the same time, nor has each country had the same number of cycles. The United States has had more cycles than England, France, the Netherlands, Sweden, and Germany. Furthermore, some countries may be in a recovery or in a prosperity stage while others are still in a recession stage.

This lack of conformity in international cycle patterns has continued in the post-World War II period. The 1949, 1953, and 1960 downturns were not experienced by most countries. The recession that began in 1957 in the United States, while relatively mild, was more severe than earlier postwar recessions. Canada and Japan had a recession at about the same time as the United States, with economic activity leveling off in most other industrial nations. The 1960–1961 recession in the United States was not generally experienced in other countries, though there was some decline in economic activity in Canada and Japan. In 1970 industrial production showed little or no growth in Canada, Japan, and most European countries. The 1973 recession affected all major industrial nations organized on a free enterprise basis.

Domestic Pattern

The cycle in the United States is also by no means an all-pervasive phenomenon which carries every economic activity with it. A sample of economic time series such as those published in *Business Conditions Digest* shows that some series are reaching their peaks at many different times during the cycle.[1] Many series do not move in complete conformity with the general business cycle but are undergoing expansion and contraction at different times. During a prosperity period many, but by no means all, of the series are expanding; and during a recession not all series are contracting.

CYCLICAL TIMING OF ECONOMIC SERIES

Most types of economic activity expand and contract in phase with overall economic activity. Some series are inverted; that is, they are moving in opposition to the direction of business in general.

---

[1] *Business Conditions Digest,* current issues.

Inverted timing occurs to a large extent because of the form in which economic data are reported. If the employment series being studied is the number of people at work, it will move with the business cycle, showing positive timing. If, instead, the employment situation is viewed from the number of people unemployed, the series will show inverted timing. Since in most cases the form in which economic data are expressed is not arbitrary but is designed for ease of use and compilation, the National Bureau has kept all of the time series it has studied in their original form. This explains the inverted position of such series as commercial failures and idle freight cars, in addition to unemployment.

Even though most economic series expand and contract with general business, they do not move in perfect unison with the cycle in overall activity. Many of them typically have leads and lags at reference cycle peaks and troughs. Such leads and lags can be measured from the reference cycle turning point dates as developed by the National Bureau. These are the dates presented as the troughs and peaks of cycles since 1854 in Table 12-2 on p. 254.

General Economic Activity

As is to be expected, indexes that reflect aggregate economic activity correspond fairly closely with reference cycle dates. Gross national product for the period for which the figures are available moved closely in harmony with reference cycle dates.[2] The Federal Reserve Board Index of Industrial Production in the post-World War II period generally had a short lead at reference peaks and reached its trough at about the same time as reference troughs.

Construction and Industrial Durable Goods

Indexes for the construction industry almost always lead reference cycle peaks and troughs. There is also a tendency for related series, such as the production of southern pine lumber, oak flooring, and plumbing fixtures, to move in about the same fashion.

Since contracts lead construction, a lead would be expected in this series even if construction moved in complete conformity with the cycle. The lead of construction itself at many upper turning points is due to several factors that are inherent in the nature of the cyclical process. The accelerator can cause construction to turn down while demand is still increasing, but at a lower rate. Innovations lead to building early in the cycle, but this slows down when plant and equipment have been built to produce the new product. The slowdown in construction before the economy turns down may also be due to overbuilding in some fields, which has often been one of the factors producing unbalance. The lead at the lower turning point is due to some of the factors at work in the economy that produce an upturn, such as an innovation, a need for more capacity in some fields as population expands, the lowering of interest rates that makes some projects profitable, and the building of plants to cut costs.

---

[2] The data on leads and lags in this section are taken from Geoffrey H. Moore (ed.), *Statistical Indicators of Cyclical Revivals and Recessions* (New York: National Bureau of Economic Research, 1950), and Geoffrey H. Moore, *Business Cycle Indicators,* Vol. I (New York: National Bureau of Economic Research, 1961), and brought up to date from data in *Business Conditions Digest.*

New orders for industrial durable goods lead at both peaks and troughs. The reasons for such leads are similar to those for construction. The movements in pig iron production and in steel ingot production are fairly coincidental with the cycle but show some lead at the troughs and some lags at the peaks. The lead at the trough is based on leads in construction and industrial durable goods. The lag at the peak is probably due to the time required to fill orders at the mill, which were placed before the downturn became apparent.

Employment and Hours of Work

Indexes of employment correspond to cyclical peaks and troughs fairly closely. Employment in nonagricultural establishments is practically coincidental with the reference cycle turns at the trough, but has at times had a short lead at the peaks due to the lead in construction and in industrial durable goods. The index of unemployment of the Department of Commerce has, in the post-World War II period, generally had a short lead at reference peaks and a lag at reference troughs. The tendency for indexes of employment to be roughly coincidental at peaks and troughs is also shown in series on employment in the durable goods field and in such industries as cement, clay, glass, iron and steel, and machinery. The Bureau of Labor Statistics index of average hours worked per week, however, shows a fairly long lead at reference peaks and a short lead at reference troughs. In other words, one of the first reactions of business to a change in economic conditions is a change in the average hours worked per week rather than in the number of workers employed.

Industrial Materials

The index of industrial materials prices has shown a tendency to lead at reference peaks and troughs. Inflationary pressures have been so strong since the 1969–1970 downturn that leads have been obscured by the strong pressures for price rises. The tendency to lead cyclical peaks and troughs is probably due in part to changes in demand arising from industries whose activity shows a cyclical lead.

Consumer Income and Spending

In the pre-World War II period there was some tendency for consumer income and spending to lag somewhat in the cyclical process. This lag has disappeared in the postwar period in part because of governmental programs to maintain purchasing power and also because of the mild nature of postwar recessions. Personal income has in recent years moved in relative harmony with turning points in the cycle and the same is true of retail sales. In recent cycles inflationary pressures have been so strong that no cyclical pattern is evident in such data in current dollars.

Profits

Since profits are a residual after all expenses have been met, they fluctuate much more widely than sales. They are already declining in some industries before business has reached a peak and increasing before business has reached a trough. In the post-World War II period the magnitude of changes in profits in such industries was large enough to give profits in total a lead at reference peaks and a short lead at troughs in some cycles, especially the earlier ones in this period.

Common Stock Prices

Common stock prices show a tendency to lead at peaks and troughs. Stock traders base their purchases on the future prospects of the economy and of a particular company whose stock they are buying, and have generally determined changes before they occur.

Business Failures

Business failures have a lead at reference peaks and at reference troughs. When the upturn begins, costs lag and profits increase. As costs catch up and as an increasing volume of goods is available from new plants constructed in the upturn, it is more difficult to operate profitably. Some weak concerns fail at this stage, and the number increases as prosperity develops. In the recession period there is also a lead because most weak concerns have failed after the full effects of lower business levels have had their impact. The concerns still in business are by and large the stronger ones that have weathered the storm.

Interest Rates

Interest rates have a tendency to lag in the cyclical process. A Federal Reserve Board quarterly index of bank rates on short-term business loans shows a lag at reference peaks and at reference troughs. This same tendency for interest rates to lag is also shown in bond yields. This is, in part, due to the contractual nature of interest payments. Loan contracts are usually signed for a minimum of 90 days, and in many cases run for years. The lag is also due to the "sticky" nature of interest rates in many situations. They are changed infrequently and only when there are clear indications that the underlying demand and supply factors have changed.

Summary

Table 12-3 presents some of the most important series that typically lead at reference cycle peaks and troughs, those which move at about the same time as the reference cycle, and those which typically lag.

CYCLICAL AMPLITUDE

This section will consider the amplitude over the cycle of various phases of economic activity. First some observations will be made on the general pattern of cyclical amplitude and then the pattern in gross national product and in industrial production will be described.

Table 12-3
Timing at Peaks and Troughs of Important Economic Series

Leading Series

Average work week, production workers, manufacturing
Average weekly initial claims, state unemployment insurance
Net business formations
New orders, durable goods industries
Contracts and orders, plant and equipment
New building permits, private housing units
Stock prices, 500 common stocks
Changes in book value, manufacturing and trade inventories
Corporate profits after taxes
Ratio, price to unit labor cost, manufacturing
Change in consumer installment debt
Change in stocks on hand and on order, 1967 dollars
Pct. change, price index for crude materials
Money supply, 1967 dollars
Percentage change, liquid assets

Roughly Coincident Series

Employees on nonagricultural payrolls
Unemployment rate, total
GNP in 1972 dollars
Industrial production
Personal income
Manufacturing and trade sales
Sales of retail stores

Lagging Series

Unemployment rate, persons unemployed 15 weeks and over
Business expenditures, new plant and equipment
Book value, manufacturing and trade inventories
Labor cost per unit of output, manufacturing
Commercial and industrial loans outstanding, weekly reporting
     large commercial banks
Bank rates on short-term business loans

Source: *Business Conditions Digest* (May, 1975), p. xv, and (February, 1976), p. 113.

General Pattern

Various phases of economic activity have different amplitudes during the cycle. In the prewar cycles for which data are available in National Bureau studies, some general patterns are evident. Prices had a lower average amplitude than production in manufacturing inasmuch as producers adjusted to changed demand primarily by reducing output. The amplitude in employment was substantially less than that in production because many workers were put on part-time employment rather than laid off. Payrolls fluctuated somewhat more than production due to changes in the work week and to overtime pay in prosperity. Profits had a much larger amplitude than production or payrolls. This is to be expected since it is a residual after all expenses are paid and fixed costs represent a large part of total business costs.

The relationships have generally held true in the postwar period. Prices have had such an upward bias that they have declined little or not at all in recession periods. An example of such postwar relationships may be seen from Table 12-4 on page 261, which shows changes in major economic variables in the 1954–1958 and the 1970–1975 cycles. Changes in the other postwar cycles show the same general pattern, but the amplitude was smaller, especially in the contraction phase.

Several other significant relationships exist. The amplitude of production of durable goods is much greater than that of nondurable goods. This would be expected from the operation of the accelerator principle and other causal factors at work in the cycle, especially those affecting the marginal efficiency of capital and interest rates. Consumer durables show a more pronounced variation than durable manufacturing in total. This was not generally true in the pre-World War II period. This is probably due to several factors. More consumers have significant amounts of discretionary income and so can buy durables in prosperity periods. They seem to have been motivated more by the changing economic outlook than by prospects for long-run changes in income. Business has done more investing than it did during the pre-World War II period on a long-run basis instead of on a short-run profit basis, and so has reduced the amplitude in the producer durable field. This has been true in part because of a desire to cut costs by introducing more modern machinery and equipment.

One of the significant factors is the very small change in personal income in the downturn, much smaller than prewar. This is due to a series of factors, such as unemployment compensation, compensatory fiscal policy, agricultural price-support programs, more stable dividend policies, and the like. These are discussed in some detail in Part 7.

Gross National Product

Inflation has been so pronounced in the most recent cycles that comparisons of changes in gross national product in recessions and recoveries are best made using constant-dollar GNP figures. In the period since 1949 the percentage increase in constant dollar GNP in recovery periods has varied between 11.7 percent and 48.0 percent. However, much of this variation is due to the varying lengths of the recovery periods. When comparison is made on the basis of the percentage increase per quarter figured at an annual rate the difference is narrowed considerably. The slowest rate was 3.9 percent per quarter in 1954–1957 and the fastest was 6.4 percent in 1949–1953. In recessions the percentage decline since 1948 has varied between 1.1 percent and

Table 12-4

Percentage Changes in the Upswing and Downturn During Reference Cycles in Selected Economic Indicators in Two Post-World War II Recessions

	Percentage Increase from Initial Trough to Peak		Percentage Decrease from Peak to Terminal Trough	
	1954–1958 Cycle	1970–1975 Cycle	1954–1958 Cycle	1970–1975 Cycle
1. GNP-Current Dollars	23.9	36.0	1.9	+6.7
2. GNP-1972 Dollars	13.2	16.0	2.5	6.6
3. Production-FRB Index	22.1	25.3	12.6	14.9
4. Nondurable goods	20.6	19.8	3.8	13.4
5. Durable goods	21.9	32.5	19.7	16.7
Nonagricultural Employment				
6. Total	8.4	9.6	4.0	0.28
Nonagricultural Employment				
7. Excluding Government	9.5	9.6	7.1	1.6
8. Wholesale Prices	6.8	27.8	+0.7	+20.1
9. Profits After Tax	29.4	100.9	21.2	15.2
10. Disposable Personal Income – 1972 Dollars	15.1	15.6	0.7	4.0
11. Consumer Expenditures on Durable Goods – 1972 Dollars	15.3	39.8	6.9	10.2

Source: Based on data in the *Survey of Current Business*.

6.6 percent. The percentage decline per quarter at an annual rate has varied between .9 percent in 1969–1970 to 6.5 percent in 1957–1958. Data for each cycle is presented in Table 12-5, page 262.

Industrial Production

The changes in industrial production are more pronounced than changes in GNP in real terms, especially in the downturn. In the post-World War II cycles the decline in industrial production has been less severe than it was on the average in the prewar period, and the expansion has been somewhat less vigorous than in minor cycles in the same period. The average per month percentage point changes in the index during the contraction phase of specific cycles in industrial production since November, 1948, were as follows:

November, 1948 – October, 1949	−1.35
July, 1953 – May, 1954	− .88
August, 1957 – April, 1958	−1.58
April, 1960 – February, 1961	− .61
December, 1969 – November, 1970	− .54
November, 1973 – March, 1975	− .93

Table 12-5

Postwar Cyclical Fluctuations in Constant-Dollar GNP

	Timing and Duration			Amplitude and Severity	
	Peak Quarter	Trough Quarter	No. of Quarters of Decline	Percentage Decline	Percentage Decline per Quarter at Annual Rate
Recessions					
1948–49:					
Fully revised	1948:IV	1949: II	2	−1.4	−2.9
1953–54:					
Fully revised	1953: II	1954: II	4	−3.3	−3.3
1957–58:					
Fully revised	1957:III	1958: I	2	−3.3	−6.5
1960–61:					
Fully revised	1960: I	1960:IV	3	−1.2	−1.6
1969–70:					
Fully revised	1969:III	1970:IV	5	−1.1	− .9
1973–75:					
Fully revised	1973:IV	1975: I	5	−6.6	−5.3

	Timing and Duration			Amplitude and Strength	
	Trough Quarter	Peak Quarter	No. of Quarters of Expansion	Percentage Increase	Percentage Increase per Quarter at Annual Rate
Recoveries					
1949–53:					
Fully revised	1949: II	1953: II	16	28.1	6.4
1954–57:					
Fully revised	1954: II	1957:III	13	13.2	3.9
1958–60:					
Fully revised	1958: I	1960: I	8	11.7	5.7
1961–69:					
Fully revised	1960:IV	1969:III	35	48.0	4.7
1970–73:					
Fully revised	1970:IV	1973:IV	12	15.8	5.0

Source: *Survey of Current Business* (January, 1976), Part I, p. 27.

The monthly increases in industrial production during expansion periods were not much different from those in contraction periods, but expansion periods were much longer than contraction periods. The average per month percentage point changes in the index during the expansion phase of specific cycles in industrial production since October, 1949, were as listed on the following page.

October, 1949 — July, 1953   1.02
May, 1954 — August, 1957   .57
April, 1958 — April, 1960   .95
February, 1961 — December, 1969   .71
November, 1970 — November, 1973   .70

FLUCTUATIONS IN INVENTORIES

Changes in inventories play a major role in changes in total economic activity. This has continued to be true in the post-World War II period even though inventories have been maintained at a lower level in relation to sales than in the prewar period. This influence was more pronounced in downturns than in expansion periods.[3] During the first postwar recession, the change in the rate of inventory purchases was somewhat larger than the decline in GNP. In the second recession, inventory adjustment was equal to about 85 percent of the change in GNP and in the third recession to about 60 percent. In the fourth postwar recession in 1960–1961, the change in inventory investment was more than seven times as great as the decline in GNP. In the 1969–1970 recession, inventories continued to increase, but the annual rate of accumulation was cut from $11.9 billion in the third quarter of 1969 to $2.6 billion in the fourth quarter of 1970.[4] In the 1973–1975 recession inflationary pressures were so strong that GNP increased by $80.9 billion from the fourth quarter of 1973 to the first quarter of 1975. Inventory liquidation was significant, however, since inventories were being built up at a $27.7 billion annual rate in the peak quarter and reduced at a $19.0 billion annual rate in the quarter of the terminal trough.

This significance of the role of inventories in the cycle is to be expected because of the causal factors at work. The accelerator principle leads to a more than proportionate change in the rate of inventory accumulation on the upswing and in the rate of liquidation in the downturn. Speculative activity also leads to inventory accumulation in a recovery period and also to liquidation in a recession.

A detailed study of several series on manufacturers' inventories was made for the National Bureau by Moses Abramovitz. He found that fluctuations in the volume of inventories conformed well with those of the reference cycle. There was, however, somewhat of a lag in inventory movements behind those of general business. Inventory series in terms of current prices showed a lag of somewhere between 3 and 6 months, while deflated series showed a longer lag that was somewhere between 6 and 12 months.[5] This lag has continued in the post-World War II recessions, but it has been somewhat shorter, especially in the earlier cycles.

---

[3] Moses Abramovitz, *The Role of Inventories in Business Cycles* (New York: National Bureau of Economic Research, 1948) and Manufacturers' Inventories in *The Study of Economic Growth,* Thirty-ninth Annual Report (New York: National Bureau of Economic Research, 1959), pp. 43, 44.

[4] Based on data in the *Survey of Current Business.*

[5] Abramovitz, *op. cit.,* pp. 87, 97.

To understand the reasons for the fluctuations in inventories during the course of the cycle, it is necessary to analyze the factors involved in holding inventories. The most common reasons cited for holding inventories are to gain the savings from buying materials and supplies in larger quantities, to achieve the cost savings resulting from smoothing production over a period of time, and to provide a buffer stock against unforeseen contingencies. These benefits from holding inventories are offset in part by the costs incurred in carrying inventories. The level of inventories that a business will normally desire to hold will depend, therefore, on a balance between costs of holding inventories and the benefits from doing so.

In determining the optimum level of inventories, the costs associated with holding different levels of inventories are first calculated on the basis that the various costs will remain constant over short periods of time and vary only with different levels of inventories. The major costs involved are such factors as interest, insurance, taxes, spoilage, obsolescence, storage, and possible price changes. A change in any of these costs will change the costs of holding different levels of inventories and, therefore, also the optimum level of inventories based upon an analysis of costs and benefits.

Two of the major costs of holding inventories have a significant cyclical fluctuation, that is, interest charges and price changes and expectations of such changes. An increase in the rate of interest will increase the cost of holding inventories and so lead to a reduction in optimum levels, and a reduction will do just the reverse. An expected rise in prices will lead to a reduction in the cost of holding inventories and so lead to an increase in optimum inventory levels, and an expected decline will have the opposite effect. Since reductions in costs of holding inventories due to price rises and expected price rises are generally greater in the early stages of expansion in business activity than increases in costs due to higher interest rates, the net effect from the cost side is to lead to an increase in inventories as expansion gets under way. The opposite is generally true of business contractions, especially in the early stages.

Changes in some of the factors that lead to cost savings from holding inventories also have a cyclical pattern. Consideration will be given in turn to savings from buying in larger quantities, savings from smoothing production, and benefits from holding buffer stocks. In most industries cost savings are usually realized by buying goods in larger quantities. These savings include quantity discounts both in the purchase price and in transportation costs and also savings from placing and processing fewer orders.

To consider the effect of these factors independently of other factors, let us assume that savings result only from buying in larger quantities and that conditions in the industries supplying the goods have not changed. Under these conditions a change in the rate of sales would not ordinarily lead to a change in the level of inventories since savings have been calculated on the basis of savings associated with quantity discounts and less frequent ordering. As the rate of sales increased, a firm would ordinarily consider one of two alternatives, either order more frequently or order in larger quantities. The effect on the level of inventories in either case would be minimal. The increases in the rate of sales associated with an upswing in business activity do not, therefore, lead to a significant increase in inventory due to cost savings arising from purchasing in larger quantities.

Inventories are also held to achieve benefits from even production. Savings result from producing goods at a more or less constant rate rather than adjusting to seasonal shifts in demand. When production is geared to sales, added costs are incurred to hire and lay off workers, to pay overtime or add extra shifts in periods of peak demand, and to pay for raw materials that are likely to be in short supply in periods of peak demand and therefore more costly. If attempts are made to spread sales more evenly and so to smooth production levels, there are added selling costs. The optimum policy balances the costs of holding inventory against the savings from maintaining smooth production. If production is almost completely smoothed, and average inventory holdings are large enough to meet seasonal needs, an increase in sales will have some effect on average inventories, but it will ordinarily not be as great as a percentage of peak stocks. This is not true, however, if production is only partially smoothed.

When sales go up cyclically in an industry, costs associated with peak periods of production will go up more than normally because of greater delays in getting raw materials, more overtime and shift work, and the like. In this situation there is a significant saving to be realized from adding to stocks early in an upswing in business. When few firms in an industry maintain smooth production fully, there are significant savings to be gained by an individual firm from increasing stocks early in an expansion period. This is another factor in explaining increases in inventory investment early in the upswing of a cycle.

A third major reason for holding inventories is to provide a buffer stock to serve as a safety factor if there is a delay in delivery of raw materials or parts and to be prepared for an unexpected surge in sales. This is true because there are significant costs associated with being out of materials and parts and having to slow production. There are also costs associated with lost sales. The relevant cost factor is the actual cost of being out of stock, multiplied by the probability that this will occur. Cyclical factors will affect the amount of inventory to be held as a buffer. An increase in the rate of sales will increase the probability of running out of finished goods and so lead to an increase in inventories. However, in industries in which stocks are relatively large in relationship to sales, the effect will not be large since the chances are good that production can be increased to meet the added demand before the inventory is depleted.

If sales go up when the supply of raw materials or other goods needed in production is tight or is expected to be, the chances of running out of stock are greatly increased and this leads to an attempt to increase inventories early in an expansion. The effect is again greater in an industry in which stocks are relatively low in relationship to production than when they are high.

In summary, the result of optimal inventory policy will be an increase in stocks in an upswing in business that is proportionately greater than the increase in sales and a similar reduction in a downturn. These effects will be greatest when significant price rises are expected and when conditions are such that raw materials and parts are expected to be tight. This is generally the situation in the early stages of an upturn.

THE GENERAL CYCLE PATTERN

Each cycle in economic activity is in many ways a unique phenomenon, but there are elements which are similar from cycle to cycle. Information on developments during a cycle is available from studies by the National Bureau of Economic Research and also from data in *Business Conditions Digest,* a monthly publication of the U.S. Department of Commerce. Some groups of items have been analyzed over a period of time during segments of the cycle and are helpful in developing information on the general cycle pattern. One such study for the pre-World War II period contains data on 34 comprehensive series analyzed by the National Bureau. These series include those on production, transportation, prices, trade, employment, income payments, investments, dealings in securities, business profits, business failures, and bank debits, and also several indexes of general business activity. They are not inclusive enough to cover all important sectors of economic activity but enough data are available to present a preliminary picture of the typical cycle.[6]

Data on the complete group of comprehensive series are not available for post-World War II cycles. Information is available, however, on the behavior of a representative group of 11 comprehensive series for the postwar period from 1945–1958 covering three complete cycles.[7] These series are:

Federal Reserve Board Index of Industrial Production
Bureau of Labor Statistics Wholesale Price Index
Federal Reserve Board Index of Department Store Sales
Bureau of Labor Statistics Production Worker Employment in Manufacturing
    Industries
F. W. Dodge Corporation Value of Construction Contracts Awarded
Number of Shares of Stock Sold on the New York Stock Exchange
Par Value of Bonds Sold on the New York Stock Exchange
Dun & Bradstreet Number of Business Failures
Bank Clearings in New York City
Bank Clearings Outside New York City
AT&T Index of Industrial Activity

Data are also available for the period from 1948 to the present on many comprehensive series in *Business Conditions Digest.*

Some data on costs, prices, and profits in post-World War II business cycles are available in a study by Thor Hultgren which covers cycles in 15 manufacturing industries and in railroads, public utilities, construction, trade, and telephone companies.[8] Most of the data is for the cycles in the 1947–1961 period. The cycles used are the specific cycles in quantity produced and in sales, but they correspond closely to the reference cycle with one exception. In

---

[6] Wesley C. Mitchell, *What Happens During Business Cycles: A Progress Report* (New York: National Bureau of Economic Research, 1951).

[7] From an unpublished research project at Washington University by Robert L. Virgil, Jr., *Comparative Patterns of Behavior by Economic Time Series during Prewar and Postwar American Business Cycles.*

[8] Thor Hultgren, *Cost, Prices, and Profits: Their Cyclical Relations* (New York: National Bureau of Economic Research, 1965).

many industries the 1949–1953 business expansion is divided into two periods since demand fell for a time after the surge in demand resulting from the outbreak of war in Korea had been met.

Some data are also available on the cyclical behavior of interest rates in the period from 1945–1961 in a study by Reuben A. Kessel.[9] This study analyzes the cyclical behavior of short-term and long-term interest rates including commercial paper rates, the yields on Treasury bills, and Moody's Aaa corporate bonds.

The Expansion Phase of the Cycle

This record of the general cycle pattern will begin at the initial trough of the cycle. The expansion phase of the cycle will be divided into four segments used by the National Bureau in describing the cycle. (See Chapter 11, page 246.)

Segment 1. The outstanding characteristic of Segment 1 of the cycle is the widespread improvement in economic activity. In the pre-World War II period all comprehensive series showed an increase in business since all series were rising except business failures, which were falling as expected. Even though all of the comprehensive series were moving with the cycle, there was a wide variation in the rates of change. The data on the monthly rates of change are expressed according to the regular method used by the National Bureau of Economic Research, based on the average monthly rate of change in reference cycle standings during a segment of the cycle.[10] Prices of all commodities were going up only 0.5 points per month in Segment 1. Production was increasing 2.0 points per month, construction 3.7 points, shares sold on the New York Stock Exchange 6.6 points, and corporate net profit 11.8 points.

In the post-World War II period all of the 11 comprehensive series were rising in Segment 1 except the number of business failures. The most rapid rate of increase in industrial production occurred in this segment just as it did prewar. This was also true of construction contracts awarded, and of employment in manufacturing industries in the early postwar cycles, but there was little increase in employment in the early months of the cycle which began at the end of 1970. In all but the 1958–1961 and 1961–1969 cycles, this is the only segment in which business failures were decreasing, whereas prewar they were decreasing throughout the expansion period.

In the 15 manufacturing industries in the Hultgren study, prices were rising in 41 percent of the observations, the smallest percentage for any of the segments of expansion, while costs per unit of output were rising in only 22 percent of the observations, which is also the smallest for any of the segments of expansion. In Segment 1 profit margins as a percentage of sales were rising in 83 percent of the observations and total profits in 89 percent, the highest figures for any of the segments of expansion.

Long-term and short-term interest rates were generally rising in Segment 1 except in the 1961–1969 cycle when bond rates were about stable. The rates of

---

[9] Reuben A. Kessel, *The Cyclical Behavior of the Term Structure of Interest Rates* (New York: National Bureau of Economic Research, 1965).

[10] See Chapter 11 for a discussion of the procedures used.

increase in commercial paper rates and in Moody's Aaa corporate bond yields were the slowest for any segment in the expansion period. Increases on Treasury bills were slower than in any segment except the last expansion segment.

Segment 2. The expansion of business continued in Segment 2. In the prewar period, all of the series with a regular cycle pattern moved with the cyclical tide except the par value of bond sales and the number of shares of stock sold on the New York Stock Exchange, which began to fall after rising rapidly in Segment 1. The other series with regular cyclical patterns moved more slowly than they did in Segment 1. The rate of increase in industrial production was only half what it was in Segment 1. Net profits still showed the largest rate of increase in any series, but the rate was less than half that in Segment 1.

The pattern in the postwar period was similar in some ways to the prewar period. Only 8 of the 11 series expanded in this segment; the value of construction contracts began falling and sales of common stock and of bonds continued to fall. The number of business failures also moved against the cyclical tide by increasing in the early postwar cycles, but in the 1958–1961 and 1961–1969 cycles the number decreased as it had prewar. No series showed the greatest rate of increase in this segment. The rate of growth clearly slowed from that of the first segment as it had prewar. This was still true in the recovery period of 1970–1973 for series expressed in real terms or in constant dollars.

The Hultgren study of manufacturing industries shows that prices rose in 63 percent of the observations compared with 41 percent in Segment 1. Costs per unit of output rose in 39 percent of the observations compared with 22 percent in Segment 1. Profit margins were still rising in 75 percent of all observations, which is somewhat less than in Segment 1, but total profits were still rising in 89 percent of all observations, the same rate as in Segment 1.

Yields on Treasury bills and commercial paper rates were rising at the most rapid rate of any segment of expansion. Yields on Moody's Aaa corporate bonds were rising more rapidly than in Segment 1, and at about the same rate as in Segment 3. Yields were still fairly stable in Segment 2 in the 1961–1969 cycle. Short-term interest rates were slow to recover in the 1971–1973 period and the 1975–1976 expansion period.

Segment 3. After the retardation in Segment 2, most of the series again rose at a faster rate as the pace of expansion quickened. In the prewar period 28 of the 32 comprehensive series having a regular cyclical pattern rose and 4 fell. The two series on business failures are expected to fall as business increases and thus were moving with the tide. Moving against the tide were the value of bond sales at par and bond prices. Most of the other series were increasing faster than in Segment 2. Those increasing faster included industrial production, fuel and electricity production, the series on transportation, all of the series on trade having a regular cyclical pattern, factory payrolls, income payments, the number of incorporations, shares sold on the New York Stock Exchange (this series fell in Segment 2 but was now rising again), and net profits of business enterprises. Liabilities in business failures also showed improvement by falling faster.

In the postwar period all of the 11 comprehensive series were rising in this segment, except the number of shares of stock sold on the New York Stock Exchange. This series was decreasing at a much slower rate than in Segment 2, whereas in prewar cycles it rose in Segment 3. The par value of bond sales was again increasing very slightly after having fallen off significantly in Segment 2 and even more rapidly in Segment 3 in prewar cycles. The value of construction contracts was again increasing in this segment, except in the 1958–1961 cycle, as it was prewar after having fallen somewhat in Segment 2. Industrial production did not increase as rapidly as it did prewar, but at only half the average rate of Segment 2. Employment in manufacturing industries went up more slowly than in Segment 2 except in the 1961–1969 cycle, and had a greater slowdown in the rate of expansion than in the prewar period. The number of business failures was going up much faster than in Segment 2 in the early postwar cycles, but dropped in the 1958–1961 and 1961–1969 cycles just as it did prewar.

In the manufacturing industry study prices were rising in 74 percent of the observations in Segment 3, and unit costs were rising in 67 percent of the observations, up materially from 39 percent in Segment 2. As a result, profit margins were rising in only 59 percent of the observations compared with 75 percent in Segment 2, but because of increased volume total profits were still rising in 70 percent of all observations.

Yields on Treasury bills were still rising but at a somewhat slower rate than in Segment 2, and commercial paper rates were rising at a significantly slower rate than in the preceding segment, except for 1961–1969 when they were rising rapidly. Yields on Moody's Aaa corporate bonds continued upward at about the same rate as in Segment 2 and started to rise more rapidly in the 1961–1969 expansion.

Segment 4. Business continued to rise during Segment 4, but fewer series participated in the rise.

In the prewar period 24 series were still moving with the tide, but 8 were already moving against it, as follows:

Liabilities of failures (moving against the tide by increasing)
Bond sales
Bond prices
Number of shares of stock sold on the New York Stock Exchange
Prices of common stock
Bank clearings in New York City
Snyder's index of deposit activity
Value of corporate security issues

Thus, most of the series on financial transactions were falling in this last segment of expansion.

In the postwar period 8 of the 11 series were still expanding in Segment 4; all but the value of construction contracts awarded, common stock sales, and bond sales. Contracts awarded dropped slowly after increasing materially in Segment 3 in the early postwar cycles but were rising in the 1958–1961, 1961–1969, and 1970–1975 cycles. This change was due to greatly increased inflation rates. The former relationships still held generally for series measured in square feet per contract rather than dollars. Stock sales continued to drop at about the same rate as in Segment 3, and bond sales dropped materially after increasing slowly in Segment 3. Stock sales and bond sales were dropping in Segment 4 in the prewar period; construction contracts awarded were still increasing but at a much slower rate than in Segment 3. Industrial production and employment continued upward at about the same rate as in Segment 3, or at a somewhat slower rate. In the 1959–1961 cycle industrial production dropped in this last segment of expansion. Thus, the more rapid increase in production and employment in the prewar cycles of Segment 4 compared with Segment 3 did not occur in postwar cycles. The number of business failures continued to increase, and at a more rapid rate than in Segment 3, until the 1961–1969 cycle in which they fell as in the prewar period.

Prices in manufacturing industries were rising in 80 percent of the observations and unit costs in 74 percent, the highest figures for any segment of expansion. Profit margins were rising in only 46 percent of all observations, the lowest figure for any segment of expansion. Because of increased volume total profits were still increasing in 70 percent of all observations.

Yields on Treasury bills went up very slowly at the slowest rate in any segment of expansion except in 1961–1969 when they rose rapidly. Commercial paper rates went up at a much slower rate, and the yields of Moody's Aaa corporate bonds went up at a somewhat slower rate than in Segment 3, again except in the 1961–1969 cycle when short-term rates also rose rapidly.

The Contraction Phase of the Cycle

The contraction phase of the cycle will be described in a similar manner to the expansion phase. In each segment the prewar pattern will be considered first, then the postwar pattern.

Segment 5. As business passes the peak, all of the regular series decline in line with the tide of contraction. In the prewar period the series that had begun to fall before the peak of the cycle all fell faster except bond prices, which were decreasing at a somewhat slower rate. The rate of decrease in commodity prices was small, as was that in income payments. Rapid rates of decrease occurred in the value of construction contracts, the value of new security issues, and the number of shares of stock sold on the New York Stock Exchange. The most rapid change for the worse occurred in corporate profits, and liabilities in business failures were also going up very rapidly.

The postwar cycles did not show the same degree of downturn in Segment 5 as did prewar cycles. In the prewar cycles all 11 series included in the postwar study moved with the tide; all decreased except business failures which went up as business turned down. Postwar increases, in addition to failures, were apparent in the value of construction contracts awarded except in the 1969–1970 downturn, in the number of shares of common stock sold, in the par value of bond sales, and in bank clearings in New York City. Employment in manufacturing had its slowest rate of decrease just as it did prewar and it even rose somewhat in the 1969–1970 downturn and the early segments of the 1973–1975 downturn.

In manufacturing industries prices were still rising in 85 percent of all observations, the highest percentage for any segment of the cycle; and unit costs were up in 85 percent of all observations, a higher percentage than in any segment of expansion. Profit margins were rising in only 28 percent of all observations, and because of decreasing volume total profits were up in only 19 percent of the observations.

Yields on Treasury bills dropped at the sharpest rate in any segment of contraction, and commercial paper rates also started to drop significantly. Yields on Moody's Aaa corporate bonds started to decline slowly except in the 1969–1970 downturn when they continued to rise.

Segment 6. There was no retardation in the rate of decline in the second segment of contraction as there was in the second segment of expansion. In the prewar period the most rapid rates of decline took place in this segment in most sectors of the economy. The only sector of the economy moving counter to the tide was the bond market.

The rate of decline was faster in this segment for most, but not all, sectors of the economy. The value of construction contracts fell somewhat more slowly, the value of corporate security issues fell much more slowly, and liabilities in business failures increased at a much slower rate.

The downturn in Segment 6 was not as pervasive in postwar cycles as it was prewar when only the par value of bond sales was moving counter to the tide. Stock and bond sales and bank clearings were still going up as they were in Segment 5. Construction contracts awarded turned down in this segment in the early postwar cycles after rising in Segment 5. In the 1969–1970 contraction, construction contracts awarded moved upward in this segment. Business failures moved with the tide by increasing in number.

The most rapid rate of decline in this segment occurred in industrial production, in employment, in manufacturing, and in the AT&T Index, just as it did prewar. In the 1960–1961 contraction, the most rapid rate of decline in industrial production was in Segment 7. Construction contracts awarded also went down most rapidly in this segment in the early postwar cycles, whereas prewar the most rapid rate of decline was in Segment 5.

In manufacturing industries prices were still rising in 78 percent of all observations and unit costs in 90 percent. Profit margins were rising in only 26 percent of all observations and total profits in the same percentage of observations.

Yields on Treasury bills continued downward at a slower rate than in Segment 5, while commercial paper rates and yields on Moody's Aaa corporate bonds continued downward at about the same rate as in the previous segment except for bonds in the 1969–1970 downturn when they were rising faster than in Segment 5.

Segment 7. The depression worsened in Segment 7, but at a slower rate. In the prewar period most series still fell and the number of business failures increased. The liabilities in failures, however, were starting to decline. The par value of bonds sold on the New York Stock Exchange continued to rise at the same rate as in Segment 6, and so did bond prices. Most series, however, fell at about the same or at a slower rate than in Segment 6. The value of corporate security issues, and shares sold on the New York Stock Exchange, were falling faster.

In Segment 7 postwar only five of the series were contracting, whereas all but bond sales and business failures went down prewar. Also expanding postwar were stock sales, construction contracts awarded except in the 1960–1961 contraction, and the two series on bank debits. No one series was going down most rapidly in Segment 7 in the early postwar contractions, but industrial production was in the 1960–1961 contraction.

Prices in manufacturing industries were rising in only 45 percent of all observations, down from 78 percent in the preceding segment; unit costs were rising in 65 percent of all observations compared with 90 percent in the preceding segment. Profit margins and total profits were rising in only 26 percent of all observations, the same percentages as in Segment 6. Yields on Treasury bills dropped somewhat faster than in Segment 6, while commercial paper rates and yields on Moody's Aaa corporate bonds dropped at about the same rate. Bond yields began to drop in this segment in the 1969–1970 downturn.

Segment 8. The decline in economic activity was no longer as pervasive as it was in the previous segment. In the prewar period 14 series with regular cyclical patterns were already rising. This group included the series on the number of failures, which was still increasing but at a slower rate than in Segment 7. The liabilities in failures, which were decreasing in Segment 7, continued to decrease at a slightly accelerated rate.

Other series that were increasing and were still moving with the cycle were those related to financial investment activity, which involves preparation for investments soon to be made. The increases show that the financial situation had become favorable and that plans were under way for a renewal of expansion.

Prewar many series already moved upward in Segment 8 and the same was true postwar. All were expanding except industrial production, manufacturing employment, and the AT&T Index. Industrial production and the AT&T Index declined at the slowest rate during this last segment, just as they did prewar. In the 1969–1970 downturn production declined rapidly in this last segment. Manufacturing employment declined at a more rapid rate than in Segment 7, but slower than in Segment 6 in the early postwar cycles; however, it declined slowly in 1960–1961 and more slowly in 1969–1970, just as was the case prewar. The expansion of construction contracts awarded, which began in Segment 7, was going on more rapidly in Segment 8 whereas prewar they began an upturn in this segment. In the 1960–1961 downturn construction contracts continued to decline during this final segment of the contraction period. They expanded somewhat during the 1973–1975 contraction, just as they did prewar.

Prices in manufacturing industries were rising in only 35 percent of the observations, the lowest rate in any segment of the cycle and unit costs in 45 percent of the observations, the lowest rate in any segment of contraction. Profit margins were rising in only 19 percent of all observations and total profits in only 11 percent, the lowest percentages in any segment of the cycle.

Yields on Treasury bills continued downward, but at a very slow rate except in 1969–1970 when they were dropping rapidly. Commercial paper rates continued downward at about the same rate as in previous segments of contraction except for 1969–1970, but yields on Moody's Aaa corporate bonds were about stabilized.

QUESTIONS

1. What has been the average length of the cycle? The most common length?
2. How do the lengths of the periods of expansion and contraction compare?
3. Describe the international pattern of business cycles.
4. Discuss the extent to which various phases of economic activity in the United States move with the cyclical tide.
5. Study the list in Table 12-3 of series which typically lead, move with the cycle, and lag. Account for the timing of (a) common stock prices, (b) new orders, durable goods industries, (c) labor cost per unit of output, manufacturing, and (d) sales of retail stores.
6. Describe and account for the general pattern of amplitude in various phases of economic activity.
7. Describe the fluctuations in GNP in cycles in the post-World War II period.
8. Describe the fluctuations in industrial production during postwar cycles.
9. How important are fluctuations in inventories over the cycle?
10. Discuss the factors that affect the level of inventories and the effect that cyclical factors have on them.
11. Describe what happens in each of the segments of the cycle during expansion. Contrast the prewar and postwar record.
12. Summarize what you feel are the most significant aspects of the behavior of cycles.

SUGGESTED READINGS

Abramovitz, Moses. *The Role of Inventories in Business Cycles.* New York: National Bureau of Economic Research, 1948.

Business Conditions Digest. Washington: U.S. Department of Commerce. Current monthly issues.

Hultgren, Thor. *Cost, Prices, and Profits: Their Cyclical Relations.* New York: National Bureau of Economic Research, 1965.

"Inflation and Stagnation in Major Foreign Industrial Countries." *Federal Reserve Bulletin,* (October, 1974), pp. 683–698.

Kessel, Reuben A. *The Cyclical Behavior of the Term Structure of Interest Rates.* New York: National Bureau of Economic Research, 1965.

Mitchell, Wesley C. *What Happens during Business Cycles: A Progress Report.* New York: National Bureau of Economic Research, 1951. Part II.

Monhollon, Jimmie R. *Manufacturers' Inventory Investment and Monetary Policy.* Washington: Board of Governors of the Federal Reserve System, 1965.

Moore, Geoffrey (ed.). *Business Cycle Indicators,* Vol. I and II. Princeton, N.J.: Princeton University Press, 1961.

"Review and Outlook 1975–76." *Business Conditions,* Federal Reserve Bank of Chicago (January, 1976), pp. 3–10.

"The Seventh Business Cycle." *Business Conditions,* Federal Reserve Bank of Chicago (March, 1975), pp. 10–15.

CHAPTER 13

OTHER FLUCTUATIONS IN ECONOMIC ACTIVITY

Business cycles are usually the most important fluctuations to analyze for the purpose of making forecasts. In some fields, however, seasonal fluctuations lead to wider swings in business activity than those due to the cycle, but they are more regular in their pattern and thus easier to predict. Several other types of fluctuations must be understood if a forecasting program is to be successfully carried out. These fluctuations will be analyzed in this chapter.

Consideration will be given first to cycles in building activity. These are treated separately from the business cycle since the movements do not coincide, and some special factors affect the volume of building at times. Special cycles in agricultural production will be studied next.

Attention will then be directed to seasonal variations that occur in different sectors of the economy. The nature of long-run developments in economic activity and the possibility of long waves in such development will then be considered. This chapter will conclude with an analysis of long-run fluctuations in prices and their relationship to long-run movements in business.

CYCLES IN BUILDING ACTIVITY

The construction field is subject to regular cyclical movements that have not always coincided with fluctuations in general business and which have often been more severe. The cycle in building activity plays an important part in economic fluctuations since the building industry is of major importance. In 1975, for example, out of a total employment of 77.0 million in nonagricultural establishments, 3.5 million were employed in contract construction. This by no means indicates the total economic influence of the construction industry since many people are employed in the development of timber, the mining of metals, the manufacture of various building materials, and the furnishing of services related to the construction field. Expenditures on new construction in 1975 amounted to over $131 billion out of total expenditures of about $1,499 billion.[1]

---

[1] *Federal Reserve Bulletin* (March, 1976), pp. A51, A52, and A54.

Characteristics of the Building Industry

Some of the characteristics of the building industry are important in explaining fluctuations in the volume of building activity. It must be recognized first of all that the building industry is a combination of different types of concerns, some of which build small homes, some skyscrapers, other specialized industrial plants and equipment and so on. The industry is also made up of an unusually large number of small firms and of a much smaller number of large contractors engaged in developing large projects or specialized buildings. There are also local differences in the industry in the way of union organization; in the types of buildings permitted under building codes; in the availability of building materials such as stone, sand, and gravel; and in the seasons in which operations are possible.

One of the most important characteristics of the building industry is that it produces a product of unusual durability. Most buildings, especially of the residential type, last for forty years or more. In fact, obsolescence is often more important than actual physical depreciation. The immobility of buildings is also of economic importance since, as population shifts, new buildings must be constructed to take care of the people who change locations. Another important factor is the variation in different buildings, which is especially pronounced in industrial units. Buildings are not directly interchangeable so that, as the pattern of production and income shifts, there is a demand for some types of buildings that are currently not in existence and a slackening of demand for some types which exist.

Building Cycles

Various students of fluctuations in building activity have found that cycles exist in almost all types of building. Clarence D. Long, Jr., made a study of building cycles for the period from 1868 through 1936, starting with one city in 1868 and increasing the number of cities studied to 27 after 1911. He has found that there are cycles in total building, in residential building, in nonresidential building, and in alterations.[2] William H. Newman found similar cycles in building activity, which he has divided into major cycles and minor cycles.

Some students of the construction industry have questioned the existence of long cycles in urban nonresidential building, believing that the work of Long was based on too limited a survey of data. A very thorough study of construction data has been made under the sponsorship of the National Bureau of Economic Research by Moses Abramovitz and published in an occasional paper under the title *Evidences of Long Swings in Aggregate Construction Since the Civil War*.[3] This study found that the weight of evidence indicates

---

[2] Clarence D. Long, Jr., *Building Cycles and the Theory of Investment* (Princeton, N.J.: Princeton University Press, 1940), pp. 226–227.

[3] Moses Abramovitz, *Evidences of Long Swings in Aggregate Construction Since the Civil War* (New York: National Bureau of Economic Research, 1964).

that a series of long cycles or waves has occurred in aggregate construction activity and in construction work in all important sectors of the industry. In aggregate construction activity each wave was not followed by a distinct long-swing decline, but it was followed by a long period of retardation in growth. Waves similar to those in aggregate construction occurred in all major sectors of the construction field. Table 13-1 shows the timing and duration of the long waves in aggregate construction activity.

Table 13-1
Timing and Duration of Long Waves in Aggregate Construction 1861–Present

			Duration in Years		
Trough	Peak	Trough	Upswing	Downswing	Cycle
1861	1871	1878	10	7	17
1878	1892	1898	14	6	20
1898	1912	1918	14	6	20
1918	1927	1933	9	6	15
1933	1941	1944	8	3	11
1944	1959	1960	15	1	16
1960	1973		13		

Source: Adapted from Moses Abramovitz, *Evidences of Long Swings in Aggregate Construction Since the Civil War* and brought up to date. (New York: National Bureau of Economic Research, 1964), p. 90.

These cycles are all between 15 and 20 years long, except for the 1933–1941 cycle. This cycle was cut short in 1941 by wartime restrictions on building. The contraction phase of the last complete cycle (1944–1960) lasted only about a year. Construction was still in the upswing phase of the current cycle in the early 1970s but a decline took place in 1974 and continued through 1975 and in real terms into 1976.

Residential construction has shown somewhat more variation during the period since 1933 than construction in the aggregate. The number of nonfarm dwelling units constructed increased sharply from 1933 until 1942 when wartime restrictions greatly reduced the level of home building. At the end of the war residential construction increased rapidly until early 1949, and a peak was reached in 1950. Then a decline began and activity levelled off until 1953–1954. A new peak was reached in 1955 followed by a rapid decline until 1957–1958. This cyclical activity continued with peaks in 1959, 1963, 1969, and 1973, followed by declines which reached the bottom in 1960–1961, 1967, and early 1970. By late 1976 housing had not recovered to 1973 levels. The low levels of housing activity in the postwar period occurred during periods of recession and in the 1967 slowdown in economic activity. Peaks were reached, however, early in the recovery period and were followed by sharp declines.

Nature of the Building Cycle

An analysis of the data on major cycles in building activity shows that they have an average length of about 18 years. Clarence Long found that the average duration for the six cycles since 1830 is 17 years and for the last three cycles is just over 18 years.[4] The average duration of the cycles identified by Abramovitz is 17 years and if the cycle cut short by the outbreak of World War II is omitted, it is 18 years.

There is no disagreement about the severity of the building cycle. Fluctuations in building cycles are usually several times as great as those in general business. It is to be expected that some individual industries would have fluctuations greater than those in total business activity, but building fluctuations are wider than those in almost any other component of business activity.

The major movements in building and in general business appear to be associated in the absence of war, but the minor cycles are not parallel. Building reached a peak in the last years of the 1860s and in the early 1870s, and a major depression began in 1873. Building reached its next peak in the middle 1880s and turned downward in the early 1890s preceding the depression of 1893. The next cycle reached a peak in 1916 and declined in 1917 and 1918 because of America's entry into World War I; but indications are that, had it not been for the war, it would probably not have reached a peak until several years later. The cycle, which began at the end of World War I, was interrupted briefly during the sharp depression in 1920; but it then rose to a spectacular peak in 1925 and started to decline rapidly after 1928. It reached a trough in 1933 when general business reached a trough. The next peak of housing construction in 1941 was not a peak in economic activity, but building was restricted due to the demands for war goods during World War II. The peaks in construction in 1959 and 1973 were also peaks in economic activity and the recession in building which followed was short just as was the recession in overall economic activity. Thus, it can be seen that major turning points in building have corresponded reasonably well with major turning points in business and have usually preceded them by one or more years.

Causal Factors

The causes of the differences in the building cycle from the general business cycle, especially the greater length and severity of the major building cycles, are inherent in the nature of the building industry. One of the major reasons for these long and severe fluctuations is the durability of buildings. The basic demand in the economy is for a certain stock of buildings, the vast majority of which are currently in existence since buildings last from 20 to 50 or more years. For example, let us suppose that a community with 10,000 people has 2,500 dwellings. Suppose further that, on the average, one new house is constructed for each increase of four persons in the population. As population increases, the need for housing in succeeding years varies, as shown in Table 13-2.

---

[4] Long, *op. cit.*, p. 159.

Table 13-2
Effect on Housing Demand of Changes in Population

Year	Population	Increase in Population	Percentage of Increase in Population	Number of Houses Required	Number of Additional Houses Required	Percentage of Difference in Additional Houses Needed
1	10,000	—	—	2500	—	—
2	10,160	160	1.6%	2540	40	—
3	10,240	80	0.8%	2560	20	−50%
4	10,300	60	0.6%	2575	15	−25%
5	10,420	120	1.2%	2605	30	+100%

Source: Hypothetical data.

The demand for houses in this example increases along with the increases in population, one house being required on the average for each four persons. As population increases by 1.6 percent in the second year, the demand for houses also increases by 1.6 percent, from 2,500 to 2,540 houses. The 160 additional people create a demand for 40 new houses in the second year. In the third year population continues to increase, but at a slower rate. The demand for houses increases at the same rate as the increase in population. The demand for new houses, however, is only half of what it was in the previous year; 20 in the third year compared with 40 in the second year. In the fifth year population and housing demand increase by 1.2 percent, but the demand for new houses doubles the amount in the fourth year. Thus, while population increases by a small amount each year but not by the same amount each year, the demand for new houses shows wide fluctuations. This is another application of the accelerator principle discussed as one of the causal factors in the cycle.

Fluctuations in the demand for new buildings are not as extreme as the above example indicates, since a certain amount of building is required for the replacement of existing structures. If buildings on the average lasted 50 years in this community, there would be a demand for about 50 houses a year for replacement. The 15 to 40 new houses a year needed to accommodate increases in population, however, is between 30 and 80 percent of the demand for replacement. In actual practice houses would not be replaced at a steady rate, and as a result fluctuations in building activity would be further magnified.

Thus, it can be seen that minor shifts in population growth can lead to large shifts in the rate of demand for new housing. Cycles may easily develop even while population continues to increase but at different rates. In most areas population does not grow at a smooth rate, and there have been fluctuations in the rate of population growth in many sections of the United States as large as or larger than those used in the above example. Local factors influence rates of population growth, and shifts of population take place as some neigh-borhoods in a city decline. In addition, changes in income lead to a demand for different types of housing, which increases the demand for new buildings.

Availability of Financing

Another factor of importance in determining the demand for buildings and hence the character of the building cycle is the availability of new financing. Most building is done on borrowed capital. It seems clear from various studies that changes in interest rates will not explain major cycles in building activity. Even when interest rates move in the same direction as building, the changes are not big enough to assign any important causal significance to them. In-terest as a cost is overshadowed by such important factors as amortization, taxes, and insurance. The availability of credit, however, rather than the cost, is a major factor in the level of activity in the housing field. During periods of recession in economic activity in which the aggregate demand for credit has eased, funds are freed for investment in mortgages. Savings institutions have a larger inflow of funds in part because of the declining rates of return on Treasury bills and issues of federal agencies. Thus, savings institutions have more money to invest in construction and mortgage loans. Mortgage rates are eased somewhat and terms of loans are made more attractive. These changes help stimulate a housing boom. As business in general picks up, the reverse process takes place and a shortage of funds develops for housing. Credit stringency was an important factor leading to the decline in home building in 1956–1957, 1960, 1966, 1969–1970, and 1973; credit availability was a major factor leading to an upturn in 1958, 1961, 1967, and 1971. The 1973–1975 recession was severe enough that home building continued to decline even after credit again became available to more than meet needs.

Other Factors

The level of activity in housing is affected in part by the level of activity in other areas of construction. During recession periods in general economic activity, some workers and equipment made idle because of declining industrial and commercial building move into the housing field, thus making a housing boom possible. As business activity picks up the reverse process takes place. Thus, the short cycle in housing is partially out of phase with the general cycle in economic activity and generally reaches a peak early in the recovery period.

Building costs, it would appear, are also one of the factors that should affect the demand for building and thus the building cycle, but studies indicate that no direct relationship exists. Costs usually move independently of changes in building activity and such relationship as does exist indicates that building activity causes changes in building costs rather than vice versa. The relation-ship between the income to be obtained from a building and the cost of the building, however, is an important factor when determining the level of construction.

AGRICULTURAL CYCLES

Fluctuations in agriculture are directly related to cycles in general business since the purchasing power of farmers forms an important part of the pattern of expenditure for consumer goods. The income of nonfarm consumers also has a substantial effect upon the demand for and price of agricultural products; however, some cycles in this field have a pattern different from that of the business cycle.

Two-Year Cycles in Agriculture

There is a tendency toward a two-year cycle in the price and production of many crop products. If extremely favorable weather makes it apparent that there will be an unusually large crop of some commodity, such as soy beans, the price will drop to a relatively low level. This price will prevail during most of the crop season and will be the one in existence when new sowings are made. As a result of the low price, some farmers may not feel that it is profitable to raise soy beans and will cut the acreage for this crop. As a consequence the price in the next crop year, barring other factors of major importance, will tend to be higher. As this higher price will prevail when another crop is sown, the tendency is to sow a larger acreage, which will lead to a larger crop and lower prices, in turn followed by a smaller crop and higher prices. Thus, there is a tendency toward two-year zigzag cycles.

The cycles result from the way in which supply and prices interact. Supply reacts to the price of a commodity only after a lag because the production period of most agricultural commodities is more or less fixed. Thus, an exogenous factor, such as the weather and the reaction of producers to prices and profit prospects, leads to cycles in production. The theory that describes such production-price cycles is called the *cobweb theorem,* which was explained in Chapter 5.

Hog and Cattle Cycles

In those fields in which the cycle of production is longer, this same tendency will lead to a longer cycle. One of the best examples is in the hog market, although cattle and other animal markets show the same general pattern. The production and slaughter of hogs has a tendency to move in a series of cycles that are three to four years in length and have been longer. These cycles did not exist during the World War II period, but have since redeveloped. These cycles were due in a significant degree to variations in corn production and the relative price of corn and hogs before the period of government price support and storage programs that helped to stabilize corn prices. In recent years these cycles have been due primarily to the reaction of hog producers to prices received for hogs, but they have been longer than the two-year agricultural cycles because of the time required to produce hogs for market. The number of hogs slaughtered in any year is determined by the number of sows that were bred in the preceding year. The spring pig crop, which is marketed from September to March, was born six to nine months previously from sows bred ten to thirteen months previously. The same time relationships hold for the fall pig crop, which is marketed from April to August.

This cycle can be explained as follows. Assume that in the first period under consideration hog slaughter is low, causing relatively high hog prices, and that the pig crop is about normal in size. Slaughter will tend to increase and prices to decrease to more normal levels in the second period as the normal pig crops come to market. The attractiveness of hog prices in period one, however, leads to an above normal pig crop in period two. In the third period this larger pig crop will produce a larger than normal rate of slaughter and prices will drop. The pig crop has, however, declined because of the normal prices in period two. As a result, slaughter and prices will return to normal levels in period four. However, the pig crop will be below normal because of the relatively low prices for hogs in period three, and forces are set in motion to start the cycle over again. These relationships may be summarized as follows:

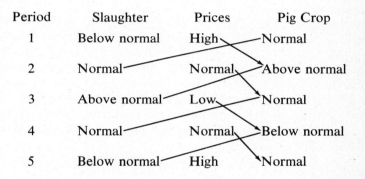

Period	Slaughter	Prices	Pig Crop
1	Below normal	High	Normal
2	Normal	Normal	Above normal
3	Above normal	Low	Normal
4	Normal	Normal	Below normal
5	Below normal	High	Normal

Hog cycles are somewhat more complicated than the above example because hog production is governed to some degree by the relative price of corn and other feeds. The production of hogs and the production of corn are interrelated, since most of the corn crop is fed to hogs and corn makes up about two thirds of the feed used in pork production. Before government price support programs helped stabilize the price of corn, changes in the corn crop had a significant effect on hog production and the cycle was a corn-hog cycle to a large degree. This relationship became significant again in 1973 when the price of corn and other feed grains soared to record levels because of poor weather in the United States during the 1972 fall harvest and poor crops abroad which led to unprecedented demands for feed grains for export.

The process worked in the following way. An unusually large corn crop, which resulted from large plantings or unusually good growing conditions, depressed the price of corn. This low price of corn made it cheaper to raise pigs and thus had a tendency to lead to larger pig crops. The most significant price was not the absolute price of corn, but the relative prices of corn and hogs, or the ratio of the price of hogs to the price of corn. When corn was cheap relative to the price of hogs, the pig crop was increased; and when corn was high, the pig crop was decreased. This led to cycles similar to those described above that are based on the price of hogs without regard to the relative price of corn and hogs. The situation was, however, somewhat more complex and less regular since weather conditions could change the expected yields from a given acreage of corn that was planted on the basis of past price relationships.

The cycle was also accentuated by variations in the length of time that hogs were kept on the farm instead of being sent to market. When the corn-hog ratio was such that it was more profitable to feed hogs and sell them than to sell corn, hogs were kept on the farm and fed longer than normally, and supplies of pork became even smaller than expected on the basis of the pig crop and prices rose further. When the point was reached at which feeding was no longer profitable, slaughter increased and prices were reduced to more normal levels. There is still some tendency for this to happen at the present time, but it has been reduced materially by more stable corn prices and by relatively stable prices of feed supplements. The hog cycle may be further complicated and increased somewhat in length by the number of sows that are available, which is, in part at least, determined by earlier price situations and price expectations.

Since the production period in raising cattle is considerably longer than that in raising hogs, the cattle cycles are of longer duration, having ranged from 9 to 16 years since 1900. It is also less regular, since the longer the time involved, the greater the possibility of outside factors affecting the cycle. Recent cycles have been shorter than earlier ones probably because of better market information. The current cycle has not followed previous patterns since the upturn which began in 1958 would typically have reached a peak in 1963 or 1964. Instead, total cattle numbers almost stabilized for several years and then continued upward.

Coffee Cycle

One of the longest of the agricultural cycles occurs in the coffee market because it takes seven years from the time that a coffee tree is planted until it yields coffee beans. Therefore, a cycle of 15 or more years occurs in this field. This cycle is no longer as clearly visible as it was some years ago because of the interference of the Brazilian and other governments in the coffee market. However, it has continued to affect coffee production and prices in the post-World War II period.

SEASONAL VARIATIONS

Seasonal fluctuations in the volume of business are important in many fields. We shall see why and look at a few examples next.

Causes of Seasonal Fluctuations

Various factors are responsible for these fluctuations in economic activity that take place during the course of the year. Some segments of the economy are affected by the yearly cycle in weather. Other segments are affected by the customs of society, especially those related to holidays. A third factor that causes data to have seasonal fluctuations is our present calendar.

Climate. Climatic conditions influence the periods of growth and the time of maturity of crops, and also to a lesser extent of livestock, and thus economic activity related to agriculture undergoes pronounced seasonal fluctuations. The weather also determines the period of ice-free navigation on various bodies of water and thus influences economic activity. For example, iron ore cannot be transported on the Great Lakes during part of the winter. In some parts of the country the weather also influences operations in the lumber industry and in some types of open-pit mining. In many places climatic conditions necessitate different types of clothing during various seasons of the year, and the manufacture and sale of clothing show the influence of these variations. In addition, the weather determines which sports are carried on at different times and so leads to a seasonal variation in the sale of sporting goods.

Customs. Human institutions and customs also materially affect the volume of business during the course of a year. Holidays materially affect retail activity, and these influences extend into the manufacturing field. There is a demand for various types of merchandise for Christmas gifts, for new clothing at Easter, for fireworks on the Fourth of July, and so on.

The Calendar. The construction of our calendar gives monthly economic data the appearance of seasonal variations greater than the actual fluctuations in business. The months of the year vary from 28 to 31 days. February, for example, is usually almost 10 percent shorter than January, and April is about 3 percent shorter than March. In addition, February has several holidays which make the comparison of the volume of business in February with that in January or March less valid as an indication of the true course of economic activity. The number of Saturdays or Sundays in a month also causes variations, and the changing date of Easter affects sales differently in different years.

Seasonal Patterns in Production

For purposes of analysis, industries with definite seasonal influences may be divided into four basic groups.

The first group consists of those industries in which the supply of raw materials is subject to large seasonal variations, while the demand for the finished product is fairly constant. Most food products are included in this classification.

The second group includes those industries in which the supply of raw materials and the demand for finished products are both subject to large seasonal fluctuations. Examples of this type of industry are the natural fibers, such as cotton and wool, in which there are definite seasonal fluctuations in the demand for the finished products as well as in their production.

The third category embraces industries that make use of raw materials with a fairly constant supply but have a final product that is subject to fairly large seasonal variation in demand. The automobile industry and industries related to it, such as the petroleum industry, are characterized by this type of fluctuation.

The fourth group includes primarily the construction industries, in which there is no necessary seasonal fluctuation in the manufacture of raw materials or in the demand for the final product.

The seasonal movements in some of the component activities of each of these four groups will be presented in general outline, and some comments will also be made on seasonal variations in phases of economic activity other than production.[5]

The supply of most food products is subject to seasonal fluctuations while the demand is not, but the seasonal fluctuations work out differently in such fields as wheat and flour, dairy products, and fruits and vegetables.

Group 1 — Wheat and Flour. The harvesting of wheat is subject to pronounced seasonal fluctuations since it usually occurs between early June in the southern part of the wheat belt in Texas to late July in the northern wheat belt. Flour milling shows a peak in activity in October but not nearly to the same extent as that for the harvesting of wheat in the summer. There is some peak in flour consumption during the winter months, which is in turn much smaller than that in flour milling.

Stocks of wheat are held at various places — on the farms, in elevators, and at flour mills. The stocks of flour, on the other hand, are usually carried by wholesalers and large bakers.

Group 1 — Dairy Products. Seasonal fluctuations in dairy products differ somewhat from those in wheat because the industry is dealing with a perishable commodity. Since more milk is produced in summer than in winter and since the demand for it shows little seasonal variation, the surplus of summer milk is converted into evaporated milk, butter, and cheese, which are then stored until needed. The summer peak in the production of durable dairy products has a tendency to lower their price and thus produces a seasonal price fluctuation.

Group 1 — Fruits and Vegetables. The demand for raw fruits and vegetables would probably remain fairly stable throughout the year in the absence of a seasonal cycle in production. However, their consumption is much heavier in summer, when the supply is large, than it is during other times of the year. The development of the frozen-food industry is tending to smooth out the seasonal fluctuation in consumption, but this industry also has a pronounced seasonal fluctuation since the freezing of food can be done only at the height of the season for each crop. This is also true of other forms of food processing, such as canning and drying; however, a large part of the seasonal adjustment in this field is made by consumers who adjust their purchases to fluctuations in production.

Group 2 — Cotton. In some ways the seasonal pattern in the movements of raw cotton and cotton textiles is similar to that in the field of wheat and

---

[5] For indexes of seasonal variation the reader is referred to the Board of Governors of the Federal Reserve System, *Federal Reserve Index of Industrial Production* (Washington: Federal Reserve System, 1943) and to Appendix B in a current issue of *Business Conditions Digest*.

flour milling. The consumption of raw cotton by textile mills does not have any major seasonal fluctuation even though the harvesting of cotton is concentrated in four months. As in the case of flour, the seasonal peak in mill activity occurs several months after the peak in the harvesting of the crop. This is the case because the farmer carries large and seasonally variable stocks of raw cotton. Cotton differs from wheat, however, since there is also a pronounced variation in manufacturing based upon the seasonal demand for cotton goods. This seasonal variation becomes greater in amplitude the closer one gets to the final consumer. In other words, the retailer has a larger seasonal fluctuation than the wholesaler, and the wholesaler a larger seasonal variation than the manufacturers in the various stages of production.

Group 3 — Automobile Field. There is some seasonal variation in the demand for automobiles. This variation is based partly on the demand during the summer for cars for vacation travel and partly on the dates new models are introduced. Increased summer demand is normally more pronounced in low-priced cars than in higher priced cars. Seasonal variation is smaller for trucks than passenger cars.

Seasonal variations in automobile purchases lead to seasonal variations in the manufacture of automobiles because the industry, as a rule, does not stock many cars. These variations are carried over somewhat into automobile parts production, spark plugs and tires for example, and to a lesser degree for the manufacture of upholstery materials and sheet steel. Seasonal variation also affects the gasoline field, but this variation is more in the amount of stock rather than in production since the technical characteristics of the industry make it difficult to vary production in response to demand.

Group 4 — Construction. In the construction field rain and low temperatures impede activity and thus lead to fluctuations in building activity. Many seasonal problems have been overcome in the construction of major buildings, such as industrial plants and office and apartment buildings, but in the construction of smaller buildings and in the laying of roads and highways some activity is still impossible in severe weather. Most contractors carry no stocks of raw materials, and consequently there are extreme fluctuations in the demand for materials as building speeds up in the summer months.

The peaks for all materials do not come at the same time since some are needed early in the process of construction and others somewhat later. Dealers stock some materials, but a large part of the task of meeting fluctuations in demand falls upon manufacturers, especially in the case of heavy equipment. Production of most construction materials proceeds at a much more even rate than the shipment of these materials; the production of some types of brick and lumber is, however, subject to changes in the weather.

LONG WAVES IN ECONOMIC ACTIVITY

A theory of long waves in economic activity was developed by N. D. Kondratieff while he was director of the Conjuncture Institute of Moscow. He studied various series, such as indexes of wholesale prices in England, France, and the United States; bond prices in France and England; and series on wages, foreign trade, and the output of coal, pig iron, and lead.[6] After smoothing out all cycles with a duration of nine years or less from the late 1780s to 1920, he found two complete long waves and the beginning of a third. The first wave began in the late 1780s, rose until 1810–1817, and then declined until 1844–1851. The second wave began at this time, rose until 1870–1875, and then declined until around 1890–1896. The third wave began at this time with an expansion which continued to the period from 1914 to 1920 and then began to decline.

This theory of long waves has not been generally accepted by economists. Economic data expressed in money terms do show fluctuations that correspond in a general way to Kondratieff's long waves. This relationship is due to the inflation which occurs during major wars, but that does not mean that there were true waves in economic activity. There is no statistical evidence in production series in the United States of any long wave fluctuations of 50 or 60 years.

Burns and Mitchell in their study of business cycles have sought to determine if there is any difference between business cycles occurring during the upswing of long waves in commodity prices and those occurring during the downswing. On the basis of a study of deflated bank clearings, pig iron production, railroad stock prices, the number of shares of stock traded, call money rates, railroad bond yields, and freight car orders, they decided that the cyclical patterns during the upswing and downswing in the long-period movements in commodity prices are broadly similar.[7]

They did find that business cycles in the United States, Great Britain, France, and Germany are somewhat longer on the average during a period of declining wholesale prices than they are when such prices are increasing. It is difficult, however, to draw any accurate conclusion from this relationship since longer business cycles may influence the direction of price movements rather than vice versa, or more complex factors may influence both the length of the cycle and the movement of prices.[8]

Joseph Schumpeter adopted the idea of long cycles in describing economic fluctuations. According to his pattern of the cycle the Kondratieff cycle of 50 to 60 years' duration contained six Juglar cycles of 9 to 10 years' duration, and each Juglar cycle contained three Kitchin cycles of about 40 months' duration.[9] Schumpeter did not always find this regular pattern in actual practice; but whenever one of the cycles was omitted, he believed that some special factor was responsible. The statistical work of Burns and Mitchell, however,

---

[6] Kondratieff's articles have been translated and summarized in the following article: N. D. Kondratieff, "The Long Wave in Economic Life," *Review of Economic Statistics* (November, 1935).

[7] Arthur F. Burns and Wesley C. Mitchell, *Measuring Business Cycles* (New York: National Bureau of Economic Research, 1946), p. 432.

[8] *Ibid.*

[9] Schumpeter named each of these cycles after the men who, in his opinion, did the first important work in describing each type.

does not bear out this relationship between cycles. In the first place less than a third of the business cycles since 1854 have a length between 37 and 43 months.[10] Furthermore, attempts by Burns and Mitchell to group monthly cycle data into patterns of three consecutive cycles produced no approximation to a Juglar cycle of 9 to 10 years.[11]

LONG-RUN FLUCTUATIONS IN PRICE

A study of prices for the last 200 years shows wide fluctuations, which have at times been described as price cycles. To the extent that such cycles exist, they are primarily related to fluctuations in prices that have occurred as the result of inflationary policies during major wars. If wars are considered as political factors impinging upon the economy, then these are not cycles in the same sense as other economic cycles. To those students of our economy, such as Karl Marx and N. D. Kondratieff, who believed that wars are an integral part of the capitalistic process, such cycles would, of course, be true economic cycles. These long-run price movements have also been influenced by major discoveries of gold as, for example, in the period after 1896. They may also have been influenced to some degree by increased demand resulting from major innovations, such as the railroads and the automobile.

In the United States prices rose to high levels during the Revolutionary War and then declined after the end of the war. They fluctuated more or less in harmony with the business cycle until the War of 1812, when they again reached high levels due to wartime inflationary finance. There was a downward trend after the war, and then prices again moved more or less in harmony with business cycles until the Civil War period. During this war wholesale prices more than doubled under the impact of wartime fiscal policy.

After the Civil War the downward movement of prices was again repeated so that by 1896 whosesale prices were not much over one third of the level of the Civil War peak. Prices then began a gradual upward movement that was greatly accentuated during World War I. From this point on prices moved downward, reaching a level in 1932–1933 of about 40 percent of the World War I peak, and then they started up again and continued upward through World War II. There was only a slight falling off in prices after the end of World War II, and prices resumed their upward movement in the summer of 1950 after the outbreak of the Korean War.

From 1958 through 1964 prices remained about stable and then started to rise again due to the demands arising from the intensification of the Vietnam War and the devaluation of the dollar in the late war and postwar periods.

A cursory examination of the history of prices may give the impression that prices have moved in long waves. More careful examination of price data, however, will show that this is not the case. Prices have moved upward sharply during wartime periods and some early postwar periods and then have generally stabilized or gradually declined. These sharp wartime peaks give price data the appearance of long waves, which is largely illusory.

---

[10] Burns and Mitchell, *op. cit.*, p. 462.
[11] *Ibid.*

QUESTIONS

1. What is the nature of the building cycle?
2. How are building cycles related to business cycles?
3. Account for the length and severity of the building cycle.
4. Why is the short cycle in housing usually out of phase with the cycle in overall economic activity?
5. Describe the hog and cattle cycles. What accounts for them? How has the situation changed since the introduction of agricultural programs to stabilize feed prices and to provide better market information?
6. Why is the coffee cycle one of the longest on record?
7. Briefly describe the factors that lead to seasonal fluctuations in business.
8. Identify the four basic types of seasonal variations in production industries.
9. Briefly analyze the Kondratieff theory of long waves.
10. Are there long cycles in price movements?
11. How is the economy affected by having various cycles in different phases of their cycle as well as the business cycle?

SUGGESTED READINGS

Abramovitz, Moses. *Evidences of Long Swings in Aggregate Construction Since the Civil War.* New York: National Bureau of Economic Research, 1964.

Burns, Arthur F. "Long Cycles in Residential Construction," *Economic Essays in Honor of Wesley Clair Mitchell.* New York: Columbia University Press, 1935.

Kondratieff, N. D. "The Long Waves in Economic Life." *Review of Economic Statistics* (November, 1935).

Long, Clarence D., Jr. *Building Cycles and the Theory of Investment.* Princeton, New Jersey: Princeton University Press, 1940.

"Meat Prices." *Review,* Federal Reserve Bank of St. Louis (August, 1969), pp. 24–28.

Newman, William H. *The Building Industry and Business Cycles.* Chicago: University of Chicago Press, 1935.

"Roller Coaster in Housing." *Monthly Economic Letter,* First National City Bank of New York (November, 1969), pp. 128–131.

"Soviet Agriculture." *Business Conditions,* Federal Reserve Bank of Chicago (June, 1976), pp. 3–10.

CHAPTER 14

BUSINESS CYCLES FROM THE PRE-WORLD WAR II PERIOD TO THE PRESENT

Economic conditions during the World War II period would have been materially different if the economy had been operating at anything near prosperity conditions in the prewar period. As things were the economy entered one of its most severe depressions in 1929 and economic activity continued downward into 1933. This depression was so severe that industrial production fell by almost 50 percent and employment by 25 percent. Consumer prices declined by about 20 percent. This depression affected all industrialized nations, but was more severe and longer in the United States than in most other countries.

Under the impetus of the various government programs designed to increase economic activity, industrial production increased after 1933 and continued upward to 1937. By the early summer of 1937 business had reached the peak of a new cycle, but it had not grown during this recovery period at anything like the rate of the 1920s. Employment was about the same as in 1929; but since the labor force had grown materially, approximately eight million people were out of work in 1937.

The failure of the economy to continue its rapid growth during the 1930s was due to several factors. For one thing there were no innovations equal in their effect on production and national income to that of the automobile and related fields in the 1920s. Electric power production did increase much more rapidly from 1929 to 1937 than in the period from 1920 to 1929, but it did not create the same derived demand for the products of other industries as did the rapid development of the automobile, and it did not account for anything like the same amount of increased employment.

Another reason for the failure of the prosperity period that ended in 1937 to achieve 1929 proportions was the reduced rate of residential construction. Since so many houses had been built during the 1920s, there was little need for replacement during the 1930s; and the low rate of economic activity did not create the demand for any large-scale new construction. Construction other than residential also failed to equal the 1928 boom. Some of the policies of the federal government, irrespective of any long-range merits, contributed to uncertainty in the business field and thus probably also delayed recovery.

THE 1937 RECESSION AND RECOVERY

Recovery had not carried the economy back to full employment levels when another recession occurred in 1937. The decline in business activity, which began in the latter half of 1937 and continued into the first half of 1938, was rapid. Industrial production dropped by over 25 percent in a short time, but it did not reach the low levels of 1932 or 1933.

The greatest decline during this depression occurred in the production of durable goods. Residential construction, which had not recovered to anything like 1929 levels, showed no new decline but continued upward in 1937 and 1938. There was a reduction in the level of wholesale commodity prices late in 1937, in 1938, and continuing into 1939.

Several factors accounted for the downturn in business activity in 1937. During the recovery period after 1933 governmental deficits added to the income stream. In 1936 the deficit of the federal government was unusually large due to the cashing of bonus certificates for veterans of World War I. In 1937 receipts of all governmental units exceeded expenditures by $685 million.

In addition to the decrease in the deficit of the federal government, funds in the hands of consumers were further reduced when Social Security tax collections increased by over $1 billion in 1937 from the 1936 level and no provision was made for paying out any funds until a later period. The net result of the operations of the federal government was a decrease in borrowing from $3.8 billion in the calendar year 1936 to about $300 million in 1937.[1] This rapid shift in government finances was a major factor leading to the downturn in 1937.

Another factor that influenced the business situation at this time was the June, 1936, Revenue Act, which contained an undistributed profits tax. This tax caused the payment of a larger sum in dividends on 1936 corporate income than would otherwise have been the case, and this added to consumer income in the latter part of 1936 and the early part of 1937. Its long-range effect on business expansion, however, was repressive in that many businesses were afraid of the implications of such a tax. Prices also played a part in the 1937 recession. Prices of agricultural commodities increased in 1936 because of the severe drought. There was a decline in speculative activity in world commodity markets in April, 1937, and the prices of raw materials declined after that time and with them the speculative demand for goods.

The reaction of the federal government to the decline in business in 1937 was to step up its public works program, which was financed by again running a deficit. More orders for airplanes and armaments were placed in this country by European countries as the international situation deteriorated, and these orders helped increase the level of business activity. Almost all phases of economic activity in the United States increased rapidly after World War II began in Europe in the fall of 1939 at which time America became the Arsenal of Democracy.

---

[1] *National Income Supplement to Survey of Current Business* (July, 1947), pp. 21–23.

THE WORLD WAR II PERIOD

When the United States entered the war in December, 1941, over five million people were still unemployed in this country. Within a short time, however, demand became so large that it was impossible for the economy to produce enough war goods without reduction of production in industries serving civilian needs and wants. The task of getting sufficient production allocated to war needs was turned over to the newly created War Production Board early in 1942. This board stopped the production of various consumer durables and issued limitation orders and set priorities on the nonwar use of metals to insure sufficient supplies for the production of war equipment. As war production increased rapidly at the end of 1942, the system of priorities proved inadequate and a controlled-materials plan was set up. Under this plan production was controlled by basing schedules on the available quantities of carbon and alloy steel, copper, and aluminum.

The increased demand for goods for military operations, as well as increased purchasing power in the hands of a much larger labor force as the unemployed were absorbed in war production, led to price control and rationing in an attempt to prevent inflation. The Office of Price Administration was set up and it rationed such items as tires, automobiles, typewriters, gasoline, bicycles, fuel oil, shoes, processed foods, and meats and fats. It also established maximum prices on various commodities, first at the wholesale level and then at the retail level, and it set ceilings on rent.

The War Manpower Commission was established on April 18, 1942, by executive order in an attempt to assure more efficient use of the nation's human resources in the war effort. It recruited workers for private industry and government service, developed lists of individuals with particular skills, set up training programs, and encouraged women to participate in the war effort.

Early in 1942 the President established a National War Labor Board to hear all controversies that might interrupt any work which contributed to the effective prosecution of the war. The wage policy used by the War Labor Board in developing its stabilization program was called the "Little Steel Formula." The War Labor Board decided in a dispute involving the workers of Bethlehem, Youngstown, Inland, and Republic Steel companies that a top wage increase on June 16, 1942, of 15 percent above the straight-time rates which prevailed on January 1, 1941, would adequately compensate employees for the increased cost of living from January 1, 1941, through May, 1942. This was the date when the President sought to stop the ruinous price-wage race. This formula was used to determine cost-of-living wage increases and above that no increases were allowed except to correct inequities.

Because of war expenditures, the total federal budget increased rapidly. In fiscal year 1941 the federal government spent $12.8 billion, of which approximately half was directly war-related. Total expenditures increased to $100.4 billion in fiscal year 1945, of which 90 percent was for war expenditures.[2]

---

[2] *Tax and Expenditure Policy for 1950,* A Statement on National Policy by the Research and Policy Committee of the Committee for Economic Development (New York: 1950), p. 38.

Part of the cost of the war was raised through increased taxation, but a substantial part was raised by government borrowing since in the seven War Loans and in the Victory Loan the United States Treasury sold almost $157 billion of securities. The Federal Reserve System facilitated the financing of the war by supplying reserves to the banking system through the purchase of over $20 billion of government securities.[3]

THE RECONVERSION PERIOD

The reconversion period was viewed with misgivings by many who felt that the economy would return to prewar depression levels. As the economy shifted back to peacetime production at the end of 1945 and in 1946, the controls were lifted one by one. Control over prices was modified shortly after the end of the war and was allowed to lapse on June 30, 1947, except for rent control in housing shortage areas. Prices rose rapidly when controls were lifted.

Production decreased in 1946 and employment decreased somewhat. Most of the difference in production, however, was accounted for by the elimination of overtime work. In 1947 production and employment again increased; the year was one of virtually full employment of labor and resources, and a strong seller's market continued. Prices continued upward during 1947 as supply and demand were seeking a new balance. During the second quarter of the year there was some tendency for domestic business to level off.

As the world agricultural situation became worse because of poor crops in 1947, the foreign demand for farm products created new pressure on prices. Demand by foreign countries increased generally and reversed the easing tendencies that were beginning to appear in some lines of business. Foreign countries drew on their dollar resources so rapidly that they soon were all but exhausted. This led Secretary of State George C. Marshall to suggest a foreign aid program; Congress passed an interim aid program late in 1947 and the European Recovery Program in the next year. These programs kept foreign demand at a high level, but not at the level of the second quarter of 1947.

Factors Leading to Inflation

Several factors accounted for the postwar increases in prices after the period of wartime price control. There was a large demand for consumer durable goods such as automobiles, refrigerators, washing machines, and radios since the output of these goods had been drastically curtailed during the war. Wartime savings, larger than usual because of patriotic appeals and the shortage of goods, were available for postwar purchases. The changed situation from a partially employed economy in the prewar period to a fully employed economy in the postwar period also made price increases likely. The most important reason for inflation in the postwar period was the method of wartime finance. As already pointed out, the government resorted to borrowing on a large scale and the

---

[3] *Federal Reserve Bulletin* (January, 1950), p. 61.

banks of the country bought government bonds from private investors in large quantities. With a greatly increased money supply and the increased demand for goods, it was inevitable that prices should rise.

The 1949 Readjustment

The economy continued to operate at close to capacity levels during 1948. Wartime income tax rates were cut in the spring of 1948, and the extra income left in the hands of consumers had an expansionary effect on the economy. In 1948 the price level increased more slowly than in 1947, and the rate of increase in consumption expenditures also began to level off. Business people did not adjust immediately to this change in the rate of increase in business activity and, as a result, found themselves with excessive inventories. Toward the end of 1948, businesses adopted cautious buying policies and during the first quarter of 1949, substantial inventory liquidation took place.

As a result of the change in inventory policies, industrial production declined about 8 percent. Durable goods production fell 10 percent, but nondurable production fell only 5 percent. Total employment declined slightly and manufacturing employment fell off 9 percent. Construction continued upward through 1949, and expenditures on producers' durable equipment were down by only about 5 percent.

One reason that business did not decline further was that personal consumption expenditures held up and even increased slightly toward the end of 1949. This was due in part to the payment of unemployment compensation to most of the workers who were out of work and also to the effects of lower federal income taxes under the 1947 Revenue Act. Perhaps most important was the willingness of consumers to keep expenditures up even in the face of some falling off in business.

It became evident in the second half of 1949 that inventory liquidation had gone too far. Buying for stock was resumed in more normal proportions and business picked up early in 1950. A new boom began later in the year as the Korean War and large-scale rearmament led to an intensified demand for goods.

THE KOREAN WAR PERIOD

The Korean War started on a small scale as a United Nations police action, but it developed into a major conflict lasting several years. This war had a significant effect on our economy because the bulk of the UN forces were American and most of the war material was supplied by this country.

The demand for goods arising out of the Korean War led to renewed inflationary pressures. Government deficits were not the cause of price rises in the last half of 1950, since the Treasury had an excess of cash income over cash outgo of almost a billion dollars in the last half of the year. The explanation lies in private spending. Consumers, fearing the shortages of World War II, spent large sums on various types of durable and semidurable goods. Business also spent heavily for inventories and capital investment.

Under these conditions Federal Reserve Bank credit increased materially. The Board of Governors of the Federal Reserve System wanted to act to restrict expansion, but could not so long as it felt obligated to support the bond market by buying all government securities at par or better. The Treasury wanted to follow a pattern of low interest rates as it did in World War II, and this, of course, required price-support operations since interest rates would have gone up in a free market as the demand for funds increased.

The controversy between the Treasury and the Federal Reserve System developed into an open conflict in the summer of 1950, especially after the Federal Reserve System had to engage in large-scale, open-market operations to assure the success of some financing at a rate the market did not find attractive. President Truman appointed a committee to study ways and means to provide the necessary restraint on private credit expansion and at the same time to maintain stability in the market for government securities. Before this committee could report, however, an agreement between the Treasury and the Federal Reserve System was announced in March, 1951. This accord was designed to check credit expansion without the use of direct controls. Government bonds were no longer bought in the market by the Federal Reserve to maintain a set pattern of interest rates. The Federal Reserve was not to stay out of the market completely but continued to buy and sell some securities so as to maintain an orderly market. As the private demand for funds increased because of a boom in residential building and in the capital markets, interest rates rose and the price of long-term securities dropped somewhat.

THE 1953 RECESSION AND RECOVERY

Business continued upward in the first half of 1953. By summer the rate of increase in business activity had slowed down, and there was some fear that a recession might occur. The Federal Reserve System eased credit to prevent a downturn or to make any downturn that might occur less serious. A downturn began in the third quarter of 1953 and continued through the second quarter of 1954. Industrial production dropped about 10 percent from July, 1953, to May, 1954, and unemployment increased to about 4 million. Gross national product decreased by only about 2 percent and personal income remained almost unchanged during the recession. Expenditures on construction leveled off in the second half of 1953 and the first quarter of 1954, and then increased rapidly during the remainder of the year.

The 1953–1954 downturn was largely a readjustment to a lower level of defense expenditures made possible by the end of the Korean War. The decreased demand for war goods also led to some decrease in business investment expenditures and to liquidation of inventories in late 1953 and 1954, whereas they were being increased before that time. Consumers also reduced expenditures on durable goods somewhat, especially on automobiles. This was due to the fact that most consumers had late-model cars because of large-scale purchases in the postwar period and also the uncertainty of the economic outlook as unemployment increased.

This readjustment to a lower level of government expenditures, especially on war goods, and the resulting decline in investment expenditures and reduction in inventories did not result in a protracted depression for several reasons. Personal income held up well during the recession because most sectors of the economy were not affected and because personal taxes were cut by over $3 billion. Unemployment compensation also helped cushion the decline in income of the unemployed.

Economic activity increased rapidly in 1955 and personal consumption expenditures increased, especially on durable goods. Automobile sales increased from about 5.5 million cars in 1954 to almost 8 million in 1955. Residential construction increased by over $3 billion from 1954 to 1955, and then declined somewhat in 1956 and 1957. Inflationary pressures began to develop during this prosperity period. To prevent serious inflation, the Federal Reserve System followed a highly restrictive monetary policy. Reserve requirements were raised, and the rediscount rate was raised several times.

THE 1957-1958 RECESSION AND RECOVERY

In the late summer of 1957 the economy experienced the beginning of the third postwar recession. This recession was in some ways the most severe of the three readjustments but the period of decline was the shortest. Industrial production dropped 13 percent between August, 1957, and April, 1958, compared with 10 percent in the two earlier recessions. By August, 1958, unemployment had increased to 7.7 percent of the civilian labor force. Gross national product declined 2.5 percent, but disposable personal income changed little.

All sectors of the economy were not affected uniformly by the recession. One of the hardest hit was the capital goods industry since business expenditures on plant and equipment dropped by 16 percent. Consumer durable goods expenditures also declined, especially those on automobiles.

One of the major factors leading to the decline in production and in gross national product was the liquidation of inventories. In the third quarter of 1957 inventories were being built up at a rate in excess of $2 billion per year. During the first quarter of 1958 inventory liquidation was at an annual rate of $9.5 billion, and in the second quarter at $8 billion.

A number of other causal factors were at work in the 1957-1958 recession. One was the slowing down of capital expenditures because plant and equipment had been expanded faster than the increase in demand for goods and services. Another was the shift in consumer expenditures. Less money was spent on durable goods and more on nondurables and services.

Shifts in foreign trade also affected the economy in the 1957 downturn. Exports of goods and services increased in the early part of 1957 because of the crisis in Egypt and the Middle East which closed the Suez Canal and disrupted some pipelines carrying oil, and then dropped again in 1958.

Business reached the low point of the recession in April, 1958, and then started upward. The boost did not come from any sharp reversals in the areas leading to the downturn. It came in part from the ending of inventory liquidation in the last quarter of 1958 and some increase of inventories in the first quarter of 1959. A major impetus for recovery came from the consumer sector as expenditures increased on nondurable goods and services. There was also an increase in residential construction as interest rates eased and mortgage funds were made more easily available under FHA and VA programs.

Increased government expenditures also helped increase business activity. Federal government expenditures increased by almost $3 billion from the third quarter of 1957 to the third quarter of 1958, and state and local government expenditures increased by almost $4 billion. By the spring of 1959 economic activity had passed the prerecession levels in most sectors of the economy. Unemployment remained a problem, however, since it was at 6 percent of the labor force and had been about 4 percent in the 1955–1957 prosperity period.

The first half of 1959 was a year of strong economic recovery that showed some signs of turning into a boom. The economy suffered a severe setback, however, when the longest steel strike on record began shortly after midyear. When the steel strike ended in November, there was a new surge in economic activity. Inventories were rebuilt rapidly through the first quarter of 1960, and production and gross national product reached new highs by midyear.

THE 1960–1961 RECESSION

The fourth postwar recession began in the second half of 1960. Industrial production dropped during the second half of the year and into early 1961. Gross national product eased somewhat during the last quarter of 1960 and fell somewhat further in the first quarter of 1961. Unemployment, however, posed more of a problem than in earlier postwar recessions. It had been more severe in the 1957–1958 recessions than in the earlier postwar downturns and continued to be a problem in the recovery period. During the 1960–1961 recession unemployment almost reached the 1958 peak even though the downturn in production was mild. One reason for the increased unemployment was the increasing size of the labor force due to an increasing birth rate after 1939. Another was the accelerated pace of automation resulting from new technological advances and rising labor costs.

The 1960–1961 recession was due to several factors. Inventories that had been depleted by the steel strike were rebuilt rapidly in the first quarter of 1960 and then more slowly in the second quarter. This build-up led to an increase in production which could not be sustained when inventory building ceased in the third quarter. Residential construction also slowed down since the huge backlog of deferred demand had been met and mortgage money for residential financing was more difficult to obtain and more costly than it had been during the 1957–1958 downturn and early recovery period. Consumer buying also weakened somewhat after midyear, especially the purchase of durable goods. Consumers had a good stock of automobiles and other durables so demand was no longer pressing. Rapid increases in the volume of consumer credit outstanding in 1959 and in the first half of 1960 led consumers to slow down purchases to increase their equity position.

THE PROSPERITY PERIOD OF THE SIXTIES

The prosperity period that followed the mild recession of 1960–1961 was the longest in our history. There was some retardation in the rate of advance in economic activity in late 1962 which was more pronounced in industrial production than in gross national product. There was some intensification of economic activity in 1965 and especially 1966 as American participation in the Vietnam War was increased greatly. Policies that were designed to slow inflation led to a slowdown in the forward movement of the economy in the first quarter of 1967, but the economy moved forward again in the second quarter and continued to advance until late 1969.

Several characteristics of the early years of this prosperity period before it was affected by the Vietnam War are somewhat unusual. Wholesale prices remained almost completely stable from 1961 through 1964 and then started to move upward slowly in 1965 as demand accelerated. Labor cost per unit of output remained relatively stable throughout the period from 1961 through 1966. This was due to wage increases that were to a large extent held within average increases in productivity and to major expenditures by industry on more efficient production plants and equipment.

The money supply was also increased gradually during most of this period rather than being decreased during the prosperity period. There was a reduction in the money supply in the early part of 1962, but the supply was increased sharply in the second half of the year as retardation in the rate of advance in economic activity took place. The federal government had a cash deficit that did not vary significantly in amount during the first four years of this period. One major reason for the unusual length of this prosperity period was that many things which lead to cyclical unbalance did not occur until 1965 and 1966.

This does not mean that the prosperity period was without problems. The unemployment rate did not fall below 5 percent of the labor force until late 1964, and unemployment was especially severe among teenagers. The Vietnam War led to additional demands for military personnel, goods, and services, but even under the impetus of war demands, the unemployment rate did not drop much below 4 percent. Many of those who were still unemployed were for all practical purposes unemployable in a highly mechanized economy without an upgrading of their labor skills.

The problem of a deficit in the balance of payments also persisted during this period of prosperity. Campaigns to increase exports had some measure of success, and foreign investment was reduced by a Voluntary Foreign Credit Restraint program. The measures taken were not sufficient, however, to solve the problem of the balance of payments.

A new problem arose in 1966 when interest rates climbed to the highest levels since the early twenties. The demand for funds from all sectors of the economy was high and increasing, especially the demand for bank loans from business. To prevent serious inflation arising out of the demands of the Vietnam War, the Federal Reserve raised the discount rate in December, 1965, and acted generally to restrict the supply of money and credit. The result was a slowdown in residential construction during the summer of 1966. The stock market also reacted to higher interest rates and reduced profit prospects; by mid-1966 the average price of industrial common stocks had dropped by some 20 percent from the high points reached in 1965.

There were signs in late 1966 that the economy was slowing down. The Federal Reserve acted to stimulate the economy by increasing the money supply at the end of the year and into the first half of 1967. Economic activity slowed down in the first quarter of 1967 when GNP in real terms did not increase over the fourth quarter of 1966. GNP in current dollars went up somewhat as price pressures continued. There was a very sharp recovery in economic activity in the second half of 1967 which continued until late 1969. Inflation continued at an accelerated rate during this period primarily because of a high level of private spending and inflationary policies followed by the federal government in the 1967 slowdown in economic activity. The federal budget for fiscal 1969 showed a slight surplus and by mid-1969 the Federal Reserve was following a policy of severe credit restraint. Interest rates rose to higher levels than in 1966 and in some cases were the highest since Civil War days.

THE 1969 RECESSION

The economy experienced another recession in late 1969 which lasted during most of 1970. This recession was as mild as, or milder, than the recession of 1960–61 and was among the mildest in our history. Gross national product in current dollars continued to expand and declined only very slightly in constant dollars. Industrial production dropped by 6.6 percent from its high point and employment by 1.6 percent. The general price level continued to increase at a high rate during this recession period. The GNP implicit price deflator rose at an annual rate in excess of 5 percent.[4]

This recession was not mild, however, in the financial markets. The prices of common stocks declined somewhat more than in the earlier postwar recessions, but not as much as in the depression of 1937 or 1929–1933. The prices of long-term debt securities were falling before the recession as interest rates rose to unusually high levels and continued to do so during the first half of the recession period. A dramatic event was the failure of the Penn-Central Railroad to meet its obligations which resulted in its filing for bankruptcy.

This recession was not caused by inventory liquidation or a decline in business capital investment. Business continued to add to inventories throughout the recession and 1970 was a record year for capital outlays. The major cause was the restrictive monetary policy followed by the Federal Reserve in the second half of 1969 and into early 1970 in an effort to slow down the rate of inflation. Consumers also increased their level of saving to near a 20-year high because of the uncertainties related to inflation and the continuation of the Vietnam War.

---

[4] Solomon Fabricant, *Recent Economic Changes and the Agenda of Business-Cycle Research* (New York: National Bureau of Economic Research, Inc., 1971), p. 27.

BOOM PERIOD OF THE EARLY SEVENTIES

The recession of 1969–1970 was unusually mild and recovery began near the end of 1970. To slow the decrease in economic activity and to stimulate recovery, the Federal Reserve adopted a policy of credit ease. Inflationary pressures were so strong, however, that prices continued to increase even during the recession. The economy entered into a period of slow recovery in 1971 under the stimulus of a rapidly increasing money supply in the first half of the year. Prices moved up sharply, with the consumer price index increasing by more than five percent during the year. To combat inflation, the President ordered a 90-day price freeze in mid-August and set up wage and price controls when the freeze ended. The goal was to cut price increases to an average of 2.5 percent per year while wages were to rise on an average of 5.5 percent. This was based on the assumption that average productivity in the economy would increase at a rate of 3 percent per year. To help restrain prices, the growth rate of the money supply was cut materially after midyear.

The economy continued to have balance-of-payments problems which had persisted for several years. To correct what appeared to be a basic unbalance in the relationship of the dollar to major foreign currencies, the dollar was devalued in December of 1971 by 12 percent.

Recovery in economic activity accelerated in 1972 and by the end of the year real growth was increasing at a rapid rate. Consumer prices went up by only about 3.5 percent, the best year for price restraint since 1967. This was due in large measure to price and wage controls. Federal Reserve monetary policy was expansive in the early part of the year, but late in 1972 money growth was slowed due to renewed inflationary pressures. Unemployment continued to be a serious problem even though employment increased as recovery continued. This was due to several factors of a structural type. The labor force was growing more rapidly than population as children born in the post-World War II baby boom reached the age to seek employment. This also meant that more teenagers were seeking employment and they generally have a higher rate of unemployment than older workers. More women, who historically have had a higher unemployment rate than men, were also seeking employment.

These inflationary pressures continued and became greater in 1973, a year in which consumer prices increased some 9 percent. It looked early in the year as if 1973 might be a good year for the economy. American involvement in the Vietnam War ended early in the year, the dollar was devalued by 10 percent in February, and the balance-of-payments problem seemed to be on the way to solution as America again developed a surplus in its trade balance with the rest of the world. Price controls of a mandatory nature were replaced in January with more-or-less voluntary controls. The growth of Federal Reserve credit was slowed and the federal government had a surplus by the second quarter of the year.

However, economic activity increased at a rapid rate and demand in many fields was in excess of supply. Price controls also led to dislocations in many sectors of the economy, thus adding to shortages in some areas. Prices moved up so rapidly that a new 60-day price freeze was put into effect in June, and at the end of this period prices were again frozen but were allowed to be increased by the exact amount of higher costs. Provisions were made for decontrol on an industry-by-industry basis.

The price situation got worse as the year progressed for several reasons. There were poor crops in many parts of the world, which raised the prices of food products. Large amounts of wheat were sold to Russia and China and this led to rapid increases in grain prices. In October another Arab-Israeli War broke out, but it was of short duration. The Arabs, however, to put pressure on the United States and other countries to support their cause, put an embargo on oil shipments and raised oil prices. The embargo was lifted after a time but prices were raised to several times their prewar levels. As the demand for credit remained high, the supply of credit was restricted, and investors feared continued inflation as interest rates reached unprecedented levels.

Early in 1973 there were reports of short supplies of many basic materials and also some finished goods. By late summer it seemed as if almost everything was in short supply. These shortages were due to the boom in economic activity which was taking place in all industrial nations. But they were also due to dislocations caused by price controls. Part of the shortage was also caused by a rapid increase in exports of goods. This was not only due to booming business activity but also to inflation in foreign countries at a greater rate than that in the United States, which made American goods a good buy. Devaluation also helped to make the prices of American goods attractive in foreign countries. The boom in 1973 was of such a nature that it could not last even if the Federal Reserve had not acted to restrict credit expansion.

THE 1973–1975 RECESSION

The recession which began late in 1973 was the most severe of the recessions in the post-World War II period and it was also the longest. According to preliminary dating it began in November, 1973, and lasted through March, 1975, a period of 16 months. Real GNP in terms of 1972 prices declined 6.6 percent, well over twice the decline in the recession of 1957–1958, which was the most severe of the earlier recessions in the postwar period. Industrial production dropped almost 15 percent, a somewhat larger decline than in the most severe recession before that in the postwar period. The other postwar recessions varied in length between 8 and 11 months.

Construction also declined significantly. Total construction contracts in early 1975 were 25 percent below the average level in 1973. Housing experienced an even more dramatic decline from a level of 2.4 million starts in 1973 to a low of 880,000 on an annual basis at the end of 1974.[5]

Inventories also created problems in the 1973–1975 recession. Inventories generally lag GNP, but the lag was unusual in this recession. Inventories increased in each quarter of 1974, but for different reasons. In the first two

---

[5] *Federal Reserve Bulletin* (February, 1976), p. A50.

quarters inventories rose in the materials and supplies fields as producers attempted to build stocks which had been in short supply. In the last two quarters inventories rose because sales declined and stocks had become excessive in relationship to sales. This was especially true in the last quarter of 1974. There was a massive liquidation of inventories in the first two quarters of 1975, and the liquidation continued at a slower pace during the remainder of the year.

Employment dropped from a record 79.9 million in October, 1974, to 76.6 million in February, 1975, and three fourths of the reduction was in manufacturing. The unemployment rate rose to a postwar high of 9.2 percent in the spring of 1975.[6] Prices rose rapidly during the recession instead of declining or the rate of increase slowing down as had happened in earlier cycles. The GNP deflator rose almost 10 percent in 1974 compared with less than 6 percent in 1973. The price level increased in each recession period after the end of the Korean War, but earlier increases were at a much slower rate than in 1974. Consumer prices also increased rapidly, going up at an 11 percent rate in 1974.[7]

Interest rates also rose to unprecedented levels in 1974. Near the end of April the Federal Reserve raised the discount rate to 8 percent and late in June and early in July the federal funds rate averaged a record 13.5 percent. On July 3 major banks raised their prime rates to a record 12 percent. The high interest rates and poor business conditions led to a major decline in stock prices. Early in December the Dow industrials closed at 578, the lowest level since October, 1962, and well below the high for the year in mid-March of 892.[8]

Several events in the financial sector also contributed to the general atmosphere of severe recession. In April, Consolidated Edison omitted a dividend for the first time in its history and in May the Franklin National Bank also omitted a dividend due to foreign exchange losses. In early October the Comptroller of the Currency declared the Franklin National Bank insolvent. New York City also had continuing problems in meeting payments on debts as they came due, but continued to find a way with federal and state help to keep from being in default.[9]

The 1973–1975 recession, like all severe recessions in modern times, was worldwide so far as industrial nations are concerned. The acceleration of output in the first half of 1973 in France, West Germany, Italy, the United Kingdom, Japan, and Canada was at an exceptionally high rate. This was followed by an equally sharp deceleration of output in all countries and a general recession.[10] In some cases the recession was the most severe in recent years, just as it was in the United States.

---

[6] *Ibid.*, p. A52.

[7] *Federal Reserve Bulletin, op. cit.*, pp. A53–A55.

[8] *Business Conditions*, Federal Reserve Bank of Chicago (January, 1975), pp. 16, 17.

[9] *Ibid.*

[10] "Inflation and Stagnation in Major Foreign Industrial Countries," *Federal Reserve Bulletin* (October, 1974), pp. 683–698.

The 1973–1975 recession also differed from earlier postwar recessions in that it consisted of two distinct phases. The first phase was a response to constraints on aggregate supply; the second stage, which began in the early fall of 1974, also reflected a reduction in demand for goods and services.

Total spending for goods and services rose substantially during the first three quarters of the recession with only a minor halt after the peak of the cycle. Money expansion continued to be rapid during the first two quarters of the recession whereas this period is usually characterized by slow monetary growth. The chief cause of the downturn during this period came from the supply side. The ability of the nation to produce was reduced by increased energy costs, unfavorable weather leading to crop reductions and higher prices, the cost of environmental and safety programs, the effect of dollar devaluations, and the unbalancing effects on production of price controls. The result was a decline in the quantity of goods available for consumption while prices went up. After the first phase of the recession the second phase was also affected by the more typical lack of demand at prevailing prices and institutional arrangements. Total spending declined sharply in the last quarter of 1974 and the first quarter of 1975.

Causes of the 1973–1975 Recession

Like all severe recessions, the recession of 1973–1975 had its immediate causal factors and longer-run causal factors. The major immediate causal factor was inflation in the United States which was part of a worldwide inflation in major industrial countries. This was due in part to relatively easy monetary and fiscal policy in the years preceding 1973. This was true not only in the United States, but in all major industrial countries. There were also several additional inflationary factors involved. Farm prices went up rapidly in 1973 due to poor crops in many parts of the world. Oil prices also went up dramatically due to the actions of OPEC countries. There was an increase in raw material prices generally as a worldwide boom ran up against a relatively fixed supply, at least in the short run. Inflation not only had an effect on interest rates and stock prices, but also on consumers. Increased prices for oil products and food left consumers with less money for other products. Higher wage rates which were to help offset inflation, at least in part, provided no greater real wages. But under our system of progressive income taxes a larger percentage of real income went to the federal government, thus creating more problems for consumers. Inventory build-up was also excessive and this helped cause recession. Goods were so scarce during the boom that many businesses failed to see signs that the boom was ending and they thus continued to build stocks. When stocks had to be liquidated demand was further reduced and this led to more severe recession.

The more basic causes of the recession of 1973–1975 go back to some of the developments in the preceding period.[11] In a real sense 1973 marked the

---

[11] This section relies heavily on a paper presented by Arthur F. Burns, Chairman, Board of Governors of the Federal Reserve System, at a meeting of the Society of American Business Writers and published in the *Federal Reserve Bulletin* (May, 1975), pp. 273–279.

end of a period which began in 1958 or as late as 1961, just as 1933 marked the end of a period which began in 1921. There were several such periods in the pre-World War II period so they are not a phenomenon of the postwar period but a general pattern in our economy. Total employment rose in every year from 1961 through 1973, as did disposable personal income and personal consumption expenditures, both on a per capita basis and in real terms.

The period from 1961 through 1964 was one of sustained expansion in which unemployment fell to 5 percent of the labor force and productivity grew rapidly. Around 1965 speculative excesses developed in several fields. One such excess was in corporate mergers and acquisitions, especially in the era of conglomerates. The effect of such actions on projected profits per share diverted management from its more basic tasks of increasing technology and profit prospects. Many conglomerates were a disappointment so far as earnings were concerned and the prices of their stocks dropped dramatically.

Other stocks were also involved in a speculative market for common stocks. The volume of trading on the New York Stock Exchange doubled between 1966 and 1971. In the two-year period of 1967–1968 the average price per share on the New York Stock Exchange went up 40 percent while earnings went up less than 2 percent. Needless to say, the stock market could not and did not sustain such a record of growth, but dropped to lower levels. Such stock speculation was aided by mutual funds of the "performance" type. A similar stock market boom took place in all major industrial countries.

A speculative wave also hit the real estate markets. Real estate investment trusts supplied high risk construction loans for condominiums, recreational developments, shopping centers, and the like. The result was overbuilding so that by 1972 the vacancy rate for office buildings reached 13 percent and many projects were in serious financial trouble.

The inventory boom has been referred to several times. It began in 1973 as several other speculative excesses were diminishing. There were signs in early 1973 that consumers were reducing spending, but these signs were missed as business rushed to get "scarce" goods before the price went even higher.

Fiscal policy was not used to stop speculative excesses but became more expansive. Taxes were cut in 1964, 1965, 1969, and 1971 and spending was increased for social programs and the war in Vietnam. Corporations allowed their equity positions to deteriorate and liquidity to decrease. Large money-market banks relied more heavily on volatile short-term funds to finance their customers and some state and local governments followed unsafe financial practices. Some resorted to excessive short-term borrowing while others issued so-called "moral obligation" bonds which some investors regarded wrongly as equal in credit rating to "full faith and credit" obligations. Such excesses could only lead to problems which needed correction and this helped intensify the 1973–1975 recession.

Recovery from the 1973–1975 Recession

Recovery from the 1973–1975 recession began in the fourth quarter of 1975. To stimulate recovery monetary policy became much more expansive early in 1975. Fiscal policy became stimulative late in 1974 and expansionary in 1975 because of an increase in expenditures and a sizable tax cut, especially for lower income groups. Interest rates declined from the high levels of 1973 and 1974 and thereby made expansion easier to finance. Inflation also slowed from the high rates of 1973 and 1974.

Consumers led the way to recovery with increased expenditures on nondurable goods. As excess inventories were worked off in field after field, production was again called for to meet current demand. The trade surplus of the United States hit a record level in 1975 as imports were reduced and exports expanded.

Economic activity continued to expand in 1976 and into 1977 as the economy recovered from the most severe recession in the postwar period. Problems remained, such as inflation at too high a level, unemployment at too high a level, a problem of access to sufficient raw materials, pollution problems, and uneasy international financial and goods and services markets. It appeared, however, that the economy was well on the way to a healthy and sustained recovery in 1977.

QUESTIONS

1. Why did business turn down in 1937 before full employment was achieved?
2. Outline the steps which were taken to adjust the economy to the demands of World War II.
3. How would economic conditions probably have differed in 1946 and 1947 if almost all of the cost of the war had been raised by taxation?
4. What led to the 1949 readjustment?
5. (a) Describe the nature of the 1953–1954 downturn. (b) Discuss the factors which led to this downturn.
6. (a) Describe the extent of the 1957 recession. (b) Which factors were responsible for this recession? (c) Why was it sharp, but short?
7. Discuss the nature of and causal factors at work in the 1960–1961 recession.
8. Describe the prosperity period of the 1960s. Why was it longer than earlier prosperity periods?
9. Discuss the nature of the causal factors at work in the 1969–1970 recession.
10. Outline the major steps taken in 1971 to correct the imbalances in the economy. What were they designed to accomplish?
11. Describe the state of the economy in 1972 and 1973.
12. Describe the character of the 1973–1975 recession.
13. How does the 1973–1975 recession compare with earlier post-World War II recessions?
14. What was the immediate cause of the recession which began in 1973?
15. Outline the basic causes of the 1973–1975 recession.
16. What led to economic recovery in 1975?
17. What was the character of the recovery after the 1973–1975 recession?

SUGGESTED READINGS

Bowsher, Norman N. "1974—A Year of Inflation, Production Cutbacks, and Oil-Induced Payments Deficits." *Review*, Federal Reserve Bank of St. Louis (December, 1974), pp. 2–10.

————. "Two Stages to the Current Recession." *Review,* Federal Reserve Bank of St. Louis (June, 1975), pp. 2–8.

"Consumer Income, Spending, and Saving, 1960–1970." *Economic Review,* Federal Reserve Bank of Cleveland (June, 1971), pp. 10–18.

Craf, John R. *A Survey of the American Economy, 1940–1946.* New York: North River Press, Inc., 1947.

Economic Report of the President. Washington: U.S. Government Printing Office, 1947 to date.

Federal Reserve Bulletin. Current issues.

"Inflation and Stagnation in Major Foreign Industrial Countries." *Federal Reserve Bulletin* (October, 1974), pp. 683–698.

Roose, K. D. "The Recession of 1937–38," *Journal of Political Economy,* LVI (June, 1948), pp. 239–248.

"The Current Recession in Perspective." *Federal Reserve Bulletin* (May, 1975), pp. 273–279.

"The Seventh Business Cycle." *Business Conditions,* Federal Reserve Bank of Chicago (March, 1975), pp. 10–15.

PROBLEMS ON PART 4

1. The following data are available on the cycle of an industry producing kitchen gadgets:

    Initial trough of the cycle...September, 1970
    Peak of the cycle...November, 1973
    Terminal trough of the cycle.....................................April, 1975

    Average specific cycle relatives for the nine stages of the cycle are as follows:

Stage I	85	Stage VI	111
Stage II	95	Stage VII	100
Stage III	102	Stage VIII	90
Stage IV	111	Stage IX	85
Stage V	120		

    (a) Plot the cycle pattern.
    (b) Calculate the timing and duration of this cycle.
    (c) Calculate the amplitude for the rise and for the fall. Also calculate the amplitude per month for the rise and for the fall.

2. Select a company for which you can get monthly sales data for January, 1962, to the present. Using this data calculate:
    (a) The trend of sales since 1962 (use annual sales data).
    (b) The seasonal pattern.
    (c) The cycle pattern (National Bureau Method). Plot this pattern.
    (d) The timing and duration of the cycle.
    (e) The cyclical amplitude.

3. Study the record of economic activity in the late 1970s from articles in the *Survey of Current Business* and the *Federal Reserve Bulletin.* Select monthly reference dates for peaks and troughs and bring Table 12-2 on page 254 up to date. How does the most recent cycle (or cycles) compare with earlier cycles in duration of expansion and contraction?

4. (a) Plot the number of nonfarm dwelling units started in each year since 1962 on ratio paper, using data from the *Federal Reserve Bulletin.* On the same chart also plot the following:
    (1) Gross national product from the *Survey of Current Business.*
    (2) Average interest rates on Treasury bills from the *Federal Reserve Bulletin.*

(b) Discuss the relationships, if any, among the three series above. Which additional factors are likely to have caused some of the fluctuations in residential construction?

5. Analyze the current situation in the economy. Which past period does the current situation resemble most? Are there any changes on the horizon that could lead to major readjustments of the 1929 type?

6. Make a table similar to that of Table 12-4 on page 261. Analyze the data for the most recent cycle or the recovery phase if that is all that is complete. Comment on similarities and differences between the most recent cycle and the 1970–1975 cycle.

PART 5

FORECASTING ECONOMIC ACTIVITY

One of the important reasons for studying the nature of business fluctuations and the causal factors that have produced them is to be able to determine the most probable future levels of economic activity. This is of significance in developing governmental policies in the monetary and fiscal areas, and it is also of primary importance to the business person who must develop plans in light of future prospects for the economy. Part 5 will deal with techniques and procedures currently used to forecast future levels of economic activity.

Chapter 15 considers various procedures for projecting the trend of activity in the economy for several years into the future and describes and analyzes various approaches to such forecasting. Chapters 16, 17, and 18 deal with short-run forecasting of economic activity for a year ahead and present procedures for building a model of gross national product for the next year. Chapter 19 discusses methods of predicting long-run price trends and of making short-run price forecasts.

Forecasting is at the stage that medicine was during its early days, but early medicine, though experimental, was a good deal better than were the witch doctors. Even today, when the practice of medicine is an applied science based on the underlying biological sciences, there is an element of art left in it. Business forecasting is largely an art, but it is developing into an applied science with an element of art just as medicine has done.

The science of forecasting is based on an understanding of the causal factors at work in the economy. Future events can only be predicted when the causal factors at work are understood. Forecasting is also based on a knowledge of past reactions to a given set of causal factors. To provide such knowledge, the record of past cycles is analyzed. If the causal factors at work and the reactions to them are fully known, an analysis of the present situation should make prediction possible. In our present state of knowledge, much is still not known about the causal factors at work in the economy and about the reactions of the economy to such factors. Therefore, a full science of prediction is not possible and a large area of judgment remains. At this stage of development, forecasts will therefore be subject to some error and may at times be completely incorrect. However, a forecast based on available techniques is, on the average, far superior to intuition, chart reading, and the like.

CHAPTER 15

PROJECTING THE TREND OF ECONOMIC ACTIVITY

In any business important decisions must be made in light of the long-term trend in sales of that business. If sales are likely to be growing over a period of time, plans must be made for the expanded facilities necessary to handle the increased volume of business and for the necessary financing for such facilities. This planning must be done on the basis of the long-term trend of the total economy, of the industry of which this business is a part, and of the business itself. Studies of these trends must take into consideration the varying rates of growth in different sections of the United States.

If the business is regional, the trend of economic activity in its region will affect its sales in the future. If the business is national, the trend of sales in different regions will affect the location of future plant additions so as to be most economically located in relationship to raw materials, labor, and future markets.

PROJECTING THE GROSS NATIONAL PRODUCT TREND

One of the best ways of making a long-range projection of total economic activity is to project the level of gross national product since this is the most comprehensive series on economic activity in general use. This is done by such organizations as the National Planning Association, the Conference Board, and the Department of Commerce. These projections are not forecasts of the actual level of economic activity to be expected in the future but projections of long-run trends in the economy, made on the assumption of full employment in the forecast year and in terms of prices current at the time they are made. Such projections are useful as a guide to the building of plant and equipment on the basis of the long-run demand for a product, not on the basis of the cyclical fluctuations.

Since trends change slowly, such projections can be made with reasonable accuracy for several years into the future. As the period of time involved is lengthened, the projections become less reliable since unforeseen factors can have considerable influence on economic activity in the future and since trends may change materially over a period of time. Projections have been made for as many as fifty years ahead, but these are only rough, general estimates of the potentialities of the economy. Fortunately for planning most types of capital expenditures, projections for five to ten years are usually sufficient and these can be made with reasonable accuracy in real terms.

Various procedures with different degrees of refinement may be used for projecting gross national product. The simplest technique is to project the trend for the past few years either on a freehand basis or by using the line of least squares. Another possibility is to find the average annual rate of growth for a period of years in the past and then project this rate of growth to the forecast year. A more complex approach is based on a determination of the number of persons likely to be in the labor force and of the most likely output per employed worker in the forecast year. This approach can be refined by determining the most likely distribution of employees by fields and also the most likely output per worker in each field. Each of these procedures will be considered more fully.

Line of Least-Squares Trend

In projecting the trend, it is necessary to consider which time period in the past shall be used for such a projection. GNP, for example, grew more rapidly from the depths of the depression in 1933 through the end of the early post-World War II period than it has since that time or can be expected to grow in the future. The period since then has not been affected by these abnormal developments. Prices rose rapidly during the Vietnam War, but this effect is largely eliminated by using GNP in constant dollars as a basis of projection. This is done since increases in real output are to be projected, not price changes. Table 15-1 gives GNP figures from 1957 through 1975 in terms of 1972 dollars. The formula for the line of least squares applied to this data for the period 1957–1975 is:

$$Y = 953.5 + 33.4x \text{ } (x \text{ is the forecast year minus 1966).}$$

Table 15-1

Gross National Product for 1957–1975
(In Billions of 1972 Dollars)

Year	GNP	Year	GNP
1957	680.9	1967	1,007.7
1958	679.5	1968	1,051.8
1959	720.4	1969	1,078.8
1960	736.8	1970	1,075.3
1961	755.3	1971	1,107.5
1962	799.1	1972	1,171.1
1963	830.7	1973	1,233.4
1964	874.4	1974	1,210.7
1965	925.9	1975	1,186.1
1966	981.0		

Source: *Survey of Current Business* (January, 1976), Part II, pp. 6–7, and (May, 1976), p. 3.

The projected 1985 GNP in 1972 dollars is $1,788.1 billion. Adjusting this to 1975 prices by means of the 1975 GNP price deflator of 127.25 gives a GNP figure for 1985 in 1975 dollars of $2,275.4 billion.

Extending Average Rates of Growth

An alternative method of making a projection of GNP is to extend the average rate of growth in a past period into the future to the forecast year. It is necessary to select a period for calculating average rates of growth just as it is necessary to do so to determine and project the line of least squares.

The average rate of growth of GNP in real terms for the period from 1957 through the 1972–1973 period was about 3.75 percent per year. The rate of growth dropped in the 1974–1975 recession period but increased again in 1976. Extending the 3.75 percent rate of growth to 1985 from the 1975 level of GNP of $1,516.4 billion gives a value of GNP of $2,191.2 billion in 1985 in terms of 1975 prices. This may be calculated by the following formula:

$$\$1,516.4 \ (1.0375)^{10} = \$1,516.4 \times 1.445 = \$2,191.2.$$

Estimating GNP from the Supply of Factors of Production

A more refined approach is to project GNP from the basis of the ability of the economy to supply goods and services. This is done by estimating the most likely level of the labor force and the GNP output per worker. The GNP output is total output of GNP arising from labor itself and also from the other factors of production.

This procedure also projects GNP in terms of current prices. Furthermore, it assumes full employment in the forecast year. This means that results will be somewhat higher than projections based on extending past growth from a period in which significant unemployment existed in some years. This will be true in the 1957–1975 period since there was unemployment of some magnitude above frictional unemployment in the second half of 1957 and 1958, in 1961 and 1962, in 1969 and 1970, and in 1974, 1975, and 1976.

Population and Labor Force. The first step in this procedure for projecting gross national product is to estimate the population at the future date selected for the forecast. This step requires a study of the trend of population and a projection of this trend into the future. Such estimates are made by the Bureau of the Census of the Department of Commerce, as well as individuals and private agencies. Table 15-2 shows the increases in population since 1920, the total labor force, the labor participation rate, and the unemployment rate.

After the size of the population has been estimated, the number of individuals who will be in the labor force must be estimated. Such projections are based upon a study of the long-term trend of the labor force in relationship to the total population and the population of working age. From 1900 until about 1950 the labor force was growing when compared with total population. It started a slow decline then which continued until the early 1960s. Since then it has increased again primarily because more married women have been seeking work. It has been going up faster since 1969 as babies born during the post-World War II baby boom have entered the labor force and the rate of population increase has slowed down. All of these factors must be considered in estimating the total labor force from an estimate of population. The Bureau of the Census estimates the size of the labor force and its probable distribution as to sex and age groups.

Table 15-2

Population and Employment, 1920–1975

Year	Population*	Total Labor Force*	Labor Participation Rate†	Unemployment Rate‡
1920	106.5	42.8	39.9	4.0
1930	123.2	50.1	40.6	8.7
1940	132.6	56.2	42.4	14.6
1950	152.3	63.9	42.0	5.1
1955	165.9	68.1	41.0	4.2
1956	168.9	69.4	41.1	4.0
1957	172.0	69.7	40.5	4.1
1958	174.9	70.3	40.2	6.5
1959	177.8	70.9	39.9	5.3
1960	180.7	72.1	39.9	5.3
1961	183.7	73.0	39.7	6.5
1962	186.5	73.4	39.4	5.3
1963	189.2	74.6	39.5	5.5
1964	191.8	75.8	39.5	5.0
1965	194.2	77.2	39.8	4.4
1966	196.5	78.9	40.1	3.6
1967	198.6	80.8	40.7	3.7
1968	200.6	82.3	41.0	3.4
1969	202.6	84.2	41.6	3.4
1970	204.8	85.9	41.9	4.9
1971	207.0	86.9	42.0	5.9
1972	208.8	89.0	42.6	5.6
1973	210.4	91.0	43.3	4.9
1974	211.9	93.2	44.0	5.6
1975	213.6	94.8	44.4	8.5

Source: Bureau of Census data and *Federal Reserve Bulletin* (March, 1976), p. A52.

* In millions of persons.
† Percentage of total population in the labor force; that is, persons who are able and willing to work, age 16 years and over (14 years and over for 1920, 1930, and 1940).
‡ Percentage of the civilian labor force which is unemployed.

The number of persons 16 years of age and over in the labor force in 1975 was 94.8 million, or 44.4 percent of the population of 213.6 million.

Assume that the population in 1985 will be 234 million, which is near the center of the range of estimates for that year. The labor participation rate will probably continue upward somewhat as more married women enter the labor force and the unusual number of children born in the post-World War II boom are absorbed in the labor force. If we assume a 46.0 percent participation rate, the labor force estimate for 1985 is 107.6 million workers.

Estimates of GNP are usually based on production of goods and services by the civilian labor force. Therefore, the number of people likely to be in the armed forces must be subtracted. This number was about 3.2 million in 1970. It had been going down gradually for several years before it increased again in the summer of 1966 due to the demands of the Vietnam War. It decreased again to about 2.2 million in 1975.[1] Let us assume it is 2.0 million in 1985. Our estimate of the civilian labor force is then 105.6 million workers.

After the size of the civilian labor force in the forecast year has been projected, the amount of frictional unemployment must be estimated. *Frictional unemployment* includes unemployed workers who are entering the labor force for the first time, who are shifting from one seasonal job to another, who are shifting the concern for which they work, who are changing their line of work, and the like. Even in such years of high business activity as 1929, 1948, 1950, 1951, 1952, 1966, and 1973, unemployment did not drop below 3–4 percent of the civilian labor force and has been over 6 percent in some prosperous years in the 1960s and 1970s. Therefore, about 4.5 percent can be used as a good approximation of frictional unemployment. The above estimate of the civilian labor force for 1985 was 105.6 million workers. If about 4.5 percent or 4.8 million workers are unemployed, civilian employment in 1985 will be about 100.8 million.

Production. After the size of the employed civilian labor force in the forecast year has been determined, the volume of goods and services that will be produced must be estimated. This estimate depends upon the number of hours that will be worked and the rate of output per hour. The long-run trend of the number of hours worked has been going down; but it is unlikely, according to most observers, that it will drop much below 40 hours a week in most fields, at least not during periods of full employment that are assumed to exist as a basis for estimating the long-term trend. The average hours worked per week were about 36.1 in 1975. This was about a half hour lower than the level in the previous year, and was more than three hours lower than the level 10 years before. The level in 1975 was somewhat lower than normal because of the recession in economic activity. The annual average is, however, likely to continue to drop somewhat because of a tendency toward more paid holidays and longer vacations. Let us assume for our projection of GNP that the average number of hours worked per week is 36.0 in 1985.

The next step is to estimate the amount of gross national product that is likely to be produced for each hour of civilian employment in the forecast year. The rate of increase in gross national product per worker-hour since 1957 has been about 3.0 percent per year. From 1957 to 1960 it was below the postwar average and this was again true in the 1966–1969 period and in 1973–1974, but in other years it was well above the average. Let us assume

---

[1] *Federal Reserve Bulletin* (March, 1976), p. A52.

that it will be 3 percent per year between 1975 and 1985. In 1975 GNP per hour of civilian employment was $9.56 [GNP of $1,516.4 billion ÷ 158.6 billion hours of work (36.1 hours average work week × 52 weeks × 84.5 million civilian employees)]. At an average annual rate of increase of about 3 percent per year, GNP per civilian worker-hour will be $12.85 in 1985. Gross national product in 1985 is then based on the following factors:

> Civilian employment — 100.8 million workers
> Average hours of work per week — 36.0
> GNP per hour of civilian employment — $12.85

The average hours of work per year per worker are 1,872 (52 × 36), and the total number of hours of work in the year is 188.7 billion (1,872 × 100.8 million workers). Multiplying by an average projected rate of output of $12.85 per worker-hour gives a GNP figure of $2,425 billion in 1975 dollars.

More Refined Estimates of GNP

Estimates of GNP based on expected employment levels and expected output per worker may be refined by making separate estimates for major sectors of the economy and totaling these to arrive at an estimate of GNP. One such refinement is to estimate the civilian and governmental contribution to GNP separately. This is done for several reasons. One is that it is impossible to measure trends in productivity in government employment since government services are not sold in the marketplace. Another is that trends in wage rates in government and private employment have not always been the same.

The private contribution to GNP is found by determining private employment, hours to be worked per year, and output per hour. Such output can be projected on the basis of trends of productivity in general, or by figuring trends in productivity of labor and capital separately. The government contribution is developed from figures on the number of workers and the average pay per worker. The number of workers in government employment is determined from past trends in the number of government employees and a qualitative evaluation of the factors likely to affect employment in the future as, for example, the smaller number of schoolteachers required in the 1970s to educate the smaller number of children of school age because of decreased birth rates in the 1960s. The average wage per government worker is likewise determined from the trends of wages and also from a consideration of qualitative factors.

A further refinement calls for estimating output in major fields of civilian employment separately. This is, at times, done only for agricultural and non-agricultural production because of varying rates of productivity and hours of work in these fields. At times nonagricultural employment is further subdivided. For example, the National Planning Association has divided the economy into the fields shown in Table 15-3, along with estimates of 1976 employment figures.

Table 15-3

Number of Jobs by Industry, 1976
(Thousands of Jobs)

All industries	90,302
Agriculture, forestry, and fisheries (SIC 01,07–09)	3,122
Mining (SIC 10–14)	733
Contract construction (SIC 15–17)	3,740
Durable manufacturing (SIC 19,24,25,32–39)	11,719
Nondurable manufacturing (SIC 20–23,26–31)	7,951
Transportation, communication, and public utilities (SIC 40–42,44–49)	4,873
Trade (SIC 50,52–59)	19,829
Finance, insurance, and real estate (SIC 60–67)	4,857
Services (SIC 70,72–3,75–6,78–82,84,86,88–9)	18,193
Civilian government (SIC 91–93)	15,246

Source: *National Planning Projections, 1961–1986* (Washington: National Planning Association, November, 1976).

ESTIMATING GNP FROM THE DEMAND FOR THE FACTORS OF PRODUCTION

Gross national product can also be estimated from the demand side by making an estimate of each of the major categories of GNP in the forecast year. This is done be estimating personal consumption expenditures, gross private domestic investment, government purchases of goods and services, and net exports of goods and services. These categories are estimated from past trends in each of its major subdivisions, from an analysis of qualitative factors, and from past relationships between them. The procedure is similar to that described in Chapters 17 and 18 for making a short-run forecast.

More refined estimates may be made by estimating receipts and expenditures in each major sector of GNP and determining the excess of receipts or expenditures in each sector. The total of these must, of course, balance *ex post,* and estimates should be evaluated and modified if need be. A lack of balance between total receipts and disbursements may indicate that some of the estimates are not accurate or that they have not been made consistently. It may also indicate that the economy will tend to behave in this way, but that forces will be put in motion to adjust the lack of *ex ante* balance between savings and investment. These factors are considered more fully in Chapters 17 and 18.

Estimates of GNP made from supply and demand sides can also be compared and differences analyzed. If the supply figure is above that from the demand side, unemployment is likely to exist; if the demand figure is the higher, inflationary pressures will exist. In making a final forecast, it is necessary to consider the most likely actions by government, business, and labor if deflation or inflation exists and to estimate the effect of these actions on GNP.

The National Planning Association has been making estimates of future levels of GNP for some time. These estimates have been made by using various approaches to projecting GNP and developing the most likely figures on the basis of the judgment of the economists making the estimates. The size of the labor force and the most likely output per hour of employment are used as one approach. Estimates are also made of the demand for GNP from purchases of goods and services by consumers, for domestic investment, by government, and from net international purchases. In developing the estimate for each sector, disposable receipts as well as purchases are estimated, and the projected excess or deficit of receipts is determined for each sector as well as the balance for the total economy. The National Planning Association has developed estimates that are in balance under each of the following sets of circumstances:

High Consumption Models	High Government Model
Slow Growth	Slow Growth
Fast Growth	Fast Growth
High Investment Models	Alternative Defense Models
Slow Growth	Low Defense
Fast Growth	High Defense

PROJECTING DISPOSABLE PERSONAL INCOME

In many areas of economic decision making and especially in projecting consumer expenditures, it is necessary to have a forecast of disposable personal income as well as a forecast of gross national product. The amount of income individuals have to spend after taxes is one of the major factors determining the level of many consumer expenditures. The following adjustments must be made to GNP to get disposable personal income:

Subtractions
    Capital consumption allowances
    Indirect business tax and nontax liability
    Current surplus of government enterprises
    Corporate profits and inventory valuation adjustment
    Contributions for social insurance
    Excess of wage accruals over disbursements
    Personal tax and nontax payments
Additions
    Government transfer payments
    Net interest paid by government and consumers
    Government subsidies to business
    Dividends

Each of these items must be estimated in the forecast year to develop a forecast of disposable personal income. Minor items, such as the surplus of government enterprises and government subsidies to business, are usually ignored. An estimate of capital consumption allowances requires estimates of the year-by-year increases in plant and equipment, and of the depreciation on them. Also needed are estimates of losses of capital by destruction and of capital expenditures charged to income currently. These estimates are made on the basis of past relationships and the qualitative factors in the present situation.

Indirect business taxes, mainly sales and excise taxes, must also be estimated and subtracted, since they are not available for consumer expenditures. These taxes are usually estimated by applying present tax rates to estimates of future increases in business and adjusting the figures for expected tax changes.

Corporate income taxes and retained earnings are not available for consumer expenditures either. Except during recession years, corporate profits after taxes have had a fairly stable relationship to gross national product. This past relationship can be used along with present and projected tax rates and qualitative factors to estimate corporate income taxes. Estimates of retained earnings and of dividend payments can also be made from an analysis of past trends in the division of profits after taxes between dividends and retained earnings.

Deductions for estimates of social insurance contributions are also necessary. These can be estimated from past trends and any expected changes in social security tax rates, as well as from projected levels of employment and increases in the income of workers.

Personal taxes must be estimated and subtracted to determine disposable personal income. This is usually done first by assuming that current tax rates will continue, and then by making adjustments for expected changes in tax rates.

Several items must also be added to arrive at disposable personal income. One of these items is government transfer payments. These can be projected from past trends and also from a thorough study of present programs for veterans, for agricultural aid, and the like. The other important item to be added is personal interest income. This involves a projection of interest rates and the levels of government and consumer debt. The level of the debt can be developed from a study of probable surpluses or deficits in government budgets and from trends and current developments in consumer borrowing. To estimate interest rates involves a study of supply and demand factors.

An alternative approach starts with a projection of national income. This is built up by projecting the trend of the various payments to the factors of production—essentially wages, interest, rent, and profits. Then the various items that must be added to and subtracted from national income to arrive at personal income must also be estimated. These items, as well as the various payments making up national income, were described in Chapter 3.

PROJECTING THE TREND FOR AN INDUSTRY

Several steps are involved in making long-range estimates of sales in various fields. One step for many consumer items is to find the relationship to disposable personal income. Sales of some items bear a more or less constant relationship to disposable personal income, some items are growing more rapidly than income, and some at a slower rate. If the relationship to disposable personal income follows a regular pattern, that relationship and a forecast of disposable personal income can be used as a basis for a projection for five or ten years in the future.

In making such a projection the trend of sales in the industry itself should also be considered. It may also be helpful to study the trend of consumption on a per capita basis. The trend is difficult to project in the early stages of an industry when sales may be growing rapidly and also irregularly. When an industry has become well established, however, and sales are growing primarily in response to changes in such factors as income, population, and price changes, projections based on past trends can be made with more confidence. Qualitative factors such as the development of substitute products or changes in consumer tastes or habits must also be considered carefully. Consideration must also be given to trends in exports and imports if they are significant.

The Department of Commerce analyzes trends in many industries and publishes such data in an annual publication called *U.S. Industrial Outlook*. This volume analyzes past trends and makes a forecast for the next year and a projection for a period some five to ten years in the future.

The soft drink industry may be used as an example of the types of projections which are made. The sale of soft drinks had been growing somewhat more rapidly in recent years than disposable personal income. Figure 15-1 shows relative changes in the value of soft drink shipments, disposable personal income, and the wholesale price of soft drinks for the 1967–1975 period.

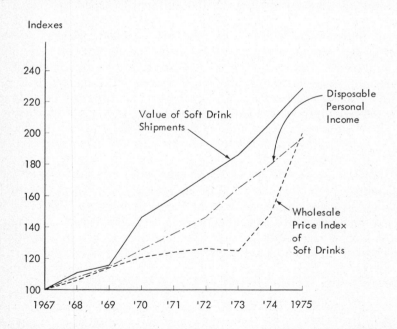

Source: *U.S. Industrial Outlook, 1975* (Washington: U.S. Department of Commerce), pp. 210–211; *U.S. Industrial Outlook, 1976* (Washington: U.S. Department of Commerce), p. 214; and *Survey of Current Business* (January, 1975), Part II, p. 35, and (June, 1976), p. 9.

Figure 15-1

Relative Changes in the Value of Soft Drink Shipments, Disposable Personal Income, and the Wholesale Price of Soft Drinks

One explanation of the somewhat greater increase in soft drink shipments than in disposable personal income is that the largest group of soft drink consumers—teenagers and young adults—has been increasing relative to the total population. Also, increased leisure time for the adult population has led to increased recreational activities resulting in increased soft drink consumption. Furthermore, the industry has been successful in introducing new products during this period. Exports and imports are insignificant and can be ignored in long-range projections. However, a new factor was added in 1974 when the price of soft drinks went up rapidly due to greatly increased sugar prices. The value of soft drink shipments went up somewhat faster than disposable income in 1974 and 1975, but not nearly as fast as the increase in the wholesale price of soft drinks. Consumers adjusted by reducing the quantity of soft drink purchases, but dollar purchases increased slightly.

Sales can be expected to grow at a faster rate than disposable personal income since many of the factors which have led to the increased rise of soft drink sales are expected to continue. But it is unlikely that sales will grow at the rate of the period of the 1970s, especially since the number of teenagers will not be increasing as rapidly as it did in that decade, and the price of soft drinks has gone up more rapidly than consumer prices generally.

In projecting the long-term trend of an industry, the best procedure is to correlate sales with projected disposable personal income, cash farm income, or gross national product, whichever is most applicable, and also to study the growth of the industry in question, considering all qualitative factors as well as its growth curve. On the basis of this information, a tentative estimate may be made of the long-term trend of the industry; but it must be kept in mind that this trend can be altered by changes in any of the factors that determine the trend. Continual study is necessary.

REGIONAL FACTORS

In developing the trend for a particular business, it is necessary to consider trends in the region and in the state or states in which the business is conducted. For national businesses such trends are also important in deciding on plant location in relationship to future markets and labor supply, as well as sources of raw materials. From time to time the Department of Commerce makes studies of trends in income payments by regions and states. They compare income for years in which economic activity was at about the same stage in the cycle. They also divide longer periods into subperiods to see if there is a continuity of trend.

According to such a Department of Commerce study there has been a relative shift in income from New England, the Middle East, the Great Lakes area, the Rocky Mountain region, and the plains to the south and west. This shift is based in part on relative shifts in population from the Northern and Central Regions to the Southwest and Far West. Since 1950 population has grown much more rapidly in the Far West than in any other region of the country. The Department of Commerce has made projections of shares of population and personal income by region for the period to 1990. Such figures for 1990 and some earlier years and estimates of changes in relative shares of personal income and population between 1969 and 1990 are presented in Table 15-4.

Table 15-4

Regional Shares of Personal Income and of Population

	1929	1950[1]	1969[1]	1990[1]	Percentage Change in Share[2]		
					1929–1950[3]	1950–1969	1969–1990
Personal Income							
Northern and central regions	**72.88**	**63.86**	**58.63**	**56.98**	**−12**	**−8**	**−3**
New England	8.22	6.56	6.33	6.27	−20	−4	−1
Mideast	32.11	26.06	23.64	22.64	−19	−9	−4
Great Lakes	23.62	22.38	21.04	20.85	−5	−6	−1
Plains	8.93	8.86	7.62	7.22	−1	−14	−5
Southern and western regions	**27.12**	**36.14**	**41.37**	**43.02**	**33**	**14**	**4**
Southeast	11.63	15.22	17.35	17.91	31	14	3
Southwest	4.96	6.54	7.10	7.24	32	9	2
Rocky Mountain	1.89	2.24	2.16	2.14	19	−4	−1
Far West	8.63	11.30	14.17	15.12	31	21	7
Population							
Northern and central regions	**61.42**	**57.73**	**54.58**	**53.88**	**−6**	**−5**	**−1**
New England	6.68	6.13	5.82	5.98	−8	−5	3
Mideast	23.17	22.21	20.90	20.50	−4	−6	−2
Great Lakes	20.68	20.10	19.82	19.89	−3	−1	0
Plains	10.89	9.29	8.04	7.51	−15	−14	−7
Southern and western regions	**38.58**	**42.27**	**45.42**	**46.12**	**10**	**7**	**2**
Southeast	22.30	22.30	21.59	21.16	0	−3	−2
Southwest	7.38	7.53	8.12	8.13	2	8	0
Rocky Mountain	2.23	2.30	2.45	2.36	3	7	−4
Far West	6.67	9.33	12.74	13.93	40	31	9

Source: *Survey of Current Business* (April, 1972), p. 24.

[1] Alaska and Hawaii included in southern and western total.
[2] Percent changes calculated from data carried to one more decimal than shown.
[3] Alaska and Hawaii are excluded from 1929 data. To achieve comparability, they were excluded from 1950 data in calculating percent change for 1929–1950 period.

The projections shown in Table 15-4 indicate that the Far West, Southeast, and Southwest will continue to increase their shares of personal income relative to other regions. However, the rates of growth in their relative shares of income will be much slower than in the 1950–1969 period.

For many economic decisions an important variable is per capita personal income rather than total personal income in a region. Average per capita income has grown rapidly in the Southeast in the period since 1950. It grew at about average rates in New England, the Plains, and the Southwest Regions; more slowly in the Mideast, Great Lakes, and Far West Regions; and much more slowly in the Rocky Mountain Region. The Department of Commerce projections indicate a trend toward a convergence of per capita personal income in the period to 1990. Projections for 1990 are presented in Table 15-5.

Table 15-5
Regional Per Capita Personal Income

	Percent of National Average				Percent Change in Relation to National Average[2]		
	1929	1950[1]	1969[1]	1990[1]	1929–1950[3]	1950–1969	1969–1990
Northern and central regions	**118.65**	**110.60**	**107.40**	**105.69**	**−7**	**−3**	**−2**
New England	123.11	106.97	108.20	104.87	−13	1	−3
Mideast	138.55	117.34	113.23	110.23	−15	−4	−3
Great Lakes	114.20	111.28	106.24	104.87	−3	−5	−1
Plains	81.96	95.40	94.56	96.14	16	−1	2
Southern and western regions	**70.30**	**85.47**	**91.10**	**93.37**	**22**	**7**	**2**
Southeast	52.19	68.28	80.24	84.85	31	18	6
Southwest	67.21	86.68	87.50	89.07	29	1	2
Rocky Mountain	85.05	97.38	87.97	90.62	14	−10	3
Far West	129.29	120.97	111.53	108.58	−6	−7	−3

Source: *Survey of Current Business* (April, 1972), p. 28.

[1] Alaska and Hawaii included in southern and western total.
[2] Percent changes calculated from data carried to one more decimal than shown.
[3] Alaska and Hawaii are excluded from 1929 data. To achieve comparability, they were excluded from 1950 data in calculating percent change for 1929–1950 period.

In using such analyses of the trends in income for the purpose of forecasting the trend of a particular business, it again is necessary to look at the qualitative factors to see why these trends have been taking place. This means that the sources of the relative gains or declines in regional income must be analyzed to determine whether they arose from shifts in manufacturing, agriculture, trade, service, government, etc. It is also necessary to see whether they are based primarily upon shifts in population or upon per capita variations in income. The reasons for the changes in each individual field must then be analyzed and estimates of the future course of each field made in light of future economic developments.

A Department of Commerce study is based on such an analysis. This study has projected data on employment and on total personal income for 1980 and 1990 for each region and also for each state in a region. It has also projected total earnings for major sectors of the economy in agriculture, mining, construction, manufacturing, transportation and utilities, trade, finance, services, and government for each region and for each state in the region. Constant study of all of these factors is required since past trends are always changing to some degree and they change abruptly at times.

On the basis of the national and regional trends of the industry, the future trend of sales in an individual business may be determined. The first step is to find the trend of sales of the business and to compare it with the industry trend. Since trends are different in different regions of the United States, the trend of sales of the business should be compared to industry sales on a region-by-region basis. The next step is to explain any differences in rates of company and industry growth. For example, little sales effort may have been put into some regions, or high transportation costs may have cut down sales. On the bases of industry trends, of past relationships to industry trends, and of future sales policies, it is possible to develop projected sales for the company in each region and in total.

QUESTIONS

1. On what assumption is a projection of the trend in economic activity based?
2. Outline the steps involved in projecting gross national product by (a) projecting the line of least squares, (b) extending past average rates of growth, (c) estimating the number of employed workers and the output per worker.
3. What problems are involved in projecting the size of the labor force?
4. How are trends in output per hour of employment determined?
5. Why is projection of GNP made by estimating the labor force and output per worker likely to give somewhat higher results than projecting the trend of GNP?
6. Outline several procedures for making more refined estimates of future levels of GNP.
7. Describe the National Planning Association procedure for projecting GNP.
8. Outline the procedure for developing estimates of disposable personal income from estimates of GNP.
9. Describe a procedure for estimating consumer expenditures in total and for major categories of expenditures from estimates of disposable personal income.
10. How do varying regional growth trends affect long-run business decisions?
11. How have population, personal income, and per capita personal income by regions shifted since 1950?
12. What changes are expected in the relative shares of personal income by regions and in per capita personal income by regions?
13. Outline a procedure for projecting sales on a regional basis.

SUGGESTED READINGS

Almon, Clopper, Jr., Margaret R. Buckler, Lawrence Horwitz, and Thomas C. Reimbold. *1985 Interindustry Forecasts of the American Economy.* Lexington, Mass.: Lexington Books (D.C. Heath and Co.), 1974.

Bretzfelder, Robert B. "State and Regional Personal Income, 1959–1972." *Survey of Current Business* (August, 1973), pp. 39–49.

Gross, Charles W., and Robin T. Peterson. *Business Forecasting.* Boston: Houghton Mifflin Co., 1976.

Growth Patterns in Employment by County, 1940–1950 and 1950–1960. Vols. 1–8. Washington: U.S. Government Printing Office, 1966.

Kendrick, John W. "Productivity and Growth Trends and Their Implications." *Pittsburgh Business Review* (Fall, 1975), pp. 2–10.

Long-Range Economic Projection, Studies in Income and Wealth, Volume 16. Princeton, New Jersey: National Bureau of Economic Research, 1954, Part I.

"State Projections of Income, Employment, and Population to 1990." *Survey of Current Business* (April, 1974), pp. 19–45.

United States Department of Commerce. *Area Economic Projections, 1990.* Washington: U.S. Government Printing Office, 1975.

United States Department of Commerce. Bureau of the Census. *Long-Term Economic Growth 1860–1970.* Washington: U.S. Government Printing Office, 1973.

Valentine, Lloyd M. "The Economy of 1984," in Henry G. Baker, *Environment 1984: Interfacing with Management and Business.* Columbus: Grid, Inc., 1975.

CHAPTER 16

SHORT-RUN FORECASTING OF GENERAL BUSINESS ACTIVITY

Since forecasting is still much more of an art than a science, it is to be expected that economists will use varying approaches in making forecasts. This is especially true in making short-run forecasts of general economic activity. Most forecasters also use several approaches to forecasting since none of them is completely accurate at this stage of development. This eclectic attitude is especially useful when economic activity is believed to be near an upper or lower turning point. The major approaches to short-run forecasting of overall economic activity will be considered in this chapter.

FAVORABLE AND UNFAVORABLE FACTORS

A simple, but valuable, starting point to forecasting is to list all of the favorable and unfavorable factors in the current situation. Favorable factors are those whose effect is likely to keep the level of overall economic activity expanding, while unfavorable factors are those that have a tendency to cause a slowing down or decline in economic activity. This procedure is worthwhile only if the current situation is carefully analyzed. The analyst must also understand the factors that are likely to lead to further expansion or to contraction. For example, a list of favorable and unfavorable factors made in the summer of 1976 might have contained the following items:

Favorable
    Increasing level of activity in residential construction
    Decrease in level of unemployment
    Inventories in reasonable balance with sales
    Federal Reserve monetary policy to provide reasonable growth and control inflation
    Decreasing rate of inflation
    Increase in capital appropriations after several quarters of decline
    Reduced rate of consumer saving
    Increasing consumer purchases, especially of durables
    Moderate rise in family formation
    Falling interest rates

Unfavorable
  Rising costs due to wage settlements in major industries
  Rising wholesale prices and threat of further inflation
  Possibility of a further price rise for oil from OPEC countries
  Balance of payments problems as imports rise with prosperity
  Lack of long-run stability in foreign exchange markets
  Continuing financial problems in local governments
  Uncertainty due to the political situation in an election year
  Continuing energy crisis

This method is valuable because it requires a thorough analysis of the current situation. When all factors are listed, judgment is used to decide what the impact of all of these factors in combination will be on the economy. This is especially difficult after economic activity has expanded for a time and unfavorable factors develop in greater number.

One of the important factors to consider in such analyses, especially in judging the severity of an impending recession, is the state of the building cycle. Recessions in business activity that have occurred when the building cycle was on the upswing have seldom led to deep or protracted depressions. When building is in a downward phase of the building cycle, however, depressions are usually of some severity.

Major depressions have usually occurred when major new industries, especially those related to the transportation field, have reached a point where their rate of growth has slowed down materially. This was true in 1929 when the automobile industry reached such a stage in its development. It was true for the railroad field in such major depressions as 1873 and 1893 and for the canal building field in 1837. It should be kept in mind that major developments in transportation have not only led to increased demand for capital goods in this field and in related fields, but have changed past living patterns and have thus stimulated investment to an even greater degree. Therefore, a study of the trend of major new industries should form a part of the process of forecasting cyclical change.

CONSENSUS OF OBSERVERS

In an area as important as forecasting is to many businesses and governmental units, and subject as it is to error, it is natural to want to get the opinion of other analysts who have studied the economic outlook. Therefore, getting the consensus of qualified observers is part of the program of almost every forecaster. For some, it is the major approach to forecasting.

Several sources of such opinions are available. At the turn of the year financial papers and journals, as well as the financial sections of many daily newspapers, publish the opinions of leaders in government, industry, and education. The Conference Board, Inc., has a discussion meeting on the outlook attended by prominent economists engaged in forecasting and publishes the proceedings in a pamphlet called the *Business Outlook*. The First National Bank of Chicago publishes the opinion on the outlook for their industry by leaders in many fields every six months. Magazines such as *Business Week*, *Fortune*, and *Dun's* have articles on the economy in almost every issue. The Federal Reserve Bank of Richmond publishes annually summaries of forecasts of a large number of prominent forecasters in its *Business Forecasts*.

As long as forecasting is subject to considerable error, it is possible for many experts to be wrong at the same time. Their reactions to the situation in their fields are, however, valuable background in developing a forecast by any method or combination of methods.

LEADING AND LAGGING SERIES

Economists have searched for years for a series that would give a signal of changes in economic activity by turning upward and downward before the overall economy turned. No single series has had such a relationship on a regular basis. Several series usually lead at turning points, however, and others usually lag. An analysis of a group of such series has been used to get an indication of the direction of economic activity.

The most complete studies of cyclical leads and lags have been made by the National Bureau of Economic Research. Geoffrey H. Moore and Julius Shiskin have chosen 88 indicators out of the large number of series studied by the National Bureau of Economic Research, 36 of which they have placed in a leading group, 25 in a roughly coincident group, 11 in the lagging group, and 16 in a group unclassified as to timing. These series cover a wide range of economic processes representing all sectors of the economy.

Of the 88 indicators, 26 have been selected as a short list of some of the most consistent indicators which involve little duplication of economic processes. This short list contains 12 leading, 8 coincident, and 6 lagging series. The series included in this list and the median lead or lag are presented in Table 16-1.

It is interesting to examine the behavior of these series in the immediate post-World War II period. All of the series in the leading group were contracting by the middle of 1948. In the prewar 1936–1937 period the peaks in these leading series came within a short space of time, but in the postwar period they were scattered over several years as such series as business failures and stock prices began to decline early in 1946. The roughly coincident series rose during 1946 and 1947 and reached their peaks in late 1947 and 1948 while the lagging group reached peaks in 1948–1949. The pattern, therefore, had been maintained.

Since the recession in 1948 was mild, took place in different fields at different times, and did not affect to any degree two major groups, namely residential building and automobile production, the various series acted as would be expected in such a situation.

The leading series forecast the 1953 recession, although somewhat less clearly than the 1949 recession. Wholesale prices turned down and business failures up about two and one-half years before the recession began. New durable goods orders and commercial construction were higher in mid-1953 than

Table 16-1

Short List of Economic Indicators

Classification and Series Title	First Business Cycle Turn Covered	Median Lead (−) or Lag (+) in Months
Leading indicators (12 series)		
Average workweek, production workers, manufacturing	1921	−5
Average weekly initial claims, state unemployment insurance, thousands (inv.)†	1945	−8[a]
Index of net business formation	1945	−7
New orders, durable goods industries	1920	−4
Contracts and orders, plant and equipment	1948	−6
New building permits, private housing units	1918	−6
Change in book value, manufacturing and trade inventories	1945	−8
Industrial materials prices	1919	−2
Stock prices, 500 common stocks	1873	−4
Corporate profits after taxes, Q*	1920	−2
Ratio, price to unit labor cost, mfg.	1919	−3
Change in consumer installment debt	1929	−10
Roughly coincident indicators (8 series)		
Employees in nonagricultural establishments	1929	0
Unemployment rate, total (inv.)†	1929	0
GNP in current dollars, Q*	1921	−1
GNP in constant dollars, expenditure estimate, Q*	1921	−2
Industrial production	1919	0
Personal income	1921	−1
Manufacturing and trade sales	1948	0
Sales of retail stores	1919	0
Lagging indicators (6 series)		
Unemployment rate, persons unemployed 15 + weeks (inv.)	1948	+2
Business expenditures, plant and equipment, Q*	1918	+1
Book value, manufacturing and trade inventories	1945	+2
Labor cost per unit of output, mfg.	1919	+8
Commercial and industrial loans outstanding	1937	+2
Bank rates, short-term business loans, Q*	1919	+5

Source: Adapted from Geoffrey H. Moore and Julius Shiskin, *Indicators of Business Expansions and Contractions* (New York: National Bureau of Economic Research, Inc. 1967), p. 68.

* Quarterly series.
† Inverted.
[a] This series has had a lead of 10 to 22 months and an average lead of 15 months at the peak, but is almost coincident at the trough.

in the fall of 1951, but were well below their peaks in early 1951. Residential construction declined in 1951, recovered in 1952, and then declined again in the first half of 1953. The average hours worked per week dropped sharply and stock prices fell somewhat before the downturn. New incorporations had only a slight drop, and this change did not come until the economy turned down. The picture of the leading series in the 1953 downturn was not as clear as it might have been because an adjustment took place in 1952 to lower levels of defense expenditures as the Korean War was stabilized and brought to a halt.

The upturn was also foretold by the leading series since, by the second quarter of 1954, four were expanding. The same was true of the 1957 downturn. By the end of 1956 five of the eight leading series had turned down. They also foreshadowed the upturn in 1958, the downturn in 1960, and the upturn in 1961. They gave false signals of recession, however, in 1962 and in 1967. These were only periods of retardation in the forward advance of economic activity although in 1967 the retardation was more serious than in 1962. The leading indicators also foreshadowed the 1969–1970 recession. The peak in several indicators expressed in monetary terms came somewhat late. However, if they are expressed in real terms, the peaks came earlier and gave a longer lead. This was also true in the 1973–1975 recession and the following recovery. In a period of rising prices such as 1969 it is necessary to study indicators in real terms to get a true picture of developments in the economy.

The staff of *Business Conditions Digest,* a monthly publication of the Department of Commerce, has developed a new list of leading indicators based on a comprehensive study of economic indicators. This list has many series in real terms to get around the problem of high-level inflation which obscures some of the changes in series in current dollars. Table 16-2 shows the series in the new index, the series in the old index, and the reason for the change. This new series showed a lead in the 1973–1975 recession and recovery on an *ex post* basis.

While one would expect that the leading series indicators would be most useful for forecasting turning points, there are some who feel that a superior indicator is the ratio of the coincident series to the lagging series. This particular ratio, which is published irregularly in *Business Conditions Digest,* has consistently given a longer warning signal of impending downturns than has the leading indicator series. One can also learn a great deal about business cycle forces by conscientious study of the lagging indicators.

DIFFUSION INDEXES

Economic time series do not all move uniformly up or down in any stage of the business cycle. Therefore, diffusion indexes are used at times to gauge the relative strength of the forces of expansion and of contraction over a time span.[1] Various time spans are used ranging from 1 to 12 months and, at times,

---

[1] The diffusion index is the percentage of the series in any group being studied that is expanding in any period of time, such as a month or a quarter. For example, if out of a group of 50 series, 30, or 60 percent, are expanding in a month, the diffusion index is 60; if 35, or 70 percent, are expanding, it is 70; and so on.

Table 16-2
New Composite Index of Leading Indicators Versus Old Index

Line	Series in New Index[1]	Series in Old Index[1]	Reason for Change
1	Average workweek of production workers, manufacturing (I)	Same (I)	
2	Index of net business formation (IV)	Same (IV)	
3	Index of stock prices, 500 common stocks (VI)	Same (VI)	
4	Index of new building permits, private housing units (IV)	Same (IV)	
5	Layoff rate, manufacturing (inverted) (I)	Average weekly initial claims for unemployment insurance (inverted) (I)	Layoff rate leads more consistently at troughs; classified L,L,L. Initial claims classified L,C,L.
6	New orders, consumer goods and materials, 1967 dollars (III)	New orders, durable goods (III, IV)	New series avoids duplication with orders for equipment. Deflation needed for better cyclical performance since late 1960s.
7	Contracts and orders for plant and equipment, 1967 dollars (IV)	Same, current dollars (IV)	Deflation needed for better cyclical performance since the late 1960s.
8	Net change in inventories on hand and on order, 1967 dollars (smoothed) (V)	Change in book value, manufacturing and trade inventories (V)	Concept of including stocks on order is better. Deflation is needed for better cyclical performance since the late 1960s.
9	Percent change in sensitive prices, WPI of crude materials excluding foods and feeds (smoothed) (VI)	Index of industrial materials prices (VI)	Percent change is better than level. Leads are more consistent, especially since the late 1960s.
10	Vendor performance, percent of companies reporting slower deliveries (III)		Best available indicator of changes in delivery lags. Good record of timing and conformity.
11	Money balance (M1), 1967 dollars (VII)		Important measure of the quantity of money in real terms. Good scores for indicator performance.
12	Percent change in total liquid assets (smoothed) (VII)		Comprehensive measure of changes in wealth held in liquid form by private nonfinancial investors.
13		Corporate profits after taxes (VI)	Quarterly and tardy (low score for currency).
14		Change in consumer installment debt (VII)	Lacks timeliness. In recent period, very erratic and more nearly coincident than leading at troughs.
15		Ratio, price to unit labor cost, manufacturing (VI)	Failed to lead at the last three business cycle troughs (1958–1970). Work continuing on developing a satisfactory substitute.

Source: *Business Conditions Digest* (May, 1975), p. X.

[1] Roman numerals in parentheses identify the economic process groups. The major types of economic process are the following: I. Employment and Unemployment; II. Production and Income; III. Consumption, Saving, and Distribution; IV. Fixed Capital Investment; V. Inventory and Inventory Investment; VI. Prices, Costs, and Profits; VII. Money and Credit; VIII. Foreign Trade and Payments; IX. Government Activities.

a 6- or 9-month time span and a 1-month span are used together. A diffusion index fluctuates between 100 percent when all components are expanding and zero when all are declining. When it is at 50 the implication is that there is no change in the aggregate series. This would, of course, only be true if all the component series had the same relative importance. A diffusion index also takes no account of the magnitude of change in the component series. An index of 80 may at one time be associated with a 10 percent rate of increase in the aggregate series and at another time with a 5 percent increase.

Even though they have limitations, diffusion indexes can be useful in predicting turning points in the aggregate series. Both the level and direction of change of a diffusion index must be considered. When a diffusion index is rising in the 50 to 100 percent range, it implies that the aggregate series is increasing at an increasing rate. An index which is falling at a rate between 50 percent and zero implies that the aggregate series is declining at an increasing rate and one that is rising at a zero to 50 percent rate implies that the series is declining at a decreasing rate. These changes may be seen in Figure 16-1.

A diffusion index of the Index of Industrial Production illustrates the use of diffusion indexes in forecasting. The index used is a six-month span of the 24

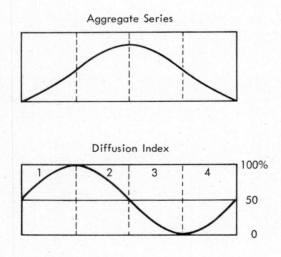

Stage	a diffusion index that is	implies that the aggregate series is
1	rising (50% – 100%)	increasing at an increasing rate
2	falling (100% – 50%)	increasing at a decreasing rate
3	falling (50% – 0)	declining at an increasing rate
4	rising (0 – 50%)	declining at a decreasing rate

Source: *Economic Review,* Federal Reserve Bank of Cleveland (January, 1971), p. 6.

Figure 16-1

Properties of a Diffusion Index

industries in the Index of Industrial Production. This diffusion index was at high levels and expanding in 1965 and early 1966 and industrial production moved upward vigorously. It turned down early in 1966 well before the slow-down in activity in 1967. It turned upward in the middle of 1967 before production moved upward. It also turned down in early 1969 before the recession which began near the end of the year, and it did the same in 1973. It turned up just before the economy did in 1975. These changes may be seen graphically in Figure 16-2, page 332.

Business Conditions Digest publishes diffusion indexes for several leading and coincident series as follows:

> Leading Indicators
>> Average workweek, production workers, manufacturing
>> New orders, durable goods industries
>> Newly approved capital appropriations
>> Profits, First National City Bank of New York, percent reporting higher profits
>> Stock prices, 500 common stocks
>> Industrial materials prices
>> Initial claims, state unemployment insurance
> Coincident Indicators
>> Employees in nonagricultural establishments
>> Industrial production
>> Wholesale prices
>> Sales of retail stores

Their turning points tend to lead the turning points of the aggregate of the items in the series on which they are based. Widespread increases in the components of a series are often associated with a period of rapid growth and widespread declines with a sharp reduction in activity.

Diffusion indexes based on these series behaved perfectly in postwar cycles. The diffusion index of leaders passed 50 percent on the way up before each peak and on the way down before each trough. The diffusion index of coincident series passed 50 near peaks and troughs. They also, however, gave a false indication of a recession in 1962 and in 1967 just as the leading series themselves did.

The diffusion indexes, along with the leading indexes, have indicated every turn in general economic activity. They have also turned for a short period when no turn occurred, however, so they cannot be used alone as a forecasting device or without judgment. They also do not tell the exact timing of turning points or the intensity of changes in economic activity. They are, nevertheless, valuable as one tool in a forecaster's kit.

RELATIONSHIP OF NEW ORDERS, INVENTORIES, SALES, AND PRODUCTION

Another method or group of methods for short-run forecasting involves a study of the relationships between sales and inventories and sales and new orders, and, in turn, the effect of changes in such relationships to changes in production. The ratio of inventory to sales for the manufacturing field as a

Roughly Coincident Indicators

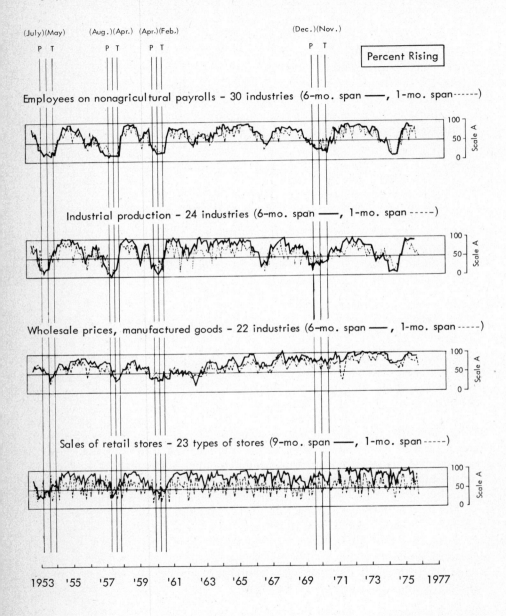

Employees on nonagricultural payrolls – 30 industries (6-mo. span ——, 1-mo. span------)

Industrial production – 24 industries (6-mo. span ——, 1-mo. span -----)

Wholesale prices, manufactured goods – 22 industries (6-mo. span ——, 1-mo. span -----)

Sales of retail stores – 23 types of stores (9-mo. span ——, 1-mo. span -----)

Source: *Business Conditions Digest* (June, 1976), p. 64.

Figure 16-2

Diffusion Index of Industrial Production
6-Month Span & 1-Month Span

whole and for major sectors of it, such as durable goods manufacturing, often gives an indication of turning points in production. During the upswing of a cycle, inventories are first reduced as sales go up faster than expected. They are then increased to bring them back into line with sales. Inventories have in the past been increased too much, and this has led to a downturn. As sales have declined, inventories have become even greater in relationship to sales until substantial inventory liquidation has occurred. These changes have been clearer and more pronounced in recessions such as 1957–1958 than in the mild recessions of 1960–1961 or 1969–1970.

Such changes in the 1956–1958 period of the downturn and the recovery may be studied from Figure 16–3. Inventories of durables, for example,

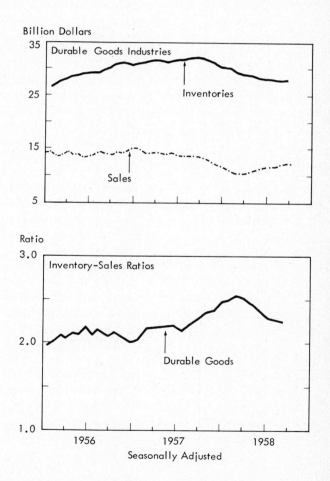

Source: *Survey of Current Business* (November, 1958), p. 4.

Figure 16-3

Manufacturers' Inventories and Sales

increased faster than sales in the first half of 1956 and again in early 1957. This led to a decrease in production at midyear as the economy went into a recession, especially in durable goods production. During the second half of 1957 and the first quarter of 1958, inventory-sales ratios went up involuntarily as inventories were not reduced as rapidly as sales. This led to a decrease in production of a greater magnitude than the decrease in sales in real terms. As sales increased, inventory-sales ratios dropped rapidly during the second and third quarters of 1958 and more slowly in 1959. This led to increases in production to meet the increased sales, as well as demand for goods to rebuild inventory levels. The pattern in 1959 was obscured by the effects of the steel negotiation deadlock and strike. The normal pattern is one of relative stability for a short period and then a new increase of inventories in relationship to sales. Inventories went up again in relationship to sales before and during the 1960–1961 recession, especially inventories of durable goods. This ratio also went up in the 1967 slowdown, but not to the levels reached in 1960–1961 or 1957–1958. In the mild recession of 1969–1970 inventories did not change much in relation to sales before the recession began, but did go up somewhat during the recession period, especially in the durable goods field. In the boom period before the 1973–1975 recession, inventories continued to go up as attempts were made to overcome shortages. By studying such relationships of inventories to sales it is possible to predict turning points in production. Since the leads are not uniform and the ratios give some false signals, judgment is still required to pinpoint changes.

An analysis of new orders and of new orders in relationship to sales and production can also be used as an indication of turning points. For example, the turning point in new orders during a recovery period is preceded by a slowdown in the rate of decrease in new orders. When new orders turn up, the turning point in production is usually only several months away.

Such relationships may be observed in the 1958 recovery period. New orders in manufacturing declined slowly in January and February of 1958 after going down rapidly in the last half of 1957. Sales were decreasing more rapidly in early 1958 than new orders. While new orders went up, inventories and production continued to decrease. In March new orders increased over the level of February and of January. This indicated that production would shortly stop decreasing and start upward if new orders kept going up. In May production was somewhat above April, and in June it was substantially above May levels. After midyear, inventories were about stabilized, and as new orders increased, production continued upward. In 1959 the building of inventories due to the threat of labor difficulties in steel obscured normal patterns (see Table 16-3).

These series were also useful in predicting increased business in the second half of 1961 as the economy recovered from the 1960–1961 recession. By June new orders had advanced 9 percent from January levels, while production was up only about 7 percent. New orders for durable goods were up over 15 percent, whereas production was up less than 11 percent. Since inventories were at low levels, the new orders could not be filled out of stock and, as a result, production had to be increased further to meet demand. These relationships were not evident in the mild recession of 1969–1970. In the period before the 1973 recession began the boom was so strong that new orders continued upward well into the recession period.

Forecasting of production for one to two quarters in the future is done by some forecasters by studying patterns of new orders, unfilled orders, inventories, sales, and production in the major sectors of durable and nondurable goods production. From past relationships and typical time intervals between new orders, production, sales, and inventory levels, it is possible to forecast what production is likely to be in the future. This cannot be done purely mechanically because relationships change and factors such as threatened strikes alter business decisions concerning inventories and production.

Table 16-3

New Orders, Production, and Inventories in Manufacturing
January, 1958 – June, 1959

Month	New Orders*	Production†	Inventories‡
1958			
January	24.4	135	52.9
February	24.1	131	52.4
March	24.8	129	52.0
April	24.5	128	51.5
May	25.0	130	50.9
June	25.8	134	50.2
July	26.5	136	49.8
August	26.1	138	49.4
September	27.0	139	49.3
October	27.9	140	49.3
November	27.8	143	49.3
December	28.4	144	49.2
1959			
January	28.5	145	49.5
February	29.7	148	49.9
March	30.2	150	50.5
April	31.2	153	51.0
May	30.5	156	51.6
June	31.4	158	52.1

Source: *Survey of Current Business* and *Federal Reserve Bulletin*.
* Department of Commerce Series, seasonally adjusted, in billions of dollars.
† Federal Reserve Index, seasonally adjusted, 1947–1949 = 100.
‡ Department of Commerce Series, seasonally adjusted, in billions of dollars.

SERIES ON EXPECTATIONS AND EXPENDITURE PLANS

Another approach to forecasting is to try to develop data on future expectations of business conditions by business executives whose decisions determine the economic outlook. This approach has been expanded to include expectations and expenditure plans for most of the major spending sectors of the economy. Information on the expectations of major executives who make business decisions is published by Dun and Bradstreet in its quarterly survey of *Businessmen's Expectations*. It is based on interviews with a sample of over 1,500 business executives regarding their expectations for their respective businesses. They are asked if they believe there will be an increase, a decrease, or no change in net sales, net profits, selling prices, the level of inventories, and the number of employees, compared with the same quarter a year ago. Data are presented for all concerns and also separately for manufacturers, wholesalers, and retailers.

The National Association of Purchasing Management, Inc., obtains the reaction of some of its members to business conditions through a monthly survey of a committee selected so as to reflect both regional and industrial diversification. These members are asked to indicate whether production, new orders, commodity prices, inventories of purchased raw materials and purchased finished materials, employment, and their level of buying were higher than a month ago, lower, or the same. The questionnaire also asks for specific commodity price changes and the reasons for them, for items that are in short supply, for business changes in the member's area, and for general business factors that may affect purchasing policies. A summary and an analysis of the answers of the purchasing agents in the Survey Committee are published in the Bulletin of the Association.

These surveys have been valuable gauges of changes in business conditions during the month since the results have been accurate and are available within two weeks or less after the questionnaires are filled out. In the period since 1947, during which the surveys were made on the present basis, they forecast the 1948, 1953, 1957, 1960, and 1969 downturns several months in advance, but were not always accurate on the magnitude of changes in business.

A major problem with this series and that of expectations of executives by Dun and Bradstreet is that they show changes in sentiment from time to time when general business conditions do not experience a turning point. They give signals of changes when overall activity changes, but they also give false signals and can, therefore, not be used alone to predict changes in the economy. They are, however, valuable to the forecaster because they provide a check on forecasts obtained by other methods.

Another way to use data on expectations is to get information on expenditure plans by major spending sectors in the economy. These plans are available for many of the major categories of expenditures into which gross national product is divided. Surveys of consumer buying plans were begun in 1946 by the Survey Research Center of the University of Michigan. The Center interviews a sample of about 2,000 families during January and February and conducts supplemental surveys at other times. The Center gathers information on consumer intentions to buy durable goods including automobiles, furniture and appliances, and also new houses. The Conference Board sponsors a monthly survey and publishes it in the *Conference Board Record*. Consumer surveys have been generally accurate in predicting changes in expenditures; that is, downturns and upturns. They have not, however, been accurate on a regular basis in predicting the magnitude of the changes in purchases of durable goods. There are no data on plans for expenditures on nondurable goods and services, but these do not change much in the short run.

Data on plans for spending by the federal government are available in the budget, which is presented by the President almost nine months before the beginning of the new fiscal year. This is generally a good guide to the direction of change in expenditures, if any, but it cannot be used without analysis and revision as an estimate of the amount of change. To date no series exists on the expenditure plans of state and local governments. The same is true of exports and imports; but the net figure, which is all that is included in gross national product, is usually so small that it makes little difference in the general direction of economic activity.

Series on expenditure plans exist for most components of gross private domestic investment. The Department of Commerce surveys plans of business executives for expenditures on plant and equipment. The McGraw-Hill Book Company also makes such surveys. They have been accurate in predicting turning points in expenditures. Series on building permits can be used to show future changes in the volume of new building. Changes in plans for the level of inventories can be obtained from surveys by the National Association of Purchasing Management, Inc., and also the United States Department of Commerce.

Thus, there are series on expenditure plans for every major sector of spending, except state and local government expenditures and consumer expenditures on nondurables and services, and these have not changed direction abruptly in the past. A study of all of these series can be used to judge the direction of business. When all these expenditures are moving in the same direction, as they are in the early stages of recovery, this procedure is relatively easy and effective. Later in prosperity, some expenditures may show increases and some a leveling off or decreases; and then it is difficult, if not impossible, to judge future business from changes in direction of spending alone. This requires estimates of the magnitude of changes which are made in model building. Chapters 17 and 18 present a technique for building a model of GNP by the expenditure approach.

CYCLES AND TRENDS

Some attempt has been made to forecast economic activity by projecting the trend and cycle. If a regular cycle with uniform duration and amplitude existed, this would be the only procedure needed for accurate forecasting. Since such a cycle does not exist, however, this procedure cannot be used with any degree of assurance of success. Some analysts have at times tried to develop a cyclical pattern in GNP or industrial production by developing a multiple correlation relationship with a series of factors that they consider to be most significant in determining the course of the cycle, such as prices, interest rates, and unit labor costs. Such techniques must be viewed with skepticism since it is possible to recreate the movement of a series, such as the GNP or industrial production, with formulas relating the past behavior of the variable to the future behavior of that same variable. The correlation method is called *auto-correlation,* and the technique based on it is called *autoregressive forecasting.*

Some forecasters have used cycles and trends to develop a general picture of the pattern of economic development for five or ten years in the future. This may be done, for example, by using a future cycle pattern based on the average duration and amplitude of postwar cycles. Such a pattern is easy to develop and can serve a useful purpose in business planning and in assessing the possible effects of cycles on plans, but it cannot be used to make forecasts. The out-standing characteristic of cycles is their variability.

ECONOMETRIC MODELS

The development of econometric models was discussed in Part 3 in the section on the theory of national income determination. Past relationships are used to determine the endogenous variables in such models from known levels of exogenous variables. The procedure by which this is done is known as correlation analysis. Correlation is similar in some respects to trend analysis; but instead of using time as one variable, other series are used as the inde-pendent variables.

In a strict sense the changes in the dependent variable should be caused by changes in the independent variable or variables. However, such a strict causal relationship seldom, if ever, holds in economic analysis. Usually a whole series of forces are at work even though one or two may be dominant. However, unless a relationship exists that has remained fairly stable over time and is likely to continue to do so, the use of measures of correlation can lead to serious errors in prediction. The only situation in which a measure of correlation can be reliably used in forecasting is when theoretical analysis leads to the conclu-sion that the changes in the variables are related.

The period used to develop a correlation relationship should cover more than one complete cycle. This is desirable to establish the validity of the rela-tionship. Generally the effects of price changes should also be removed by putting value series in real terms. This is sometimes essential when correlating a value series with a physical volume or other nonprice series.

In developing correlation relationships between time series, it is often desirable to correlate year-by-year changes in the series rather than the original data. The trend of many time series is so strongly upward that a high degree of relationship exists because of this factor alone. If a significant relationship exists in the year-by-year changes in each series, it is frequently more useful for prediction than the relationship between the series themselves.

The development of a measure of correlation is similar to the determination of the trend in that it is a curve-fitting operation. The line of relationship is usually developed in one of two ways. The line of least squares may be used just as for the trend. The straight line relationship between two variables is ex-pressed by the formula $y = a + bx$ just as for the trend, only x is the independent variable instead of time. When used to develop the relationship among variables rather than the relationship of one variable over time, the method of least squares is called *regression analysis*.

Frequently a relationship exists between a series and two or more other series. Such a multiple correlation relationship should be developed mathematically, but it may be done graphically at least as a first step. A regression line is developed between the dependent variable and the most important independent variable. Deviations from this line are plotted against a second independent variable, and a regression line developed from these relationships. The relationship between these factors must then be expressed by the appropriate equations.

The relationship between a series and two or more series may still at times best be expressed by a straight line. But the relationship is often a more complex one and may require more complex mathematical formulas. It may at times be useful to express the factors in the form of logarithms because certain relationships which are nonlinear become linear in log form.

One of the forms of multiple correlation is that in which time is one of the variables that is used in developing the relationship. If technological, population growth, or other factors have affected the relationship so as to introduce a time trend, the deviations from the first line of regression may be plotted year by year on a second chart to see if a consistent pattern appears. This is true in the case of consumer expenditures on clothing and shoes in constant dollars that show a relationship to disposable personal income, but one that has been decreasing gradually for some years. When there is a trend in the relationship over time, a formula must be used in which time measured from a base year is introduced as a factor. Econometric models have been used with increasing success as a basis for forecasting gross national product and its major components. The Research Seminar on Quantitative Economics at the University of Michigan has been making forecasts for some time with the Klein-Goldberger model.[2] This model has been revised and improved on a regular basis since it was first used to make forecasts in 1953. The results have been good in most years so far as total GNP is concerned, but not as good on individual components.[3]

The Bureau of Economic Analysis of the Department of Commerce has done research and experimentation with a quarterly economic model of GNP that is based on a variant of the model developed by Professor Lawrence Klein. This model is based on 63 equations on each of the major components of GNP, and on factors such as prices, the labor force, income to the factors of production, monetary factors, taxes and transfers, and output and capacity utilization. This model has been developed for the period from 1953 on and has been used on an *ex post* basis to make forecasts for each year. In most years the error in total GNP was $3 billion or less, but errors in the components were larger than in GNP, as is generally true of all forecasts. Turning points were generally

---

[2] L. R. Klein and A. S. Goldberger, *An Econometric Model of the United States, 1929–1952* (Amsterdam: North Holland Publishing Co., 1955).

[3] Daniel B. Suits, "Forecasting and Analysis with an Econometric Model," *American Economic Review* (March, 1962), pp. 104–132.

forecast within one quarter plus or minus the actual turning points.[4] This model has been used by the Bureau of Economic Analysis as one of its tools of forecasting since 1965. Its record has been about as good as that of other models, especially when the judgment of the forecasters is used along with the model rather than using the model mechanically.

The Federal Reserve Board, MIT, and the University of Pennsylvania have jointly developed a large-scale model of the economy. It puts more stress on monetary, price, and wage factors than most other models. The current model is developed and kept current as the MIT, Penn.-SSRC model by the Massachusetts Institute of Technology, the University of Pennsylvania, and the Social Science Research Council. The Federal Reserve has developed a Minnie version which has 149 stochastic coefficients and 21 equations, which is only about a third the number of the larger model. After some study it has been decided that Minnie's short-run responses are similar to those of the larger model. In recent years, a large number of additional econometric models have been developed, including a number of proprietary models such as the Chase Econometrics, Inc., model.

An analysis of the forecasts of econometric models for the postwar period made under the sponsorship of the National Bureau of Economic Research concluded that they have not been able to forecast the levels of aggregate economic activity as well as some forecasts based on more general methods. The errors have resulted primarily from the forecasts of price movements that have often been wide of the mark. The forecasts of changes in economic activity, which exclude price movements, have been about as accurate as the better forecasts made by other methods.[5]

The National Bureau of Economic Research has continued to analyze the results of forecasts made by various methods. It has cooperated with the American Statistical Association in conducting a quarterly survey of forecasts of members of the ASA who are professionally engaged in a continuing analysis of the economic outlook. An analysis of the surveys led to the conclusion that no systematic differences appeared between the accuracy of the forecasters who used principally the informal GNP model, an econometric model, or the leading indicator approach.[6]

MONETARY FACTORS AND MODELS

Monetary factors can be used to give some indication of changes in business conditions. Changes in the money supply have in the past led to changes in business activity. This is true whether the money supply is defined as demand deposits plus currency adjusted for seasonal variation, or defined in the broader

---

[4] Maurice Liebenberg, Albert A. Hirsch, and Joel Popkin, "A Quarterly Econometric Model of the United States: A Progress Report," *Survey of Current Business* (May, 1966), pp. 13–41, and Albert A. Hirsch, Maurice Liebenberg, and George R. Green, *The BEA Quarterly Economic Model* (Washington: U.S. Department of Commerce, 1973), pp. 1–5.

[5] *Forty-Fifth Annual Report* (New York: National Bureau of Economic Research, 1965), p. 60.

[6] *Fifty-First Annual Report* (New York: National Bureau of Economic Research, 1971), p. 67.

concept to include time deposits. A good leading series is the M_1 measure of the money supply expressed in constant 1967 dollars. Its record in postwar cycles is as follows: [7]

Recession	Lead at Peaks (In Months)	Lead at Troughs (In Months)
1949	5	4
1953–1954	2	7
1957–1958	16	1
1960	9	8
1970	10	9
1973–1975ᵖ	10	1

p—preliminary. Like all leading indicators, this series also turned down during the period of retardation in the rate of growth in 1952 and in 1966–1967, so it must be used with care.

The St. Louis Federal Reserve Bank has developed a model of the economy based on the monetarist approach to economic analysis. This model is designed to provide information on the most likely course of development of strategic economic variables in response to monetary and fiscal actions. It is not designed to provide exact information on quarter-by-quarter changes in economic activity, but on the effect of money and monetary aggregates on spending, output, and prices. According to this model total spending is determined by monetary and fiscal actions. Fiscal actions are defined as federal spending financed by taxes or borrowing from the public. The change in total spending is combined with potential output at full employment to provide a measure of demand pressure. Anticipated price change, which depends on past price changes, is combined with demand pressure to determine the change in the price level. The change in total spending and the change in the price level can be used to find the change in output. The model can also be used to predict market interest rates and the unemployment level. The workings of this model are summarized as a flow diagram in Figure 16–4, page 342.

The change in total spending in this model is a function of two key exogenous variables. One is current and past changes in the money stock defined as demand deposits and currency held by the nonbank public. The other is current and past changes in high-employment federal expenditures defined as expenditures on goods and services plus transfer payments adjusted to remove the influence of variations in economic activity on unemployment benefit payments. The period from 1953–1969 is one which has been used to develop the relationships. The pattern of coefficients of relationship for this period indicates a large and rapid influence of monetary actions on total spending when compared to that of fiscal actions.

The St. Louis model has been in use for too short a time to confidently judge its success. It did succeed in giving good indications of the changes in real product, prices, unemployment, and interest rates during the recession period of 1969–1970 and the recovery period of 1971. It did not work well in

_____

[7] _Business Conditions Digest_ (May, 1975), p. XII.

the period before the 1973 recession primarily because price controls obscured the effect of monetary factors. It should be included in the forecaster's kit, however, and used along with other tools.

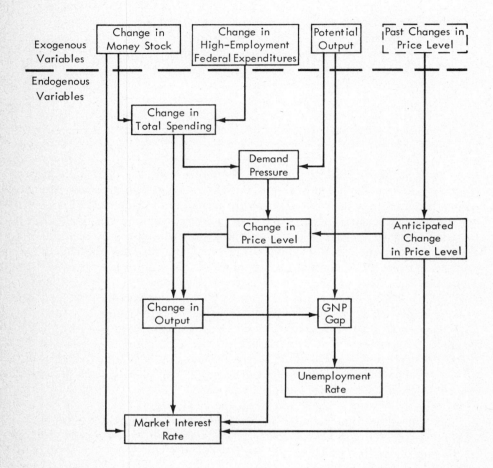

Source: *Economic Review,* Federal Reserve Bank of St. Louis (April, 1970), p. 10.

Figure 16-4

A Monetarist Model of the Economy

JUDGMENT MODELS

At this stage of knowledge of the economy it is impossible to use an econometric model to develop a completely accurate forecast. Therefore, models are also built that use the judgment of the forecaster to determine the most likely figure for each sector in the model. Such models have been developed primarily for gross national product and for industrial production. A gross national product model is generally developed by the expenditure approach. All available data are gathered on each major sector of GNP, including expenditure plans, analysis of supply and demand factors using formulas based on past experience, monetary factors, and leading series. A preliminary figure is developed for each spending sector based on the best judgment of the forecaster. These figures are then checked for consistency based on past relationships among them and revised if need be. A step-by-step approach to such model building to forecast GNP by the expenditure approach is presented in the next two chapters.

At times a judgment model of GNP is developed from the income or receipt of money flow approach. This involves many more estimates and is a more complex procedure. It adds several valuable items of information, however. For one thing, it provides forecasts of income payments for wages, interest, rent, and profits. These are needed by the Treasury Department when it forecasts budget receipts for the year since the major sources of revenue of the federal government are personal and corporate income taxes. A judgment model of GNP developed from this approach is also helpful as a cross-check on a model developed from the expenditure approach.

Models are also developed from the Federal Reserve Board Index of Industrial Production. The divisions of the index itself can be used to build up a model. They are at times reclassified into groups that have similar factors affecting them. One such classification uses the following groups:

Consumer perishable goods	Capital goods
Consumer semidurable goods	Fuels
Consumer durable goods	Materials and supplies
Construction materials	

A judgment figure is developed for each sector using techniques similar to those used to build up a model of GNP by the expenditure approach. When adequate productive capacity exists, the major emphasis is put on demand factors.

An alternative approach, which is often used at the same time as an analysis of changing demand factors, is a study of new orders and production in each sector of the economy into which the model is divided. Time lags that occur between changes in new orders and production are studied for a period covering several of the most recent cycles. In some cases it is easier to get data on new orders and on sales or expenditures rather than on production. Time lags between production and sales must then be determined in each sector of production into which the model is divided. Then changes in new orders can be used to predict changes in production based on past relationships. A study must continually be made of any tendency for past relationships to change.

QUESTIONS

1. Describe and evaluate the use of a listing of favorable and unfavorable factors as a method of forecasting.
2. How may the consensus of qualified observers be used in forecasting?

3. Describe the use that can be made of leads and lags in forecasting.
4. Evaluate the record of the National Bureau's statistical indicators in the post-World War II period.
5. What is a diffusion index? How may it be used in forecasting?
6. How are new orders, inventory, production, and sales series used in forecasting?
7. How may expectations about future business conditions be used in forecasting?
8. Describe and evaluate the use of series on spending plans as a method of forecasting.
9. Of what value is a projection of cycles and trends in forecasting and in business planning generally?
10. What is the record of econometric models as forecasting devices?
11. Discuss the use of monetary factors as a means of forecasting income.
12. Describe the St. Louis model for forecasting total spending, prices, and output.
13. What is a judgment model? How is it developed?

SUGGESTED READINGS

"A Monetarist Model for Economic Stabilization." *Review,* Federal Reserve Bank of St. Louis (April, 1970), pp. 7–25.

Battenberg, Douglas, Jared Enzler, and Arthur Havenner. "MINNIE: A Small Version of the MIT-PENN-SSRC Econometric Model." *Federal Reserve Bulletin* (November, 1975), pp. 721–726.

Business Conditions Digest. U.S. Department of Commerce, monthly.

Business Outlook. Conference Board, Inc., annually.

Butler, William F., and Robert A. Kavesh (eds.). *How Business Economists Forecast.* Englewood Cliffs, N.J.: Prentice-Hall, Inc., 1966.

Butler, William F., Robert A. Kavesh, and Robert B. Platt (eds.). *Methods and Techniques of Business Forecasting.* Englewood Cliffs, N.J.: Prentice-Hall, Inc., 1976.

Chisholm, Roger K. and Gilbert R. Whitaker, Jr. *Forecasting Methods.* Homewood, Ill.: Richard D. Irwin, Inc., 1971, Chapters 2–6.

de Menil, George, and Jared Enzler. *Prices and Wages in the FRB-MIT-PENN Econometric Model.* Published in mimeographed form by the Board of Governors of the Federal Reserve System, undated.

"Diffusion Indexes and Economic Activity." *Economic Review,* Federal Reserve Bank of Cleveland (January, 1971), pp. 3–17.

Hirsch, Albert A., Maurice Liebenberg, and George R. Green. *The BEA Quarterly Economic Model.* Washington: U.S. Department of Commerce, 1973.

Pindyck, Robert S., and Daniel L. Rubinfield. *Econometric Models and Economic Forecasts.* New York: McGraw-Hill Book Co., 1976.

Press, S. James. *Applied Multivariate Analysis.* New York: Holt, Rinehart and Winston, 1972.

Silk, Leonard S. and M. Louise Curley. *A Primer on Business Forecasting.* New York: Random House, 1970.

"What Businessmen Expect." Quarterly in *Dun's.*

Also see the "Business Roundup" section of *Fortune* and the "Business Situation" section of the *Survey of Current Business* for current analyses of inventories, sales, and new orders.

CHAPTER 17

SHORT-RUN FORECASTING OF GNP BY BUILDING AN EXPENDITURE MODEL

This chapter will consider the procedures involved in forecasting gross national product by estimating government purchases of goods and services, private construction, and producers' durable equipment for the ensuing year. The next chapter will consider the procedures for forecasting the remaining sectors of GNP and for checking and refining the overall forecast.

In making forecasts of gross national product, it is necessary to keep in mind the major factors that cause shifts in economic activity. Money flows through the economy in a circular fashion since expenditures of one group are income for another. Changes in economic activity occur because individuals, businesses, private institutions, and governmental units change the amount of their spending or change the relationship of such spending to the amount of income received. Changes may also occur because the spending units decide to spend their income in a pattern different from that in which goods are being produced and, as a result, demand exceeds supply in some fields and is less than supply in others. Since labor and capital are not completely mobile, these changes lead to shifts in the level of economic activity.

The circular flow of economic activity may appear to create a problem in forecasting since there is no clear-cut starting or stopping point. However, since time elapses between various economic activities, such as an increase in production due to an increase in sales with the receipt by consumers of income from such production and the resultant further increase in sales, it is possible to break into the process at any point and to determine what is likely to happen during a future period of time. As long as the proper time relationships between the variables are considered, it makes little difference at what point in the economic cycle forecasting is begun.

The most commonly used procedure is to build up forecasts of gross national product for a year ahead by estimating expenditures by consumers, business, government, and foreigners. Such forecasts must include factors due to the trend and the business cycle. Seasonal variations do not affect the annual forecasts, and quarterly forecasts are usually made at seasonally adjusted annual rates. Therefore, the effect of the seasonal variations can be ignored in a GNP forecast.

Before this analysis is begun, the general state of the economy and the direction of economic activity should be studied. The analyst should also check the relationship of economic activity to the capacity of the economy to produce goods and services by comparing the current level of activity with an estimate of full employment GNP.[1] It is also desirable to check unemployment levels and the indexes of manufacturing capacity utilization to see if slack exists in the economy. The trend of prices in the recent past should also be studied along with trends in the growth of the money supply and the full employment deficit or surplus in the federal government budget to get some idea of price trends and price pressures.

The factors involved in estimating levels for the next year of government purchases of goods and services will be analyzed first because they are, in part at least, based on decisions that are not related to the circular flow of economic activity. The level of these items, nevertheless, affects general business activity materially.

GOVERNMENT PURCHASES OF GOODS AND SERVICES

Government purchases of goods and services have fluctuated widely, especially since 1929. However, since they are to a large extent not dependent upon the general level of business activity and since the democratic process requires a great deal of time, especially when money is being appropriated, it is possible to forecast government expenditures with a reasonable degree of accuracy for a year ahead. Attention will first be directed to federal expenditures and then to state and local government expenditures.

Federal Government Purchases of Goods and Services

The level of governmental purchases of goods and services can be forecast by analyzing the budget of the federal government and political and international factors in the current and future situation. The government of the United States uses a fiscal year that runs from October 1 to September 30. The fiscal year is designated by the number of the calendar year in which it ends; thus, fiscal 1977 ran from October 1, 1976, to September 30, 1977.

The President must submit a budget to Congress in January of each year. The budget as submitted is in great detail and involves a large amount of work by the Bureau of the Budget. The salient features of the budget are contained in a pamphlet called *Budget in Brief,* which is available as soon as the budget is transmitted to Congress. Some aspects of the budget are analyzed in a companion volume to the budget entitled *Special Analyses Budget of the United States Government.* The economic implications of the budget are analyzed a few days later in the *Economic Report of the President.* The budget and its economic implications are also analyzed in the February issue of the *Survey of Current Business* and budget progress is reviewed from time to time in later issues.

---

[1] Refer to Chapter 15 for procedures in estimating full employment GNP.

The Federal budget process was revised significantly by the Congressional Budget Act of 1974, which set up new congressional budget procedures. The early stages are still the same, calling for the President to submit a budget in January based on budgets proposed by the various agencies, reviewed in detail by the Office of Management and Budget, and modified to conform to overall outlay and receipt levels considered appropriate by the President. The Act sets up new House and Senate Budget Committees and requires them to receive reports on individual budget requests by the various agencies from congressional committees. They also get a fiscal policy report by April 1 from the new Congressional Budget Office. By May 15 Congress must adopt a concurrent resolution which sets budget targets. Congress then works on bills providing budget authority and on September 15 passes a second concurrent resolution on budget ceilings. By September 25 Congress must reconcile appropriations to conform to the second concurrent resolution ceilings.

Budget authority is voted by Congress, but this total is different from outlays for the year. This is because the budget authority for major projects covers the full cost when a project is started even though funds may be spent over several years. This is also true for many loan, guarantee, and insurance programs, as well as for some trust funds which are used as needed over a period of years. New authority is therefore divided into outlays for the current year and funds to be spent in future years. Part of the unspent authority from prior years will also be spent in the current year. The Office of Management and Budget provides estimates of the amount to be spent in the current year from new and unspent obligational authority.

Types of Budget Data. In working with the contribution of the federal government to overall economic activity, three sets of budget figures must be distinguished. These are the unified budget, the national income accounts budget, and the full employment budget.

The *unified budget* is the government's financial operating plan and includes total spending, lending, and financing activities.

The *national income accounts budget* is more useful than the unified budget in making economic forecasts since it is consistent with the general national income and product account framework. Financial transactions and lending activity are excluded since they make no direct contribution to economic activity. In the national income accounts budget government receipts are generally recorded on an accrual basis, that is when the tax liability is incurred, except for personal incomes taxes, which are recorded when payment is received. On the expenditure side most purchases of goods and services are recorded when delivery is made, but other expenditures, including transfer payments, are recorded on a cash basis. In the unified budget all receipts and expenditures are recorded on a cash basis, but the plan is to put them on an accrual basis in the future.

The *full employment* (or high employment) *budget* is the budget as it would be if the economy were operating at an assumed level of full employment, generally considered to be the level based on a 4 percent unemployment rate.

The main difference between the national income budget and the full employment budget is on the revenue side since in the full employment budget revenues are estimated on the basis of GNP at full employment. The only difference on the expenditure side is for unemployment compensation, which is estimated on the full employment basis.

Forecasting Government Purchases of Goods and Services. The figures in the unified budget are not in the same form as in the national income accounts due to such items as different handling of geographic coverage, netting differences in financial transactions, and timing differences. National income account figures are also on a calendar year basis. The *Survey of Current Business* usually shows such relationships in its February issue. Table 17-1 shows such relationships for calendar years 1975, 1976, and 1977.

Table 17-1
Relation of Federal Government Expenditures in the National Income and Product Accounts to the Unified Budget
(Billions of Dollars)

	Fiscal Year			
	1975	1976	Transition Quarter	1977
Unified budget outlays	**324.6**	**373.5**	**98.0**	**394.2**
Less: Coverage differences:				
Geographic	2.0	2.4	.6	2.3
Other	−9.7	−9.5	−4.1	−11.3
Financial transactions:				
Net lending	12.3	12.7	5.1	12.3
Other	−.3	−.3	−.1	−.4
Net purchases of land:				
Outer Continental Shelf	−2.0	−2.6	−.3	−5.4
Other	.4	.4	.1	.4
Plus: Netting differences:				
Contributions to government				
employee retirement funds	5.1	5.6	1.5	6.1
Other	2.4	2.4	.6	2.7
Timing differences:				
Purchases of goods and				
services (increase in				
payables net of advances)	−.6	.5	−1.5	−.5
Other	−.2	−.3	.0	−.1
Miscellaneous	.1	.1	−.1	.0
Equals: Federal Government expenditures, national income and product accounts	**328.7**	**378.7**	**97.2**	**404.5**

Source: *Survey of Current Business* (February, 1976), p. 18.

The forecast of government purchases of goods and services should begin with an analysis of the budget for the remainder of the current fiscal year and for the next fiscal year. The budget review can be used to get the final figures for the current fiscal year. As early as the first part of December, the size of the budget to be proposed to Congress is usually reported in the press. When the budget is available, it cannot be taken as presented as a forecast of what will happen. This is true because Congress is unlikely to go along with all items and because of some bias in the budgetary process itself. Expenses of items included in the purchase of goods and services are usually overestimated somewhat, especially on new programs. In the postwar period final expenditures have usually been within 10 percent of the President's budget and in most years within 5 percent. More accurate estimates are possible if based on an analysis of the budget along with an analysis of the current situation.

One factor that needs consideration is an analysis of appropriations for new programs or agencies. When a new agency is set up or appropriations are made for a new program, expenditures are often below the budget in the early stages. This is due to such factors as overestimating the speed with which a new program can be set up, delays in getting the proper employees, delays in getting equipment, and the like.

To forecast the appropriate figure for government purchases of goods and services it is necessary to adjust budget figures on the basis of an analysis of the major items of equipment to be produced, the overall military situation, and the use of judgment. It is possible to use data on new obligational authority as a lead series to gauge the future trend of expenditures.

Two members of the staff of the Board of Governors of the Federal Reserve System, Harvey Galper and Edward Gramlich, developed models for forecasting defense spending using regression techniques. They estimated the lag between awards and expenditures so as to show variation of the lag in response to measures of supply bottlenecks, demand urgency, and the mix between short-lag and long-lag items. Supply bottlenecks are measured by the Federal Reserve index of the capacity utilization rate and demand urgency is measured by the rate of growth or decline of the armed forces. This model has had a good measure of success in predicting spending on equipment and appears to be a promising aid to short-run forecasting in this field.

In addition to considering the effects on spending of new programs or agencies and of purchases of major items of equipment, requests for changes in governmental expenditures should be considered carefully in light of the present and prospective political and international situation. Adjustments should be made in the budgeted figures for items the analyst feels Congress will raise or cut, especially when the analyst believes that Congress will not follow the budget recommendations for military spending or for pay rates of federal government employees.

The budget expenditure figure as presented should therefore be adjusted for three types of factors:

1. Bias in estimates of spending when new programs are introduced.
2. Other cases in which spending on purchases of major items may not be as great as estimated by the Office of Management and Budget.
3. Estimates of changes Congress will make in the President's budget.

State and Local Government Purchases of Goods and Services

If data and resources were available, it would be possible to forecast state and local government expenditures in the same way as federal government expenditures. However, there are well over 100,000 such governmental units, and many do not publish budget figures and others have little classification of items in their budget. Since 100 of the largest spending units account for about half of all spending at the state and local level, an analysis of their budgets can be made to get some idea of what is happening. This may be supplemented by analyzing a sample of the budgets of smaller spending units.

The most generally used approach in recent years has been to extend the trend of the last several years into the future for one year. This trend line may be modified if recent elections and political trends have shown a tendency to either defeat or pass tax increases, new bond issues, etc. This procedure is likely to be reasonably accurate for some years to come. Increased population in the past has increased the need for governmental services. This has also increased the need for capital expenditures that are likely to be spread out due to limits on the debt governments can incur, limits on taxes, and the like. Until some research organization develops figures on state and local government expenditure plans, the average analyst must rely on a projection of recent trends that are modified by an analysis of qualitative factors when necessary.

GROSS PRIVATE DOMESTIC INVESTMENT

The most volatile component of gross national product is gross private domestic investment, which includes new construction, producers' durable equipment, and the net change in business inventories. These categories are all difficult to forecast, but procedures have been developed that make it possible in most years to develop reasonably accurate forecasts.

Only the value of private construction is included in gross private domestic investment. Government construction is included under government purchases of goods and services.

Private building is usually divided into several categories for forecasting purposes. The major categories are the following:

Residential building, nonfarm
Nonresidential building, nonfarm
Farm construction
Public utility construction
   Railroads
   Telephone and telegraph
Other public utilities
   Local transit
   Petroleum pipelines
   Electric light and power
   Gas

Procedures for forecasting residential construction will be considered first, and then other construction.

Residential Construction

The level of residential construction may be estimated in several different ways. One method is based upon data on building starts developed by the Bureau of the Census. Since 1959 building starts are being measured directly rather than estimated from building permits. This data covers all residential buildings both in areas requiring permits and in those that do not. It is subject to sampling error since it is based on sample data. The Bureau of the Census also develops data on the value of housing under construction. Figures are available for single-family and for multi-family units. These figures are published monthly in the *Construction Review* by the Department of Commerce.

In developing patterns of construction from permit data, it is necessary to work with single-family and multi-family units separately since the factors affecting them are different. The availability and cost of financing may also be different in the short run for different types of housing and the pattern of construction expenditures is different for different types of housing. The first step in developing an estimate of construction volume for single-family dwellings is to develop patterns of construction spending from the housing starts and permit value data. A study of past construction activity will show the average expenditures over the period of construction for various types of projects. For example, a project costing $40,000, which is begun in January, may typically involve expenditures of $4,000 in January, $8,000 in February, $16,000 in March, $8,000 in April, and $4,000 in May. In making such estimates, it is necessary to consider qualitative factors, such as a shortage of materials or labor, or work stoppages due to strikes, that may lead to a stretching out or perhaps even some speeding up of activity. Sone analysts prefer to work with data which are not seasonally adjusted in making expenditure projections. This is done because the weather may be such in some years that average seasonal patterns do not hold. A mild February, for example, may allow housing starts to begin early in some sections of the country and therefore make seasonal adjustments misleading.

Estimates of expenditures for multi-family units based on starts are not very helpful because there are very few "starts" as such in large projects. Therefore, estimates must be developed from permit data. These estimates are not as accurate as estimates based on single-family units because the quantity of data is not as great for multi-family as for single-family units. While the proportion of multi-family units has been increasing in recent years, the length of time for which data is available is not as great as for single-family units. Also, figures may need to be adjusted on the basis of value of multi-family housing under construction because past patterns may not develop due to strikes, material shortages, financing problems, or slow sales. Some analysts prefer to use data on permits and starts to gauge direction of movement, and thus develop some indication of volume changes, rather than developing a detailed forecast.

The demand for residential construction may also be forecast from an analysis of the most significant demand and supply factors. The starting point in such a forecast is an estimate of net family formation and net household formation. Net family formation can be forecast with accuracy for a year ahead since the age at which persons marry and the percentage of persons of marriageable age who marry change slowly. To develop estimates of net household formation, it is necessary to make allowances for changes in doubling up of families in one housing unit and for the net change in single-member families and nonfamily households. The Bureau of the Census publishes projections of the number of families and of households up to twenty years into the future.

New houses may also be demanded for reasons other than new household formation. Houses may be demolished due to accidents, such as fires and tornadoes. Houses are torn down because of housing projects resulting in slum clearance, to make way for commercial centers, for highways, and the like. Additional houses are also needed because population is shifting, thus leading to vacant houses in some sections and the need for new houses in others. This demand has been largely due to a shift from rural to urban areas in the post-World War II period. A small housing demand also exists for second houses. These factors may be summarized as follows:

Net family formation
     + or − Undoubling or doubling
     + or − Changes in single-member and non-family households
     =   Net household formation
     + or − Net change in vacancies
     =   Housing units required based on demand changes
     +   Replacement demand
     +   Net demand due to population shifts
     +   Net demand due to an increase in two-house families
     =   Total housing units required
     −   Forecast for mobile home sales
     =   Permanent housing units required

The unit forecast for permanent housing units can be put on a dollar basis by a fairly simple procedure. The dollar value of housing for the past year can be divided by the number of houses built to get the average cost per house. This figure can be adjusted for expected changes in construction costs and in the size of houses to arrive at an average unit cost and total cost for the forecast year.

A preliminary forecast of housing expenditures based on demand must be adjusted in light of qualitative factors on the demand side and on the basis of supply factors. Individuals buy houses somewhat more easily when income is rising than when it is falling. Housing demand is increased significantly when vacancy rates are lower than normal because building in the past has not kept up with demand. Housing demand increases when credit terms on government underwritten mortgages are favorable and financing is easily available, and it drops when credit is harder to get. Housing demand is increased when monthly payments are less than rentals for comparable units. Housing demand is slowed somewhat by rising costs of new houses. Some indication of the effects of changing rental rates and construction costs may be obtained by comparing rates of change in the rent index section of the consumer price index and a residential construction cost index. Housing demand will also be slowed when demand is close to, or somewhat ahead of, available supplies of building materials. This has a tendency to slow construction and so reduce the number of houses built in a year. The effect of these factors cannot be put into quantitative terms, but judgment must be used by the analyst to raise or lower the forecast in light of the analysis of these factors.

The effect on housing of the cycle in housing construction must also be taken into consideration, especially in the short cycle discussed in Chapter 13 in which housing activity has been almost counter-cyclical. This pattern is based to a large degree on availability of financing and to some degree on the shift of labor from other construction. Therefore, a complete analysis of the financial markets and prospects for housing credit must be made and their effect on prospective housing used to modify a forecast based on demand factors and other qualitative factors. It is also necessary to consider the effect of shifts of resources to housing if the forecast for other construction shows a decline. The analyst must study current and new programs for housing credit since these programs modify the shortage of housing funds as the economy expands and will thus change the housing cycle.

The effect on demand for housing of the permanent type due to competition from sales of mobile homes must also be considered. Some mobile homes are used for second homes but the vast majority are used for low-cost housing. In 1972 a record number of such homes were sold when the total reached 575,000 compared with just over 100,000 in 1960. The number in 1973 was almost as large, but the number dropped during the ensuing recession to only 225,000 units in 1975.[2] Mobile homes are bought primarily by young persons in their mid-twenties to mid-thirties whose family incomes are generally considerably below average incomes. Almost all new housing units sold in the under-$10,000 price range are mobile homes.

A sum must be added to the forecast of expenditures for new houses for additions, alterations, and structures, such as new garages. This category is an increasing one on which complete data have only recently become available. It probably responds closely to changes in consumer income, to the cost of the work, and to the ease of getting it done.

Forecasts prepared from analysis of demand, permit data, and the index of consumer purchase projections for single-family housing, can well be compared to see to what extent they are in harmony. Any significant differences call for a thorough analysis of all factors in the forecasts and such revisions as seem necessary to bring the forecasts into line. The analyst will also want to check other forecasts such as that published in *Construction Review,* usually in the November issue.

Other Construction

Private nonfarm, nonresidential building may be forecast in much the same way as housing from contract data of the F. W. Dodge Company. Several adjustments must be made in their data to use them as a basis for a forecast. The F. W. Dodge Company reports cancellations or corrections in the month in

---

[2] *U.S. Industrial Outlook 1976* (Washington: U.S. Department of Commerce), p. 11.

which they are ascertained. It is necessary to make such adjustments to the data for the month in which the contracts were reported. The F. W. Dodge Company data include permits for offices, warehouses, and other buildings constructed by public utilities that are usually estimated separately and must therefore be excluded.

The same pattern that was used for residential construction can be used to forecast nonresidential construction from a record of permits. A study of the progress of past projects of various types, such as the construction of retail establishments, office buildings, schools, hospitals, and churches, is used to determine the rate at which building is likely to take place. Qualitative factors are again considered and these, along with the past patterns, are used to develop the final forecast. Since construction of most of the structures in this category takes a relatively long period of time, forecasts may be made on the basis of general relationships between permit data and construction data without analyzing construction spending patterns in detail. Some analysts use a different technique for forecasting construction of retail establishments. Since these have followed residential construction with only a short lag, they have used forecasts of residential construction to develop retail construction forecasts. A general demand factor is also used at times to help forecast the demand for office buildings. Since office buildings are used primarily to house white-collar employees, there is a relationship between trends in such building and trends in white-collar employment. A projection of such past relationships is used to arrive at a demand for office building. Such a demand forecast must be modified, however, for added demands due to shifts in centers of employment of a trend toward new, more modern buildings. The relationship of the level of industrial construction to the Federal Reserve Board Index of Industrial Production is also used at times to develop a demand factor for new industrial structures. But shifts in production patterns and processes, and the trend toward greater efficiency, make such demand projections of limited usefulness.

Estimates of farm construction are developed from forecasts of farm income. There has been a high degree of relationship in the past between the trend of cash farm income and the amount of building done on farms. Some analysts prefer to use the relationship between farm construction and net farm income per farm. This may prove to be more useful in the future as farming becomes more a business and less a way of life. By using the past trend and studying qualitative factors, such as the relationship of building costs to farm prices, it is possible to forecast farm building.

Forecasts of the level of construction activity by railroads and public utilities are made somewhat differently. The Interstate Commerce Commission prepares monthly estimates of expenditures for all Class I railroads. These must be adjusted upward on the basis of past experience to make allowance for expenditures by smaller railroads. From developments in the past year or so and from a study of plans of the major railroad systems, it is possible to project construction levels for a year ahead with reasonable accuracy and a quarter ahead with a fairly high degree of accuracy.

Data for capital expenditures of electric light and power, gas, and petroleum pipeline companies are published quarterly by the Securities and Exchange Commission. Since such projects often take several years to complete, changes do not occur quickly. From a study of the figures for the past five or six quarters and from a study of expansion plans that are made several years ahead, it is possible to arrive at reasonable forecasts.

Local transit expenditures on construction have not been large in recent years and have followed the trend of expenditures by other utilities. The American Telephone & Telegraph Company publishes monthly estimates of construction by its subsidiaries and by independent companies. Since the AT&T system accounts for the bulk of the construction, its plans for the coming years form the basis for forecasting the level of activity. These must be raised on the basis of past experience to allow for construction by independent companies. Since AT&T plans several years ahead, such forecasts for a year ahead are reasonably accurate. A similar procedure is followed in regard to Western Union Telegraph Company construction. The *Construction Review* contains forecasts of the most likely volume of construction in each of these areas.

Producers' Durable Equipment

Forecasts of private construction include only business plant, not expenditures on producers' durable equipment. The latter are treated as a separate subcategory of gross private domestic investment and must be projected independently if a separate figure is to be developed for both plant and equipment. The next section discusses techniques for forecasting expenditures on plant and equipment together.

A statistical method of forecasting the demand for domestic producers' durable equipment has been developed by the late C. F. Roos, of the Econometric Institute. He did this by studying the factors that influence business executives to invest in such equipment. There is an incentive to invest in equipment when the expected return from that equipment in relationship to its supply price is greater than the interest rate. Since it is impossible to determine accurately the future rate of return, Roos believed that most executives solve this problem by projecting the present rate of profit and he, therefore, used current profits in his calculations. To determine a measure of the interest rate that is significant in business decisions, he worked with both AAA bond yields and a combination of AAA bond yields and short-term interest rates, since some capital equipment is financed by short-term borrowing. Since he found that adding short-term rates made little difference in the accuracy of his forecasts, he used only AAA bond yields.

No index is available to show changes in the supply price of capital assets. The closest approximation to it is an index of machinery and machinery products prices. Unfortunately this index is not available for a long enough period to make an adequate study but, for the period for which it is available, it fluctuates in much the same way as the Bureau of Labor Statistics index of the price of metals and metal products. Therefore, this index was used by Roos as a proxy for changes in the supply price of capital assets.

He found, furthermore, that changes in real wage rates influence the demand for investment goods. This relationship may well be twofold since, as real wages go up, there is a greater demand for capital equipment to cut production costs. At the same time, increases in wages also lead to an increase in the demand for consumer goods and thus in the derived demand for capital equipment. Since there was no index available to measure changes in real wage rates, Roos used the Bureau of Labor Statistics index of nonfarm prices as the best approximation of such changes. The relative prices of consumer goods to producer goods also influence the level of demand for investment goods; a high level of consumer goods prices to producer goods prices encourages investment, whereas a low level discourages it. From this data he calculated capitalized profits based upon corporate profits and the supply price of capital assets and adjusted them for changes in nonfarm prices. This capitalized relative profits factor is calculated as follows:

$$X = \frac{\text{Corporate profits}}{\text{AAA bond yields}} \times \frac{\text{Nonfarm prices}}{\text{Price of metals and metal products}}$$

This factor is then correlated with producers' durable equipment six months later.

The lag in the production of producers' durable equipment is to be expected, since some time must elapse between the decision to invest in new equipment and the fabrication of this equipment. The formula that expresses this relationship is as follows:[3]

$$Y \text{ (Producers' durable equipment} = .021X + 2,500 \text{ million}$$
$$\text{6 months in the future)}$$

Thus, from this formula it is possible to make a preliminary forecast six months ahead with some degree of accuracy. Forecasts for a year ahead can also be made fairly accurately, since it is necessary to forecast the four factors involved in capitalized relative profits for only six months in the future.

Roos found that the demand for producers' durable equipment is greater than that which would be expected from past relationships when the economy is operating at or near capacity levels. At such times upward adjustments must be made in the figures to take the effects of this capacity "squeeze" into consideration.

Some analysts develop their forecasts of producers' durable equipment by following new orders, unfilled orders, inventories, and shipments. This is the method frequently used to forecast the Federal Reserve Index of Industrial Production, which was discussed in the previous chapter.

---

[3] Charles F. Roos, "The Demand for Investment Goods," *American Economic Review* (May, 1948), pp. 314–316.

QUESTIONS

1. Describe the relationship that exists between the circular flow of economic activity and forecasting?
2. Describe the preliminary analysis which should be made before beginning to build a judgment model of GNP by analyzing major sectors.
3. Describe the budget process of the federal government.
4. Distinguish between the unified budget, the national income accounts budget, and the full employment budget.
5. How are expenditures for defense systems and other major equipment items handled in the federal government budget?
6. Describe procedures for forecasting the effect of defense expenditures on government purchases of goods and services.
7. Explain the role of new and unused obligational authority in the budget process.
8. Describe the adjustments needed in federal budget figures to use them as a basis for developing a forecast.
9. Explain how a forecast of federal government purchases of goods and services may be developed from adjusted budget figures.
10. Explain a procedure for forecasting state and local government purchases of goods and services.
11. Outline a division of private building for forecasting purposes.
12. Describe, step-by-step, two alternative procedures for forecasting the volume of residential construction.
13. How do developments in the mobile home field affect a housing forecast?
14. Explain how other, nonresidential construction may be forecast.
15. Explain a procedure for forecasting the volume of producers' durable equipment.

SUGGESTED READINGS

See the Suggested Readings at the conclusion of Chapter 18.

CHAPTER 18

BUILDING AN EXPENDITURE MODEL

This chapter concludes the procedures for developing an expenditure model of gross national product. First, we will consider the remaining items in the investment sector, that is, new plant and equipment, other capital items, and the change in business inventories. The factors involved in forecasting the net export of goods and services are considered next and then procedures for forecasting personal consumption expenditures. The last section of this chapter discusses the steps involved in developing the final forecast of GNP.

NEW PLANT AND EQUIPMENT

The value of new construction and producers' durable equipment is often broken down differently for forecasting purposes than it is in national income statistics. Business firms do not as a rule differentiate clearly in their planning between new buildings and new equipment. Therefore, business expenditures on new plant and equipment are often projected as one unit. This reduces the number of classes of new construction that must be projected separately to the following:

Capital outlays by business
Residential construction
Nonresidential construction for nonbusiness purposes, such as institutions
    and private schools
Farm construction

Expenditures on farm machinery and equipment must also be projected separately since they are included in producers' durable equipment, but not in business expenditures on plant and equipment. The same is true of expenditures on professional equipment and that for private institutions.

The Department of Commerce and the Securities and Exchange Commission have in the post-World War II period surveyed business plans for expenditures on new plant and equipment. Data are gathered by the SEC on plans of all corporations registered with them under the Securities Acts, and the Department of Commerce uses a large sample in order to get data from nonregistered corporations. Beginning in 1972 the Bureau of Economic Analysis of the Department of Commerce assumed responsibility for all aspects of the survey.

McGraw-Hill also conducts a similar survey and publishes the results in *Business Week*. It is based on a smaller sample that is somewhat less representative, since it concentrates to some extent on larger concerns. The sequence of these surveys is as follows:

Fall (usually a November issue of *Business Week*)
> Preliminary McGraw-Hill report for the coming year.

December
> Commerce revised report for the current quarter and report for the first two quarters of the coming year.

January
> Commerce report on plans for the coming year.

March
> Commerce revised report for the current quarter, the second quarter, and the current year.

April
> McGraw-Hill revised report for the current year.

June and September
> Commerce revised report for the current quarter and the rest of the year.

A Department of Commerce forecast for 1976 is presented in Table 18-1.

Table 18-1
Plant and Equipment Expenditures 1974–1976
(Billions of Dollars)

				Percentage Change	
	Actual 1974	Actual 1975	Expected 1976	1974 to 1975	1975 to 1976
	(Billions of dollars)				
ALL INDUSTRIES	112.40	112.79	120.06	.3	6.5
Manufacturing	46.01	47.95	51.85	4.2	8.1
Durable goods	22.62	21.84	22.93	−3.4	5.0
Nondurable goods	23.39	26.11	28.92	11.6	10.8
Nonmanufacturing	66.39	64.82	68.21	−2.4	5.2
Mining	3.18	3.79	3.88	19.4	2.3
Railroad	2.54	2.55	2.08	.2	−18.4
Air transportation	2.00	1.84	1.33	−8.1	−27.7
Other transportation	2.12	3.18	2.82	50.0	−11.1
Public utilities	20.55	20.14	23.24	−2.0	15.4
Communications	13.96	12.74	13.56	−8.8	6.5
Commercial & other	22.05	20.60	21.30	−6.6	3.4

Source: U.S. Department of Commerce *News* (March 9, 1976), p. 3.

These surveys have established a good record in anticipating the change in investment expenditures. The Department of Commerce-SEC annual surveys from 1947 through 1975 had a median deviation from actual expenditures of only 3 percent. In 20 of the 29 years for which the annual survey was conducted, anticipated expenditures have been within 3 percent of actual expenditures. In only two years, 1947 and 1950, were the deviations in excess of 6 percent. The direction of change was predicted accurately in all years except 1950. In the boom year of 1955 the survey was low by 6 percent, in the recession year of 1958 it was high by 5 percent, and in the 1961 and 1970 recession years it was high by 4 percent.

The 1947 figure was low because of the rapidly rising prices during that year as industry emerged from a period of price control. The larger volume of expenditures in 1950 was due largely to the impact of the Korean War on the economy, which could not have been foreseen at the beginning of the year. The survey would probably have been off, however, even if the Korean War had not occurred, since in the first two quarters outlays approached the 1949 levels and business firms had scheduled a rise in output in the third quarter before the war began. The 1951 and 1952 figures were again somewhat low because of events related to the Korean War. Large increases in defense expenditures required more plant and equipment than anticipated. Prices of capital equipment also increased faster than foreseen.[1] Under more normal conditions such errors should not occur.

In the fall of 1956 the National Industrial Conference Board introduced a new survey, which is published quarterly in the Conference Board publication *Investment Statistics*. This is based on a survey of capital appropriations of the 1,000 largest manufacturing companies. The survey gives data on newly approved capital appropriations and on total outstanding capital appropriations. The difference between spending plans and new appropriation is analogous to that between new appropriations and expenditures in the government budget. Thus, the Conference Board survey gives additional information that should prove useful in projecting capital spending more accurately several quarters ahead. This survey predicted the 1957 downturn and the following upturn and also the 1960 downturn, the slowdown in 1967, and the 1970 downturn.

Economists at the Federal Reserve Bank of Cleveland have developed relationships between new capital appropriations and expenditures on plant and equipment. The procedures are similar to those for defense spending based on new authorizations and for construction expenditures based on permit data. The basis for these relationships is a seven-quarter relationship between appropriations and expenditures. Estimates for spending for each quarter are based on some portion of new appropriations for that quarter and for each of the previous six quarters. In manufacturing, for example, during the 1961–1969 period 14 percent of new appropriations was spent in the first quarter and this amount accumulated as follows:

[1] Murray F. Foss and Vito Natrella, "Ten Years' Experience with Business Investment Anticipation," *Survey of Current Business* (January, 1957), pp. 16–24.

Within Quarter	Cumulative Percentage of New Appropriations Spent
1	14
2	35
3	56
4	74
5	86
6	92
7+	100

In utilities, however, only 6 percent was spent in the first quarter and only 62 percent in six quarters.[2]

The figures reported in the surveys of expenditures on plant and equipment should be analyzed in light of conditions in the economy and revised if need be. It is impossible to check them quantitatively with building permit data, but an analysis of such data for several quarters will show if the surveys are in conformity with future building as shown in permits. The same kind of check can be made with the Department of Commerce series on new orders and order backlogs in the durable goods manufacturing industries. If these series have been moving in the same direction as the expenditure surveys indicate that expenditures on plant and equipment will move, they help substantiate the survey figures. If not, they raise serious questions about the figures in the survey and may call for some revision of these figures in making the forecast for this sector of the economy.

The survey figures should also be checked in light of their feasibility, both from a physical and a financial point of view. If the construction and equipment industry is operating at or near full capacity, additional spending plans cannot be fully met on time and the figures should be adjusted downward. This, for example, was the situation in 1956. If indications are that money will become extremely tight, some downward revision may also be necessary. Large concerns usually can get the funds to carry out plans for the current year, but some of the smaller firms may have to postpone some expenditures because of difficulties in financing. The effects of tight money are probably felt primarily in making plans for the next year, not in completing those for the present year. Downward revision may also be necessary if stock prices are dropping or have dropped significantly since this will cause some business to defer new financing.

Expenditure plans may also have to be changed because the analyst believes sales and profits will be substantially different from those which business executives expected at the time of the survey. Minor changes in sales do not affect spending decisions significantly, but a sharp drop in sales and profits will. There is, however, a lag of three or four quarters before significant changes occur. The analyst has information on the sales picture expected because the Commerce Department report for the year asks business executives about their expectations of sales for the year.

---

[2] *Economic Review,* Federal Reserve Bank of Cleveland (October, 1970), p. 9.

OTHER CAPITAL ITEMS

After expenditures on plant and equipment have been forecast from surveys of business plans, it is necessary to estimate the levels of the remaining items. Capital outlays charged to the current account fluctuate in about the same way as capital outlays in general. They are usually forecast by adjusting the figure for the past year by the same percentage by which the expenditure survey shows that spending on plant and equipment will change. Methods of forecasting residential construction, nonresidential construction for nonbusiness purposes, and farm construction have already been considered.

Expenditures on farm machinery and equipment show a reasonable degree of correlation with cash farm income or net income per farm. They can therefore be forecast by adjusting levels in the past year by expected changes in these factors. Expenditures on professional equipment are not a large part of total investment expenditures and do not change rapidly. They can be estimated from expenditures during the past year and trends over the past five years or so.

CHANGE IN BUSINESS INVENTORIES

The last item in the gross private domestic investment group to forecast is the net change in business inventories. This has often been the most volatile series of all and so, in many ways, the most important one to forecast accurately, especially in minor recessions. It is also one of the most difficult to forecast.

In analyzing inventory changes it is well to keep in mind the adjustments companies are trying to make in inventory levels. In the retail and wholesale fields, and in major segments of the manufacturing field, goods are no longer made to order but are kept in stock and sold out of stock. The competent business manager has a pretty good idea of the optimal relationship of inventory to sales. Inventory acts as a cushion for unexpected changes in sales levels since it is depleted as sales increase more than expected in an upturn and is allowed to increase when sales decrease in a downturn.

In such fields as the manufacture of major types of industrial equipment, goods are still made to order. In these industries, for example in machine tools, sales and production are almost the same. The cushion is in unfilled orders because new orders are above sales in an upswing and below sales in a downturn. In most manufacturing industries some goods are made to order, but enough goods are kept in stock so that inventories perform a major cushioning function.

The attempt to adjust inventories to sales has been reasonably successful, but there is usually a lag. In those industries in which sales are made primarily out of finished goods inventories, production lags behind sales when unexpected changes in sales occur. Unexpected increases in sales are limited in the short run by the availability of inventories.

Total inventories in manufacturing and trade cannot be changed rapidly because concerted efforts to build or to liquidate stocks are in part self-defeating. If a retailer wants to increase inventory because less inventory than planned is on hand due to higher sales than expected, more is ordered from wholesalers and manufacturers and this ordering reduces their stocks. The result has been a lag of several months between sales and inventories in manufacturing and trade. The change in the book value of inventories in manufacturing and trade is, however, a leading series, as is to be expected from attempts by business executives to adjust planned inventory levels to planned levels of future sales.

The relationship of inventories to sales has continued on a more or less stable basis in recent years. There has been a trend toward lower inventories in relation to sales in recent years due to better methods of inventory control and higher costs of financing inventories. A close relationship exists between average monthly sales in manufacturing and trade and the book value of inventory (see Figure 18-1). This relationship holds for retail trade inventories and for the volatile durable goods sector of manufacturing as well as for nondurable goods.

The relationship of inventories to average monthly sales on an annual basis is effective for showing the ratios businesses would like to have when they consider stocks to be normal. Quarterly figures show variations around these levels as inventories move out of balance and are brought back into line.

FORECASTING INVENTORIES

The first step in forecasting inventories is to develop an estimate of the level of inventories expected from past relationships and to compare them with current levels to see the size and direction of changes that are likely to occur.

Forecasting such changes involves an analysis of the cyclical and price factors which have affected inventories over the past several quarters. The analysis of optimal inventory policy in Chapter 12 shows that there is a tendency for inventories to increase more rapidly than sales in the early expansion phase of a cycle. This is especially true when significant price rises are expected and when raw materials and parts are expected to be short. The opposite tendency holds in a downturn; that is, inventories decrease less rapidly than sales. The result is that inventory-to-sales ratios rise rapidly in recession periods and drop significantly early in recovery periods. If such changes are occurring or are likely to occur on the basis of the overall forecast being developed, they must be considered in projecting changes in inventories from past relationships. Such adjustments are significant when a recession is in progress or is being forecast, or when an upturn is being forecast or is in its beginning stages. The price situation should also be considered when the economy is in a period of rapid price rises in the materials stage which have not as yet been fully reflected in finished goods prices. In such a situation the book value of inventories may for a time rise faster than past relationships would indicate.

The GNP figures on nonfarm business inventories are somewhat more inclusive than manufacturing and trade inventories, but the two series move together. Therefore, the percentage change expected in manufacturing and trade inventories can be applied to nonfarm business inventories. Changes in farm inventories then remain to be forecast. They are small and the change can generally be forecast from an extrapolation of the trend during the past seven or eight quarters. This trend projection should be adjusted up or down if an analysis of qualitative factors indicates that unusual forces are at work.

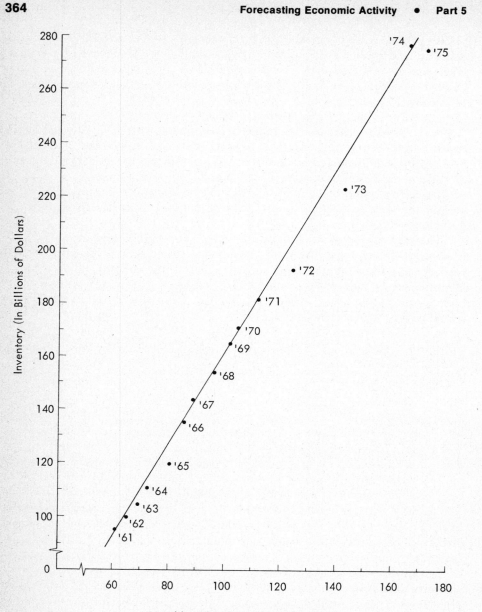

Source: U.S. Department of Commerce, *1971 Business Statistics,* pp. 23, 24; and *Survey of Current Business* (July, 1973), p. S-5, (January, 1976), p. S-5, (June, 1976), p. S-5, and (January, 1977), p. S-5.

Note: Numbers beside points represent years 1961 through 1975.

Figure 18-1

**Relationship of Inventory to Average Monthly
Sales in Manufacturing and Trade, 1961–1975**

Such forecasts of inventory changes should be compared with manufacturers' inventory and sales expectations as reported in the quarterly survey by the Department of Commerce. This survey shows manufacturers' expectations for changes in inventories and in sales for the next two quarters. It also gives their evaluation of their inventories as about right, too high, or too low; and an estimate of the net amount and percentage of inventory imbalance. If the analyst is expecting a level of sales different from that expected by manufacturers, appropriate changes can be made in the inventory figures. The data on the condition of inventories will also help to adjust a forecast of inventory levels based on past relationships, since it will show any tendency to change inventory-sales relationships.

Econometric models are used by some analysts to help forecast inventory investment. A simple model correlates the book value of inventories with sales in the second preceding quarter. More complex models use such factors as the change in inventory investment from the preceding period, the change in final product sales in the preceding period, the change in plant and equipment outlays from the preceding period, and the change in manufacturing and unfilled orders from the preceding period. Such models have proven helpful but results have generally not been as good as those based on less formal procedures or as forecasts using a combination of procedures.

Before making a final forecast of the change in inventories, it is desirable to look at inventories in major fields. It is especially significant to study the inventory situation in the automobile and steel fields because significant changes often take place here. This has been especially true in years in which a steel strike threatens or in which sales have not been up to expectations. In periods following a major build-up in the defense field, it is also necessary to look at prospective changes in defense inventories. The relationship of such inventories to government purchases was described earlier in this chapter. For example, as the Vietnam War heated up, defense stocks more than doubled during the 1965–1968 period. They were reduced by about 15 percent between the third quarter of 1969 and mid-1971 as war goods were delivered in large quantities and defense spending was cut.

NET EXPORT OF GOODS AND SERVICES

Net exports of goods and services do not constitute a large item. Therefore, even sizable errors in this forecast would have a negligible effect on the total forecast. In 1946, 1947, 1948, and 1949, however, the sums involved were about 4 percent, 5 percent, 3 percent, and 2 percent, respectively. This situation resulted from heavy foreign purchases in the United States, in part because of pent-up war demand and in part because exchange rates were so regulated as to make some American goods cheaper than domestic goods in many countries. In each year large amounts of long-term foreign investments were liquidated to help pay for the goods purchased here.

Since net exports of goods and services are such a small percentage of GNP, the accuracy of a forecast will not be affected much by some margin of error. Therefore, some analysts give very little consideration to this sector and make changes in levels in the immediate past only on the basis of qualitative factors which they feel will affect foreign trade materially. Other analysts spend a great deal of time on this sector since they are interested in balance-of-payments problems. Forecasts are likely to be somewhat more accurate if an analysis is made of the factors affecting both imports and exports.

The Department of Commerce breaks down import and export categories into great detail. It categorizes imports as follows:

Merchandise, excluding military
Direct defense expenditures
Payments on income of foreign investments in the United States
Other goods and services

The volume of merchandise and service imports is related to the volume of domestic business activity. It is affected by the level of overall economic activity in the United States since raw materials and materials used in production are imported as well as finished goods. The volume of merchandise and service imports is also affected by the relative prices of domestic and imported goods. In the period from 1960 to 1970 imports generally fluctuated between 4.5 and 6.0 percent of gross national product. Since 1970 the percentage has risen steadily until it was 9.7 percent in 1974. Relationships since 1960 are shown in Table 18-2.

Table 18-2
The Relationship of Merchandise and Service
Imports to Gross National Product, 1960–1976
(Billions of Dollars)

Year	Gross National Product	Merchandise and Service Imports	Percentage of Imports to GNP
1960	506.0	23.2	4.6
1961	523.3	23.1	4.4
1962	563.8	25.2	4.5
1963	594.7	26.4	4.4
1964	635.7	28.4	4.5
1965	688.1	32.0	4.7
1966	753.0	37.7	5.0
1967	796.3	40.6	5.1
1968	868.5	47.7	5.5
1969	935.5	52.9	5.7
1970	982.4	58.5	6.0
1971	1,063.4	64.0	6.0
1972	1,171.1	75.9	6.5
1973	1,306.6	94.4	7.2
1974	1,413.2	136.9	9.7
1975	1,516.3	127.6	8.4
1976	1,692.4	155.1	9.2

Source: *Survey of Current Business* (January, 1976), Part II, pp. 8, 69; (July, 1976), p. 24, and (January, 1977), p. 9.

Imports have generally grown somewhat more rapidly than GNP in periods of rapid growth. For example, in the several years after 1965 inflation in the United States made imports more desirable from a price standpoint. Domestic prices rose more rapidly during the Vietnam War than prices in many foreign countries and the dollar became overvalued. Costs were also increasing in many fields on a long-run basis because labor in some fields in the United States was getting wage increases at a faster rate than increases in productivity. Also, consumer preferences in many fields had shifted to foreign-made goods.

A forecast of merchandise imports should begin with an analysis of trends of imports to GNP. Modification of recent figures should be based on the expected growth in GNP and in the relative price trends of domestic and imported goods. Other qualitative factors, such as overstocking in some fields that may lead to price cuts and thus tend to lower foreign purchases, should also be considered.

Foreign purchases of items for military establishments and troops abroad do not change rapidly in peacetime. They can be forecast from the past trend, modified by expected changes in the number of troops abroad. Some attention should also be given to pressures to use more American goods to supply troops and military establishments abroad since this may cut direct expenditures.

Income from foreign investments in the United States can be forecast by projecting the trend. Consideration should be given to any factors which might lead to significant short-run changes in foreign investment and also significant changes in the trend of dividend rates.

Payments for services except for tourist expenditures are largely related to the import of merchandise and can be forecast by applying the same percentage to them by which merchandise imports are expected to change. Tourist expenditures can be forecast by projecting the trend of the past several years.

The Department of Commerce categorizes exports as follows:

Merchandise, excluding military
Transfers under U.S. military agency sales contracts
Receipts of income on U.S. investments abroad
Other goods and services

Merchandise exports depend on business conditions in foreign countries and fluctuate to a large degree in relationship to industrial production in such countries. To analyze demand factors in each country is an almost impossible task. Therefore, analysis is generally restricted to such countries as Canada, France, Italy, Japan, the United Kingdom, and West Germany.

Prospective changes in foreign production are used as a basis for projecting changes in export purchases. Past relationship must be modified if relative prices are expected to change materially. *Business Conditions Digest* publishes monthly charts on industrial production and consumer prices in each of these countries or groups of countries. Some analysts study exports by commodity groups and their trends and use projections on a commodity group basis to check forecasts made on an area basis. In recent years exports of agricultural products have been large and must be analyzed separately to get a good picture of the projected level of exports. Transfers under military agency sales can be forecast by projecting the trend. This should be modified if military aid programs are likely to change during the next year. Action in Congress can be used as a guide to such potential changes.

Receipts on income from U.S. investments abroad can be forecast by projecting the trend modified by significant business changes expected in the next year. Foreign dividend policies are more erratic than those in the United States so such a check is more important on the export side than on the import side. Services can be forecast much as in the case of imports. Tourist expenditures should be treated separately and forecast on the basis of the trend of the recent past. This trend should be modified if economic conditions are expected to be materially better or worse since personal expenditures on travel are made from discretionary income and are easy to defer.

PERSONAL CONSUMPTION EXPENDITURES

The forecast of the major sectors of gross national product can be completed by forecasting personal consumption expenditures. It is possible to develop estimates of consumer expenditures in each of the major subcategories in the durable goods field, the nondurable goods field, and the service field by studying changes in the recent past and the effect that foreseeable changes in current conditions will have upon them. This can also be done for all individual categories that form the 12 major subdivisions of consumer expenditures used in national income accounting, but it becomes a formidable undertaking. A common procedure is to develop separate forecasts for expenditures on durable goods, nondurable goods, and services.

The surveys of consumer buying intentions discussed in Chapter 16 are of some help in forecasting expenditures on durable goods, since they have generally gauged the changes in the direction of consumer expenditures accurately. Studies have been made to determine which factors cause consumer purchases to vary from intentions.

Some analysts calculate a normal volume of automobile sales by figuring a total of expansion demand and replacement demand. Expansion demand can be calculated from the trend in the number of cars in use over the last several years. The trend must be modified to account for significant changes in the number of households, and the number of households adding a second and third car. Replacement demand can be calculated from the trend in automobile scrappage for five or more years in the past.

This procedure, however, will not in itself give an accurate year-by-year picture of automobile demand, but it does give a fairly good picture of average demand over a period of years. Replacement in any one year is determined to a large extent by changes in income and psychological factors. When more new cars are purchased, more used cars are available, thus depressing prices on the used-car market. This drops the value of older used cars to the point where selling them as scrap is the most profitable course. Thus, years of high car sales are also years of high scrappage.

In developing forecasts of new car sales, the sales picture of the last few years should be analyzed, especially in relation to long-run demand. Then the effect of probable changes in income must be considered. The Department of Commerce has found that on the average an increase of 1 percent in real disposable income has been associated with a rise of 2.5 percent in automobile sales. Prices of automobiles must also be considered, since a change in auto prices in comparison with general consumer prices has led to a greater percentage change in car sales.[3]

Sales figures must also be adjusted for psychological factors. Major changes in new models have a stimulating effect on sales. The extent, of course, depends on consumer acceptance. The general attitude of optimism or pessimism on the part of consumers also has an effect, and in any model year car manufacturers can push sales and get dealers to move cars as they did in 1955 and 1973–1974. This may, of course, reduce sales below long-term levels the next year or two.

The sales of other durables depend, to a large degree, on the trend in the number of households and disposable income and on changes in disposable income. Thus, expected income changes are a major factor in forecasting changes in demand and sales. Years of major increases in home building are also likely to show more than normal increases in sales of home furnishings and appliances. In determining sales levels, increases in prices due to cost increases must also be considered.

In making a forecast of demand for all consumer durables, the financial position of consumers must be considered. Years in which consumer debt has increased markedly are followed by years of a smaller increase as consumers get into a more liquid position. The total of consumer expenditures on durables and personal saving that includes net repayments on consumer credit is more stable than either series alone. Thus, when consumers go into debt at an unusually rapid rate, a slowdown in new debt and also durable goods sales is to be expected as consumers plan their finances. This factor must be considered in making the forecasts of automobile and other consumer durable goods sales.

The general availability of credit also has an effect on the purchase of durable goods. The staff of the Federal Reserve has developed a model for projecting expenditures on automobiles and parts and also one for other durables, both of which use a vector of interest rates, income, and the price of durables relative to other consumer goods and service prices as demand factors. Other models and factors involved in forecasting sales for automobiles and for furniture are considered in Chapter 20.

Forecasts of demand for nondurable goods and services are easiest to make. The volume of these purchases is little affected by small changes in income. Even in years of severe depression the effect is negligible until economic activity has been declining for a year or more. Such sales have increased in the postwar period in line with changes in real income, population, and the price level. These factors can be analyzed separately, or the trend of several

---

[3] The factors affecting automobile sales and sales of other durables are discussed in more detail in Chapter 20.

years in the past can be projected. When this is done, allowance must be made for expected price changes different from the average for the last few years. Some upward adjustment is also desirable because of an above average increase in expenditures on household operation in recent years. This is likely to continue in years when high levels of residential building are maintained.

Since expenditures on nondurable goods and services do not fluctuate unduly but move in relationship to changes in total economic activity, they can also be forecast on the basis of other factors for which forecasts are available. Expenditures on nondurable goods and services bear a more or less linear relationship to disposable personal income, but one which has a declining trend. The relationship since 1960 may be seen in Table 18-3. This relationship can be projected for the year being forecast from annual trends and quarterly figures for the last seven or eight quarters.

Table 18-3

Expenditures on Nondurable Goods and Services in Relationship to Disposable Personal Income, 1960–1976
(Billions of Dollars)

Year	Disposable Personal Income	Nondurable Goods Spending	Services Spending	Total Spending	Percentage of Income
1960	349.4	151.1	130.7	281.8	80.7
1961	362.9	155.3	138.1	293.4	80.8
1962	383.9	161.6	147.0	308.6	80.4
1963	402.8	167.1	156.1	323.2	80.2
1964	437.0	176.9	167.1	344.0	78.7
1965	472.2	188.6	178.7	367.3	77.8
1966	510.4	204.7	192.4	397.1	77.8
1967	544.6	212.6	208.1	420.7	77.2
1968	588.1	230.4	225.6	456.0	77.5
1969	630.4	247.0	247.2	494.2	78.4
1970	685.9	264.7	269.1	533.8	77.8
1971	742.8	277.7	293.4	571.1	76.9
1972	801.3	299.3	322.4	621.7	77.6
1973	901.7	333.8	352.3	686.1	76.1
1974	982.9	376.2	389.6	765.8	77.9
1975	1,080.9	409.1	432.4	841.5	77.9
1976	1,181.8	440.3	482.0	922.3	78.0

Source: *Survey of Current Business* (January, 1976), Part II, p. 45, (July, 1976), pp. 32, 33, and (January, 1977), pp. 12, 13.

Disposable personal income in turn has a predictable relationship to personal income. Since 1960 it has generally fluctuated between 84.5 and 88.2 percent of personal income, as can be seen from Table 18-4.

Table 18-4

Relationship of Gross National Product, Personal Income, and Disposable Personal Income, 1960–1976
(Billions of Dollars)

Year	GNP	PI	PI/GNP	DPI	DPI/PI
1960	506.0	399.7	79.0	349.4	87.4
1961	523.3	415.0	79.3	362.9	87.4
1962	563.8	440.7	78.2	383.9	87.1
1963	594.7	463.1	77.9	402.8	87.0
1964	635.7	495.7	78.0	437.0	88.2
1965	688.1	537.0	78.0	472.2	87.9
1966	753.0	584.9	77.7	510.4	87.3
1967	796.3	626.6	78.7	544.6	86.9
1968	868.5	685.2	78.9	588.1	85.8
1969	935.5	745.8	79.7	630.4	84.5
1970	982.4	801.3	81.6	685.9	85.6
1971	1,063.4	859.1	80.8	742.8	86.5
1972	1,171.1	942.5	80.5	801.3	85.0
1973	1,306.6	1,052.4	80.5	901.7	85.7
1974	1,413.2	1,153.3	81.6	982.9	85.2
1975	1,516.3	1,249.7	82.4	1,080.9	86.5
1976	1,692.4	1,375.4	81.3	1,181.8	85.9

Source: *Survey of Current Business* (January, 1976), Part I, p. 51, Part II, p. 35, (July, 1976), pp. 26, 32, and (January, 1977), pp. 9, 12.

There is some evidence of a declining trend, but the rate of decline is not rapid. Figures for the last several years and quarterly figures for the past seven or eight quarters can be used to project the relationship for the next year.

Personal income also has a predictable relationship to gross national product. As can be seen from Table 18-4, the median figure is about 79 percent. This can be used in a forecast, but greater accuracy is possible if cyclical deviations are considered. In a period of moderate expansion the figure will generally be in the 79–80 percent range; it has recently been somewhat above 80 percent. In the recession period of 1973–1975 it was above 81 percent in 1974 and above 82 percent in 1975. Past figures and a general indication of the state of the economy in the forecast year can be used to derive a percentage figure for that year.

These relationships can be used to relate expenditures on nondurables and services to GNP as follows:

$$\frac{PI}{GNP} = x \qquad\qquad \frac{DPI}{PI} = y \qquad\qquad \frac{C_{NS}}{DPI} = z$$

Then $C_{NS} = xyzGNP$

And $GNP = G + I + F + C_D + xyzGNP$

or $GNP - xyzGNP = G + I + F + C_D$

or $GNP = \dfrac{G + I + F + C_D}{(1 - xyz)}$

GNP = Gross national product
PI = Personal income
DPI = Disposable personal income
G = Government expenditures on goods and services
I = Gross private domestic investment
F = Net export of goods and services
C_D = Consumer expenditures on durables
C_{NS} = Consumer expenditures on nondurable goods and services
$x, y,$ and z are relationships projected for the forecast year.

All of the factors are available to find GNP in the equation above. And GNP times xyz is equal to the forecast for expenditures on nondurable goods and services.

DEVELOPING THE FINAL FORECAST OF GNP

After figures for each sector of GNP have been developed, the resulting product will not necessarily be the final forecast of GNP; in fact, it is very unlikely to be. The whole forecast should be cross-checked and revised as needed. The first step calls for a comparison of the total of GNP with the level of activity considered most likely when such sectors as residential construction and consumer durable goods purchases were forecast. If it appears that total economic activity will be greater or less than originally expected, these estimates should be revised.

Then the forecast can be cross-checked in several ways, using past relationships. One such check uses the relationship between real disposable income and real consumer expenditures on goods and services. Price developments may be such that prices will rise or fall more than was assumed as forecasts were made. The effect of various factors on the general price level and methods of forecasting prices are considered in Chapter 19. These factors and past relationships can be used to revise consumer expenditure forecasts which, when revised, are a first approximation. Past relationships of real durable sales, nondurable sales, and service expenditures to real disposable income can be used to divide the adjustments among these categories. These relationships are considered more fully in Chapter 20.

A second approximation calls for adjustment in other factors, such as capital goods expenditures, that are likely to be affected as consumer sales levels change. These changes affect GNP and, in turn, call for more revision of consumer expenditures. This process could go on indefinitely, but rather than do it mechanically the best judgment of the analyst should be used and all revisions made in one step.

A last check is worthwhile before the forecast is accepted as final. This involves an analysis of the excess of receipts or expenditures for each sector of the economy. The sum of these must, of course, in actual fact balance out to zero. A good form for doing this is that of the Council of Economic Advisers as published in its annual report.

At this stage the analyst has most of the figures necessary for making such a check and those not available are reasonably easy to forecast. Interest paid by persons can be forecast from past trends and developments expected in the durable consumer goods field. Transfer payments to foreigners are small and can be forecast by projecting the trend. Government tax and nontax receipts can be forecast from budget data and from past relationships to personal consumption expenditures. Government transfers can be forecast from budget data and past trends and the same is true for interest payments if the trend of debt and interest rate developments are also considered.

The only complex item to forecast is business retained earnings. This involves a forecast of profits, of corporate income taxes, and of dividend payments. Dividends change slowly and can be forecast from trends for the past seven or eight quarters. Profit is a volatile factor which bears some relationship to GNP and has a pronounced cyclical pattern. Past relationships and the stage of the cycle can be used to develop a preliminary forecast. This can be adjusted for qualitative factors such as the trend of costs and prices, governmental attitudes and policies, and the labor situation. Corporate profits taxes can be forecast from past relationships to profits and any prospective changes in tax rates.

Any significant lack of balance of the excess of receipts or disbursements calls for adjustments since the economy will set forces into motion that will balance them. No set rules can be given for doing this. The analyst must make needed adjustments based on knowledge of the economy, past cycles, and the causal factors at work in the cycle.

Such cross-checking helps refine a forecast to make it internally consistent. At this stage of knowledge of the cycle, it cannot assure accuracy because the economy does not always react as it did in the past. Forecasting is still to a large degree an art even though the amount of guesswork is being reduced.

QUESTIONS

1. How is the Department of Commerce series on new plant and equipment related to the construction and producers' durable equipment series?
2. What has been the record of the Department of Commerce series on projected expenditures on new plant and equipment?
3. Explain a procedure for forecasting expenditures on new plant and equipment using the Department of Commerce series.
4. Describe the use of the series on new appropriations as a forecasting device.
5. How are the remaining capital items forecast?
6. Explain a procedure for forecasting inventory investment. How do developments in the defense procurement field offset inventory changes?
7. Explain a procedure for forecasting each major sector of net imports of goods and services; of net exports of goods and services.
8. How may durable goods sales be forecast?
9. Describe the process for forecasting nondurable goods and service expenditures directly.
10. How can relationships between gross national product, personal income, disposable personal income, and consumer expenditures for nondurable goods and services be used to forecast expenditures for nondurable goods and services?
11. Describe the process of checking a forecast for consistency and revising it in light of such checks.

SUGGESTED READINGS

Almon, Clopper, Jr., Margaret R. Buckler, Lawrence Horwitz, and Thomas C. Reim-
  bold. *1985 Interindustry Forecasts of the American Economy*. Lexington, Mass.:
  Lexington Books (D. C. Heath and Co.), 1974.
"Business Investment and Sales Expectations." *Survey of Current Business* (annually
  in March issue).
Butler, William F., and Robert Kavesh (eds.). *How Business Economists Forecast*.
  Englewood Cliffs, N.J.: Prentice-Hall, Inc., 1966.
Butler, William F., Robert A. Kavesh, and Robert B. Platt (eds.). *Methods and Tech-
  niques of Business Forecasting*. Englewood Cliffs, N.J.: Prentice-Hall, Inc., 1976.
Chou, Ya-lun. *Probability and Statistics for Decision Making*. New York: Holt,
  Rinehart, and Winston, Inc., 1972.
"Consumer Income, Spending, and Saving, 1960–70." *Economic Review*, Federal
  Reserve Bank of Cleveland (June, 1971), pp. 10–18.
Federal Budget Trends. Federal Reserve Bank of St. Louis, quarterly.
Galper, Harvey, and Edward Gramlich. *A Technique for Forecasting Defense Ex-
  penditures*. Washington: Board of Governors of the Federal Reserve System,
  1968, and *The Review of Economics and Statistics* (May, 1968).
Hamburger, Michael J. *Interest Rates and the Demand for Consumer Durable Goods*.
  Washington: Board of Governors of the Federal Reserve System, 1967.
"Manufacturers' Inventory and Sales Expectations." *Survey of Current Business*.
  Washington: Department of Commerce, annually in March and later issues.
McKinley, David H., Murray G. Lee, and Helene Duffy. *Forecasting Business Con-
  ditions*. New York: American Bankers Association, 1965.
The Federal Budget—Its Impact on the Economy. New York: National Industrial
  Conference Board, annually.
"The Relationship Between Capital Appropriations and Expenditures." *Economic
  Review*, Federal Reserve Bank of Cleveland (October, 1970), pp. 3–11.
Wolfe, Harry D. *Business Forecasting Methods*. New York: Holt, Rinehart, and
  Winston, Inc., 1966.

CHAPTER 19

FORECASTING PRICE CHANGES

A forecast of probable price changes is frequently necessary or desirable as part of a forecasting program. It may be necessary as a basis for converting a dollar forecast into a unit forecast. On the other hand, if the basic forecast is in units, a price forecast is needed to put it on a dollar basis.

The government needs price forecasts in planning monetary and fiscal policy. Such forecasts are needed to estimate both expenditures and income in governmental budgets, especially those of the federal government. Price forecasts are also needed in planning programs in the agricultural area. Federal price forecasts often provide a basis for action to prevent an unfavorable situation from arising.

Price and unit forecasts are usually needed in business too—the unit forecast to plan production and the dollar forecast to plan finances. Data on prospective price changes are also useful in other phases of business operations. Price forecasts are necessary to set prices months ahead for inclusion in a catalog; they are useful in planning raw materials purchases. A forecast of changes in the general price level may be helpful in bargaining with labor on wages. Data on long-term price trends aid in effective long-range planning of capital expenditures. Thus, a price forecast is an integral part of any forecasting program.

Methods of determining price trends and forecasting price changes will be considered in this chapter. Consideration will first be directed to projecting the trend of prices, since short-run price forecasts are affected by the general direction in which prices are moving. Then the factors involved in forecasting short-run changes in the general price level will be considered. This discussion will be followed by an analysis of the factors involved in forecasting prices of specific commodities. A final section will consider some of the schemes that purport to forecast common stock prices. Forecasting in this area is all but impossible because of the changing psychological reactions of a changing group of investors.

ANALYZING AND PROJECTING PRICE TRENDS

In projecting price trends, it is necessary to consider the basic factors that affect prices in the long run and the effect those factors have had on price levels over the years. Several factors seem to indicate that the long-run price level in the United States should have a downward bias. Prices should move downward gradually because increases in technology and in the skills of the labor force and of management are making it possible to produce increased quantities of goods and services per capita at a lower per unit cost. A study of long-run price movements, however, fails to show such a downward trend.

This is true primarily because prices have been inflated substantially during the major wars and have not in all cases dropped to prewar levels before new forces have caused them to go up again. Since 1900, prices have increased materially, primarily as a result of the inflationary financing of World War I and World War II. Even at the low point in the 1933 depression, they were well above prosperity levels in 1900. After World War II there was no tendency for prices to decline materially because the government continued to pursue inflationary policies. New demand pressures and supply problems also pushed prices upward.

Factors Determining Long-Run Prices

As was pointed out in the description of the salient features of the American economy, there are several important sources of new purchasing media in the American monetary system. The stock of money is supplied by the Treasury, the Federal Reserve System, and the system of commercial banks; the bulk of it is in the form of demand deposits that are liabilities of commercial banks. Coins are provided by the Treasury and currency by the Federal Reserve Banks. The size of the money supply depends on the action of these three supplier agencies and is determined in part by the constraints placed upon them by laws and by the procedures developed to administer the programs of these agencies. The money supply also depends upon the actions of governmental units, households, business units, and the rest of the world in demanding credit to meet their needs. The potential for monetary expansion depends on excess reserves that are available in the banking system and on the monetary expansion multiplier. This multiplier is based on reserve requirements but is reduced by such factors as increased demand for currency in circulation and time deposits, and increased demand by banks for vault cash and excess reserves when the money supply is increased. These factors were discussed in Chapter 9.

In the discussion of the quantity theory in Chapter 4, it was pointed out that changes in the money supply can lead to changes in the price level. The cash balances which spending units desire to hold or the level of goods and services that are produced, or both, may also change. The institutional arrangements on which cash balances depend to a large degree are not likely to change rapidly; but the desire to hold cash is also affected by such factors as expectations of price level changes and of interest rate changes, the relative attractiveness of near money substitutes, such as savings accounts, and the ease of borrowing money. If the desire to hold cash balances or its reciprocal, the velocity of money, does not change, either the general price level or the output of goods and services must change. Output is likely to increase in part, at least, so long as there are unused resources. But as full utilization of plant and equipment and full employment are approached, the major impact of an increase in the money supply will be on the price level.

This has happened during wartime when the money supply has been increased by the creation of credit for the government in the form of credits to the Treasury checking accounts arising out of bank purchases of government bonds with excess reserves or newly created reserves. When government deficits are financed in this way, the effect on the economy is potentially inflationary because the money supply is increased without increasing the supply of goods. This type of action was used in part to finance World War II expenditures. Prices were held in check by price control laws, but the basis was laid for an increase in the price level. The money supply was increased about threefold between 1939 and 1947, while physical output went up somewhat less than 50 percent. In other words, the supply of money went up somewhat over twice as fast as the supply of goods. Prices went up by only about 75 percent by 1947, since the velocity of money slowed down. When the velocity of money increased in 1948, 1949, and 1950, the full impact of the increased money supply was brought into play.

Projecting Price Trends

A projection of price trends involves a projection of the supply of purchasing media, the velocity of circulation of money, and also a projection of the level of output of goods and services. The level of output can be projected several years ahead by the methods described in Chapter 15. The projection of the money supply involves an analysis of many factors, but most of them generally change slowly except in unusual periods such as wartime. The level of coins and currency in circulation can be projected from past trends, and this is also true to a large degree of the level of demand deposits held by businesses and consumers. However, such factors as the general state of the money markets and the level of interest rates must be considered since these affect the degree to which businesses and some individuals invest idle short-term funds in short-term obligations. Policies being followed by the Treasury and the Federal Reserve must also be analyzed, and the effect of likely changes must be projected. Changes in the velocity of circulation of money can also be projected from past trends. These must be modified by an analysis of the factors that may lead to a change in desired cash balances, such as the relative attractiveness of short-term obligations like commercial paper; the attractiveness of keeping liquid funds in other institutions, such as savings and loan associations; and the ease of obtaining credit in emergencies.

So many variables are involved that it is difficult to work with all of them at one time. Part of the difficulty may be overcome by working with rates of change in two basic series; that is, the output of goods and services and the money supply, since the velocity of money circulation does not change materially except in unusual periods such as World War II and the early post-war period when controls were phased out. Data on all of them are published in the *Federal Reserve Bulletin* and information on rates of change of many monetary and related series is available in a monthly release of the St. Louis Federal Reserve Bank called *Monetary Trends*.

This method of estimating changes in the general price level involves many broad estimates and cannot be expected to give completely accurate results. It can determine the level of prices in a general way by a comparison of the trend of output with the trend in the size of the supply of purchasing media. The analyst must be on the alert constantly for changes in other factors, such as velocity, which could occur in a period of price controls.

Effect of Production Costs on Prices

A rise in the price level may also be caused by an increase in the costs of production. Increases in productivity have in the past reduced total costs, especially in manufacturing. In recent years, however, labor unions have had sufficient bargaining power to win wage increases in some industries at a faster rate than increases in overall productivity. The expected result from this is increased costs to the industry employing the unionized labor and increased prices of the products. The higher factor expense and the higher product price would be expected to lead to less employment and lower output in the affected firms. If there are rigidities (which there are) preventing the un-employed workers and other resources from moving quickly to other areas of the economy, the result is an increase in prices and a decrease in aggregate output. This is one possibility in a class of events referred to as "cost-push" or "administered-price" inflation. In terms of the equation of exchange ($MV = Py$), MV has remained constant and the changes in P and y have offset each other.

Inflation generated through this cost-push mechanism is typically ratified by the monetary authority allowing the money supply to increase, permitting real output (y) to rise to its original level. Thus, it would appear that M and P have increased in approximate proportionality, with V and y remaining essentially unchanged.

There are many other examples of cost-push (a better term would be supply side inflation) factors which have led to overall price increases in recent years. Among them are the higher cost of imported resources such as oil and the greater amount of resources needed to produce domestic energy sources, governmental rules on environmental concerns, rules on occupational safety and health, the outlawing of a number of inputs (and outputs) such as DDT, low auto and truck speed limits, and increased governmentally-required record keeping. The number of examples could be expanded, but the important point to remember is that each of them has its impact by shifting production functions downward, such that for any given level of labor employment a smaller total output will be produced. Again, in terms of the equation of exchange, if real output (y) falls, given MV as constant, P must rise.

SHORT-RUN PRICE FORECASTING

The direction of prices in the short run may be determined in a fashion similar to that for projecting long-run price developments. In the long run it is usually sufficient to know the general direction of prices and to have some idea of the average rate at which they are moving, whereas in the short run it is often desirable to have more definite information about future prices.

Use of Supply and Demand Factors

In forecasting the level of prices, general measures of supply and demand are called for. The supply of all goods is determined by the supply of the factors of production, that is, natural resources, real property, capital goods, and labor. The supply of real property is not a significant variable, since for all practical purposes it remains constant in the short run. The capacity of capital equipment to turn out goods is, however, an important variable. It is almost impossible to arrive at a general measure of the productive capacity of all plants and other capital improvements used in producing goods and services. An index is available, however, of manufacturing capacity utilization based on 1969 output as 100.[1]

The supply of labor is continually measured by the Bureau of the Census, and figures on the size of the labor force and on unemployment are regularly published by the Bureau of Labor Statistics. The measure of manufacturing capacity utilization and figures on the labor force and unemployment thus provide a measure of the utilization of the supply of the factors of production. Changes in these measures will show the degree to which pressure on price is changing because of the rate of utilization of labor and capital.

It is impossible to find a true measure of the aggregative demand of the community. It is, however, possible to use GNP figures to show changes in demand that have taken place, since the demand for goods is translated into expenditures. Many analysts prefer real GNP figures, which can be especially important in a period in which significant price changes are taking place. Some analysts feel that it is better to use the Federal Reserve Board Index of Industrial Production as a measure of past changes in demand. Production in the manufacturing field is adjusted rather quickly to changes in demand; therefore, changes in the Index of Industrial Production provide a reasonable measure of current changes in demand. If goods are being produced for inventory rather than for sale, total demand is increased and this results in pressure on prices; but if stocks are being depleted, the situation is reversed. Changes in real GNP or in the Index of Industrial Production provide a fairly good measure of changes in the aggregative demand for goods.

The third group of factors that must be considered are changes in the monetary factors which affect the general price level. These could be measured in

---

[1] For a description of this index, see the *Federal Reserve Bulletin* (November, 1966), pp. 1605–1615, and (October, 1971), pp. 779–781.

detail, but such a procedure adds too many factors for practicable forecasting. Therefore, changes in the money supply and in the velocity of circulation have been used as a general measure of monetary influences on prices.

The first step in developing a forecast of prices from these supply, demand, and monetary factors is a study of past relationships of these factors. This may be done in several ways. One technique is to plot supply, demand, and monetary factors on ratio paper and analyze past relationships between them and wholesale prices as changes in the various series take place. Another possibility is to develop a multiple correlation relationship between wholesale prices and supply, demand, and monetary factors.

The next step is to forecast each of the major factors that affect prices. Methods of forecasting GNP, industrial production, the size of the money supply, and the velocity of circulation have already been considered. The size of the labor force changes slowly and factors affecting it are continually studied by the Bureau of Labor Statistics. Forecasts of the size of the labor force are made regularly by the Bureau of the Census. The index of manufacturing capacity changes slowly, but not necessarily at a regular rate. Changes can be forecast from past trends and from data on plans for capital expenditures in manufacturing. A forecast of each of these factors for several quarters in the future and past relationships can be used to arrive at a preliminary forecast of wholesale prices.

Factors other than those considered in studying past relationships between supply, demand, and monetary factors also have an effect on prices, and the preliminary forecast must be adjusted in light of them. This is especially true of such factors as foreign aid programs that stimulate exports and wartime price controls and materials allocation. It is also true of general increases in costs, such as increases in raw material prices due to import restrictions and increases in labor costs resulting from general wage increases that are greater than increases in productivity. It is, therefore, necessary to study all qualitative factors in the situation before making a final forecast of wholesale prices. Continual study of the relationships among the basic forecasting factors is also needed, since past relationships among so large a group of variables can change readily.

The St. Louis Model

The economic model of the St. Louis Federal Reserve Bank described in Chapter 16 is designed to measure changes in the price level as well as changes in total spending and changes in output. The general nature of this model can be seen from Figure 16-4 on page 342. It estimates price changes on the basis of current and past demand pressure and anticipated price changes. To measure demand pressure on prices, the change in total spending is related to the potential change in output; that is, full employment GNP in constant prices. The use of these two variables provides a measure of the total demand for goods and services in relation to the capacity of the economy to provide such goods and services. The change in prices is in part a positively related linear function of this measure of demand pressure. Demand pressure, D_t, is defined as:

$D_t = \Delta Y_t - (X^F_t - X_{t-1})$
where: ΔY_t is the change in total spending in quarter t
X^F_t is full employment GNP in 1958 prices in quarter t
X_{t-1} is real GNP in the previous quarter

The factor $X^F_t - X_{t-1}$ is the GNP gap, that is, full employment GNP in 1958 prices in quarter t minus real GNP in the previous quarter.[2] If the GNP gap is given, the larger the change in total spending, the greater will be the spillover into higher prices. If the change in total spending is given, the larger the GNP gap, the greater the expansion of output, and the less the spillover into higher prices.

The price equation includes past measures of demand pressure as well as current values. This allows for lags in the response of prices to changes in output and for changes in demand resulting from changing input prices and costs of production.

The other variable in the price equation is anticipated price changes. This is included because anticipation of future price changes has an effect on current price decisions. There is no observable measure of price anticipation so one has to be constructed. To do so, past changes in prices are adjusted by a measure of current economic conditions. Price changes tend to lag behind changes in total spending so the degree of utilization of resources as measured by the unemployment rate is used as a leading indicator of future price movements. To get at the price anticipation factor, the price change in each quarter is divided by an index of the unemployment rate for the quarter. These changes are calculated for several quarters and values are determined for the lag period and the relative weights to give to each earlier period. The price equation, omitting scripts for time periods and lags, is $\Delta P = f(D, \Delta P^A)$

where: D = demand pressure
ΔP^A = anticipated price change[3]

It is still too early to tell if the St. Louis model has real value for predicting general price changes on a consistent basis under all types of conditions.

Other Methods

Leading series and series on expectations may also be used in short-run price forecasting either independently or in conjunction with forecasts based on supply, demand, and monetary factors. One of the leading series is the

---

[2] Anderson, Leonall C., and Keith M. Carlson, "A Monetarist Model for Economic Stabilization," *Review*, Federal Reserve Bank of St. Louis (April, 1970), p. 12.

[3] *Ibid*, p. 22.

sensitive industrial materials index, a subgroup of the Wholesale Price Index.[4] This index usually leads the Wholesale Price Index, but the time period of the lead is not uniform. Price increases in sensitive industrial materials that are rapid or sustained tend to be followed by price increases in other industrial materials and these, in turn, by price increases in finished goods. The daily spot price index of 13 raw industrials may also be used as an indicator of present and future price developments. This index must be studied for basic underlying movements since it is subject to erratic movements on a day-by-day basis. This index, like all leading series, must be considered along with other factors in the situation since it often gives false signals.

Price diffusion indexes may also be used to help gauge future price developments. When a diffusion index moves above 50 percent, price increases are outnumbering price decreases and this is usually an indication that the aggregate price index will rise. Diffusion indexes can be used to gauge the direction of price changes, but they cannot be used to determine the timing or magnitude of such changes. One such index is based on the National Association of Purchasing Management, Inc., monthly survey of price developments. The index shows the percentage of purchasing agents reporting higher prices from the previous month, plus one half the percentage reporting unchanged prices. When this index has fallen below 50 percent, the industrial section of the Wholesale Price Index has declined or shown weakness; when it has passed 50 percent, prices have firmed or risen. Another diffusion index, which is published monthly in *Business Conditions Digest,* is that of industrial materials prices based on the Index of Industrial Materials Prices of the Bureau of Labor Statistics. This index has also foreshadowed major price movements, but it must be used with care since it can give false signals.

Another approach to price forecasting is the use of series on price expectations. Dun and Bradstreet in its quarterly survey asks over 1,500 executives what they expect will happen to prices in the next quarter in relation to the same quarter a year ago. The net percentage of those expecting price increases, that is, the percentage expecting increases minus the percentage expecting decreases, gives some indication of future price developments. These executives are more often right than wrong about future price changes. But this series must be used with care since expectations at times lag behind price developments, especially in periods when prices are declining.

FORECASTING THE PRICE OF AN INDIVIDUAL COMMODITY

In forecasting the price for an individual commodity, such as a farm product, it is necessary to consider the same three groups of factors; that is, supply

---

[4] The sensitive industrial materials index includes iron and steel scrap, nonferrous metals, lumber, plywood, wastepaper, rubber, hides, leather, textile fibers and intermediate products, and residual fuel oil.

factors, demand factors, and monetary factors. The specific items used are different from those for the general price level because only one commodity is involved.

As far as the supply is concerned, the most important factor is the volume of production. If the commodity is purely a domestic one, United States production is all that need be studied; but if it has a world market, foreign production must be studied also. Inventories also have an effect when they are unusually large or small, especially in the case of agricultural raw materials.

Disposable income is one of the basic demand factors. Other demand factors are consumption in the United States and, for a product having a world market, consumption outside the United States. It is often desirable, especially for farm products, to use consumption per capita.

Monetary factors can be measured, as was done in the forecasting of the general level of prices, by determining the degree of credit expansion. For commodities having a worldwide market it is necessary to study monetary and credit expansion in the major trading nations of the world. For individual commodities which have a market that is largely domestic, however, it is usually satisfactory to use disposable personal income as a measure of such changes, since such changes reflect the monetary factors that have been at work. Thus, it can be seen that disposable income should be a significant factor in forecasting the prices of many individual commodities because it is related to demand factors and monetary factors at the same time.

Agricultural Prices

The first step in forecasting annual price changes of agricultural commodities is to decide upon the dating of the year to be used. For such a commodity as butter, which is produced continually throughout the year, the calendar year may be used for convenience. For crops such as wheat, which are produced only once a year, it is best to use the crop year, beginning with the month in which the new crop is harvested. For livestock there is a fairly distinct marketing year that should be used.

Selection of Factors for Study. The next step is the selection of the supply, demand, and monetary factors to be analyzed. As has already been indicated, consumer disposable income is one of the most important of these factors. Next in importance is the annual variation in supply. This variation may be analyzed as one factor, that is, production plus carry-over, or the two may be treated separately. If the amount of carry-over has a significant influence upon price, it should be considered as a separate factor. Consumption may also be considered as one of the factors in the analysis. If most of the product is consumed in the United States, domestic consumption may be utilized. If not, a separate measure of consumption outside the United States may be needed.

To determine which factors to use in correlation analysis, it is usually best to plot several of the most significant factors on a line graph, plotting past price variations of the commodity at the top of the graph and the related factors underneath. The two or three factors which fluctuate most nearly like that of the price in question should be selected for correlation. In forecasting individual prices, it is seldom practicable to use more than three related factors and two are often enough.

Past Relationships of Selected Factors. The past relationships between these factors may be determined by multiple correlation analysis. However, graphic correlation analysis can also be used quite effectively with about the same degree of accuracy and it has the added advantage of visual presentation. The period selected for correlation analysis should be long enough to cover several business cycles so that almost any conceivable combination of factors which may affect prices is included. If graphic correlation is to be employed, the factor fluctuating most nearly like that of the price being forecast should be used first and deviations from it then plotted against the factor having the next closest variation. In this way it is usually possible to explain past variations by two or three variables, usually disposable personal income and some measure of production or consumption or both. In those cases in which stocks are extremely important in determining price, it may be advantageous to use disposable personal income, production, and inventories or stocks as the three variables to be correlated.

Forecast Procedure. After past relationships have been established, it is necessary to forecast the related factors to obtain the price forecast. Methods of arriving at disposable personal income have already been considered. For basic agricultural raw materials, the Department of Agriculture and private organizations make continuous crop forecasts. Changes in consumption may be estimated from past changes in relationship to disposable personal income, and future stocks of goods may be estimated from the differences between estimated production and consumption. Qualitative factors in the situation, such as government controls and changes in them, unusual demands due to war, and shifts in consumer tastes should also be continually studied and forecasts modified in light of these studies.

After annual prices have been forecast, it is necessary to superimpose a forecast of seasonal movements on them to describe prospective price changes during the year. Seasonal variations in raw material prices may be determined by the method described in Chapter 11, watching carefully for changes in seasonal patterns. This is important because changes such as the gradual introduction of improved methods of cold storage have materially affected the seasonal variations of some prices. Of more significance, however, are different seasonal patterns that occur under different conditions. For example, there may be one seasonal variation in years following a small crop of a commodity and another one in years after a large crop. There may also be different variations in years in which national income is increasing or decreasing.

The relationship in some fields may be still more complex. Since the price of corn is related to the price of hogs, when the major price trend of hogs is downward there are different patterns in the years following a large corn crop and the years following a small corn crop; and other patterns following large and small crops when the major hog price trend is upward. Some of the most accurate price forecasting on a seasonal basis has been done by a very careful study of the different seasonal patterns under different conditions. Of course, the use of too many seasonals will limit the number of past examples of each type and the patterns will not be representative.

Manufactured Goods Prices

In forecasting the price of manufactured goods in which administered prices hold to some degree, it is necessary to forecast not only the price of the basic raw materials used but also changes in labor costs and overhead costs. This involves estimates of wage increases to be granted and also a study of internal business costs. Past patterns between costs and prices can be used to arrive at preliminary price forecasts from future cost estimates. This procedure will indicate the prices that businesses would like to charge. Whether they can or not depends upon the prospective demand for their product. A forecast of demand and a study of past relationships between the level of demand and prices in relation to costs can be used to make the needed adjustments in the price forecast.

FORECASTING COMMON STOCK PRICES

The value of a share of stock should theoretically be the present discounted value of a stream of earnings over a period of years. It is easy to develop the theory but difficult to measure the variables and the relationships among them. The stream of earnings is very difficult to forecast since it depends on factors in the economy at large and in the business in question. The time period is also difficult to estimate since it cannot be infinite and earnings in the near future are worth more than in later years. Economists talk of earnings to the "period of the horizon," but this period cannot be determined precisely and is probably different for different investors. The interest rate at which to discount earnings is also indefinite and different analysts use different rates. In addition, expectations of future conditions play a large role in the decisions of investors. Therefore, all that can be done on the basis of the factors involved is to make general observations. Profits have a positive impact on the stock market and have the impact with some lead. Interest rates also have an impact, but an inverse one since, when the discount rate is higher, the value of a share of stock is less and vice versa. It is all but impossible, however, to determine reliable relationships in more than a general way.

Nevertheless, no phase of economic activity has received as much study as the fluctuations in the security markets. Spurred on by a desire to make profits in the stock market, a large number of individuals and institutions have attempted to forecast the future course of stock prices. Many of the forecasting services have proved to be of little value, and some individuals have sold forecasts that were not even based on a study of stock market behavior. For example, in 1947 an individual who had a large number of clients for his forecasting service was arrested in New York. The authorities became suspicious because he claimed to have inside information. Upon checking they found that he claimed that he obtained his information through his sister who insisted that she had contacted the spirits of some of the great speculators of the past and that they had given her the secret of the security market. According to this source of information, the market was rigged every day, and clues to the security market could be found in the Maggie and Jiggs cartoon. The amazing thing about this situation was that many of the clients of this forecasting service maintained that it had an unusual degree of accuracy.

It should be recognized that a forecaster could be right a number of times purely on a chance basis. For example, if 100 people are forecasting the direction of the market, 50 could be right the first time purely by chance. Of those 50, 25 could be right the second time, 12 the third time, 6 the fourth time, 3 the fifth time, and at least 1 the sixth time, purely by chance. About 11 of the forecasters would be expected to be correct at least 5 times out of the 6 chances even if they were all to flip coins to make their choices. There can, therefore, be no acceptance of a system for forecasting the market on its record of calling four or five turns correctly without a study of the scientific basis underlying it. To demonstrate that chance relationships can exist, one analyst (with tongue in cheek) found a high degree of relationship, for the 1960–1966 period, between year-end prices of the Dow-Jones Industrial Index stocks and the number of times players on the Washington Senators baseball team struck out each season.

Numerous attempts have been made to forecast the security market by finding a number of economic series which, when combined over a past period, have moved in conformity with an average of stock prices. For example, one such service was inaugurated in 1948 on the basis of a study of the market from 1919 through 1947. By combining several series, a line was developed which gave buy and sell signals that had been correct in practically every case over the past test period. The hypothetical results if money had been invested beginning in 1919 and held through 1947 were phenomenal, since a fund would have increased by over six hundred times. In the first year in which the line was used to make actual forecasts, however, it gave a major sell signal at a point below the last buy signal and several false indications in between.

This has happened frequently because by combining several series and weighting them properly it is possible to pass through or near almost any series of points. In fact, it can be shown mathematically that a combination of three curves properly weighted can be made to pass through or near ten points chosen almost at random. Therefore, little faith should be placed in any forecasting service in which the series chosen and the weights used in combining them are not based upon a logical study of the movements of the market but only upon the excellence of past fit.

Other approaches to forecasting the level of stock prices are based on the technical approach that assumes that a relationship exists between prices in one period and prices in another period. This assumption has been questioned and some have suggested that stock price movements are more like a *random walk;* that is, that past price behavior is no indicator of future price behavior. A major statistical study to test this hypothesis has been carried on at the Center for Research in Security Prices at the University of Chicago. This Center has made use of computer analysis to study various aspects of the stock market.

One study was designed to test two of the major theories of market behavior. The chartist approach holds that past market behavior gives information on future behavior because price patterns develop and such patterns tend to recur. If this is true and the patterns can be identified, it should be possible to develop a forecasting technique based on past developments. The random walk approach holds that no regular pattern exists and that the future of prices is no more predictable than the path of a series of random numbers which have been cumulated. In other words, successive price changes are independent, random variables with no identifiable pattern. To test these hypotheses, the daily prices of each stock in the Dow-Jones Industrial Average were used. The time periods were usually from the end of 1957 to September 26, 1962. For each of the 30 stocks in the Industrial Average, there were between 1,200 and 1,700 observations. The price changes were found to be distributed in a frequency distribution which was similar to that based on chance, but had a long tail because there were more scattered large increases in price than small ones. This data thus supported the random walk hypothesis since this is the shape of frequency distributions of most economic series which are not causally related to each other.[5]

Dow Theory

Some techniques that are used to forecast the security markets have met with some degree of success. The best known of these is the Dow theory. The Dow theory was named after Charles H. Dow, who was the founder of Dow-Jones & Comapny and the original editor of *The Wall Street Journal,* the first of the financial publications of his concern. Dow wrote a series of articles in *The Wall Street Journal* in which he analyzed and attempted to explain past actions in the stock market. William P. Hamilton, who was an assistant to Dow and succeeded him as editor, continued these studies in his column in *The Wall Street Journal,* "The Stock Market Barometer." Various individuals have elaborated on the writings of Dow and Hamilton and have stressed different phases of their work or have added their own interpretations so that there is really no one Dow theory.

From a study of stock market averages developed by the Dow-Jones Publishing Company beginning in 1885, Dow recognized that there were three major movements in the security markets: the primary movement, which has

---

[5] Eugene F. Fama, "The Behavior of Stock Market Prices," *The Journal of Business,* Vol. XXXVIII (January, 1965), pp. 34–105.

varied from less than a year to several years in duration; the secondary reaction, which has lasted from three weeks to three months or more and has retraced from one third to two thirds of the preceding primary swing; and the day-to-day fluctuations. This observation was based on averages of railroad stocks and industrial stocks. Today practically all Dow theorists still work with the Dow-Jones Industrial Average and the Dow-Jones Railroad Average.

Forecasting by the Dow theory is based upon the study of the primary fluctuations and the secondary reactions. Usually a primary upward movement has had two or more secondary reactions, and a primary downward movement has had two or three upward reactions. According to the Dow theory, stocks should be bought on a primary upswing when the high point of the last secondary reaction has been exceeded. Since it is impossible to forecast accurately the low point of the cycle, the best policy is to wait for a secondary reaction to run its course so as to establish clearly that the primary trend is up. When the market, after a secondary reaction, passes the high point from which this reaction began, it is an indication to Dow theorists that the primary movement is upward and that a new bull market is in progress. For a positive signal to buy, it is necessary for this to happen in both the rail and the industrial averages. Figure 19-1 shows such buy signals.

To sell at the high point of the cycle is also impossible, since the peak cannot be forecast. Therefore, under the Dow theory the investor takes no action on the first downturn in prices when the primary trend is reversed because it is not possible to be sure that this may not be another secondary reaction on the upswing. When the market has moved downhill substantially for a period of three or more weeks, has revived and moved upward from one third to two thirds of its previous drop, and again turned downward, indications are that a secondary reaction on the downswing is in progress. When the market on the downturn exceeds the low point from which the last secondary revival began, a sell signal is given. The determination of the point of such a sell signal is shown in Figure 19-1. It is again necessary for the two averages to corroborate each other for a positive signal.

This technique, when followed in major market swings, has often been used quite successfully. The Dow system, however, has given many false signals, especially in more recent years. In a market in which wide swings occur, it provides a method for an individual to buy stocks at relatively low prices and to sell them at relatively high prices without trying to forecast the exact tops or bottoms of the market. It cannot work, however, when the market is not subject to large up-and-down movements, since it is easily possible in such a case to have a buy signal at a higher point than a subsequent sell signal. The system has also in part defeated itself, since it has had many adherents and their actions have influenced the course of the market at times.

Since the Dow theory has given false signals, Dow theorists have also used other market factors in conjunction with it. For example, some of them are on the alert for a line being formed in the market. This occurs when for a period of several weeks both the rail and the industrial averages fluctuate within narrow limits of about 5 percent. If both of the averages break out above the line, there

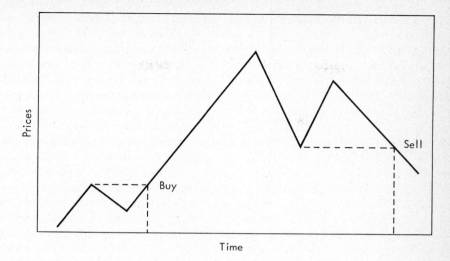

Source: Hypothetical data.

Figure 19-1

Dow Theory — Major Buy and Sell Signals

is an indication of higher prices, according to Dow theorists. If they break out below the line, the indication is for lower prices. There does not appear to be much logical basis for this phase of the Dow theory, and it has given many false signals.

More recently, stress has been placed on the relationship of volume to price movements. For example, according to this theory a market that has been over-bought becomes dull on rallies and develops activity on declines; and bull markets tend to terminate with excess activity after beginning with a comparatively low volume. There is undoubtedly something to the relationship between volume and price, since these factors are important in determining the total demand for stocks, but little of true forecasting value has been developed to date.

Other Techniques

In recent years a large number of other services that attempt to forecast prices in the security markets have appeared. One such service is based on the principle that in a strong market there will not only be an increase in the averages but also a large number of individual stocks advancing in price. When the number of stocks advancing declines while the market averages are continuing upward, or vice versa, there is an indication of a reversal in movement.

Other services have tried to use odd-lot data, that is, data on sales of less than a round lot, as a basis for forecasting. When odd-lot sales are moving in a direction different from that of the general market, bullish or bearish signals are given. When in a market upswing or downswing the odd-lot traders significantly change their behavior and switch from buying to selling or vice versa, this is a signal to do the opposite. The main difficulty with this system is not only that it has given wrong signals, but it has also given no signal when a signal has been called for. It will, as a rule, give a dependable signal to sell in those speculative markets in which the general public has done a large amount of speculative buying, but such markets have not existed often in recent years.

Some analysts have used a confidence index to try to gauge the general direction of the stock market. One such index is calculated by dividing high grade bond yields by lower grade bond yields. For example, the yield on Aaa bonds may be divided by the yield on Baa bonds or Ba or B bonds. The basic idea is that the smaller the spread, the greater the level of investor confidence in the future of the economy. A rise in this index indicates that stock prices will go up, a decline indicates that they will fall. This is again too simple a device to be used alone since many factors other than investor confidence affect the market, and the change in relative bond yields may be due to factors other than changes in investor confidence.

Some analysts have used the ratio of the number of new highs to new lows of stocks on the New York Stock Exchange to gauge future price movements. An increase in the ratio of highs to lows is bullish, a decrease is bearish. Some analysts believe that if the number of new lows exceeds the number of new highs, it is a signal of the end of a bull market. The basic idea of this technique is similar to that of a diffusion index, but it is too simple a technique to be used alone as a forecasting device and can serve only as one of several factors to gauge general price movements.

Attempts to forecast stock price changes will no doubt go on. These prices are, however, among the most difficult to forecast because psychological factors influence them to a large extent. From time to time, also, the uninitiated enter the market and accentuate price swings. The average investor would do well to base any purchase of common stock on an analysis of the worth of individual stock based on forecasts of the future prospects of particular companies rather than on price forecasts of the stock market in general. In this way the investor is assured of a reasonable return and relative safety, irrespective of market movements.

QUESTIONS

1. Discuss the factors that lead to price changes in the long run.
2. Describe a procedure for projecting price trends.
3. What effect do costs have on price trends?
4. Describe and evaluate the use of supply and demand factors for forecasting prices.
5. Describe the St. Louis model for forecasting the general price level. Relate it to the analysis of the quantity theory in Chapter 4.

6. Describe procedures for forecasting prices based on leading series, expectations, and diffusion indexes.
7. Describe the procedures used to forecast prices of agricultural commodities.
8. How may monthly price forecasts for such commodities as cotton be developed from annual price forecasts?
9. How can prices of manufactured goods be forecast?
10. Describe the chartist and the random walk theories of stock price movements. What are the implications for the investor of the random walk theory?
11. Describe the workings of the Dow theory for forecasting stock prices.
12. Under what conditions would the Dow theory work reasonably well?
13. Discuss several other methods for forecasting stock price changes.

SUGGESTED READINGS

Bolton, Steven E. *Security Analysis and Portfolio Management,* Part Five. New York: Holt, Rinehart and Winston, Inc., 1972.

Chase, Richard H. Jr., William C. Gifford Jr., Richard S. Bower, and Peter J. Williamson. *Computer Applications in Investment Analysis.* Hanover, N.H.: The Amos Tuck School of Business Administration, Dartmouth College, 1966.

Fama, Eugene F. "The Behavior of Stock Market Prices." *The Journal of Business,* Vol. XXXVIII (January, 1965), pp. 34–105.

Handbook of Agricultural Charts (annually). Washington: U.S. Department of Agriculture.

Karnosky, Denis S. "The Link Between Money and Prices: 1971–1976." *Review,* Federal Reserve Bank of St. Louis (June, 1976), pp. 17–23.

Rhea, Robert. *Dow's Theory Applied to Business and Banking.* New York: Simon and Schuster, Inc., 1938.

Waugh, Frederick V. *Demand and Price Analysis.* Washington: U.S. Department of Agriculture, 1964.

PROBLEMS ON PART 5

1. Project GNP ten years into the future by:
   (a) Projecting past trends.
   (b) Projecting the number of employees and output per employee.
2. From data on regional trends in the economy furnished by the Department of Commerce and the *Survey of Current Business,* study the trend of population, income, and retail sales in your section of the country. What effect are such trends likely to have on the growth of gross private product in your area in the period to 1985?
3. Study the following factors in the current business situation:
   The segment of the typical cycle business is in at the present time.
   An analysis of the leading, coincident, and lagging series.
   Consumer buying intentions as developed in the Survey Research Center surveys.
   Business plans for expenditures on plant and equipment.
   Analysis of business executive's expectations.
   Analysis of the monetary and fiscal situation.

4. Prepare a forecast of GNP for each of the next four quarters following the procedures for forecasting each sector of the economy described in Chapters 17 and 18. Cross-check the forecasts and prepare a final forecast for each sector and for GNP.
5. Plot the Bureau of Labor Statistics Wholesale Price Index for each year from 1965 to the present. Account for the changes that have taken place.

PART 6

FORECASTING SALES

This part shows how forecasting is used in business to forecast sales. Many factors must be forecast in addition to sales, including costs, capital requirements, and labor requirements. The starting point in all of these forecasts is, however, a forecast of sales. Such forecasts need to be stated in dollars and also in units to provide a basis for business planning.

Sales forecasts should not be made entirely from an analysis of the situation in an individual business or in the industry of which that business is a part. All business is affected to some degree by general economic activity. Therefore, before a forecast for an industry or an individual business is made, it is desirable to have a forecast of overall economic activity. This background is used to help develop a forecast for an industry, and an industry forecast is generally useful in developing a forecast for an individual business. The steps in developing a sales forecast are usually to forecast (1) general economic activity, (2) the level of sales in the industry, and finally (3) the sales of an individual business. Chapter 20 discusses methods used to forecast sales for an industry, while Chapter 21 looks at sales forecasting for an individual business.

CHAPTER 20

FORECASTING SALES FOR AN INDUSTRY

In addition to a forecast of general economic activity, it is desirable to have forecasts of the volume of business in major industries. Such forecasts can help cross-check forecasts of total activity. They also are valuable in helping to determine if unemployment is likely to occur in an industry, to decide if additional workers must be recruited, and to estimate the amount of new capital that will be required. The managers of a business will find a forecast of industry sales helpful in forecasting sales of their business and in planning operations for the next several quarters.

STEPS IN FORECASTING INDUSTRY SALES

In forecasting cyclical movements in an industry, it is necessary to study the factors that have been responsible for changes in sales in the past. The first step in this process is the careful selection of the specific sales items that are to be analyzed. It is necessary to decide whether the sales should be analyzed as a whole or divided into subcategories for study. The latter should be done if different factors affect different classes of sales. For example, in analyzing the factors that have affected sales in the clothing field, better results are obtained by studying women's, men's and children's clothing separately since trends are different in each field and since changes in birth rates affect the last category materially.

The second step is to select the measure of aggregative economic activity that is most closely related to changes in sales of the products being studied. In some cases in which a good is sold to consumers, producers, and the government, the most important factor to study is the relationship to gross national product. In other cases in which a product is sold primarily to consumers, it is probably the relationship to disposable personal income, or in rural areas to cash farm income. In still other fields, such as building hardware, the volume of construction activity may be the most important factor and in some manufacturing fields the Federal Reserve Board Index of Industrial Production may be the best measure.

The third step in forecasting cyclical movements in an industry is to study the trend of sales over the past 10 to 15 years. This trend should be compared with trends in gross national product, industrial production, disposable personal income, or other appropriate measures of aggregative economic activity to see in a general way how sales have been growing and how they have fluctuated in relationship to changes in total economic activity. A thorough study and analysis should be made of factors which have affected the trend of sales, especially in periods in which activity in the industry may not have been following the trend.

The fourth step is to develop a preliminary forecast based on the relationships of industry sales to general economic activity and other factors which affect the demand for the product. Any business can easily list 15 or 20 factors that affect sales in its field. It is seldom practicable, however, to work with more than three or four of the most important variables on a quantitative basis. It is extremely important in selecting these variables to work only with those that are logically related to the series being studied and as nearly as possible directly related causally. These include such factors as changes in the level of income from the past year and earlier years, changes in price, changes in the expected life of the product, and changes in population.

After having selected the most important variables, it is necessary to consider the nature of the relationships that have occurred in the past. This can be done by charting these relationships or by the techniques of correlation analysis. The correlation approach has the advantage of being definite since, once the general formula is decided upon, any analyst will arrive at the same specific formula. The graphic approach, however, is simpler and is easier for most business people to comprehend.

To use relationships of general measures of economic activity as a basis for forecasting industry sales, it is, of course, necessary to have a forecast of such series. This approach of basing a forecast on such general measures is feasible for a business because private organizations and government agencies have spent millions of dollars in developing such forecasts. Many of these are available at little or no cost, and even those bought from research organizations cost far less than it would cost to develop forecasts by other methods. Another reason for using relationships of aggregative measures is that they are often easier to develop than sales forecasts for industries made by other methods.

A fifth step is to analyze all of the qualitative factors in the past, present, and future to determine if past relationships will continue. In general, consumer buying habits do not deviate radically from the pattern of the past in the short run, nor do methods of business operation change rapidly in the absence of marked technological innovations. Changes do take place, however, and it is necessary to study the effects of changes in governmental policies, technological innovations, and the like before deciding that past relationships will continue into the immediate future.

A sixth step, or in some cases an alternative to steps two, three, four, and five, is to develop a forecast by end-use analysis. This technique starts with a grouping of products or services by end uses, such as for direct personal consumption, as a material or part for further manufacture in a specific industry, or as a product or service sold to the federal government. It is necessary to determine the relationship of activity in the end-use industries to sales in the industry being forecast. A next step is to forecast the level of sales in each of the end-use industries and then develop an industry forecast from such forecasts and past relationships.

This method is practicable only if the end use is distributed over a few major industries. It is used, for example, in the industrial chemical industry in which most of the sales go to a limited group of users. Detailed information on the end use of industry sales is available in input-output tables, which are discussed in the last section of this chapter. In cases in which it is practicable, industry forecasts may be developed both by end-use analysis and by relationships to aggregate measures of economic activity and the two forecasts used as a crosscheck on each other. If the two methods have given similar results in the past and now give significantly different results, it is an indication that all factors need to be studied carefully since chances are good that some significant factors have been overlooked or that past relationships are changing.

The last step is to develop an awareness of the error that will be involved in any forecast which is made. No relationship based on the past can be expected to work perfectly in the future, since there are scores of factors other than the variables used that affect sales, and since new factors also come into play. The effects of these other factors may tend to balance out in most years, but at times there may be an unusual number of them working in the same direction so that the error may be greater than the average.

FORECASTING DEMAND IN CONSUMER NONDURABLE GOODS AND SERVICES INDUSTRIES

The demand for consumer nondurable goods is usually easier to forecast than that for consumer durable goods because the former are usually purchased more frequently and because they do not last for long periods of time; therefore, the demand cannot be transferred to the future to any great extent.

The Department of Commerce has developed the relationship between disposable personal income and personal consumption expenditures for detailed categories of nondurable goods and services. The sensitivity of personal consumption expenditures to disposable personal income is expressed by a figure showing the average change in expenditures in relationship to changes in income. For example, the figure for gasoline and oil for the post-World War II period is 1.6, indicating that expenditures on gas and oil have changed on the average 1.6 times as fast as changes in income. Some figures for the prewar and postwar period for the major categories of consumer expenditures are shown in Table 20-1. This table shows the sensitivity of a group of expenditures in real terms based on 1957 dollars, thus eliminating the effect of price changes.

A study by the Harvard Economic Research Project under a contract with the United States Bureau of Labor Statistics has also developed relationships based on past data which are helpful in forecasting consumer expenditures. This study developed the relationships in constant dollars of expenditures of 82 categories of personal consumption expenditures to total consumption expenditures. This was done using 1929–1964 data and also 1946–1964 data. They concluded that relationships based on the pre-World War II and postwar periods were better than those for the postwar period alone, especially since many post-war series had a persistent upward movement and the results were largely due to the trend rather than changes in personal income for 11 broad expenditure groups used by the Department of Commerce based on data for the 1929–1964 period. The long-run income sensitivity of some of these groups is also shown in Table 20-1. [1]

Table 20-1

Sensitivity* of Personal Consumption Expenditures to Changes in Disposable Personal Income

Group	Prewar	Postwar **	Both ***
	Based on Constant (1957) Dollars		
Total personal consumption expenditures.....	0.8	1.0	
Durable goods..................................	2.1	1.2	
Nondurable goods.............................	.7	.9	
Services	.5	1.0	
Automobiles and parts.........................	2.8	1.1	1.5
Furniture and household equipment	1.6	1.0	1.3
Clothing and shoes.............................	‡0.9	#0.5	0.9
Food and alcoholic beverages	§ .8	#0.8	0.9
Gasoline and oil	‡ .6	#1.6	1.9
Household operation	.9	1.5	—
Housing	.2	1.3	2.0
Transportation.................................	1.0	.3	0.4

Source: *Survey of Current Business* (March, 1959), p. 25; and H. S. Houthakker and Lester D. Taylor, *Consumer Demand in the United States: Analyses and Projections* (Cambridge: Harvard University Press, 1970), pp. 189–190.
* Based on least squares using $C = aI^a(1 + r)^t$ for the period 1929–1940 and $C = aI^a$ for the postwar period where C = personal consumption expenditures, I = disposable personal income, and t = time. The exponent a derived from the data is an approximate measure of the income sensitivity of the expenditure items.
** In the case of total goods and services, durable goods, nondurable goods, and services, the sensitivity coefficients in this column were based on the twenties and the postwar period.
*** From the study by Houthakker and Taylor for the period 1929–1964.
‡ Based on period 1929–1940 and postwar year including income and time as factors. The postwar relations using income alone give a coefficient of 0.5 for clothing and 2.0 for gasoline.
§ Based on period 1933–1941 and postwar years.
# Based on current dollars.

During the pre-World War II period the changes in sales of most nondurable goods were determined largely by changes in disposable personal income. The high degree of correlation between sales of nondurable goods and

---

[1] H. S. Houthakker and Lester D. Taylor, *Consumer Demand in the United States: Analyses and Projections*. (Cambridge: Harvard University Press, 1970), pp. 189–190.

disposable personal income was disturbed somewhat during World War II because of shortages, especially of gasoline. In the early postwar period, sales of nondurables were somewhat above the level indicated by prewar relationships but many have about returned to levels indicated by past experience. Personal consumption expenditures for services have grown more rapidly than personal consumption expenditures for durable and nondurable goods. Expenditures on housing and household operation have also shown a marked upward shift from the prewar to the postwar period. It is necessary, therefore, to study changes which have taken place or are in progress when forecasting most likely sales levels.

It may also be helpful to correlate per capita sales deflated either by the Consumer Price Index of the Bureau of Labor Statistics or by the appropriate subcategory of the Bureau of Labor Statistics Wholesale Price Index, such as textiles or shoes and leather goods, with per capita disposable income deflated by means of the Consumer Price Index. If possible, it is also desirable to correlate the unit sales in a field with an index of the volume of production, such as the Federal Reserve Board Index of Industrial Production. Greater accuracy can be obtained by using the index for nondurable manufactures or subdivisions of this index, such as leather and products, manufactured food products, textiles and products, or tobacco products. It is probably best to make calculations by all three of these methods before deciding on the sales to be expected in a particular field from a forecast of disposable personal income.

FORECASTING DEMAND IN THE CONSUMER DURABLE GOODS INDUSTRIES

Forecasting the demand for consumer durable goods is usually somewhat more complex than projecting the demand for nondurables, since sales change more rapidly and to a greater degree and more factors must be taken into consideration because buying decisions are more complex. The most important influence upon the demand for durable goods, just as in the case of nondurable goods, is disposable personal income. Since the purchase of a consumer durable good usually involves a larger expenditure than does the purchase of a nondurable good, the direction of change in income from the preceding year and earlier years is also important. Purchases from any given income tend to be greater when income has been rising from the level of the year previous than when it has been falling. This is probably due in part to the optimism associated with rising income and to the pessimism associated with falling income, and to a lag that probably exists in adjusting expenditures for major items when income is changed.

Also important in determining the demand for many durables is the rate of population growth and the growth in the number of families. Demand is likewise affected by the relative price of the durable good in relationship to the general price level. Changes in the length of the life of the good, such as the increasing length of life of automobiles, also influence current demand significantly. The factors involved in determining the demand for automobiles and for furniture will be used as illustrations.

Forecasting Automobile Sales

The most significant item to forecast in the automobile sales field is the demand for new passenger cars by U.S. consumers. This demand is a derived demand arising out of the primary demand for automotive transportation service. Such a demand may be satisfied for a considerable period of time without purchases of new cars, since the automobile is a durable good.

Factors influencing automobile demand can be divided into three groups: long-term factors, factors influencing yearly changes in demand, and seasonal factors, as listed by S. L. Horner of the General Motors Corporation.[2]

Long-Term Factors

1. The improvement in the product and the lowering of real price.
2. The decrease in the cost of operation.
3. The increased mileage of good roads.
4. The increasing length of car life.
5. The greater availability of service.
6. The increase in installment buying.
7. The increase in population.
8. Improved standards of living.

Year-to-Year Change Factors

1. General business activity and national income (considering both the level and direction of change).
2. The distribution of national income.
3. The cost of living.
4. The psychological atmosphere — whether optimistic or pessimistic.
5. The extent and character of model changes.
6. The age of cars in the hands of new car buyers.
7. The number of cars scrapped.
8. The used car stocks in dealers' hands and the dealers' working capital position.
9. Financing terms — both the required down payment and the length of time over which monthly installments may be spread.
10. Used car prices and trade-in allowances.

Seasonal Factors

1. Seasonal variation.
2. The dates of new model announcements and new model stimulus.
3. The trend of general business activity and national income.
4. New car stocks.
5. Used car stocks and deliveries.
6. Price change anticipation.
7. Weather conditions.
8. Abnormal interruptions in production.
9. Sales campaigns for both new and used cars.
10. The relative prosperity of different geographical regions and different sections of the population.

---

[2] C. F. Roos, et al., *The Dynamics of Automobile Demand* (New York: General Motors Corporation, 1939), pp. 6, 7.

Only a few of the most important of these factors can be utilized specifically in studying past sales relationships as a basis for forecasting, but the effect of all of them must be analyzed constantly.

A landmark study of automobile demand was made in the late 1930s by C. F. Roos and Victor von Szeliski. In their study of automobile demand, Roos and von Szeliski developed a system that is based upon the maximum owner-ship level of automobiles, which is changing continually in response to all of the factors that affect the demand for cars. They have outlined their basic idea in the following five steps: [3]

1. The central point is that the demand for new automobiles is a derived demand, since the primary demand is for transportation service. This is furnished by the total car population, only a part of which consists of cars sold during any given year. New car demand may thus be considered as dependent upon consumers' decisions regarding the number and quality of the cars to be maintained in operation.
2. Consumers are thought of as continuously adjusting the number of cars in operation toward some particular car population called "the maximum ownership level." This concept of a maximum ownership level appears to be of major importance in durable goods studies.
3. The maximum ownership level is regarded as changing continually in response to the economic status of consumers and such other factors as car durability and price.
4. Consumers are likewise continuously adjusting the quality of the car population toward an optimum level by replacements.
5. The rate at which consumers adjust the car population toward the maximum ownership level and the optimum quality level depends upon both general and specific economic conditions.

The results of the research by Roos and von Szeliski have shown that the most important factors affecting the maximum ownership level are the number of families in the United States, the real discretionary income per capita, and the replacement cost of new automobiles.[4] The use of replacement cost as a factor indirectly takes into consideration also the effect of operating costs, since automobile prices have closely paralleled the prices of automobile parts, tires, and gasoline. Replacement cost also considers durability, since it is derived from an index of the price of new cars divided by the average life of cars.

On the basis of past relationships between these items, a series of formulas has been developed to express the maximum ownership level as inferred from such relationships. The difference between the maximum ownership level at any time in the future and the current number of automobiles in use gives the potential demand for new automobiles. The number of families in the United States changes slowly and thus can be forecast quite accurately. Indexes on the prices of automobiles are available, and the manufacturers set new car prices when announcing new models. The average life of an automobile changes

---

[3] *Ibid.*, p. 22.
[4] *Ibid.*, pp. 87, 88.

slowly. The major item to forecast is, therefore, real discretionary income per capita, and this can be derived from a forecast of disposable personal income. Thus, all of the data to forecast automobile demand by this method are available.

The Department of Commerce has used a somewhat different basis for determining the demand for new cars. They have developed the relationship between new private passenger car registrations per 1,000 households and a combination of real disposable income per household in terms of 1939 dollars, the percentage of the real disposable income per household of the current year to that of the preceding year in 1939 dollars, and the relationship of the average retail price of cars to consumer prices. A downward trend has also been introduced into the equation because of the substantial rise in the average useful life of automobiles.

According to the Department of Commerce formula, a 1 percent increase in real disposable income was associated with a rise of 2.5 percent in automobile sales, and each increase of 1 percent in the ratio of the current to the preceding year's income was associated with a rise in sales of 2 percent. The effect of the other factors was smaller but nevertheless significant, since a rise of 1 percent in the ratio of automobile prices to the level of general consumer prices was associated with an average decline in the number of cars sold of 1.3 percent. The trend correction for the increase in the average usable life of automobiles showed that there would have been a gradual decline of about 1.5 percent a year in the sale of automobiles per 1,000 households had there been no change in income per household or in relative prices.[5]

These two methods of determining the demand for automobiles are basically similar. The Department of Commerce method is based upon real disposable income and changes in that income, while the Roos method uses real discretionary income. It is probably more logical to use discretionary income, and that figure can be arrived at fairly accurately from budget studies. Both methods take account of changes in population, since the one is based on the number of households and the other on the number of individuals in the United States. Both formulas introduce the cost element, one as a basic factor standing alone and the other by relating automobile costs to the general price level.

The increasing life of automobiles has also been taken into consideration in both cases. The Department of Commerce has a declining time factor due in large part to this change. Roos determines the maximum ownership level from his formula and then subtracts cars currently in use; this automatically adjusts for the increased life of automobiles, since more cars from past production will be in use as their life increases.

Such past relationships can be used as a starting point to determine demand factors, but they cannot be used alone as a basis for a forecast. This involves a careful analysis of all qualitative factors in the current and prospective situation and a forecast based on judgment concerning the effect of these factors. This has been especially true in the post-World War II period. In 1950 automobile sales increased much faster than demand factors would have indicated, but this

---

[5] L. J. Atkinson, "The Demand for Consumer Durable Goods," *Survey of Current Business* (June, 1950), p. 6.

increased buying was due to a fear of shortages and higher prices arising out of the Korean War. In 1955 sales increased faster than demand factors would have indicated due to new styling that consumers liked and to easier credit terms. When sales are above long-run demand factors for a year, there will be compensatory downward adjustments in the following years. In 1957–1958 sales dropped somewhat faster than demand factors had indicated. Consumers were shifting expenditure patterns as real per capita income first ceased growing and then declined, and they also reacted against the trend toward bigger and more expensive cars. During the 1960s a new problem arose in forecasting domestic automobile sales; that is, the increasing share of the market taken by imports. Imported automobiles made up about 5 percent of the market in the middle 1960s and increased to about 15 percent by 1970. This was due in large part to the popularity of small foreign cars and also consumer preference for some sport models. The percentage of imports held about constant in 1971, 1972, 1973, and 1974, but declined somewhat in late 1975 and 1976 as American car manufacturers entered the small car field with some success. Thus, any forecast can start with basic demand factors, but it must be based on a careful analysis of all factors in the field.

Forecasting Furniture Sales

The demand for furniture differs in some respects from the demand for automobiles. The response to changes in income is pronounced, and recession years are somewhat lower in relationship to income than prosperous years. Demand is also affected by changes in the number of families, by the rate of construction of new homes, and by price changes in furniture in relationship to changes in the general level of consumer goods prices.

Expenditures for household furniture have not grown as rapidly in recent years as expenditures for consumer durable goods in total, and consumer expenditures on goods of all kinds have not grown as fast as disposable personal income since expenditures on services have taken an increasing share of consumer income. Furthermore, sales are affected materially by declines in housing such as those which occurred in 1966, 1969, and 1973 when credit became unusually tight. This explains the slower recovery of furniture sales than durables in total after the 1969–1970 recession. Housing starts did not increase materially until the second half of 1970 and furniture sales for new houses lag housing starts by several quarters. Those developments may be seen graphically in Figure 20-1.

The Department of Commerce has developed formulas that explain the demand for furniture based upon the relationship between these items. In making its estimates, the Department of Commerce developed the multiple correlation relationship between expenditures for furniture in dollars per household and disposable personal income per household, value per household of private residential construction, and the ratio of the price index for furniture to the index of prices for all goods.

It must be remembered that various factors affecting the demand for furniture which have not been included in the formula are changing and may therefore lead to somewhat different relationships in the future. One of these is the

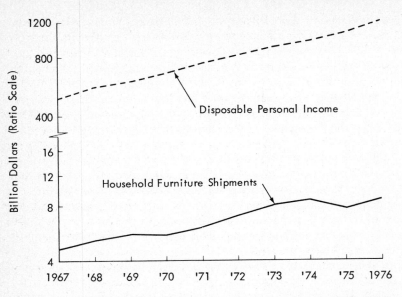

Source: *U.S. Industrial Outlook 1976* (Washington: U.S. Department of Commerce), p. 254.

Figure 20-1

**Disposable Personal Income and
Household Furniture Shipments,
1967–1976**

large increase in the liquid assets of individuals, which makes it somewhat easier for them to buy furniture than when it was necessary to save the purchase price over a longer period of time or to use credit.

The unusually high marriage rates in the early post-World War II period have been represented in the formula to a large extent by putting it on a per household basis and by including the value of residential construction. The increasing average age of the population may gradually affect the demand for furniture, although it is not clear at present just what the change will be. The use of consumer credit also has an effect on furniture sales, and so does any possible restriction of such credit by the Federal Reserve System. A forecast of furniture sales must consider these and other qualitative factors in the present and future situations as well as demand factors which are based on past relationships.

FORECASTING DEMAND IN INDUSTRIES THAT SELL GOODS USED BY PRODUCERS, CONSUMERS, AND GOVERNMENT

Although the changes in demand for most nondurable goods used by consumers can be explained by changes in disposable personal income, it is better to use gross national product, national income, or industrial production when measuring changes in the production of products used by producers, consumers, and the government. For example, paper production in total shows a high degree of correlation with gross national product. This is true since there is a substantial demand for paper by the ultimate consumer, by retailers, wholesalers, and manufacturers, and by the government; in fact, by every segment of the economy. There is also a good fit when paper production is correlated with the Federal Reserve Board Index of Nondurable Goods Production.

On the basis of a forecast of gross national product, it is thus possible to forecast paper production by using past relationships and by studying the current situation. Such a forecast can be cross-checked by a forecast of the Federal Reserve Board Index of Nondurable Goods Production and the past relationships of paper production to it.

Such forecasts of total paper production are of value to the producers of basic paper raw materials and of a diversified line of paper products. Many individual producers, however, will have to study the demand for a particular type of paper, such as book paper, wrapping paper, tissue paper, container board, and various papers used by the building trades. In each sector of the industry it is necessary to find that component of gross national product or industrial production which most closely explains changes in sales in the past. It may also be necessary to study technological changes that have led to the substitution of one type of paper for another and price changes that may have led to shifts in paper usage.

The demand for paperboard fluctuates in relationship to economic activity just as the demand for paper does. Since paperboard is used primarily for packing manufactured products it correlates best with industrial production. Until the middle 1950s paperboard production was growing more rapidly than industrial production since packing was shifting from the use of wooden containers to paperboard containers. After 1955 the growth of paperboard production was only slightly more than industrial production growth, and for a period of time in the middle and late 1960s the rate of growth was practically the same. Figure 20-2 shows the relative growth of demand for paper and paperboard in relationship to industrial production during the 1961–1975 period.

A forecast of paper and paperboard consumption can start with an analysis of such past relationships. It is also necessary to study carefully all factors in the current and prospective situation as well as the possibility of a change in past relationships.

FORECASTING DEMAND IN PRODUCER GOODS AND BUILDING MATERIALS INDUSTRIES

Many of the techniques already discussed in other fields are used in forecasting the demand in the producer goods and building materials fields. Procedures for forecasting overall demand in these fields were considered in forecasting gross national product and industrial production. Since the demand for producer goods is a derived demand, a basic approach is to study demand for producer goods in relationship to changes in demand and production in the related consumer goods or service field. The demand for some types of railroad

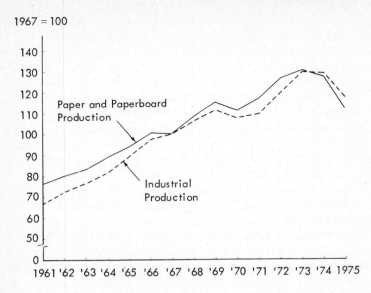

1967 = 100

Source: U.S. Department of Commerce, *1971 Business Statistics,* p. 172; *Survey of Current
Business* (February, 1974), p. S36, (January, 1976), Part II, p. S36, and (June, 1976),
p. S36; and *Federal Reserve Bulletin* (July, 1976), p. A50.

Figure 20-2

**Growth of Paper and Paperboard Production
in Relationship to Industrial Production,
1961–1975**

cars, for example, is related to the demand for transportation of freight by railroads and correlates with industrial production. In a recession period new cars
are not needed, and railroads are reluctant to buy ahead of needs when profits
are declining. As an upturn proceeds, additional demand for cars exists and
funds are available to finance these purchases. Past patterns of freight-car
demand in relationship to industrial production and a forecast of such production can be used as a basis for developing a forecast of demand for such
freight cars.

In some producer goods fields, pressure indexes may be used to indicate
increases or decreases in the demand for a particular product. A pressure index
shows the relationship between the rate of production or output in a field and
the amount of capital equipment used to produce such output. For example,
the present rate of use of existing electric power-generating equipment gives
some indication of demand for it at a future time; and the ratio of seasonally
corrected carloadings to the number of cars owned by railroads gives a reasonable indication of the number of cars railroads will order six months to a year
in the future. Such pressure indexes based upon present usage give an indication of the demand in the near future for many types of durable producer goods.

In many individual industries it is desirable to employ relationships between
new orders, production, and inventory series in a manner similar to that used in

forecasting various sectors of overall economic activity. The Department of Commerce has series of this kind available for an increasing number of fields. Trade associations in increasing numbers also gather these figures for their fields.

In some industries it may be possible to arrive at reasonably accurate timing of the changes in demand from lead-lag relationships. This is true in most of the fields that produce construction materials. For example, the sales of manufacturers of plumbing supplies have usually followed by three or four months the F. W. Dodge Company series on residential contracts awarded. The sales of many of the items used in the construction of homes have followed this index in a pattern that follows the use of these materials in building, since supplies are not stocked to any great extent. In looking for lead-lag relationships, only those with a logical basis should be considered since spurious relationships may hold for a period of time. Continuous study is needed even in the case of logically related series since past relationships may change.

As in all cases of forecasting, it is necessary to study qualitative factors in the industry before arriving at a definite forecast of the volume of business. Such factors as the trend of past sales, the relationship of costs to price, the labor situation, and the general state of confidence must be carefully checked. In addition, an analysis should be made of competing products to see what effect they will have upon demand and also of potential new products that may affect the industry.

USE OF INPUT-OUTPUT DATA IN INDUSTRY FORECASTING

The Bureau of Economic Analysis of the Department of Commerce is working on a major new program that involves the periodic preparation of interindustry tables that can serve as a basis for industry forecasts. These tables provide a comprehensive picture of the interaction between the various industries and the final market demand in the economy. The input-output tables show final product flows and value added just as is the case with the National Income and Product Accounts. The final product flows are shown as sales by each industry to consumers, investors, government, and foreigners; and the value added is shown by the industry in which it originates. The input-output accounts also cover the flow of raw materials, semifinished products, and services among industries. The tracing of these flows is the major contribution of input-output accounts.

The tables that are currently available in detailed form are based on data for 1967 and cover 370 separate industries. Data are also available on 85 industry categories which are aggregates of the data for the 370-industry analysis. Earlier input-output analyses are available for 1947, 1958, and 1963. The Bureau of Economic Analysis plans to develop input-output data as a regular part of an integrated system of national accounts.

Input-output data are usually presented in a table in which each industry is represented by a row and a column, each final market by a column, and value added by one or more rows. The row for an industry shows the distribution of

Table 20-2

Total Requirements (Direct and Indirect) per Dollar of Delivery to Final Demand, 1967

(Producers' prices)

Each entry represents the output required, directly and indirectly, from the industry named at the beginning of the row for each dollar of delivery to final demand by the industry named at the head of the column.

Industry No. / Name	14 Food and kindred products	15 Tobacco manufactures	16 Broad and narrow fabrics, yarn and thread mills	17 Miscellaneous textile goods and floor coverings	18 Apparel	19 Miscellaneous fabricated textile products	20 Lumber and wood products, except containers	21 Wooden containers	22 Household furniture	23 Other furniture and fixtures	24 Paper and allied products, except containers	25 Paperboard containers and boxes	26 Printing and publishing	27 Chemicals and selected chemical products
1 Livestock and livestock products	0.35807	0.01892	.02652	.05585	.01147	.01806	.01133	.00613	.00648	.00425	.00652	.00420	.00429	.00622
2 Other agricultural products	.20677	.24390	.12385	.04719	.04301	.05868	.02552	.01151	.01356	.00610	.00754	.00462	.00442	.00685
3 Forestry and fishery products	.00671	.00045	.00061	.00081	.00987	.00104	.10884	.04141	.01564	.00754	.00967	.00444	.00195	.00154
4 Agricultural, forestry and fishery services	.01705	.01189	.00648	.00347	.00260	.00326	.00404	.00126	.00126	.00066	.00083	.00053	.00053	.00063
5 Iron and ferroalloy ores mining	.00124	.00036	.00075	.00079	.00048	.00077	.00113	.00106	.00260	.00738	.00083	.00127	.00070	.00416
6 Nonferrous metal ores mining	.00070	.00038	.00097	.00106	.00060	.00081	.00071	.00063	.00176	.00268	.00083	.00110	.00074	.00670
7 Coal mining	.00252	.00132	.00419	.00364	.00233	.00328	.00204	.00197	.00308	.00510	.00799	.00456	.00247	.00745
8 Crude petroleum and natural gas	.01201	.00770	.01424	.01319	.00823	.00987	.01240	.00883	.00778	.00684	.01313	.01213	.00719	.05708
9 Stone and clay mining and quarrying	.00204	.00157	.00175	.00156	.00087	.00120	.00173	.00138	.00165	.00151	.00535	.00267	.00136	.00503
10 Chemical and fertilizer mineral mining	.00145	.00131	.00400	.00394	.00191	.00245	.00110	.00079	.00126	.00108	.00426	.00283	.00169	.03554
11 New construction														
12 Maintenance and repair construction	.01980	.01080	.01790	.01612	.01202	.01390	.01549	.01348	.01418	.01440	.01967	.01862	.01555	.02459
13 Ordnance and accessories	.00016	.00010	.00020	.00021	.00015	.00020	.00024	.00082	.00169	.00394	.00019	.00017	.00040	.00082
14 Food and kindred products	1.26514	.00805	.01480	.01655	.00950	.01097	.00785	.00794	.00819	.00645	.01642	.01018	.00987	.01749
15 Tobacco manufactures	.00028	1.26746	.00025	.00025	.00030	.00027	.00020	.00032	.00032	.00027	.00025	.00024	.00042	.00030
16 Broad and narrow fabrics, yarn and thread mills	.00396	.00223	1.50769	.30275	.49411	.67435	.00599	.00487	.09034	.02406	.02158	.01070	.00938	.00318
17 Miscellaneous textile goods and floor coverings	.00247	.00136	.04790	1.07989	.02437	.12750	.00555	.00282	.02768	.02271	.00667	.00416	.00428	.00147
18 Apparel	.00145	.00070	.00615	.02101	1.26344	.02864	.00228	.00263	.00556	.00506	.00171	.00242	.00181	.00091
19 Miscellaneous fabricated textile products	.00193	.00066	.00557	.01503	.02348	1.02747	.00125	.00174	.00469	.00714	.00185	.00107	.00091	.00134
20 Lumber and wood products, except containers	.00671	.00415	.00449	.00551	.00367	.00840	1.37635	.52241	.19575	.09353	.12001	.05415	.02241	.00858
21 Wooden containers	.00261	.00195	.00062	.00032	.00027	.00037	.00386	1.03428	.00102	.00081	.00049	.00034	.00016	.00016
22 Household furniture	.00018	.00006	.00019	.00130	.00016	.00189	.00327	.00845	1.01626	.02068	.00041	.00024	.00014	.00009
23 Other furniture and fixtures	.00009	.00005	.00009	.00026	.00009	.00048	.00092	.00081	.00353	1.02568	.00025	.00024	.00030	.00008
24 Paper and allied products, except containers	.03741	.02268	.01946	.02870	.01859	.03272	.01589	.01659	.01971	.01937	1.21526	.51005	.21367	.02745
25 Paperboard containers and boxes	.02924	.01184	.01289	.01114	.01223	.02454	.00512	.00932	.01846	.01771	.02806	1.03796	.01002	.01002
26 Printing and publishing	.02705	.02354	.01216	.01459	.01262	.01236	.00996	.01013	.01310	.01348	.02301	.02432	1.14708	.01588

No.	Industry														
27	Chemicals and selected chemical products	.04088	.04031	.13538	.13491	.06420	.08114	.03417	.02373	.03625	.02730	.07719	.06840	.04610	1.26870
28	Plastics and synthetic materials	.00724	.01843	.16339	.21939	.08301	.10324	.00746	.00538	.02943	.01820	.02568	.01802	.01070	.04225
29	Drugs, cleaning and toilet preparations	.00625	.00413	.00550	.00518	.00324	.00491	.00127	.00119	.00197	.00186	.00317	.00235	.00185	.01893
30	Paints and allied products	.00242	.00106	.00321	.00478	.00186	.00259	.00777	.01195	.01817	.01485	.00336	.00323	.00246	.00654
31	Petroleum refining and related industries	.02280	.01539	.02562	.02409	.01445	.01708	.02383	.01568	.01354	.01125	.02235	.02171	.01247	.11357
32	Rubber and miscellaneous plastics products	.01680	.01296	.01362	.02974	.01000	.03169	.01115	.00758	.05432	.04988	.02819	.01887	.01274	.01158
33	Leather tanning and industrial leather products	.00013	.00008	.00016	.00044	.00457	.00424	.00016	.00012	.00106	.00060	.00016	.00016	.00012	.00016
34	Footwear and other leather products	.00032	.00016	.00019	.00043	.00082	.00070	.00033	.00023	.00039	.00039	.00027	.00040	.00029	.00017
35	Glass and glass products	.01588	.00051	.00753	.00343	.00291	.00400	.00272	.00166	.00840	.01126	.00111	.00112	.00079	.00170
36	Stone and clay products	.00267	.00151	.00397	.00624	.00209	.00328	.01209	.01049	.01077	.00678	.00587	.00362	.00218	.00675
37	Primary iron and steel manufacturing	.02284	.00540	.00886	.00974	.00671	.01167	.02082	.01998	.05000	.14652	.01306	.02228	.01178	.02734
38	Primary nonferrous metal manufacturing	.00789	.00344	.00744	.00892	.00573	.00788	.00848	.00793	.02496	.03606	.00816	.01308	.00929	.03392
39	Metal containers	.03013	.00144	.00265	.00284	.00170	.00200	.00356	.00234	.00252	.00206	.00226	.01032	.00969	.01521
40	Heating, plumbing and structural metal products	.00168	.00088	.00162	.00152	.00109	.00148	.00318	.00205	.00246	.00677	.00194	.00173	.00131	.00253
41	Stampings, screw machine products and bolts	.00593	.00149	.00178	.00231	.00182	.01187	.00806	.00601	.00857	.02443	.00268	.00286	.00226	.00280
42	Other fabricated metal products	.00821	.00555	.00442	.00492	.00468	.00620	.02390	.02106	.06672	.05834	.01954	.01620	.00913	.00930
43	Engines and turbines	.00070	.00050	.00058	.00053	.00038	.00048	.00068	.00055	.00064	.00117	.00062	.00056	.00039	.00100
44	Farm machinery and equipment	.00257	.00283	.00153	.00071	.00063	.00086	.00047	.00031	.00112	.00220	.00027	.00026	.00021	.00034
45	Construction, mining and oil field machinery	.00093	.00077	.00087	.00085	.00062	.00074	.00078	.00072	.00099	.00139	.00108	.00090	.00076	.00196
46	Materials handling machinery and equipment	.00054	.00026	.00079	.00063	.00042	.00059	.00132	.00108	.00081	.00327	.00174	.00105	.00055	.00192
47	Metalworking machinery and equipment	.00280	.00190	.00254	.00726	.00208	.00551	.00342	.00549	.00609	.00930	.00328	.00986	.00209	.00316
48	Special industry machinery and equipment	.00255	.00074	.01111	.00862	.00462	.00597	.00286	.00349	.00204	.00148	.00364	.00293	.00236	.01397
49	General industrial machinery and equipment	.00292	.00133	.00272	.00278	.00156	.00218	.00317	.00292	.00392	.00468	.00628	.00423	.00207	.00731
50	Machine shop products	.00132	.00078	.00128	.00150	.00090	.00131	.00287	.00174	.00220	.00534	.00128	.00130	.00094	.00211
51	Office, computing and accounting machines	.00052	.00043	.00041	.00045	.00042	.00044	.00034	.00034	.00043	.00142	.00068	.00052	.00061	.00068
52	Service industry machines	.00066	.00047	.00052	.00091	.00044	.00084	.00091	.00249	.00090	.00600	.00064	.00060	.00054	.00075
53	Electric industrial equipment and apparatus	.00153	.00089	.00168	.00187	.00122	.00171	.00164	.00169	.00219	.00464	.00173	.00186	.00137	.00418
54	Household appliances	.00052	.00031	.00038	.00044	.00062	.00063	.00062	.00067	.00063	.00180	.00100	.00067	.00052	.00053
55	Electric lighting and wiring equipment	.00077	.00040	.00071	.00071	.00054	.00070	.00125	.00101	.00186	.00212	.00100	.00092	.00068	.00117
56	Radio, television and communication equipment	.00063	.00038	.00060	.00072	.00059	.00075	.00055	.00061	.00103	.00530	.00061	.00061	.00128	.00081
57	Electronic components and accessories	.00069	.00048	.00070	.00367	.00067	.00118	.00055	.00060	.00098	.00235	.00085	.00077	.00106	.00084
58	Miscellaneous electrical machinery, equipment and supplies	.00098	.00060	.00061	.00050	.00041	.00050	.00114	.00070	.00068	.00087	.00045	.00046	.00039	.00063
59	Motor vehicles and equipment	.00258	.00113	.00153	.00223	.00128	.00227	.00316	.00289	.00283	.00626	.00170	.00183	.00154	.00294
60	Aircraft and parts	.00094	.00040	.00076	.00092	.00058	.00099	.00161	.00131	.00141	.00723	.00102	.00103	.00076	.00118

Source: *Survey of Current Business* (February, 1974), p. 51.

its output to itself, to other industries, and to final markets. These final markets are the familiar personal consumption expenditures, gross private domestic investment, net inventory change, gross exports, federal government purchases, and state and local government purchases. The column for an industry shows its consumption of goods and services from the various industries and the value it has added.

Three types of tables have been prepared as part of the input-output accounts. The basic table shows the percent distribution of gross output of each industry to other industries and to final demand. This table and other input-output tables are developed in terms of producers' prices. A second table is in dollar terms and shows the direct requirements from each of the various industries for each dollar of gross output of an industry. It shows, for example, that the household furniture industry purchased $0.01529 from itself for each dollar of final demand. If, for example, it produced $1,000,000 of goods for sale to consumers it would require over $15,000 from its own industry ($1,-000,000 × .01529). It would, for example, also require fabrics, wood products, and the like. But if the fabrics industry is to produce fabrics for furniture, it, in turn, will require some products from its own industry, and so on. These demands would in turn lead to still other demands.

A third table shows the total of all such indirect as well as direct requirements. A portion of such a table is reproduced as Table 20-2, pages 408–409.

The example of household furniture can again be used since this industry is shown in Column 22 of Table 20-2. To provide for the final demand from an additional $1,000,000 expenditure on household furniture requires $1,016,260 from the industry [$1,000,000 × 1.01626 (from Line 22)]. Over $90,000 is required from the fabrics industry shown in Line 16 ($1,000,000 × .09034) and over $195,000 from the lumber and wood products industry, as shown in Line 20 ($1,000,000 × .19575).

The rows in Table 20-2 can be used to determine the requirements for the product of an industry due to final demand from other industries. Line 37, Primary Iron & Steel Manufacturing, can be used as an example to show the demand for steel arising from a $1 increase in demand for the products of some of the industries in Columns 14 to 27. A $1 increase in demand for household furniture leads to a 5 cent increase in demand for steel; a $1 increase in demand for other furniture and fixtures, to a 15 cent increase in demand for steel; and a $1 increase in demand for chemical products, to a 3 cent increase in demand for steel.

These tables can be used to get a first approximation of the change in demand for the products of an industry resulting from changes in demand in other sectors of the economy. If the demand for household furniture is expected to go up by $1,000,000, the demand for lumber and wood products would go up by $195,000 if all factors remain as they were in 1967. Adjustments, however, must be made for various factors which have changed in the years since 1967. The relative prices of household furniture and wood products and the relationships between the two industries may have changed. Adjustments will become easier when input-output data are developed regularly on a current basis.

The Bureau of Economic Analysis has also prepared a table showing the output attributed to final demand by major sectors of GNP for each industry. This data is shown in terms of producers' prices and purchasers' prices. This information can be used, along with a forecast of changes in major sectors of GNP, to get an approximation of changes in the household furniture industry arising from changes in GNP. A final forecast must, of course, be made only after an analysis of changes that may have occurred in relationships which held in 1967 and after a study of all factors that may affect demand.

It is also possible to develop a table showing the demand for each industry in dollar terms that would correspond to a given set of forecast figures for each major category of GNP. This is of doubtful value so long as current input-output data are not available. However, when current data are available, this should prove to be a most valuable tool of forecasting for an industry. This will be especially true when current tables for 370 industries are available.

As was pointed out earlier, all figures in the input-output table are in terms of producer prices, whereas figures used in the national income accounts are in terms of final purchase prices. The differences are shown in input-output accounts primarily under two industry groupings, the transportation and warehousing industry and the wholesale and retail trade industry, and in some cases also under the finance and insurance industry. Household furniture may again be used as an example. In 1967 expenditures on household furniture by consumers totaled $7,077 million. This represented $3,812 million at producer prices, $142 million in transportation charges, and $3,123 million in gross margins in wholesale and retail trade.[6] These relationships are helpful in shifting from figures for final purchases to output figures at the producer level and vice versa.

QUESTIONS

1. Discuss the steps in forecasting cyclical movements in an industry.
2. What is end-use analysis? How may it be used to make an industry forecast?
3. Describe the possible procedures for forecasting the demand for nondurable consumer goods and services.
4. (a) Which factors are involved in a forecast of demand for consumers' durable goods?
   (b) Why are some of these different from those used to forecast nondurable goods demand?
5. Show how the factors cited in question 4 have been used to forecast sales of such durables as automobiles and furniture.
6. Discuss the problems of forecasting demand for paper and paperboard.
7. How can the demand for freight cars be forecast?
8. What is a pressure index? How can it be used in forecasting demand for producers' goods?
9. How can the demand in the building materials field be forecast?
10. Discuss the role of qualitative factors in forecasting for an industry.
11. Describe input-output accounts and tables. How can they be used to forecast industry sales?

---

[6] *Survey of Current Business* (February, 1974), p. 30.

SUGGESTED READINGS

Almon, Clopper, Jr., Margaret R. Buckler, Lawrence M. Horwitz, and Thomas C. Reimbold. *1985 Interindustry Forecasts of the American Economy.* Lexington, Mass.: Lexington Books (D. C. Heath and Co.), 1974.

Chou, Ya-lun. *Probability and Statistics for Decision Making.* New York: Holt, Rinehart, and Winston, Inc., 1972.

General Motors Corporation. *The Dynamics of Automobile Demand.* New York: General Motors Corporation, 1939. Part 1, Statement of the Problem; Part 2, Factors Governing Changes in Domestic Automobile Demand, Sections 4 and 5.

Gross, Charles W., and Robin T. Peterson. *Business Forecasting.* Boston: Houghton Mifflin Co., 1976.

Houthakker, H. S., and Lester D. Taylor. *Consumer Demand in the United States: Analyses and Projections.* Cambridge: Harvard University Press, 1970, pp. 189–190.

"Input-Output Structure of the U.S. Economy: 1967." *Survey of Current Business* (February, 1974), pp. 24–56.

Jolson, Marvin A., and Richard T. Hise. *Quantitative Techniques for Marketing Decisions.* New York: The Macmillan Co., 1973.

Leontief, Wassily W. "The Structure of the U.S. Economy." *Scientific American* (April, 1965), pp. 25–35.

Murdick, Robert G. *Mathematical Models in Marketing.* Scranton, Pa.: Intext Educational Publishers, 1971.

Paradiso, Louis J. "Consumer and Business Income and Spending Patterns in the Postwar Period." *Survey of Current Business* (March, 1963), pp. 12–17.

———, and Mabel A. Smith. "Consumer Purchasing and Income Patterns." *Survey of Current Business* (March, 1959), pp. 18–28.

"Personal Consumption Expenditures in the 1963 Input-Output Study." *Survey of Current Business* (January, 1971), pp. 34–38.

Press, S. James. *Applied Multivariate Analysis.* New York: Holt, Rinehart, and Winston, Inc., 1972.

Turley, James E. "Automobile Sales in Perspective." *Review,* Federal Reserve Bank of St. Louis (June, 1976), pp. 11–16.

U.S. Industrial Outlook. Washington: U.S. Department of Commerce, annual.

CHAPTER 21

FORECASTING SALES FOR AN INDIVIDUAL BUSINESS

Forecasts of total economic activity and of sales in an industry are useful in determining the general business climate and the direction of sales. For setting sales quotas, scheduling production, and ordering raw materials, however, it is necessary to have a sales forecast for an individual business and for each of its major lines of products if it is a multiproduct firm. General business and industry forecasts constitute a basis for making such a forecast, but other important items must also be considered.

PRODUCT CLASSIFICATION

The first step in forecasting sales for an individual business is a classification of the products sold by that concern. The classification should group products that have common factors affecting the level of sales. If a system of product classification is used for inventory and production control, many of the same classes can probably be used. Additional classifications needed for forecasting purposes can often be added to such a system, or some of the classes in that system can be combined.

One of the first classifications required is the division between basic products and by-products since the planned level of production of the basic product determines the prospective supply of the by-products that will have to be sold. If the demand for the by-products is elastic, adjustments can be made in price so as to move all of them. If the demand is not elastic, it is necessary to try to develop a market for the projected volume of by-products.

The basic products should be divided into groups for which the factors determining demand are about the same. Differences in demand may be due to the degree of development of products from raw materials to finished goods since changes in consumer demand will affect the various stages in the production and selling process at different times. Therefore, different classifications should be set up for raw materials, products used in further manufacture, and finished consumer goods.

Differences in demand may also occur because different types of consumers buy the products or because a different set of factors motivates their purpose. For example, a manufacturer of electrical controls found that the basic divisions for the firm's products were heating controls and air-conditioning controls. Heating controls were further subdivided into controls for industrial and residential users. Each of these controls was further broken down into controls for gas, oil, and coal units. Significant variations, especially in the field of gas heating, were found between controls for conversion burners and those for new units.

Whenever a study of past sales experience shows appreciable differences in demand determinants, it is necessary to set up a separate category for forecasting purposes. Other factors also affect the production and the sales of a product, and these should be noted and checked in grouping products for sales forecast purposes. A factor that is especially important when business is in a downturn is the degree to which demand may be deferred. For example, the demand for furnace controls for the repair and replacement market may not be deferred for any period of time, but the demand for those for new installations may be put off as disposable personal income decreases.

It is also desirable to make separate lists of those products for which production is based to a significant extent upon contracts received in advance and those products that are sold from current stock. If firm contracts are received well in advance, it may not be necessary to forecast external factors. Even if contracts are received shortly before shipment is expected or if trade practices permit cancellations or postponement of shipment, contracts can still be useful in developing a forecast.

The forecasting department should also have available information on the average size of sale for each of its basic product categories. This information is necessary because sales will tend to be more uneven if made to a few large accounts. The effect on sales of losing one or more of these accounts will be large.

Products should also be analyzed according to the basic raw materials which are used in them so that different influences affecting the price and the availability of raw materials may be considered in forecasting.

ANALYSIS OF THE TREND OF SALES

After the products that are sold by the business have been grouped into categories that have about the same demand determinants, the trend of sales of these products for the last 10 to 15 years should be studied. This trend can be compared with trends in gross national product, in disposable personal income, or in industrial production to see in a general way how sales have been growing in relationship to the growth in total economic activity.

The trend in sales should also be compared with that in the industry of which this product group is a part. This may be difficult if the industry is not homogeneous. For example, each major chemical company produces a different product mix, and the trends in sales of different products have been quite different. The demand for some plastics has been growing much faster than that for heavy chemicals, and some companies have divisions which are producing new drugs which have rapidly increasing sales. However, in such cases it is usually possible to obtain sales figures for major products or groups of products from trade association or governmental sources and to compare company sales of these products in the past with sales nationally.

After the trend for the product group has been established and compared with trends in the economy and in the industry, the results must be analyzed. A thorough study should be made to determine the relationship between company policies and the trend of sales. Changes in price policies, sales policies, production policies, and the like may have caused company sales to grow slower or faster than industry sales.

ANALYSIS OF CYCLICAL VARIATIONS IN SALES

In forecasting sales, it is desirable to study past cyclical fluctuations in sales of each group of products. One of the first steps is to find the relationship between such sales and general business activity.

Relationship to General Business Activity

The basic procedure for finding the relationship between the sales of a company and a logically related measure of general economic activity is the same as it is for an industry. The relationship may at times not be as clear, however, since many factors affect the sales of an individual company to a much greater extent than they do those of the industry. This is true of such factors as strikes in individual plants, local shortages of materials or labor, changed business policies, and the like. It is still worthwhile, however, to see what past relationships have been and to study any deviations from typical patterns in the past.

The following are some of the most frequently used relationships with general economic activity or some major segment of it:

Product Group	Related Series
Service	Disposable personal income
Nondurable consumer good	Disposable personal income
Consumer good or service sold largely to farmers	Cash farm income
Durable consumer good	Discretionary income or disposable personal income
Producer good	Gross national product or gross private product
Raw material or parts	Federal Reserve Board Index of Industrial Production or a related subindex
Construction material	F. W. Dodge Company Index of Construction Contracts Awarded or a related subindex

In studying past relationships, the trend of sales of the company in relationship to the trend in the related variable must be considered carefully. A
company in a growing industry, such as chemicals, may find that its sales are
related to changes in gross private product but the rate of growth is much
faster. For example, since 1940 sales of some plastic products have been
growing at a rate which is several times the growth rate of gross private
product.

In some cases the most accurate relationships may be found by making the
correlations after deflating both the sales of the product in question and the
measure of aggregative income by appropriate price indexes to obtain the
relationship in real terms.

Even if it is not necessary to deflate the series to obtain patterns of past
relationships, it may be necessary to deflate the forecast of the dollar volume
of sales to put it on a per unit basis. If a concern has an index showing the
changes in price of the product being forecast, this is, of course, the best
index to use for deflation. If it does not have such an index, the appropriate
subdivision of the consumer price index or the wholesale price index may be
used.

In some situations best results may be achieved by means of correlation
with the Federal Reserve Board Index of Industrial Production, or its durable
or nondurable goods component, or one of the subdivisions of these. For most
accurate forecasting it may be worthwhile to make such a correlation, even if a
close relationship has been found with disposable personal income or one of the
other dollar measures of aggregative economic activity. In this way a comparison can be made between the value forecast and the quantity forecast to see if
they yield similar results. If such forecasts disagree, it is necessary to study
again all of the factors in the situation carefully, for indications are either that
past relationships have changed or that factors which were of minor significance in the past are currently of much greater importance.

Regional Factors

If a group of products for which a forecast is being developed is not sold
nationally, then it is also necessary to consider the different trends of sales in
different regions. This factor may be taken into consideration in several ways.
It may be possible to obtain data on past relationships of sales to a related
variable, such as disposable personal income, for that section of the country
in which a company does business. For example, shoe sales for a concern doing
business in Missouri, Illinois, and Arkansas could be related to personal income in those states for a period of years covering several cycles. Personal
income figures on a state-by-state and regional basis are developed regularly
by the Department of Commerce and published in the *Survey of Current
Business*. This method of finding relationships to state or regional personal
income can also be used to set up regional or state sales quotas for products
sold nationally.

An alternate method is to find the relationship of company sales to disposable personal income for the nation and to adjust for any changes expected from past relationships in the state or region being analyzed. The comparison of the trend of sales of the product with the trend of disposable personal income is helpful in making such adjustments. If the reasons for past relationships have been analyzed fully and if the present situation is studied carefully, it should be possible to make a reasonable forecast of sales for the coming year using such past patterns. This method will probably take somewhat less time than a state-by-state or regional analysis, but it is somewhat less useful because it provides no basis for setting sales quotas.

Relationship to Industry Sales

A study should also be made of the relationship of the sales of the concern or of its major product groups to those of the industry in the past. It may be possible to find a regular relationship between sales in the business in question and those in the industry and so devise a forecast from an industry forecast. This method is probably satisfactory if the industry consists of fairly homogeneous units, all producing an essentially similar line of products. This is true of large segments of the shoe industry in which factories produce a complete line of family shoes. A manufacturer of women's shoes alone will probably find, however, that the relationship of the firm's sales to those of the industry is not regular.

The relationship of the sales of the firm or of one of its product groups to those of the industry may follow one of several patterns. The firm may do a more or less constant percentage of the total business in the field. In other cases the firm may be getting a gradually increasing share of the business, or a gradually decreasing share. If there is such a trend in this relationship, it can usually be found by plotting the percentage of business the concern does in the field. In some cases there may be cyclical divergences in the amount of business done; that is, the percentage of business in the field may be higher when business in general is rising and the percentage may be lower when business is in recession.

Other Factors

The individual business may also develop reference-cycle patterns and specific cycle patterns of past sales as an aid to forecasting, following the technique of the National Bureau of Economic Research. Any constant reference-cycle leads or lags will aid in forecasting. Information thus obtained about the average duration of the cycle, amplitude of the cycle, and conformity to the reference-cycle pattern will also prove valuable. It may be possible to develop such patterns for major cycles and minor cycles independently and thus increase their usefulness as a forecasting device.

An analysis should also be made of cyclical variations in sales in relationship to the cycle in general economic activity or in a related segment of the economy. This should be done to see if there is any tendency for cyclical variations in sales of the company to become more or less severe than those in the industry or in general economic activity.

Another factor that should be checked is the relationship of the trend of prices in the field being studied to the general trend of consumer prices. In many consumer goods fields sales will be higher when prices in a field are relatively more favorable than consumer prices in general and lower when the reverse is true. The effect of such divergent price trends may be studied as part of the correlation pattern and expressed on a numerical basis, or treated as a qualitative factor that is used to modify statistical calculations based on past relationships.

FORECASTING SALES

The factors affecting sales in the past, both over the long term and during past cycles, and an analysis and forecast of industry sales and of total economic activity serve as a basis for making a company forecast of sales. The first step is to forecast sales on the basis of economic factors. This should be modified by special information on sales, if any, that may be available to the sales department. Then top management should review the forecast and alter it if they feel that policies should and will be followed which will change the forecast. These three stages, called the first approximation, the second approximation, and the forecast, will be considered in turn.

The First Approximation

In developing the first approximation the starting point is a forecast of total economic activity and industry sales. Past relationships can be used to develop a tentative forecast from industry and general economic forecasts. This should be done for each group of products into which the company's products have been grouped for forecasting purposes.

A complete survey must be made of all qualitative factors in the situation. Economic variables are continually changing, and such changes must be considered in developing a forecast from past relationships. A survey of this kind should include an analysis of the company's marketing activities and any changes in such activities. It should also contain marketing programs of competitors and the effects of any other actions or potential actions of competitors. Also included should be any changes in the competitive picture and any possibility of the development of substitute products.

In checking a forecast, it is usually worthwhile also to study trends of costs and profits in the field and in the business in question. If profit margins are being squeezed, the possibility of price increases to the ultimate consumer and their effects on sales should be considered. Low profit margins are likely to affect the expansion of existing businesses and the introduction of new concerns into the field, and so affect future supply.

Before any forecast for a company selling its products to other businesses is complete, trends in each one of the major fields using the product must be checked. Some concerns have found it desirable in forecasting their sales to make forecasts of sales in several of the major fields using their products.

The conditions in each of the fields supplying raw materials to the company must also be studied to see if there will be shortages of raw materials or any changes in their prices that will change the prices of finished goods and thus lead to a change in demand and sales.

The Second Approximation

A forecast of sales based upon a study of past patterns of relationships and upon an analysis of all qualitative factors must be adjusted to take special factors affecting the sales of the company into consideration. A major sales drive may be planned early in the year, which from past experience will raise sales 10 percent through June. It may be planned to eliminate a product, to change it materially, or to cut prices to move old stock quickly. All such programs must be considered and forecasts of specific product sales changed to meet expected results.

It is usually desirable to obtain an estimate of expected sales from the sales force once or twice a year. For such a survey to be most valuable, it must be carefully planned. The sales force should have had time to study all plans for sales promotion during the time of the forecast. Figures should be supplied for sales for the comparable period last year for all regions and for all customers for whom forecasts are desired. A separate forecast is usually desirable for any region in a sales representative's territory in which sales experience has varied materially from the rest of the area, and also a separate forecast for each major customer. In cases where sales are expected to be different from those of the preceding year, the sales representatives should be asked to give their reasons.

Such information, if carefully developed, is extremely useful. The sales representative knows whether customers are moving into a sales area or out of it. The representative also knows whether major new accounts are likely or if some current accounts are likely to be lost. The representative may also know whether inventory is piling up in the hands of some customers.

Some companies make a more formal users' survey in determining the sales expectations of customers. Customers may be surveyed by mail, by telephone, or by personal interviews. To get a reasonable response, companies usually assure the respondents that their information will be kept confidential and that the results of the overall survey will be made available to them. Some companies have attempted to improve the accuracy of a users' survey by asking for responses from more than one official in the company as, for example, the production manager as well as the purchasing agent. Experience has proved that it is generally better to ask how much of a product the customer plans to buy in total rather than just from the company making the survey. Past experience can then be used to estimate the company's share of the total.

The forecast made from a study of past relationships should be adjusted to bring it into line with any changes that are required by the sales or users' survey. Such a revised forecast becomes the second approximation, which is ready for analysis by top management.

The Forecast

The second approximation should be reviewed by a committee from top management, including representatives from each of the major functional areas. If they feel that it is a proper basis for planning next year's business, they may accept it. If they feel it calls for unattainable levels, they may reduce it. If they feel it is too low to meet their objectives for profit and other factors, such as market position in the next year, they may develop promotion plans to raise the sales level and adjust the forecast in line with such programs.

After the level of sales has been projected for a year ahead, it is necessary to put it on a quarterly basis and a month-by-month basis for at least one or two quarters ahead. This projection requires the calculation of a typical seasonal pattern showing the percentage of the year's business normally done in each month. Before any past seasonal pattern is projected, a study should be made to determine if anything has occurred that might change past patterns. With this information it is possible to break down an annual sales forecast into monthly and quarterly forecasts.

Review and Revision

Since the economic climate can change quickly at times, the forecasting section should study the situation continually and recommend changes in the forecast if that becomes desirable. Except in unusual situations, such as the buying sprees during the first year of the Korean War, it is sufficient to revise a forecast quarterly in most businesses. Before any major change is made, the sales force should be consulted. In addition, the revised forecast should always be approved by the committee of top management that approved the original forecast.

The last step in any forecasting procedure is to study the record of all past forecasts. When a forecast is off, every attempt should be made to ascertain the reason. Such a procedure will increase the analysts' awareness of unusual factors that affect sales. The procedure will also readily show up changing or new relationships.

SUMMARY OF FORECASTING PROCEDURES

The steps in forecasting for an individual concern may be summarized as follows:

Preparation
1. Group the products into classes which have about the same demand characteristics.
2. Study the trend of sales of each forecasting group. Account for this trend.
3. Compare trends with those of gross national product, disposable personal income, or industrial production and with the industry trend. Account for these relationships.
4. Find a relationship to a logically related general economic variable, nationally if sales are on a national scale, or by the states or regions in which sales are made. Explain all deviations from the general pattern of relationship.
5. Find the relationship of sales to industry sales. Account for the general pattern and for any deviations from it.

First Approximation
6. Using past relationships, general business and industry forecasts, and a knowledge of all qualitative factors in the present situation, project company sales for a year ahead by product groups.

Second Approximation
7. Study all plans for sales promotions and the like and determine their probable effect on sales.
8. Obtain estimates of sales from sales representatives by territories and from customers and revise the forecast, if need be, in view of this new information.

Forecast
9. Have a committee of top management reivew the forecast and adjust it if they see fit.
10. Calculate the seasonal pattern. Check to see if there are any factors that might cause it to change. Put the annual forecasts on a monthly and a quarterly basis.

Review and Revision
11. Review the forecast at least quarterly. Continually study factors that might make it advisable to change the forecast.
12. Review all past forecasts and determine, if possible, the reasons for errors.

THE ROLE OF THE FORECASTING PROGRAM IN BUSINESS MANAGEMENT

Forecasting is organized differently in both large and small corporations, but a few generalizations can be drawn that will serve as a guide to sound practice. Most of the forecasting organizations report to top management or top financial management. A few report to the chief sales official. It is usually sound to have the forecasting section report to top management so as to give it independence from influence by sales, production, or budgeting.

A market research section making studies of consumer product acceptance and consumer preferences properly belongs in the sales department. If possible, this section should be kept separate from the forecasting department. In a small business, however, the two may have to be combined because of cost considerations. Such a combined section may be placed in the sales department if proper recognition is given to the possibility of bias.

The forecasts of sales in the next year and over a longer period of time are the basis for planning the operations of a business. The long-range forecast is used to plan capital expenditures and long-run financing. The forecasts for a year ahead and for the next quarter are used for top management planning to develop the budget, for sales planning and promotion, for production scheduling and purchasing, and for short-run financing.

Top Management Planning

The forecast is used by top management as a basis for planning for the next year. The projected sales figures may be too low to utilize all facilities of the company and the decision may, therefore, be made to introduce new or expanded programs of promotion. In other situations the decision may be made to introduce new products during the coming year. The forecast may, on the other hand, call for a sales volume that cannot be met from production facilities currently in use. A decision will have to be made to expand facilities, add another shift, or to try to buy parts or even finished goods from others. In some situations the decision may be to raise prices to improve profit margins.

Top management also uses a forecast as a basis for review of operations after the period of the forecast is over. Sales are compared with the forecast and the reasons for deviations are studied. The forecast may have been a poor one, and an analysis of the reasons for being inaccurate should help improve the results in the future. But sales in the total economy and in the industry in general may have developed about as forecast, while sales of the company may have been below expectations. This could be due to such factors as the inability to meet orders, a poor promotion program, new sales personnel, too restrictive a credit program, and the like. An analysis of such factors can determine the cause of the problem and provide the information needed to correct it. In some situations the general forecast may have been accurate, but sales for the company may have exceeded the forecast level. The causal factors again need careful study since increased sales may have been due to temporary factors in the programs of one or more competitors. In short, top management can use a forecast as a basis for overall planning and control of the operations of a business.

The expenditures on a forecasting program must be watched carefully to make certain that they are contributing to the overall profitability of a company. A forecasting program can in most cases be made more accurate or more useful in planning and control if enough money is spent on it. But such expenditures must be compared with the benefits to be derived from them in the form of greater income or lower expenses. Increased expenditures are only justified so long as the benefits are greater than the costs.

Budgeting

The data from the forecast are used by the accounting department to develop the budget. The budget includes estimates of sales income by departments that can be obtained from the forecasts of sales by products. Expenses are also estimated by departments for all major subcategories of labor, materials, and overhead. These estimates are derived from a knowledge of the quantities to be produced, the amounts of each factor required to produce various products, and cost estimates for each factor. Such cost estimates usually are based on data about future costs supplied by the forecasting department. When significant seasonal variations exist, such figures are usually developed for each month of the year and they may even be developed week by week.

The estimated figures are usually organized into projected income statements for the year and by months for at least a quarter ahead. These show expected profit from operations and, after allowance for financial expenses and income taxes, show projected net profit.

The budget is usually presented to top management for approval and revision if they feel it is in need of changes. After the budget has been approved by top management, it serves to control expenditures since they must be kept in line with the budget.

Some concerns use a flexible budget program based upon the range of the forecast. If past experience shows that a range of 10 percent above and below the estimated sales figure is usually wide enough to include the actual sales figure, the budget may be based on the most likely sales estimate and on 90 percent, 95 percent, 105 percent, and 110 percent of it. Such a procedure is expensive, but it provides cost control regardless of the level of business. In other concerns the same results are obtained by means of an annual budget of income and expenses and a detailed budget for the next quarter revised quarterly as the latest quarterly forecast becomes available. Another possibility is always to have an up-to-date budget for a quarter ahead by revising the budget each month for the next three months on the latest forecast.

Sales Planning

The sales department, which should have had a voice in setting the sales figure used in the forecast, makes use of the budget in planning its operations. On the basis of estimated sales, it sets sales quotas by products and by territories, and in many cases for individual sales representatives. These quotas may be set somewhat above the budget so as to provide an incentive to do better than economic factors indicate will be done.

Sales quotas by products can usually be derived directly from the forecast, since a complete forecast is broken down into product categories. Additional work is required, however, to set realistic quotas by territories because the sales of all products do not grow or decline at the same rate in all parts of the

United States nor are they equally sensitive to changes in income in all regions. Therefore, in setting sales quotas by territories, the trend of sales of the product in each territory must be studied. It is even more important to study the relationship between changes in sales and changes in income in each territory. In some regions sales may be much more responsive to changes in income than in others. Only by taking these factors into consideration can realistic sales quotas be developed by territories.

Sales Promotion

The sales department must also integrate its sales promotion program with the sales forecast. Special promotional projects must be considered in developing the product-by-product sales forecast. Products whose potential is rising must be pushed if it is desired to hold or increase the share of the market for such products. Campaigns may also be initiated to change consumer preferences in favor of a product for which the potential is decreasing.

General advertising outlays designed to keep the company name, product name, or trademark before the public are often geared to sales by being set as a percentage of sales. Since such advertising has long-run value, it is generally felt that it should be done when it can best be afforded. The most logical way to accomplish this is to set such expenditures as a percentage of the forecasted sales.

The sales department can use the sales forecast and its advertising budget as a basis for determining its need for personnel for the year. In this way an adequate force can be provided and trained for the job when it is needed.

Scheduling Production, Personnel, and Purchasing

The production department must develop a production schedule from the sales forecast. If no significant seasonal pattern exists, the forecast can be used directly as the basis for a production schedule. Adjustments must be made if current inventory is either too high or too low for the expected sales level. Schedules must also be geared to practicable levels of operation based on assembly-line time, machine time, and other technical factors in the plant.

When a pronounced seasonal pattern in sales exists, it is usually desirable, if it is at all practicable, to smooth out production and to let changes in inventory absorb a large part of the fluctuation. Under present-day conditions, with unemployment compensation taxes based largely on a concern's employment record and with the high cost of training new employees, it is usually cheaper to carry sizable inventories part of the year to regularize production.

Such regularization of production can be done safely only if a good forecasting program exists, which implies a continuous revision of forecasts in view of changing conditions. The forecast of sales by months is the basis for the production schedule. Total production needed during the year is then planned on a regular basis. It may not be exactly $1/12$ of projected sales each month or $\frac{1}{52}$ each week, since the various products of the company may have different seasonal patterns and the goal is to regularize overall production. The difference between planned production and forecasted sales shows the projected inventory.

Constant study of present and future sales is needed to make such a program work. At least quarterly, or better yet monthly, sales forecasts and production schedules should be reviewed and changed as needed. If this is done, changes can be planned carefully and made over a period of several weeks or months.

The production schedule provides the basis for calculating workforce requirements. When calculated in a general way a year ahead and in detail at least a quarter ahead, there is time to recruit personnel carefully and to train new employees adequately. Schedules of machine time required are also developed from production schedules. Machines can be used most effectively when requirements are known for a period of time in the future.

The production schedule is also the basis for placing orders for raw materials and parts. Since it takes time to obtain many of the items needed, efficient planning can be done only when a sales forecast exists. Data on probable future price movements supplied by the forecasting staff also enable the purchasing department to buy at the most advantageous time.

A production schedule based on a sound forecast also improves the shipment of finished products. Sufficient quantities of standard items should be on hand at all times to meet the demand. This should make it possible to develop a shipping schedule providing for more or less regular work in that department. It should also be possible to give accurate shipping dates for any orders accepted for special products, since production is planned at least a quarter ahead.

Financing

The finance department can use the forecast, budget, production schedules, and shipping schedules to plan the financing of the business. The shipping schedule, based on the sales forecast and a knowledge of credit terms and experience in collecting accounts, can be used to develop estimates of the flow of cash receipts. Production schedules and cost estimates provide the basis for calculating expenditures month by month. It is also possible to estimate the amount of funds that will be tied up in inventory.

From these estimates the adequacy of the cash position at any time can be determined. It is also possible to determine when short-term borrowing will be necessary, how much is needed, and for what period, and thus to plan the financing program in advance.

EXAMPLES OF FORECASTING PROCEDURES

Several examples will show how forecasting programs are developed and used in business. The first example is a steel company that uses many of the techniques described in this chapter. The second is a plumbing supplies manufacturer that has successfully developed a less elaborate procedure. The third is an electric light and power company that forecasts on the basis of the trend, since it is not materially affected by the cycle, and the last is a chemical processing company.

A Steel Company

A large company engaged in producing steel and steel products uses many of the techniques described in this chapter. A staff group consisting of economists, a market analyst, and a statistician is responsible for economic forecasting and sales forecasting. This group is headed by an economist who is under the supervision of the manager of a business research division.

An economic forecast is prepared each year for the economy and for the company. A forecast is made of GNP and such underlying trend factors as population growth, labor conditions, and productivity. The level of activity in the steel industry is forecast for the next year. On the basis of these forecasts and of the past relationships, company sales are forecast for the next year, for each quarter of the year, and for each of the company's products.

A long-range forecast is also developed, but in less detail. Forecasts are always available for each year of a five-year period beyond the current year's forecast. The whole series of forecasts are reviewed annually when a forecast for the next year is made in detail. To aid in making long-range forecasts, trends in various sectors of GNP are studied, especially as they relate to the demand for steel.

A Plumbing Supplies Manufacturer

A company manufacturing plumbing supplies uses a less elaborate procedure, since it has found a reliable indicator of sales. It found that its sales lagged four months behind the F. W. Dodge Company figures on the value of residential construction contracts. The first step in its forecasting procedure is to find the relationship between its sales in each of its sales territories and the F. W. Dodge contract figures for that territory. Since contracts show a four-month lead, the relationship is studied with sales lagged four months behind contracts. The ratio is then found between company sales and F. W. Dodge residential contracts in the area. Some territories show a more or less constant ratio and some a trend up or down for which allowance must be made in forecasting. This ratio of sales to contracts is applied to contracts for the past twelve months. This gives an estimate of sales for the twelve months ending four months in the future. By subtracting sales for the past eight months, a forecast for the next four months is obtained.

The sales managers review all forecasts and make any adjustments they feel are needed before the forecasts become official. Forecasts are compared with actual performance, and the reasons for all deviations are analyzed carefully.

An Electric Light and Power Company

The forecasting procedure of an electric light and power company is based primarily on a projection of long-run trends. Since the building of a large steam or nuclear power generating plant takes three or four years or more, it is necessary to plan almost entirely on the basis of the trend rather than on cyclical variations in demand. The first step is to estimate residential revenues. This is done from a projection of the trend in the number of users and the trend in the number of kilowatt hours of electricity per user.

To estimate the number of users, it is necessary to make careful estimates of the trend of population in the area being served. Plans for new residential building must also be studied carefully. The forecast of the use of electricity per user can be made by extending the trend line of such use. The forecast of kilowatt hours is converted into revenues on the basis of present and prospective rate structures. A similar procedure is used to forecast sales to and revenue from industrial and commercial users. The trend in this case is checked carefully by an analysis of the pattern of industrial development in the area to find any probable changes in the past rate of growth. Large users are asked to provide information on expansion plans and on their needs for the next several years.

The effect of changes in general business on the industrial and commercial use of electricity in the area served by the company is considered in making an annual forecast of industrial sales and revenue. The effect is not considered for residential users because, for all practical purposes, it is nonexistent. The seasonal pattern is used to put annual forecasts on a monthly basis.

A Chemical Processing Company

A chemical processing company that is engaged in the manufacture of specialized cleaning compounds for industrial use makes use of several economic indicators as a basis for developing forecasts. This company has five major sales divisions including a metal industrial division, a food producers' division, a railroad division, a petrochemical producers' division, and a general industries group. This company found that total sales correlated well with gross national product in current dollars, with total manufacturing sales, and with the Federal Reserve Board Index of Industrial Production. Since increased industrial production leads to an increased demand for cleaning compounds and this demand only exists after industrial production has been increased, the FRB Index has a short lead over sales of the company.

The company purchases forecasts of the three series from an economic consulting service. Forecasts are made using all three of the series, and any differences are reconciled by an analysis of all qualitative factors. Such differences that do exist are usually readily explainable as, for example, an increase in the price level which gives the GNP figures a higher value than those developed from the FRB Index. The company pays special attention to shifting patterns in the major sectors of industrial production and uses these factors along with forecasts of total sales in order to develop sales forecasts for the five divisions.

FORECASTING THE MARKET FOR A NEW PRODUCT

Economic analysis cannot be used as the basic tool for forecasting the demand for a new product. It can help, however, by indicating what general business conditions will be and by showing how similar products have developed in the past. Such forecasting is primarily a project in market research and will therefore not be treated fully here. However, the general methods by which it may be done will be considered.

Sometimes a new product replaces an old product in whole or in part, and forecasting can be done on the basis of the old product. For example, color television is gradually replacing black and white. Some idea of the demand pattern for color television can be gained from the black and white television market in the past and at the time the forecast is made for color. Field surveys of buyers' intentions will help gauge the speed of the shift.

Even when a product does not replace another, a field survey will often help establish the demand for it. This may be done in the case of industrial products by showing a sample of prospective users' drawings and specifications, but actual samples are needed for most consumer products. In fact, it is usually best to offer a consumer product for sale in sample markets and then to estimate demand from such sales experience.

In some cases growth curves of similar products may be used as a general guide for sales. For example, the growth curve for refrigerators can be used to estimate the growth curves for other generally accepted appliances.

All sales forecasting is based on a series of estimates and projections and therefore cannot be completely accurate. The margin of error can be kept within reasonable limits for established products so that forecasts can be used as a basis for production planning if revised quarterly. Forecasts of the demand for new products are less reliable, but even so they are better than basing production on hunches or guesses. Additional study of the factors affecting consumer expenditure patterns should help in time to improve such forecasts.

QUESTIONS

1. Why is product classification important in developing a forecast?
2. Which factors must be considered in classifying products?
3. Why is the trend of sales important in a short-run forecast?
4. How may sales be studied in relationship to some measure of aggregative economic activity?
5. What use is made of regional trends in forecasting sales?
6. How can the relationship of the sales of a particular business to industry sales be used in forecasting?

7. What effect do sales promotions, actions of competitors, and the like have on sales forecasts?
8. How can users' surveys be used in a forecasting program?
9. Summarize the steps involved in forecasting sales for a particular business.
10. Outline the preferred organization of the forecasting department for effective business planning.
11. Describe the uses of the forecasting program in the following areas: top management, budgeting, sales planning, sales promotion, production scheduling, and financing.
12. Discuss several examples of forecasting procedures currently in use.
13. What is involved in forecasting the demand for a new product?

SUGGESTED READINGS

Butler, William, Jr., and Robert A. Kavesh (eds.). *How Business Economists Forecast*. Englewood Cliffs, N.J.: Prentice-Hall, Inc., 1966, Parts Three and Five.

Butler, William F., Robert A. Kavesh, and Robert B. Platt (eds.). *Methods and Techniques of Business Forecasting*. Englewood Cliffs, N.J.: Prentice-Hall, Inc., 1976.

Controllership Foundation. *Business Forecasting*. New York: Controllership Foundation, Inc., 1950. Part IV.

Crawford, C. M. *Sales Forecasting: Methods of Selected Firms*. Urbana: University of Illinois Press, Bureau of Economic and Business Research, 1955.

Goodman, Oscar R. *Sales Forecasting*. Madison: University of Wisconsin Press, Bureau of Business Research and Service, 1954.

Gross, Charles W., and Robin T. Peterson. *Business Forecasting*. Boston: Houghton Mifflin Co., 1976.

Jolson, Marvin A., and Richard T. Hise. *Quantitative Techniques for Marketing Decisions*. New York: The Macmillan Co., 1973.

Murdick, Robert G. *Mathematical Models in Marketing*. Scranton, Pa.: Intext Educational Publishers, 1971.

National Industrial Conference Board. *Forecasting Sales*. New York: National Industrial Conference Board, 1964.

PROBLEMS ON PART 6

1. (a) For the same business used in Problem 2 in Part 4, page 305, plot the following:
   Annual sales.
   Annual sales in real terms. (Deflate the sales figures by using a subindex of the Bureau of Labor Statistics Wholesale Price Index or Consumer Price Index.)
   Sales as a percentage of industry sales since 1962.
   (b) Prepare a scatter diagram showing the relationship of industry sales to disposable personal income, a subindex of the Federal Reserve Board Index of Industrial Production, or other appropriate index.
   (c) Analyze past changes in sales in the industry and in your business accounting, insofar as possible, for all past changes. Forecast sales for the industry and for your company for the next year basing your forecast upon your analysis of past relationships, of the causal factors at work, and the present and prospective status of these factors.

2. (a) Plot automobile sales for each year since 1963.
   (b) On the basis of the factors that affect automobile sales and of the economic factors at work during the period, account for the yearly changes in sales insofar as possible.
3. (a) From data in *Business Statistics, Supplement to the Survey of Current Business,* and the *Survey of Current Business,* plot the following on ratio paper:
      (1) Paper and paperboard production for each year from 1963 to the present.
      (2) Gross national product for the same period.
      (3) Federal Reserve Board Index of Industrial Production.
   (b) Discuss the relationships between these series.
   (c) Using past trends and relationships project paper and paperboard production to 1985.

PART 7

PROPOSALS FOR ACHIEVING ECONOMIC GROWTH AND STABILITY

Major fluctuations in the level of economic activity and in price levels create some of our most serious economic, social, and political problems. In the present state of world affairs, a serious depression or a major period of inflation in the United States would have serious repercussions not only in this country but also in most of the other nations of the world. A growing humanitarian concern for the plight of those afflicted by economic reversals, an awareness of the international as well as domestic political impact of fluctuations, and a faith in the efficacy of policy to cure economic ills have all combined to bring about increased attention toward devising means to stabilize economic activity.

Programs to stabilize economic activity affect all sectors of the economy, both in the short run and in the long run. In the long run, the goal of stability must be balanced with the goal of assuring a rising trend of real income. Both long-run and short-run programs must be politically and socially acceptable to our society to be put into effect. To achieve stability but to simultaneously lose a significant measure of our freedom is to win a battle but lose the war. Thus, programs to achieve stability involve political decisions that are as important or perhaps more important than economic decisions.

The first chapter in this part looks at the goals and some of the issues and problems in developing overall aggregate economic policies for growth and stabilization. The last chapter is a survey of the tools and methodology of the major approaches used, namely monetary policy and fiscal policy and their interrelationships.

CHAPTER 22

PROBLEMS IN ECONOMIC POLICY FOR GROWTH AND STABILITY

Intelligent discussion of economic policy is possible only among those who have an understanding of how an economy functions. This is the reason our chapters on policy come at the end of the book rather than at the beginning, after a theoretical framework for understanding has been constructed and some insights from the historical record have been gained. In this chapter we consider some of the major problems in developing government programs to promote growth and stability and the role of the private sector in that endeavor. Chapter 23 is devoted specifically to the primary tools of aggregate economic policy — monetary and fiscal policy.

THE NATURE OF ECONOMIC GROWTH AND STABILITY

Economic growth may be judged from the growth in total output of the economy as measured by annual increases in net national product in constant dollars. Such a measure tells us how much bigger the total economy is becoming over a period of time, but it tells us nothing about changes in the standard of living of the people in the economy. The more significant measure is the growth in real output per capita as measured by increases in real net national product divided by the number of people in the population.

The Nature of Economic Growth

A rising level of real output per capita can be achieved in several different ways. It may be done by using a larger quantity of the factors of production in proper combination or by improving these factors so that more output results from using the same quantity. The factors of production may also be combined more effectively so that a larger output results from their use. The role of each of the factors of production in achieving real growth per capita will be considered first, then attention will be directed to the gains from a better combination of these factors. In the case of labor, growth can be achieved by using more labor so long as the amount of capital per unit of labor is not reduced in doing so. More labor may be used because a larger percentage of the population of active working age is engaged in gainful employment. This may be achieved by having fewer people idle either voluntarily or involuntarily because of unemployment, sickness, or accident. It may also be achieved by lengthening the number of years individuals work during their life span. More labor may also be used by working more hours per week. This has limited possibilities because in many fields, as hours of work increase much beyond the present work week, output per hour drops rapidly.

Growth is also fostered by improving the skills of the labor force. This is done through formal education during school years and on-the-job and off-the-job training after a person begins to work. To obtain maximum growth, it is necessary also to use the skills of all workers to the maximum. This requires the proper motivation to achieve the optimum output per worker. It also calls for proper job placement, including programs to promote labor mobility. It means no discrimination because of race, color, sex, or creed, which prevents using all available skills to the fullest.

Growth also requires an adequate and balanced supply of labor to meet the needs of the expanding economy. The need for various types of skilled labor must be projected, and a program must be developed to assure the training of the needed workers.

One of the major factors leading to growth is the use of more capital equipment since machines provide many times the power of human beings. Most significant is the use of better and better machines that turn out more and more goods in relation to the economic resources used to build and run the machines. This requires research and development to produce the machines and trained scientists and engineers to do such work.

The use of more and more machinery and equipment is possible only if sufficient capital is available for investment. This may necessitate programs to stimulate saving to make the capital available.

Significant, too, is the better utilization of natural resources. This may be done in such ways as getting more usable ore from a mine, finding ways to use low-grade ores, replacing scarce materials with those that are more plentiful, and using less material to do the same job. Growth requires an adequate source of raw materials to meet expanding needs. These needs are met through better exploration for materials, the conservation and replacement of present supplies where this is possible, and the development of substitute materials for those that are scarce.

Growth also requires an adequate supply of trained managerial talent. It is furthered by better management methods and by the more effective use of such methods by present and prospective managers. Management is responsible for combining the factors of production so as to achieve the greatest possible output. This is done when more and better capital is made available to labor trained to use this capital. Growth is achieved when labor and capital are used to the optimum. Mobility of labor and of capital help to achieve the optimum combination.

The optimum combination may be achieved when procedures are developed to reduce material handling, expedite the flow of goods in a plant, and the like. These factors are as important in the field of distribution as they are in production. Of equal importance are more efficient procedures for handling work in planning, engineering, accounting, and other white-collar fields.

Stability

To achieve the maximum practicable rate of growth, it is necessary to have stability. This does not mean a perfectly smooth rate of growth, but one that is not interrupted by recessions and depressions. In other words, the optimum in stability means the end of the business cycle as we have known it in the past. There would still be some changes in the rate of growth but no periods of cumulative contraction in economic activity.

Many feel that this is an impossibility since they believe that the business cycle is an integral part of the growth process in a free enterprise economy. This has been true in the past, and some fluctuations in the rate of growth no doubt will always occur in a free economy. But the cumulative nature of the cycle is based on the reactions of individuals and groups to real changes and is therefore subject to modification.

The nature of economic development has also lessened the impact of individual changes. Innovations such as the canal, the steamboat, the railroad, and the automobile had a very great effect on the overall economy in their day, but today so many areas exist in which industry and the consumer use machinery and equipment that an innovation is likely to affect a smaller part of the economy. Research has led to so many new things that their impact is more regular than in the past. Therefore, it may be possible to achieve a large measure of stability without hampering growth.

THE GOALS OF POLICY

The habit of assuming that we are all in agreement on the goals of policy or that the goals are obvious is at the root of much of the debate on the wisdom of particular proposals. Economists are in agreement that a policy that leads to the result of more goods and services for everyone is preferred to one that results in fewer goods and services for everyone. Even here we recognize a degree of arbitrariness since such policies may bring about a change in the relative welfare of the individuals of the society. Being the richest poor person may be preferable to being the poorest rich person.

The economist, as an economist, is rigorously limited to the value judgments implicit in the concept called "Pareto optimality," named for the great Italian sociologist-economist, Vilfredo Pareto. *Pareto optimum* exists when it is not possible to make anyone better off without someone else being made worse off. Consensus is readily achieved in those instances where a particular policy leads to this optimal position. These present no problem. But major problems, in particular the kind considered under the heading of stabilization and growth policy, cannot lay claim to this solution. Still, we can use this criterion to make choices among alternative policies, not in any precise sense, but in some acceptable or workable sense.

Evaluation of any policy involves the evaluation of all the effects of that policy. Most actions have elements which will be judged beneficial, but there will also be results that are undesirable. The question then becomes one of deciding, on the basis of the total impact, the relative merits and demerits associated with the proposal or program.

Economic policy always involves technical problems that the economist is trained to answer, and questions of value judgments that the economist is trained to discover, but not to answer. Suppose, for example, that economic analysis concludes that a particular tax reduction policy will reduce unemployment by one million workers, but that it will also result in a 5 percent increase in the price level. Would this policy be superior to the continuation of a constant level of unemployment and prices? A conscientious answer demands that one be aware of the costs of unemployment to the families of the unemployed as well as to the rest of society. Are there any benefits to society? Surely everyone will agree that the costs of unemployment far exceed the benefits. But it is also necessary to analyze the impact of inflation. What difference does it make if we have a 5 percent growth in the price level? Who is hurt? Who benefits? Do these cancel out? Are there ramifications of price level changes on production?

It is too simple to say that unemployment is bad and inflation is evil. We must sometimes choose between the two evils. This is too heavy a burden to put on economists. It must be left to the public at large. It is to be hoped that the economist will be helpful in educating the public to the nature of the choices it must make.

GOALS OF A GOVERNMENTAL PROGRAM FOR PROMOTING ECONOMIC GROWTH AND STABILITY

The pressure to attain economic stability in our economy is so strong that measures to promote stability have been established by law as a goal of national policy. At the end of World War II, after a debate of about a year, Congress passed the Employment Act of 1946, thereby recognizing the relationship of the government to fluctuations in the economy. In this act Congress declared that it was the continuing policy and responsibility of the federal government, with the assistance of industry, agriculture, labor, and state and local governments, to use all practicable means consistent with national policy and the free enterprise system to promote maximum employment, production, and purchasing power. The Employment Act provides that the President shall submit to Congress at the beginning of each regular session a report on the current levels of economic activity and the levels needed to carry out the full employment policy. The President is also to present information on current trends and on the present economic program of the federal government and its effects. In light of such data, a program is to be presented for carrying out the objectives of the full employment policy whenever indications are that they will not be achieved otherwise.

A Council of Economic Advisers, composed of three members, was set up to aid the President in developing such a report, and a Joint Congressional Committee on the Economic Report has been established to provide economic information and analysis for Congress, especially for the use of other committees. Since the passage of this bill, unemployment on the scale of that of the 1930s has not been a problem, though for brief periods in 1949, 1957–1958, 1960–1961, 1969–1970, and 1974–1976, it was of some concern. Most of the recommendations have dealt with methods of avoiding inflation since that has been the major problem in the postwar period. Up to the present time, however, neither the Council of Economic Advisers nor the Joint Committee on the Economic Report has instituted any plans for coordinating government activities affecting the economy.

Growth and stability are so closely related that the economic policy of the government should include both of them. It is desirable to develop goals to guide government policies in the economic sphere. This should be done democratically by a discussion of the basic issues carried on from the grass roots level to the halls of Congress. Business and labor can plan on a long-run basis much more effectively if they know what to expect from government. Consumers can make long-run decisions more effectively, such as buying a home or planning a savings program, if they know what to expect in the way of economic policies. The development of a set of goals for government economic policy would in itself help promote growth and stability.

In his 1955 Economic Report, President Eisenhower stated the goals of our national economic policy as follows: [1] "Our economic goal is an increasing national income, shared equitably among those who contribute to its growth, and achieved in dollars of stable buying power." Such a goal has several important elements. One is a rising trend of real income, a second is full employment, a third is stable prices, and a fourth is the equitable sharing of a growing national income among those who have contributed to producing it. Most Americans will readily agree with these goals in a general way. There is some difference of opinion, however, as to the exact meaning of each goal and the degree to which it is desirable to achieve it.

Problems in Promoting Economic Growth

Let us examine the goal of a rising trend of real income first. There is some question about the rate of growth that should be achieved. Some feel that an annual rate of growth of about 3 percent in gross national product is adequate because this is in line with the trend since the turn of the century and has produced our present high standard of living. Others feel that it is not only possible to grow at a rate of around 5 percent per year but also essential in the

---

[1] *Economic Report of the President,* transmitted to the Congress January 20, 1955. (Washington: U.S. Government Printing Office, 1955), p. 2.

present world situation. They argue that the growth of 5 percent per year that was achieved in several of the post-World War II years shows that such a goal is attainable. They also feel it is essential if we are to meet our world-wide military and economic commitments.

There is some disagreement about the possibility of achieving a rate of growth of 5 percent a year and at the same time achieving a stable price level. Some economists believe that such a rate of growth would make it all but impossible to keep prices stable because demand would probably be constantly at or somewhat in excess of current supply.

The biggest disagreement exists about the role of the government in stimulating a high rate of growth. Some feel that its role should be restricted to providing a favorable climate for growth and providing incentives through such steps as rapid amortization of new plant and equipment or other tax benefits. Others feel that government should increase its investment expenditures to a level needed to insure a high rate of growth. There is still considerable disagreement about government investment programs in many areas, such as public housing and federal funds for school construction.

At this point we might pause to ask the question that may come as a shock to some readers: Is growth, in fact, a desirable goal at all? Of course, we can't answer the question since it would be necessary to be able to answer other questions, such as whether the people of the United States in 1800 were happier or better off than those of today. We obviously don't know, though most of us might be willing to make a judgment.

In recent years there has been a sizable and respectable minority of economists who have proposed that along with zero population growth we should deliberately establish a policy of zero economic growth. These economists are concerned about the rate at which a growing economy uses up exhaustible and irreplaceable resources, such as fossil fuels. They also seem to feel that the quality of life deteriorates with economic growth as such concomitants as pollution and congestion occur.

Growth of per capita income requires capital expansion—improvements in the quality or in the quantity of capital goods, in the quality or quantity of "natural" resources, or in the quality of the contribution of the human factor. None of these can be achieved without cost. The nature of the cost is emphasized in the classical expression for saving, namely waiting or abstinence. In other words, we can have more goods and services in the future only if we give up goods and services in the present. This may not appear to be a very great sacrifice to an American student of the 1970s, but in many countries of the world a significant increase in saving could be accomplished only with a serious shortening of the average life span as current consumption declined.

The key question for a well-developed society as well as for the underdeveloped is: Who should make the decision as to what the rate of growth of the economy should be? Should this be a collective decision, or should each individual determine a personal rate of asset growth and thus, in the aggregate, determine the rate of growth of national income? Should industries engaged in growth-promoting activities be given special encouragement or subsidies, and should industries producing less urgent or even frivolous commodities be penalized in some way?

As a general proposition, most economists would argue in favor of allowing the free market system to determine the rate of growth. If interference with the freedom of the individual to make choices is to be abridged, some quite powerful arguments must be marshalled. Are there such arguments?

There would appear to be two major justifications for attempting to induce a rate of growth faster than might be natural without a specific growth policy. First is the requirement that growth be sufficient to absorb into meaningful employment the additions to the labor force out of a growing population and to reemploy those who would otherwise be replaced by capital. The other justification is the political one of growing at a rate fast enough to continuously maintain the nation's military and political strength relative to any potential enemy nations.

The most profound question in growth policy is what society's attitude toward population growth should be. Is a larger human population an absolute good? If not, is there a rate of population growth that is optimum? We know that serious problems arise if population grows at a faster rate than the rate of expansion of economic output. Many nations of the world, particularly in Asia and Africa, can attest to this side of the problem. On the other hand, the governments of many of our most mature economies have felt that the source of some of their most fundamental problems is that population has not grown at a fast enough rate. Probably the safest attitude for an economist to take on this subject is to accept the rate of population growth as given and to suggest policies that move in the direction of maximizing the per capita income of the actual population.

In the last paragraph we raised the question of optimum population. One approach is the following: An increase in population is desirable if, on the average, any new entrant to the society could be expected, over a lifetime, to contribute more to the society than the individual would take from the rest of the society. If the individual's contribution were accurately measured by lifetime income (equal to production; i.e., creation of value) and if the lifetime consumption (i.e., destruction of value) could accurately be measured, then proof that on balance an increase in population would be a positive contribution to the rest of the population could be inferred if people had positive wealth at the time of death over and above any inherited assets. This is so because an increase in wealth is, by definition, the difference between income and consumption. If the wealth of society were to decrease as population increased, this would be proof that the population was too large. Thus, the optimum population would be that population at which the expected wealth of society remained constant. For this approach to be useful we would have to include all of the nonmarket benefits and costs as well as those with market prices. Disagreements over the nonmarket aspects naturally are quite severe. Some people hate crowds; some love crowds. Some people love children; some don't. We often can't even agree on whether a particular development is a cost or a benefit, let alone measure it.

Full Employment

There is general agreement on the goals of full employment and stable price levels, but disagreement on the exact meaning of such goals. Full employment does not mean that no one is out of work in a free enterprise economy. The *demand* for labor shifts from field to field, and workers must shift jobs. People may be out of work for a time when they first enter the labor force or change jobs voluntarily. A committee of the American Economic Association has developed the following workable definition of full employment:

> Full employment means that qualified people who seek jobs at prevailing wage rates can find them in productive activities without considerable delay. It means full-time jobs for people who want to work full time. It does not mean that people like housewives and students are under pressure to take jobs when they do not want jobs, or that workers are under pressure to put in undesired overtime. It does not mean that unemployment is ever zero.[2]

The amount of unemployment that is consistent with this definition of full employment is not a constant. It depends on the rigidities to employment adjustments, on the costs of information to employers and employees, on expectations about future employment conditions, and in general on the attitudes of workers about the trade-offs between employment and its alternatives. In the United States, in recent years, the figures which are usually heard vary between about 3 percent and 5 percent as the target for aggregate economic policy.

Increases in aggregate demand lead to the expansion of the money value of national income, but this will be beneficial to the society only if the real output increases and unemployment is reduced. When unemployment is very large, we expect any growth in national income to be primarily in real output and very little in the price level. It depends a great deal, however, on the nature of those who are unemployed. If all of the unemployed were very mobile geographically and flexible in their occupational skills, inflation would not be likely to occur until employment was nearly 100 percent of the labor force. The other extreme is also conceivable. Even if the unemployed were a very large percentage of the labor force, if they were unable or unwilling to move to new locations or other occupations, expansion of aggregate demand might result only in inflation rather than in the diminution of unemployment.

Another important element in the employment versus the inflation problem is the degree of wage flexibility. If, for example, the legal minimum wage were set at a rate well above the marginal revenue product of a large percentage of the labor force, a considerable amount of inflation of product prices would have to take place before these workers could find employment. Any other institutional rigidities imposed on money wages, such as union contracts or industry custom, would have the same effect.

It would be extremely valuable to us to have knowledge of the true relationship between levels of unemployment and price inflation. We would like

---

[2] Committee of the American Economic Association, "The Problem of Economic Instability," *American Economic Review,* Vol. 40 (September, 1950), p. 506.

to be able to answer such questions as the amount of inflation that would be required to reduce unemployment by a given amount if the rate of unemployment were 8 percent, 6 percent, 3 percent, 2 percent, and so on. Figure 22-1 shows a graph of such a relationship estimated by Samuelson and Solow from 25 years of American data.[3] Such a curve is usually called a Phillips curve, after A. W. Phillips, who studied the inflation-unemployment relationship for the United Kingdom with such a chart.

The Samuelson-Solow estimate is that price stability in the United States could be achieved only at the cost of unemployment of about $5\frac{1}{2}$ percent. This is shown as point A. Point B can be interpreted as saying that a rate of unemployment of 3 percent would cost about $4\frac{1}{2}$ percent in annual inflation. Improvement would be defined as a shifting of the function to the left so that at

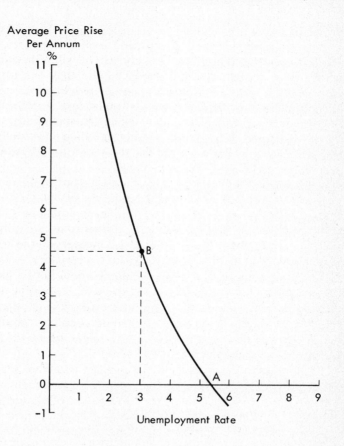

Figure 22-1

A Phillips Curve

[3] Paul A. Samuelson and R. M. Solow, "Analytical Aspects of Anti-Inflation Policy," *American Economic Review*, Vol. L (May, 1960), pp. 177–194.

any given level of unemployment, a lower rate of inflation would be experienced. Such gains can be achieved by increasing the mobility of labor through education and training, by improving information on employment sources, and by other methods instituted by labor, management, and government.

Stable Price Level

The goal of a stable price level does not mean a completely fixed price level. Individual prices, of course, will and should fluctuate in response to changes in supply and demand, both in the short run and in the long run. Not all are agreed on a goal of price stability, however. Some favor a gradually rising price level with prices moving up a maximum of 2 or 3 percent a year in boom years and remaining relatively stable in recession years. They feel that a gradually rising price level makes it easier to achieve full employment and an acceptable rate of growth, especially in an economy of strong labor unions, imperfect competition among large concerns, and administered prices.

We have just seen that there may be a conflict between the two desirable goals of relative price stability and full employment. There is also, at times, a conflict between stable prices and stable interest rates. This was particularly evident during the latter half of 1966 when the pressure on rising prices was held in check somewhat by monetary policy which allowed interest rates to rise significantly. At that time, interest rates could have been held steady at low rates, but the price for low rates would have been considerably more inflation of commodity prices and wages. The actual response of the monetary authority was a compromise: some inflation and some increase in interest rates.

During World War II and up to 1951 when aggregate demand was increasing more rapidly than the ability to produce, interest rates were kept at stable and low levels, and inflation was allowed to progress. In the early 1970s, while inflation was generally felt to be the most serious economic problem, market interest rates rose significantly. Had interest rates been held down, it is probable that inflation would have been even more severe than it actually was.

There is no final answer to the question of which route is superior. Inflation and high interest rates both are harmful to some people and helpful to other people. If real output is the same in the two cases, the choice between high prices and high interest rates is a matter of the distribution of income and wealth and the equity thereof.

Equitable Sharing of National Income

The last goal, an equitable sharing of a growing national income among those who helped to produce it, is open to more debate. Opinions differ widely on what is equitable and, of course, self-interest and group interest become involved. The extremes range from advocates of a return to more or less unregulated free enterprise, such as we had in the 1920s, to government programs of welfare economics to assure a "good life" for all groups. Most individuals are agreed that in developing a program to share the fruits of production equitably, the basic political freedoms must be preserved. This is also generally true of such economic freedoms as the choice of goods to be purchased, the field of labor to be entered, and the type of business to be established. Differences in this field are largely based on differing social and political views and are only, in a small part, based on differences in the analyses of the economic effects of various programs affecting the economy.

Almost any important economic policy has some effect on the distribution of income and wealth. Some attempt to determine this effect should be made even if it is true that as economists we cannot say that one distribution is better or worse than another. There are extreme cases where virtual unanimity would exist. Almost all economists agree that there are extreme distributions of income that are unacceptable both from the standpoint of equity and from the standpoint of the viability of the economic and political systems.

Choices of Governmental Policies

At various points in previous sections we have spoken of reasons for our economy behaving in an undesirable manner, creating unemployment, inflation, and many other problems. These are problems we do not expect to encounter in a world fitting our theoretical ideal of the purely competitive model. One approach then, it would seem, would be to have a series of government policies designed to make the real world economy more closely approximate the theoretical one.

No one seriously believes that a perfect correspondence is possible, but there are many who feel that a great deal can be accomplished in this direction. At a minimum, current policies by government which prevent the operation of the free price mechanism from making the necessary adjustments could be altered. Such programs as farm support prices, minimum wage laws, and many public utility regulations are grist for such criticism. Antitrust enforcement aimed at ensuring free entry into markets and flexible competitive price and wage behavior would be an important aspect of this type of structural policy.

It seems that almost invariably the arguments in favor of those government actions which distort the operations of the economic system are based on a criticism of the distribution of wealth or income in the system as it exists. Humane concern for the hardships suffered by the economically disadvantaged provide justification for giving up some of the benefits of a capitalistic economy. Thus it is that many economists who are defenders of free enterprise and yet sympathize with the plight of the underprivileged believe that government interference with the free operation of the system can be eliminated only if the income distribution problem can be solved first. To this end the negative income tax plan is usually proposed. This plan would guarantee a minimum income for everyone and, at the same time, make it advantageous to work at whatever an individual is capable of doing.

Positive programs and policies aimed at increasing the mobility of labor and other resources, increasing and improving the flow of information to households and other decision makers, and encouraging persons to take risks in forming new businesses and undertaking innovations would be important elements of structural strategy. Presumably this class of economic policies should be the continuing effort of government. To the degree to which they are effective, the macro-level policies will be less needed; and when aggregative programs are undertaken, they should be more successful in accomplishing their goals without undesirable side effects.

INCOMES POLICIES AND DIRECT CONTROLS

The category of policy actions referred to by the term *incomes policies and direct controls* are the antithesis of the structural policies discussed immediately above. They are advocated by those who are skeptical about the real world ever being represented realistically by the theorists' model. Or they are favored by those who are impatient with the slow working of the system itself. They are particularly attractive to noneconomists who can see the particular problem, such as inflation, but are unable to see the problems associated with direct controls on wages and prices.

After all, as these people view things, if rising prices cause hardship, why not pass a law making price increases illegal? If interest rates are "too high," pass a law saying they must be lower. In unemployment is high, have the government employ the people or pay business to employ them.

Incomes policies range from voluntary compliance and wage-price guideposts to the complete freeze on wages and prices imposed in 1971 by President Nixon. Are such programs effective in preventing inflation? The answer is that they are never completely successful if strong pressures for price increases continue to exist. There seem to be an infinite number of ways for those who wish to avoid compliance to do so. Starkly illegal black markets spring up, and many other questionable practices develop. Where discounts might have been granted to purchasers before, full list price is charged. Where certain services were rendered without charge, a fee is imposed. The quality of products, and even the quantity of the unit product, will be reduced. Tie-in sales will be demanded. Anyone who has observed periods of price controls could enumerate a long list of such subterfuges to push up the effective price while ostensibly keeping the official price unchanged. If the enforcement agents are large enough in numbers and have sufficient legal backing, many of these practices can be curtailed. But if workers are diverted to management of the controls, the output of desirable goods and services will be reduced, which in itself would inject more inflationary pressure.

There may be some beneficial results from overall price controls. Under some circumstances inflation will be fed by inflationary expectations, in which case the dramatic announcement of a control program might lead people to revise their beliefs about the inevitability of increasing prices. Of course, the opposite result is at least conceivable, in which the imposition of controls would be viewed as an admission that the administration is unable to control price level behavior through conventional tools, thus generating more firm convictions that price increases are in store. A second possible positive result of direct controls would be the achievement of a breathing spell wherein the pressures to supply the banking system with additional reserves would be relaxed and thus permit a slowing down of the growth of the money stock.

Suppose, for the moment, that controls are completely effective in preventing price and wage increases. Would our problems be solved? For a short period of time, they might seem to be; but as changes take place in the underlying conditions of supply and demand, new difficulties arise. When prices are allowed to vary, and the demand for a particular commodity increases, the price rises and encourages additional output to satisfy the new demand. If the price is not permitted to rise, the added output will not be forthcoming and so shortages appear, and resources will continue to be used to produce goods which are desired less. The other side of the problem occurs when conditions of supply change. Suppose, for example, that petroleum reserves are found to be reduced, or are more costly to recover. In a free market system the price of petroleum products would rise and their use would be curtailed by limiting consumption to more urgent needs, saving the resources for future needs. If the price is not allowed to rise, these resources will be used excessively or producers will cut back production and again "shortages" will be evident.

In the price control environment there will be fewer goods of many kinds than people wish to buy at the control price. Then the question arises as to how the limited quantities should be allocated among the prospective buyers. It can be accomplished extra-legally by any number of forms of favoritism—to the strong, to the attractive, to "good customers," to someone who has favors to grant to the seller, to whoever comes first, etc. The government can decree who gets priorities, or can outlaw certain uses, or can allocate by means of ration coupons, in which case people with little desire for the product can get as much as those with a strong desire for it.

It is certainly relevant to ask whether the evils of inflation are more or less serious than the evils of the attempts at direct price control. A responsible answer requires knowledge of the consequences of both events. This becomes even more urgent in the present time period when more knowledgeable observers are talking about inflation as a chronic ill of the modern economy.

MONETARY AND FISCAL POLICY

The main burden of aggregate economic policy must fall on either monetary policy or on fiscal policy or a combination thereof. In the next chapter we will review the theory and the nature of the tools, and the techniques available in the two classes of policy actions. Here we wish to take up the controversy described as the monetarist-fiscalist debate.

The polar positions, which very few economists would admit holding, are, on the monetarist side, that only the money stock matters in determining the behavior of the national income and that fiscal policy is impotent; on the fiscalists (or post-Keynesian) side, exactly the reverse statements would be true. The debate has been productive. Fiscalists have been forced to study and to concede that money does matter, and that the impact of fiscal policy is greatest when it is accompanied by alterations in the stock of money. On their side, the monetarists have been forced to study and to concede that the method by which the money stock changes is of some significance in evaluating the effect on the economy. For example, money created as a result of a budgetary deficit may have a greater impact than money created through open market operations.

The post-Keynesian interpretation of the impact of money on the economy is that when the money stock is increased by the action of the monetary authority, the public will readjust its portfolio holdings of money and bonds. In the process, the interest rate will fall as the price of bonds rises. Then, to the extent that spending on capital goods is sensitive to interest cost conditions, aggregate spending will increase. The monetarist views money stock changes as being more pervasive than this, arguing that if the money stock increases, *all* of the assets in the public's portfolio will have to adjust to reach a new optimum, and so all forms of spending will increase, not just interest-sensitive categories.

Fiscalists consider government expenditure to be a powerful force on national income because it is a direct contributor to aggregate demand, and taxes are important because they influence consumer spending via changes in disposable income. The monetarist denegration of fiscal policy is based on the belief that if a deficit is financed by borrowing, without resort to a monetary expansion, interest rates would rise and resources would be diverted from private use. Thus, the increase in aggregate demand by government would be offset, at least in some degree, by a reduction in private demand.

The difference between the monetarist and the fiscalist is often expressed as a difference in opinion about the slopes of the I-S and the L-M functions. Thus, if the L-M function is very flat (infinitely or very elastic with respect to interest rates), then the fiscalist case holds; whereas if the L-M function is perpendicular (infinitely or very inelastic with respect to interest rates), the monetarist case is powerful. On the other hand, given an intermediate L-M curve, the more elastic the I-S curve, the stronger the monetarist case is; the steeper the I-S curve, the stronger is the fiscalist case. By the criterion of this paragraph the dispute would be settled by empirical estimates of elasticities of the relevant relationships. Notice that the framework of this discussion has been the Keynesian one, and thus the one favored by the fiscalists.

Monetarists are more likely to utilize some version of the quantity theory to appraise the relative merits of monetary versus fiscal policy. The issue then turns on the stability of cash balance demand or velocity. The monetarist case is strongest when velocity is unaffected by changes in the money stock, and the monetarist argument would collapse if V varied perfectly inversely with changes in the amount of money in existence. The fiscalist case would be verified if velocity varied directly with government expenditures and inversely with taxes.

Two monetarists, Milton Friedman and David Meiselman, conducted a study to determine whether the Keynesian multiplier or the velocity variable of the quantity theory would serve better as a forecaster of the movements of national income.[4] They did this by testing the stability of the two variables,

---

[4] Milton Friedman and David Meiselman, "The Relative Stability of Monetary Velocity and the Investment Multiplier in the United States, 1897–1958" in *Stabilization Policies, A Series of Research Studies Prepared for the Committee on Money and Credit* (Englewood Cliffs, N.J.: Prentice-Hall, Inc., 1964).

reasoning that if the velocity of money is relatively stable, changes in the money stock would result in predictable changes in national income and would support the monetarist view. If the investment (or government expenditure) multiplier was more stable, it would indicate that a change in aggregate demand imposed by fiscal policy would result in a more predictable change in national income. The results were clearly in favor of monetary policy and the quantity theory, but the debate was not ended. Economists at the Federal Reserve Bank of St. Louis tested more directly the predictive power of changes in money versus changes in fiscal policy. Again, the evidence was in favor of monetary policy, but the debate was not ended. Post-Keynesians have not accepted these findings entirely, partly because they are critical of the methodology used, partly because of their strong attachment to the logic of their own position, and partly because of the considerable success they have had in forecasting using econometric models built along Keynesian lines.

Where does all of this leave the reader? Hopefully, with an open mind. We don't have all of the answers in economics. We still have to be very cautious in our policy prescriptions. There is a good deal of talk about "fine tuning" the economy with just "the right mix" of monetary and fiscal policy. It is, perhaps, a bit premature at this stage in our scientific development to take such talk very seriously.

QUESTIONS

1. What do you conceive to be the role of the economist in determining national economic goals and policies?
2. Compare the real costs in achieving economic growth of a relatively affluent society, such as the United States, with the costs to a society in which the majority of the population is at or near a subsistence level of income.
3. Explain how you would go about deciding for yourself what your "trade-off" rate would be regarding the conflict between increased employment and inflation. Relate your discussion to the Phillips curve on page 441.
4. If policy makers must choose between inflation and higher interest rates, what would be the nature of the considerations that should be made?
5. Discuss the following policy issues with reference to Pareto optimality.
   (a) Tariff reductions.
   (b) Highway construction during periods of full employment.
   (c) Highway construction during periods of serious unemployment.
6. How do you react to the observation that the hurt caused some people by inflation is perfectly offset by benefits derived by others?
7. Explain the most important methods of promoting economic growth.
8. Can you construct a definition of optimum population or optimum growth of population? What would be the important elements in evolving such a definition?
9. This chapter and the following chapter stress policies of aggregate demand expansion to reduce unemployment. What other approach seems promising?
10. Many government policies to promote economic growth and stability have an impact on the distribution of wealth and income. Can you formulate criteria by which you can determine that one distribution is better than another? Is it possible to argue that change in the distribution is either good or bad?
11. Describe the purpose and basic provisions of the Employment Act of 1946.

SUGGESTED READINGS

Andersen, Leonall C. "The State of the Monetarist Debate" with "Commentary" by Lawrence R. Klein and Karl Brunner. *Review,* Federal Reserve Bank of St. Louis (September, 1973).

———— and Jerry L. Jordan. "Monetary and Fiscal Actions: A Test of Their Relative Importance in Economic Stabilization." *Review,* Federal Reserve Bank of St. Louis (November, 1968).

Culbertson, J. M. *Full Employment or Stagnation?* New York: McGraw-Hill Book Co. Inc., 1964.

The Economic Report of the President. Washington: U.S. Government Printing Office, annually.

Knorr, Klaus, and William J. Baumol (eds.). *What Price Economic Growth?* Englewood Cliffs, N.J.: Prentice-Hall, Inc., 1961.

Novack, David E., and Robert Lekachman (eds.). *Development and Society: The Dynamics of Economic Change.* New York: St. Martin's Press Inc., 1964.

Phelps, Edmund S. *Inflation, Policy and Unemployment Theory.* New York: W. W. Norton & Co., Inc., 1972.

Samuels, Warren J. *The Classical Theory of Economic Policy.* Cleveland, Ohio: The World Publishing Co., 1966.

Turner, R. C. "Problems of Forecasting for Economic Stabilization," *American Economic Review,* Vol. 45 (March, 1955).

CHAPTER 23

MONETARY AND FISCAL POLICIES FOR ECONOMIC GROWTH AND STABILITY

This chapter is devoted to an analysis of monetary and fiscal policies that are designed to promote economic growth and stability. Present programs and policies will be analyzed, and proposals for revisions or for new policies will be considered.

The question arises as to whether a clear-cut distinction can be made between policies which are to be termed "monetary" and those which are to be called "fiscal." The truth is that considerable ambiguity about these terms exists, and this ambiguity often leads to useless debate and confusion. No difficulty would arise if policies were purely monetary (those which have their impact directly on the quantity or cost of money) or purely fiscal (government spending and taxing programs). But any federal budget has some implications for the money supply. A budgetary deficit requires a decision about its financing, and this will have an impact on the supply or cost of money. A surplus requires a decision about its disposition—again, this will influence the supply or cost of money.

The point is not that we need rigorous definitions of monetary versus fiscal, but that we should recognize the interrelations between the policies called by those names. We should also be aware that many users of these words use them differently.

An approach that is often used is to declare arbitrarily that actions by the central bank (the Federal Reserve System) are monetary policies, and actions by the Treasury are fiscal actions. This works fairly well for the United States, but it is hardly useful in those countries where the treasury and the central bank are under the control of the same officers.

Our organization of the discussion will be based on the proposition that Federal Reserve policy is mainly monetary and Treasury policy mainly fiscal. We, of course, will try to keep the interrelationships in proper perspective.

THE NATURE OF MONETARY POLICIES

The nature of our monetary system and the tools of monetary policy were described briefly in Chapter 9. The theoretical framework was discussed in Part 2. It should be clear that any policy proposal must be based on some theory. There is no alternative. The hope is that the theory we choose is the most accurate picture available of the economy the policy will affect.

The money supply theory presented in Chapter 9 concerned the relationship between the variables which can be directly determined by the monetary authority, the monetary base (B), which is mainly member bank reserves and currency, and the money supply (M). We used the expression $M = KB$, where K is the relationship called the money multiplier. Recall that K involved the behavior of the public and the commercial banks. It also incorporated the significance of reserve requirements that are controlled by the Federal Reserve Board of Governors.

Once we have a theory which explains how the money supply is affected by monetary policy, we then need a theory which explains how changes in the money supply influence the economy. We considered two basic approaches to this problem. The classical quantity theory approach concludes that changes in the money supply directly influence the level of absolute prices and, when unemployment exists, directly affect the level of real national income. The Keynesian approach concludes that the direct effect of changes in the money supply is on interest rates, which, in turn, affect the rate of investment and thereby, through the multiplier process, affect national income.

We should emphasize that the analytical apparatus used — classical or Keynesian — is not the source of differences of opinion on the effectiveness of monetary policy. Rather, conclusions differ primarily because of differences in judgment about what the real world is like — the degree of flexibility of wages and prices, the degree to which interest rate changes influence the level of investment or saving, the degree to which money supply changes will change interest rates, and so on.

FEDERAL RESERVE POLICY

Robert V. Roosa divides the responsibilities of the Federal Reserve System into what he calls the defensive and the dynamic responsibilities.[1] Defensive actions are taken by the Federal Reserve System in response to changes in the reserve position of commercial banks caused by others. Defensive actions simply offset such reserve status changes. Dynamic policy aims at either increasing or decreasing the ability of commercial banks to expand the money supply and credit.

The major factors, not involving Federal Reserve action, affecting member bank reserves are gold flows and foreign transactions, currency in circulation, Treasury balances in the Federal Reserve Banks, and the float. In addition to these, the volume of required reserves changes as deposits shift among banks with different reserve requirements, between member and nonmember banks, and between time deposits and demand deposits.

If all of these factors were to behave in such a way that the excess reserves in the banking system were to increase by, say, $2 billion, the Federal Open-Market Committee in its defensive posture would sell $2 billion worth of securities. Selling less than that amount would amount to a dynamic action of

---

[1] Robert V. Roosa, *Federal Reserve Operations in the Money and Government Securities Markets* (New York: Federal Reserve Bank of New York, 1956).

promoting monetary ease and expansion. Selling more than $2 billion worth of securities would be a dynamic action of curtailing the ability of banks to expand or forcing them to contract money and credit.

In an economy where money was left to manage itself, serious instability would be generated by virtue of these changes in the reserve position of commercial banks. Indeed, in Chapter 6 we looked at the purely monetary theory of the business cycle where the basic cause of the cycle was the flow of reserves into and out of the banks in the form of currency movements and gold flows. Much of the instability experienced in this country during the time of the independent treasury system, from 1846 until the Federal Reserve System took over the fiscal agency function, was due to the flow of funds between the Treasury and commercial banks as the Treasury collected taxes in cash and paid for its expenditures.

Very little controversy surrounds the defensive actions of the Federal Reserve System. A serious snowstorm that would slow the mails and increase the amount of the float shouldn't be allowed to disrupt the money market and the economy. Similarly, just because the public uses more currency in the month or two before Christmas is not justification for a large contraction of the money supply.

The important question at any time is whether it is appropriate to increase or to decrease the money supply to counter the cyclical movement of the economy or to promote growth in real output. If something should be done, there are the further questions of how much and what particular policies should be used.

USING THE INSTRUMENTS OF MONETARY POLICY

The Federal Reserve System uses the various instruments of monetary policy at its disposal to help smooth out seasonal and cyclical fluctuations in economic activity and to meet the needs of the economy for growth. Seasonal variations in the reserves of member banks are principally offset by open-market operations. Some banks may offset seasonal pressures by borrowing from their Federal Reserve Banks, but this happens primarily when pressures on a bank or a group of banks are due to special or unusual seasonal fluctuations.

The provision of bank reserves to meet the needs of a growing economy is partly through open-market operations, partly through changing reserve requirements, and partly through lending to member banks. Reserve requirements are frequently lowered during a period of recession when long-run growth indicates the need for additional reserves. This is done to help provide the stimulus for expansion. Reserve requirements also may be changed when large international movements of gold need to be offset to keep reserves in line with the demands of the economy.

The role of the Federal Reserve in helping stabilize cyclical fluctuations is carried on primarily through the use of open-market operations and by altering the ability or the willingness of commercial bank borrowing through the discount window. When economic activity is expanding rapidly and inflationary pressures develop, restraint on monetary expansion is called for to promote stability. The Federal Reserve under such circumstances resorts to open-market operations to provide banks with a smaller amount of reserves than needed to meet all demands for credit. The first reaction is for individual banks that are short of reserves to sell government bonds to obtain funds. Such sales provide funds for the individual bank, but do not increase the supply of reserves since other banks lose them as checks are drawn against deposits to pay for the bonds.

As the monetary authorities continue the policy of restraint, more and more banks become short of reserves. This leads an increasing number of banks to borrow from their Federal Reserve Banks to meet shortages in required reserves. As loans are retired and not renewed and funds are used to repay the loans from the Federal Reserve Banks, other banks experience a shortage of reserves. Thus, an increase in borrowing from the Federal Reserve Banks is a normal reaction to a restrictive monetary policy. This borrowing provides an offset to the reduction in reserves brought about by open-market sales, but it does not nullify the effects of monetary restraint. The borrowing will be offset by open-market operations to keep total reserves at the level desired by Reserve authorities.

The cost of borrowing or the discount rate will also be raised to help discourage borrowing. Furthermore, banks in debt to their Reserve Bank use any reserves that they acquire to repay their loans and thus restrict credit expansion. Their lending policies also become more stringent since they are under pressure to repay their indebtedness. Actions of one bank to free itself of indebtedness to the Federal Reserve, however, cannot correct a reserve shortage situation, because the reserves one bank gains are lost by others. As long as the Federal Reserve maintains pressure on bank reserve positions, member banks will remain conservative and even become cautious in their lending policies.

This process is just reversed when economic conditions call for a policy of monetary ease. Reserves are supplied through open-market operations and at times through lowering reserve requirements when long-run expansion requires a larger volume of reserves. The first action of member banks is to reduce their debt to the Federal Reserve Banks. When this phase has come to an end, excess reserves become available for bank loans and investments.

EFFECT OF MONETARY POLICY ON THE ECONOMY

When bank reserve positions are under pressure, banks sell government securities and so reduce their supply of secondary reserves. As their reserves are reduced and they are forced to borrow from their Reserve Bank, they become more conservative in their lending policies. The loan requests of marginal borrowers are refused or are reduced in amount. This forces business firms to spend less to increase inventory or plant and equipment. Banks are less willing to make loans on residential real estate and to consumers for purchasing durable goods. Banks are also less willing to lend to other financial institutions, such as sales finance companies, consumer finance companies, and mortgage loan companies. The lessened availability of credit puts a brake on increased spending.

This is reinforced by the increase in interest rates that results when the supply of loanable funds is restricted while demand continues to increase.

The actions of banks also affect other credit markets. As banks try to increase reserves, they sell securities. This takes funds from the money markets at the very time when demand for funds is high. This also helps raise interest rates. Rising interest rates make borrowing less attractive, and marginal projects are canceled or at least postponed.

In periods of credit ease, the effect is largely the reverse. Banks have an adequate supply of funds and are willing to make funds available to other financial institutions. Lower interest rates also encourage investment and raise the price of existing securities, and in this way make the sale of securities more advantageous.

When the new money comes into existence the public will have more money than it had before so adjustment to a new equilibrium position with respect to cash balances is necessary. As we have seen, this adjustment involves the attempts by money holders to shift into other things, securities or real goods. Through this process the prices of goods will rise and interest rates will fall unless unemployment is serious, in which case output will increase instead of the prices of securities, goods, and services.

Reduction of the money supply would be expected to have the opposite effect of money expansion, although there is the general belief that prices are less flexible downward. If this is true, the impact will be more heavily on output and employment rather than on prices.

Monetary policy has an indirect effect through its effect on the expectations of consumers and business people. If consumers feel prices are likely to rise, they will speed up purchases of durables; if they expect prices to decline, they will defer them. Business people react in a similar fashion to expectations of price changes, to difficulties in financing expansion projects, and to other changes in the economic outlook.

SELECTIVE VERSUS GENERAL MONETARY CONTROLS

The discussion of monetary policies up to this point has been in terms of general controls over the amount of credit available. Selective controls of various types also have been used from time to time, and several of them are still in use. One selective credit control at present in the hands of the Federal Reserve is that over stock market credit. By changing margin requirements on stock purchases, the Federal Reserve is able to influence directly the amount of credit used in the stock market. This is a highly volatile type of credit affected by speculative activity in the market. Selective controls in this area moderate the degree of general credit action that is necessary to offset speculation and the use of credit in the stock market.

The Federal Reserve, together with the Federal Deposit Insurance Corporation, determines the maximum interest rates payable on savings or time deposits through regulation Q. Whenever this rate is less than it would be if it were free to rise, there is a flow of funds out of time deposits and demand deposits would be expected to grow. This increases the money stock but decreases bank credit. That is, bank earning assets are less. This hits the home mortgage market particularly hard.

The Federal Reserve had power to control consumer credit during World War II, and again briefly in the postwar period, and for a time also had control over real estate credit; but these powers have not been renewed. Selective credit controls of a limited type are in operation, however, in other credit markets. When the Housing and Home Finance Agency makes it easier to buy houses on credit because it wants to encourage building or more difficult because it wants to discourage building, it is engaging in selective credit controls. This has also been done, to some degree, when the Small Business Administration has made it easier to obtain loans in a period of recession than in a boom period.

There is a basic difference of opinion about the role of selective credit controls as a permanent instrument for influencing economic growth and restraining inflationary pressures. Those who argue against selective credit controls do so largely on the basis of the efficiency of the market mechanism. They believe that competitive markets can best determine interest rates and the allocation of resources to various lenders. Any government interference can at best produce results that are less desirable in the long run than those established in the market.

Another argument against selective controls arises out of the administration of such controls. They are difficult to enforce in many cases, especially in the field of consumer credit. This is, in part, due to the large number of merchants and dealers involved in selling consumer durables on credit and to the difficulty of establishing true prices and down payments due to the widespread practice of giving inflated allowances for trade-ins as a means of cutting list prices.

One of the major arguments against selective credit controls is that they are not effective. Margin requirements in the stock market do not appear to have any significant influence on stock prices, the volume of stock trading, or even on the amount of credit used in the stock market. To the degree, if any, that selective controls are effective in the segment of the economy in which they are imposed, they only shift the inflationary problem rather than solve it. The funds made idle in one segment of the economy are transferred to other segments, and price pressure develops there.

The proponents of such controls argue that any monetary policy involves discrimination and that there is no real choice between general monetary controls and selective monetary controls from a free economy point of view. They feel that selective controls can prevent maladjustments that lead to instability more easily than general controls. For example, if housing is in a boom while unemployment exists in other areas, these advocates feel that control of housing credit can prevent undue expansion and later collapse; whereas general credit controls are powerless unless the whole economy is to be restrained at a time when such a policy is not required.

There has also been some advocacy of selective controls as a means of stimulating or retarding long-run growth in a sector of the economy so as to establish balanced patterns of growth. Under such a proposal, consumer credit could be used to increase or decrease automobile demand, for example, if it were out of line with what seemed to the regulatory authorities to be balanced growth with the rest of the economy. Such a use of selective controls would, of course, intensify the argument over control by regulation or by market forces.

ANALYSIS AND EVALUATION OF MONETARY POLICY

There is considerable disagreement about the efficiency of monetary policy in helping to promote full employment and a stable price level. Since economic forces are extremely complex and are based on many interrelated factors, it is difficult, if not impossible, to determine the real effect of any policy in isolation. Therefore, we cannot determine exactly what would have happened if monetary policies of a different type had been followed or if the timing of changes in monetary policy had been different.

Favorable Effects of Monetary Policy

Several advantages are claimed for monetary controls over other policies for stability. One important advantage is that monetary controls are impersonal; the monetary authorities determine the total volume of bank reserves, and banks ration the available credit. Such controls do directly affect various groups, however. Since monetary controls affect the volume of and interest rates on bank loans and investments, bank profits are directly affected. Changes in interest rates also redistribute income between those who pay interest and those who receive it. Many individuals and organizations, of course, are in a position to determine in which group they will be; whether lender or borrower. This is, however, not universally true nor is it true at all times even for those for whom it is generally true.

Monetary policy can be very flexible. A powerful and immediate impact need not be instituted. This is particularly true of open-market operations where the impact can be spread out in any desired amounts without any change in laws or announcements. Indeed, very few are likely to even know what is going on. Reversal of the direction of policy can very easily be accomplished if it is discovered that the initial action was in error.

It takes some time for monetary policy to influence the economy, but the time lag is probably shorter than for most other policy actions, particularly those requiring action by Congress and the executive branch of government.

Many economists believe that monetary policy is more effective in combating inflation than it is in stimulating recovery from depressed conditions. The statement defending this opinion is that during inflationary periods the banks usually have negligible amounts of excess reserves and, therefore, they will be forced to contract earning assets and demand deposits following any contractionary actions by the Federal Reserve. On the other hand, during depressions, since banks usually hold significant amounts of excess reserves, any expansionary Federal Reserve policy will simply permit but not force the banks to expand.

In addition, as was pointed out in our earlier discussion, Keynesians feel that the liquidity preference function is so elastic that any increase in the money supply during depressed periods will have virtually no effect on interest rates. Since the Keynesian analysis makes interest rates important only to the extent that they influence investment demand, if interest rates are not lowered significantly, the impact on investment and national income will be negligible. The other string to the Keynesian bow is the judgment that at the low interest rates which prevail during depressions, investment demand is not responsive to further rate reductions.

Since the people responsible for monetary policy seem to have accepted this line of argument, they have had little faith in the power of their tools to bring the economy out of depressions. Consequently, expansionary monetary policy has been somewhat halfhearted during such periods. At least, so argue the defenders of monetary policy.

The negative side of the argument is countered point by point by those who do believe in the effectiveness of monetary policy. First, on the question as to whether banks with large excess reserves will increase earning assets and hence the money supply, these economists contend that under the prevailing economic and banking conditions, equilibrium for banks requires a large volume of excess reserves, but if they are provided with additional amounts, they will seek profitable outlets for them. In particular, when large volumes of risk-free government securities can be purchased and if the monetary authorities act aggressively to promote expansion, it is felt that banks will not continuously allow nonearning cash to build up.

Rebuttal to the interest rate and investment argument is that Keynesians have excessively stressed interest as a cost to investors. They have neglected to observe that at low interest rates, even a minute reduction in the rate has a very large impact on capital values, and for that reason an increase in the money supply would be very expansionary even if the interest rate effect were small. Ultimately, of course, the answers to these questions are not to be found in a priori speculation but must be found from empirical tests. Perhaps we have never adequately tested the power of monetary policy in bringing about expansion from a serious depression.

Unfavorable Effects of Monetary Policy

Major criticism of monetary policy lies in the area of timing. The tendency is not to act until it is clear that action is needed. This means that action is usually too late to do the most good. For example, in the beginning of a recovery period, there is a hesitancy to restrict credit for fear of reversing the recovery. When action is taken, inflationary pressures are already built up.

Another criticism of monetary policy is that it tends to slow down the rate of growth. In a period of tight money, financing of new projects is more difficult than is the case in a period of monetary ease. New businesses based on new ideas and growing small businesses find it harder to get funds. The forced saving arising in the early stages of a cycle may lead to short-run inequities, but it promotes growth by increasing investment faster than voluntary savings.

The argument is frequently made that the high interest rates resulting from monetary restraint slow down investment. This of course is true, and this is what they are designed to do. Price stability can only exist when investment takes place from voluntary saving, not from forced saving. In the long run, lower interest rates will stimulate investment if they arise because the supply of funds for investment has been increased through saving. When interest rates are kept abnormally low, prices will rise and offset much of the real effect on investment.

Monetary policy is also criticized at times because it works a hardship on various groups in society. In a period of monetary ease, it reduces the income of those trying to live on the income from bond investments. It also increases the cost of insurance and pensions. Problems are created for financial institutions since their income from interest is cut. In a period of monetary restraint, other problems arise. The cost of financing a home increases, and the burden falls primarily on young people buying their first home. Small business finds it harder to get funds and therefore feels it is being put at a disadvantage. Financing costs of state and local governments and private institutions, such as hospitals, go up. Those who have to finance at the period of greatest monetary pressure are hardest hit. Such policy is, of course, designed to postpone projects, but some plans cannot be postponed without serious consequences.

PROPOSALS FOR CHANGES IN MONETARY INSTRUMENTS OF CONTROL

Various proposals have been made for changing the monetary instruments used for control of the economy. Some would make relatively minor changes, others more drastic changes. Several such proposals will be considered briefly.

Discretionary Monetary Control

First, consider the major current Federal Reserve tools. Open-market operations, per se, are almost never criticized. They can be as powerful as needed; they are flexible, they are impersonal, there are no "announcement effects," and the impact is quite predictable. Indeed, a number of monetary economists contend that open-market operation is so ideal a tool that the other methods are not needed and, in fact, are harmful. Changing reserve requirements, it is said, are too upsetting to the banking system; their impact is less predictable, they are not flexible, and the announcement effects are dramatic and uncertain. Changing the discount rate is judged to be a weaker tool. With the development and growth of the federal funds market and other financial instruments, there is no longer any need for the discount facilities of the Federal Reserve Banks. Bank borrowing or repayments of loans to the Federal Reserve can offset the effects of open-market operations. Thus, if open-market action takes away reserves, the member banks can get them back by borrowing, frustrating the intent of the policy. Defenders of the discount mechanism point out that that is the virtue of the tool; it allows for an escape valve and an orderly adjustment to a new reserve situation. Even those who advocate keeping the discount mechanism usually feel that it should be more closely attuned to market interest rates, rather than lagging seriously behind them as has been the practice.

Automatic Monetary Control

A fairly drastic proposal calls for an end to discretionary monetary policy. Several reasons are offered for this change. First, it is felt that the Federal Reserve's record in preventing the extremes of business cycle swings has been worse than what would have happened in the absence of any action. Second, and as a partial explanation of the first statement, the lags in monetary policy are believed to be so long that by the time the action takes effect, the economy may already have reversed direction and would need the opposite prescription. Advocates of automatic monetary policy further argue that discretionary monetary policy depends upon a degree of accuracy in forecasting which is beyond our present capabilities.

The proposal itself involves the rule that the money supply should be allowed to grow at approximately the same rate as the long-run rate of growth in productivity. The reason for choosing this rate of growth, of course, is to maintain relatively constant prices over the long term, though it is said that the particular growth rate chosen is not of critical importance to the proposal.

The basic reasoning behind the plan is that a constant rate of growth in the money supply will act as an automatic stabilizer. During an expansionary period when aggregate demand is increasing at a more rapid rate than is aggregate output, interest rates would rise, discouraging investment demand and, to some extent, consumption. It is felt that depressions could not become very severe or last very long if the money supply were to increase continuously, and that aggregate demand would have to turn up when the money stock becomes large enough. In the depression, the interest rate would fall to promote increased investment and consumption demand.

Some proponents of this type of plan advocate Congressional establishment of the required rate of monetary growth, making elected officials responsible for the policy. Others would advise the Board of Governors of the Federal Reserve System to establish the rate as a guide to policy, leaving some flexibility for unusual circumstances. Having such a clear-cut rule of policy would eliminate one important source of uncertainty in the economy. Whereas discretionary policy requires planners to forecast what the monetary authorities will do, a rule requires planners to forecast only the more fundamental variables of the economy.

There are, of course, objections raised to this proposal. Advocates of flexible monetary policy feel it is needed to adapt to different growth conditions and changes in the world economic scene. They also argue that discretionary monetary policy has functioned well when given a chance to work. They feel that a fixed growth rate subject to change by Congress would become a political "football." It would not achieve the advantages claimed for it, but would create new uncertainty in trying to figure out what Congress would do.

The implication that stable growth in the money supply would lead to a more even rate of growth is also open to question. As was seen in Part 2 on causal factors in the cycle, real changes take place in supply and demand, and these lead to changes in economic activity. The cycle would be different if the money supply were set at a fixed rate of growth, but it would not be eliminated.

FISCAL POLICY AND OTHER PROGRAMS FOR ECONOMIC GROWTH AND STABILITY

In this section attention will be directed to fiscal and other governmental programs designed to promote economic growth and stability. These include measures designed to help stabilize disposable income, to influence the propensity to consume out of a given level of income, and to influence the level of investment of all types. This may be done indirectly by means of fiscal policy or by more direct controls, such as price and wage controls. Government policies can also be used to stabilize the level of economic activity arising out of international transactions.

Automatic Stabilizers

The workings of a free, frictionless economic system are characterized by a multitude of automatically stabilizing forces. When unemployment occurs, wages fall to restore full employment. Excesses or deficiencies of aggregate demand are self-correcting by rising or falling price levels. Imbalances in international transactions are automatically adjusted by international reserve flows or exchange rate fluctuations. Such equilibrating mechanisms are at the core of most of the great body of economic theory. If these adjustment variables are fully operative, the need for economic policy by government is lessened considerably.

However, to the extent that rigidities in prices, wages, interest rates, and so on exist, and to the extent that factors of production are not completely mobile, the automatic stabilizers of the economy fail to produce the precise results of competitive theory. One view of the role of government in the economy is to break down the frictions that arise and restore, as much as possible, the self-adjusting economy. Others are pessimistic about the ability of government to bring about this result and call for more direct action to cure the resulting evils.

Still another approach is to design the federal government receipts and outlays in such a way as to provide automatic stabilizers for the economy. To accomplish this function, receipts must fall and outlays rise when the economy is moving downward; and receipts must rise and outlays fall when the economy is expanding. We demand somewhat more than this of our fiscal policy since our goal is not simply stability, but stability at a high (near full employment) level of activity.

Our "pay-as-you-go" progressive income tax structure provides us with our most important automatic stabilizer in the sense that as income increases, the withdrawal of purchasing power from the private sector gets progressively greater; and, conversely, during periods of declining income, the withdrawals or taxes decrease more than proportionally. With the progressive income tax then, disposable income will increase and decrease as the GNP increases and decreases but the variation in the former will be much less than in the GNP. For this reason, consumption demand is less volatile than it would be expected to be if taxes were less progressive; and if consumption expenditures are relatively stable, this situation will have a stabilizing influence on investment expenditures.

The best example of an automatic stabilizer in the complete sense is the unemployment insurance program because it is tied directly to the social goal of full employment. As long as people are out of work, payments from the unemployment compensation fund will continue. Such payments are injections into the flow of national income — large when unemployment is great, small but still positive even when unemployment is small. Contributions into the fund are withdrawals from the income stream and vary as income varies. Thus, the entire program acts to stabilize disposable income and serves as a depressant to national income when full employment exists and inflation threatens, but it is a stimulant to national income whenever the economy is operating at less than full employment.

The corporate income tax also is an automatic stabilization force even though the rates are not progressive in any very significant way. The reason is that corporate profits themselves tend to increase more than proportionally when national income increases, and decrease more than proportionally when national income decreases. In this way government withdraws spending power from the private economy progressively as income increases.

Other government programs contribute stability to the economy automatically, such as the agricultural price support programs and the Social Security programs. However, none are as important as those we have already mentioned.

The Full Employment Surplus Concept. The Council of Economic Advisers has developed a very interesting technique by means of which one can evaluate and distinguish clearly those elements of government activity that are called the automatic stabilizers, and those which are not automatic but are instead discretionary acts. The focus of this tool is on the surplus or deficit in the federal budget under the given set of laws and regulations and various levels of national income.

It was shown in Chapter 8 that a deficit financed by monetary expansion was multiplicatively expansionary to the national income, and that a surplus, together with money contraction, was multiplicatively contractive to the national income. Since, as we have just seen, some government expenditures and some government revenues depend upon national income, the size of the deficit or surplus cannot be known unless the size of national income is known. This is shown in Figure 23-1.

Figure 23-1 shows that under Fiscal Program *A,* a surplus of 1 percent of GNP will occur in the event that GNP is at its full potential, and a balanced budget will take place if GNP is 95 percent of potential GNP. At lower levels of actual GNP, budget deficits will come about.

Each of the fiscal programs charted reflects the tax and spending plans of a particular set of laws. The lines all have positive slopes because of the assumption that tax revenues and/or expenditures always vary positively with GNP. Since the horizontal axis is GNP as a percentage of potential GNP, we can compare the degree of "drag" on national income expansion of two budget plans at different times or places, or, most significantly, of any two proposed fiscal programs.

Fiscal programs with steep slopes are powerful in their counter cyclical effects. Falling incomes bring about rapid decreases in surpluses or increases in deficits; and rising incomes precipitate large decreases in deficits or increases in surpluses. In Figure 23-1, Programs *A, B,* and *E* all have the same slope; Program *C* is a weak counter cyclical plan; and Program *D* is the extreme in its strong anticyclical impact since surpluses and deficits increase at an increasing rate.

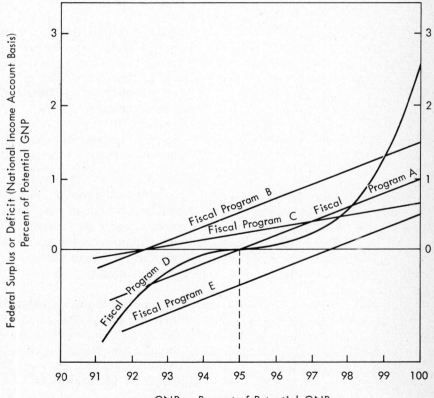

Figure 23-1

Full-Employment Surplus Budgets

The line shifts upward whenever an increase in taxes is included in the budget or when a reduction of spending plans is programmed. Shifting the program lines is called discretionary fiscal policy. If, for example, the economy were operating at about 90 percent of its potential and Fiscal Program *B* were in effect, there would be great pressure to include new spending proposals and/or tax cuts to help stimulate the economy. The function would then shift to Program *A* or, if the action were still more dramatic, to Program *E*.

It is very important to realize that a change in spending or taxes that will produce a given increase in the size of the deficit at the current level of GNP will result in a much smaller deficit, since the action itself would be expected to increase GNP. What that actual deficit would be could only be forecast, which could be done in the manner of our models in Part 3 supplied with the statistical values of the parameters.

The utilization rate at which the fiscal program line crosses the balanced budget line presumably should be about at that point where it is estimated that further increases in GNP would be largely through inflation.

Balanced Versus Unbalanced Budgets. Since the 1930s most economists have struggled to gain acceptance for the idea of planned divergences from the balanced federal budget. Most of the population thought of deficits as immoral or at least as very poor business practice and dangerous. It needed pointing out that deficits could bring about desired expansion of the economy, and it was important to analyze unemotionally the significance of growth in the national debt. As a matter of fact, deficits can be very harmful but so can budget surpluses and even balanced budgets. Under different business conditions, each budget situation can be appropriate.

The balanced budget principle does serve the important function of acting as a disciplinary device. At or near full employment, any use of resources by the federal government implies the giving up of desired goods or services by the private sectors of the economy. In this condition two basic questions need to be answered. First, does government use render a greater "social" utility than private use? This question has an answer only through the (hopefully democratic) political process. The second question is: Are taxes the best way to induce the private sector to give up the necessary resources? It should be clear that there are alternatives.

The two alternatives to taxation as a means of financing government expenditures are borrowing from the public by issuing interest-bearing bonds or other forms of indebtedness, and borrowing from the public by issuing non-interest-bearing debt, namely, money. How different are these two methods from each other and from taxes?

When government acquires its ability to command resources by taxation of individuals, all evidence indicates that the taxpayer's demand for goods and services is reduced. The balanced budget multiplier theory indicates that the public does not voluntarily give up quite as much as the government spends so that at full employment an increase in government expenditures matched by increased taxes will have some inflationary effect.

If government acquires its ability to command resources by the sale of bonds, it is not necessarily true that the bond buyers reduce their demand for goods and services at all. The buyers may simply shift from private security holdings to government security holdings, but the result will be for interest rates to rise, which will reduce demand by business for investment and may increase saving (decrease consumption demand) somewhat. If an increase in government spending is matched by an increase in government debt without a change in the money supply, the result on aggregate demand is not greatly different from the increased tax case. There is a difference on the balance sheets of the public in that more government securities are outstanding, and this may influence future consumption behavior.

If increased government spending is made possible by an increase in the money supply, the situation is quite different from the tax and debt expansion method. The money supply will increase if the Treasury borrows from the Federal Reserve System,[2] spends out of its past accumulation of deposits in the Federal Reserve, or issues new gold certificates or new Treasury currency. The money supply may or may not increase if the Treasury borrows from commercial banks, depending upon the reserve position of the banks. When the money supply does increase to allow the additional government spending, the public will give up resources but it must be done by rising prices, the process we referred to earlier as "forced saving."

Inflation redistributes the use of resources from the private to the government sector just as does taxation or borrowing, but it does it in capricious ways. The people who pay may or may not be the ones society's principles would decree ought to pay. In particular, inflation strikes without reference to economic contribution, equity, ability to pay, or any other criterion.

The situation is considerably different if the economy is experiencing serious unemployment. Then any action that increases aggregate demand can increase output without increasing prices. This is the reason for recommending a deficit, and, if real impetus is needed, the reason for financing it in such a way as to increase the money supply. In less than full employment conditions, government may be able to increase its use of resources without the private sector giving up any because the resources might otherwise be unused.

To insure that expenditures, planned or started while the economy was suffering from unemployment, are important enough that the public is willing to pay for them when they must, it is sometimes proposed that tax rates be set to cover the spending at full employment. In terms of Figure 23-1, the fiscal program line would rotate to become steeper but would still intersect the balanced budget line at the same point.

We have been speaking here as if the question of balanced versus unbalanced budgets were purely an economic question. In fact, as our news media often remind us, the political implications of taxing and spending are often controlling.

---

[2] The Treasury does not normally borrow directly from the Federal Reserve, but the effect is the same if, as the Treasury is selling to the public, the Federal Reserve is buying from the public.

The Dual Budget

Some countries, notably Denmark and Sweden, have adopted a dual budget in which the ordinary operating expenses of government and capital expenditures are separated. Under such a budget system, tax rates are set high enough so that on the average in good years and bad the operating budget is in balance. With fixed tax rates there is, of course, a surplus in prosperity and a deficit in depressions. Capital expenditures for all types of public construction are planned on a long-term basis and budgeted separately. The funds are raised initially by borrowing, but interest payments and depreciation are added to the operating budget. Only such public construction is carried on as the public is willing to pay for over its life in the operating budget. In short, the same accounting and cost determination practices used in private businesses are used in government accounting and financial planning. Insofar as possible, capital expenditures are made in years of recession and depression.

A dual budget is not necessarily related to the use of fiscal policy for growth and stability. It is primarily a device to put government operations on a basis of sound planning. Public construction is carried out only if the electorate is willing to assume the full cost of it over its life. It prevents deficits for which no repayment procedure exists. A dual budget, however, facilitates compensatory fiscal planning. It also helps remove many fears of the evil consequences of growing deficits since plans are made to meet the costs of all expenditures over their period of usefulness.

Long-Run Growth Policy

Until recently the role of the government in promoting short-run stability has received more attention than its role in promoting long-run growth. The analysis of growth in Chapter 22 indicated that growth depended on some factors in the public sector as well as some in the private sector of the economy. If optimum growth is to be achieved, services provided by the government must also grow to meet the needs of the economy. This includes all of the services regularly provided by state and local governments. If some areas cannot afford adequate services, such as education, growth would be aided by having the overall economy provide them. This raises questions about states' rights and government interference in education, but there is little question about it as a means of promoting growth. Services provided by the federal government must also keep pace with the economy. This includes federal highways, waterways, and other major projects called "social capital." It also includes such programs as the United States Employment Service, the activities of the Department of Labor to promote labor peace and help settle strikes, and the work of the Federal Trade Commission.

The need for a growing government program in these areas, growing as the economy grows, is by and large not subject to much disagreement. Some disagreement arises over who will do it—local units, the states, or the federal government—and there is some hesitancy in paying for it. Some hold that the government contribution to growth ends with providing the needed services for an expanding economy. Beyond this, they believe that the greatest contribution government can make is to provide an environment in which private investment can grow. Government programs to stimulate private investment, including aid to research, have been discussed. Some have advocated government investment programs, which are greatly increased in scope and in the volume of funds involved. Such programs have long been advocated by those who feel they are sound in themselves. But recently some have advocated programs of increased government investment as a means of speeding up economic growth. They would increase government investment in such fields as public housing, schools, hospitals, public buildings, and power projects, not only to meet needs in these fields, but primarily to speed up the rate of growth.

Increased government investment programs can, of course, only speed up the rate of growth when it is not at optimum levels. Those who advocate an expanded government investment program on a regular basis feel this is generally true, or true so much of the time that the loss of goods to the private sector would not be material.

Growth Policy for Underdeveloped Economies

Promotion of long-run growth in underdeveloped societies is usually hamstrung by an insufficiency of saving. It is difficult to ask a people whose standard of living is already far below that of people of well-developed economies to reduce their current consumption even more. Aside from gifts or loans from other countries, more saving is needed to increase the rate of capital building.

There are steps a government can take to encourage growth in saving aside from the obvious one that so many of such governments seem to favor; that is, to tax the public (a form of saving) or cause inflation (forced saving), and build capital projects with the proceeds. Making the business environment attractive to foreign investors is a relatively painless way to encourage economic development without domestic saving, but this process is frequently hampered by the political popularity of extreme nationalism. Political instability also militates against economic growth by directing resources to the creation of armies and other monuments. It may even lead to the export of the resources saved by the portion of the population that does save.

Financial institutions and instruments fitted to the particular needs of the people can be a significant stimulus to saving as well as to an efficient direction of saving into the right forms of investment. Actions that lead to smaller families may have the effect of raising per capita income and thus make saving less painful. In fact, anything which results in a larger proportion of productive workers to the total population ought to expand savings. Education and propaganda informing the population of the benefits of thrift and how to accomplish saving may ultimately be an important policy which governments of developing nations must formulate.

Governmental Programs to Influence Sector Behavior

Up to this point we have dealt with the overall impact of the federal budget on economic activity. Here we shall consider what can be done to influence the spending behavior of the other economic sectors — consumption by households, investment by business, and foreign trade with the rest of the world. Here, the focus is not upon the amount of spending or taxing that may be involved, but upon the particular method or direction the spending or taxing may take. Furthermore, some of the programs require little or no taxing or spending.

The Propensity to Consume out of a Given Level of Disposable Income. The government can use its powers to influence the propensity to consume out of a given level of income and has done so to some extent. This has been true primarily in wartime when programs in this area were designed to reduce inflationary pressures, but some programs of this type have been used in peacetime and others have been advocated.

The propensity to consume can be affected by changing the relative relationship between the level of wages and profits. This has been done on a limited basis by laws favorable to union bargaining positions. Since the marginal propensity to consume (*MPC*) out of wages appears to be greater than the *MPC* out of profit, such actions are defended by some when the assumption is made that the long-run problem is too low a level of consumer demand. Excess profits taxes also alter the division of the national income, but they have usually been instituted during wartime on emotional rather than on economic grounds. Direct price, wage, and production controls, along with rationing, also have an important effect on the propensity to consume and have been used in wartime. In the early 1970s, the Nixon administration imposed price controls and freeze phases somewhat halfheartedly in an attempt to break what was considered to be an inflation expectations psychology.

Another possibility that has not been used to date is to tax consumption and saving at different rates. In periods of inflation, a tax on consumption has been advocated in the form of a federal sales tax or a value added tax (VAT).

Excise taxes on particular commodities have been imposed during inflations and reduced or eliminated during slack periods as counter cyclical acts. In depressions some have advocated taxing saving so as to encourage spending. The proposal to tax spending in an inflationary period has been given serious consideration in the World War II and postwar period, but it has not been used to date.

Another possibility is to stimulate saving so as to reduce the propensity to consume. This has been done through campaigns to buy bonds, especially through payroll savings plans. This worked reasonably well during World War II, but it has had little effect in the postwar period of inflation. Proposals have been made for compulsory savings programs in inflationary periods, but they have received little support except during wartime. Pronouncements by the President and other major government officials to encourage or discourage consumption spending are made at different times. It is not likely that this kind of "jawbone fiscal policy" is very effective.

The Social Security program probably has had a long-run effect on the propensity to consume. If some of the economic uncertainties of life due to unemployment, sickness, and old age are lessened, there is less need for current saving. To the extent that a single, large-scale insurance type program is more efficient than many individual programs, the propensity to consume is increased. Guaranteed annual incomes and guaranteed financing of education would presumably have the same effect. These programs could not be used countercyclically, but could be used as secular stimulants to consumption.

Investment Expenditures. Government programs also have an influence on investment expenditures, primarily on expenditures for plant and equipment and for housing, but also to a limited degree on expenditures for inventories. Tax incentives have been used to some extent to stimulate investment in plant and equipment. Rapid amortization of facilities needed to meet defense needs stimulated such construction. There have been proposals to use rapid amortization in a period of recession to stimulate capital goods demand, especially in the 1957–1958 downturn. A conscious effort to encourage investment in durable capital goods was the 7 percent tax credit granted to firms making such expenditures. It was instituted in 1962 when it was thought that such stimulation was needed, and it was revoked in 1966 when the fear of an overheated economy prevailed. More powerful variants of this technique are obviously possible up to a 100 percent tax credit on income used for investment purposes.

The effect of corporate income taxes and changes in the corporation tax on investment is different from the effect of the personal income tax and changes therein on consumption. Actually, the important effect of the corporation tax is likely to be on consumption since it lowers the disposable income of stockholders and/or of the other suppliers of resources.[3] It is true that any tax change which influences expectations of future consumption will have an effect on investment spending, but we shall now proceed to demonstrate that any direct effect on investment by corporate income taxes is likely to be very small.

This conclusion, which is initially surprising, can be demonstrated with a simple example. Suppose a firm has an investment opportunity under consideration that is expected to yield a net return of 10 percent. If we can show that the decision to invest or not invest is the same if the corporate tax is 50 percent or if the tax is zero, we should agree that the tax has no effect on investment. For this example, we will assume that the firm borrows the $10,000 needed to buy a machine at 5 percent interest, although the same principles are involved if the financing is through internal funds or by issuance of additional equity capital.

The pertinent figures are the following:

$10,000 cost of machine
$ 2,500 gross annual return

---

[3] The incidence of the corporate profits tax is not entirely resolved in the theoretical literature of the subject. For our purposes, identification of the final bearer of the tax is unimportant.

$ 1,000 annual depreciation
$ 500 annual interest cost
$ 1,000 net annual return if taxes are zero ($2,500 − $1,000 − $500)
$ 500 net annual return if taxes are 50 percent [($2,500 − $1,000 −
         $500) × .50]

This example shows that the firm is better off with no taxes than with taxes, but this is completely irrelevant to the question asked. Will the firm invest in both cases? The answer is yes. This may be objected to on the grounds that the firm is not likely to risk $10,000 to earn just $500 annually under these conditions. But that is exactly the point. If the tax rate is 50 percent, the firm risks only 50 percent of the initial capital. This can be seen in two ways. First, if the gross return were zero instead of $2,500 in our first case, the loss to the firm when no taxes exist is $1,500; but if taxes are 50 percent, the loss to the firm is just $750. Thus, while a firm gains more profit when profits are positive if there are no taxes, it also bears the full loss when there are losses. When the corporate tax rate is 50 percent, the government absorbs 50 percent of all losses.

The second way to see the issue involved is to assume that the machine becomes obsolete or is physically destroyed before operations can start. If there are no taxes, the firm has lost the full $10,000. If the taxes are 50 percent, the firm can deduct $5,000 of the loss from its other income so that its actual loss is just $5,000. In other words, the government is a full partner in both gains and losses, and the private firm's decision is unaffected by the proportion of the investment the two partners undertake. Returning to our original example, the return on risked capital is 10 percent in both the tax and the no-tax case,

$$(\text{@ } 50\% \text{ tax: } \frac{\$500}{\$5,000} = 10\%; \text{@ no tax: } \frac{\$1,000}{\$10,000} = 10\%.).$$

Relating the simple example to the real world, some qualifications are necessary. For the example to work as presented, it is necessary to assume: (1) that the tax is not progressive, which with only minor qualifications is true of the corporate income tax in the United States; and (2) that either the firm has other income which can be offset by any losses, or that unlimited carry forward and back of profit and loss is permitted, which is also quite close to the case in the United States.

Accelerated depreciation allowances for tax purposes is a stimulant to investment, but not to the extent that is frequently assumed. If, as is typically the case, exactly 100 percent depreciation is permitted, then the only difference between fast and slow "writeoffs" is that the taxpayer is permitted to use the tax funds for a longer or shorter period of time. The amount of the tax over the lifetime of the capital is the same in both cases. To calculate the advantage of accelerated depreciation to the firm, it is necessary to multiply the difference in after-tax profit by the interest rate for the period of time involved. The most effective way to use this instrument is to create the impression that depreciation schedules will be shortened if increased investment is desired. The best way to create that impression is to shorten them "temporarily." Similarly, if excessive demand pressure seems to be the problem, a lengthening of depreciation schedules may induce some investors to wait until more favorable rules abide.

Capital investment is also encouraged by government programs that make financing more easily available to business firms than would be the case without them. This is done on a long-run basis by such agencies as the Small Business Administration. It is also done on a cyclical basis by making larger amounts of funds available to the SBA in a recession period and by establishing general financing programs as was done when the Reconstruction Finance Corporation was set up during the depression of the 1930s. Capital investment could be stimulated, and has been to a limited degree, by government programs of research. These have been restricted to the fields of health and scientific developments related to defense and space age needs. But they could be used more generally not only to develop new products and industries and so create more demand for capital goods, but also to do basic research that is needed to make applied research possible.

During inflationary periods it is generally desirable to depress capital goods construction. This is done primarily through monetary policy. It has been done during wartime through direct controls by requiring special permits to get scarce materials for building. This could, of course, be used in highly inflationary periods in peacetime, but it has not been to date. Demand for housing in our economy is also affected by governmental programs. During the depression of the 1930s, steps were taken to stabilize mortgage markets by taking low quality mortgages out of the hands of private investors and by setting up government guarantees of new mortgages that met preestablished standards. In more recent years the terms of financing on government guaranteed mortgages have been varied to stimulate or depress housing demand. This is done by changing down payments and repayment periods as well as interest rates.

Direct government construction of public housing can also be used to stabilize total housing demand. In a general way, it has been used in this way, but some public housing has been built even in years of a housing boom. Government programs of urban redevelopment to replace slums with planned housing projects could also be used to foster stability. The pressure for such programs on a long-run basis, however, has kept their use as a stabilization device minor up to the present time.

Inventory investment is largely unaffected by fiscal policies. Monetary policy has an important effect on inventory investment, however. When credit becomes tight in recovery, funds are not available for investment in additional inventory without cutting other uses, and this is difficult because all demand is high. Since inventories are financed to a significant degree by short-term bank credit, monetary policy is especially restrictive. Monetary policy is only partially successful, however, in stabilizing inventory investment. Easy credit in recession encourages inventory build-ups, and stocks usually are being built up at a rate that cannot be sustained by increases in demand before credit becomes tight. This has led to a search for other programs to supplement monetary programs. The government has done little in this area, but it has helped management control stocks more adequately by making current data available on the level of inventories by basic fields and by stages of manufacture. These data help show when inventories are out of line with past relationships to sales. This has been helpful, but fluctuations in the rate of inventory holding have continued to be one of the major factors leading to changes in economic activity in minor cycles.

Foreign Trade and Investment. Governments have been engaged in efforts to influence foreign trade and foreign investments since early modern times and even before. They have had only a very limited measure of success with such programs, however, in promoting growth and stability in foreign trade. In the worldwide depression of the late 1920s and early 1930s, foreign trade and investment collapsed almost completely.

In the absence of government restrictions, a boom or severe depression in a major industrial country has a tendency to spread to other industrialized countries. For example, if a boom exists in the United States, imports are likely to rise. Since imports from England are substantial, the demand for English goods is increased. This creates increased demand and increased price pressure in England. If these are great enough, they can initiate an upward movement in business after a recession. If a boom already exists, they can add to inflationary pressures. The situation is just the reverse in a depression.

For example, assume that England and the United States are both experiencing a period of prosperity and that a severe depression develops in the United States. Imports from England will be cut, and this will cut demand for English goods. It will also cut the means of payment for goods from the United States. To pay for these imports from the United States, gold and other reserves will have to be transferred to the United States. This will reduce the money supply and lead to deflation. The Bank of England will take steps to stop the outflow of gold and this will tend to reduce business further. Thus, depression will spread to England, from England to countries with which it trades, and so on.

Further problems arise in a severe depression. Traders in a country experiencing low demand will try to sell goods in foreign markets at a price low enough to move them. This helps demoralize business in the foreign countries.

This spread of business cycles from one country to another led most nations to take steps to insulate their economy from the rest of the world during the 1930s. This was done by means of high tariffs, trade quotas, bilateral trade agreements, barter arrangements, and the like. It was also done by changing the value of domestic currency in relation to gold to make exports cheaper in world markets and imports more expensive and, therefore, less desirable. The result was an almost complete breakdown of world trade and investment in the 1930s.

Stability of trade is furthered by the International Monetary Fund. The Fund provides for short-term credits to take care of temporary imbalances in foreign trade. It also provides an orderly procedure for changing the value of currencies when this is necessary to promote long-run trade equilibrium. Various steps have been taken to make funds available for foreign investment. The American government has made loans through the Export-Import Bank. The World Bank has financed capital development projects in many countries.

It gets its funds by selling bonds that are guaranteed by the member countries. Proposals have been made with increasing frequency for guarantees by the American government of foreign investments. Some call for a general guarantee, others would only guarantee losses due to confiscation of property by foreign governments, confiscatory taxes, and changes in exchange rates.

A related proposal would use tax incentives to stimulate foreign investment. Income from foreign investment could be taxed at a lower rate or not at all. One proposal would not tax any income reinvested in foreign projects.

With the heavy outlays by the federal government in foreign military and economic aid and in prosecuting the conflict in Southeast Asia in recent years, the problem has been of the opposite type. Gold has been flowing out, and a balance of payments deficit has become significant. In an attempt to mitigate this situation, a penalty rate has been imposed upon foreign private investment.

The last series of proposals to be discussed provide for some form of international stockpiling of goods. This could be done by coordinating domestic stockpiling programs. It could also be done by a world agency to buy stocks in periods of surpluses and dispose of them in periods of excess supplies. More extreme proposals call for international quotas for production of basic materials. These have had a poor reception in the United States, except for international agreements to stabilize wheat production and prices. Some propose using international stockpiles as collateral for currency issued by a world bank to be used for settling international balances. Such proposals have received little serious consideration in the United States.

INTERRELATIONSHIP OF FISCAL AND MONETARY POLICY

The discussion in this chapter and in the preceding chapter shows clearly that monetary policy and fiscal policy are operating to meet similar objectives. Since this is true, these policies should be coordinated. If the government is adding to purchasing power by means of a deficit, it makes little sense to have a monetary policy of restraint. Both should usually be working in the same direction. This is just as true in a period of inflation as in recession. The only reason a question arises at all is because in the American economy these two groups of policies are in the main administered by two separate agencies. Monetary policies are largely the responsibility of the Board of Governors of the Federal Reserve System, a nonpolitical board to which members are appointed for 14-year terms and cannot succeed themselves. Since only one member is appointed every two years, there is at no time a wholesale shift in board membership. Fiscal policy is determined by Congress and by the Treasury Department. Congress and the Treasury usually work in harmony, but may not do so completely when Congress is controlled by one political party and the President is from the other party.

Conflicts have arisen from time to time between fiscal and monetary policy. In recent years the conflict has been largely one over interest rates. Federal Reserve monetary policy has raised interest rates materially, and this has also raised the cost of financing the public debt. Since Congress has by law put a ceiling on interest rates on government bonds, the Treasury has been forced to resort to short-term borrowing. Ceilings on the national debt also regularly force the Treasury to act in ways that are inconsistent with its stabilization goals. In such circumstances the Federal Reserve is forced into being the active agent.

Such conflicts of interest and the possibility of more serious conflicts have led to repeated proposals for a central agency to coordinate monetary and fiscal policy. One proposal calls for a national monetary authority. This agency would be comprised of representatives of both the Federal Reserve and Treasury and would develop policies that both groups would carry out. Other proposals would put the Federal Reserve Board under the Treasury or would make it a board appointed by the President on a political basis. To date, the desire to keep monetary policies out of politics and to keep inflation from becoming a political tool has kept the Federal Reserve Board of Governors an independent, nonpolitical agency.

Management of the national debt is another tool that can be used to promote economic stability. There is some question as to whether debt management should be considered monetary policy or fiscal policy since it is the responsibility of the Treasury, but its impact is on the liquidity of the economy.

By debt management we mean the changing of the composition of the debt, mainly in its term structure, but also other terms such as marketability, callability, interest rates, ownership restrictions, denominations, redeemability characteristics, and other actual and potential terms. The absolute size of the debt is not viewed as a part of debt management, although when the debt is expanded or a portion is retired, important questions of debt management do arise.

There are many considerations the Treasury must keep in mind, such as cost and legality, but we shall restrict our attention to the role that debt management can play in a stabilization program. The general proposition is that long-term and less liquid government securities should be increased when inflation is the devil; and when depressed conditions exist, the debt should be shifted to a larger proportion of short-term and more liquid forms of securities. Issues must be tailored to fit the needs of particular classes of potential holders, such as insurance companies, commercial banks, wage earners, and industrial concerns.

With a national debt of close to $700 billion, its maturity structure is likely to have some impact on the term structure of interest rates of private borrowers. There are times when it seems desirable to try to increase rates at the short end and decrease long-term rates. Debt management can play a part in such an attempt.

Management of the public debt is so closely related to the activities of the Federal Reserve System, particularly in its open-market operations, that coordination is absolutely essential. Significant gains could undoubtedly be achieved by making the Federal Reserve System completely responsible for debt management.[4]

---

[4] A. G. Hart and P. B. Kenen, *Money, Debt, and Economic Activity* (3d. ed.; Englewood Cliffs, N.J.: Prentice-Hall, Inc., 1961), pp. 454–457.

QUESTIONS

1. Distinguish between Roosa's defensive and dynamic policies of the Federal Reserve.
2. Outline the connection between: (a) the monetary authority, the monetary base, the money supply, and (b) real income, price levels, interest rates, and employment.
3. Contrast the flexibility of prices and wages, upward and downward.
4. What kind of time lags exist between the time the need for monetary policy occurs and the time the effect of monetary policy on the economy takes place?
5. Evaluate the several tools of monetary policy.
6. Describe the factors that affect bank reserves. Which of these does the Federal Reserve control?
7. Evaluate arguments for and against the use of selective credit controls to combat inflation and influence growth.
8. Which factors are used to support the case for a long-run inflationary bias?
9. Explain the concept of "automatic stabilizers."
10. Explain the full employment surplus concept.
11. Explain the concept of "social capital."
12. Evaluate the principle of annually balanced budgets for the federal government.
13. Do you think that the individual states should engage in counter cyclical fiscal policy to the same extent and with the same techniques as the federal government?
14. Evaluate the statement that counter cyclical fiscal policy is necessary only because of the imperfections of the free enterprise system and such rigidities in wages, prices, and immobility of resources as are characteristic of our economy.
15. What considerations are involved in determining whether a particular amount of increased government spending should be handled by additional taxes, by increasing the national debt, or by increasing the money supply? State in each case what major effects would be expected and the relative merits or evils of these effects.

SUGGESTED READINGS

American Bankers Association. *Proceedings of a Symposium on Federal Taxation.* New York: The American Bankers Association, 1965.

American Bankers Association. *Proceedings of a Symposium on Money, Interest Rates, and Economic Activity.* New York: The American Bankers Association, 1967.

American Economic Association. *Readings in Business Cycle Theory.* Homewood, Illinois: Richard D. Irwin, Inc., 1944. Chapters 13 and 14.

American Economic Association. *Readings in Fiscal Policy.* Homewood, Illinois: Richard D. Irwin, Inc., 1955.

Anderson, Clay J. *A Half-Century of Federal Reserve Policymaking, 1914–1964.* Philadelphia: Federal Reserve Bank of Philadelphia, 1965.

Balassa, Bela, and Richard Nelson. *Economic Progress, Private Values, and Public Policy.* New York: Elsevier North-Holland Publishing Co., Inc., 1977.

Brunner, Karl, and Allan H. Meltzer (eds.). *Stabilization of the Domestic and International Economy.* New York: Elsevier North-Holland Publishing Co., Inc., 1977.

Clark, John J., and Morris Cohen (eds.). *Business Fluctuations, Growth and Economic Stabilization,* Part IV. New York: Random House, Inc., 1963.

Commission on Money and Credit. *Money and Credit: Their Influence on Jobs, Prices, and Growth.* Englewood Cliffs, New Jersey: Prentice-Hall, Inc., 1961. Parts I–III.

The Economic Report of the President. Washington: U.S. Government Printing Office, annually.

Lundberg, Erik. *Instability and Economic Growth.* New Haven: Yale University Press, 1968.

Mitchell, William E., *et al. Readings in Macroeconomics: Current Policy Issues,* edited by J. S. Dietrich. New York: McGraw-Hill Book Co., 1974.

Musgrave, Richard A. *The Theory of Public Finance: a Study in Public Economy.* New York: McGraw-Hill Book Co., 1959.

Peston, Maurice Harry. *Theory of Macroeconomic Policy.* New York: Halsted Press, a div. of John Wiley & Sons, Inc., 1975.

Phelps, Edmund S. *Inflation, Policy and Unemployment Theory: The Cost-Benefit Approach to Monetary Planning.* New York: W. W. Norton & Co. Inc., 1972.

Ritter, Lawrence S. (ed.). *Money and Economic Activity, Readings in Money and Banking,* 3d ed. Boston: Houghton Mifflin Co., 1967.

Roosa, Robert V. *Federal Reserve Operations in the Money and Government Securities Markets.* New York: Federal Reserve Bank of New York, 1956.

Tobin, James. *National Economic Policy.* New Haven, Connecticut: Yale University Press, 1966.

Walker, Pinkney C. (ed.). *Essays in Monetary Policy in Honor of Elmer Wood.* Columbia, Missouri: University of Missouri Press, 1965.

PROBLEMS ON PART 7

1. Critically evaluate the following quotation from a Federal Reserve study:

"In one sense, full employment is a political concept rather than a statistical one. In our economic system, where government has only the residual responsibility for providing full employment and private enterprise has the major responsibility, full employment really means that enough jobs are and will be available to make unnecessary government action to create additional jobs. What number of jobs is considered enough will depend on political attitudes as well as on economic facts. Political attitudes about unemployment and employment will vary with time, location of unemployment, cause of unemployment, and who is affected."

2. Explain in your own words the meaning of the following quotation from a Federal Reserve study:

"Declining Rate of Growth. A more difficult problem arises if the secular percentage rate of growth declines. If this development is not caused by a shortage of productive capacity, but only by the failure of monetary expenditures to expand at the proper rate, the remedy is still relatively simple (at least in theory): larger expenditures (both public and private) should be made. Failure to do so simply means that the productive powers of the economy go unused, creating unemployed workers and resources. But if it is the productive powers that fail to expand at a sufficiently rapid rate, the situation is more serious. It means that technological progress has not been sufficiently rapid to offset the limitations imposed on income growth by a stationary population and existing natural resources. Therefore further additions to our productive equipment increase its capacity at a diminishing rate."

3. Outline a program which you believe business, labor, and the government should follow at the present time to promote economic growth and stability.

4. Suppose you observe the following features exhibited by the economy:
   (a) Prices are rising at a fairly rapid rate (say 6 percent per year).
   (b) Interest rates are near the historical highs (say 7 or 8 percent on public utility bonds).
   (c) Unemployment persists at an uncomfortably high level (say 7 or 8 percent of the labor force).
   How do you diagnose the reasons for this state of affairs, and what policy prescriptions would you suggest? Include in your discussion the role of monetary policy, fiscal policy, and other government policies.

5. Some economists (most notably Professor Friedman) argue that increasing the money supply results in increasing interest rates rather than decreasing interest rates as has been generally argued in this book. We have been assuming "other things remaining constant," but in the real world other things are not constant. What other factors do you think could be introduced into the analysis to bring about the result Friedman says is characteristic of the empirical evidence?

INDEX

E

F